129.95

Race, Crime and Justice

Edited by

Barbara A. Hudson

Reader in Criminal Justice and Socio-Legal Studies
University of Northumbria at Newcastle

Dartmouth
Aldershot • Brookfield USA • Singapore • Sydney

Published by
Dartmouth Publishing Company Limited
Gower House
Croft Road
Aldershot
Hants GU11 3HR
England

Dartmouth Publishing Company
Old Post Road
Brookfield
Vermont 05036
USA

British Library Cataloguing in Publication Data
Race, crime and justice. – (The international library of
    criminology, criminal justice and penology)
    1. Discrimination in criminal justice administraton 2. Crime
    3. Criminal justice, Administration of 4. Race relations
    5. Justice
    I. Hudson, Barbara A.
    364'.089

Library of Congress Cataloging-in-Publication Data
Race, crime, and justice / edited by Barbara A. Hudson.
        p.   cm.— (The international library of criminology, criminal
    justice and penology)
        Includes bibliographical references and index.
        ISBN 1–85521–660–4
        1. Discrimination in criminal justice administration.   2. Criminal
    justice, Administration of.   3. Minorities—Legal status, laws, etc.
    I. Hudson, Barbara, 1945– . II. Series: International library of
    criminology, criminal justice & penology.
    HV7419.R33 1996
    364'.08'693—dc20   95–52504
                                                                                                       CIP

ISBN 1 85521 660 4

Printed in Great Britain by Galliard (Printers) Ltd, Great Yarmouth

Contents

PART III BLACK CRIME: PERSONALITY, CULTURE OR STRUCTURAL CIRCUMSTANCES?

PART IV RACE AND GENDER

Acknowledgements

The editor and publishers wish to thank the following for permission to use copyright material.

Academic Press Limited for the essays: Paul Gordon (1988), 'Black People and the Criminal Law: Rhetoric and Reality', *International Journal of the Sociology of Law*, **16**, pp. 295–313. Copyright © 1988 Academic Press Limited. Tony Jefferson (1988), 'Race, Crime and Policing: Empirical, Theoretical and Methodological Issues', *International Journal of the Sociology of Law*, **16**, pp. 521–39. Copyright © 1988 Academic Press Limited.

American Sociological Association for the essay: Gary Kleck (1981), 'Racial Discrimination in Criminal Sentencing: A Critical Evaluation of the Evidence with Additional Evidence on the Death Penalty', *American Sociological Review*, **46**, pp. 783–805.

Blackwell Publishers for the essay: Maureen Cain and Susan Sadigh (1982), 'Racism, the Police and Community Policing: A Comment on the Scarman Report', *Journal of Law and Society*, **9**, pp. 87–102.

Carfax Publishing Company for the essays: Barbara Hudson (1989), 'Discrimination and Disparity: The Influence of Race on Sentencing', *New Community*, **16**, pp. 23–34; Robert Reiner (1989), 'Race and Criminal Justice', *New Community*, **16**, pp. 5–21.

The Institute of Race Relations for the essays: Lee Bridges (1983), 'Policing the Urban Wasteland', *Race & Class*, **XXV**, pp. 31–47; Cecil Gutzmore (1983), 'Capital, "Black Youth" and Crime', *Race & Class*, **XXV**, pp.13–30.

Kluwer Academic Publishers for the essay: William J. Sabol (1989), 'Racially Disproportionate Prison Populations in the United States: An Overview of Historical Patterns and Review of Contemporary Issues', *Contemporary Crises*, **13**, pp. 405–32. Copyright © 1989 Kluwer Academic Publishers. Reprinted by permission of Kluwer Academic Publishers.

National Association of Probation Officers for the essay: Ruth Chigwada (1989), 'The Criminalisation and Imprisonment of Black Women', *Probation Journal*, September, pp. 100–105.

Oxford University Press for the essays: Simha F. Landau and Gad Nathan (1983), 'Selecting Delinquents for Cautioning in the London Metropolitan Area', *British Journal of Criminology*, **23**, pp. 128–49; Benjamin Bowling (1993), 'Racial Harassment and the Process of Victimization: Conceptual and Methodological Implications for the Local Crime Survey', *British Journal of Criminology*, **33**, pp. 231–50.

Sage Publications, Inc. for the essays: Joan Petersilia (1985), 'Racial Disparities in the Criminal Justice System: A Summary', *Crime & Delinquency*, **31**, pp. 15–34. Copyright © 1985 by Sage Publications, Inc. Reprinted by permission of Sage Publications, Inc. Michael Tonry (1994), 'Racial Politics, Racial Disparities, and the War on Crime', *Crime & Delinquency*, **40**, pp. 475–94. Copyright © 1994 by Sage Publications, Inc. Reprinted by permission of Sage Publications, Inc. John Hagan (1985), 'Toward a Structural Theory of Crime, Race, and Gender: The Canadian Case', *Crime & Delinquency*, **31**, pp. 129–46. Copyright © 1985 by Sage Publications, Inc. Reprinted by permission of Sage Publications, Inc.

Social Justice for the essays: Leslie Inniss and Joe R. Feagin (1989), 'The Black "Underclass" Ideology in Race Relations Analysis', *Social Justice*, **16**, pp. 13–34; Coramae Richey Mann (1989), 'Minority and Female: A Criminal Justice Double Bind', *Social Justice*, **16**, pp. 95–114.

Sweet & Maxwell Limited for the essays: Michael McConville and John Baldwin (1982), 'The Influence of Race on Sentencing in England', *Criminal Law Review*, pp. 652–8; Tony Jefferson and Monica A. Walker (1992), 'Ethnic Minorities in the Criminal Justice System', *Criminal Law Review*, pp. 83–95.

University of Colorado Law Review for the essay: Alfred Blumstein (1993), 'Racial Disproportionality of U.S. Prison Populations Revisited', *University of Colorado Law Review*, **64**, pp. 743–60. Reprinted, as abridged, with permission of author and the University of Colorado Law Review.

University of Texas Press for the essay: Grace Hall Saltzstein (1989), 'Black Mayors and Police Policies', *Journal of Politics*, **51**, pp. 525–44. By permission of the author and the University of Texas Press.

Every effort has been made to trace all the copyright holders but if any have been inadvertently overlooked, the publishers will be pleased to make the necessary arrangement at the first opportunity.

Series Preface

The International Library of Criminology, Criminal Justice and Penology, represents an important publishing initiative designed to bring together the most significant journal essays in contemporary criminology, criminal justice and penology. The series makes available to researchers, teachers and students an extensive range of essays which are indispensable for obtaining an overview of the latest theories and findings in this fast changing subject.

This series consists of volumes dealing with criminological schools and theories as well as with approaches to particular areas of crime, criminal justice and penology. Each volume is edited by a recognised authority who has selected twenty or so of the best journal articles in the field of their special competence and provided an informative introduction giving a summary of the field and the relevance of the articles chosen. The original pagination is retained for ease of reference.

The difficulties of keeping on top of the steadily growing literature in criminology are complicated by the many disciplines from which its theories and findings are drawn (sociology, law, sociology of law, psychology, psychiatry, philosophy and economics are the most obvious). The development of new specialisms with their own journals (policing, victimology, mediation) as well as the debates between rival schools of thought (feminist criminology, left realism, critical criminology, abolitionism etc.) make necessary overviews that offer syntheses of the state of the art. These problems are addressed by the INTERNATIONAL LIBRARY in making available for research and teaching the key essays from specialist journals.

GERALD MARS
Professor in Applied Anthropology, University of Bradford
School of Management

DAVID NELKEN
Distinguished Research Professor, Cardiff Law School,
University of Wales, Cardiff

Introduction

The essays collected in this volume represent the most significant findings, theoretical perspectives and controversies which have been published in North American and British journals during the 1980s and 1990s on the important and politically contentious topics of race, crime and criminal justice.

The starting point for enquiries into the linkages between race, crime and criminal justice is the fact that in England, the US, Canada, Australia and Western European countries such as France and The Netherlands, the numbers of minority ethnic persons found in the criminal justice system – and especially in prisons – are disproportionate to their presence in the general populations of these societies (Hudson, 1993; Dholakia and Sumner, 1993). In 1992 in England and Wales, minority ethnic groups constituted about 5 per cent of the general population, but 18 per cent of the prison population (Dholakia and Sumner, 1993: 29), whilst in the US, African Americans make up about 12 per cent of the general population, but account for one-third of all arrests and one-half of all incarcerations (Hagan and Peterson, 1995). Incarceration rates for black Americans in 1991 were seven times higher than those for white Americans (Tonry, 1995: 4).

These disproportionate, and disturbing, imprisonment rates have prompted a great deal of investigation of one question in particular: is the high minority imprisonment rate the result of disproportionately high rates of black crime, or is it the result of discriminatory processing by police, courts and other criminal justice agencies such as probation services? Research evidence on this question is summarized in this volume by Blumstein, Hudson, Kleck, Petersilia and Reiner (Chapters 1–4 and 7).

The rather tentative consensus that has emerged is that there is some, but not much, excess imprisonment which is clearly attributable to discrimination at sentencing; in other words, some of the disproportion is the result of minority defendants being sentenced to imprisonment in circumstances where white, majority group defendants would receive non-custodial sentences. On the other hand, much of the disproportion is held to be explained by the fact that the crime rate for Afro-Caribbeans in England and Wales, blacks and hispanics in the US, indigenous minorities in Canada and Australia, and migrant workers in northern European countries such as Germany and The Netherlands – in other words, economically disadvantaged minority groups – as measured by arrests and convictions, is higher than for white majority populations. Only in cases of rape, and first-degree homicide in the US, is there acknowledged to be substantial disparity in sentencing. Kleck's review of US studies is a frequently-cited early statement of this view in the US, as is McConville and Baldwin's study of sentencing based on British data (Chapters 3 and 5). To date, no important study has challenged the view that discriminatory sentencing by courts produces only a small amount of the excess imprisonment of minority ethinic groups: rather, researchers have emphasized that, even if discriminatory sentencing is responsible for only a small part of the disproportionate incarceration, it is nonetheless important and needs to be investigated and eradicated. A second issue has also been raised: to what extent are arrest and conviction rates a good representation of crime rates?

To the extent that there is direct discrimination – i.e. differences in outcomes such that certain groups can be shown to have been treated unfavourably because of one particular characteristic (all other characteristics being equal) – this has been explained by abuse of discretion by individual judges and magistrates. Much official or officially-sponsored research has been concerned to measure this kind of discrimination, acknowledging as 'discrimination' only such differences in outcomes that cannot be 'explained away' by factors such as variations in charges, in previous criminal histories, in employment records or ties to the community. It has been conceded that individual judges may hold prejudiced views, and that these views may lead them to abuse their discretionary powers. This explanation of discriminatory outcomes is persuasive for less serious offences, where judges do have discretion either to send defendants to prison or to impose community sanctions. As Blumstein states in Chapter 4:

> For the less serious crime types, the fraction of blacks in prison tends to be larger than the fraction of blacks at arrest. For these crimes, there is more room for discretion at the various stages of decision-making within the criminal justice system (p. 68).

Blumstein was referring here to a study of criminal justice decision-making in 1983. A British study in the 1980s also concluded that, in cases of lesser seriousness where there was not a strong presumption of custody, black defendants were more likely than whites charged with similar offences to receive either a custodial sentence or a high-tariff alternative to custody (Moxon, 1988). My own research, summarized in Chapter 7, supports this view.

Sentencing is, of course, not the only criminal justice decision point at which discretion could adversely affect outcomes for black defendants. In American studies, it is plea-bargaining – the decision about what to charge – that is perhaps the most significant decision. In England and Wales, where plea-bargaining has not been such a feature of criminal justice processing, discriminatory use of discretion has been identified in decisions about remand, whether to ask for a pre-sentence report, and in the recommendations made in such reports. In England and Wales also, the decision to ask for a jury trial in the Crown Court, rather than accepting the jurisdiction of magistrates, has been shown to affect outcomes since Crown Court judges are much more likely than magistrates to impose custodial sentences; their greater powers also enable them to impose longer sentences.

An authoritative, large-scale study of sentencing in England and Wales by Hood (1992) brings together and reinforces these various findings: the influence of remand, plea and mode-of-trial decisions; also the identification of a measure of differential sentencing which can only be explained by the discriminatory practices of one or two individual judges. Current thinking on the extent of discrimination by courts in England and Wales and in the US, then, is that some, but not much, of the disproportionate minority imprisonment is attributable to abuse of discretion by some criminal justice practitioners.

Race and Policing

Black minorities, indigenous minorities and groups, such as migrant labourers, are arrested proportionately more frequently than members of white majority communities. There has been a considerable amount of research attention focused on the question of whether high minority arrest rates reflect high minority crime or whether they reflect police racism.

Radical criminologists and sociologists in England, in particular the authors of the influential book *The Empire Strikes Back* (Centre for Contemporary Cultural Studies, 1982), have analysed the 'new racism' which, they claim, developed in England from the mid-1970s. This 'new racism' saw black people as threatening the socially stable, law-abiding culture of England and Wales and, say Gilroy and his colleagues, involved among other manifestations a recasting of the 'black crime problem'. This social problem was no longer perceived as being that of helping black parents and communities deal with a small minority of delinquent youth, but instead one of maintaining order in communities where most people were hostile to authority and were either involved in crime or indifferent to criminality. For these theorists, the style of policing of black communities that emerged during the 1980s marked the prioritization of preventing disorder over preventing or solving crime. This focus on disorder rather than crime was heightened during the 1980s after riots and disturbances in several British cities. Police racist stereotyping means that black people, especially young black males, are continually stopped and searched, their homes are entered, their clubs and cafes are raided; higher black crime rates are a construction resulting from greater police attention. Other writers argue that, although policing styles in black communities may indeed be confrontational and coercive, the police presence is a response to a real problem of high black crime rates (Lea and Young, 1984).

An interactionist analysis of the effect of suspects' demeanour and attitudes on the outcomes of interactions between young people and police (Piliavin and Briar, 1964) is often drawn upon to explain the differences in cautioning and arrest rates reported, for example in Chapter 11 by Landau and Nathan. Racist stereotypes may lead police officers to target black people as suspects; this disproportionate targeting is resented by black people; their consequent hostility confirms the stereotype of them as anti-police, aggressive and uncooperative. A racist 'canteen culture' is thus perpetuated.

American studies have in the past, been less concerned than British research with this racist 'canteen culture'. Patterns of policing black and other minority ethnic groups have been shown to be associated (1) with historical relations between the communities, (2) with whether the black population in a state or county is perceived as threatening to public order, and (3) with factors such as the level of participation of minorities in the political structures of the area. These American and British perspectives are reviewed by Cashmore and McLaughlin (1991) and are represented here by the essays in Part II, 'Crime, Policing and Racial Unrest'. The greater acceptance by American analysts of arrest rates as reasonable reflections of crime rates (see, for instance, Chapters 2 and 4) could well of course be shaken by incidents such as the Rodney King case and by revelations of police racism in the Mark Furhman tapes introduced in the O.J. Simpson trial.

Race, Crime and the Underclass

In the late 1980s and into the 1990s, most commentators, however, seem to agree that, even if arrest rates and imprisonment rates are inflated by discriminatory decision-making, high crime rates are a real and serious problem for black communities. As well as arrest statistics, evidence for high black crime rates has come from victim surveys (Hagan and Peterson, 1995, using American data; Bottomley and Pease, 1986, using English data). A high percentage of victims report their assailants to have been black; self-report studies show higher proportions of black than white young men reporting involvement in violent incidents, and minority groups have higher officially recorded victimization rates than white citizens. Indeed, it is a frequent complaint of minority communities that their victimization is not taken seriously enough: black neighbourhoods may be over-controlled, but they are under-protected. Accordingly, the advocates of the 'non-discrimination thesis' – the view that excessive black imprisonment is (almost) entirely due to excessive black crime – have gained prominence in recent years (Wilbanks, 1987).

Wilbanks (1989) acknowledges that some law enforcement and criminal justice officials make decisions on a racist basis, but insists that the more urgent challenge for criminologists – and for policy makers – is to accept the reality of the black crime problem and to try to do something about it.

For all those who accept this reality of crime as a problem which particularly affects black neighbourhoods, the question then becomes whether these high crime rates result from some sort of innate differences between black and white persons; whether they arise because of cultural differences between black and white communities; or whether they are associated with structural factors which happen to affect black communities more than white, but would produce the same results – high crime rates – in white communities if the latter were afflicted by the same circumstances. These individual, cultural and structural perspectives are summarized by Reiner in Chapter 1 and are presented in more detail in the essays in Part III, 'Black Crime: Personality, Culture or Structural Circumstances?'

Explanations of High Black Crime Rates

Biological explanations of crime are persistent: every new generation seems to produce a new biological theory, from Lombroso's cataloguing of cranial shapes and features, through endomorphic and mesomorphic body types, the XYY chromosome theory and the contemporary discovery of a 'crime-gene'. A debate conducted in the *Canadian Journal of Criminology* between those who claim and those who refute the existence of a gene found in black races linked to high crime rates is included in Part III (Chapters 16 and 17). Such bald assertions of genetic explanations for crime rates are less common than correlations of certain personality characteristics, such as impulsiveness, that really or stereotypically are linked to race (Wilson and Herrnstein, 1985).

More influential than genetic theories are the various formulations of 'underclass' theory. According to this theory, in certain districts of the inner cities the inhabitants have developed lifestyles and value systems which are quite different from those of mainstream North America and Western Europe. Theories of social disorganization and differential organization have a long pedigree in criminology, and there is much continuity between descriptions of the underclass and, for example, Chicago-School depictions of 'zones of transition'. Although there is no standard definition of the underclass or an underclass area, certain elements are common to most variants of the idea: a high proportion of single-headed households; a high proportion of female-headed households; a high and persistent rate of unemployment; high rates of welfare dependency; a prevalent 'informal economy' centred on drugs and crime. According to the more conservative formulations of the theory, for example the writings of Charles Murray (1984), members of the underclass develop distinctive values and subcultures which are tolerant of crime and hostile to authority. Even during an economic upturn, argue Murray and other theorists of the same persuasion, underclass members would not re-enter employment because they have become de-skilled, de-motivated and, having embraced a 'culture of dependency', are quite content to remain dependent on benefits; they have, in short, rejected the work ethic.

A more liberal version of underclass theory, which has many adherents in Britain, stresses not so much the existence of an underclass of persons who are permanently cut adrift from the rest of society, but the dangers of creating such a class if social inequalities are not reduced. This 'marginalization' thesis stresses the similarities in aspirations between impoverished and affluent citizens, drawing on a version of anomie theory to suggest that, when society stresses material goods but restricts access to these for some people, when the mass media and the proximity of affluent and impoverished districts means that the have-nots are very much aware of the lifestyle of the haves, high crime rates are bound to result. If, moreover, minority groups face racism in their daily lives and if they feel excluded from the mainstream economic, social and political life of the wider society, then their impoverishment and alienation produce a 'marginalization' which will loosen their adherence to the laws of society. Such a theory has been developed by the so-called 'left realist' criminologists in England (Lea and Young, 1984).

An important difference between the marginalization thesis and underclass theory is that, in the former, crime is not considered as an outcome of an entrenched, inherited culture. Whereas Murray sees some of the roots of underclass culture in the values and lifestyles of hispanic migrants and similar groups, marginalization theorists point to differences between the crime rates of younger minority citizens and those of their parents. Pitts, for example, has described how young black offenders in England often come from families with no history of involvement with social welfare or criminal justice agencies, unlike their white counterparts where the whole family may well be known to the authorities (Pitts, 1986). This points to a link between high crime rates and economic circumstance, rather than culture. Immigration was originally encouraged, explains Pitts, at a time of high demand for labour; employment rates among migrant groups started off high and crime rates were (therefore) low. However, subsequent generations find that, in periods of recession, minority groups are discriminated against in the allocation of such jobs as are available and crime rates consequently rise. This explanation, which emphasizes economic over cultural arguments and which links race to a more class-based perspective on crime, seems to fit the experiences of minority groups in England and also of Western Europe. It may also be a better explanation than underclass theory of the rise in black crime rates in the ghettoized areas of 'rust-belt' America. On the other hand, it may indicate that the American underclass theory is not relevant to the situation in Europe.

The rise of a black middle class in America has been cited as evidence for the declining significance of race as a variable in social life generally, and in crime and criminal justice in particular. Poverty, rather than culture or genetics, is the key factor in producing high black crime rates, according to William Julius Wilson (1978, 1987). In this he is at one with Pitts, who urges that the black chartered accountant is no more likely than the white chartered accountant to commit crime (Pitts, 1993). Moreover, if s/he did commit a crime, it would more likely be the suite crime typically associated with white, middle-class defendants, rather than the street crime of the underclass. It is concentration of poverty, claims Wilson, which produces the demoralized, disorganized culture of the underclass, with its high levels of drug trafficking and other forms of violent crime (Sampson and Wilson, 1995). The concentration of poverty idea certainly fits the English case better than the race-linked underclass theory; as Inniss and Feagin indicate in Chapter 19, impoverished, high-crime areas in Britain are as likely to be white as black.

In recent work concern with the crimes of the underclass is linked to concern with the extent of discrimination in the criminal justice system, particularly to the effects of current crime policies (especially the 'war on drugs') on racial disproportions in prison populations. Michael Tonry has examined this in his recent book (1995) the main arguments of which are summarized in Chapter 10. As Tonry and others point out, the war on drugs has been waged on crack/cocaine which is much used in black, underclass areas. It is not unreasonable to expect that, had there been similar offensives against possession and trading in heroin or marijuana, favoured by middle-class white youth, there would have been an outcry from parents about the criminalization and imprisonment of their offspring. A somewhat similar 'war on crime' strategy which can be expected to impact black people disproportionately was launched in England in the summer of 1995 with the approach made by Sir Paul Condon, Commissioner of the Metropolitan Police in London, to black communities for assistance in reducing the incidence of street robbery or 'mugging' – said to be a racially-correlated crime.

This investigation of the effects of 'war on crime' policies brings consideration of race and criminal justice almost full circle. Earlier studies pinpointed discretion as the cause of direct discrimination; in the 1980s, however, criminal justice legislation in most Western countries has been in the direction of reducing discretion by criminal justice professionals. This has occurred through the introduction of sentencing laws and guidelines, guidelines to police on cautioning, bail guidelines, as well as rules for the granting of parole or remission. Rather than looking for direct discrimination due to discretion, scholars such as Tonry are concerned with indirect discrimination through the application of policies and strategies which, though not expressly targeted at racial or ethnic groups, impact on some groups more than on others. In Chapter 9, Sabol too raises concerns about the implications for race differences in imprisonment rates of policy developments which, among other objectives, reduce discretion.

Black Victims and Black Women

The literature on race, crime and criminal justice has concentrated very heavily on black men and, furthermore, on black men as offenders rather than as victims. As mentioned above, victimization rates are higher for minority than for majority ethnic groups; indeed 'homicide is the leading cause of death among African-American youth' (Hagan and Peterson, 1995: 16. Much attention in recent years has been given to victimization in law-and-order politics, in crime policy and in criminological theory, as evidenced by the rise of victims' rights movements, policy orientations towards prevention of victimization (Elias, 1986; Fattah, 1986), and the upsurge in theoretical work centred on the victim rather than the offender

(Walklate, 1989; Young and Rush, 1994). In spite of this, there remains very little work on race and victimization. The high rates of black victimization (quoted in this Introduction and in the essays included in the volume) are frequently cited, but used as evidence for the high rates of black offending: racial victimization is not widely studied as a problem in its own right.

Bowling's essay (Chapter 20) raises issues of racial victimization, arguing that, as well as acknowledging the incidence of racial harassment and racial violence, more qualitative understanding of the dynamics and the contexts of racial violence needs to be developed. Such understandings would still, however, need to be integrated with the main body of work on victimization.

Black women are another group who tend to be lost in the statistical surveys favoured as the primary method of establishing both discrimination and high black crime rates. Imprisonment rates in England and Wales consistently reveal that the ethnic disproportion in prison populations is higher for females than for males (Dholakia and Summer, 1993); this imbalance is also found in the US. Studies of other criminal justice processes also reveal that the ethnic imbalances in cautioning/arrest rates, in the use of community sanctions and in commitment to psychiatric institutions are greatest for females.

Chapters 21 and 22 by Chigwada and Richey Mann explore these disparities. Each demonstrates how black women suffer from the 'double bind' of both racist and sexist stereotyping. Elsewhere, Chigwada has shown how contacts between black women and control officials are often cast as involving mental health problems, with black women vulnerable to psychiatric confinement or confinement to the psychiatric wings of prisons (Chigwada, 1991).

In her book *Unequal Justice: A Question of Color* (1993), Richey Mann summarizes the many studies of the treatment of females by law enforcement and criminal justice agencies; she shows how the findings of leniency towards females that emerge from many comparisons of cautioning, arrest, acquittal and sentencing apply to conventional, respectable women – in other words, to white women. This work raises important theoretical and methodological questions. In relation to research methods, Richey Mann argues against over-reliance on between-group comparisons (black/white, male/female) and urges more use of within-group studies: which women, which black people, which minorities?

Discovery that it is *black* women who are treated more severely by the criminal justice system; that is it *poor* minority communities which have high crime rates; that it is black *men* who are highly vulnerable to street crime whilst black *women*, like white women, are highly vulnerable to domestic crime – all these results link the race variable to other variables. Whilst the proponents of marginalization and other relative deprivation theories, as well as writers such as Julius Wilson, have urged the priority of economic factors over race and ethnicity, other analysts have tried to develop more dynamic models of the interactions between race, class and gender. Rather than privileging one factor over others, the 'multiple inequalities' analysis shows factors such as race, gender, class and age combining in various ways in different situations. Chapter 23 by Hagan was an early formulation of such a perspective.

The class–race–gender approach resonates with postmodernism in the social sciences, rejecting as it does unitary notions such as 'woman' or 'black people'. As Kathleen Daly has argued (1993, 1995), what is needed is a way of studying issues such as crime and criminal justice which acknowledges that, for example, black men's and black women's experiences will be different (as will white women's and black women's, rich black men or women and poor black men or women), but still allows for empirical investigation and for the bringing to light of race-, gender- or class-based injustice. There is also a need to avoid over-emphasizing differences in people's experiences and situations, so that similarities between them – patterns of differential involvement with crime and justice, for instance – become obscured.

References

Bottomley, A.K. and Pease, K. (1986), *Crime and Punishment: Interpreting the Data*, Milton Keynes: Open University Press.

Cashmore, E. and McLaughlin, E. (eds) (1991), *Out of Order? Policing Black People*, London: Routledge.

Centre for Contemporary Cultural Studies (1982), *The Empire Strikes Back*, London: Hutchinson.

Chigwada, R. (1991), 'The policing of black women' in Cashmore and McLaughlin, op. cit., pp. 134–50.

Daly, K. (1993), 'Class-race-gender: sloganeering in search of meaning', *Social Justice*, **20** (1–2), 56–71.

Daly, K. (1995), 'Where feminists fear to tread? Working in the research trenches of class-race-gender', paper given to the British Society of Criminology conference, Loughborough, July.

Dholakia, N. and Sumner, M. (1993), 'Research, policy and racial justice' in D. Cook and B. Hudson (eds), *Racism and Criminology*, London: Sage, pp. 28–44.

Elias, R. (1986), *The Politics of Victimization: Victims, Victimology and Human Rights*, New York: Oxford University Press.

Fattah, E.A. (ed.) (1986), *From Crime Policy to Victim Policy*, London: Macmillan.

Hagan, J. and Peterson, R.D. (eds) (1995), *Crime and Inequality*, Stanford: Stanford University Press.

Hood, R. (1992), *Race and Sentencing: A Study in the Crown Court*, Oxford: Clarendon Press.

Hudson, B.A. (1993), *Penal Policy and Social Justice*, Basingstoke, Macmillan.

Lea, J. and Young J. (1984), *What is To Be Done About Law and Order?* Harmondsworth: Penguin.

Moxon, D. (1988), *Sentencing Practice in the Crown Courts*, Home Office Research Study no. 103, London: HMSO.

Murray, Charles (1984), *Losing Ground – American Social Policy, 1950–1980*, New York: Basic Books.

Piliavin, I. and Briar, S. (1964), 'Police Encounters with Juveniles', *American Journal of Sociology*, **70**, 206–14.

Pitts, J. (1986), 'Black young people and juvenile crime: some unanswered questions' in R. Matthews and J. Young (eds), *Confronting Crime*, London: Sage.

Pitts, J. (1993), 'Thereotyping: anti-racism, criminology and black young people' in D. Cook and B. Hudson (eds), *Racism and Criminology*, London: Sage.

Richey Mann, C. (1993), *Unequal Justice: A Question of Color*, Bloomington: Indiana University Press.

Sampson, R.J. and Wilson, W.J. (1995), 'Toward a theory of race, crime and urban inequality' in Hagan and Peterson, op. cit., pp. 37–54.

Tonry, M. (1995), *Malign Neglect – Race, Crime and Punishment in America*, New York: Oxford University Press.

Walklate, S. (1989), *Victimology: The Victim and The Criminal Justice Process*, London: Unwin Hyman.

Wilbanks, W. (1987), *The Myth of a Racist Criminal Justice System*, New York: Brooks-Cole.

Wilbanks, W. (1989), 'Response to the critics of *The Myth of a Racist Criminal Justice System*', *Critical Criminologist*, **1**, 3.

Wilson, J.Q. and Herrnstein, R. (1985), *Crime and Human Nature*, New York: Simon and Schuster.

Wilson, W.J. (1978), *The Declining Significance of Race*, Chicago: University of Chicago Press.

Wilson, W.J. (1987), *The Truly Disadvantaged: The Inner City, the Underclass and Public Policy*,

Chicago: University of Chicago Press.

Young, A. and Rush, P. (1994), 'The law of victimage in urbane realism: thinking through inscriptions of violence' in D. Nelken (ed.), *The Futures of Criminology*, London: Sage.

[1]

new community 16(1): 5−21   October 1989

Race and criminal justice

Robert Reiner

Abstract Black people are disproportionately represented in
the British criminal justice system. This article reviews the
research literature with a view to assessing explanatory
frameworks. The evidence about prejudice, about differential
and discriminatory practices in criminal justice and about
black involvement in crime are considered in turn. In
conclusion an assessment is made as to the explanatory value
of respectively individualist, cultural or structural
frameworks of analysis.

On 30 June 1988 there were 7,200 people in Prison Service establishments who
were 'known to be from the ethnic minority communities' (Home Office 1989b:
Table 6). This number constituted 14.5 per cent of the total prison population.
Of these the overwhelming majority (4,850 or 67 per cent) were classified as of
West Indian or African origin, the rest being roughly equally divided into those
from the Indian sub-continent, and those of 'Chinese, Arab or mixed origin'. The
proportion of ethnic minority people who are incarcerated is evidently far higher
than their representation in the population as a whole.[1] This is primarily because
of the grossly disproportionate incarceration rate of Afro-Caribbeans. The
disproportion remains when age and gender are controlled for — indeed, the
disproportion is greatest amongst women: 19 per cent of the female prison
population 'were known to be of West Indian or African origin'. In many prisons,
primarily those located in the South-East, the proportion of ethnic minority
prisoners is now regularly over 25 per cent.

The ethnic imbalance is greater the further back in the criminal justice process
one looks. Thus recently published statistics indicate that 18 per cent of those
arrested in the Metropolitan Police District are 'black-skinned' compared with
a population proportion of about 5 per cent. (Home Office 1989a Table 5). For
some offences the disproportion is vastly greater: over 60 per cent of those arrested
for 'street robbery' or 'theft from the person — snatches' are 'black-skinned' (Home
Office 1989a). Of those proceeded against for indictable offences at magistrates'
courts in the Metropolitan Police District, 19 per cent are black[2] (Home Office
1989a: Table 1). All the statistical sources show that the ethnic imbalance has
become steadily larger over time on every count.

The data on the disproportionate black representation in the criminal justice
process constitutes the bedrock of information around which the flourishing debate
about race and criminal justice has come to be constituted. This has become the
single most vexed, hotly controversial and seemingly intractable issue in the politics
of crime, policing and social control. The official statistical picture is the starting

---

Robert Reiner is Lecturer in Criminology at the London School of Economics.

point for all perspectives, although its meaning can be interpreted in sharply polarised ways. Is the problem the menace of a growing black criminal and dangerous class as the Right would portray it? (Powell, cited in Solomos 1988, Part Four, *passim*). Or the criminalisation of young black people through the discriminatory prejudices and practices of a racist system of criminal injustice, as it is portrayed by many on the Left? (Gordon 1983; Gilroy 1982; 1988). Or is there an interaction between these processes, as the beyond either/or analysis of the 'new realists' urges? (Lea and Young 1984, Chapter Four). Underlying all the concrete analyses are three diverse explanatory paradigms: individualistic, cultural and structural. If there is disproportionate black involvement in criminal behaviour, what explains this: genetically programmed individual constitutional proneness to criminality (Wilson and Hernstein 1985: 103), the historically generated and sustained peculiarities of 'underclass' culture (Murray 1984; Leman 1986), or the present social structural position of ethnic minorities as the essential condition precedent (Lea and Young 1984; Reiner 1985b: 175–8)? If there is racial discrimination in and by the criminal justice process, why does this occur? Is it the predisposing psychological peculiarities of those recruited into authoritarian occupations (Colman and Gorman 1982) and de facto exclusion of ethnic minority individuals from official roles in the systems (Wilson, Holdaway and Spencer 1984; King and May 1985; Oakley 1989)? Or the racist norms of the occupational cultures into which recruits are socialised (Smith *et al* 1983; Holdaway 1983; Genders and Player 1988; Graef 1989)? Or the structurally determined role of criminal justice organisations (Brogden *et al* 1988, Chapter Six; Jefferson 1988)? Or do these processes interact? (Reiner 1985b; Lea 1986).

This article will review the research literature on criminal justice in Great Britain, with a view to assessing these various explanatory frameworks. The material will be organised into three sections, considering in turn the evidence about: (a) prejudice, (b) differential and discriminatory practices in criminal justice, and (c) black involvement in crime.[3] The conclusion will consider whether individualist, cultural or structural frameworks of analysis most plausibly account for the evidence.

Prejudice and criminal justice

This section will consider the research evidence concerning the attitudes of personnel in the criminal justice system towards black people, and vice versa. It will assess the extent of racial prejudice which exists, defining this as a negative stereotype of an ethnic group as a whole, by which its members are perceived as certain or at least very likely to be criminal or disorderly.

Police

The police are by far the most researched group in the criminal justice system in the context of race relations, and arguably the most significant because of their gate-keeping function in the process. Most research to date has been on the perspectives of the rank-and-file, but I will also report some preliminary findings from my recent study of chief constables in England and Wales.

Rank-and-file-attitudes

There is a plethora of research evidence, dating back to the earliest studies of the police, both in Britain and the USA, documenting racial prejudice as a prominent feature of street-level police culture. (Examples are Westley 1970 and Skolnick 1966 for the USA and Lambert 1970; Cain 1973; Reiner 1978; Smith *et al.* 1983; Holdaway 1983 for the UK. The literature is reviewed in Reiner 1985a; b; Benyon 1986; Lea 1986; Jefferson 1988; Brogden *et al.* 1988).

It has often been pointed out that the common rank-and-file perception of black proneness to crime (which these studies document) pre-dates any official recording of this. Lambert's study of Birmingham in the late 1960s (Lambert 1970) showed that Afro-Caribbean people were prosecuted for indictable offences at a rate lower than their proportion of the population. The Select Committee on Race Relations and Immigration concluded in 1971–2, on the basis of information provided by many chief police officers, that 'the West Indian crime rate is much the same as that of the indigenous population' (*Police/Immigrant Relations* Vol. 1 Report, HC 471, London: HMSO, 1972, para. 242). The only research support for the rank-and-file view before and mid-70s is a study of crimes of violence in London in the 1950s which found that the proportion of people convicted for these offences who were black immigrants had risen from 6.2 per cent in 1950 to 13 per cent in 1960 (McClintock 1963).

Is racial prejudice still prevalent in rank-and-file police culture after nearly a decade of Scarman-inspired efforts to extricate it, by appropriate selection, training and discipline? One commentator has claimed on the basis of four months' observation in East London during 1986 that he heard 'only two racist epithets in this period? (Brown 1988: 51). This is at odds with the earlier findings of the celebrated Policy Studies Institute (PSI) study of the Metropolitan Police that 'racialist language and racial prejudice were prominent and pervasive' (Smith *et al* 1983: 109). Is the difference between these accounts evidence of miraculously successful reforms in the intervening period? There is no extensive recent research which can answer this question, but it would seem implausible (and at odds with my own observations of policing culture during recent field-work in the Metropolitan Police) to suppose that prejudice had been extirpated from canteen culture. Roger Graef's recent book based on interviews with a very large and varied though unsystematically drawn sample of police officers certainly suggests that racial prejudice remains rife in police ranks (Graef 1989, Chapter Four).

One academic evaluation of the Metropolitan Police's recent efforts at 'Human Awareness Training' reports that the number of officers who 'revealed negatively stereotype opinions' about ethnic minorities was small, but gives us no indication of how small small is, nor of how it reached this conclusion (Bull and Horncastle 1989:112). Another study conducted as part of the same research programme, specifically rebutted this 'one bad apple' approach and found racism to be structurally embedded in operational policing practices and perspectives (Pearson *et al* 1989).

Command-level attitudes

While the evidence of substantial racial prejudice at the rank-and-file level of police forces has seldom been questioned, it is often assumed that it is a problem of the culture of street cops not the managerial strata. This consensus was clearly articulated by Lord Scarman: 'Racial prejudice does manifest itself occasionally in the behaviour of a few officers on the streets. I am satisfied, however, that such a bias is not to be found amongst senior police officers' (Scarman 1981: para 4.63).

My recent research study of chief constables in England and Wales suggests that this assumption may be somewhat too optimistic (Reiner 1988; 1989; forthcoming). The majority of chief constables I interviewed saw the development of divisions between ethnic groups as a major problem (often *the* major problem) facing the police. At one level this could be taken as merely a statement of fact from the chief constable's hot-seat. Tensions and conflicts associated with race *have* been a major headache for many police forces. But in the majority of cases, the chiefs articulated an analysis in which the source of the troubles was located in the black population, *not* in the difficulties of achieving multi-cultural harmony, and certainly not in white prejudice. It should perhaps be underlined that the perception of black people as a cause of crime and disorder was *not* displayed by most of the chief constables who police the metropolitan areas in which the majority of the ethnic minority population live. But nonetheless amongst a majority of the chief constables there was a view of black people themselves as a potential source of policing problems, ranging in a few cases to clear dislike. The following perspectives on the problems of policing and race are characteristic of the majority of chief constables:

> The shortcomings of Scarman were that he was looking at the large conurbations
> . . . and therefore on a political basis it was said we'll blanket the whole country.
> The dangers are there in the eyes of the junior policeman who finds himself in
> the centre of -shire, where we've got a fairly substantial coloured community and
> sees himself being prevented from doing it the way he was taught by the training
> school . . . the danger today is saying Scarman says this and Scarman says that
> and the particular circumstances of thinking that most usually with a coloured
> community with a different and somewhat effervescent and occasionally violent
> type of personality' (County Chief Constable).
>   We in -shire have one of the lowest ratios of policemen to population and are
> under pressure now. We have a fairly volatile town in x, where rising 7 per cent,
> which comes as a surprise to many people, rising 7 per cent of the population
> literally is black . . . we have a black and white problem in x . . . and when we
> meet the leaders, the minority group leaders, it is quite amazing. It is a marvellous
> exercise in restraint when they make outrageous statements. They complain bitterly
> about harassment and what have you . . . we have had our problems here, certain
> pubs used by certain groups for drug-trading, and taken over if you like by blacks
> . . . we have a much more cosmopolitan society. Whereas before one occasionally
> saw perhaps a Roman Catholic Church, now you see not only the odd synagogue
> but now even here in x you find mosques, temples and people, it is very sad to
> see them not integrating, hardly at all (County Chief Constable).

While it must be emphasised that these sort of views depicting black people as a source of crime, tension and disorder tend not to be found amongst metropolitan chief constables, they are characteristic of the majority around the country. The perspective on policing which sees prejudice as a phenomenon of street-cop not management-cop culture is oversimplistic. Prejudice is rooted in the structural position and role of police forces as a whole, not just at rank-and-file level.

Race and criminal justice 9

Prosecutions

The *Prosecution of Offences Act* 1985 established the Crown Prosecution Service (CPS) to take over from the police the process of instituting and conducting criminal proceedings. There is as yet no research on the perspectives of those employed by the CPS, so no conclusions can be drawn about the extent of racial prejudice. It might be hypothesised that the CPS would reflect the prejudices found in the legal profession generally, from whose ranks the staff of the CPS is drawn (cf. the essay by Israel and King in the present issue). However, this might be mitigated to the extent that the CPS disproportionately recruits from those who are unable to compete effectively for more lucrative opportunities in private practice, who are likely to include a higher proportion of ethnic minority lawyers.

Probation Service

The attitudes of the staff of the Probation Service towards ethnic minorities is crucial in two ways. Firstly, the views and recommendations expressed in the Social Inquiry Report (SIRs) they write are an important ingredient in the sentencing process. Secondly, the attitudes of probation officers are crucial to the experience of those they supervise.

Considerable concern has been expressed because of this about the disproportionately low number of Probation Service staff who are from ethnic minorities,[4] and there has been official encouragement of ethnic minority monitoring, equal opportunity policies, and the development of racism awareness training for the Probation Service (NACRO 1986, Chapter Four; NACRO 1989, Chapter Four).

There is no systematic evidence about the racial attitudes of Probation Service staff. Studies of the content of SIRs have had contradictory findings. Whitehouse (1983), Pinder (1984), and de la Motta (1984) all suggest that these reports do tend to offer more negative views of black defendants. De la Motta found a tendency to make no specific recommendations for sentence more frequently in the case of black people, leaving the courts with fewer sentencing options, while Pinder claimed that the offending behaviour of blacks was characteristically attributed to a refusal to follow legal rules rather than personal inadequacies as with white defendants.

Some more recent studies call into question the notion of a tendency for negative images of black people to appear in SIRs. Mair (1986) found that the recommendations in SIRs were similar for all ethnic groups (although they were asked for by courts proportionately most with Afro-Caribbean defendants and least with Asians, and there was a complex relatonship to sentencing outcome). Waters (1988) found in a sample of 41 SIRs written on Afro-Caribbean defendants that nearly half these reports (46.3 per cent) made no reference to race at all, and only a small minority depicted blacks in a negative way. (There was also some evidence of positive bias in favour of ethnic minorities.) However, a subtle process of differentiation was found in a recent West Yorkshire study, leading to disproportionate incarceration and fining of black offenders (Voakes and Fowler 1989).

The judiciary

There is no systematic evidence about the racial attitudes of the judiciary in general. The study of black magistrates by King and May in 1985 did find 'evidence of racial prejudice among some of the members of the Lord Chancellor's advisory committees' who are responsibile for magistrates' recruitment. 'This takes the form of negatively stereotyping African and Afro-Caribbean people, and applying such stereotypes in their expectations of black people's behaviour' (King and May 1985:135). There is certainly ground for concern about the small proportions of ethnic minority judges at any level, and the lack of training in issues concerning race (NACRO 1986, Chapter 3).

The prison service

An important recent study of race relations in prisons (Genders and Player 1989) has documented the extent of racial stereotyping amongst a representative sample of prison officers. This seems to echo the canteen culture of the police, in both the pervasiveness and the virulence of racial prejudice.

> What emerged were clearly defined and widely endorsed racial stereotypes which categorised and stigmatised inmates on the basis of the colour of their skin ... Black prisoners were described by all but a handful of officers in at least one of the following negative terms: arrogant, hostile to authority, estranged from the institutions of 'law and order', alienated from the values associated with hard work, and having 'chips on their shoulders' (Genders and Player 1989: 50).

It is worth noting that such provocative views of ethnic minorities were not found amongst prison governors, probation officers or education staff (Genders and Player 1989: 61). They were, however, echoed by members of Boards of Visitors, a third of whom thought a high proportion of black prisoners led to increased disruption, either because of their innate 'hot-bloodedness' or 'belligerence', or because of problems of inter-cultural communication (1989: 61–2).

Discriminatory practices in criminal justice

There is evidently substantial differentiation in the treatment of ethnic groups by the system of criminal justice, as the statistics cited at the beginning of the paper show. Afro-Caribbeans in particular are arrested and imprisoned far more than in proportion to their representation in the population. The previous section has documented the existence of prejudiced attitudes towards black people amongst the personnel of the system, especially those working at the beginning and end points of the process, in police forces and prisons.[5] The issue addressed in this section is the relationship between these two facts. To what extent is the differential treatment of blacks the result of prejudice? In other words, to what extent is there racial *discrimination* by the criminal justice system, defining this as differential handling of black people which is not justified with reference to legal standards. For example, if proportionately more blacks than whites receive sentences of imprisonment, this can be counted as discrimination to the extent that it is not accounted for by relevant legal factors such as the seriousness of the offences committed or the past criminal record of those sentenced.

Race and criminal justice   **11**

There are thorny methodological problems in establishing that a pattern of differentiation in the use of legal powers is in fact discriminatory. Research on this issue can be based either on the analysis of the statistical pattern of use of legal powers, or on the observation of the use of these powers in action.

Statistical methods

The question addressed by statistical analyses is whether blacks are treated worse than whites by the criminal justice system, holding constant legally relevant variables. There are four main methodological problems in inferring that this is so on the basis of a pattern of differentiation.

(i) What are 'legally relevant' variables, and how can they be adequately measured and controlled for? For example, in the decision whether to caution rather than prosecute a suspect, or to bail them rather than jail them, the likelihood of further offending is a 'legally relevant' variable. But if the indices taken as signifying greater likelihood of further offending are themselves statistically related to ethnic group, then is their use discriminatory, or 'legally relevant'? One study of the cautioning of juveniles found, for example, that the indices used to typify 'bad risks', such as being a 'latch-key' child, coming from a single-parent or disrupted family, or having an unemployed father, were more prevalent amongst black than white juveniles. Their use means that proportionately fewer black juveniles were cautioned than white juveniles who had committed similar offences and had similar past records (Landau and Nathan 1983). Is this racial discrimination or a legally justifiable distinction?

(ii) What constitutes 'worse' treatment by the criminal justice system? It is not always clear that one disposition would be regarded as less desirable than another by everyone, or in every way. To take the above mentioned study of the cautioning of juveniles as an example again, it is assumed that cautioning is a more preferable outcome than prosecution, and the lower cautioning rate for black juveniles thus constitutes at least prima facie evidence of discrimination (Landau 1981). However, one factor in this is said to be a lesser willingness of black suspects to accept a caution with its attendant admission of guilt. It may be that this is part at least reality-based, and that prosecution carries some probability of acquittal (Walker 1988). In this light, a caution with its associated necessity to admit guilt may not really be the preferable outcome (Walker 1987: 50) nor may prosecution signify 'worse' treatment.

(iii) If discrimination is established, in the sense of worse treatment of blacks than whites in the criminal justice system holding constant legally relevant variables, this may not result from discrimination by the criminal justice system itself. There is evidence, for example, that the preferences and attitudes of victims or complainants are an important influence on police decisions to arrest, holding constant the legal quality and quantity of evidence (Black 1980, Chapter Four). If complainants are more likely to prefer arrest when suspects are black, then the result will be discriminatory use of the arrest power in the sense of a differentiation between the treatment of black and white suspects which is not justified by the legal evidence. But the discrimination is not due to the actions of the criminal justice systems in an active sense: the police are passively transmitting a pattern of discrimination by citizens who complain to them of offences.

(iv) Finally, suppose a pattern of discrimination is established in which the criminal justice system does treat black people worse in ways not accounted for by legally relevant factors. It does not follow necessarily that the system is treating blacks worse because of their race. Race could be a proxy for other variables which are the effective determinant of the discrimination, such as youth or class. The disentangling of the web of relationships between class, age, gender and race is complex and fraught with methodological difficulty (Walker 1983; Hagan 1988, esp. Chapter Five).

Observational methods

Research based on observation has found it even harder to pinpoint discrimination. How can discrimination be observed in individual cases unless the discriminator is foolish enough to reveal verbally that the ground for their action is racial bias? Without verbal admissions, discrimination could only be directly observed if cases which are construed as identical in terms of the observer's categories are treated differently. However, given the tense and mutually suspicious character of relations between blacks and criminal justice practitioners, notably the police, the demeanour of black people is not likely to be the same as whites. Numerous observational studies of the police, for example, while documenting widespread police prejudice, fail to find observable differences in the quality of the handling of similar cases (Black and Reiss 1967; Reiss 1971; Smith *et al* 1983; Holdaway 1983). In so far as the outcome of encounters involving black people is more likely to involve the invocation of legal powers, this is partly the product of interaction during the encounter itself, the perceived greater 'disrespect' shown by black suspects (Black 1980).

Nonetheless there is a large volume of evidence documenting differentiation in the treatment of blacks and whites at almost every stage of the criminal justice process. While given the methodological caveats above it is impossible to establish this beyond doubt, the quantity and quality of this evidence is such as to render any doubts about discrimination fanciful rather than reasonable.

The evidence of racial differentiation and discrimination

This section will review the now copious evidence of a pattern of differentiation and discrimination in the handling of black people at each stage of the criminal justice process.

The public

The pattern of reporting victimisation by members of the public to the police displays racial differentiation and arguably discrimination (Tuck and Southgate 1981; Smith 1983). According to a Home Office Statistical Bulletin published on 10 March 1989,[6] 'non-whites' were reported by victims as the perpetrators for some offences in proportions far greater than their representation in the population. For recorded offences or 'robbery and other violent theft' in the Metropolitan Police District during 1980–5, the proportion of assailants said to be 'non-white' was over 50 per cent (although only around 20 per cent of the population in the age-group 10—20 is 'non-white'). The statistics recorded for assaults in general do not show the same 'non-white' over-representation, with around 17 per cent of perpetrators reported as 'non-white' by victims.

The Home Office bulletin notes that these statistics on victims' assessment of the ethnic origin of their assailant 'are of more limited value' than most such figures. In a substantial proportion of inter-personal crimes no assessment of the ethnic appearance of the offender could be made. But even when it was, it 'could be unreliable and possibly biased. The reliability of the victims' assessment is inevitably limited by the circumstances of the offence — the difficulty of recalling accurately a sudden event and the possibly limited opportunity to see the assailants; for instance, the offender may only be seen when running away, many offences occur at night in ill-lit places, the offender may wear a mask etc.' (*Home Office Statistical Bulletin*, 10 March 1989:5).

There is some limited evidence that the propensity of white victims to report violent crimes is greater when the offender is black. (Carr-Hill and Drew 1988:40—3). Thus one study by the Home Office Research and Planning Unit shows that in 50 per cent of the cases where white victims suffered an attack by a 'coloured' person no injury was sustained, while this was true of only 22 per cent of cases with white victims and white attackers. In 12 per cent of the white victim/white attacker cases, the injuries sustained were fatal or serious, but this was true of only 4.5 per cent of cases with white victims and 'coloured' attacker (Stevens and Willis 1979, Table 7). The implication is that white victims might have a higher threshold of reporting attacks by white than black assailants, and/or the police have a greater readiness to record them. In any event, the reporting of some offences already disproportionately feeds black people into the criminal justice process as suspects.

The police

Numerous studies have shown that the police disproportionately exercise their powers against black people.[7] This has been documented with respect to stop and search in the street, arrest, and decisions to prosecute (when these were the province of the police).

(a) *Street Stops*: One Home Office study of stops in four police stations (two Metropolitan, two provincial) found that annual recorded stop rates for blacks were markedly higher than those for the population as a whole, and this was particularly true for young blacks (Willis 1983: 14). The British Crime Survey found in its national sample that young black males had a higher chance of being stopped than other people (Southgate and Ekblom 1984: 19).

The PSI study in London shows striking evidence of this disparity. 'Among men aged 15—24, the proportion stopped is 63 per cent for West Indian, 44 per cent for whites, and 18 per cent for Asians. Those young West Indian males who have been stopped at all over the past 12 months have been stopped four times on average, compared to 2+ times for whites' (Smith *et al* 1983, Volume 1: 95—101). The only studies of stop and search which do not confirm this pattern of disproportionate use of the power against young black males were both carried out in inner-city areas, one in Manchester and one in Liverpool (Tuck and

Southgate 1981; Brogden 1981). It has been argued that this might indicate that
the disproportionate black stop rate elsewhere is primarily due to class factors rather
than race *per se*, as in homogeneously deprived areas the racial difference largely
disappears (Jefferson 1988: 528–30). The Islington Crime Survey, conducted in
an inner-city area of London, does record a disproportionate stop rate for black
males under 25 (52.7 per cent) compared to whites (31.6 per cent) (Jones *et al*
1986: 148–9). However, as Islington is far from homogeneous in social class terms,
it cannot be determined whether this supports the view that there is a separate
element of racial discrimination involved. The most plausible interpretation is that
blacks are more likely to be subject to police attention than whites even if class
could be held constant, as indicated by anecdotal evidence about the treatment
of middle-class or professional blacks, and by American survey evidence (Jefferson
1988: 529–305; Hagan 1988: 137–41).

(b)   *Arrests*: Numerous studies document a disproportionate arrest rate for young
blacks (Stevens and Willis 1979; Smith *et al* 1983, Volume 1: 121–2; Volume 3:
96–7). There is, however, a heated and vigorous debate about the extent to which
this reflects police discrimination as distinct from a higher rate of offending by
blacks, and the relationship of both to socio-economic considerations (Hall *et al*
1978: 358–81; Lea and Young 1981; 1984; Bridges 1983a; b; Gilroy 1982; 1983;
1987; Gutzmore 1983). This debate will be considered in the last section below.

(c)   *Prosecution by police*: A number of studies also show that black people were
prosecuted disproportionately after arrest, when the police were in most cases solely
responsible for this decision (Cain and Sadigh 1982; Landau 1981; Landau and
Nathan 1983). The Landau study of the cautioning of juveniles by the Metropolitan
Police is especially noteworthy, as it purports to establish a degree of discrimination
which cannot be accounted for by legally relevant variables which are meticulously
controlled for. As noted earlier, however, there is some room for doubt as to
whether cautioning should necessarily be regarded as the less punitive outcome
(Walker 1987: 50).

Prosecution

There is no research evidence as yet on whether the introduction of the Crown
Prosecution Service will affect the disproportionate prosecution rate of black people.
However, it is likely that the factors which underlie the differential prosecution
rates of black and working-class people will remain operative, especially as the
CPS decisions will be made on the basis of case papers initially constructed by
the police as before (Sanders 1985; 1987).

The jury

There is little empirical evidence about the determinants of decision-making by
juries, due to the formidable legal and other access problems facing researchers
in this area (Baldwin and McConville 1979: 16). A major British study has,
however, raised the possibility that juries might be 'prejudiced against the defendant

on racial grounds' (Baldwin and McConville 1979: 80–83). On the basis of examination of case-papers by a professional panel of judges, lawyers and police officers, Baldwin and McConville identified a group of 'doubtful convictions', those which were regarded as questionable by the professional scrutineers. 'No fewer than eight out of fifteen involved black defendants . . . the figures do suggest that the possibility of racial prejudice by some juries is one that deserves serious attention' (1979: 81).

The judiciary

The evidence on decision-making by the judiciary, either in terms of reaching verdicts or in sentencing, is scanty. Overall what there is does not suggest that there is further discrimination against black people at this stage of the process. This is broadly indicated by the fact that according to the Home Office Statistical Bulletins in the Metropolitan Police area at any rate the ethnic distribution of those found guilty roughly matches that for arrests.

One study of 1,476 Crown Court cases in London and Birmingham (of which 339 involved non-whites) found 'no evidence of direct systematic bias on racial lines in sentencing in the Crown Court. The implication is that defendants are treated equally once they attain the status of convicted persons' (McConville and Baldwin 1982: 658). A later study looked at nine courts in different parts of the country (four juvenile, three magistrates' and two Crown Courts). It concluded also that 'the different ethnic groups present similar patterns of crime, their cases are handled in similar ways and the sentences they are given are similar' (Crow and Cove 1984: 416).

A later study of two magistrates' courts in West Yorkshire did find some complex differences in the sentencing of black offenders. They were less likely to receive probation orders, more likely to get community service orders, and less likely to be sentenced to prison. The fact that black defendants were usually younger than white was taken as suggesting that they were more likely to be arrested and prosecuted in the first place (Mair 1986).

A recent study of the court disposition of young males in London, supports the latter finding, but finds that black defendants were more likely to receive custodial sentences[8] (Walker 1988: 457). This was partly because they were sentenced for violence or robbery offences more often, but even within this category were more likely to receive custodial sentences. It could not be established that this signified discrimination, as details of the seriousness of the specific offence and the prior records of those sentence were not available. On the other hand, this study did show that a higher proportion of blacks were acquitted after trial, and that judges dismissed relatively more cases with black defendants before trial due to insufficient evidence. This suggests either that black people are more likely to be prosecuted on insufficient evidence, or that courts require more convincing evidence to convict black people, or both. None of the studies of the courts, for all the variations in their results, establishes a finding of discrimination against blacks at that stage of the criminal justice process.

Prisons

Once black people reach prison (which as shown above they do disproportionately) there is evidence that they are further discriminated against within the walls. Although sensitive to the thorny problems of proof, a recent study of race relations in prisons does provide at any rate prima facie evidence of discrimination against black prisoners in four areas: in disciplinary proceedings, the writing of assessments of prisoners, the allocation of accommodation, and the allocation of jobs and training courses (Genders and Player 1989, Chapter Five).

Black involvement in crime

There is evidence therefore of racial differentiation and discrimination at most points of the criminal justice process. The most controversial issue of all, however, is the extent to which black people are disproportionately involved in offending, as well as being discriminated against by the system.

It is impossible to conclusively resolve this issue because of the limitations of official crime statistics, the fact that they are certainly an incomplete and almost certainly a biased sample of offending and offenders (Walker 1983; Bottomley and Pease 1986; Carr-Hill and Drew 1988). Victim surveys, which normally allow some penetration behind the officially recorded date, do not help here because of the dangers of victim stereotyping of offenders. *Any* conclusions about the racial pattern of offending can only be tentative speculation.

Supporting the view that much of the disproportionate processing of black people is the product of discrimination is the fact that the disproportion tends to be greatest in some offences which are maximally open to police discrimination and stereotyping, such as the old 'sus' law and minor public order offences (Stevens and Willis 1979; Cain and Sadigh 1982). On the other hand, the sheer volume of the disparity makes it implausible to attribute it all to discrimination. Lea and Young support the view that there is a real difference in offending rates (in addition to discrimination in arrests) by two arguments:

(i) If the disparity in arrests was entirely the product of police prejudice, how is the sharp difference to be explained between 1972, when the Select Committee Report on *Police/Immigrant Relations* interpreted the dominant police view as being that blacks were not over-involved in crime, and 1975 when the Metropolitan Police created a 'moral panic' by releasing statistics on arrests for robbery analysed by race? (Lea and Young 1984: 138). It is implausible they argue to claim that the sudden shift is due to an explosion of prejudice. It is, however, equally implausible to see it as a result of a sudden explosion of black crime. Rather there is a long and complexly intertwined process of shifting balances of power within the police, between factions seeing blacks as responsible for proportionately more crime and a more liberal element denying this, each using contradictory facets of official statistics. The change in the mid 1970s is best interpreted as signifying a strategic eclipse in the more liberal position within senior police circles (Benyon 1986: 28–32).

(ii) A more convincing argument advanced by Lea and Young points to the fact that the black population of Britain became ever more characterised during

the 1970s by social conditions of a criminogenic kind: they became disproportionately a youthful population, and increasingly subject to high unemployment
and economic (and perhaps political) marginality. 'If these sorts of deprivations
are not crucial factors leading to increasing crime rates then what are?' (Lea and
Young 1984: 167–8).

It must be underlined that it is impossible to apportion with any certainty the
contributions of racial discrimination and real offending patterns to the growing
involvement of black people in the criminal justice system. It is suggested, however,
that the most plausible interpretation is that both play a part, and furthermore
that criminal justice system prejudice and discrimination on the one hand, and
black crime on the other, reinforce and feed off one another in a vicious circle
of amplification.

Conclusion

Both criminal justice system discrimination and black crime have been analysed
by three contrasting frameworks of explanation; individualist, cultural and
structural.

Individualist explanations

Individualist explanations of racial crime patterns are significant in popular and
political discourse, and that of some criminal justice practitioners. In the USA
there has been a major recent attempt to revive such accounts within academic
criminology (Wilson and Herrnstein 1985 — This has been subject to withering
critiques by amongst others Kamin 1986; Jencks 1987; Curtis 1989).

While individualist interpretations of crime are not prevalent in academic
discourse, they do figure large in academic explanations of criminal justice practices,
especially in the extensive debate over whether or not there is a distinctive 'cop
personality' (For critical reviews see Reiner 1985a: 101–3; Brogden *et al* 1988,
Chapter Two.) The weight of empirical evidence is against the view that police
work attracts measurably authoritarian personalities. Only one (much criticised)
recent study supports this conclusion (Colman and Gorman 1982). However, even
if it were true that policing attracts distinct personality types, it would be necessary
to explain this attraction in terms of the culture and character of police work (Reiner
1985b: 173–5).

Cultural explanations

An influential line of argument claims that there are particular aspects of black
culture which generate criminal activity (Murray 1984; Leman 1986). The evidence
on black attitudes towards crime and criminal justice certainly documents
considerable suspicion of, even hostility to, personnel in the system and its current
practices. The PSI study of Londoners found for example that 'the lack of
confidence in the police among young West Indians can be described as disastrous'
(Smith *et al* 1983, Volume 1: 326). However, it is clear that hostile or critical

views of criminal justice practices do not amount to a rejection of the values or aims of the system (Smith *et al* 1983, Volume 4: 332; Gaskell and Smith 1981; Gaskell 1986; Gifford 1986, Chapter Seven). Black people are *not* alienated from the criminal justice system and its values. Furthermore, their more critical views of its practices are largely a function of their economic and social position. As a recent analysis of attitudes towards the criminal justice system in the USA shows, racial variation in these is largely explicable by the fact that black people occupy disproportionately those social positions which have historically been the main grist to the criminal justice mill, in the economically marginal 'surplus population' of the inner-city (Hagan 1988, Chapter Five). Thus any 'cultural' difference is not due to the intrinsic attributes of an alienated underclass, but are generated by the structural position of black people in society. (Currie 1985; Curtis 1989: 143–5).

Similarly, the culture of the criminal justice system is not a free-floating and independent source of its practices. To be sure there is evidence that police officers, for example, are socialised into a 'canteen culture' which may include racial prejudice as an element. (Brown and Willis 1985; Fielding 1988). However, this is more plausibly interpreted as a culture which develops as a way of facilitating the adjustment of criminal justice personnel to their structurally determined roles than as an autonomous and original source of their practices.

Structural explanations

From both sides therefore we are driven to seeking a structural account of the relations between ethnic minorities and the criminal justice system (Reiner 1985b: 175–7; Jefferson 1988). The basic trigger for what can become a vicious circle of spiralling conflict is societal and institutionalised racism. This forces discriminated-against ethnic minorities to acquire those characteristics upon which 'normal' policing bears down most heavily, and it is the policing element which is crucial for feeding disproportionate numbers of black people into the system.

The structural position of black people essentially exposes them to becoming 'police property' (Lee 1981), whose control is left to the police by the dominant groups in society. Indeed, the criminalisation of black people may benefit the majority group directly in times of shrinking economic opportunities, as it further disadvantages blacks in the competition for scarce resources in the job and offer markets (Johnson 1976: 108). Cultural hostility between prejudiced police and black people suspicious of the justice of the system further exacerbates but is not the ultimate source of the conflict.

A structural analysis at least offers more hopes of change than an individualist account rooted in fixed aspects of human nature. But it casts doubt on the prospects of reforms directed merely at changing individual or cultural attitudes by personnel methods like selection and training processes. It underlines the futility of policies directed at the criminal justice system by itself.

Notes

1   Approximately 5 per cent for all ethnic minorities, and 2 per cent for Afro-Caribbeans, (NACRO 1986: 3).

Race and criminal justice   19

2 The appropriateness of the term 'black' to refer generically to all non-white ethnic minorities is itself politically and conceptually contested terrain. I will adopt it as the most familiar usage, while making more precise distinctions between groups when relevant.

3 There is also a copious literature on discrimination within the criminal justice system in terms of appointment and advancement of personnel. This will not be examined in detail, because it is the focus of several papers in this issue, e.g. King and Israel. It will also not directly consider the evidence about the alleged under-policing of racial attacks or inadequate protection of black victims.

4 According to the Home Office Statistical Bulletin 24/88 'The Ethnic Origins of Probation Service Staff', only 1.9 per cent of probation officers of all grades were from ethnic minorities (1 per cent being Afro-Caribbean). Only three of the 127 non-white probation officers were seniors, and none was in the chief officer grades.

5 For earlier reviews of the evidence on racial discrimination in criminal justice see Reiner 1985b; Gordon 1983; Gilroy 1983; 1988; Crow 1987; Benyon 1984; 1986; Benyon and Solomos 1987; NACRO 1986; 1989; Lea 1986; Brogden *et al.* 1988, Chapter Six; Solomos 1988 Chapters Three, Six and Seven; Carr-Hill and Drew 1988; Holdaway 1988, Chapter Six; Jefferson 1988; Walker 1983; 1987; 1988.

6 *Home Office Statistical Bulletin*, 'Crime Statistics for the Metropolitan Police District by Ethnic Groups 1987', 10 March 1989.

7 Black people are also more likely to make serious complaints against the police, but less likely to have them sustained (Stevens and Willis 1981).

8 This is further confirmed in a recent West Yorkshire study of sentencing: Voakes and Fowler 1989.

References

Baldwin, J. and McConville, M. (1979) *Jury Trials*, Oxford: Oxford University Press

Benyon, J. (ed) (1981) *Scarman and After*, Oxford: Pergamon Press

Benyon, J. (1986) *A Tale of Failure: Race and Policing*, Policy Papers in Ethnic Relations No. 3, Coventry: University of Warwick

Benyon, J. and Solomos, J. (eds) (1986) *The Roots of Urban Unrest*. Oxford: Pergamon Press

Black, D. (1980) *The Manners and Customs of the Police*, New York: Academic Press

Black, D. and Reiss, A. (1967) *Studies of Crime and Law Enforcement in Major Metropolitan Areas*, Washington D.C.: Government Printing Office

Blom-Cooper, L. and Drabble, R. (1982) 'Police Perception of Crime', *British Journal of Criminology* 22(1): 184–7

Bottomley, A.K. and Pease, K. (1986) *Crime and Punishment: Interpreting the Data*, Milton Keynes: Open University Press

Bridges, L. (1983a) 'Extended Views: The British Left and "Law and Order"', *Sage Race Relations Abstracts*, February: 19–26

Bridges, L. (1983b) 'Policing the Urban Wasteland', *Race and Class*, XXV(2): 31–48

Brogden, A. (1981) '"Sus" is Dead: But What About "SAS"?', *New Community* 9(1): 44–52

Brogden, M., Jefferson, T. and Walklate, S. (1988) *Introducing Police Work*, London: Unwin Hyman

Brown, A. (1988) *Watching the Detectives*, London: Hodder and Stoughton

Brown, L. and Willis, A. (1985) 'Authoritarianism in British Police Recruits: Importation, Socialisation or Myth?', *Journal of Occupational Psychology* 58: 97–108

Bull, R. and Horncastle, P. (1989) 'An Evaluation of Human Awareness Training', in R. Morgan and D. Smith (eds), *Coming to Terms with Policing*, London: Routledge: 97–117

Cain, M. (1973) *Society and the Policeman's Role*, London: Routledge

Cain, M. and Sadigh, S. (1982) 'Racism, The Police and Community Policing: A Comment on the Scarman Report', *Journal of Law and Society* 9(1): 87–102

Carr-Hill, R. and Drew, D. (1988) 'Blacks, Police and Crime' in A. Bhat, R. Carr-Hill and S. Ohri (eds), *Britain's Black Population*, Aldershot: Gower: 29–60

Colman, A. and Gorman, L. (1982) 'Conservatism, Dogmatism and Authoritarianism in British Police Officers', *Sociology* 16(1): 1–11

Crow, I. (1987) 'Black People and Criminal Justice in the UK', *Howard Journal of Criminal Justice* 26(4): 303–314

Crow, I. and Cove, J. (1984) 'Ethnic Minorities and the Courts', Criminal Law Review: 413–417

Currie, E. (1985) *Confronting Crime*, New York: Pantheon

Curtis, L. (1989) 'Race and Violent Crime' in N.A. Weiner and M.E. Wolfgang (eds) *Violent Crime, Violent Criminals*, Beverly Hills: Sage: 139–170

de la Motta, K. (1984) *Blacks in the Criminal Justice System*, Aston University: M.Sc. Thesis

Fielding, N. (1988) *Joining Forces*, London: Routledge

Gaskell, G. (1986) 'Police and Black Youth', *Policing* 2(1): 26–34

Gaskell, G. and Smith, P. (1981) 'Alienated Black Youth: An Investigation of Conventional Wisdom Explanations', *New Community* 12(1): 66–74

Genders, E. and Player, E. (1988) *Race Relations in Prisons*, Oxford: Oxford University Press

Gifford, Lord (1986) *The Broadwater Farm Inquiry*, London: Karia Press

Gilroy, P. (1982) 'The Myth of Black Criminality', *Socialist Register 1982*, London: Merlin Press: 47–56

Gilroy, P. (1983) 'Police and Thieves' in Centre for Contemporary Culture Studies, *The Empire Strikes Back: Race and Racism in 1970s Britain*, London: Hutchinson: 143–82

Gilroy, P. (1987) *There Ain't No Black in the Union Jack*, London: Hutchinson

Gordon, P. (1983) *White Law*, London: Pluto Press

Graef, R. (1989) *Talking Blues*, London: Collins

Gutzmore, C. (1983) 'Capital, "Black Youth" and Crime', *Race and Class* XXV(2): 13–30

Hagan, J. (1988) *Structural Criminology*, Oxford: Polity Press

Hall, S., Critcher, C., Jefferson, T., Clarke, J. and Roberts, B. (1978) *Policing the Crisis, Mugging the State and Law and Order*, London: Macmillan

Holdaway, S. (1983) *Inside the British Police*, Oxford: Basil Blackwell

Holdaway, S. (1988) *Crime and Deviance*, London: Macmillan

Home Office (1989a) 'Crime Statistics for the Metropolitan Police by Ethnic Group', *Home Office Statistical Bulletin*, 10 March

Home Office (1989b) 'The Prison Population in 1988', *Home Office Statistical Bulletin*, 6 April

Jefferson, T. (1988) 'Race, Crime and Policing: Empirical, Theoretical and Methodological Issues', *International Journal of the Sociology of Law* 16: 521–539

Jencks, C. (1987) Review of 'Crime and Human Nature', *New York Review of Books*, 12 February: 33–41

Johnson, B. (1976) 'Taking Care of Labor', *Theory and Society* 3(1): 89–117

Jones, T., MacLean, B. and Young, J. (1986) *The Islington Crime Survey*, Aldershot: Gower

Kamin, L. (1986) 'Is Crime in the Genes?', *Scientific American*, March: 22–27

King, M. and Israel, M. (1989) 'The Pursuit of Excellence, or How Solicitors Maintain Racial Inequality', *New Community* 16(1)

King, M. and May, C. (1985) *Black Magistrates*, London: Cobden Trust

Lambert, J. (1970) *Crime, Police and Relations*, Oxford: Oxford University Press

Landau, S. (1981) 'Juveniles and the Police', *British Journal of Criminology* 21(1): 27–46

Landau, S. and Nathan, G. (1983) 'Selecting Delinquents for Cautioning in the London Metropolitan Area', *British Journal of Criminology* 28(2): 128–49

Lea, J. (1986) 'Police Racism: Some Theories and their Policy Implications' in R. Matthews and J. Young (eds) *Confronting Crime*, London: Sage: 145–166

Lea, J. and Young, J. (1981) 'The Riots in Britain 1981' in D. Cowell, T. Jones and J. Young (eds) *Policing the Riots*, London: Junction Books: 5–20

Lea, J. and Young, J. (1984) *What is to be done about Law and Order?* Harmondsworth: Penguin

Lee, J.A. (1981) 'Some Structural Aspects of Police Deviance in Relations with Minority Groups' in C.D. Shearing (ed) *Organisational Police Deviance*, Toronto: Butterworths: 49–82

Leman, N. (1986) 'The Origins of the Underclass', *Atlantic Monthly*, June: 31–55; July; 54–68

Mair, G. (1986) 'Ethnic Minorities and the Magistrates' Courts', *British Journal of Criminology*, 26(2): 147–155

McClintock, F.H. (1963) *Crimes of Violence*, London: MacMillan

McConville, M. and Baldwin, J. (1982) 'The Influence of Race on Sentencing in England', *Criminal Law Review*: 652–8

Race and criminal justice   21

Murray, C. (1984) *Losing Ground*, New York: Basic Books

Natonal Association for the Care and Resettlement of Offenders (1986) *Black People and the Criminal Justice System*, London: NACRO

National Association for the Care and Resettlement of Offenders (1989) *Race and Criminal Justice: A Way Forward*, London: NACRO

Oakley, R. (1989) *Employment in Police Forces: A Survey of Equal Opportunities*, London: Commission for Racial Equality

Pearson, G., Sampson, A., Blagg, H., Stubbs, P., Smith, D. (1989) 'Policing Racism', in R. Morgan and D. Smith (eds), *Coming to Terms with Policing*, London: Routledge: 118–137

Pinder, R. (1984) *Probation Work in a Multi Racial Society*, University of Leeds: Applied Anthropology Group

Reiner, R. (1978) *The Blue-Coated Workers*, Cambridge: Cambridge University Press

Reiner, R. (1985a) *The Politics of the Police*, Brighton: Wheatsheaf

Reiner, R. (1985b) 'Police and Race Relations', in J. Baxter and L. Koffman (eds) *Police: The Constitution and the Community*, Abingdon: Professional Books: 149–187

Reiner, R. (1989) 'Where the Buck Stops' in R. Morgan and D. Smith (eds), *Coming to Terms with Policing*, London: Routledge

Reiner, R. (forthcoming) 'Social Portrait of a Criminal Justice Elite: Chief Constables in England and Wales', in R. Reiner and M. Cross (eds), *Beyond Law and Order: Criminal Justice Policy and Politics into the 1990s*, London: Macmillan

Reiss, A.J. (1971) *The Police and the Pubic*, New Haven: Yale University Press

Sanders, A. (1985) 'Class Bias in Prosecutions', *Howard Journal of Criminal Justice* 24(3): 176–199

Sanders, A. (1987) 'Constructing the Case for the Prosecution', *Journal of Law and Society* 14(2): 229–253

Scarman, Lord (1981) *The Brixton Disorders*, Cmnd. 8427, London: HMSO

Skolnick, J. (1966) *Justice Without Trial*, New York: Wiley

Smith, D. and Gray, J. (1983) *Police and People in London*, London: Heinemann/Policy Studies Institute

Solomos, J. (1988) *Black Youth, Racism and the State*, Cambridge: Cambridge University Press

Southgate, P. and Ekblom, P. (1984) *Contacts Between Police and Public: Findings from the British Crime Survey*, Home Office Research Study 77, London: HMSO

Stevens, P. and Willis, C. (1979) *Race, Crime and Arrests*, Home Office Researchs Study 58, London: HMSO

Stevens, P. and Willis, C. (1981) *Ethnic Minorities and Complaints Against the Police*, Research and Planning Unit Paper 5, London: HMSO

Tuck, M. and Southgate, P. (1981) *Ethnic Minorities Crime and Policing*, Home Office Research Study 70, London: HMSO

Voakes, R. and Fowler, Q. (1989) *Sentencing, Race and Social Inquiry Reports*, West Yorkshire Probation Service

Walker, M. (1983) 'Some Problems in Interpreting Statistics Relating to Crime', *Journal of the Royal Statistical Society* (Series A), 146(3): 281–293

Walker, M. (1987) 'Interpreting Race and Crime Statistics', *Journal of the Royal Statistical Society* (Series A), 150(1): 39–56

Walker, M. (1988) 'The Court Disposal of Young Males By Race in London in 1983', *British Journal of Criminology* 28(4): 441–460

Waters, R. (1988) 'Race and the Criminal Justice Process: Two Empirical Studies on Social Inquiry Reports and Ethnic Minority Defendants', *British Journal of Criminology*, 28(1): 82–94

Westley, W. (1970) *Violence and the Police*, Cambridge, Mass.: MIT Press

Whitehouse, P. (1983) 'Race Bias and Social Inquiry Reports', *Probation Journal* 30: 43–49

Willis, C. (1983) *The Use, Effectiveness and Impact of Police Stop and Search Powers*, Research and Planning Unit Paper 15, London: HMSO

Wilson, D., Holdaway, S. and Spencer, C. (1984) 'Black Police in the UK', *Policing* 1(1): 20–30

Wilson, J.Q. and Herrnstein, R. (1985) *Crime and Human Nature*, New York: Simon and Schuster

[2]

Racial Disparities in the Criminal Justice System: A Summary

Joan Petersilia

This article summarizes a comprehensive examination of racial discrimination in the criminal justice systems of California, Michigan, and Texas. In each of those states, judges typically imposed heavier sentences on Hispanics and blacks than on whites convicted of comparable felonies and who had similar criminal records. Not only did these minorities receive harsher minimum sentences but they also served more time. It is chiefly at the sentencing stage where differential treatment is most pronounced. I discuss what could account for differences in sentencing, and suggest areas for future policy and research attention.

The United States criminal justice system allows policemen, prosecutors, judges and parole boards a great deal of discretion in handling most criminal cases. The statistics on minorities in prison have convinced many people that this discretion leads to discrimination. These statistics are, indeed, alarming.

As Figure 1 shows, blacks make up only 12% of the United States population, but 48% of the prison population. This seemingly outrageous disparity has prompted allegations that the police overarrest minorities, prosecutors pursue their cases more vigorously, judges sentence them more severely, and corrections officials make sure they stay incarcerated longer than whites. However, it is difficult to believe that discrimination in the United States is so vast as to produce such a disparity. Logic suggests and statistics show that much of this disparity is simply due to the much greater prevalence of crime among minorities than among whites. As Alfred Blumstein (1982) recently concluded, "racial differences in arrest alone account for the bulk of racial differences in incarceration."

The facts about traditional street crimes support this conclusion. An astonishing 51% of black males living in large cities are arrested at least

JOAN PETERSILIA: Senior Researcher, Criminal Justice Program at Rand Corporation, Santa Monica, California.

CRIME & DELINQUENCY, Vol. 31 No. 1, January 1985 15-34

16   **CRIME & DELINQUENCY / JANUARY 1985**

STUDY MOTIVATION

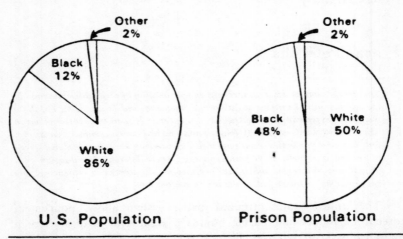

Figure 1:   Racial Distribution in the United States and the Prison Population

once for an index crime during their lives, compared to only 14% of white males. Fully 18% of black males serve time in prison or jail, either as juveniles or adults, compared with 3% of white males (Greenfield, 1981). Murder is the leading cause of death for young black males, and is almost as high for young black females.

Crime is a fact of life in the ghetto. Blacks and other minorities must cope with both crime and the criminal justice system much more than whites, with devastating effects on families, employment, and self-respect. This situation raises a vital question for criminal justice research: Does the American judicial system intensify the problem by discriminating against minorities in any way? The central issue for this study is not whether blacks and hispanics (in the general population) commit a disproportionate amount of crime, but whether, once arrested, the criminal justice system compounds the problem by treating them differently from whites.

The National Institute of Corrections supported this two-year study to answer three basic questions:

(1) Does the criminal justice system treat minorities differently from whites;

(2) If so, does that treatment reflect bias or the extent and seriousness of minority crimes;

(3) If the treatment reflects bias, how can that be corrected?

This article summarizes the study's main findings and policy implications. However, because the study deals with a complex and sensitive issue, interested readers are urged to read the full report, *Racial Disparities in the Criminal Justice System,* which describes the data, methodology, and findings in considerable, technical detail.[1]

DATA AND METHODS

Over the last three decades, social science researchers have addressed repeatedly the possibility of racial discrimination. Studies have offered evidence both for and against racial bias in arrest rates, prosecution, conviction, sentencing, corrections, and parole. There are many reasons for these contradictions. Some studies have data bases too small to permit any generalization. Others have failed to control for enough (or any) of the other factors that might account for apparent racial discrimination. Most studies have looked at only one or two levels of the system. And no studies have examined criminals' prearrest contact with the system—the point at which many believe the greatest racial differences in treatment exist.

We attempted to overcome those shortcomings by using data from official records and prisoner self-reports, by examining the evidence for discrimination throughout the criminal justice system, and by controlling for the major variables that might create the appearance of discrimination. Whenever the data were sufficient to do so, we used multiple regression analyses of system decisions and criminal behavior to control for the most obvious variables.

The study data came from two sources: the California Offender-Based Transaction Statistics (OBTS) for 1980, and the Rand Inmate Survey (RIS). The OBTS is a computerized information system maintained by the California Bureau of Criminal Statistics. It tracks offenders from arrest through sentencing (or presentencing release). Once an offender enters the system, a number of social and legal variables are recorded (e.g., sex, race, age, prior record, criminal status, and the original arrest offense). The OBTS also records the date of arrest and offense, conviction offense, date and point of disposition, type of proceeding, type of final sentence, and length of prison sentence.

The Rand Inmate Survey consists of data obtained from a self-administered questionnaire completed by a total of 1380 male prison inmates in California, Michigan, and Texas in 1978. Together, these three states house 22% of the national population of state prisons. In each state, the survey procedures produced a sample of inmates whose characteristics approximated the statewide intake of male prisoners. The self-reports elicited information about inmates' crimes, arrests, criminal motivations, drug and alcohol use, prior criminal record, participation in prison programs, institutional infractions, and the like.[2]

Because self-reports inevitably raise questions about the respondents' veracity, the survey was constructed to allow for both internal and external validity checks. The questionnaire included pairs of questions, widely separated, that asked for essentially the same information about crimes the respondents had committed and about other topics. This made it possible to check for internal quality (inconsistency, omission, and confusion). Over 83% of the respondents filled out the questionnaire accurately, completely, and consistently. The responses were not anonymous, and the official records serve not only as part of the analysis but also as an external check on the validity of the self-reports. Although the external check revealed more inconsistencies than the internal check, 59% of the respondents had an external error rate of less than 20%. However, for most disparities, the records were as questionable as the respondents' veracity. Records are often missing or incomplete, through no fault of the prisoners.[3]

The Rand Inmate Survey data permitted us to examine racial differences in crime commission rates—as opposed to arrest rates—and the probability of arrest. This information gave the study a considerable edge over much prior research because it provided a standard for assessing charges that minorities are overarrested. It also enabled us to examine questions of discrimination in corrections and length of sentence served, and of racial differences in crime motivation, weapon use, and in-prison behavior.

MAJOR FINDINGS

As Table 1 indicates, we found some racial differences in the criminal justice system's *handling* of offenders, but few statistically significant

TABLE 1
Summary of Study Findings

Element Studied	Evidence of Racial Differences[a]
Offender Behavior	
Preference for different crime types	+
Volume of crime committed	0
Crime motivation	++
Type of weapon preferred and extent of its use	++
Victim injury	+
Need for drug and alcohol treatment	0
Need for vocational training and education	+
Assessments of prison program effects	0
Arrest	
Probability of suffering arrest	0
Whether arrested on warrant or probable cause*	+
Probability of having case forwarded to prosecutor*	+
Prosecution and Sentencing	
Whether case is officially filed*	+
Type of charges filed*	0
Reasons for nonprosecution*	+
Whether the case is settled by plea bargaining*	+
Probability of conviction*	0
Type of crime convicted of*	0
Type of sentence imposed*	++
Length of sentence imposed	+
Corrections	
Type of programs participated in	0
Reasons for not participating in programs	0
Probability of having a work assignment	0
Length of sentence served	++
Extent and type of prison infractions	++

SOURCES: The OBTS for starred (*) items; the Rand Inmate Survey for all others.
a. 0 = none; + = suggestive trend; ++ = statistically significant.

racial differences in *criminal behavior* of active offenders. However, strong trends in some of the data raise important issues for policy and future research.

Racial Differences in Case Processing

As for racial differences in the disposition process, the OBTS data revealed an interesting pattern in California. As Table 2 shows, at the front end of the process, the system seems to treat white offenders more

TABLE 2
Racial Differences in Case Processing

| | Percentage At Each Stage | | |
Stage	White (N = 90, 865)	Black (N = 58, 683)	Hispanic (N = 39, 753)
Arrested "on warrant"	9	6	6
Arrested "on view"	91	94	94
Released without charges	20	32	27
Felony charges filed	38	35	35
Misdemeanor charges filed	41	33	37
Felony convictions	20	20	19
Convicted by plea bargain	92	85	87
Tried by jury	7	12	11
Sentenced to probation	21	15	12
Sentenced to prison	6	8	7

SOURCE: OBTS data for 1980.

severely and minority offenders more leniently; at the back end, the reverse is true.

White suspects are somewhat more likely than minority suspects to be arrested on warrant, and considerably less likely to be released without charges. Whites are also more likely than blacks or Hispanics to have felony charges filed. However, a greater percentage of whites arrested on felony charges are subsequently charged with misdemeanors, whereas blacks and Hispanics are less likely to have the seriousness of their cases thus reduced.

Once charged, offenders of all races have about the same chance of being convicted of a felony, but white defendants are more likely than minorities to be convicted by plea bargain. In contrast, minority defendants are more likely than whites to have their felony cases tried by jury. Although plea bargaining, by definition, ensures conviction, it also ensures a reduced charge or a lighter sentence, or both. Moreover, prior research indicates that defendants receive harsher sentences after conviction by juries. These differences may contribute to the racial difference in sentencing. The study found that after a misdemeanor conviction, white defendants had a greater chance than minority defendants of getting probation instead of jail. After a felony conviction, minority defendants were somewhat more likely to get prison instead of jail sentences.

These aggregate findings treat all felonies as if they were the same. If minority defendants had committed more serious felony offenses and had more serious prior records, we would expect their treatment to be more severe. Actually, minorities in the 1980 OBTS did have more serious prior records; a greater proportion of them had been charged with a violent crime; and a greater number were on probation or parole. However, by controlling for these factors using multiple regression techniques, we determined that the racial differences in postarrest and sentencing treatment still held.[4] White arrestees were more likely than minorities to be officially charged following arrest. Black arrestees were more likely to have their cases dismissed by either police or prosecutor. After charges were filed, the conviction rates were similar across the races, but more black defendants than whites or Hispanics were sentenced to prison.

Length of Court-Imposed Sentence Using RIS Data

Our analysis of the OBTS data yielded evidence of racial disparities in postarrest release rates and in type of sentence imposed. The latter, especially, seems to substantiate charges that the criminal justice system does sentence minorities to prison more often than it does whites. But what of sentence length? Critics have also repeatedly claimed that judges sentence minorities to longer terms. Although the scope of the study did not permit us to analyze all aspects of case processing in all three states, it did allow us to analyze and compare length of court-imposed sentences. Considering the seriousness of the issue, we preferred to use the Rand Inmate Survey data rather than limit the findings to one state.

To establish the minimum and maximum sentence imposed by the court for each inmate who completed the Rand Inmate Survey, we consulted his official corrections records. We used this information in separate regression analyses for the three states to assess possible racial disparities in those sentences. The regression models controlled for race, age, type of conviction crime, and number of previous juvenile and adult incarcerations. In all three states, we found that prior criminal record was not significantly related to *length* of court-imposed sentence. However, sentence length was significantly related to age and type of conviction crime. Further, the regression results indicate that, controlling for the defendant's age, conviction crime, and prior record, race made a difference in each state.

Although the relative lengths are not consistent for particular groups or states, these findings support charges that minorities receive longer

22   **CRIME & DELINQUENCY / JANUARY 1985**

TABLE 3
Additional Months Imposed and Served for Minorities

State	Court-Imposed Sentence	Length of Sentence Served
California		
Blacks	+1.4 months	+2.4 months*
Hispanics	+6.5 months*	+5.0 months*
Michigan		
Blacks	+7.2 months*	+1.7 months
Hispanics	(small sample)	(small sample)
Texas		
Blacks	+3.7 months	+7.7 months*
Hispanics	+2.0 months	+8.1 months*

*Statistically significant

sentences. In all three states, minority status alone accounted for an additional one to seven months in sentence length (see Table 3).

CORRECTIONS AND LENGTH OF SENTENCE SERVED

From arrest to sentencing, the system duly records most major decisions involving offenders. Consequently, it is rather easy to examine racial differences in handling. However, once a person is sentenced to prison, he is potentially subject to a range of decisions that are not systematically recorded. Prison guards and staff make decisions that influence strongly the quality of an offender's time in prison, and parole boards and other corrections officials decide how long that time lasts. The possibility of discrimination enters into all these decisions, but length of time served is the only one certain to be recorded. In other words, corrections is a closed world in which discrimination could flourish.

That charge has frequently been brought against the system, and the steady increase of prison racial problems makes it imperative to examine the treatment that different races receive in prison and at parole. We examined prison treatment and length of sentence served using the Rand Inmate Survey and the official records of our sample, where available. Our analysis revealed some racial differences for participation in work and treatment programs, but they were largely determined by the prisoners, not by guards or staff.

To create a larger framework for assessing possible discrimination, the study established criteria for identifying inmates who needed education, vocational training, and alcohol and drug treatment programs. We then compared the percentage who had need with the percentage that participated for each racial group.

Although there were no significant racial differences in the overall rate of program participation, there were some differences in participation, relative to need. In all three states, participation matched need most closely for education. In all three states, a greater percentage of minorities than of whites were identified as having high need for education. However, in Texas, blacks received significantly less education treatment. Moreover, in two of the study states, blacks had a significantly higher need for vocational training than whites or Hispanics, but did not have significantly higher participation rates. Compared with the other racial groups, blacks who needed alcohol treatment had a significantly lower participation rate.

Nevertheless, the reasons respondents gave for *not participating* suggested that minorities were discriminating against the programs, not vice versa. Prisoners most often said they were "too busy" or "didn't need" to participate; few said that they did not participate because staff discouraged them. The findings for work assignments were similar.

We found, however, that although minorities received roughly equal treatment in prison, race consistently made a difference when it came time for release. In Texas, blacks and Hispanics consistently served longer than whites—and the disparity was appreciably larger than the disparity in court-imposed sentences. In California, blacks served slightly longer sentences, but the disparity largely reflected the original sentencing differences. In Michigan, the parole process evidently worked in favor of blacks. Although their court-imposed sentences were considerably longer than those of whites, they did not actually serve longer (Table 3).

CRIME COMMISSION RATES AND PROBABILITY OF ARREST

To estimate whether minorities are overarrested *relative to the number of crimes they actually commit,* analysts need comparable "prearrest" information—variety of crimes committed, incidence of crime or crime commission rates, and the probability of arrest—-for white and minority arrestees. Although official records provide information on the crimes for which people are arrested and convicted, they provide no information on the number of other crimes these offenders commit. To overcome this problem, we used data from the RIS on the actual types and number of crimes that offenders reported committing in the 15-month period preceding their current imprisonment. Inmates also reported on the number of arrests for each kind of crime they had committed during the same period. Using this information, we estimated each offender's annualized crime rate. Our purpose was to estimate separately the range of crime types in the different racial groups, and then to estimate the probability that a single crime would result in arrest for members of that group. We found strong evidence that *in proportion to the kind and amount of crime they commit,* minorities are not being overarrested.[5]

There are racial differences in the range of crime *types* committed:

- More Hispanics reported committing personal crimes—both personal robberies and aggravated assault.

- More whites and Hispanics reported involvement in both drug dealing and burglary.

- Significantly more whites committed forgery and credit card and auto thefts.

We found few consistent, statistically significant, differences in *crime commission rates* among the racial groups. However, there were differences in rates for two particular crimes.

- Blacks reported committing fewer burglaries than whites or Hispanics.

- Hispanics reported fewer frauds and swindles than whites or blacks.

- Black and white offenders reported almost identical rates of robberies, grand larcenies, and auto thefts.

- Black and white offenders were involved in more drug deals than Hispanics, but the differences were not statistically significant.

That last finding illustrates the difference between range of criminality and incidence of crime. The findings on range indicate that more

Hispanics than blacks reported being involved in at least one drug deal. However, the annualized crime rates, which represent incidence, indicate that once involved in drug dealing, blacks committed more of it than Hispanics did.

Even though minorities are not overarrested relative to the number of crimes they commit, it is still possible that they have a higher *probability* than whites of being arrested for those crimes. Critics of the system have argued that this explains why blacks are "overrepresented" in the arrest and prison populations. We found, however, that the probability of being arrested for a crime is extremely low regardless of race. For example, only 6% of the burglaries, 21% of the business robberies, 5% of the forgeries, and less than 1% of the drug sales reported by these offenders resulted in arrest. This finding held for all racial groups. We found no statistically significant racial differences in arrest probability for the crimes we studied with the exception of personal robbery. For personal robbery, blacks and Hispanics did report suffering more arrests relative to the number of crimes they committed.

MOTIVATION, WEAPON USE, AND PRISON BEHAVIOR

Motivation, weapon use, and prison behavior seem likely to influence the impression a prisoner makes on probation officers, judges, and parole boards. Using RIS data, we examined these characteristics for racial differences that might help explain the differences we observed in sentencing and time served. The statistically significant differences were few and not very helpful in explaining those decisions.

All three racial groups rated economic distress as the primary motive for committing crime, with "high times" second and "temper" third. However, there was only one statistically significant difference in motivation: Whites rated "high times" much higher than blacks and Hispanics did. Nevertheless, there were some other, suggestive, differences. Blacks rated economic distress considerably higher than high times, whereas whites rated it only slightly higher. This suggests that socioeconomic conditions among blacks may be more consistently related to crime than they are among whites. That comes as no particular surprise; but if probation officers, judges, and parole boards

26   **CRIME & DELINQUENCY / JANUARY 1985**

see unemployment as an indicator or recidivism—rather than as a mitigating circumstance in crime—blacks or any unemployed offenders are likely to receive harsher sentences and serve longer.

In weapons use, the data revealed a few clear racial differences, but if those differences influence sentencing or parole decisions, they do so inconsistently. Hispanics are more likely than whites to be sent to prison and to stay there longer, and Hispanics show a statistically significant preference for using knives in all crimes. Moreover they indicated a greater tendency to injure their victims seriously. In contrast, the proportion of blacks in prison for burglary is considerably higher than the proportion of blacks arrested for that crime. Yet, in our sample, blacks were the least likely to be armed during burglaries. Indeed, they were less likely than whites to use guns and less likely than Hispanics to use knives. If these differences indicate that blacks are less violent and, perhaps, less "professional" than other groups, probation officers and judges apparently do not recognize it. Our findings on prison violence raise similarly conflicting suggestions.

The percentage of inmates with behavioral infractions differs markedly across states—significantly for five of the seven infraction types we studied. We therefore examined each state separately. Racial differences were pronounced for prison behavior. However, in all three states, age was most strongly, and negatively, correlated with higher infractions. Younger prisoners in all three states got into the most trouble. After age came race, but not consistently for all states. In California, white inmates had the highest infraction rate; in Texas, blacks did. The high-rate infractors had the following profiles:

- California: a young white inmate who has had limited exposure to treatment programs, and who currently has no prison work assignment.
- Michigan: a young inmate serving for nonviolent crime.
- Texas: a young black inmate with few serious convictions, who has had limited exposure to treatment programs and currently has no prison work assignment.

Racial differences in prison behavior had no apparent relation to length of sentence served. In California, whites have significantly higher infraction rates than blacks. In Texas, the reverse is true. Yet, in both states, blacks serve longer sentences. (In Michigan, where there were no statistically different racial differences in prison behavior, race also had no bearing on length of time served.)

We again advise the reader that, whenever the data were sufficient to do so, our analyses of system decisions and criminal behavior controlled for the major variables that could reasonably account for apparent racial differences. Because of data limitations, however, we were unable to control for all important factors such as strength of the evidence. We also want to stress again that both our findings and our conclusions reflect data from only three states. Further, our self-report data come from prisoners, and conclusions drawn from those data are not applicable to the criminal population at large.

EXPLAINING DISPARITIES IN CASE PROCESSING AND TIME SERVED

Our analysis of the RIS data found that minorities are not overrepresented in the arrest population, *relative to the number of crimes they actually commit,* nor are they more likely than whites to be arrested for those crimes. Nevertheless, the OBTS analysis raised a question that the study could not answer: If blacks and Hispanics are not being overarrested, why are police and prosecutors so much more likely to let them go without filing charges? One possibility is that the police more often arrest minorities on "probable-cause" evidence that subsequently fails to meet the filing standards of "evidence beyond a reasonable doubt."

Prior research may shed some light on this phenomenon. Earlier studies have shown that arrests depend heavily on witnesses' or victims' identifying or carefully describing the suspect (Greenwood, Chaiken, and Petersilia, 1977). Prosecutors may have a more difficult time making cases against minorities "beyond a reasonable doubt" because of problems with victim and witness identifications. Frequently, witnesses or victims who were supportive at the arrest stage become less cooperative as the case proceeds. Witness problems may be more prevalent in minority defendant cases.

In addition to "evidentiary" problems, the study found another racial difference in case processing that may help explain a small proportion of the high release rates for minorities. A slightly higher percentage of white suspects than blacks were arrested with a warrant in the study period. Because the criteria for issuing warrants are essentially the same as the criteria for filing charges, cases involving warrants would be less

28   **CRIME & DELINQUENCY / JANUARY 1985**

likely to develop evidentiary problems after arrest. However, there is only a 3 percentage point difference between whites and minorities for warrant arrests.

Nevertheless, the difference raises a provocative question. Why are the police more hesitant to arrest white than minority suspects without a warrant? From the release rates, it appears that the police and prosecutors have a harder time making a "fileable" case against minorities. Yet, by getting warrants more often to arrest whites, the police implicitly indicate that the reverse is true. Or, they may assume that minority suspects are less likely than white suspects to make false arrest charges or other kinds of trouble if a case is not filed.

Whatever their reasons, the racial differences in warrant arrests and release rates suggest that the police operate on different assumptions about minorities than about whites when they make arrests. Other study findings tend to reinforce the suggestion that the system regards minorities differently. Controlling for the factors most likely to influence sentencing and parole decisions, the analysis still found that blacks and Hispanics are less likely to be given probation, more likely to receive *prison* sentences, more likely to receive longer sentences, and more likely to serve a greater portion of their original time.

Possibly, the racial differences in type and length of sentence imposed reflect racial differences in plea bargaining and jury trials. Fully 92% of white defendants were convicted by plea bargaining, compared with 85% for blacks and 87% for Hispanics. Those numbers imply the percentage that engaged in plea bargaining since, by nature, plea bargaining virtually ensures conviction. However, it also virtually guarantees a reduced charge and/or lighter sentencing. Defendants who go to trial generally receive harsher sentences, and our study found that only 7% of whites prosecuted in Superior Court were tried by jury, compared with 12% for blacks and 11% for Hispanics.

However, even if these mechanisms did account for the apparent racial differences in sentencing, the implication of bias simply shifts to another node in the system. Why should minorities plea bargain less and go to jury trial more than whites? If the differences represent defendants' attitudes and decisions, then the system is not actively responsible for this racial difference. If these differences reflect decisions by prosecutors or decisions by default, then the issue of bias returns.

The suggestions that the system regards whites and minorities differently may enter into sentencing in another way. Judges may hesitate to send white defendants to prison for two reasons. First, research indicates that in prisons where whites are the minority, they are often victimized by the dominant racial group, whether black or Hispanic. In most states, blacks now outnumber whites in the prison population. Second, judges may regard whites as better candidates for rehabilitation.

INFORMATION USED IN SENTENCING AND PAROLE

Putting aside the ambiguity of findings about post-arrest release, the study found strong racial differences only in length and type of sentence imposed and length of time served. If there is discrimination in the system, it is inconsistent. Minorities are no more likely than whites to be arrested or convicted of crimes or to be treated differently by corrections. Yet, they are given longer, harsher sentences at conviction and wind up serving longer terms than whites in two of our study states. It may be possible to explain these inconsistencies by considering who makes decisions at key points in the system and what kinds of information they use to make those decisions.

As the accused moves through the system, more information about him is attached to his folder and that information is weighted differentially. Police and prosecutors are primarily concerned with "just desserts." Their legal mission is to ensure that criminals are convicted. They concentrate on the information they need to make arrest and conviction stick—primarily information about the crime and about the offender's prior record—according to strict legal rules. Judges also consider the nature of the crime and prior record in weighing just desserts, but they are further concerned with the defendant's potential for rehabilitation or recidivism. In other words, will returning him to society through probation or a lighter sentence endanger society? In deciding on probation, jail, or prison for an offender, they consider his conviction crime, prior record, and his personal and socioeconomic characteristics.

To provide the latter material, probation officers in most counties prepare a presentence investigation report (PSR), which contains a sentence recommendation. Probation officers are more concerned with analyzing and understanding the person and his situation, and they tend to deemphasize the legal technicalities necessary to assess guilt and convictability. The PSR describes factors such as the subject's family background, marital status, education and employment history, past encounters with the law, gang affiliation, and drug and alcohol abuse. In most states, it is the key document in sentencing and parole decisions. Its recommendations are generally followed by the sentencing judge, and its characterization of the defendant becomes the core of the parole board's case-summary file.

The influence of the PSR may help explain the racial differences in sentencing and time served. Minorities often do not show up well in PSR indicators of recidivism, such as family instability and unemployment. As a result, probation officers, judges, and parole boards are often impelled to identify minorities as higher risks.

These conjectures are supported by the comparison between length of sentence imposed and time served. In California, determinate sentencing practices make length of time served depend primarily on length of sentence imposed. Thus, racial differences in time served there, especially for Hispanics, reflect racial disparities in sentencing. Minority defendants also receive longer sentences than whites in Texas, and parole decisions there lengthen those sentences even more, relative to time served by whites. In Michigan, we found a reverse effect. Blacks received sentences 7.2 months longer than white defendants, but they served roughly equal time.

This contrast can perhaps be explained by the parole practices in Texas and Michigan. Texas has a very individualized, highly discretionary, parole process that incorporates the full range of an inmate's criminal history and personal and socioeconomic characteristics. Since 1976, Michigan parole decisions have been based almost exclusively on legal indicators of personal culpability such as juvenile record, violence of conviction crime, and prison behavior. Evidently, this practice not only overcomes racial disparities in time served, but also even overcomes racial disparities in sentencing. Nevertheless, overcoming racial disparities in sentencing is neither the primary, nor perhaps the proper, concern of parole boards. Their major responsibility is to decide whether an inmate can safely be returned to society. By putting aside the socioeconomic and other extra-legal indicators of recidivism, they may be setting potential recidivists loose.

ASSESSING THE INDICATORS OF RECIDIVISM

If the indicators of recidivism are valid, the criminal justice system is not discriminating against minorities in its sentencing and parole decisions: it is simply reflecting the larger racial problems of society. However, our research suggests that the indicators may be less objective (and certainly less "race-neutral") than past research and practice have indicated.

The overrepresentation of minorities in aggregate arrest statistics has tended to obscure the fact that the criminal justice system and criminal justice research are, nevertheless, dealing with a criminal population that is half white and half minority. Unless minorities in *that* population have had higher recidivism rates than whites, there is no reason why minorities should consistently be seen as presenting a higher risk of recidivism. There is clearly a much higher *prevalence* of crime within the minority portion of the national population—that prevalence largely accounts for their equal representation with whites in the criminal population. But there is no evidence that they have a higher recidivism rate.

The Rand Inmate Survey data indicate that, once involved in crime, whites and minorities in the sample had virtually the same annual crime commission rates. This accords with Blumstein and Graddy's (1982) finding that the recidivism rate for index offenses is approximately 0.85 *for both whites and nonwhites*. Thus, the data suggest that large racial differences in aggregate arrest rates must be attributed primarily to differences in *ever becoming involved in crime at all* and not to different patterns among those who do participate.

Under these circumstances, any empirically derived indicators of recividism should target a roughly equal number of whites and minorities. The reason this does not happen may be the relative sizes and diversity of the base populations. The black portion of the criminal population draws from a population base that is much smaller and more homogeneous, socioeconomically and culturally. That is, black criminals are more likely than their white counterparts to have common socioeconomic and cultural characteristics. The white half of the criminal population comes from a vastly larger, more heterogeneous base. Individuals in it are motivated variously, and come from many different cultural, ethnic, and economic backgrounds. Consequently, the characteristics associated with "black criminality" are more consistent, more visible, and more "countable" than those associated with white criminality. Moreover, because *prevalence* of crime is so much higher than incidence of crime (or recidivism) among minorities, characteristics associated with prevalence of crime among blacks (e.g., unemployment, family instability) may overwhelm indicators of prevalence for the entire criminal population. They may also mask indicators of recidivism common to both blacks and whites.

The findings on criminal motivation and economic need lend support to this hypothesis. Blacks rated economic stress much higher than "high times" and much higher than "temper" as their motive for committing crime. They also rated it more highly than either whites or Hispanics did. Moreover, the black inmates were consistently identified as economically distressed by the study's criteria for economic need. These findings imply that socioeconomic characteristics are more consistent and more consistently related to crime among blacks than they are among whites. Considering that blacks make up approximately half of the criminal population, their characteristics may have the same effect on indicators of prevalence and recidivism that the extremely high crime rates of a few individuals have on average crime rates.

This is a real vicious circle. As long as the "black experience" is conducive to crime, blacks will be identified as potential recidivists, will serve prison terms instead of jail terms, will serve longer time, and will thus be identified as more serious criminals.

IMPLICATIONS FOR FUTURE RESEARCH AND POLICY

These findings and conclusions suggest some important research needs and policy initiatives. Among the research priorities are the following:

- documenting the reasons for postarrest/prefiling release rates and controlling for race of the offender and type of arrest;
- analyzing postarrest problems with witnesses to discover whether and how the race of the suspect and/or of the witness affects cooperation;
- determining the relation of plea bargaining and jury trials to race, and why minority defendants are less likely to plea bargain; and
- establishing the reasons why minorities receive and serve longer sentences, paying particular attention to effects that length of court-imposed sentences, gang-related activities in prison, and prison infractions have on time served.

Although these and other issues deserve research attention, we believe that understanding why recidivism indicators more often work against minorities has particular priority. The system is moving to heavier reliance on these indicators precisely to render sentencing and parole decisions more objective. Paradoxically, just the opposite may result if, as we suspect, some of these indicators overlap with race in ways largely unrelated to recidivism.

Definitive policy recommendations will not be possible until some of these research tasks are completed, but three interim policy initiatives may be useful:

- Police and prosecutors should take into account the obstacles to filing charges after minority arrests, particularly the problems with witnesses, and try to find ways of ensuring that prearrest identifications will hold firm.

- Plea bargaining needs close monitoring, perhaps by a single deputy, for indications that minority defendants are consistently offered less attractive bargains than whites.

- Until the quality and predictive weight of recidivism indicators can be tested, probation officers, judges, and parole boards should give more weight to indicators of personal culpability than to indicators based on group classifications, such as education and family status.

Although this study shows that minorities are treated differently at a few points in the criminal justice system, it has not found evidence that this results from widespread and consistent racial prejudice in the system. Racial disparities seem to have developed because procedures were adopted without systematic attempts to find out whether they might affect various races differently. Consequently, future research and policy should be concerned with looking behind the scenes at the key actors in the system and their decisionmaking process, primarily at the kind of information they use, how valid it is, and whether its use affects particular racial groups unfairly.

NOTES

1. Copies of the complete report can be obtained by writing Joan Petersilia, The Rand Corporation, Santa Monica, California, 90406-2078.

2. For researchers with a special interest in Rand's inmate survey itself, a discussion of the method and content and a description of the objectives are detailed by Mark Peterson et al. (1982).

3. For a complete discussion of the validity of the Rand Inmate Survey, see Chaiken and Chaiken (1982) and Marquis and Ebener (1981).

4. Previous research using the OBTS file has shown significant differences in the processing of defendants from different counties and arrested for different crimes.

Consequently, for the regression analysis, we wanted a sample from the same county and charged with the same crime. We were able to obtain a large homogeneous sample (n = 6652) by selecting defendants who were charged with robbery in Los Angeles County in 1980.

5. The Rand Inmate Survey has certain limitations as a means of calculating crime rates and of detecting racial differences in these rates. All the respondents were in prison and the sample was chosen to represent each state's male prison population. Therefore, it is not appropriate to view these crime rates as applicable to offenders in the community. They refer only to a cohort of incoming prisoners in the states chosen for this study. Selection effects and other factors cause these rates to be substantially higher than those for "typical" offenders (Rolph, Chaiken, and Houchens, 1981).

REFERENCES

Blumstein, A.
   1982   "On the racial disproportionality of United States prison populations." The J.
           of Criminal Law and Criminology 73: 3.
Blumstein, A. and E. Graddy
   1982   "Prevalence and recidivism in index arrests: A feedback model approach." Law
           and Society Rev. 16: 2.
Chaiken, J. and M. Chaiken
   1982   Varieties of Criminal Behavior. Santa Monica, CA: Rand Corporation.
           R-2814-NIJ.
Greenfeld, L.
   1981   "Measuring the application and use of punishment." Washington, DC:
           National Institute of Justice.
Greenwood, P., J. Chaiken, and J. Petersilia
   1977   The Criminal Investigation Process, Lexington, MA: D. C. Heath and
           Company.
Marquis, K. and P. Ebener
   1981   Quality of Prisoner Self-Reports: Arrest and Conviction Response Errors.
           Santa Monica, CA: Rand Corporation, R-2637-DOJ.
Peterson, M. et al.
   1982   Survey of Prison and Jail Inmates: Background and Method. Santa Monica,
           CA: Rand Corporation, N-1635-NIJ.
Rolph, J., J. Chaiken, and R. Houchens
   1981   Methods for Estimating Crime Rates of Individuals. Santa Monica, CA: Rand
           Corporation, R-2730-NIJ.

Part I
Do the Courts Discriminate?

[3]

RACIAL DISCRIMINATION IN CRIMINAL SENTENCING: A CRITICAL EVALUATION OF THE EVIDENCE WITH ADDITIONAL EVIDENCE ON THE DEATH PENALTY*

GARY KLECK
Florida State University

Reevaluation of published research on racial bias in criminal sentencing and of data on execution rates by race from 1930 to 1967 and on death-sentencing rates from 1967 to 1978 indicates that, except in the South, black homicide offenders have been less likely than whites to receive a death sentence or be executed. For the 11% of executions imposed for rape, discrimination against black defendants who had raped white victims was substantial, but only in the South. Evidence for noncapital sentencing also largely contradicts a hypothesis of overt discrimination against black defendants. Although black offender–white victim crimes are generally punished more severely than crimes involving other racial combinations, this appears to be due to legally relevant factors related to such offenses. Crimes with black victims, however, are less likely than those with white victims to result in imposition of the death penalty. The devalued status of black crime victims is one of several hypothetical explanations of the more lenient sentencing of black defendants.

The legitimacy of the legal systems of modern democracies depends heavily on the degree to which the systems operate in a manner consistent with their own stated procedural standards of justice. It has been argued that Western societies, including the United States, are undergoing a "legitimation crisis" and that this is occurring specifically in criminal justice systems at least partly because they fail to live up to their stated commitments to treatment of defendants without regard to ascribed personal characteristics such as race, ethnicity, and gender or partially ascribed characteristics such as status or class position (Quinney, 1974; Chambliss and Seidman, 1971).[1]

It is widely believed, and frequently stated, that the criminal justice system has been in the past, and remains, racially discriminatory (e.g., Sutherland and Cressey, 1970; Clark, 1970). The most frequently cited category of evidence for this assertion has been research indicating more severe sentencing of black criminal defendants than white defendants, especially in imposition of the death penalty. As there have been at least sixty empirical studies of adult criminal sentencing published which refer to race, it is not surprising that at least one critic of the criminal justice system has asserted that evidence on racial discrimination in sentencing is probably the strongest evidence of racial bias in the criminal justice system (Overby, 1971:575). Because the outcomes of sentencing decisions are among the most visible of legal processing, the legal system's claim to legitimacy is especially dependent on the public's perception of the pattern of such outcomes. Therefore, it seems particularly important to take a close look at evidence bearing on this issue.

The first part of this paper attempts a comprehensive assessment of the published scholarly empirical research on racial bias in criminal sentencing in the U.S. in connection with both capital punishment and noncapital sentencing. One of the principal sources of distortion regarding this issue in the past has been selective citation of studies supporting one position or another; therefore, great care has been

---

* Direct all correspondence to Gary Kleck, School of Criminology: Florida State University, Tallahassee, Florida 32306.

[1] As used in this paper the word "race" is socially defined, referring to 'a human group that defines itself and/or is defined by other groups as different from other groups by virtue of innate and immutable physical characteristics" (van den Berghe, 1967:9).

taken to be as exhaustive as possible in finding relevant studies. The second part of the paper presents new evidence on race and capital punishment, consisting of an analysis of execution rates for blacks and whites over the period 1930 to 1967, for the United States as a whole and for the South, and of death-sentencing rates for the period from 1967 to 1978.

The Varieties of Racial Bias: Some Conceptual Distinctions

At least five different practices can produce racial differentials in criminal sentences which are likely to be viewed as illegitimate or unjust.

(1) *Overt racial discrimination against minority defendants.* This refers to the imposition of more severe dispositions on members of a subordinate racial group, independent of their legally relevant individual merits, and primarily as a direct result of the conscious or unconscious racial prejudice of the sentencing decisionmakers.

(2) *Disregard for minority crime victims.* This would include the failure to sentence offenders (of any race) who victimize minority-group members as severely as those who victimize nonminority-group members.

(3) *Class discrimination.* This refers to more severe treatment of lower-class defendants as a consequence of class prejudice. It may be due to hostility or indifference of middle-class decisionmakers toward culturally different defendants, or because lower-class defendants better fit popular stereotypes of serious or dangerous criminals. Because blacks in the United States are disproportionately members of the lower class, class discrimination would affect them more heavily than whites, independent of any overt racial discrimination. This assumes that among the set of criminal defendants blacks are more likely to be lower class than whites, a debatable assumption considering the overwhelmingly lower-class character of criminal defendants of all races.

(4) *Economic discrimination.* When a society's legal system is structured so that significant private economic resources are required in order to effectively obtain full legal protection, this constitutes economic discrimination, even where there is no class discrimination (as defined above). If low-income defendants receive more severe sentences than middle-income defendants because they cannot afford to hire an outside private attorney or cannot make bail, this constitutes economic discrimination and could produce racial differentials in sentencing outcomes.

(5) *Institutional Racism.* This refers to the application, possibly in a universalistic fashion, of decisionmaking standards which in themselves have considerable consensual support (possibly even among minority members) but which result in less favorable outcomes for minority defendants. As used in the past, the term seems to have referred to, among other things, practices (2) through (4); but institutional racism in sentencing can take other forms as well. For example, if racial-minority defendants are likelier to have prior criminal convictions, then the use of prior record as a criterion for sentence determination will tend to produce less favorable outcomes for minority defendants and would therefore be an instance of institutional racism (for this view, see Burke and Turk, 1975, or Farrell and Swigert, 1978a). The establishment, by legislatures, of higher statutory penalties for crimes committed more frequently by racial-minority members than by others (such as violent interpersonal crimes) would also constitute institutional racism, regardless of the behavior of judges, prosecutors, and others who influence sentencing outcomes.

For the sake of verbal and conceptual clarity, it is misleading to label either (3) or (4) "racial" bias or discrimination. Although clearly unjust and certainly related to race in the United States, these practices are not directly racial in themselves, since they affect whites as well as blacks and could occur in jurisdictions or societies where no racial distinctions of any sort were made. Therefore, although reference will be made to them in examining the evidence regarding overt racial discrimination, these practices are not themselves primary objects of the analysis.

RACIAL DISCRIMINATION IN CRIMINAL SENTENCING 785

The concept of institutional racism is highly problematical. It is so flexible that any practice producing unfavorable sentencing outcomes for racial-minority members can be characterized as racist, no matter how the outcomes were produced, whether they were intentionally sought, and regardless of what criteria were involved in the decisions producing the outcomes. Any pattern of sentencing involving the crimes commonly dealt with by U.S. criminal courts could be construed as institutional racism, since blacks commit a disproportionate share of such crimes relative to their share of the population (see Hindelang, 1978, for a thorough discussion of the evidence for this statement) and therefore are bound to receive a disproportionate share of the criminal punishment, no matter how fairly the sentencing process is administered. Only an alteration of the social conditions producing differentials in the racial distribution of criminal behavior or a radical redefinition of which crimes the courts focus on could eliminate institutional racism of this sort. For these reasons, neither this study nor any other study of sentencing per se could reject the hypothesis of institutional racism in sentencing. Consequently, attention in this analysis will be primarily focused on overt racial discrimination and secondarily on disregard for minority crime victims.

ASSESSMENT OF PRIOR RESEARCH

This review is intended to be an exhaustive assessment of all scholarly empirical studies of race and criminal sentencing of adults in the United States published up through 1979. It does not cover the few studies relating ethnicity and sentencing, such as Castberg (1971) or Hall and Simkus (1975), nor studies of conviction, as opposed to sentencing, such as Forslund (1969). It does cover studies of the determination of degree of homicide of which defendants were convicted, such as Farrell and Swigert (1978a; 1978b), since such a determination is tantamount to determination of sentence. Also included are studies of commutations of death sentences, as these have commonly been cited as sentencing studies.

When two or more studies of the same data set, using very similar methods, have been published, only one is included, or the studies are treated as a single study (e.g., Wolfgang and Riedel, 1973 and 1975; Farrell and Swigert, 1978a and 1978b, and Swigert and Farrell, 1977; Lotz and Hewitt, 1977 and Hewitt, 1976). Studies of juvenile court dispositions are excluded since, properly speaking, juveniles are not sentenced to criminal penalties and determination of disposition is in any case substantially different from the adult sentencing process.[2] Further, the following kinds of studies are excluded: anecdotal or journalistic accounts, case studies, hypothetical-case sentencing studies (e.g., Johnston et al., 1973), purely theoretical studies, and other reviews of the literature. The review also ignores studies such as those of Sellin (1928, 1935) which simply compare sentence lengths of persons sentenced or executed, without any comparison to numbers arrested, convicted, etc. Finally, unpublished studies such as dissertations are excluded because the availability of such material is limited.[3]

Studies which fit the selection criteria were located through an iterative search process. An initial list of relevant studies was compiled through a search of Sociological Abstracts, Crime and Delinquency Abstracts, Legal Abstracts, and Hagan's (1974) bibliography. (About one-third of the studies reviewed here were also included in Hagan's review.)

---

[2] Liska and Tausig (1979) reviewed eight studies which examined race and juvenile court dispositions, noting that five of them show a significant race effect in the conventionally expected direction. However, only two of the five simultaneously controlled for offense seriousness and prior record. The crude state of research in this field is also indicated by the almost complete absence of attention to controlling for effects of juveniles' family circumstances or disposition. Although the philosophy of the juvenile court explicitly defines family stability as a legitimate factor to be considered, Liska and Tausig do not say a word suggesting that racial differences in family intactness could account for differences in juvenile court dispositions.

[3] However, for a sampling of recent doctoral dissertation on the subject the reader may consult Dison (1976), Hutner (1977), and San Marco (1979). A reading of their abstracts indicates findings highly congruent with the conclusion of my review.

Then the references listed in each of these studies were examined for further relevant studies, and so on, until no further leads were uncovered.

Capital Punishment Sentencing Studies

Table 1 summarizes in compact form the prior scholarly empirical research on racial discrimination and use of the death penalty, first regarding murder and then rape. The last column indicates whether racial differences were statistically significant and in the predicted direction. In a minority of studies my assessment of the evidence presented in a study differs from that of the authors. Two examples of this are noteworthy.

Bedau (1964) concluded that there was racial bias in the final disposition of persons sentenced to death, despite his own acknowledgment that his data showed no significant relationship between race and final disposition, and despite the fact that the observed relationship was in the opposite direction to that indicating discrimination against nonwhites. In New Jersey 66.2% of nonwhites sentenced to die were executed, compared to 68.4% of whites (Bedau, 1964:19). Further, Bedau claimed there was no significant relationship between race and execution when felony and nonfelony murders were separated, but reanalysis of his data reveals that in fact nonwhite murderers were significantly less likely to be executed for felony killings than were white felony murderers (χ^2 = 8.114, 1 degree of freedom, p = .01). There was no race difference for nonfelony killings.

Bowers (1974:81–107) claimed to have found evidence which pointed "unmistakably to a pattern of racial discrimination in the administration of capital punishment in America" (p. 10). His conclusion was not limited to the South or to use of the death penalty for rape, although he laid particular stress on these areas. Regarding racial bias in use of the death penalty for murder, the evidence that Bowers produced was of two kinds: he argued first that the lower mean age at execution of nonwhites compared to whites was evidence of racial discrimination, and, sec-

ond, that the lower percentage of cases appealed by nonwhites compared to whites indicated discrimination. While Bowers acknowledged that the age differentials at execution may simply reflect age differences at commission of the offense and arrest, he argued that the difference at arrest was not as large as that at execution. In fact, there was a 2.4 year difference in mean age at execution in Bowers' data (p. 80), while Wolfgang's (1958:70) homicide arrest data indicate an almost identical 2.3 year difference in the median age of black and white male homicide arrestees. Regarding the data on appeals, racial differentials in percentage receiving appeals of death sentences for murder since 1940 are largely confined to the South (see especially Bowers' Table 3–9), consistent with our interpretation of the findings of previous death-penalty discrimination studies. Nevertheless, Bowers concludes that, as indicated by age differentials at execution and differentials in percentage receiving higher appeals, "racial discrimination in northern and western states began to rival that in the South, at least for the period of decline in capital punishment" (1974:104).

Probably the most serious shortcoming of death-penalty discrimination studies is that they nearly all fail to control for prior criminal record. The one study which introduced such a control, Judson et al. (1969), found no evidence of racial discrimination, suggesting that apparent racial differences in other studies may actually have been due to racial differences in prior criminal activity. This hypothesis is supported by Wolfgang's (1958:175–6) findings that black homicide offenders were significantly more likely to have previous criminal arrest records than white homicide offenders. It is further supported by Hagan's (1974:366–8) reanalysis of Nagel (1969), which indicated that where crude controls for prior record (record/no record) were introduced, racial effects shrank. Where more adequate controls for prior record (number of prior convictions) were introduced, the racial difference disappeared altogether (Judson et al., 1969:1366–76), suggesting that the dichotomous measure of prior record may be inadequate for

Table 1. Empirical Studies of Racial Discrimination and the Death Penalty

Study	Jurisdiction(s)	Time Period Covered	Dependent Variables	Variables Controlled	Race Relationship Significant?
Murder:					
Mangum (1940)	9 Southern States	1909–1938	Executed/commuted	None	Yes
Johnson, G. (1941)	N. Carolina	1933–1939	Sentence; executed/commuted	None	Sentence, yes/no[a]; exec./commuted, no
Garfinkel (1949)	N. Carolina	1930–1940	Charge, conviction, sentence	Degree of Homicide	Yes/No[a]
Johnson, E. (1957)	N. Carolina	1909–1954	% executed, admissions to death row	None	Yes
Bensing & Schroeder (1960)	Cleveland	1947–1953	Death sentence/other	Degree of Homicide	No
Bridge & Mosure (1961)	Ohio	1950–1959	Executed/commuted	None	Yes
Wolfgang et al. (1962)	Pennsylvania	1914–1958	Executed/commuted	Felony/nonfelony, type of counsel[b]	Felony, yes; nonfelony, no
Bedau (1964)	New Jersey	1907–1960	Executed/commuted	Felony/nonfelony	No
Wolf (1964)	New Jersey	1938–1961	Death sentence/life imprisonment	Felony/nonfelony	No
Bedau (1965)	Oregon	1903–1964	Executed/commuted	None	No
Judson et al. (1969)	California	1958–1966	Death sentence/other sentence (imposed by penalty jury)	Prior record, occupation, characteristics of offense, and others	No
Bowers (1974)	U.S.	1864–1967	Appeal of death sentence	Region	In the South, yes; elsewhere, no
Rape:					
Johnson, O. [1951] (1970)	Louisiana	1900–1950	Executed/commuted	None	Yes
Johnson, E. (1957)	N. Carolina	1909–1954	% executed, admissions to death row	None	No
Florida Civil Liberties Union (1964)	Florida	1950–1964	Death sentence/other	None	Yes
Partington (1965)	Virginia	1908–1963	Death sentence/other	Type of rape	Yes
Wolfgang & Reidel (1973; 1975)	6 Southern States[c]	1945–1965	Death sentence/other	Contemporaneous offense/no contemporaneous offense	Yes

[a] There were no significant differences between black killers as a group and white killers as a group, but when offender/victim racial relationship was examined, blacks who killed whites were found to have received significantly more death sentences than the other three groups.

[b] Not controlled for simultaneously.

[c] Data were gathered on 11 states, but published results refer only to 6 states for some tables, 5 for other, 3 for yet other tables. Reidel has informed the author that the data for this study were partially destroyed in a fire, accounting for the fragmented data analysis. The 1975 study is simply an analysis of a subset of the data analyzed in the 1973 study; therefore, the two are treated as a single study.

control purposes (see also Green, 1961:11 on this point).

All of the studies purporting to find racial bias in use of the death penalty for murder failed to control for income, class, or occupation of the defendants.[4] However, the most methodologically sophisticated study of the subject, which did control for defendant's occupation, found no racial effect on whether or not a death sentence was imposed for murder by California penalty juries (Judson et al., 1969:1366–76). Further, they found no relationship between the victim/offender racial relationship and sentence imposed, suggesting that the findings of Johnson (1941) and Garfinkel (1949) may have reflected regional and temporal peculiarities characteristic of North Carolina (or more generally, the South) in the 1930s and earlier.

Several points should be noted about the pattern of findings on discrimination in use of the death penalty for murder. First, every single study consistently indicating discrimination towards blacks was based on older data from Southern states, and three of these four studies were based on overlapping data from North Carolina. Second, all of the studies finding discrimination in administration of capital punishment for murder were not in fact studies of sentencing, although most of them have been cited in the research literature as if they were. Mangum (1940), Johnson (1957), Wolfgang et al. (1962), and Bridge and Mosure (1961) all studied commutation of death sentences, not sentencing itself, while Bowers' (1974) data largely concerned appeals of death sentences. Third, all of these studies failed to control for prior criminal record of the defendant, for the defendant's class or income, or for the distinction between felony and nonfelony killings. Since studies which do introduce such controls find that they reduce the sentencing differentials between blacks and whites (Green, 1961;

---

[4] Although both Wolfgang et al. (1962) and Johnson (1957) had data on occupation of offenders as well as race, they did not attempt to simultaneously control for race and occupation. No explanation of this conspicuous omission was offered in either study.

Judson et al., 1969; Nagel, 1969), even in the South the racial differential may have been due to differences in criminal record, income, or type of homicide committed rather than discrimination. The evidence considered as a whole indicates no racial discrimination in use of the death penalty for murder outside the South, and even for the South empirical support for the discrimination hypothesis is weak.

Regarding the use of capital punishment for rape, the evidence strongly suggests overt discrimination against black defendants. Four of the studies of this issue found evidence of discrimination, while the relationship between race and the carrying out of the death sentence (as opposed to commutation of the sentence) was not significant in the Johnson (1957) study, according to Hagan's (1964:370) reanalysis. The relationships found in the other four studies (Johnson, 1970; Florida Civil Liberties Union, 1964; Partington, 1965; Wolfgang and Reidel, 1973, 1975) are very strong, and the evidence indicates that the death penalty for rape was largely used for punishing blacks who had raped whites. Although all of these studies were methodologically crude, it is doubtful if additional controls could eliminate the huge racial differentials in use of the death penalty. The importance of this conclusion, however, is limited by several facts. First, the death penalty has rarely been used to punish rape. Only 11.8% of the executions from 1930 to the present were for rape. Virtually all the rest were for murder. Second, the use of the death penalty for rapes has always been, at least since national data on executions were first gathered in 1930, strictly a peculiarity of the South. Not a single execution for rape occurred outside the South or the border states during that period (U.S. Federal Bureau of Prisons, 1970). Third, the imposition of death sentences for rape has virtually disappeared. Of the 183 persons who were sentenced to death during 1978, only one was sentenced for rape (U.S. NCJISS, 1979:25). Thus, the rape discrimination conclusion is of historical significance with regard to capital punishment in the South, but has limited relevance to current debates over capital punishment, especially since the United

RACIAL DISCRIMINATION IN CRIMINAL SENTENCING 789

States Supreme Court declared, in Coker vs. Georgia (1977), that the use of the death penalty for the rape of an adult woman was a disproportionate penalty and therefore unconstitutional (U.S. NCJISS, 1979:2).

Noncapital Punishment Sentencing Studies

Table 2 summarizes the empirical research on sentencing involving penalties other than the death penalty. The results of each study are simply summarized in the last column of the table ("Discrimination?"), with each study characterized as to whether its findings largely supported a discrimination hypothesis (indicated by "Yes"), were mostly inconsistent with such a hypothesis ("No"), or were only partially consistent with the hypothesis ("Mixed"). Mixed findings most frequently occurred when more than one crime was studied, when sentencing patterns of a number of judges were reviewed, or when more than one measure of sentencing outcome was examined.

Studies were classified, in somewhat arbitrary fashion, according to what proportion of their findings were in favor of the discrimination hypothesis. They were characterized as mixed if from one-third to one-half (inclusive) of the findings favored the discrimination hypothesis and as favorable to the hypothesis if more than one-half of the findings favored it. For example, if a study examined eight different offenses, it would be labelled "Yes" if evidence of bias against black defendants was found for four or more offenses, as "Mixed" if such evidence was found for three of the offenses, and as "No" if two or fewer offenses showed such evidence. Since it could be argued that evidence of discrimination even for one crime or sentence-outcome measure out of many is evidence worth taking very seriously, readers must judge for themselves the significance of the "mixed" findings.[5]

Under the heading "Sentencing Measure" in Table 2, the dependent variable in each study is noted. The term "disposition" indicates that the dependent variable distinguished between categories like probation, jail sentence, prison sentence, etc., while "sentence severity" denotes a single scale of severity of disposition or sentence constructed by the researcher. The other terms are self-explanatory.

Table 2 also indicates whether the authors of these studies in any way controlled for the type of criminal offense involved. In those studies where only one type of crime was involved, or where several very similar offenses were studied, such a control was obviously unnecessary. However, where several different offense types were lumped together, as in Cargan and Coates (1974) or Pope (1975a), differences in sentence received by black and white defendants could be at least partly attributable to differences in the seriousness of the types of offenses for which they were prosecuted.

Of the 40 studies listed in Table 2, only eight consistently support the racial discrimination hypothesis, while 12 are mixed and the remaining 20 produced evidence consistently contrary to the hypothesis. Since a study's findings were characterized as mixed even if as few as a third of them favored the discrimination hypothesis, this means that a substantial majority of all of the findings of these 40 studies contradicted the hypothesis. However, the evidence for the hypothesis is even weaker than these numbers suggest, since of the minority of studies which produced findings apparently in support of the hypothesis, most either failed completely to control for prior criminal record of the defendant, or did so using the crudest possible measure of prior record—a simple dichotomy distinguishing defendants with some record from those without one. This is probably the most important flaw in studies drawing a conclusion of racial discrimination,

---

[5] Use of these standards occasionally resulted in characterizations of findings which differed from those of the original authors (e.g., Bedau, 1964). Since I attempted to accurately reflect the studies' theoretical or ideological preferences, when the original authors' conclusions did not seem congruent with their data, their conclusions were discounted. Skeptical readers are encouraged to examine the original studies in order to judge for themselves the accuracy of my characterizations.

Table 2. Race and Noncapital Sentencing

Study	Jurisdiction(s)	Time Period Covered	Sentencing Measure	Offenses Involved	Control for Offense Type?	Measure of Prior Record	Discrimination?
Martin (1935)	Texas	1930	Sentence	Various	Yes	None	Yes
Lemert & Rosberg (1948)	Los Angeles	1938	Prison sentence/other; sentence length	Various	Yes	No record/minor record/prior felony	Mixed
Bullock (1961)	Texas	1958 & before[a]	Prison sentence less than 10 yrs./over 10 yrs.	Burglary, rape, murder	Yes	None	Mixed
Green (1961)	Philadelphia	1956–57	Sentence	Burglary, robbery, theft misdemeanor	Yes	0–1 prior conviction/2+ prior convictions	No
Jacob (1962)	New Orleans	1954–60	Prison sentence greater than 1 yr/other	Various	Yes	None	Mixed
Cameron (1964)	Cook County (Chicago)	1943–50	% jail sentences; % 30 days or more	Shoplifting	+	None	Yes
Green (1964)	Philadelphia	1956–57	Sentence length	Robbery, burglary	Yes	Prior convictions	No
Howard (1967)	Baltimore	1962–66	Sentence length, type	Rape	+	None	Yes
Janos & Mendelsohn (1967)	Detroit	1966	% jailed, average fine	Traffic	No	None	No
Baab & Ferguson (1968)	27 counties in Texas	1966	Sentence severity	Various felonies	Yes	No. prior felony, misdemeanor convictions	No
Southern Regional Council (1969)	7 Southern states	1967 & before[a]	Sentence length	Various	Yes	1st offender/recidivist	Yes
Nagel (1969)	194 counties in 50 states; Federal	1962; 1963	Prison sentence/other; % prison sentence greater than 1 year	Assault, larceny	Yes	Prior conviction(s)/no prior convictions	Mixed
Atkinson & Newman (1970)	A major midwestern metropolitan center	c. 1968?	Fine, jail sentence/other	Nontraffic misdemeanors	No	None	No
Gerard & Terry (1970)	8 Missouri counties	1962	% prison/probation/fine	Various felonies	Yes	None	Yes
Mileski (1971)	"Middle-sized Eastern City"	c. 1969	Incarceration/other	Intoxication	+	Length and recency of prior record	No
Conklin (1972)	Boston	1964; 68	Disposition	Robbery	+	None	No
Levin (1972)	Minneapolis, Pittsburg	1966	Sentence length	Various	Yes	"prior record"	No
Rau (1972)	Federal	1967–70	% sentenced to prison, mean sentence length	Various	Yes	None	Mixed
Greenwood et al. (1973)	Los Angeles	1970	Sentence level (felony/misdemeanor)	Theft	+	None	No
Cargan and Coates (1974)	Montgomery County, Ohio	c. 1971–72	% sentenced to prison	Various felonies	No	None	Mixed

Study	Location	Years	Dependent variable	Offense type	Control variables	Controlled	Discrimination
Burke & Turk (1975)	Indianapolis	1964	Disposition	Various	Prior arrest/none	Yes	No
Chiricos & Waldo (1975)	N. Carolina / S. Carolina / Florida	1969–73 / 1969–70 / 1969–70	Sentence length	Various	Felony conviction/none, ≥5 arrests/<5 arrests, juvenile institutions/no record	Yes	No
Kulig (1975)	Douglas County, Nebraska	1970–72	Mean sentence, % receiving probation	Various	Low/med./high arrest record	Yes	Yes
Pope (1975a)	12 California counties	1969–71	Disposition	Various felonies	No arrests/some arrests; no prison/previous prison	No	Mixed
Pope (1975b)	12 California counties	1969–71	Disposition: sentence length	Burglary, assault	Same as above	Yes	No
Tiffany et al. (1975)	Federal	1967–68	Sentence length	Various	"Prior record"	Yes	Mixed
Clarke & Koch (1976)	Charlotte, N.C.	1971	Prison sentence/other	Burglary/larceny	Prior arrests	Yes	No
Kelly (1976)	Oklahoma	1974 & before[a]	Sentence length	Burglary, homicide	No prior convictions	Yes	Mixed
Rhodes (1976)	Minneapolis, St. Paul	1970	Prison sentence/other disposition	Various	Number & seriousness of prior convictions	Yes	Mixed
Zimring et al. (1976)	Philadelphia	1970	Death or life sentence/other prison	"Felony" murder	None	†	Yes
Bernstein et al. (1977)	City in N.Y. State	1974–75	Sentence disposition (7 levels)	Various	Weighted index of prior convictions	Yes	No
Lotz & Hewitt (1977)	King County, Washington	1973	Prison or jail/deferred, suspended sentence	Felonies	"Prior record"	Yes	No
Perry (1977)	U.S. Military	1972 & before	Sentence length	Various military offenses	None	Yes	No
Uhlman (1977)	"Major metropolitan center"	1968–74	Sentence length	Various	None	Yes	Yes
Farrell & Swigert (1978a; b)	"Large urban jurisdiction in N.E."	1955–73	Degree of homicide assigned	Homicides	None	†	No
Gibson (1978)	Atlanta	1968–70	% "severe sentences"	Various	Felony conviction/none	Yes	Mixed
Lizotte (1978)	Chicago	1971	Sentence length	Various	Arrest record/no record	Yes	Mixed
Sutton (1978)	Federal	1971	Disposition, sentence length	8 felonies	Conviction, incarceration	Yes	No
Foley & Rasche (1979)	Missouri	1959–74	Sentence length	Various felonies	None	Yes	No
Myers (1979)	Indianapolis	1974–76	Prison sentence/other sanction	Various felonies	Arrest/conviction/incarceration	Yes	No

[a] Sample of prisoners' records were examined in the year indicated, but the prisoners had been sentenced in that year and previous years.

† Only one offense type was studied, or offenses were so homogeneous that control for offense type or seriousness was unnecessary.

since the most methodologically sophisticated sentencing studies have consistently shown various measures of prior record to be either the strongest predictor, or among the strongest predictors, of sentences received (Chiricos and Waldo, 1975; Bernstein et al., 1977; Lotz and Hewitt, 1977; Lizotte, 1978). It appears to be the case that the more adequate the control for prior record, the less likely it is that a study will produce findings supporting a discrimination hypothesis.

Table 3 summarizes the whole body of prior research on race and sentencing, both capital and noncapital. Simply adding up the number of studies favoring or not favoring the discrimination hypothesis could be somewhat misleading, since some studies are clearly better than others and should therefore be weighted more heavily than others in assessing the body of evidence as a whole. Therefore, although it would be difficult to assign exact weights, some simple quality distinctions can be made, such as distinguishing between studies which control for prior criminal record and studies which do not. Regarding noncapital punishment, Table 3 makes clear the importance of such controls—one-third of the studies without a control for prior criminal record support a discrimination conclusion, while less than a tenth of those with such controls support a discrimination conclusion. Regarding capital punishment, separate tallies of studies with and without such controls are unnecessary, since only one study, that of Judson and his colleagues (1969), controlled for prior record, finding no evidence of racial discrimination either in the sentencing of black defendants in general or in sentencing of those who had victimized whites.

Interracial Relationship of Offender and Victim

It has long been argued that racial bias in sentencing is not to be detected only by looking at the race of the defendant, but by noting the racial relationship of the offender and the victim (e.g., Johnson, 1941). Specifically, it is asserted that crimes involving black offenders and white victims are punished more severely

Table 3. Summary of Prior Research

	Results			
	Yes	Mixed	No	Total
Capital Sentencing				
All Studies	7	4	6	17
Murder	3	4	5	12
Rape	4	0	1	5
Noncapital Sentencing				
All Studies	8	12	20	40
Control for prior record	2	8	13	23
No control for prior record	6	4	7	17

NOTE: See the discussion of prior literature in the text for an explanation of the classification of studies by their results.

than crimes involving the other three racial combinations, either because crimes involving black victims are taken less seriously or because the crossing of racial lines in the commission of a crime is taken very seriously (Johnson, 1941; Garfinkel, 1949). While black offender–white victim crimes, especially homicides and rapes, are punished more severely than crimes with other racial combinations, it is unclear whether this is due to the racial character of the crime, or to related, confounding factors. Black offender–white victim killings are more likely than other killings to involve an offender and a victim who are strangers to each other, and such killings are much more severely punished regardless of the races involved (Lundsgaarde. 1977:232). Such killings are also more likely to be committed in connection with some other felony, like robbery. Data in Block and Zimring (1973:8) indicate that for Chicago homicides in 1970, 38% of killings with black offenders and white victims were robbery killings, while only 5% of the white offender–white victim killings were robbery killings. Felony killings are punished more severely than other homicides, regardless of races involved (Wolfgang et al., 1962; Bedau, 1964; Wolf, 1964). Finally, black-white killings are less likely than black-black killings to be victim-precipitated, and victim-precipitated killings in turn are less likely to be premeditated (Wolfgang. 1958), leading one to expect less severe punishment of black-black killings for this reason, rather than the racial relationship per se. Eleven

RACIAL DISCRIMINATION IN CRIMINAL SENTENCING 793

studies have examined sentencing outcomes by racial combination, and of these, seven (Johnson, 1941; Garfinkel, 1949; Florida Civil Liberties Union, 1964; Howard, 1967; Southern Regional Council, 1969; Wolfgang and Reidel, 1973; Zimring et al., 1976) found more severe punishment for black-white offenses.[6] However, none of these studies controlled for the possibly confounding factors we have mentioned. The only four studies which did introduce such controls (Green, 1964; Judson et al., 1969; Farrell and Swigert, 1978b; Myers, 1979) all found no evidence of such sentencing patterns. Thus, consideration of the pattern of findings as a whole strongly suggests that the interracial relationship itself does not affect the sentencing decision, except in connection with the punishment of rape in the South (Florida Civil Liberties Union, 1964; Howard, 1967; and Wolfgang and Reidel, 1973, 1975 support this limited assertion of discrimination).

Examination of prior studies on the question of racial discrimination and use of the death penalty for murder has suggested that many of their conclusions may be seriously time-bound and region-bound. Their findings may not be generalizable to areas outside the South, considering the generally contrary findings of studies of non-Southern jurisdictions using more recent data. Given these considerations, it would seem reasonable to study national sentencing practices, making regional comparisons, using data covering as long a period of time as possible.

EXECUTION RATES AND DEATH SENTENCING BY RACE

It has been claimed that "racial discrimination is strongly suggested by the national execution figures" (NAACP, 1971: 51-2). Clearly, blacks have been executed in numbers far out of proportion to their numbers in the population. Over the period 1930–1976, 53.6% of all legally executed persons in the United States were black, although blacks constituted only about 10–11% of the U.S. population during that period (U.S. Federal Bureau of Prisons, 1971:8; U.S. Bureau of the Census, 1977:25). This disproportion, however, cannot in itself be taken as evidence of racial discrimination, since blacks also commit a large proportion of U.S. homicides, the crime most frequently punished by death. A more meaningful measure of capital punishment sentencing outcome would be an indicator of execution risk, i.e., an execution rate. A true rate compares a number of events (such as executions) with the number of times the event could have occurred. Therefore, the ideal base for the execution rate could be the number of persons convicted of a capital offense, i.e., a crime for which, in a given jurisdiction, the offender could be sentenced to death. However, there are no national data on the number of such crimes committed or on persons arrested for the crimes. Therefore, a surrogate measure is needed.

In this analysis, execution risk by race is measured as the number of executions (for murder) of persons of a given race in a given year, divided by the number of homicide victims of that race who died in the previous year. The number of homicide victims of a given race is used as an approximation of the number of persons of that race who committed a homicide, whether a capital murder or a noncapital murder.[7] Since 92–97% of all homicides involve killers and victims of the same race (Garfinkel, 1949:371; Harlan, 1950:745; Wolfgang, 1958:379; Bensing and Schroeder, 1960:51; U.S. Federal Bureau of Investigation, 1977:9), the racial distribution of homicide victims can be used to describe the racial distribution

---

[6] Although Bullock (1961) has been cited in connection with the issue of sentencing and interracial relationships (e.g., Hindelang, 1969 and Baab and Ferguson, 1968), his study did not actually contain any data on victim-offender racial relationships.

[7] Execution rates for rape cannot be computed because there are no comparable data to use for the base of the rate. There were no national data on rape victimizations by race up until 1973 (by which time the judicial moratorium on execution had begun and even the imposition of death sentences for rape had virtually disappeared). In any case, the evidence showing discrimination in capital punishment of rape is fairly conclusive, making the computation of such rates redundant.

of homicide offenders with very little error (Wolfgang, 1958:223).

Since there is a median lag between arrest and a court trial for criminal homicide of slightly under six months (Wolfgang, 1958:296, 299), and a mean lag of about one year between conviction and execution (Lunden, 1962:1043; McCafferty, 1967:95; U.S. Federal Bureau of Prisons, 1970), the appropriate comparison for our purposes is between the executions in year t and arrests in year t−1, or possibly year t−2. For the sake of simplicity, the execution rates assume a one-year lag between commission of the homicide and execution of the offender over the time period studied. In any case, the results assuming a two-year lag would be substantively identical.

Table 4 presents the computed execution rates for blacks and whites, covering the entire period for which national execution data is available, 1930–1967.[8] In the final column, a ratio greater than one indicates a black execution rate higher than the white execution rate; therefore, for 25 of 38 of the years examined, the black execution rate was lower than the white execution rate. Since they are based on fairly small numbers of executions, race-specific execution rates and ratios of execution rates are somewhat unstable for single years, especially for the later years in the time series. Therefore the rates for the entire period were computed. For the period 1930–1967 there were 1,663 executions of whites for murder and 1,638 executions of blacks, while for the period 1929–1966 (lagged one year behind the other period) there were 159,482 white homicide victims and 168,518 black homicide victims (and presumably roughly equal numbers of homicide offenders). Therefore, the white execution rate for the entire period was 10.428

executions per 1,000 homicides and the black rate was 9.720 executions per 1,000 homicides. Thus, over the entire period, blacks were subject to a lower execution risk than whites.[9]

Given the regional pattern of discrimination findings of previous studies of capital punishment sentencing, it may be the case that execution rates are higher for blacks than for whites in the South and that this fact is obscured in national data. It is also possible that the relative execution risks of blacks and whites changes over time and by region. These possibilities are addressed using the data in Table 5.

These data indicate that the execution risk of black homicide offenders (actually nonwhites in this analysis) has indeed been greater than that of white homicide offenders in the South, while the opposite has been true in the rest of the United States. However, the excess of the black execution risk over the white execution risk in the South has declined over time, to the point where execution rates were roughly equal in the period since 1950. The evidence, considered in combination with prior research on capital punishment sentencing outcomes, suggests that use of the death penalty is not inevitably or inherently discriminatory, but rather that racial discrimination in its administration has been highly variable over time and between regions. These data support the racial discrimination hypothesis in connection with death penalty sentencing only for the South. Of particular interest is the somewhat surprising finding that in the recent past, outside of the South, the white execution risk has been substantially higher than the nonwhite risk, a fact which apparently has gone unnoticed in the literature. Possible explanations of this phenomenon will be discussed later in the paper.

---

[8] The number of homicide victims of each race excludes executions and killings committed by policemen in the line of duty. Executions are excluded because it is undesirable to have a common component in the numerator and denominator of the execution rate. Police killings are excluded because they are nearly always considered justifiable homicides and therefore not criminal. These exclusions make the homicide victim figures somewhat better surrogates for figures on criminal homicide offenders.

[9] It is debateable whether statistical tests of significance are appropriate where population data are involved, although Blalock (1972:238–9) has argued that they can serve to rule out an alternative explanation of a set of results—that the data could have been generated by chance processes rather than causal ones. A two-sample test of the difference between the proportions of persons executed among blacks and whites indicates the difference is significant at the .05 level (two-tailed test, Z = 2.03).

RACIAL DISCRIMINATION IN CRIMINAL SENTENCING 795

Table 4. Execution Rates by Race, 1930-1967

Year	Black Executions for Murder	Black Homicide Victims[a]	White Executions for Murder	White Homicide Victims[a]	Black Execution Rate[b]	White Execution Rate[c]	Ratio of Black to White Execution Rates
1967	1	—	1	—	0.168	0.191	0.880
1966	0	5,945	1	5,230	0.000	0.205	0.000
1965	1	5,408	6	4,879	0.203	1.336	0.152
1964	4	4,926	5	4,492	0.893	1.197	0.748
1963	6	4,478	12	4,176	1.375	2.918	0.471
1962	15	4,364	26	4,112	3.583	6.468	0.554
1961	15	4,187	18	4,020	3.568	4.688	0.761
1960	26	4,204	18	3,840	6.394	4.826	1.325
1959	26	4,066	15	3,730	6.619	4.260	1.554
1958	20	3,928	20	3,521	5.040	6.073	0.839
1957	22	3,968	32	3,293	5.479	9.718	0.564
1956	31	4,015	20	3,239	8.105	6.240	1.299
1955	24	3,825	41	3,205	5.954	12.387	0.481
1954	33	4,031	37	3,310	8.317	11.315	0.735
1953	25	3,968	25	3,270	5.840	7.492	0.779
1952	36	4,281	35	3,337	9.217	10.965	0.841
1951	31	3,906	55	3,192	7.463	16.965	0.456
1950	32	4,154	36	3,362	7.402	9.882	0.749
1949	56	4,323	49	3,643	12.216	12.626	0.967
1948	61	4,584	32	3,880	13.475	8.095	1.664
1947	89	4,527	40	3,953	18.924	10.005	1.891
1946	61	4,703	45	3,998	15.877	12.879	1.233
1945	52	3,842	37	3,494	14.790	12.445	1.188
1944	48	3,516	45	2,973	13.829	14.227	0.972
1943	63	3,471	54	3,163	14.593	16.162	0.903
1942	58	4,317	57	3,341	13.075	16.681	0.784
1941	46	4,436	55	3,417	10.426	14.773	0.706
1940	61	4,412	44	3,723	13.610	11.429	1.191
1939	63	4,482	79	3,850	14.338	18.283	0.784
1938	63	4,394	89	4,321	13.011	20.408	0.638
1937	62	4,842	67	4,361	12.086	13.405	0.902
1936	93	5,130	86	4,998	18.383	15.826	1.162
1935	66	5,059	115	5,434	12.028	18.338	0.656
1934	89	5,487	64	6,271	17.056	9.672	1.763
1933	74	5,218	75	6,617	16.122	12.093	1.333
1932	63	4,590	62	6,202	13.322	10.003	1.332
1931	57	4,749	76	6,198	12.800	12.722	1.006
1930	57	4,453	90	5,974	13.106	16.474	0.796
1929	—	4,349	—	5,463	—	—	—

SOURCE: U.S., Federal Bureau of Prisons, *National Prisoner Statistics, Bulletin No. 46* (1971), p. 8; U.S., National Center for Health Statistics, *Vital Statistics of the U.S.: Mortality,* (annual issues, 1937–1966); U.S. Bureau of the Census. *Mortality Statistics,* (annual issues, 1929–1936).

NOTE: There were no executions in the U.S., 1968–1976; complete execution figures by race for the U.S. before 1930 are not available. Mortality figures for 1929–1932 refer to the death registration area rather than the entire U.S. (95.7% of the U.S. population was covered in 1929; 96.3% was covered in 1932). In 1929–1932 black homicide victim figures were estimated from "colored" homicide figures; the difference is very slight.

[a] Excluding executions and killings by policemen in the line of duty for 1950–1967. Figures before 1950 exclude executions but include killings by police.

[b] Black execution rate is number of black executions in year t per 1,000 black homicide victims in year t−1.

[c] White execution rate is number of white executions in year t per 1,000 white homicide victims in year t−1.

Possible Biases in Computation of Execution Risk

Our estimates of execution risk by race could be biased if the homicides which blacks commit are less likely to be capital murders than those committed by whites. If this were true, using the number of homicide victims of each race as the base of the execution rate would be misleading for comparative purposes, since a smaller proportion of the black offenders could be

Table 5. Execution Rates for Groups of Years by Region and Race

Years	United States		
	White	Black[a]	Black Rate/ White Rate
1930–1939	14.38	14.24	0.99
1940–1949	12.80	14.07	1.10
1950–1967	5.94	4.57	0.77
1930–1967	10.43	9.72	0.93
	White	Nonwhite[a]	Nonwhite Rate/ White Rate
	South		
1930–1939	11.01	14.41	1.31
1940–1949	11.24	14.26	1.27
1950–1967	5.02	5.30	1.06
1930–1967	8.39	10.47	1.25
	Non-South		
1930–1939	15.08	12.56	0.83
1940–1949	13.61	13.78	1.01
1950–1967	6.11	3.34	0.55
1930–1967	11.00	9.32	0.85

[a] In regional and state breakdowns of mortality by cause of death, the data refer only to white/ nonwhite, while the published cumulations for the United States refer to white, black, and other races.

considered to be at risk of execution, compared to white offenders. In this case, the black execution would be understated relative to the white rate.

Three studies report figures on the percentage of criminal homicides designated as first degree (capital) murders, by race. One found the percentage designated first degree murder, both at indictment and at conviction, to be higher for blacks than for whites (Garfinkel, 1949:372), and one found the opposite (Bensing and Schroeder, 1960:43, 45, 88), while the third study found no significant difference (Wolfgang, 1958:302–03). Thus, no consistent relationship was found between race and proportion of criminal homicides designated first degree murder.

However, it has been argued that the designation of degree of homicide could itself be racially biased (Garfinkel, 1949). Would there be a racial difference if the degree of homicide were designated without bias? Given the hypothetical nature of the question, this is not easy to answer directly; however, we can evaluate it indirectly. It is generally agreed that there are a number of factors which can legitimately affect the designation of degree, including whether or not the homicide was committed in connection with another felony (called "felony killings"), whether the killing involved excessive violence or brutality, and of course whether or not the crime seemed to be premeditated. There is no direct evidence on premeditation by race. Wolfgang's (1958:376) data indicate that a higher proportion of killings committed by whites are committed in connection with robberies than are killings by blacks, suggesting that a higher proportion of white killings might be felony killings, compared to killings by blacks. However, the difference is slight, and this finding has not been corroborated elsewhere. On the other hand, Wolfgang (1958) found no significant relationship between race and the tendency to inflict multiple acts of violence, while black homicide arrestees were significantly more likely to have prior arrest records than white homicide arrestees (Wolfgang, 1958:160, 175–6). Therefore, there is little evidence that would indicate that killings committed by blacks are significantly less likely to be capital murders than those committed by whites.

There is another potential source of bias peculiar to the use of victim data by race as a surrogate for offender data by race. It was assumed that the number of offenders of one race would be roughly equal to the number of victims of that race. This assumption could be substantially incorrect, if, for example, killings involving black victims and white killers were more numerous than killings with white victims and black killers. If such were the case, the number of black victims would overestimate the number of black killers relative to white killers, and therefore underestimate the black execution rate relative to the white execution rate. Data relevant to this question are contained in the 1976 Uniform Crime Reports, which reported offender-victim racial relationships for murders and nonnegligent manslaughters (U.S. F.B.I., 1977). These data indicate that black offender–white victim killings are more numerous than white offender– black victim killings. They further indicate that while only 53.2% of the 10,538 homicide victims were black, 55.8% of the known offenders were black. This finding

RACIAL DISCRIMINATION IN CRIMINAL SENTENCING 797

suggests that use of victim data by race involves a bias whose correction would only strengthen our findings. Similar conclusions on victim-offender racial relationships could be drawn from data reported in smaller scale studies of criminal homicide (Garfinkel, 1949:371; Wolfgang, 1958:379; Bensing and Schroeder, 1960:51; and the seventeen-city study of Curtis, 1974:21).

Death-Sentencing Rates

Execution rates, as we have measured them, reflect not only rates at which defendants are sentenced to death, but also the extent to which such sentences are successfully appealed or commuted to a lesser penalty. Therefore, a purer measure of the rate at which defendants are sentenced to death is desirable. Annual data on the number of persons sentenced to die has been compiled, by race of the offender, for the United States since 1967. While this does not allow computation of death-sentencing rates for a very long period of time, it does update our analysis by providing information on the administration of capital punishment since the de facto moratorium on executions began in 1967.

Death-sentencing rates were first computed in a fashion similar to the computation of execution rates: the number of death sentences (actually, persons received by U.S. prisons from the courts, sentence of death) for murder is compared with the number of homicides in the previous year, for each race. Then a second measure of the death-sentencing rate was computed. It could be argued that a better measure of the risk of receiving a death sentence would use persons arrested for, or convicted of, capital crimes as the base for the rate, since it is only such persons who are actually at risk of receiving a death sentence. While there are no national data on convictions for murder, there are national figures on persons arrested for murder or nonnegligent manslaughter. Therefore, rates were computed using these figures for the base of the death-sentencing rate, again in a manner similar to the computation of execution rates.

Table 6 shows the computation of death-sentencing rates. The resulting rates, whether based on homicide deaths or homicide arrests, indicate that nonwhites were subject to a lower risk of being sentenced to death than whites over the period from 1967 to 1978. Because of the small numbers of death sentences each year, rates for single years are somewhat unstable, especially for 1972 and 1973. Nevertheless, the findings are on the whole quite consistent with the findings for execution rates.

This aggregate-level analysis does not show that there is never overt racial discrimination in the administration of the death penalty for murder outside of the South. There may be discrimination in particular jurisdictions, in specific individual cases, or at specific, previously unstudied, stages in the legal process leading up to execution, although a close reading of previous studies of various stages in this process, such as arrest, indicate that, at least outside the South, overt racial discrimination may be more apparent than real, just as seems to be the case with sentencing (regarding arrest, see Green, 1970; Black, 1971; Monahan, 1972; Lundman et al., 1978).

What the present analysis does show is that regardless of whatever discrimination there may or may not be at particular stages in the legal process, the outcome is a lower execution rate for blacks than for whites. If there is discrimination against blacks at one or more stages, then, given the observed net result, it seems that there must also be some compensating effects, favoring blacks, at other stages.[10] Likewise, if there is discrimination against blacks in one or more regions, jurisdictions, or specific cases, or with particular subtypes of homicides, then there must be some counterbalancing effects elsewhere.

The simple computation of execution and death-sentencing rates obviously does not in any way control for differences in prior criminal record (or other legally relevant variables, for that matter). Consid-

---

[10] This possibility of a pattern of compensating discriminatory effects has been raised by Nagel and Neef (1977:185–8).

Table 6. Death-Sentencing Rates by Race, 1967–1978

Year	Nonwhite	White	Ratio: Nonwhite/White
	Sentences per 1,000 Homicide Deaths[a]		
1978	74/ 9,230 = 8.02	108/ 10,730 = 10.07	0.80
1977	64/ 9,439 = 6.78	68/ 10,115 = 6.72	1.01
1976	88/ 10,377 = 9.51	136/ 10,973 = 12.39	0.69
1975	143/ 10,817 = 13.22	121/ 10,648 = 11.36	1.16
1974	65/ 10,291 = 6.32	67/ 9,789 = 6.84	0.92
1973	23/ 10,498 = 2.19	11/ 8,840 = 1.24	1.76
1972	40/ 10,226 = 3.91	26/ 8,561 = 3.04	1.29
1971	51/ 9,045 = 5.64	45/ 7,803 = 5.77	0.98
1970	52/ 8,461 = 6.15	64/ 7,016 = 9.12	0.67
1969	36/ 7,880 = 4.57	49/ 6,806 = 7.20	0.63
1968	45/ 7,027 = 6.40	51/ 6,009 = 8.49	0.75
1967	38/ 6,077 = 6.25	36/ 5,230 = 6.88	0.91
1967–78	719/109,328 = 6.58	782/102,529 = 7.63	0.86
	Sentences per 1,000 Homicide Arrests[b]		
1978	74/ 9,256 = 7.99	108/ 7,866 = 13.73	0.58
1977	64/ 7,083 = 9.03	68/ 5,792 = 11.74	0.77
1976	88/ 8,592 = 10.24	136/ 6,581 = 20.67	0.50
1975	143/ 7,567 = 18.90	121/ 4,879 = 24.71	0.76
1974	65/ 7,677 = 8.74	67/ 5,236 = 12.80	0.66
1973	23/ 8,661 = 2.66	11/ 5,145 = 2.14	1.24
1972	40/ 8,586 = 4.66	26/ 4,716 = 5.51	0.85
1971	51/ 7,344 = 6.94	45/ 4,503 = 9.99	0.69
1970	52/ 6,669 = 7.79	64/ 3,743 = 17.10	0.46
1969	36/ 5,922 = 6.08	49/ 3,536 = 13.86	0.44
1968	45/ 5,018 = 8.97	51/ 3,200 = 15.94	0.56
1967	38/ 4,203 = 9.04	36/ 2,911 = 12.37	0.73
1967–78	719/ 86,578 = 8.30	782/ 58,126 = 13.45	0.62

Sources: Persons sentenced to death: U.S., NCJISS, *Capital Punishment* (1971–72; 1973; 1974; 1975; 1976; 1977; 1978).
Homicide deaths, 1966–76: U.S., NCHS, *Vital Statistics of the United States: Mortality (Year)* (1968–79).
Homicide deaths, 1977: U.S. NCHS, *Monthly Vital Statistics Report: Advance Report: Final Mortality Statistics 1977* (1979).
Arrests, 1966–77: U.S., F.B.I., *Crime in the United States (Year)* (1967–1978).
[a] Death sentences for murder, year t, per 1,000 homicide deaths, year t−1.
[b] Death sentences for murder, year t, per 1,000 homicide arrests, year t−1.

ering the stress laid on controlling for prior record earlier in the paper, this omission might seem to undercut confidence in the death penalty findings. However, because introduction of such controls has consistently reduced differences in sentencing outcome attributable to racial discrimination, correcting this omission would only tend to strengthen the conclusion of no overt discriminatory effect of homicide offenders' racial identity. In connection with capital punishment of rape, controlling for prior criminal record would reduce the apparent discriminatory effect to some degree, but this effect is so large to begin with that it is doubtful if the conclusion of discrimination would have to be altered.

Conclusions

The conclusions which can be drawn from the available evidence on the racial patterning of sentencing may be briefly summarized as follows:

(1) The death penalty has not generally been imposed for murder in a fashion discriminatory toward blacks, except in the South. Elsewhere, black homicide offenders have been less likely to receive a death sentence or be executed than whites.

(2) For the 11% of executions which have been imposed for rape, discrimination against black defendants who had raped white victims was substantial. Such discrimination was limited to the South and has disappeared because death sentences are no longer imposed for rape.

(3) Regarding noncapital sentencing, the evidence is largely contrary to a hypothesis of general or widespread overt discrimination against black defendants, although there is evidence of discrimination for a minority of specific jurisdictions, judges, crime types, etc.

(4) Although black offender–white victim crimes are generally punished more severely than crimes involving other racial combinations, the evidence indicates that this is due to legally relevant factors related to such offenses, not the racial combination itself.

(5) There appears to be a general pattern of less severe punishment of crimes with black victims than those with white victims, especially in connection with imposition of the death penalty. In connection with noncapital sentencing, the evidence is too sparse to draw any firm conclusions.

None of these findings are inconsistent with the assertion of institutional racism or income discrimination in sentencing. It is quite possible that low income makes it more difficult to make bail, hire a private attorney genuinely independent of the court, etc., for both blacks and whites, and that these factors in turn result in more severe sentencing outcomes, as Lizotte's (1978) research indicates.[11] If black criminal defendants are poorer than white criminal defendants, then income discrimination would produce racial differentials in sentences received. Nor are the data inconsistent with a hypothesis of overt discrimination at earlier stages of the criminal justice process. We might expect violations of stated values such as equal protection and justice for all to occur most commonly in connection with the least visible decisions, such as the decision to arrest, charge, prosecute, or release a defendant on bail (e.g., see Hagan, 1975 on the decision to charge). However, these decisions are less well studied than the sentencing decision, so the evidence

for discrimination is necessarily even weaker than that regarding sentencing, quite apart from the actual prevalence of discriminatory practice.

The findings of this study do not suggest a different explanation for a well-known phenomenon. Rather they point to a phenomenon to be explained which differs from that conventionally addressed by American students of the legal reaction to crime and criminals. Students of the criminal justice system, concerned with the contemporary consequences of a historical pattern of racism, have sought to explain patterns of more severe treatment of blacks, while overlooking or downplaying the pattern of more lenient treatment of black defendants.

Blacks in the United States, both in the recent and more remote past, have been less likely than whites to receive a death sentence if they committed a homicide. Furthermore, this pattern is apparently not entirely limited to the sentencing of capital offenders. For a variety of specific crimes, jurisdictions, and judges, various researchers have produced data indicating more lenient treatment of black defendants than whites, although the admittedly scattered findings were usually deemphasized or discounted as merely anamalous results attributable to some flaw in the analysis or research design.[12] For example, Bullock (1961) found significantly shorter prison sentences were assigned to blacks convicted of murder; Levin's (1972) Pittsburgh data indicate that blacks received more lenient dispositions than whites for eight out of nine offense categories; and Bernstein and her colleagues (1977) found that blacks received significantly less severe sentences than whites. Gibson (1978:469) studied sentences given by individual judges and found that seven of eleven judges gave a higher percentage of severe sentences to whites than to blacks.

---

[11] It is interesting that Lizotte's path-analysis findings indicate that defendant's race affects whether the defendant makes bail (which in turn affects sentence), but that it does not affect the bail amount set. This suggests that there is no overt racial discrimination in bail setting, but that there is income discrimination. Since Lizotte had no measure of defendant's income, it is possible that the race effect was found simply because the race variable was serving as a rough surrogate for defendant income.

[12] This may be one of the more important subsidiary findings of the literature review. It is a chronic problem in this area, and perhaps in sociology as a whole, that researchers fail to recognize the significance of anomalies, which should alert them to the possible need for alterations in their fundamental assumptions rather than just their methods (See Kuhn, 1962: ch. VI on this issue).

The specification of phenomena to be explained is in a way a more fundamental scientific task than the development of explanations, since the former obviously must occur before the latter can even be imagined. The pattern of lenient treatment of black defendants in the South was recognized in the 1940s and before by observers such as Dollard (1937) and Myrdal ([1944] 1972), and various explanations were developed to account for it. Today, however, this phenomenon is largely disregarded.

A number of factors which may help account for this pattern can be briefly outlined.

(1) *Blacks as devalued crime victims.* Perhaps the most plausible explanation of lenient treatment of black offenders who commit predominantly intraracial crimes such as homicides. assaults, and rapes is that crimes with black victims are considered by predominantly white social-control agents to be less serious offenses, representing less loss or threat to the community than crimes with white victims (Myrdal, [1944] 1972:551). Thus, paradoxically, racist sentiments would produce more favorable treatment for members of the subordinate racial group who commit intraracial crimes.

(2) *White paternalism.* Students of criminal justice in the South have suggested a widespread view among whites of blacks as child-like creatures who were not as responsible for their actions as whites were, and who therefore could not be held accountable to the law to the extent that whites are (Dollard, 1937; Myrdal, [1944] 1972; Garfinkel, 1949). Therefore their perceived diminished responsibility presumably earned them more lenient sentences.

(3) *Sociology-based tolerance.* White paternalism may account for Southern sentencing patterns of the past but not patterns in the rest of the country in more recent times. However, it may have been replaced by a new form of white tolerance for black crime, involving the following line of reasoning: "Blacks commit crimes because of poverty, racism, and/or the resulting black poverty-subculture, which accepts or encourages criminal behavior. Their crimes are due to forces beyond

their control or at least are to be expected in this light. Therefore blacks should not be held as responsible for their actions as whites." Of course, this is largely speculative; however, criminal court informants questioned by Bernstein and her colleagues (1977:753) stated that "some judges and prosecutors assume that non-whites commit crimes because the non-white subculture accepts such behavior. These subcultural differences are considered by the judges and prosecutors, thereby making the offenses of nonwhites seem less pernicious."

(4) *Affirmative action in the courts.* White guilt over acknowledged past discrimination could motivate liberal criminal-justice decisionmakers to consciously or unconsciously compensate with more lenient treatment of black defendants.

(5) *Compensation for institutional racism.* Recognizing the handicaps of low income and greater prior criminal records which black defendants bring into court, some decisionmakers may attempt to compensate in determining sentence.

(6) *Compensation for unconscious prejudice.* Johnston et al. (1973) conducted a study involving criminal court judges sentencing hypothetical defendants and found that the hypothetical white "defendants" were sentenced more severely than the black "defendants." Two of the judges who participated in the study explained that they consciously sought to compensate in their sentencing for any unconscious prejudice on their part against minorities (p. 870).

Various combinations of these explanations can be used to account for less severe sentencing of blacks when and where it has occurred. Factors (1) and (2) may be primarily responsible for lenient sentencing in intraracial cases in the South in the 1940s and before, while different combinations of factors (3) through (6) account for leniency when it occurs elsewhere today and in the relatively recent past—say, since the late 1960s. Only future research designed to test the hypotheses can determine which of these are more than merely plausible and actually produce the patterns observed.

The findings of this paper should not be

RACIAL DISCRIMINATION IN CRIMINAL SENTENCING 801

interpreted as being incompatible with conflict, critical, or Marxist approaches to law, but rather only with the more simplistic, instrumentalist versions of these perspectives, which heavily stress the failure of the criminal justice system to operate according to its own stated standards of equity and proper procedure (e.g. Quinney, 1974; Chambliss and Seidman, 1971). In contrast, Beirne (1979) has pointed out the partial autonomy from particular social classes which the legal system enjoys, and has stated that "The capitalist class *as a whole* cannot be well served by frequent and visible abuses of due process" (p. 379). The criminal justice system can routinely operate to further legitimate the existing order through an obedience to its own rules and limits to its power, even when overt class or race bias in specific situations would otherwise aid particular segments of the ruling class. Clearly then, a more intellectually mature version of conflict theory would not necessarily predict overt class or race bias in the allocation of penalties among criminal defendants.

However, there are forms of class bias in the legal system which are not so clearly a threat to the legitimacy of the system. For example, the American legal system openly permits differing economic resources to be used in mounting a criminal defense, and such differences render legal advantages in avoiding conviction or obtaining lenient sentences if convicted, even though the advantages may operate indirectly and may involve no intentional prejudice on the part of any system decisionmaker. Lizotte (1978) has demonstrated how criminal sentence is affected by whether the defendant made bail and by the type of attorney the defendant had (private attorneys who were not courtroom regulars were more successful in negotiating light sentences than other types). While Lizotte had no measure of income, these are both clearly advantages more available to defendents with greater income. If equal protection of the law is a commodity which must be purchased, then this "equality" cannot be anything more than a legal fiction as long as the resources for such a purchase are distributed in an unequal fashion.

Serious though this economic or income discrimination in court processing may be, there is a far more fundamental bias in criminal sentencing. No studies of court processing of criminal defendants can address the issue of how legislatures criminalize behaviors common to lower-class persons, while either failing to criminalize or assigning slight penalties to equally harmful behaviors common among middle- or upper-class persons, such as poisoning of the air and water, manufacture of food, drugs, and other products harmful to human health, price-fixing, and consumer fraud. Detailed study of the use of wealth and power in controlling the ideological composition of legislatures and enforcement agencies, thereby influencing selection of behaviors to be criminalized, the original setting of penalty ranges, the determination of enforcement priorities, and allocation of enforcement resources, is likely to reveal far more about why blacks and lower-class persons are over-represented in arrest, court, and prison data than studies of processing within the criminal justice system. The focus on the influence of ascribed characteristics of individual criminal defendants on processing decisions has, at least up to now, failed to yield the empirical support which would justify the attention that continues to be lavished on the subject.

REFERENCES

Atkinson, David N. and Dale A. Newman
1970 "Judicial attitudes and defendant attributes: some consequences for municipal court decisionmaking." Journal of Public Law 19:68–87.
Baab, G. A. and W. R. Ferguson
1968 "Texas sentencing practices: a statistical study." Texas Law Review 45:471–503.
Bedau, Hugo Adam
1964 "Death sentences in New Jersey." Rutgers Law Review 19:1–55.
1965 "Capital punishment in Oregon 1903–1964." Oregon Law Review 45:1–39.
1967 "Criminal justice: the general aspects." Pp. 405–14 in Hugo Adam Bedau (ed.), The Death Penalty in America. Garden City, N.Y.: Doubleday.
Beirne, Piers
1979 "Empiricism and the critique of Marxism on law and crime." Social Problems 26:373–85.
Bensing, Robert C. and Oliver J. Schroeder
1960 Homicide in an Urban Community. Springfield, Ill.: Charles Thomas.

Bernstein, Ilene Nagel, William R. Kelly, and Patricia A. Doyle
1977 "Societal reaction to deviants: the case of criminal defendants." American Sociological Review 42:743–55.

Black, Donald
1971 "The social organization of arrest." Stanford Law Review 23:1087–111.

Blalock, Hubert A.
1972 Social Statistics. New York: McGraw-Hill.

Block, Richard and Franklin E. Zimring
1973 "Homicide in Chicago, 1965–1970." Journal of Research in Crime and Delinquency 10:1–12.

Bowers, William J.
1974 Executions in America. Lexington, Mass.: D.C. Heath.

Bridge, Franklin M. and Jeanne Mosure
1961 Capital Punishment. Staff Research Report No. 26. Columbus, Ohio: Ohio Legislature Service Commission.

Bullock, H. A.
1961 "Significance of the racial factor in the length of prison sentences." Journal of Criminal Law, Criminology and Police Science 52:411–7.

Burke, Peter and Austin Turk
1975 "Factors affecting postarrest dispositions: a model for analysis." Social Problems 22:313–32.

Cameron, Mary Owen
1964 The Booster and the Snitch. New York: Free Press.

Cargan, Leonard and Mary A. Coates
1974 "Indeterminate sentence and judicial bias." Crime and Delinquency 20:144–56.

Castberg, A. Didrick
1971 "The ethnic factor in criminal sentencing." Western Political Quarterly 24:425–37.

Chambliss, William J. and Robert B. Seidman
1971 Law, Order, and Power. Reading, Mass.: Addison-Wesley.

Chiricos, Theodore G. and Gordon P. Waldo
1975 "Socioeconomic status and criminal sentencing: an empirical assessment of a conflict proposition." American Sociological Review 40:753–72.

Clark, Ramsey
1970 Crime in America: Observations on Its Nature, Causes, Prevention and Control. New York: Simon and Schuster.

Clark, Stevens H. and Gary G. Koch
1976 "The influence of income and other factors on whether criminal defendants go to prison." Law and Society Review 11:57–92.

Conklin, John E.
1972 Robbery and the Criminal Justice System. Philadelphia: Lippencott.

Curtis, Lynn A.
1974 Criminal Violence. Lexington, Mass.: D.C. Heath.

Dison, Jack Everitt
1976 "An empirical examination of conflict theory: race and sentence length." Ph.D. dissertation. Department of Sociology, North Texas State University, Denton, Texas.

Dollard, John
1937 Caste and Class in Southern Town. New Haven: Yale University Press.

Farrell, Ronald A. and Victoria Lynn Swigert
1978a "Prior offense as a self-fulfilling prophecy." Law and Society Review 12:437–53.
1978b "Legal disposition of inter-group and intra-group homicides." Sociological Quarterly 19:565–76.

Florida Civil Liberties Union
1964 Rape: Selective Electrocution Based on Race. Miami: Florida Civil Liberties Union.

Foley, Linda A. and Christine E. Rasche
1979 "The effect of race on sentence, actual time served and final disposition of female offenders." Pp. 93–106 in John A. Conley (ed.), Theory and Research in Criminal Justice: Current Perspectives. Cincinnati: Anderson.

Forslund, Morris A.
1969 "Age, occupation and conviction rates of white and negro males: a case study." Rocky Mountain Social Science Journal 6:141–6.

Garfinkel, Harold
1949 "Research note on inter- and intra-racial homicides." Social Forces 27:369–81.

Gerard, Jules and T. R. Terry
1970 "Discrimination against negroes in the administration of criminal law in Missouri." Washington University Law Quarterly 1970:415–37.

Gibson, James L.
1978 "Race as a determinant of criminal sentences: a methodological critique and a case study." Law and Society Review 12:455–78.

Green, Edward
1961 Judicial Attitudes in Sentencing. London: MacMillan.
1964 "Inter- and intra-racial crime relative to sentencing." Journal of Criminal Law, Criminology and Police Science 55:348–58.
1970 "Race, social status, and criminal arrest." American Sociological Review 35:476–90.

Greenwood, Peter W., Sorrel Wildhorn, Eugene C. Poggio, Michael J. Strumwasser, and Peter De Leon
1973 Prosecution of Adult Felony Defendants in L.A. County: A Policy Perspective. Law Enforcement Assistance Administration, Washington, D.C.: U.S. Government Printing Office.

Hagan, John
1974 "Extra-legal attributes and criminal sentencing: an assessment of a sociological viewpoint." Law and Society Review 8:357–83.
1975 "Parameters of criminal prosecution: an application of path analysis to a problem of criminal justice." Journal of Criminal Law and Criminology 65:536–44.

Hall, E. L. and A. A. Simkus
1975 "Inequality in the type of sentences received by native Americans and whites." Criminology 13:199–222.

RACIAL DISCRIMINATION IN CRIMINAL SENTENCING 803

Harlan, Howard
1950 "Five hundred homicides." Journal of Criminal Law and Criminology 40:736–52.

Hewitt, John D.
1976 "Individual resources, societal reaction, and sentencing disparity." Western Sociological Review 7:31–56.

Hindelang, Michael J.
1969 "Equality under the law." Journal of Criminal Law, Criminology and Police Science 60:306–13.
1978 "Race and involvement in crimes." American Sociological Review 43:93–109.

Howard, Joseph C., Jr.
1967 Rape death penalty study reported in the New York Times, September 18, 1967, p. 33.

Hutner, Michael
1977 "Sentencing in Massachusetts Superior Court." Ph.D. dissertation, Department of Sociology, Syracuse University, Syracuse, N.Y.

Jacob, Herbert
1962 "Politics and criminal prosecutions in New Orleans." Tulane Studies in Political Science 8:77–98.

Janos, Dean and Robert I. Mendelsohn
1967 "The judicial role and sentencing behavior." Midwest Journal of Political Science 11:471–88.

Johnson, Guy
1941 "The negro and crime." The Annals of the American Academy of Political and Social Science 217:93–104.

Johnson, Elmer H.
1957 "Selective forces in capital punishment." Social Forces 36:165–9.

Johnson, Oakley C.
[1951] "Is the punishment of rape equally administered to negroes and whites in the state of Louisiana?" Pp. 216–28 in William L. Patterson, (ed.), We Charge Genocide. New York: International Publishers.

Johnston, Barbara L., Nicholas P. Miller, Ronald Schoenberg, and Laurence Ross Weatherly
1973 "Discrimination in felony sentencing—a study of influencing factors." Washington Law Review 48:857–89.

Judson, Charles J., James J. Pandell, Jack B. Owens, James L. McIntosh, and Dale L. Matschullat
1969 "A study of the penalty jury in first degree murder cases." Stanford Law Review 21:1297–431.

Kelly, Henry E.
1976 "Comparison of defense strategy and race as influences in differential sentencing." Criminology 14:241–9.

Kuhn, Thomas S.
1962 The Structure of Scientific Revolutions. Chicago: University of Chicago Press.

Kulig, Frank
1975 "Plea bargaining, probation, and other aspects of conviction and sentencing." Creighton Law Review 8:938–54.

Lemert, Edwin M. and Judy Rosberg
1948 The Administration of Justice to Minority Groups in L.A. County. Berkeley: University of California Press.

Levin, Martin A.
1972 "Urban politics and judicial behavior." Journal of Legal Studies 1:220–1.

Liska, Allen E. and Mark Tausig
1979 "Theoretical interpretations of social class and racial differentials in legal decisionmaking for juveniles." The Sociological Quarterly 20:197–207.

Lizotte, Alan J.
1978 "Extra-legal factors in Chicago's criminal courts: testing the conflict model of criminal justice." Social Problems 25:564–80.

Lotz, Roy and John D. Hewitt
1977 "The influence of legally irrelevant factors on felony sentencing." Sociological Inquiry 47:39–48.

Lunden, Walter A.
1962 "Time lapse between sentence and execution: the U.S. and Canada compared." ABA Journal 38:1043–5.

Lundsgaarde, Henry P.
1977 Murder in Space City: A Cultural Analysis of Houston Homicide Patterns. New York: Oxford University Press.

Lundman, Richard J., Richard E. Sykes, and John P. Clark
1978 "Police control of juveniles: a replication." Journal of Research in Crime and Delinquency 15:74–91.

Mangum, Charles S., Jr.
1940 The Legal Status of the Negro. Chapel Hill: North Carolina Press.

Martin, Roscoe
1934 The Defendant and Criminal Justice. University of Texas Bulletin No. 3437. Austin, Texas. Bureau of Research in the Social Sciences.

McCafferty, James A.
1967 "The death sentence, 1960." Pp. 90–103 in Hugo Adam Bedau, (ed.), The Death Penalty in America. Garden City, N.Y.: Doubleday.

Mileski, Maureen
1971 "Courtroom encounters: an observation of a lower criminal court." Law and Society Review 5:473–538.

Mohahan, T. P.
1972 "The disposition of juvenile offenders by race and sex in relation to the race and sex of police officers." The International Review of Modern Sociology 2:91–101.

Myers, Martha A.
1979 "Offended parties and official reactions: victims and the sentencing of criminal defendents." Sociological Quarterly 20:529–40.

Myrdal, Gunnar
[1944] An American Dilemma. New York: Pantheon.
1972

National Association for the Advancement of Colored People (NAACP)
1971 "Legal defense fund brief for Aikens 1971." Cited on p. 71 in William J. Bowers (ed.), Executions in America. Lexington, Mass.: D.C. Heath.

Nagel, Stuart
  1969 The Legal Process From a Behavioral Per-
         spective. Homewood, Ill.: Dorsey Press.
Nagel, Stuart and Marian Neef
  1977 The Legal Process: Modeling the System.
         Beverly Hills: Sage.
Overby, Andrew
  1971 "Discrimination against minority groups."
         Pp. 569–81 in Leon Radzinowicz and Mar-
         vin Wolfgang (eds.), Crime and Justice, Vol.
         II: The Criminal in the Arms of the Law.
         New York: Basic Books.
Partington, Donald
  1965 "The incidence of the death penalty for rape
         in Virginia." Washington and Lee Law Re-
         view 22:43–75.
Perry, R. W.
  1977 "Justice system and sentencing: the im-
         portance of race in the military." Criminol-
         ogy 15:225–34.
Pope, Carl E.
  1975a Sentencing of California Felony Offenders.
         National Criminal Justice Information and
         Statistics Service, Washington, D.C.: U.S.
         Government Printing Office.
  1975b The Judicial Processing of Assault and
         Burglary Offenders in Selected California
         Counties. National Criminal Justice Infor-
         mation and Statistics Service, Washington,
         D.C.: U.S. Government Printing Office.
  1977 "The influence of social and legal factors on
         sentence dispositions: a preliminary
         analysis of offender based transaction
         statistics." Journal of Criminal Justice
         5:203–41.
Quinney, Richard
  1974 Critique of Legal Order. Boston: Little,
         Brown.
Rau, Richard M.
  1972 Sentencing in the Federal District Courts.
         Law Enforcement Assistance Administra-
         tion, Washington, D.C.: U.S. Government
         Printing Office.
Rhodes, William M.
  1976 "The economics of criminal courts: a
         theoretical and empirical investigation."
         Journal of Legal Studies 5:311–40.
San Marco, Louis Robert
  1979 "Differential sentencing patterns among
         criminal homicide offenders in Harris
         County, Texas." Ph.D. dissertation, De-
         partment of Sociology, Sam Houston State
         University, Huntsville, Texas.
Sellin, Thorsten
  1928 "The negro criminal: a statistical note." The
         Annals 140:52–64.
  1935 "Race prejudice in the administration of jus-
         tice." American Journal of Sociology
         41:212–17.
Southern Regional Council
  1969 Race Makes the Difference. Atlanta:
         Southern Regional Council.
Sutherland, Edwin H. and Donald R. Cressey
  1970 Principles of Criminology. Philadelphia:
         Lippincott.
Sutton, Paul
  1978 Variations in Federal Criminal Sentences:

A Statistical Assessment at the National
         level. National Criminal Justice Informa-
         tion and Statistics Service, Washington,
         D.C.: U.S. Government Printing Office.
Swigert, Victoria Lynn and Ronald A. Farrell
  1977 "Normal homicides and the law." American
         Sociological Review 42:16–32.
Tiffany, Lawrence, Yakov Avichai, and Geoffrey
     Peters
  1975 "A statistical analysis of sentencing in Fed-
         eral courts: defendants convicted after trial,
         1967–1968." Journal of Legal Studies
         4:369–90.
Uhlman, Thomas H.
  1977 "The impact of defendant race in trial-court
         sanctioning decisions." Pp. 19–51 in John
         A. Gardiner (ed.), Public Law and Public
         Policy. New York: Praeger.
U.S. Bureau of the Census
  1929– Mortality Statistics. Washington, D.C.:
  1936 U.S. Government Printing Office.
  1975 Historical Statistics in the United States,
         Colonial Time to 1970. Washington, D.C.:
         U.S. Government Printing Office.
  1977 Statistical Abstract of the United States.
         Washington, D.C.: U.S. Government
         Printing Office.
U.S. Federal Bureau of Investigation
  1954– Crime in the United States. Washington,
  1978 D.C.: U.S. Government Printing Office.
U.S. Federal Bureau of Prisons
  1970 National Prisoner Statistics, Bulletin No.
         47, Capital Punishment, 1930–1970. Wash-
         ington, D.C.: U.S. Government Printing
         Office.
  1971 National Prisoner Statistics, Bulletin No.
         46. Washington, D.C.: U.S. Government
         Printing Office.
  1976 National Prisoner Statistics, Capital
         Punishment, 1975. Washington, D.C.: U.S.
         Government Printing Office.
U.S. National Center for Health Statistics
  1937– Vital Statistics of the United States (year),
  1979 Mortality, Vol. I, Vol. II, Part A. Wash-
         ington, D.C.: U.S. National Printing
         Office.
U.S. National Criminal Justice Information and
     Statistics Service (NCJISS)
  1971– Capital Punishment. Washington, D.C.:
  1979 U.S. Government Printing Office.
  1976 Criminal Victimization in the United States:
         1973. Washington, D.C.: U.S. Government
         Printing Office.
van den Berghe, Pierre L.
  1967 Race and Racism: A Comparative Perspec-
         tive. New York: Wiley.
Wolf, Edwin D.
  1964 "Abstract of analysis of jury sentencing in
         capital case." Rutgers Law Review
         19:56–64.
Wolfgang, Marvin E.
  1958 Patterns in Criminal Homicide. Philadel-
         phia: University of Pennsylvania Press.
Wolfgang, Marvin E., Arlene Kelly, and Hans C.
     Nolde
  1962 "Comparison of the executed and com-

STABILITY OF PUNISHMENT HYPOTHESIS   805

muted among admissions to death row."
Journal of Criminal Law, Criminology, and
Police Science 53:301–11.

Wolfgang, Marvin E. and Marc Riedel
1973   "Race, judicial discretion, and the death
penalty." The Annals of the American
Academy of Political and Social Science
407:119–33.

1975   "Rape, race, and the death penalty in Georgia." American Journal of Orthopsychiatry
45:658–68.

Zimring, Franklin E., Joel Eigen, and Sheila O'Mal-
ley
1976   "Punishing homicide in Philadelphia: perspectives on the death penalty." University
of Chicago Law Review 43:227–52.

[4]

RACIAL DISPROPORTIONALITY OF U.S. PRISON POPULATIONS REVISITED

ALFRED BLUMSTEIN*

INTRODUCTION

Over the past two decades, the growth in prison populations in the United States has been astonishing. The trend in prison populations over the fifty year period from the mid-1920s to the mid-1970s (shown in Figure 1) had been impressively stable. The nation's incarceration rate averaged about 110 per 100,000 population, with a coefficient of variation[1] of only about eight percent.[2] Indeed, the phenomenon was sufficiently stable, both in the United States and elsewhere, that it encouraged two hardy souls to publish a paper that developed a theory of the "stability of punishment."[3] That theory attempted to explain the trendless pattern in incarceration rates in terms of shifting thresholds of the seriousness of offenses that warrant imprisonment. When crime rates increase, the threshold goes up and formerly punished offenses end up being dealt with less severely than through imprisonment; and when crime rates come down, there is spare capacity for punishment that can be used to punish offenses (like child sexual abuse, for example) that were previously viewed as only marginal.

When the period following the mid-1970s is added to the picture (see Figure 2), one must be impressed by the much more dramatic growth of the incarceration rate subsequent to that period, a growth rate that has averaged about eight percent per year since 1980.

One of the distressing aspects of the United States's prison populations is the very high degree of disproportionality in the incarceration rates for blacks compared to whites, with a ratio of about seven to one. An earlier article based on data from the

---

* H. John Heinz III School of Public Policy and Management, Carnegie Mellon University. The author wishes to note that he has discussed these issues with Jacqueline Cohen and Angela Williams but that they, of course, have no responsibility in this article.

1. The coefficient of variation is the ratio of the standard deviation of the annual readings to their mean.

2. *See* Alfred Blumstein & Jacqueline Cohen, *A Theory of the Stability of Punishment*, 64 J. CRIM. L. & CRIMINOLOGY 198, 201 (1972).

3. *Id.* at 198.

Figure 1

U.S. Imprisonment - 1925-1975

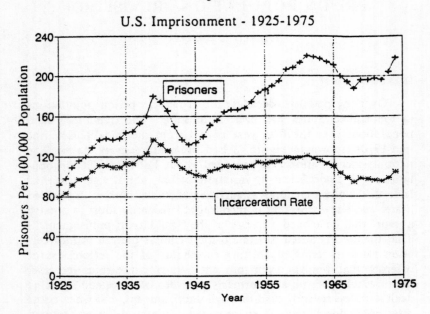

1970s expressed considerable dismay not only at the magnitude of the seven to one incarceration rate ratio, but also at the absolute magnitude of the incarceration rate of black males in their twenties, which was then about 3000 per 100,000, or about three percent of that population group.[4] As incarceration rates have grown through the 1980s, so has this absolute magnitude of the prevalence of this group in prison.

Recent reports have focused on statistics regarding this same high-risk group—black males in their twenties—but have examined the broader issue of the fraction of that group who are under the control of the criminal justice system on any day. The forms of control include not only prison, but also jail, probation, and parole. These have been reported as twenty-five percent in the nation as a whole,[5] forty-two percent in the District of Columbia, and fifty-six percent in Baltimore.[6] These numbers compare with

---

4. Alfred Blumstein, *On the Racial Disproportionality of United States' Prison Populations*, 73 J. Crim. L. & Criminology 1259 (1983).

5. Marc Mauer, Young Black Men and the Criminal Justice System: A Growing National Problem (1990).

6. Jerome G. Miller, Hobbling a Generation: Young African American Males in Washington, D.C.'s Criminal Justice System (1992).

Figure 2

U.S. Incarceration Rate

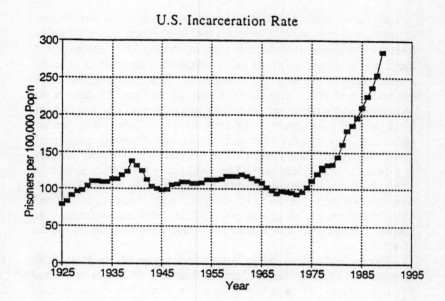

2.35% of the adult population under correctional supervision (primarily probation, which accounts for sixty-two percent of those under supervision) in 1990.[7] Thus, the concern expressed in the earlier paper about the sweep of the criminal justice system over young black males continues to be even more distressing in terms of the scope of intervention by the criminal justice system with so large a fraction of that particular population.

This large and expanding scope of intervention intensifies the concern about the degree to which the gross racial disproportionality in incarceration rates is a consequence of discrimination within the criminal justice system—in contrast to the degree to which it is merely a true reflection of differential involvement in crime, and particularly in those kinds of crime that result in incarceration.[8]

---

7. LOUIS W. JANKOWSKI, U.S. DEPARTMENT OF JUSTICE REPORT No. NCJ-134946, CORRECTIONAL POPULATIONS IN THE UNITED STATES, 1990, at 1259 (1992).

8. Even if all of this incarceration is totally legitimate in terms of law violation, it still must give rise to major concern about the undesirability of so broad a use of this otherwise poorly regarded instrument with so large a segment of an important part of the nation's population. That is an extremely important question that this paper does not attempt to address.

I. EARLIER STUDY

An earlier study by this author compared the racial distribution at arrest for the various crime types that comprise the major fractions of prison populations (predominantly felonies) with the racial mix in prison for those same offenses.[9] The analysis involves a calculation of the expected fraction of black prisoners based on the fraction of black arrestees for each crime type. If there is no discrimination after arrest, then one would expect the fraction of black arrestees for each crime type to be reflected in a similar racial mix in prison for that crime type. The expected fraction of black prisoners is then compared to the fraction of blacks actually in prison for that crime type. The 1983 study results are shown in Table 1. The two serious crimes of murder and robbery, which were the two most prevalent crime types in prison, then comprised about forty percent of prison populations; both had a fraction of blacks in prison that was almost identical to the fraction of blacks at arrest.

For the less serious crime types, the fraction of blacks actually in prison tends to be larger than the fraction of blacks at arrest. For these crimes, there is more room for discretion at the various stages of decision-making within the criminal justice system. That discretion could invoke considerations other than the seriousness of the crime, which is most likely to dominate the sentencing decision for murder and robbery. These other considerations include some that are clearly appropriate (such as prior conviction record) and some that are at least arguably legitimate (such as prior arrest record or current employment status), that might differ between the races. Of course, the room for discretion also offers the opportunity for the introduction of racial discrimination.

The general conclusion of the analysis was that eighty percent of the disproportionality in prison was explained just by the differential involvement in arrest. Furthermore, it was noted that even if the racial mix in prison precisely equaled the racial mix at arrest for each crime type, the fraction of blacks in prison would be reduced, but not dramatically (from forty-nine percent to forty-three percent, or a reduction of about 10,000 out of a total of 131,000 black prisoners).

An analysis of race ratios in prison compared to the ratios at arrest reflects only a measure of the aggregate equality of treatment

---

9. *See* Blumstein, *supra* note 4.

Table 1

Table 1
Comparison of Crime-Type-Specific Percentages of Blacks in Prison and in Arrests

Crime Type	Prisoners		Arrests		Crime Type Distribution in Prison (Fj)	Black Percentage		Percent Disproportionally Unexplained (100-Xj)
	Black	White	Black	White		Prisoners (Actual=Qj)	Arrests* (Expected=Rj)	
Murder & Non-Negligent Manslaughter	24,577	22,399	8,413	7,882	17.7	52.3	51.6	2.8
Forcible Rape	6,261	4,852	11,134	11,709	4.2	56.3	48.7	26.3
Robbery	41,022	26,003	51,401	38,604	25.2	61.2	57.1	15.6
Aggravated Assault	9,193	12,516	85,236	123,210	8.2	42.3	41.0	5.2
Other Violent	2,924	3,310	237,932	370,621	2.3	46.9	39.1	27.3
Burglary	20,383	27,765	74,676	152,396	18.1	42.3	32.9	33.1
Larceny/Auto Theft	8,678	8,916	235,519	445,710	6.6	49.3	34.6	4.3
Other Property	7,313	13,239	127,464	240,986	7.7	35.6	34.6	4.3
Drugs	5,966	9,141	110,518	331,629	5.7	39.5	25.0	48.9
Public Order	4,028	6,413	81,331	183,938	3.9	38.6	30.7	29.5
Other	234	592	452,870	889,380	.3	28.3	33.7	-28.7
Total	130,579	135,146				49.14	43.45b	20.5

*The percentage of blacks arrested is also the expected fraction of blacks in prison if there is no post-arrest discrimination.

bThe expected percentage of blacks in prison, 43.45%, is calculated by the method used in Table 3.

This table originally appeared in Alfred Blumstein, _On Racial Disproportionality of United States Prison Populations_, 73 J. of Crim. L. & Criminology n.3 (1983) and is reprinted with the permission of the journal.

within the criminal justice system from arrest to imprisonment.
But that still leaves open the question of whether arrest is a good
indicator of the race of those who commit the crimes—in other
words, whether there is discrimination (or even unintended bias)
by the police reflected in who they arrest. That question can be
addressed by comparing the distribution of the offender's race as
reported by victims, with the race of arrestees for the same type
of crime. Indeed, this is the kind of analysis Hindelang performed
in eight cities.[10] His results showed a strong correspondence between the race of offenders as reported by the victims, and the
race of arrestees.[11] We know that there are important racial disparities in arrest for minor crimes like disorderly conduct because
of police patrol practices (they tend to patrol more heavily in
lower-income areas where crime rates are higher, and so are more
likely to detect such offenses), and that there are disparities also
in general patterns in the exercise of police discretion to arrest.
However, for the serious crimes that are likely to lead to imprisonment, the Hindelang study does show a strong relationship
between the race of offenders and the race of arrestees.

Accepting the eighty percent figure still leaves one concerned
about what happens to the "remaining" twenty percent. Aside
from discrimination, it is entirely possible that some of this residual
is attributable to differences in other factors that differ between
white and black offenders that might contribute to the imprisonment decision; these factors could include prior record or employment status, for example.[12]

It is also possible that there are other effects that could work
in the opposite direction—benefiting black offenders—that could
thereby counteract the other factors or could serve to mask racial

---

10. Hindelang's study compared the race distribution at arrest for robbery and for
aggravated assault (two crimes in which there is usually a face-to-face confrontation between
the victim and the offender) in eight cities with the race distribution as reported by the
victims in those cities in the National Crime Survey, and found very close concordance
between the corresponding race distributions. Michael Hindelang, *Race and Involvement in
Common Law Personal Crimes*, 43 AM. SOC. REV. 93 (1978).

11. His analysis was necessarily limited to those crimes where there was a personal
confrontation between the offender and the victim—robbery and aggravated assault in
particular.

12. In considering such factors that might differ between black and white offenders,
it is important to recognize that factors that distinguish between blacks and whites in the
general population (e.g., unemployment status) are not necessarily different between the
blacks and whites who become offenders; in general, those differences in the general
population are likely to be diminished among an offender population, or possibly even
reversed.

discrimination. These factors include the presence of relatively greater punitiveness in rural areas compared to the urban areas, where most crimes by black offenders occur. There is also a phenomenon of "victim discounting," a form of racial discrimination that diminishes the punishment if the *victim* is black (a phenomenon documented by Baldus and others[13] for the imposition of capital punishment). Since most crime is intra-racial, such discounting of the seriousness of the offense when the victim is black would tend generally to *benefit* black offenders.

Racial discrimination is part of the residual not accounted for. Such discrimination could account for a part, or all, of the twenty percent not accounted for by the differential involvement in arrest—or perhaps for even more than twenty percent. There have been a number of attempts to isolate racial discrimination in various particular aspects of the sequence from arrest to imprisonment broadly covered in this analysis. Any such study is subject to concern over the effects of "selection bias" at an earlier stage of the criminal justice system. Thus, for example, if a white prosecutor displayed racial bias, then the cases coming to trial would involve a representative group of black defendants, but a selectively more serious group of white defendants. If that were to occur, then if a judge was totally even-handed at trial, the white defendants would appear to be getting convicted more often than would the blacks. Alternatively, if the judge were also to display discrimination, the selection bias reflected in the more serious white defendants would mask all or part of the discrimination displayed by the judge.[14]

Most of these single-stage studies have focused on the sentencing stage, where the presumption of differential sentencing is greatest. One very thorough study, by Klein, Petersilia, and Turner, found no evidence supporting a presumption of racially different treatment of cases at sentencing.[15] Of course, any such result could always be attributable to the selection bias of the cases presented for sentencing.

---

13. David C. Baldus et al., *Comparative Review of Death Sentences: An Empirical Study of the Georgia Experience*, 74 J. CRIM. L. & CRIMINOLOGY 661, 709 (1983) (discussing victim discounting in homicide).

14. These issues are explored in detail by Steven Klepper et al., *Discrimination in the Criminal Justice System: A Critical Appraisal of the Literature*, in SENTENCING RESEARCH: THE SEARCH FOR REFORM 55 (Alfred Blumstein et al. eds., 1983).

15. Steven Klein et al., *Race and Imprisonment Decisions in California*, 247 SCIENCE 812 (1990).

The principal conclusion of the earlier Blumstein paper was not that racial discrimination does not exist—there are too many anecdotal reports of such discrimination to dismiss that possibility—but, rather, that the bulk of the racial disproportionality in prison is attributable to differential involvement in arrest, and probably in crime, in those most serious offenses that tend to lead to imprisonment.[16] Over a decade has passed since the earlier study, so it is important to examine whether the conclusions based on data from the 1970s are still valid, or whether these conclusions have changed in any significant way.

II. UPDATE OF THE 1983 STUDY

Table 2 presents data for 1991 that are comparable to those presented in Table 1 for the four crime types that account for at least ten percent of the prison population, and for the aggregate of all other crime types—which collectively account for 38.6% of the 1991 prison population.[17] Most of the principal results shown for 1991 in Table 2 are reasonably similar to the comparable results for 1979, which are also shown for the same four crime types in Table 2.

The important exception is reflected in the dramatic growth in the number of drug offenders in prison; their fraction increased from less than six percent in 1979 to 21.5 percent in 1991. Because of the general growth in prison populations, the total number of white and black drug offenders in prison grew almost ten-fold, from 15,107 in 1979 to 145,225 in 1991. Other than this difference, most of the other components of race ratios at arrest and in prison that are important (in the sense of being associated with a large fraction of the prisoners) have not changed significantly over the twelve years between the two studies.

The analysis of the 1991 data show that the racial disproportionality in incarceration rates is still about seven to one, and that

---

16. Blumstein, *supra* note 4.

17. The data on prisoners comes from the BUREAU OF JUSTICE STATISTICS, SURVEY OF PRISON INMATES (1991). Lawrence Greenfeld of the Bureau was most helpful in making those data available prior to their formal publication. The data on arrests comes from the FEDERAL BUREAU OF INVESTIGATION, UNIFORM CRIME REPORTS (1990) ("UCR"). The UCR for the earlier year was chosen to impose a one-year lag to accommodate the time from arrest to appearance in prison. However, the black-white ratios at arrest were examined for the period of the 1970s, and were found to be quite stable over time. Indeed, comparison of the race ratios at arrest by crime type in Table 1 and Table 2 indicates a similar stability.

Table 2

Explanation of Racial Disproportionality through
Differential Involvement in Arrest: 1991 and 1979

1991

	Percent of Prisoners	Percent of Blacks		Percent of Disproportion- ality Explained by Arrest
		Prison	Arrest	
Homicide	12.5	47	55	135
Robbery	14.9	64	61	89
Burglary	12.5	41	34	75
Drugs	21.5	58	40	50
All Other	38.6			
Total	100	49.3	42.6	76

1979

	Percent of Prisoners	Percent of Blacks		Percent of Disproportion- ality Explained by Arrest
		Prison	Arrest	
Homicide	17.7	52	52	95
Robbery	25.2	61	57	84
Burglary	18.1	42	33	67
Drugs	5.7	40	25	51
All Other	33.3			
Total	100	49.1	43.5	80

racial differences at arrest account for seventy-six percent of this disproportionality, a number only slightly below the eighty percent that was calculated for 1979. The race distribution in prison for robbery (14.9 percent of prisoners) still very closely matches the race distribution at arrest. For homicide (murder and manslaughter), blacks are significantly *under*-represented in prison compared to their presence in arrest. For most of the other crime types, there is some degree of over-representation of blacks in prison, but of a comparable aggregate magnitude to that in the 1970s.

The striking new issue in 1991 is the saliency of drug offenders in prison. Blacks comprise 57.7 percent of the prisoners for drug offenses, but they are only 40.4 percent of the arrestees for drug offenses, so that they are over-represented in prison by forty-three percent compared to arrest. This difference is comparable to that found in 1979, but the problem is profoundly exacerbated by the fact that the presence of drug offenders has increased almost four-fold in the percentage of the prison population (from 5.7 percent to 21.5 percent), far more than any other crime type.

This growth in processing of drug offenders through the criminal justice system is reflected in Figure 3, which presents the race-specific arrest rate for drug offenses.[18] The striking growth for non-whites (primarily blacks) in the period since the mid-1980s (coinciding with the growth in the crack trade) is certainly evident. But it is also clear that the growth rate in incarceration has been even more dramatic. Thus, based on Table 2, the rate of imprisonment for drug offenses is the most poorly correlated to the rate of arrest of all the crime types, and arrests for blacks for drugs has grown dramatically in the late 1980s.

The issue is further aggravated by the recognition that arrests for drug offenses are far less likely to be a good proxy for offending patterns than they are for aggravated assault, murder,

Figure 3

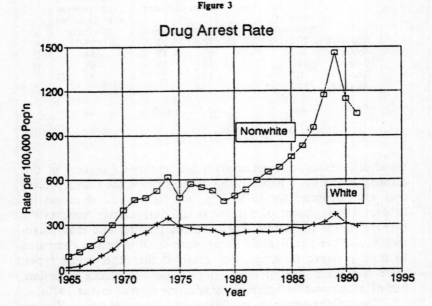

18. The data for these graphs is derived from the FEDERAL BUREAU OF INVESTIGATION, AGE-SPECIFIC ARREST RATES AND RACE-SPECIFIC ARREST RATES FOR SELECTED OFFENSES, 1965-1985 (1986) (subsequent data was provided by staff of the Uniform Crime Reporting Program of the Federal Bureau of Investigation).

and robbery. This can be attributed to the fact that non-whites are more vulnerable than whites to arrest for drugs. First, there does tend to be a more dense police presence where blacks reside because of the greater amount of crime there. There have also been reports of race being used at least implicitly in police profiles of drug couriers. Also, according to personal reports from police officials involved in narcotics enforcement,[19] markets operated by blacks tend much more often to be outdoors and vulnerable to police action, whereas markets operated by whites tend much more often to be clandestine and indoors, and thereby less visible and more protected from police surveillance and arrest. Further, the dramatic growth in arrests of blacks since 1985 also reflects the growth of crack-cocaine use, a growth that has occurred predominantly in black communities, and the associated enforcement focus on that drug.[20]

If one examines the racial disproportionality in prison for all offenses other than those involving drugs, the situation is somewhat improved compared to the earlier study. For the full array of crimes, including drugs, the fraction of blacks actually in prison is 49.3 percent, compared to an expected value based on arrest of 42.6 percent, and these figures give rise to the assessment that 76.3 percent of the disproportionality is explained by differential arrest; this is marginally worse than the 1979 situation presented in Table 1. If one examines the crime types other than drugs, the fraction of blacks actually in prison drops to forty-seven percent, and the expected fraction of blacks based on arrest increases to 45.4 percent. These two numbers are sufficiently close that the crime type distribution at arrest thereby accounts for 93.8 percent of the racial disproportionality in prison. This number is as high as it is because of the high under-representation of blacks in prison for homicide compared to arrest, which compensates for the other crime types, where the representation in prison compared to arrest is roughly comparable to the situation in 1979.

---

19. Personal communication.

20. The Minnesota Supreme Court, in State v. Russell, 477 N.W.2d 886 (Minn. 1991), struck down as unconstitutional a Minnesota statute which provided a presumptive sentence of 48 months for possession of three grams of crack cocaine but only 12 months for possession of 10 grams of powder cocaine. The ruling, based on equal protection grounds, found that the legislative distinction was racially discriminatory in its impact: In 1988, 100% of those sentenced under the crack cocaine statute were black, while 66% of those sentenced under the powder cocaine statute were white. In part because of evidence that crack and powder cocaine are pharmacologically identical, the court held that there was no rational basis for the differential treatment of blacks and whites. (The assistance of Michael Tonry in developing the information on this ruling is much appreciated.)

754   UNIVERSITY OF COLORADO LAW REVIEW   [Vol. 64

Thus, the racial disproportionality situation for the crimes other than drugs is roughly comparable in 1991 to what it was in 1979. The situation appears to have improved for homicide, but the greatly increased prevalence of drug offenders in prison and the race differences in arresting and imprisoning black offenders for drug offenses combine to make the disproportionality in 1991 worse than in the earlier period. The concern over this situation is aggravated by the fact that drug arrests are not necessarily indicative of offending patterns and probably are associated with over-arresting of blacks compared to whites. These facts, combined with the high prevalence of young black males under control of the criminal justice system, must raise serious questions about the degree to which the policy associated with the drug war has significantly exacerbated the racial disproportionality in prisons.

III. STATE-SPECIFIC ANALYSIS

Although the aggregate disproportionality in the United States is about seven to one, this varies considerably across the states, with some states showing a disproportionality greater than seven to one, and some less. Table 3 shows the state-specific ratios of black-to-white incarceration rates in 1990.[21] The results are presented only for those forty-two states with enough of a black population in the state (more than ten thousand) and in prison (more than one hundred) to provide meaningful rates. It is interesting to note the extremes of the range, 20.4 at the high end, and 1.5 at the low end—a very broad range that aggregates to seven to one for the nation. It is particularly interesting to note which states occupy these ends. The high end, including Minnesota, Connecticut, Utah, and New Jersey, is composed primarily of Northeastern and Midwestern states that might generally be viewed as liberal, whereas the low end includes Hawaii and Alaska (both of which are likely to be very distinctive), and a large number of Southern states, including Tennessee, South Carolina, Georgia, Mississippi, Alabama, West Virginia, Louisiana, and North Carolina. This distribution of the state-specific ratios would certainly not be consistent with the commonly-held stereotype that it is southern states that practice racial discrimination.

---

21. The data for Table 3 are derived from the BUREAU OF JUSTICE STATISTICS, REPORT No. NCJ-137003, CENSUS OF STATE AND FEDERAL CORRECTIONAL FACILITIES, 1990 (1992) (providing the race-specific count of prisoners by state); United States Bureau of the Census, News Release, *Census Bureau Completes Distribution of 1990 Redistricting Tabulations to States* (Mar. 11, 1991) (providing race-specific population counts for each state).

Table 3
State-Specific Ratios of Black-to-White Incarceration Rates

State	Ratio of Black-to-White Incarceration Rates	State	Ratio of Black-to-White Incarceration Rates
Minn	20.4	*US*	*7.1*
Conn	17.5	Indiana	6.9
Utah	15.0	Missouri	6.9
NJ	14.5	Calif	6.9
Neb	14.4	Kentucky	6.9
Iowa	14.3	Nevada	6.9
Wisc	13.0	Oklahoma	6.3
Penn	12.6	Ariz	6.3
NY	11.7	Texas	6.2
Oregon	10.1	New Mex	6.0
RI	10.0	Arkansas	6.0
Ill	9.6	NC	5.4
Mass	9.4	La	5.4
Colo	9.2	W Va	5.2
Ohio	9.0	Alabama	5.1
Mich	8.8	Miss	4.8
Wash	8.4	Georgia	4.5
Kansas	8.3	SC	4.2
Maryland	8.1	Tenn	4.0
Florida	7.6	Alaska	3.7
Del	7.4	Hawaii	1.5
Va	7.1		

This surprising result[22] warrants some inquiry into the factors contributing to the state-to-state variation. A number of possibilities exist, and it is difficult to unambiguously distinguish among them. It might be that blacks in the South in the 1980s are those who remained following the massive migrations of African-Americans from the South over the past fifty years, and so they are more likely to be compliant and socialized

---

22. Surprising, at least, to those who believe that the racial disproportionality is largely attributable to racial discrimination, and that racial discrimination is more likely to be displayed in southern states than in generally liberal states.

to local mores. Conversely, those who left for new communities are likely to be more aggressive, to have weaker local roots in the communities to which they moved, and so the forces exercising social control over them would thereby be diminished compared to those who remained in the South. Furthermore, those who moved into the North and the Midwest tended to move into urban areas where crime rates are higher, perhaps also because of the weaker social control in the atomized urban areas compared to rural areas.

It is also possible that the differences reflect different punishment policies between the South and the North/Midwest. We do know that incarceration rates in the South tend to be high, and those in the liberal states much lower (one reflection of their liberal political attitudes). One consequence of those differences in punishment policies could be that the mix of offense seriousness in prison increases as the incarceration rate decreases. This could result because the most serious offenders (say, the robbers and murderers) are very likely to be incarcerated everywhere, and the differences in incarceration rates result in larger differences in the more marginal offenses. But the race ratio at arrest is most extreme for the most serious crimes (murder and robbery) and less so for the less serious crimes. Thus, a state that sent *only* robbers and murderers to prison (presumably a liberal state) would end up displaying the highest racial disproportionality.

This issue is illustrated in Figure 4, which shows the relationship between the incarceration rate and the ratio of the black-to-white incarceration rates for each of the states represented in Table 3. The regression line through the graph has a strong and statistically significant (t > 3) negative slope, certainly confirming the fact of the inverse relationship between the incarceration rate and the disproportionality rate.

Of course, this is only one possible explanation. Indeed, it incorporates some of the considerations discussed above, but only partially so. Other explanations are certainly possible. It is important that one try to identify the causes of these state-specific differences in order to help illuminate the factors other than crime-type differences that contribute to the serious racial differences in incarceration rates.

IV. THE DRUG STUDY

One of the sad commentaries of criminal justice policy that is contributing in a major way to the racial disproportionality in

Figure 4

Disproportionality vs. Incarceration Rate

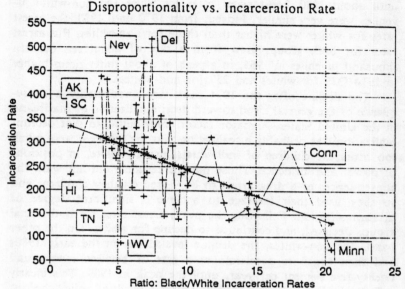

Ratio: Black/White Incarceration Rates

prison is the war on drugs. Despite clear indications that attacking the supply-side of the drug markets is futile, that has been the major strategy, and one that has increased dramatically since about 1985, with a particularly severe effect on racial minorities.

The futility of the strategy is clear from basic criminological theory. Incapacitation cannot work because the offender removed from the street does not take his crime off the street with him; his transactions are replaced by a substitute as long as the demand remains. Similarly, deterrence fails (even when large numbers are indeed deterred) as long as there is a queue of replacements to substitute for those who are deterred. Nevertheless, sanction levels have been cranked up so high that a majority of the offenders in federal prisons[23] and almost one-quarter of those in state prisons[24] are there on drug charges.

This growth in incarceration of drug offenders has certainly contributed to the racial disproportionality in prison. Figure 3 showed the arrest distribution by race. The figure for juvenile

---

23. U.S. DEPARTMENT OF JUSTICE, LAW ENFORCEMENT ASSISTANCE ADMINISTRATION, SOURCEBOOK OF CRIMINAL JUSTICE STATISTICS: 1991, at 657 (1992).

24. *See* Table 2.

arrests (Figure 5) shows the consequences on juveniles from 1965 until about 1980. Most arrest rates for white and non-white juveniles were very similar. Indeed, from 1970 until 1980, the arrest rates for whites were higher than those for non-whites. But arrest rates for both groups grew from a rate of about ten per ten thousand juveniles in 1965, to a peak of about thirty times higher in 1974 (329 for whites and 257 for non-whites).

The decline after the 1974 peak was undoubtedly a consequence of the general trend toward decriminalization of marijuana in the United States. A major factor contributing to that decriminalization was probably a realization that the arrestees were much too often the children of individuals, usually white, in positions of power and influence. Those parents certainly did not want the consequences of a drug arrest to be visited on their children, and so they used their leverage to achieve a significant degree of decriminalization. Following the peak, arrest rates for both racial groups declined, and continued to decline for whites. On the other hand, for non-whites, the decline leveled out in the early 1980s and then began to accelerate at a rate of between twenty and twenty-five percent per year, until the peak in 1989. This clearly reflects the fact that drug enforcement is a result of policy choices,

Figure 5

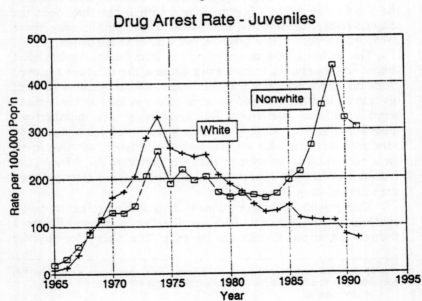

Drug Arrest Rate - Juveniles

which need not have been intended to be racially discriminatory, but which do appear to have had a major differential consequence between the races.

Conclusion

It should be clear that it is not the conclusion of this paper or the earlier one that there is no racial discrimination in the criminal justice system. There are too many anecdotal incidents and analysis of particular jurisdictions reflecting blatant discrimination to reach so naive a conclusion.

It is the conclusion, however, that the bulk of the disproportionality is a consequence of the differential involvement by blacks in the most serious kinds of crime like homicide and robbery, where the ratio of arrests is between five and ten to one. For these crimes, the race ratio in prison is still very close to that at arrest. For the less serious crimes, there is greater disparity between the race ratio at arrest and that in prison, probably because there is more room for the exercise of discretion, which could reflect legitimate factors other than the offense itself, or could reflect racial discrimination.

For the drug crimes, the race ratio in prison is much larger than that at arrest, and furthermore, there are strong reasons to believe that the race ratio at arrest does not necessarily reflect the race ratio at "offending," whatever that might mean with respect to drug offenses. The futile supply-side war on drugs has contributed significantly to the growth in prison populations and to its racial disproportionality.

Comparison of state-level black-to-white incarceration ratios suggests that the lowest ratios occur in Southern states, and the highest ones in "liberal" states, probably reflecting differences in aggregate incarceration rates, rather than differences in racial discrimination.

Finally, and perhaps most importantly, we must recognize that the U.S. displays distressingly high rates of intervention with blacks by the criminal justice system, particularly in terms of incarceration. In that context, it is only of secondary consideration that this is not so much due to racial discrimination, but to other factors outside the criminal justice system. These other factors could well include racial discrimination in many other aspects of black people's lives, but must also include the many factors that contribute to the limited opportunities available to them in the American economy and society. Our nation's social stability de-

pends critically on our ability to identify those factors and to find
means to redress them somehow.

[5]

The Influence of Race on Sentencing in England

[1982]

By Michael McConville

Lecturer in Law, University of Birmingham.

and John Baldwin

Director, Institute of Judicial Administration, University of Birmingham.

No empirical research has ever been conducted in this country into the relationship between the race of an offender and the severity of the sentence received. Nor, it seems, is any such research being planned. This apparent lack of interest in the subject is in sharp contrast to the position in the United States where there is a long research tradition in this field spanning over half a century to which over 50 individual researchers have made contributions.

It is true that a good deal of the American research has been of poor quality, with generalisations sometimes based on small and unrepresentative samples [1] and with crude methods that have failed adequately to take into account the complex interplay of legal and social variables which distort any comparisons made. But the research effort in the United States has been impressive and, though early findings were somewhat equivocal in nature,[2] much more clearcut results have emerged in recent years. Indeed, it is probably true to say that, as methods have become more satisfactory, so the results have tended increasingly to show minimal racial bias in court dispositions. As the authors of a well-conceived study conducted in Denver and Memphis write in a passage which closely parallels conclusions drawn by a good many recent American researchers:

> " our analysis offers little support for the argument that race or class bias directly affect the dispositions given to juveniles . . . Our evidence suggests that offence and prior record are the major determinants of the severity of disposition "[3]

Conclusions of this kind are strikingly at odds with those drawn by earlier writers on the subject, whose methods, though crude and inadequate, were

---

[1] Several studies, which include those most often quoted in this field, deal only with the narrow question of racial bias in decisions relating to the commutation of sentences of those on Death Row. On this, see particularly Wolfgang, Kelly and Nolde, " Comparison of the Executed and the Commuted Among Admissions to Death Row " *Jo.Crim. Law, Crim. and Pol.Sc.* Vol. 53 (1962) pp. 301–311, and Wolfgang and Reidel, " Race, Judicial Discretion, and the Death Penalty " *Annals of the Amer.Acad. of Pol. and Soc.Sc.* Vol. 407 (1973), pp. 119–133.

[2] The early studies are critically reviewed by Hagan, " Extra-Legal Attributes and Criminal Sentencing: An Assessment of a Sociological Viewpoint " *Law and Society Rev.* Vol. 8 (1974) pp. 357–383.

[3] Cohen and Kluegel, " Determinants of Juvenile Court Dispositions: Ascriptive and Achieved Factors in Two Metropolitan Courts " *Amer.Sociol.Rev.* Vol. 43. (1978) pp. 162–176 at pp. 173–174.

nonetheless used to support far-reaching inferences, such as that " equality before the law is a social fiction." [4]

But on questions of this kind English researchers have been silent. This may be explained in terms of political and cultural differences, although there has been no shortage of research in England on similar questions such as relations between the black population and the police. Quite a lot has been written in the recent past about dissatisfaction on the part of racial minorities with the way courts operate (particularly in the light of proceedings following the urban disturbances in 1981), but little of this concern has found expression in empirical research. Having ourselves amassed a good deal of information on Crown Court cases tried in Birmingham and in London in recent years, we thought it worthwhile to attempt to shed some light on the question of the extent to which the race of defendants involved in criminal trials influenced the severity of the sanctions imposed.

The research that we conducted in Birmingham and London was initiated some eight years ago and has been funded by the Home Office and, more recently, by the Royal Commission on Criminal Procedure. The research has covered a number of somewhat disparate issues but has been primarily concerned with the outcome of cases tried by jury, the role of oral and written statements in Crown Court trials, and the determination of guilty pleas.[5] In the course of conducting this research, we have drawn material from a number of sources, and built up a considerable body of information about cases which have passed through the Crown Courts of Birmingham and London. This has allowed us to re-analyse certain parts of the information we have collected to examine specific issues that have arisen from time to time. The influence of race in sentencing is one example of how the material has proved useful in examining a question that was not part of our original plans.

This examination is to some extent based upon inspection of large numbers of sets of committal papers which were kindly made available to us by the Midland and Oxford Circuit and by the Metropolitan Police. In addition, we have made use of information extracted from court registers relating for instance to demographic and social characteristics of defendants, and material supplied by police officers concerning the criminal records of defendants and the charges they faced.

Our examination of the racial factor in sentencing was based upon four random samples of Crown Court trials drawn from Birmingham and London and comprising:

  (i) 500 contested cases heard in Birmingham in 1975 and 1976;
 (ii) 500 guilty plea cases heard in Birmingham in 1975 and 1976;
(iii) 271 contested cases heard in London in 1978 and 1979; and
 (iv) 205 guilty plea cases heard in London in 1978 and 1979.

There were many black defendants involved in these trials and we extracted

---

[4] Sellin, " Race Prejudice in the Administration of Justice " *Amer.Jo.Sociol.* Vol. 41 (1935), pp. 212–217 at p. 217.

[5] Details of the research that we have undertaken are given in McConville and Baldwin, *Courts, Prosecution, and Conviction* (1981).

the relevant cases from each category. The numbers of black defendants (for this purpose those of West Indian, Asian or African origin) falling within each sample were as follows: 141 (of whom 93 were convicted), 124, 40 (of whom 21 were convicted) and 34 respectively.

In order to establish whether there is any relationship between race and sentence severity, it is clearly unsound to draw inferences from the fact that overall sentencing differentials exist. And that is so even where, as in some jurisdictions in the United States, the disparity is large. The fact that the black defendants in our samples were on the whole given more severe sentences than their white counterparts (the disparity being much less marked than has been noted in America [6]) is, therefore, of no significance in itself. The important question concerns the extent to which the disparity is explicable in terms of factors that might reasonably be expected to affect the nature of sentences imposed.

There are a number of techniques that one might use to examine this. The simplest and most appropriate method that we could devise involved attempting to match, on a group basis, the black defendants within each sample with white defendants.[7] In this way, we sought to ensure that we had two samples to compare—one consisting of all black defendants and a control group of the same size consisting of white defendants, and including the same number of females, individuals charged with the same types of offence, of the same age, criminal experience, and so forth. The aim in this was to control for all those factors thought likely to influence the nature of the sentence finally imposed. In this way we would be able to establish whether there were differentials in sentence as between black and white defendants after the legitimate considerations in sentencing had been taken into account. In other words, we sought to test the hypothesis that, if there were residual differences in sentencing as between black and white defendants, then these would be attributable to racial bias.

The criteria on which we attempted to match defendants were as follows:

(1) sex;
(2) age;
(3) type of offence;
(4) the number of counts in the indictment;
(5) the defendant's criminal record;
(6) the length of time the defendant had previously served in prison;
(7) the pre-trial bail status of the defendant; and
(8) plea.

We took great care to ensure that the groups were matched as closely as possible, and in line with this we sub-divided each of the legal factors for which we controlled into a number of categories. Thus age was broken down into eight subgroups, type of offence into 20, the number of counts in the indictment into nine, criminal record into five and time spent in prison

---

[6] In London, for example, 54 per cent. of blacks received immediate custodial sentences compared to 49 per cent. of whites.

[7] On the procedures adopted, see Hood and Sparks *Key Issues in Criminology* (1970) at pp. 146 *et seq.*

into seven. The degree of complexity introduced by this discrimination meant inevitably that it was not possible to match each paired sample on every single category within each control variable. It was still possible, however, to produce an almost complete match so that the slight differences that remained could not reasonably be said to have created any distortion in the results.

None of this means of course that the method adopted is perfect. The major limitation of this approach, and it is one that is shared by most other research into sentencing disparity, is that it is only appropriate for examining whether any systematic, institutional bias exists in the sentencing decisions of the court. The method is not suited for teasing out bias in individual sentencers.[8] We shall return to this point later but it is important to remember that the objective of this study is to examine whether, in the sentencing decision, institutional bias exists based upon racial factors.

Although four different samples of cases were used and the matching procedures employed complex, the results are clearcut and on the whole consistent for each of the samples. Tables 1 and 2 below give the details of the results obtained.

TABLE 1

The sentences received by black and white defendants who pleaded guilty

(i) London cases

Sentence received	Black defendants	%	White defendants	%
Discharges	1	2·9	0	0·0
Fines	4	11·8	1	3·0
Probation orders	3	8·8	8	24·3
Suspended prison sentences	7	20·6	7	21·2
Prison—under 1 year	5	14·7	3	9·1
—1–2 years	1	2·9	0	0·0
—over 2 years	4	11·8	5	15·1
Borstal or detention centre	8	23·6	8	24·3
Other measures	1	2·9	1	3·0
Not known	0	—	1	—
	34	100·0	34	100·0

Prison and Borstal percentages bracketed: Black 53·0%, White 48·5%.

---

[8] An exception is the study by J. L. Gibson, "Race as a Determinant of Criminal Sentences: A Methodological Critique and a Case Study" *Law and Society Rev.* Vol. 12 (1978) pp. 455–478. Gibson found no evidence of racial discrimination at the institutional level in one of the Georgia Supreme Courts but he did find that certain judges treated blacks a great deal more severely than they treated whites. The apparent contradiction in the results is explained by the fact that "blacks are the victims of discrimination by some judges but the beneficiaries of discrimination by others" (p. 470).

(ii) Birmingham cases

Sentence received	Black defendants	%	White defendants	%
Discharges	16	14·4	5	4·4
Fines	11	9·9	19	16·7
Probation orders	10	9·0	14	12·3
Suspended prison sentences	19	17·1	17	14·9
Prison—under 1 year	6	5·4 ⎫	8	7·0 ⎫
—1–2 years	5	4·5 ⎪	9	7·9 ⎪
—over 2 years	13	11·7 ⎬ 46·0%	20	17·5 ⎬ 48·2%
Borstal or detention centre	27	24·4 ⎭	18	15·8 ⎭
Other measures	4	3·6	4	3·5
Not known	13	—	10	—
	124	100·0	124	100·0

TABLE 2

The sentences received by black and white defendants convicted after a not guilty plea

(i) London cases

Sentence received	Black defendants	%	White defendants	%
Discharges	1	4·7	1	5·0
Fines	4	19·1	4	20·0
Probation orders	2	9·5	0	0·0
Suspended prison sentences	4	19·1	6	30·0
Prison—under 1 year	4	19·1 ⎫	2	10·0 ⎫
—1–2 years	1	4·7 ⎪	2	10·0 ⎪
—over 2 years	2	9·5 ⎬ 47·6%	2	10·0 ⎬ 45·0%
Borstal or detention centre	3	14·3 ⎭	3	15·0 ⎭
Other measures	0	0·0	0	0·0
Not known	0	—	1	—
	21	100·0	21	100·0

(ii) Birmingham cases

Sentence received	Black defendants	%	White defendants	%
Discharges	4	4·3	5	5·4
Fines	6	6·5	11	11·8
Probation orders	3	3·2	7	7·5
Suspended prison sentences	19	20·4	15	16·1
Prison—under 1 year	5	5·4 ⎫	10	10·8 ⎫
—1–2 years	12	12·9 ⎪	11	11·8 ⎪
—over 2 years	29	31·2 ⎬ 65·6%	17	18·3 ⎬ 59·2%
Borstal or detention centre	15	16·1 ⎭	17	18·3 ⎭
Other measures	0	0·0	0	0·0
Not known	0	—	0	—
	93	100·0	93	100·0

Although the tables show certain variations in sentence as between black and white defendants, in no instance do these differences reach a level of statistical significance. Indeed, the figures show that, regardless of plea and regardless of whether cases were tried in London or in Birmingham, black defendants did not receive significantly heavier sentences than did white defendants. Perhaps the crucial distinction from a defendant's viewpoint (particularly when his case is tried in the Crown Court) relates to whether or not he receives a custodial sentence. Though there are again certain differences apparent in the tables in the proportion of defendants receiving custodial sentences, these are not consistent and in any event fail to reach a level of statistical significance. In short, it is clear that there is no support for the proposition that black defendants are sentenced more severely than white defendants in the Crown Courts in these cities.

Few researchers have tried to grapple with the complexities of the English sentencing system. One problem with research in this area is that, for all practical purposes and with the exception of murder, the judge's sentencing discretion is virtually unfettered so that the researcher is confronted by the difficult task of identifying the factors that are given weight in the sentencing decision and isolating their influence. Many researchers who have looked at the issue of the relationship between race and sentence in the United States have failed to take into account even the most important variables, such as whether or not black defendants are convicted of more or less serious offences or have lengthier or shorter criminal records than white defendants. Though controlling for such factors makes for a complex analysis, the effort is worthwhile since allegations of bias in our system of criminal justice are frequent.

These allegation have been given added force and intellectual respectability by a number of theorists, particularly those of the conflict school.[9] To take only one example, Richard Quinney writes:

> "Obviously judicial decisions are not made uniformly. Decisions are made according to a host of extra-legal factors, including the age of the offender, his race, and social class. Perhaps the most obvious example of judicial discretion occurs in the handling of cases of persons from minority groups. Negroes, in comparison to whites, are convicted with lesser evidence and sentenced to more severe punishments." [10]

Challenges of this kind (which contain testable hypotheses) must be taken into account when analysing the criminal system, and they contrast markedly with the assumption in standard books on sentencing[11] that the English system does not (and presumably should not) permit extra-legal variables such as race to affect the sentencing decision.

Although we have indicated that the results of the exercise we have undertaken are clearcut, it has to be borne in mind that no attempt could be made to examine the possibilities of bias on the part of individual judges.

[9] See, particularly, Turk, *Criminality and Legal Order* (1969); Quinney, *The Social Reality of Crime* (1970), and Chambliss and Seidman, *Law, Order and Power* (1971).
[10] *The Social Reality of Crime* (1970) pp. 141–142.
[11] Cross, *The English Sentencing System* (3rd ed., with Andrew Ashworth) (1981) does not, for example, discuss the question of race in relation to sentencing at all.

As has been noted, it is possible for some judges to be prejudiced against black defendants in sentencing but for this bias to be masked by the effect of other judges being correspondingly lenient in similar cases.[12] Furthermore, it should not be assumed that, because this study uncovered no evidence of direct racial bias in sentencing, racism is not in evidence at other stages in the criminal process as, for example, in connection with policing, arrest patterns, bail status or jury selection. The high proportion of defendants who were black, particularly in our Birmingham samples, is itself a matter that needs explanation.

What emerges from our analysis is a single, tentative but important finding: that there appears to be no evidence of direct, systematic bias on racial lines in sentencing in the Crown Court. The implication is that defendants are treated equally once they attain the status of convicted persons [13]: not necessarily fairly or appropriately, but equally.

---

[12] This phenomenon emerged clearly in the study by Gibson *op. cit.*

[13] There is evidence to suggest that some sentencing disparity in America can be explained in terms of the effect of race and occupation and the indirect effects they have on defendants not being able to afford bail: A. J. Lizotte, " Extra-Legal Factors in Chicago's Criminal Courts: Testing the Conflict Model of Criminal Justice " *Social Problems* Vol. 25 (1978), pp. 564–580.

[6]

Crim.L.R.

Ethnic Minorities in the Criminal Justice System

By Tony Jefferson

Reader in Criminology, University of Sheffield

and

Monica A Walker

Research Fellow, University of Sheffield

Summary: *This article presents a longitudinal study of the treatment in the Criminal Justice System of Blacks, Whites and Asians in a provincial city. The results are complex, and highlight the problems of interpreting cross-sectional studies. The study also emphasises the importance of attending to areal factors. A survey examined experiences and attitudes in the more socially deprived areas of the city. The differences between Blacks and Whites were fewer than have been found in other surveys, though Blacks' attitudes tended to be less favourable. Asian experiences were significantly different, and their attitudes were consistently more favourable.* *

1. Introduction

There has been some concern, over the last 10 years, about the involvement of the ethnic minorities in Great Britain in the Criminal Justice System. This has tended to be focussed on Afro-Caribbeans (hereinafter called Blacks) and considerable publicity has been given in the press to their over-representation in the arrest statistics collected by the Metropolitan Police District (M.P.D. *i.e.* London).[1] They comprised about 16 per cent. of those arrested in 1987, whereas in the whole of London Blacks comprised about 5 per cent. An analysis of early data[2] found that Blacks were over-represented in each main offence group and each age group, whereas Asians (from the Indian sub-continent) were roughly proportionately represented. Crude explanations of this over-representation are that either the police are more readily arresting Blacks than Whites for similar behaviour, or more Blacks are indulging in criminal behaviour than Whites.

However, taken over such a large area, it is undoubtedly the case that Whites have higher socio-economic status than Blacks, and since social deprivation tends to be associated with criminal behaviour it is not surprising to find Blacks are over-represented among those arrested. A more valid comparison would be

---

* The authors wish to thank Mary Seneviratne and Halina Szulc for their assistance in this research.

[1] "Crime statistics from the Metropolitan Police District, by ethnic group, 1987, victims, suspects and those arrested, "*Home Office Statistical Bulletin* 5/89. Later statistics are not available.

[2] Stevens, P. and Willis, C.F. *Race, Crime and Arrests* (1979) Home Office Research Study No. 58. London: H.M.S.O.

between Black and White arrest rates of those living in the same small areas, because their living circumstances are more likely to be similar, as is their policing.

The second striking feature of published official statistics is the high proportion of black people in prison.[3] About 8 per cent. of male prisoners were Black in 1985, increasing to 11 per cent. in 1990, compared with 1 per cent. in the population of the United Kingdom. Once again this cannot be easily interpreted, and the two possible face-value interpretations—that Blacks are being sentenced more harshly than Whites, or the Blacks are more criminal—oversimplify the situation.

Research on this topic has been piecemeal. There have been few detailed research studies that have examined arrest rates of those living in the same areas[4] or sentencing in both the magistrates' courts and the Crown Court in one study. One of the difficulties of carrying out research on this topic is the need to follow through cases from arrest onwards, as studies of what happens at one stage in the process may be misleading. For example Landau and Nathan[5] found, in a study of juveniles in London, that Blacks were more likely than Whites to be prosecuted by the police, rather than cautioned. However, Farrington and Bennett,[6] in a study in another part of London, did not confirm this result. This would seem to demonstrate not only that studies in different areas or at different times have produced different results, but that a follow through of the cases prosecuted might have found, for example, that Blacks had a different (possibly higher) rate of "not guilty" pleas, with acquittal rates which might have justified them in not accepting a caution. There may also have been earlier differences in the decision whether to take "no further action" after arrest, or indeed in the decision by the police to arrest.

Examination of sentencing in either the magistrates' courts *or* the Crown Court on their own may also be misleading. Mair,[7] for example, in his study of sentencing in West Yorkshire magistrates' courts found quite small differences between the race groups in sentences, but he did not incorporate committals to the Crown Court for sentence or for trial. That this is important was shown by one of the authors[8] in two studies analysing sentences in the London courts in 1983. It emerged that in the magistrates' courts the distribution of sentences did not differ greatly between Blacks and Whites, and this was also the case in the Crown Court. However, Blacks had significantly higher proportions committed for trial in the Crown Court, where custodial sentences are more likely. This resulted in Blacks overall receiving proportionately more custodial sentences. It

---

[3] "The Prison population in 1990", *Home Office Statistical Bulletin* 9/91.

[4] A survey carried out in Moss Side Manchester (Tuck M. and Southgate P. 1981, entitled "Ethnic Minorities, Crime and Policing", Home Office Research Study No. 70) found few differences between Blacks and Whites.

[5] Landau, S.F. and Nathan, G. "Selecting delinquents for cautioning in the London Metropolitan Area". (1983) *British Journal of Criminology 22*, at pp. 28–49.

[6] Farrington, D.P. and Bennett, T. "Police cautioning of juveniles in London". (1981) *British Journal of Criminology 21*, at pp. 123–35.

[7] Mair, G. "Ethnic minorities, probation and the magistrates' courts: a pilot study". (1986) *British Journal of Criminology 26*, at pp. 147–55.

[8] Walker, M.A. "The court disposal of young males, by race in London in 1983." (1988) *British Journal of Criminology 28*, at pp. 141–60. Walker, M.A. "The court disposal and remands of White, Afro-Caribbean and Asian men (London) 1983." (1989) *British Journal of Criminology 29*, at pp. 353–67.

appeared, on examining the offences involved, that Blacks had more "indictable only" offences,[9] and also more "triable-either-way" offences for which they were committed for trial. It was not possible to know from the data available whether this was the defendants' choice or magistrates declining to try them.

Three important factors emerged from this discussion, and these gave rise to a research project[10] in which some of these problems were addressed. In the first place, since little research had taken place outside London, we chose to investigate a provincial city.[11] Secondly, to try to increase the validity of inter-racial comparison we decided to compare arrest rates of Black, Asian and White males[12] who lived in the same small areas. Thirdly, to avoid the problems of "single stage" studies, we adopted a processual approach and followed up a sample of those arrested through to final outcome. There were considerable methodological difficulties, not all of which were overcome. An aspect we were not able to cover was details of behaviour (of suspect and the police) leading up to the arrest. We did, however, manage to carry out a certain amount of court observation and also to interview solicitors who dealt with some of the cases. We were also allowed to observe a juvenile cautioning panel in its decision making, and to interview its members.

Besides this, we carried out a survey of males aged 10–35, among the general population, living in areas where more than 10 per cent. of the non-whites lived.[13] The purpose of this was to compare the experience of and attitude to the police of Blacks, Asians and Whites living in roughly the same conditions. The results will be described only briefly here.[14]

2. Arrest rates (Leeds study)[15]

The population of Leeds was made up of 3 per cent. Blacks, 4 per cent. Asians and 93 per cent. Whites, at the time of this research (1987). We confined our arrest data to males aged 10–35, as this would contain the bulk of the offenders. We found that Blacks were over-represented, although not to the same extent as in London, 6 per cent. being Black, 3 per cent. Asian and 91 per cent. White. This can also be expressed in terms of arrest rates—the numbers arrested over the six month period per 100 in the resident population. The rates were Blacks

---

[9] Whether or not an offence is indictable only depends on the charge, which may itself depend on the perception of the police. For example "robbery", which is indictable only and has to be tried in the Crown Court, may result in conviction for the lesser offence of "theft from the person". White people, in similar circumstances, may possibly have been charged initially with this lesser offence and so tried in the magistrates' courts.

[10] Walker, M.A., Jefferson, T., and Seneviratne, M. *Ethnic minorities, Young People and the Criminal Justice System* (1990) (Main Report). Centre for Criminological and Socio-Legal Studies, University of Sheffield. This research was funded by ESRC Ref E0625(0)23.

[11] The research described here took place in Leeds, with the full co-operation of the West Yorkshire Police, the West Yorkshire Probation Service and Leeds courts.

[12] Given limited resources, we decided to focus on males because of their far greater involvement in official criminal justice statistics.

[13] This was based on the 1981 census. See *op. cit.* n. 10, Chap. 5. The sampling scheme results in roughly equal numbers of males in each race group.

[14] See *op. cit.* n. 10, Chap. 5.

[15] See Walker, M.A. "Arrest rates and Ethnic Minorities: a study in a provincial city" (forthcoming) *Journal of the Royal Statistical Society A*

8.5 per cent., Asians 3.9 per cent. and Whites 4.7 per cent. The offences for which people were arrested did not differ greatly. Blacks and Asians had more offences of violence than Whites, but Whites had more burglary and criminal damage. We recorded the address of each person arrested over the six month period—a total of over 5,000 people—and, using maps, we ascertained the enumeration district or ward in which the arrestee lived. Since we wished to compare arrest rates between people living in the same small areas, we needed to obtain population numbers for these areas. We were able to obtain data from the 1981 census[16] for enumeration districts (average about 150 households). These enabled us to estimate numbers of resident males aged 11–21 and 22–35.[17] Where the population was too small to calculate reliable rates, enumeration districts were combined to form larger areas, in some cases whole wards.[18] The enumeration districts with sufficient non-whites in them for reliable rates were those with 10 per cent. or more non-whites, so we divided all areas into those with less or more than 10 per cent. non-white, and called these lighter and darker areas respectively. The results had several interesting features, as shown in Table 1.

Table 1

Arrest rates by age group and area type

Ratio†	Age 11–21				Age 22–35				All males 11–35	
	Black	Asian	White	All	Black	Asian	White	All	Population	%
< 10%	15.0	5.0	6.9	7.0	8.9	3.2	2.9	3.0	79235	90
> 10%	8.9	4.4	13.3	9.9	4.4	2.4	3.9	3.7	9175	10
All areas	11.7	4.7	7.2	7.2	6.3	3.1	3.0	3.1	88410	100

* Rate = (total number of offenders in all relevant areas/total estimated population in these areas) × 100.

† Ratio = (all black households + all Asian households)/all households.

When we looked at the lighter and darker areas separately we found considerable differences. In the *lighter* areas (top line, Table 1) we can see that, again, Blacks have the highest arrest rates, and the Asian rate is close to that of Whites. The *darker* areas present a different picture. In the younger group it is the Whites who have a much higher arrest rate than Blacks—13.3 per cent. compared with 8.9 per cent., and Asians have the lowest rate at 4.4 per cent. In the older groups Blacks and Whites have virtually the same rate (4.4 per cent. and 3.9 per cent. respectively) with Asians, once again, having the lowest.

Table 2 gives a more detailed analysis, for Blacks and Whites only. It shows, in the first two columns (younger group) how the Black arrest rates increases steadily as the areas change from over 33 per cent. non-white to less than 2 per cent. At the same time the White rate decreases steadily.

---

[16] A special tabulation was obtained from the Office of Population, Censuses and Surveys.

[17] These age groups were chosen as the census gave numbers in age groups 5–15, and 16–29, six years earlier.

[18] Excluding certain wards on the outskirts of Leeds.

Table 2

Arrest rates related to census variables (Blacks and Whites)

	Arrest rates				Census data (1981)					
	Age 11–21		Age 22–25		% Privately rented		% Unemployed		No. of households	
Ratio†	Black	White	Black	White	Black	White	Black	White	Black	White
< 2%	16.5	5.4	6.1	2.4	5	4	7	18	420	90900
2–10%	11.1	8.3	9.0	3.2	15	13	25	19	1055	76820
10–33%	9.5	12.6	4.1	3.6	10	27	21	27	500	4460
33% +	7.8	14.4	4.6	7.3	3	26	41	39	915	1340
All Areas	11.7	7.2	6.3	3.0	9	9	24	19	2890	173520

* Rate = (total number of offenders in all relevant areas/total estimated population in these areas) × 100.

† Ratio = (all black households + all Asian households)/all households.

Three interesting questions arise: why do Blacks have higher arrest rates in the lighter areas than in the darker areas? Why do they have higher rates than Whites in these areas? And why do Whites have higher rates than Blacks especially among the young in the darker areas?

Part of an answer to these may be found in the fact that a personal visit (by the researchers) to the areas where the black arrestees lived revealed that these were pockets of very poor houses in large wards of predominantly good class housing. It may also be the case that reporting *by* Blacks of offences *against* Blacks was lower in the darker areas; or that police are more inclined to "cuff" (*i.e.* not record) Black offences in these areas, in the interests of improving race relations. The answer to the third question may lie in the socio-economic characteristics of Blacks and Whites living in these areas, which suggest we were not in fact comparing "like with like." Table 2 shows data for two characteristics—proportions living in privately rented housing and unemployment (1981 data). The Whites had over a quarter in the darker areas (third and fourth lines of Table 2) in privately rented housing, whereas the Blacks had 10 per cent. or less. This suggests the Whites were a more transient, less stable population. The unemployment rates did not differ significantly in these darker areas, being high for both groups. It should be noted that the darker areas contained only 6 per cent. of the white population but between 50 per cent. and 60 per cent. of the Blacks and Asians.

3. Outcome of arrest

It was intended to follow up, through the records, all the Blacks and Asians who had been arrested, and a sample of the Whites. This material was to have been obtained from files returned to the police after the completion of the case (in the courts, or otherwise). Unfortunately, in the time period available, there was considerable shortfall due either to delays in the courts or the file having been impossible to trace for some reason. However, we were able to obtain details of all Crown Court cases from the Probation Service. It seems likely that the files of cases which had "no further action" or were cautioned would be returned to the police quickly, so we inferred that those cases not followed-up had been tried in the magistrates' courts. However, we were not able to know the outcome of those that had been tried (which probably had a high proportion of not guilty pleas, this being the likely explanation for the delayed return of at least some of the files), so our data were, to this extent, incomplete.

Table 3

Outcome of arrest

	Age 10–16			Age 17–35		
	Black	Asian	White	Black	Asian	White
Intended sample	95	56	280	255	126	756
% No Further Action	9	4	8	7	15	9
Total dealt with	86	54	261	237	107	687
Of these:						
% Cautioned	31	72	41	4	5	7
% Magistrates Court trial	54	20	52	57	66	62
[followed up]*	[11]	[9]	[19]	[21]	[30]	[23]
[not followed up]*	[43]	[11]	[33]	[36]	[36]	[39]
% Crown Court trial	14	7	7	39	29	31

* These figures are estimated and probably include a few cautioned and NFAed whose files had not been returned by July 1988 (see text).

We found among juveniles (aged 10–16) that about 8 per cent. had "no further action," with no difference between races. Of the remainder, significantly more Asians were cautioned (72 per cent. Asians compared with Blacks 31 per cent. and Whites 41 per cent.) About half of the Blacks and Whites were tried in the magistrates' courts and one-fifth of the Asians (see Table 3). In our sample we had details of only eight Blacks, five Asians and 43 Whites sentenced in the magistrates' courts. As many as a third of these received a custodial sentence, but the numbers were too small to detect differences in sentencing patterns. Blacks had significantly more tried in the Crown Court (14 per cent. compared with 7 per cent. of Asians and Whites). However, the numbers were small and examination of the data showed that several of the Blacks were arrested on one day (during riots) and at least one was charged with robbery, probably with adults; this one incident could have accounted for the larger percentage of Blacks going to the Crown Court.

For adults the pattern was somewhat different. Asians had significantly more "no further action," 15 per cent. compared with 7 per cent. Blacks and 9 per cent. Whites. Once again, the reason is unclear. Possibly the Asians had been arrested too readily or the police thought the matter would be dealt with within the Asian community. However, the proportions cautioned were about the same (at about 6 per cent.) The most interesting finding was once again that

Blacks had significantly more tried in the Crown Court (39 per cent. compared with about 30 per cent. of the other groups. See Table 3).

We were able to examine the records to explore the reason for this difference. The proportion of "indictable only" offences was small (about 3 per cent), about the same for each race. The triable-either way offences were classified as "Summary Trial Not Available"—that is, the magistrate thought the case too serious to be dealt with in the lower courts—or "Defendant Elects Jury Trial." We found for each of the races 75 per cent. fell into the former category and 25 per cent. into the latter. Thus although it is true to say more Blacks chose to be committed to the Crown Court for trial this was certainly not a complete explanation of the difference, as magistrates also committed more cases.

With regard to acquittal rates in the magistrates' courts, our data are too uncertain to draw firm conclusions as they are incomplete. This is also true to some extent for the Crown Court cases. The indications are, however, that in both types of court a higher proportion of Blacks pleaded "not guilty" and of these a higher proportion of Blacks were acquitted.[19]

An analysis of sentencing in the magistrates' courts and in the Crown Court (where the data were available) showed that differences between the races in sentencing were not significant. Details are given in Table 4. About 5 per cent. in the magistrates courts received immediate custody, and about 40 per cent. in the Crown Court.

Table 4

Distribution of sentences (age 17–35) (percentages)

Sentences	Magistrates' Court			Crown Court		
	Black	*Asian*	*White*	*Black*	*Asian*	*White*
Custody	5	3	5	44	40	32
Suspended Sentence	2	3	7	11	12	9
Detention Centre			0*	1		3
Community Service Order	5		5	12	20	16
Probation	2		5	14	8	13
Fine	70	70	57	4	12	4
Discharge, Other	15	23	21	13	8	6
N = 100%	40	30	141	76	25	206

* Less than 0.5%, but not zero.

4. Observation and interviews

The collection of data from the police files formed an important part of this research, but it was thought that a look at "what went on" behind the statistics might help explain any statistical differences that emerged. The main difference between the races in the data so far discussed was that in the arrest rates of Blacks and Whites living in the same areas. As has been mentioned, our limited resources made it impossible to examine the circumstances leading up to the

[19] Details of these results are given in the Main Report *op. cit.* Chap. 2.

arrest which might, or might not, explain this finding, and we were also unable to interview the police on this matter.

However, with regard to the follow-up of arrests, one of the research team was able to sit in on a Juvenile Case Referral Panel, which recommended whether juveniles should be cautioned, and another member made observations in the magistrates' courts. Lastly, interviews were carried out with panel members, and with some of the solicitors who had had black clients, to explore their perceptions.[20]

(a) A Juvenile Case Referral Panel

A Juvenile Case Referral Panel in one police subdivision was observed in its decision making. One member of the panel of five was black. In 12 cases of the 23 observed there was clear indications that the child concerned was black, and three were identified as Asian by their names. But no specific reference was made to the race of the children, nor did it appear to affect deliberations. Thirty-nine per cent. of the cases observed received a caution with no significant difference between races. This appears to be a relatively low figure (The percentage for West Yorkshire was 77 per cent. in 1987,[21] though our figures, gleaned from police statistics, were much lower, see Table 3). The members of the panel were interviewed. There was unanimous agreement that race did not affect the panel's work, "even though some thought racial identification would prove useful for monitoring purposes."[22] Our observations confirmed this: race did not seem to affect panel decision-making.

(b) Court room observations

A total of 135 cases were observed in the magistrates' courts: 46 Blacks; 7 Asians; and 82 Whites. The majority of cases were dealt with in a routine, bureaucratic fashion and suffered at least one adjournment. "Harsh" treatment was observed in only a small number of cases (18 per cent.) and was usually attributable to particular benches. Racial discrimination was not observable, though proportionately slightly more Blacks and Asians were subject to harsh treatment. This was also true of lenient treatment, which was less common (13 per cent.) and more randomly distributed across benches. A "cocky" demeanour, one possible explanation for harsher treatment, was only rarely observed, more often with white than black youths.

Our overriding conclusion was that racially discriminatory behaviour was not an obvious or noticeable feature of court-room interactions. However, we thought bail and custodial remands, of which we observed few, might repay a closer look. And we stress that the absence of noticeable discriminatory behaviour says nothing about how defendants *perceived* their treatment.

---

[20] See Main Report *op. cit.* Chap. 4 for more details. Only brief summaries are presented here.

[21] *Criminal Statistics, 1987.* Home Office (1988) H.M.S.O. London.

[22] Main Report *op. cit.* n. 10 at p. 64.

(c) Interviews with solicitors:

Nine solicitors were interviewed for between 20 and 50 minutes about the treatment of ethnic minority defendants. Each had some dealings with black clients, though few had a caseload of more than 25 per cent. black or Asian clients. Experiences and perceptions of black clients differed, though mention was made of greater intelligence, more alienation, a greater tendency to plead not guilty, and to be "excitable" or "cocky" in court. Asian clients tended to be seen as less criminal, to lack credibility as witnesses, and to be industrious and family-minded.

The police were the agency criticised most in their dealings with black clients, and belief in police harassment was widespread. Courts were generally regarded as fair, and in some cases as attempting to compensate for racial disadvantage. However, some thought courts were very variable, and that particular courts were "out of touch." Mention was made by some of a belief that Blacks get custodial sentences more often. The efforts of probation and social services were praised, whilst lawyers were not exempted from charges of racial prejudice. Black and Asian clients were recognised as having special needs, resulting from, for example, cultural differences.

Overall, though the various criminal justice agencies were seen as differentially culpable with regard to racial discrimination, racially prejudiced *attitudes* were thought to be widespread. Sometimes these were regarded as the product of individuals, sometimes of institutions.

5. Survey[23]

The survey was carried out in Leeds to compare the three race groups— Blacks, Asians and Whites—in their attitudes to the police and their experiences of them. We wished to compare those living in the same areas (as we did for arrest rates) and decided to exclude areas with less than 10 per cent. non-whites. We were thus able to control, to some extent, for socio-economic characteristics of the environment, and for the amount of policing. The respondents in the survey cannot be regarded as representative of the general population as these areas contained only 58 per cent. of Blacks and 55 per cent. of Asians and even less Whites (6 per cent.) in the city. Besides this we confined our survey to males aged 10–35, the full questionnaire being given to those aged 16–35. The latter group contained 171 Blacks, 199 Asians and 271 Whites (totalling 641). Only 225 boys were interviewed and their results, while interesting (and, so far as we know, possibly unique), will be mentioned only briefly.

(a) Attitude to the police

Attitude to the police was explored in several ways, the main measures being called "approval," "perception" and "co-operation." We measured approval by asking respondents to say if they broadly agreed with several general statements about the police (*e.g.*, police do a good job). We found Blacks were more disapproving than Whites, who in turn were more disapproving than Asians. With

---

[23] Full details of methodology and questionnaire are given in Main Report *op. cit* n. 10, Chap. 5.

regard to "perception" we asked if the police were thought to indulge in certain types of misconduct, such as using unnecessary violence.[24] Blacks and Whites were remarkably similar on this item, with Asians having a better perception of the police. This was also the case when we asked about whether the police discriminated against certain groups, two-thirds of Blacks and Whites believing this but only about one-third of Asians. The measure of co-operation was obtained by asking if the respondent would probably report to the police an offence he had witnessed. In this case Blacks were clearly less co-operative than Asians and Whites, who did not differ significantly.

These results, which show that Blacks and Whites are similar in some aspects of their attitude to the police, tend to differ from those in some other studies (such as the P.S.I. Survey of Londoners) carried out on samples representative of very large areas, in which Whites will have higher proportions in the higher socio-economic groups than Blacks. These found, in the main, that Blacks had a consistently more hostile attitude to the police. Our most striking finding was that Asians differed consistently from Blacks, and this emphasises the need to consider these two racial groups separately. (We cannot, of course, assume that there was no differences between Asians in different parts of the country—or, indeed, that particular events at any one time do not affect their attitude.)

(b) Experience of the police

We asked respondents whether they had been stopped (on foot or in a vehicle) or had their house searched in the last year, and whether they had been arrested in the last five years (called here, "stopped, etc.") It emerged that, if anything Whites had had more such experiences than Blacks, and Asians less than both. Besides this, we asked about contacting the police for help. Whites had contacted the police more than Blacks, and Asians less than both, Whites tending to be more satisfied with the result.

In relating these results to our measures of attitude to the police we found those who had been stopped etc., had a less favourable attitude to the police on all three measures. But, besides this we found those who had not been stopped etc. at all still reflected the overall differences between races—Blacks being least favourable, Asians most favourable, with Whites being sometimes closer to Blacks and sometimes closer to Asians.

Other experiences of the police emerged from follow up questions to perception of the police. For example, a large number (16 per cent.) thought that the police had used unnecessary violence towards themselves, or that an acquaintance had experienced or witnessed this. Both the Blacks and the Whites interviewed contained several people who had had some unpleasant experience of the police, though this only occasionally (for the Blacks) included a racial element. Once again, fewer Asians had had unpleasant experiences.

---

[24] These items were copied from Policy Studies Institute *Survey of Londoners*, D. Smith (1983) London: Policy Studies Institute. For a recent, in-depth, small-scale study of black and white experiences of the criminal justice system, see Smellie, E. and Crow, I. *Black People's Experience of Criminal Justice*, (1991) London: NACRO.

(c) Other items

We investigated several other topics to see in what ways the race groups differed. We found that the Blacks had more unemployed than Asians and Whites, and of those who were employed Whites had less in semi- and unskilled jobs. Whites had significantly more in privately rented accommodation (confirming the census, Table 3) and had over half who had lived in their house less than three years, compared with about a quarter of Blacks and Asians; they also had more than academic qualifications. This shows that the groups of Blacks and Whites differed in certain important respects.

We attempted to investigate, briefly, some aspect of "way of life" and found Blacks and Whites had, on average, gone out just under three evenings in the previous week and Asians only one and a half times. We also looked at their transport, destination and time they returned home, which revealed some slight differences. Only for Whites was if found that those who went out more were likely to have been stopped. We also talked about experiences of being victims of offences and found Blacks had significantly less, and had reported fewer of these to the police.

(d) The boys

We found that the pattern of boys' attitudes to the police were consistent with those of adults, Blacks and Whites tending to be similar, and Asians slightly more favourable than the others. In some cases Blacks were less favourable than Whites. For example, when asked if they would like to be a policeman 47 per cent. of Blacks said "definitely not" compared with 36 per cent. of Whites and 23 per cent. of Asians. A fairly high proportion, 18 per cent. (nearly one in five) had been stopped by the police in the street.

It is interesting to speculate whether the boys' attitudes are a result of their own experiences or are simply a reflection of the attitudes of the adults in their household.

6. Summary and conclusions

(a) Summary

The research that has been carried out in Leeds illustrates the complexity of the data regarding the comparative involvement of Blacks and Whites in the Criminal Justice System. With Asians the picture in Leeds appears more straightforward: they tended to be less involved at every stage.

(i) *Arrest rates.* The analysis of arrest rates (males aged 11–35) showed that in the whole city, Blacks had higher rates than Whites, but when the areas were grouped into those with less than 10 per cent. non-white and those with more than 10 per cent. (*lighter* and *darker* areas, respectively), it was found than in the *darker* areas Whites had *higher* arrest rates than Blacks. These areas tended to be socially deprived, with more unemployment, more manual workers, etc., *i.e.* those characteristics that tend to be associated with a high offender rate.[25] How-

---

[25] See Baldwin, J. and Bottoms. A. E. *The Urban Criminal* (1976) London: Tavistock.

ever, there were two big differences: Whites had more in privately rented accommodation and had lived there for a shorter time; these areas contained only 6 per cent. of the White population in the city. The Black households in these areas (58 per cent. of those in the city) were evidently a more stable population, although both groups had high unemployment rates. It is possible the low rates for Blacks were due to under-reporting by black victims of black offenders in these areas, or under-recording by the police. The absence of these factors might also explain the higher arrest rate of blacks in the *lighter* areas.

(ii) *Follow-ups.* It appeared that, among the juveniles, Asians had more cautions, and among the adults Asians had more with "no further action." Apart from this, it was found that sentencing in the magistrates' courts and sentencing in the Crown Court did not differ significantly. However, more Blacks were tried in the Crown Court where custodial sentences are more likely. Blacks had more pleading not guilty and more acquitted than Whites. These results are similar to a finding of M.P.D. statistics of sentencing, 1983.[26] This study confirms the need to carry out a follow-through of all persons arrested and not look simply at discrete "moments" in the process.

(iii) *The survey.* This was confined to areas where more than half the non-white population lived, and where all the areas had more than 10 per cent. non-white. Comparisons between the three race groups were between those living in the same small areas *i.e.* in roughly the same circumstances, rather than over a whole city or London borough. This made the differences found more meaningful.

Instead of finding Whites had more favourable attitudes to the police than Blacks, and had been stopped, etc., less (as found in the studies of larger areas), we found that on some measures Whites were similar to Blacks in their attitude and experience, though there was still a tendency for Blacks to be less favourable to the police. Asians tended to be more favourable on every measure, and to have had less experience of stops, etc.

(b) Conclusions

Our decision to take a more detailed comparative look at the throughput of males from different ethnic backgrounds from arrest to final outcome within a provincial city would appear to be vindicated. Though it provides no final answers to our starting questions, it demonstrates the difficulties—of methodology and interpretation—involved in comparative work of this sort, and the need for research designs to take these into account. It also identified certain "moments"—decisions about charging and type of trial, for example—which would clearly benefit from closer analysis. Finally, our research indicates that area of residence needs to be taken into account in comparing the experiences of the police of Blacks and Whites. Overall differences, which have been found in

---

[26] See Walker *op. cit.* n. 8.

other studies, may be partly due to black people tending to live in areas of social deprivation. Besides this we found that there are important differences between the Black and Asian experience of criminal justice, and that this needs to be taken into account in ethnically-based studies.

[7]

new community 16(1): 23—34

October 1989

Discrimination and disparity: the influence of race on sentencing

Barbara Hudson

Abstract Although it has been established by official statistics that Afro-Caribbeans are over-represented in the prison population, research into sentencing decisions has yielded little evidence of discrimination. This article reviews existing research, and presents results of a survey which does suggest some race influence on sentencing. The article suggests that understanding of race effects could be advanced in relation to other known characteristics of sentencing, for instance that there are disparities in the sentences given by different courts to people convicted of similar offences. Strategies for further research are suggested.

Disparity of sentencing between courts, and between regions of the country, and discrimination by the courts against black[1] people are both areas of concern to those working within the criminal justice system, and to academics reflecting upon the system. Both are areas where, although much disquiet is voiced by people at all levels, and where official statistics have provided evidence that the phenomena are real, little empirical research has been accomplished to establish either the dimensions of disparity and discrimination, or the mechanisms by which they are produced. To the extent that they have been studied, they have been treated as completely separate outcomes of criminal justice processes. Seldom is it argued that the disparity which is apparent between courts and areas in sentencing in relation to offence categories is the product of patterns of consistent discrimination against certain types of offenders, notably black people, and in particular unemployed, male Afro-Caribbeans.

Disparity and discrimination have both aroused the concern of practitioners and policy-makers, and it is only in applied, policy-oriented briefing papers, or statistical exercises with little interpretive discussion, that these two characteristics of the criminal justice system are addressed together. The National Association for the Care and Resettlement of Offenders (NACRO), the Lord Chancellor and Home Office officials, as well as bodies such as the Magistrates Association and the National Association of Probation Officers have addressed both issues, but on different occasions and without any attempt to link the two together. Evidence for disparity is given by regional statistics, which show for instance that the rates of custody differ considerably between such ostensibly similar regions as Oxford and Cambridge or Greater Manchester and Merseyside, whereas evidence for discrimination is derived from aggregated national statistics, where differences between regions are lost.

Barbara Hudson is Senior Lecturer in the Department of Social Work and Social Policy, Newcastle upon Tyne Polytechnic.

If discrimination and disparity are separated at the practice-policy level, they are still more hermetically sealed against each other when considered theoretically. Discrimination on the basis of race and other personal-social characteristics of offenders (gender, unemployment, etc.) has been analysed within a sociological framework, the problematic being the state's repression of potentially threatening groups of people, as for example in the work of Box (1983; 1987), where aggregate data links 'capitalism' with the imprisonment of black people and unemployed and other potential dissidents, and where England and Wales during the last 20 years becomes the most detailed unit of analysis, so that differences between individual industrial-capitalist societies, let alone between courts or regions, are not addressed. Disparity, on the other hand, has been discussed by scholars coming from a legal or jurisprudential background (e.g., very influentially by Ashworth 1983), whose concern is that present disparities between different courts within the same jurisdiction can threaten fairness, an important legal value, and can engender disrespect for the legal system: such critics generally do not relate sentencing to general levels of difference between one country and another in terms of offences taken seriously, nor do they relate disparities to the characteristics of the offenders coming before the courts in the different regions of the country. Discrimination then, has been ascribed to functional necessities of 'the capitalist state' and not at all to the prejudices of individual sentencers; disparity, on the other hand, has been explained entirely in terms of the whims and tempers of sentencers, with explanations sought in terms of the social backgrounds of judges, and even the states of their livers or their relations to their wives, and never in relation to structured discrimination against ethnic minority or other disadvantaged defendants.

The purpose of this paper is first of all to look at some of the evidence of discrimination against black people in the sentences passed by English courts; secondly to suggest that disparity and discrimination have some relationship to each other, and thirdly to point to some directions for future research.

Do British courts discriminate against black people?

Discrimination against black people in our courts is something that can very easily be observed or experienced, but seems curiously unamenable to endorsement by systematic research. For many years this was also the case with the search for proof of discrimination by the criminal justice system generally. Anyone visiting one of our prisons, for example, and especially one of our young offender institutions, was likely to be struck by the sight of a disproportionate number of black faces (Kettle 1982), but official statistics on the ethnic composition of prison populations were unobtainable. With the publication in 1986 of data from a prison census taken on 30 June 1985, the Home Office acknowledged that the proportion of prisoners with ethnic minority backgrounds was substantially higher than their proportion in the general population.

The proportions of West Indian, Guyanese or African origin were substantially higher than in the general population but the proportions of prisoners from the Indian subcontinent were similar to, or even slightly lower than, the general population (Home Office 1986). Subsequent editions of the annual *Prison Statistics* have shown the disproportionate Afro-Caribbean presence to have risen still higher. Given that people are imprisoned by a decision of magistrates or crown court judges, the question immediately begged by the prison statistics is whether these figures represent discriminatory sentencing, or higher black crime rates.

So far, the balance of findings has tended to favour the idea that there is little if any discrimination at the sentencing stage of the criminal justice process, because a disproportionately high number of black people – particularly young black males – find themselves in court charged with serious offences, so that even though black custody rates may be higher than white, when all the variables such as offence seriousness, existing court orders breached, previous convictions, etc. are taken into account, little direct discrimination that could be attributed to race remains. As one of the most frequently cited studies summarises in relation to Crown Courts: '... defendants are treated equally once they obtain the status of convicted prisoners: not necessarily fairly or appropriately, but equally' (McConville and Baldwin 1982: 658).

Table 1 *Ethnic minority prisoners as a proportion of all prisoners (30 June 1985) (per cent)*

	Prisoners under sentence	Unconvicted prisoners	General population
Young males (17–21)	12.0	16	6
Adult males	11.5	15	5
Young females (17–21)	12.0	23	6
Adult females		23	5

Source: Home Office 1986

Similar findings have been reported for magistrates courts (Crow and Cove 1984). The lack of what may be called 'residual discrimination', or the excess use of custody or severity of sentence for black defendants that cannot be explained away by offence types or previous criminal/criminal justice history, is supported by a recent Home Office study of sentencing in the Crown Courts:

> This evidence, although limited, suggests that overall differences in the use of custody between ethnic groups could be accounted for by differences in offences and criminal history. The results therefore support McConville and Baldwin's finding that there are no significant differences in the use of custody for different racial groups sentenced at the Crown Court (Moxon 1988: 60).

Another recently published study of sentencing in the courts in the Metropolitan Police District finds higher black than white custody rates, but does not include data on seriousness of the offences involved or on previous convictions, and therefore does not claim to have found any evidence of discriminatory sentencing (Walker 1988).

Taken together, these studies provide evidence of higher black custody rates and of black defendants being present in the overall sentenced population in higher proportions than in the general population. They are particularly likely to be present in certain offence groups. Three explanations of the high black imprisonment rates acknowledged by Home Office prison statistics are therefore possible:

(i) proportionately more black people than white are committing crimes
(ii) black people commit proportionately more of those offences which carry high risk of custody
(iii) black people are more vulnerable than their white counterparts to apprehension and prosecution by the police.

These three possibilities are, of course, not posed as mutually exclusive; commentators generally suggest that all three may contribute to such a high percentage of the Afro-Caribbean population coming before the courts on charges for which the outcome is normally a custodial sentence.

Arrest statistics provide support for the first two propositions. For instance, a study of arrests in the Metropolitan Police District found black people to be contributing extensively to police crime statistics, and especially in the more serious offence categories (Stevens and Willis 1979). These authors found that although black people formed only 4.2 per cent of the area's population, they accounted for 37.1 per cent of arrests for violent theft and 28.7 per cent of robbery arrests. Moxon also reports Afro-Caribbeans as being very highly represented in robbery and drugs offences in his sample of Crown Court cases (Moxon 1988). Sociological or criminological discussions of these and other findings have suggested that black people (particularly young, unemployed Afro-Caribbeans) are driven to crime because they are marginalised by white society and are denied legitimate access to income, pleasure and status (Lea and Young 1984). On the other hand, it is sometimes claimed that black people are no more criminal in their actual behaviour than are their white counterparts, but over-representation is a reflection of stereotyping and rampant racism, which leads the police to stop, or to investigate, black people known to them when there is any crime requiring clearing up (Gilroy 1982; 1987). Support for this latter view can be found in studies of police cautioning, where white youths have been found to be twice as likely to be cautioned as black youths for auto-crime, public order offences and crimes of violence, while white youths with previous convictions are four times as likely to be cautioned as blacks apprehended for similar offences (Landau and Nathan 1983). In another study amongst adults, Afro-Caribbeans were five times as likely to be stopped and searched as whites (Tuck and Southgate 1981).

I have discussed these issues at greater length elsewhere (Hudson 1987: Chapter Four); for the purposes of the present paper, my starting point is that it is implausible at a common-sense level to believe that there is a segment of the criminal justice system (or, indeed, a segment of British institutional life in any sphere) which is totally devoid of discrimination. Sentencing may not be as blatantly discriminatory as policing or, for example, decision-making in regard to the granting of parole, but this is not to say that it is completely absent. Rather than sentencing being perfectly rational, offence determined and non-discriminatory, it could be that inappropriate research techniques have been used, or the wrong questions asked, or misleading definitions been used.

Greater London sentencing survey: preliminary analysis

As well as looking at existing studies, I have also analysed data from a survey of sentencing carried out in 14 courts (both magistrates' courts and Crown Courts) in the Greater London area, to see if these data would yield evidence of discrimination (Hudson 1989). It must be stated here that looking for a race influence on sentencing was not the sole or even the primary purpose of this research; rather, it was designed to illuminate the sentencing behaviour of the courts with respect to their rate of usage of various sentences; the types of offence and offender particularly vulnerable to custody in the different courts; the 'tariff' position of probation and community service in the various courts, and the degree of influence of developments such as Court of Appeal guideline judgements, and Home Office penal policy documents. Race became an important focus of interpretation of the findings as equality of service delivery is one of the objectives of the agency for which I worked. The study was conducted over a three-year period, with each court annually monitored for three months, and information amassed on some 8,000 sentencing decisions. Questions included on the monitoring forms covered the type and length of sentence, the value of any property involved, the number of charges, and current court orders breached. Also recorded were the recommendations of the social enquiry report (if any) and the age, gender, racial appearance, employment, accommodation and family status of the defendant.

There were differences in the sentences given to Afro-Caribbeans when compared with other defendants, and although some variation can be explained away by reference to other factors, differences in sentencing (and other decisions made by the courts) remained that cannot be attributed to offence seriousness or other factors. Similar findings were also contained in most of the works cited above, but have generally been given less prominence than the 'no discrimination' conclusions. The custody rates which emerged from the sentencing decisions were 1 in 10 offenders for Afro-Caribbean males, and 1 in 27 for white European males. This appears fairly startling, but like other studies, it becomes less clear-cut if other factors are examined. A substantial number of the sentences of immediate custody involved drugs importation and almost all these cases involved Afro-Caribbean defendants. Black defendants were also over-represented in robbery cases. Like Moxon, I was less interested in these cases, where the seriousness of the offence suggests little judicial discretion in choosing a non-custodial sentence, than in more run-of-the-mill cases, where there is scope for a choice from a wide range of sentences. For common offence types for which custody is a probability but by no means a certainty, I found the use of custody to be higher for Afro-Caribbeans than for white Europeans in the crown courts included in the survey.

Table 2 *Offenders sentenced to unsuspended custody by race (per cent)*

Offence	White European	Afro-Caribbean
Abh/assault	50	75
Burglary	49	64

On looking at the actual cases producing these statistics, I also found that Afro-Caribbeans had fewer previous convictions, a finding congruent with the NACRO report *Black People and the Criminal Justice System* (NACRO 1986) which claimed that Afro-Caribbeans are going to prison earlier in their criminal careers than white offenders. This discrepancy was even more marked with the magistrates' court sample, particularly in the assault/actual bodily harm offence category, which produced the same disparities in the rate of custody as the crown court cases. Taking out those cases producing serious injury to the victims (both black and white defendants), there were no cases where custodial sentences were given for white first-time offenders, but several on Afro-Caribbeans.

After reading Moxon's crown court study (1988), I re-examined my own data to see whether any of the factors he cites as influencing judges towards custody could account for my findings: age of the victim, abuse of a position of trust, lack of a settled way of life, etc. I found that although these factors could account for some of the difference in custody rates, a small amount of 'residual discrimination' remained, especially in relation to the more mundane offences against the person, and minor robbery cases. (It may seem perverse to describe any robbery as minor, but as Moxon points out, the range of behaviour which is described by this legal classification extends from the snatching of small amounts of money or property, to very dangerous, brutal robbery with violence, maybe with the use of weapons.)

One feature of the cases included in my survey which is also present in reports of other studies although given less prominence than the 'no-discrimination' policy, is that when the defendant is Afro-Caribbean, offences are most likely to be described in such a way that they come into the most serious possible legal category. Crow and Cove, whilst finding little discrimination at the sentencing stage, also remark that with Afro-Caribbeans charged with assault, there were more cases where the victim had suffered no actual injury, than when the defendants were white (1984). There must, presumably, have been scope for a reduction of such charges to threatening behaviour or breach of the peace or for non-prosecution. This accords with evidence from the USA, where studies have found that cases with black assailants, especially if the victims are white, are less likely to be downgraded than in the opposite case (Radelet and Pierce 1985).

Legal variables, such as offence type and previous criminal history, are not the only factors which affect sentences. Unemployment and lack of a permanent address, family or other community ties have also been shown to affect sentences given by both magistrates' courts and crown courts (see Moxon 1988 for a discussion of crown courts; Crow and Simon 1987 in relation to magistrates' courts). Writers within the legalistic framework see the effect of employment as working primarily through being allowed as a mitigatory factor in cases where the seriousness of the offence would indicate a custodial sentence (Thomas 1979). The sociology of control perspective suggests that the harshness of sentencing the unemployed is part of the repression of disaffected groups (Box 1983) as well as an historical continuation of the use of prisons and reformatories to resocialise the workshy and reclaim the indigent as well as to punish criminals (Blom-Cooper 1988). Studies of the effect of unemployment on imprisonment rates in both England and Wales and the USA were reviewed by Box and Hale, who also find some evidence that unemployment affects sentencing independently of rises in crime rates (1982). Box also looked at studies which investigate both race and unemployment, and reports some independent effect on sentencing for both factors (1983; 1987).

Black unemployment rates are, of course, higher than white unemployment rates, and so it is a point of interest in sentencing research to ask whether it is because so many black defendants are unemployed that they seem to receive harsher sentences. One could, of course, reverse the question and ask whether it is because so many unemployed people are black that employment status is correlated with sentencing. This seems not to have arisen as a major research interest.

The major effect of unemployment on sentencing may be related to the decline over the last decade in the use of the fine as a percentage of all sentences. Other sentences such as conditional discharge and probation have increased proportionately. If one looks at disparities in rates of custody throughout the country, it is those regions which have the most unemployment which have consistently come top of the custody league. Regions like Cleveland, for example, which have well-developed programmes of 'Alternatives to Custody', regularly produce very high rates particularly for young offender custody, whereas areas like Surrey produce much lower rates. People can still be fined in Surrey, where unemployment is so much lower than in the north east. I wanted to look in my own data, therefore, at whether there was any difference by race in the sentencing of unemployed offenders for similar offences.

To investigate this, I looked at theft cases where there were no more than two previous convictions, where there were not multiple charges, and where there was property involved to the value of £100 or less, and where the theft did not involve a breach of trust. This was to try to isolate cases which would normally attract a fine, and indeed in almost all such cases where the defendant was employed, the result was a fine. With unemployed offenders, the results were:

Table 3 *Sentencing of unemployed offenders (per cent)*

Sentence	White European	Afro-Caribbean
Conditional discharge	23	14
Probation	10	14
Community service	3	7

The point here is not custody, but that the sentencing of the black defendants is more interventionist than that of white defendants, producing the effect that NACRO describe, of black offenders going through the non-custodial options more quickly than white. In fact most of the probation orders for theft obtained on Afro-Caribbeans in my study were for females. I found a race-gender effect such that black females received a disproportionate number of supervisory sentences — probation, suspended sentence with a supervision order — and in addition the few community service orders made on females were on black females. Conversely, black males were unlikely to receive probation, receiving either community service or custody for cases similar to those in which the outcome for white European defendants was a fine or probation. In general, Afro-Caribbean defendants can be said to have a shorter tariff than white, largely missing out conditional discharge and fine, and with males tending to miss out probation as well. Moxon also reports black males being less likely to receive probation (Moxon 1988: 60). Both his study and my own data suggest that unemployment is correlated with high use of probation, and since a greater proportion of black defendants are unemployed, this would lead one to expect much higher numbers of black offenders being placed on probation. This does not happen in practice.

Another factor which Moxon and other researchers point to as being associated with custodial sentencing is the defendant being in breach of a current court order. Suspended sentences are activated when a subsequent offence occurs during the period of suspension and it has been suggested that this has meant that the introduction of the suspended sentence has added to, rather than reduced, the use of custody. Only about half of the original suspended sentences would have been given in place of custody rather than another non-custodial alternative, so any activation may be of sentences which may not have been of imprisonment in the first place (Bottoms 1981). Even where a suspended sentence is not actually in force at the time of sentence, the fact that it has already been used is very readily taken by judges to mean that only a sentence of immediate imprisonment will be taken seriously by the offender; similarly, having already been on probation or community service is often viewed as showing that the individual will only be deterred from future crime by a custodial sentence; that is, that non-custodial options have been tried and proved ineffective. Thus this 'up-tariffing' of black offenders for fairly run-of-the-mill crimes is an extremely important form of discrimination which feeds into the process by which disproportionate numbers of Afro-Caribbeans, with comparatively few previous convictions, come to be in prisons or young offender institutions.

Although I have by no means finished analysing the data produced by my survey, I feel that the evidence points, tentatively at the moment, to the idea that:

(1) in cases of offences against the person, there is a direct race effect on sentencing which produces custodial sentences in circumstances where white defendants would receive non-custodial disposals;

(2) with property offences, the impact of employment on sentences where custody is not considered appropriate is greater than the influence of race, but the latter influences the choice amongst non-custodial alternatives with the effect of producing more interventionist sentencing for Afro-Caribbeans;

(3) for very serious offences, offence gravity is the major influence on sentencing.

Discrimination and disparity

Amongst both the crown courts and the magistrates courts in my sample, there was considerable disparity of sentencing for offences of intermediate seriousness. Custodial sentencing by magistrates for burglary, for instance, ranged from 5 per cent in one court to 36 per cent in another, whereas in the crown courts the offences and criminal histories which resulted in probation and community service outcomes were very different. The vulnerability of the unemployed to custody, of black people to high-tariff, very interventionist sentencing in run-of-the-mill cases and to custody for even minor offences against the person, accompanied by the low use of probation for black males, was, however, entirely consistent between courts. Also consistent was the lower incidence of social enquiry reports presented on black defendants (also found by Moxon) which of course contributes to the low use of probation. This can be attributed in part to black defendants being more likely to contest cases, but even where reports are presented, there are fewer probation orders resulting. In follow-up work to the sentencing survey, I have looked at social enquiry reports, and in a borough whose courts are generally restrained in their use of custody, found a custody rate for those where reports have been presented of 34 per cent for the black and 8 per cent for the white defendants. In these cases the court has discretion to impose a non-custodial sentence so some race bias is suggested.

The borough which produced the highest custody rate has the highest percentage of ethnic minority populations in Greater London. On first examination, this borough's custody figures looked equally high for black and white defendants, but when sentences of less than one month given for motoring offences were subtracted, the result was much higher custody rates for Afro-Caribbeans than for white defendants. All the boroughs which produced high rates of custody and of high-tariff alternatives to custody for burglary, theft and assault/abh had high percentages of Afro-Caribbeans in these offence categories.

Looking at demographic data for the Greater London boroughs (by no means all of which were encompassed by my study), one finds that those boroughs which produce high custody rates also have the highest percentages of ethnic minority – particularly black – residents. Although I have not analysed this systematically and have no data on offences, criminal history or other factors, it is at least suggestive of the proposition that the racial and economic characteristics of the sentenced population in different areas are contributing to the production of regional sentencing disparities. Analysis of demographic and imprisonment data in the USA has produced evidence of a relationship between the two:

> ... there is no significant correlation between a state's racial composition and its crime rate but there is a very great positive relationship between its racial composition and its imprisonment rate (Nagel 1977: 162).

Conclusions

Research has so far failed to produce methodologically sound evidence of either the existence of or the extent of race influence on sentencing in the courts of England and Wales, and yet there is a widespread perception among those involved in the criminal justice system that this does occur. On this occasion, officialdom seems to be in advance of academia, with senior Home Office officials perceiving race matters as problems of real and urgent concern. Moreover, the Lord Chancellor recently suggested that all magistrates should receive race awareness training.

Research seems to have been impeded by deficiencies in three crucial aspects: definitions of discrimination, statistical evidence of discrimination, and any theoretical frame of reference within which to interpret findings. Without this being explicit, most studies seem to mean by discrimination, different rates of custodial sentencing for similar offences. This appears perfectly reasonable, until one remembers that the relationship between offence and sentence is not always very strong in any case and therefore to use it as a test for discrimination is questionable. The sensitivity of the subject demands statistical differences at a high level of significance drawn on a large sample of cases (Walker 1988). To date, there has not been a large, multi-factorial study which handled all the variables needing to be taken into account if a race effect on sentencing is to be isolated.

A large part of the difficulty in studying race and sentencing is that our knowledge of the behaviour of sentencers, and the factors which influence their decisions, is in any case very poor, so that it is difficult to know what variables should be included. Moxon's crown court (1988) study is thus an extremely valuable contribution with its multi-factorial analysis which reveals various characteristics associated with the use of different sentences. Particularly welcome is his inclusion of both offence-related and offender-related variables.

Progress could now best be made by looking at hypotheses from what we already know about black people and the courts, taking account of what we can learn from American and other studies. A need exists for middle-range research which fills the gap between observational studies, and large-scale surveys where the aggregating of data obscures the nuances of sentencing behaviour. Experiential knowledge might be regarded as too soft to be counted as 'methodologically sound', but it can feed into the formulation of hypotheses for testing. Some examples of things on which we do have evidence are that

(i) even where offences are similar, Afro-Caribbeans are receiving custody, and harsher alternatives to custody, with fewer previous convictions than whites;

(ii) Afro-Caribbeans have a shorter tariff than whites, with less likelihood of receiving fines or probation orders;

(iii) courts are less likely to ask for a social enquiry report in cases with black defendants, and are therefore less likely to pass a non-custodial sentence.

Research is needed not only to confirm this emergent factual mapping of discrimination, but also to demonstrate and theorise about the processes by which it occurs. This will necessarily take the study of race and the criminal justice system not only beyond the realm of the statistical interrogation of data, but also beyond the legal-jurisprudential paradigm where sentencing is thought of as responsive to the aims of penal policy, the seriousness of the offence, the previous criminal history of the person concerned and the individual subjectivity of the sentencer. Court decision-making will have to be seen as a process which, like all other social behaviour, is influenced by social-structural factors as well as legal definitions and individual beliefs. A sociological perspective will have to be introduced into the analysis, and social-structural variables such as the demographic and economic characteristics of the sentenced population taken into account in the study of any differences in the behaviour of sentencers or in the treatment received by different defendants.

The finding that Afro-Caribbeans receiving custodial sentences have fewer previous convictions, for example, has obvious resonances with the analysis of stereotyping advanced in one analysis of mugging (Hall *et al* 1978). It may be that in the case of offences against the person, the imagery of the black assailant is so strong that other, potentially mitigating, factors, such as previous good

The influence of race on sentencing   33

character, do not have the same impact as they do for white offenders. In the case of the shorter tariff, high black unemployment rates probably contribute greatly to the relatively low proportion of fines given to Afro-Caribbeans, but both the comparatively low number of probation orders and the relative infrequency of social enquiry reports also point to the stereotyping of black people. There is also some evidence of this being applicable to probation officers in the production of social enquiry reports, as well as to magistrates and judges (Pinder 1984; Hudson 1988).

It is to be hoped that present levels of official concern about the treatment of black people in the criminal justice system will be sustained, and that one of the outcomes of this concern will be the greater availability of data. Researchers should, however, also address themselves to undertaking smaller-scale studies to test specific forms of disadvantage within the criminal justice system, especially at the point of sentence. Priority should be given not just to showing the scale of discrimination, but also to understanding the processes by which it is produced.

Note

1   The term 'black' is used to refer to people of Caribbean, African and Asian origin.

References

Ashworth, A. (1983) *Sentencing and Penal Policy*, London: Weidenfeld and Nicholson

Blom-Cooper, L. (1988) *The Penalty of Imprisonment*, London: Prison Reform Trust and Howard League for Penal Reform

Bottoms, A.E. (1981) 'The suspended sentence in England, 1967–78', *British Journal of Criminology* 21(1): 1–26

Box, S. (1983) *Power, Crime and Mystification*, London: Tavistock

Box, S. (1987) *Recession, Crime and Punishment*, London: Macmillan

Box, S. and Hale, C. (1982) 'Economic Crisis and the Rising Prisoner Population in England and Wales, 1949–1979', *Crime and Social Justice* 16: 20–35

Crow, I. and Cove, J. (1984) 'Ethnic minorities and the courts', *Criminal Law Review*, 413–417

Crow, I. and Simon, F. (1987) *Unemployment and Magistrates Courts*, London: National Association for the Care and Resettlement of Offenders

Gilroy, P. (1982) 'Police and Thieves' in Centre for Contemporary Cultural Studies, *The Empire Strikes Back: Race and Racism in 1970s Britain*, London: Hutchinson

Gilroy, P. (1987) 'The Myth of Black Criminality' in P. Scraton (ed.), *Law, Order and the Authoritarian State*, Milton Keynes: Open University Press

Hall, S., Critcher, C., Jefferson, T., Clarke, J. and Roberts, B. (1978) *Policing the Crisis*, London: Macmillan

Home Office (1986) 'The Ethnic Origins of Prisoners: the Prison Population on 30 June 1985 and Persons Received, July 1984–March 1985', *Home Office Statistical Bulletin* 17/86

Hudson, B. (1987) *Justice Through Punishment*, London: Macmillan

Hudson, B. (1988) 'Content Analysis of Social Enquiry Reports Written in the Borough of Haringey', unpublished

Hudson, B. (1989) *Court Sentencing Survey: Final Report*, London: Middlesex Area Probation Service

Kettle, M. (1982) 'The Racial Numbers Game in Our Prisons', *New Society* 16(1037): 535–537

Lea, J. and Young, J. (1984) *What is to be Done about Law and Order?*, Harmondsworth: Penguin

McConville, M. and Baldwin, J. (1982) 'The Influence of Race on Sentencing in England', *Criminal Law Review*, pp. 652–658

34   Barbara Hudson

Moxon, D. (1988) *Sentencing Practice in the Crown Courts*, Home Office Research Study No. 103

Nagel, W.G. (1977) 'On Behalf of a Moratorium on Prison Construction', *Crime and Delinquency* 13(2): 154–172

National Association for the Care and Resettlement of Offenders (1986) *Black People and the Criminal Justice System*, London, NACRO

Pinder, R. (1984) *Probation Work in a Multi-Racial Society: A Research Report*, Leeds: University of Leeds

Radelet, M.C. and Pierce, G.L. (1985) 'Race and Prosecution Discretion in Homicide Cases', *Law and Society Review* 19(4): 587–621

Stevens, P. and Willis, C.F. (1979) *Race, Crime and Arrests*, Home Office Research Study No. 58

Thomas, D. (1979) *Principles of Sentencing* (2nd edition), London: Heinemann

Tuck, M. and Southgate, P. (1981) *Ethnic Minorities, Crime and Policing*, Home Office Research Study No. 70

Walker, M. (1988) 'The Court Disposal of Young Males, by Race, in London in 1983', *British Journal of Criminology* 28(4): 441–460

International Journal of the Sociology of Law 1988, **16**, 295–313

Black People and the Criminal Law: Rhetoric and Reality

PAUL GORDON

The Runnymede Trust, 178 North Gower Street, London NW1 2NB, U.K.

Introduction

Discussions of the criminalisation of black people in Britain [1] have so far been confined to accounts of relations between the police and black people. The evidence of the innumerable studies which have been carried out is incontrovertible and supports the conclusion offered by Stuart Hall nearly a decade ago that "the police have undertaken, whether willingly or not, to constrain by means which would not long stand up to inspection within the rule of law, an alienated black population and thereby, to police the social crisis of the cities" (Hall, 1979, p. 13). Yet, it is as if policing was an end, rather than a beginning—a beginning of a *process of criminalisation* which continues from the point of arrest through the courts and beyond (Gordon, 1983). Our knowledge of this process to which the black community in Britain has been subjected remains partial. We know comparatively little, for instance, about what happens after the point of arrest by the police. We know little, too, about the decision to prosecute black people, the kinds of charges brought, the grant or refusal of bail; we have little hard evidence about the treatment of black people in the courts, about the conduct of trials, the behaviour and attitudes of court personnel including magistrates and judges, the sentencing process, the probation and after-care services, and so on.

At the same time we *do* know of the suspicion with which many black people regard the agencies of the criminal justice system. As a black youth put it to one of the few researchers who has bothered to look at this issue:

> Goin' to court is frightenin' 'cos you know you're not goin' to get justice, no chance. We're black ... and that's enough to put you down. It's nothin' for the police; they come round here givin' us trouble, arresting us and draggin' us off to court—they just see it as a job but we see it different. We know that they're all in it together—coppers, probation officers, solicitors, magistrates—the lot (Hil, 1980, p. 173).

We know too, if we care to remember, of the many major trials during the

1970s and 1980s which form part of the history of black people in Britain, of racism and of resistance. Our knowledge is partial, but is nevertheless considerable. This article, which is based on reports of major trials involving black defendants since the early 1970s, and on research of a more academic nature, attempts to examine the meaning of the 'rule of law' for black people, to assess the rhetoric of the law—that justice is not only blind but colour-blind, undiscriminating in its application—against the reality of the black experience of the British criminal justice system.

The Criminalisation Process

At least since the early 1970s black people have faced serious criminal charges and what they have alleged is discriminatory treatment at the hands of the criminal law and the criminal process in Britain. In 1971, for instance, serious charges of incitement to riot and affray were brought against eight men and women following a demonstration against police harassment in the Notting Hill area of west London. Although the incitement charges were rejected by magistrates at committal hearings, new charges of riotous assembly were brought the following day. These were also rejected, but the charges of affray were allowed to stand and when the cases came to court in 1972, new charges of riot were brought by a special procedure which circumvented the normal committal process through the bringing of charges against a ninth defendant. Eventually, however, the nine defendants were acquitted of the riot charges and only two of the affray charges were upheld. Undeterred by the collapse of this case, the public prosecution authorities the same year brought serious charges of affray against several black defendants who had been arrested during a police raid on a black youth club, the Metro in Notting Hill in London. Again, however, the prosecution case collapsed and none of the charges of affray, causing grievous bodily harm or possession of offensive weapons was upheld. Three years later in 1975, charges of affray, along with other serious charges were brought against 12 black people who had been arrested following another raid on a club, this time the Carib club in Cricklewood, but again all the defendants were acquitted, nine at the trial itself, one after a re-trial and two on appeal. The following year, charges of affray were again brought against black defendants, this time against people arrested during disturbances which followed police intervention at the Bonfire Night celebrations in Chapeltown, Leeds. Although the prosecution this time secured three convictions, 21 of the 24 charges brought were dismissed.

In addition to having faced serious public order charges, black people have also been the subject of serious conspiracy charges which, until the law was changed in 1977, carried more severe penalties than specific offences. Such charges were also more easily proved since they required less by way of evidence than substantive charges and could be brought even where no evidence of the actual offence had been obtained. Such conspiracy charges had long been favoured charges of the state in political cases and the cases of black defendants joined those of, for instance, the editors of the underground magazine *Oz* in 1971, the Angry Brigade and anti-apartheid campaigner, Peter Hain, in 1973, the Shrewsbury pickets and the editors of *International Times* in 1973, and the British Withdrawal from Northern Ireland Campaign in 1975 (Spicer, 1981).

In the 1972 case of Kamara, for instance, which was brought after students had occupied the High Commission of Sierra Leone in London, the defendants were convicted not just of unlawful assembly but of conspiracy to trespass. The students' appeal that such an offence was not known to English law because there was at the time no criminal offence of trespass, was rejected. Conspiracy charges were also used against the Islington 18, black youths who were arrested following the Notting Hill Carnival in 1976 which had ended in street fighting between carnival goers and the police. After jury deliberations lasting 170 hours, then the longest in the history of the Central Criminal Court, and a case costing some £250,000 of public money, all the conspiracy charges were dismissed although some charges of theft and robbery were upheld. The year after the trial of the Islington 18, 19 black youths, the Lewisham 19, were convicted of charges of conspiracy to rob after a jury was shown secretly taken video film. In 1982, 12 black youths in Bradford, were acquitted of charges of conspiracy to damage property and to endanger the lives of others and of conspiracy to cause grievous bodily harm. The 12 had all been involved in the making of petrol bombs which, they argued and the jury accepted, had been done solely to protect themselves and their community against an attack by fascists which they believed to be imminent. The collapse of the case against the Bradford 12 did not, however, deter the prosecution authorities from bringing conspiracy charges the following year in another case involving the right of the black community to defend itself against racial violence.

In all these cases it would seem, the use of conspiracy charges was a clear attempt not just to criminalise black protest and black people, but to maximise the chances of the police and prosecution in securing convictions in the absence of hard evidence. They were attempts to ensure that the defendants, if convicted, received heavy sentences. That they did not always succeed was frequently due to juries who were prepared to make up their own minds as to the evidence. Indeed, the failure of these and other conspiracy cases led directly to attacks on the jury system and calls for restrictions on the right to jury trial, a point to which I return later. In addition, such conspiracy cases were being widely seen as clearly political and became the focus for high profile, community-based defence campaigns. As such, it seems reasonable to surmise, they were seen by the prosecuting authorities as counter-productive and the year after the Bradford 12 trial, another case involving the issue of community self-defence against racial violence illustrated the changing prosecution practice. In 1983, charges of conspiracy to assault persons unknown were brought against eight Asians in east London, the Newham 8. The charges were

298   *P. Gordon*

brought after the formation of a self-defence group following a series of attacks on Asian school pupils. These conspiracy charges were later changed to charges of affray, of which four of the eight were convicted. The dropping of the conspiracy charges was significant for it indicated that the prosecuting authorities had learned, albeit belatedly, the lesson of the previous conspiracy trials. Instead of risking another unsuccessful and embarrassing prosecution, they substituted charges which were less likely to be seen as political. Not only that, but the prosecution chose to use a charge. that of affray, which would be unlikely to fail. Since there had been fighting between the defendants (or some of them) and the police, then there had been an affray, and those involved were inevitably guilty.

'Riot Trials'

Any account of the criminalisation of black people by the criminal law and the criminal justice system must also look at the trials which have followed major demonstrations or civil disturbances which have occurred in Britain since the late 1970s and which are usually referred to as riots. It must be emphasised, however, that none of the instances discussed below was 'racial' in the sense of involving only black people: they were clearly multiracial, involving black people of both Afro-Caribbean and Asian origin and white people. Nevertheless, each instance was seen at the time as 'racial' and has been remembered as such.

In April 1979, for instance, several hundred people were arrested during a major mobilisation against fascists in the west London area of Southall and some 342 people were charged. The trials of these people were not heard in the Ealing courts which normally deal with cases arising in the area in question but in Barnet, some 20 miles away. Locating the trials so far away from where the events had taken place was itself seen as a form of punishment by the defendants. In addition, the vast majority of the trials concerned charges which could not be heard by juries but were dealt with by magistrates. As a result, the defendants had to make long journeys across London to reach the court only to face what one defence lawyer described as "a striking and well-observed example of the subjectivity and inconsistency which permeates the magistrates court system". Indeed, the rate of conviction by the magistrates was so high that defence lawyers took the unprecedented step of protesting to the Lord Chancellor of a "magisterial bias against the defendants as a whole". The number of arrests, the lawyers argued, the decision to remove the cases from people's home areas and the ability of magistrates to "consistently and unconditionally accept the evidence of police officers in the face of credible defence evidence", combined to intimidate the Asian community. Although these claims were rejected, the conviction rate did drop significantly after the lawyers' protest but by then the courts had shown themselves to be "the final stage in a process of victimisation" (Lewis, 1980. p. 27).

After the Bristol riot of 1980, the first of what was to become a series of major confrontations between the police and black (and white) people in Britain's inner cities, more than 100 people were charged with offences such as theft, threatening behaviour and possession of offensive weapons. As happened after Southall, most of these charges were heard by magistrates and most of the defendants were convicted and fined heavily. But three months after the disturbances, 16 people had the charges against them changed to the serious offences of riotous assembly, charges which were described by one defence lawyer as 'intensely speculative' but which were defended by the Director of Public Prosecutions. Despite this, charges against four of the defendants were dismissed at committal stage, three defendants were acquitted on the directions of the judge and the jury acquitted five others. Charges against the other four were dropped when the jury failed to agree (Joshua *et al.*, 1983).

The behaviour of the magistrates in the cases which followed the Bristol 'riot' was a sign of how magistrates would respond to other civil disturbances. In 1981, it is clear that magistrates responded with considerable haste and panic to the events of April and July. Bail was frequently denied to people arrested during the disturbances. For intance only 35 per cent of those arrested in Brixton, south London, were granted bail with conditions attached and only 17 per cent given unconditional bail. In Nottingham only 16 per cent of those charged were granted bail on their first appearance in court, in Leeds the figure was only 4 per cent. Where bail was granted it was generally subject to strict conditions including curfews and the requirement of substantial monetary sureties.

By July 1982, three-quarters of those who had been dealt with had been convicted. The police had clearly learned the lesson of the Bristol riot trial and had pursued lesser charges against those arrested so that they could not be tried in front of juries. The policy appeared to pay off in that the overriding tendency appeared to be for magistrates to accept the evidence of police officers and reject the testimonies of defendants even when these were convincing. Particularly in the early cases, many of those convicted were sent to prison, even where they had no previous convictions. Overall, 40 per cent of those convicted of the more serious offences were sentenced to terms of imprisonment, while only 20 per cent of those convicted of summary offence were sent to prison. Those who were unemployed were more likely to be sent to prison than those in work, 46 per cent compared to 29 per cent. Those described as 'West Indian/African' by police were more likely than whites to be sent to prison, 38 per cent compared to 34 per cent. Asians, however, were less likely than either to be sent to prison, 23 per cent (Home Office, 1982).

In relation to the various civil disturbances in 1985 even this very limited data does not exist and there appears to have been no systematic monitoring of the courts' responses to the events of that year. In relation to the Broadwater Farm riot, of October 1985, however, some useful information was compiled by the Broadwater Farm Defence Campaign. In all, 69 people were charged in connection with the disorders, 20 of whom pleaded guilty often as a result of plea bargaining in which the prosecution agreed to drop more serious charges if defendants would plead guilty to lesser charges. Of those who contested the charges against them, 27 were acquitted and 22 convicted. Most of these defendants had been charged with affray and several with riot. It would have been reasonable to expect that those charged with affray would be tried in groups since affray necessarily involves several people acting together. In fact, all those charged were tried individually. It is likely that the decision to have individual trials was influenced by the experience of the 1984/85 miners' strike in which several major trials involving groups of miners collapsed in the face of concerted and co-ordinated defences. The point was made by the United States judge, Margaret Burnham who was asked to observe the trials by Haringey Council. She concluded:

> One must surmise that the cases have been separated for trial so as to deprive the defendant of [the] ... advantages to be gained from consolidation. It will be difficult to maintain an effective, co-ordinated defence campaign for the duration of 70 trials. Potential jurors will be prejudiced by news reports of repeated convictions as the trials proceed. Further, stretching the trials over a long period will no doubt have the effect of heightening anxiety and mistrust within the community. (quoted in Rose & Kavanagh, 1987, p. 6.)

Judge Burnham also observed the case of the six people who were charged with the murder of a police officer during the riot. The case against three of the accused, all juveniles, was dismissed by the trial judge who ruled that confessions they were alleged to have made to the police were not admissible in court, but three others were convicted of murder and sentenced to life imprisonment. In her report on the case, Judge Burnham said that while the trial itself had been conducted in an even-handed manner, this did not mean that the defendants had been dealt with fairly by the criminal justice system. She pointed in particular to the treatment of the defendants by the police who had denied them access to a solicitor, had conducted interrogations which were "lengthy, dishonest and otherwise oppressive" and had created a "climate of intense fear throughout the whole of the community". Burnham also pointed to the insufficiency of the evidence against the principal accused, Winston Silcott, arguing that the jury probably convicted because it knew that he was from the start the main target of the police investigation. Judge Burnham, also stressed the importance in this respect of the press reporting of the trial which "seemed to be operating under a presumption of guilt rather than of innocence" (Burnham, 1987, p. 16).

The trials of those involved in the civil disturbances since 1979 illustrate not just the degree of panic which overtook the criminal justice system, but show too the extent to which the state, by means of the criminal justice system, is prepared to go to abandon normality and adopt 'special measures' in its efforts to restore 'law and order'. The parallels here with the situation which has pertained in Northern Ireland, which has been government by 'emergency' measures since the late 1960s, are considerable, as are those with the treatment of miners and their supporters arrested during the 1984/85 miners' strike. That it could do so and come up against very little political opposition indeed is a point to which I return in the conclusion.

Bail and Remand

In theory, people facing criminal charges are presumed to have a right to be freed on bail pending trial. In practice, the presumption is easy to rebut and even where bail is granted it may be subject to stringent conditions laid down by the court. In the 1977 case of the Islington 18 who were arrested following the 'riot' at the Notting Hill Carnival, for instance, eight of the defendants were still in prison when their cases came to trial eight months after their arrest. The others had been released on bail only in the face of determined police opposition and claims that witnesses would be intimidated, that the accused would abscond and that the accused had previous convictions. (In one case, the previous conviction in question was of theft of a sandwich some four years previously.) One of the accused was required to find a surety of £3000, all had to report to the police daily—one 14-year-old had to report twice daily—and virtually all had curfews imposed.

Even more stringent conditions were imposed in the case of the Brandford 12 some years later. Initially, all of the accused were refused bail and some were held in prison for three months. When they were released, sureties of up to £20,000 were demanded, passports had to be surrendered, a curfew from 10 p.m. to 7 a.m. was imposed, and daily reporting to the police was required. In addition, the defendants were prohibited from meeting one another except in the presence of a solicitor and were banned from taking part in any political activity, conditions which were clearly aimed at weakening the formation of a united defence campaign which was gaining widespread local and national support. These were clearly exceptional cases but they reflect the daily imposition of bail conditions on black defendants, conditions which can include curfews, geographical restrictions, sureties and so on. In any case, black people seem less likely than whites to be granted bail in the first place. Home Office figures show that black people, particularly those of Afro-Caribbean origin are over-represented in the remand prisoner population. Thus, the proportion of Afro-Caribbeans among untried males in prison was 7 to 10 per cent, somewhat higher than among the males received into prison under sentence, 6 to 7 per cent. (Both these figures are, of course, considerably higher than the proportion of Afro-Caribbeans in the population as a whole which is about 1 per cent for men aged 14 to 64.) The Home Office explains this by arguing that it is due in part to the higher proportion of those of Afro-Caribbean origin among untried prisoners in custody who were known later to have been found

302   *P. Gordon*

not guilty. But this does not explain why so many black people are being remanded into custody in the first place, particularly when so many are either acquitted in court or not proceeded against (17 per cent of Afro-Caribbeans, 3 per cent of Asians) and particularly when the proportions of those acquitted or not proceeded against is considerably higher than among whites, 6·5 per cent of Afro-Caribbeans, 5 per cent of Asians but only 3 per cent of whites (Home Office, 1986). Although there have been no studies of the effect of race on bail decisions (other than these bare figures) research has shown that the most significant factor in the courts' decision to grant bail or to remand in custody before trial is the decision by the *police* whether to grant bail or to hold in custody before appearance in court. This factor is followed by the nature of the offence and court policy (Jones, 1985). In other words, a decision by the police to refuse release influences the court in its decision whether to grant bail and if the police are exercising their discretion in a racist manner this will be further compounded, rather than alleviated, by the decision of the court.

Juries

Black people have continually had to fight for any right to be tried by a jury of their peers which has for so long been supposed to be right for all people in Britain. In 1969, for instance, the black political activist Michael X objected to being tried by an all-white jury but the court usher, when asked by the judge to find any black people in the court, could find only one man who had been called for jury service. In this case, the judge at least seemed prepared to acknowledge the unfairness of the situation to the defendant, but only a few months later the same judge refused to allow defence objections to an all-white jury. Similarly, in 1971 defence applications by barristers acting for people in the Mangrove trial for black people to serve on the jury were rejected and it was only through extensive use of the challenge by the nine defendants that two black men were called as jurors (Gordon, 1983).

As a result of such cases and the unwillingness of the courts to ensure that juries were genuinely multi-racial, black defendants resorted to the use of the peremptory challenge to try to ensure that at least some jury members were black. In the trial which followed the 1980 Bristol riot, for instance, challenges were used to ensure that the defendants, all of whom were black, had their case heard by a jury which included a number of black people. All the defendants were either acquitted or had the charges against them dropped, but the case elicited a reaction from the judiciary and politicians which questioned the very idea of trial by jury and the right of defendants to challenge potential jurors. Conservative Member of Parliament Alan Clark (now a government minister), for instance, claimed that the proceedings showed that "black jurors, whether out of racial loyalty, fear of intimidation or a combination of both, are highly unlikely to convict accused black persons of offences connected with civil disturbance" (*Hansard* 19 May 1981) and only a few months later Lord

Denning, then Master of the Rolls, told an audience of judges that the "abuse of the right of challenge" by the defence at Bristol had been used to get a "jury of their own choice or at any rate a jury on which there would be disagreement by more than two". Conviction could therefore be avoided. The following year, Denning took the attack further, directly questioning the fitness of black people to serve as jurors. In his book, *What Next in the Law?*, Denning said that the English were no longer a 'homogenuous race':

> They are white and black, coloured and brown ... some of them come from countries where bribery and graft are accepted ... and where stealing is a virtue so long as you are not found out. They no longer share the same code of morals or religious beliefs.

Using the Bristol trials as example of what he called "jury packing", Denning claimed that not all British citizens were suitable to sit as jurors and that "black, coloured and brown people do not have the same standards of conduct as whites". In the face of the furore which followed the reporting of these passages and the threat of legal action from two of the black jurors in the Bristol trial, Denning's book was withdrawn and amended. In addition, Denning announced his retirement.

But this did not mean an end to the official concern at the use of jury challenges. In 1986, a government White Paper proposed the complete abolition of the right to challenge potential jurors and the Criminal Justice Bill before parliament at the time of writing will enact this. Just as the victories of the 1971 Mangrove 9 trial, the 1975 Carib Club trial and the 1975 Chapeltown bonfire night trial were followed by the Criminal Justice Act of 1977 which restricted the right to elect trial by jury and reduced the number of peremptory challenges from seven to three, so the important black trials of the 1980s—Bristol, Bradford, Newham and others—which illustrated the importance of the jury to black defendants were to be followed by new restrictive measures and a further reduction in the right of defendants to be tried by juries of their peers. This is not to suggest that restrictions on the right to jury trial have come about solely because of cases involving black defendants. There are numerous other factors, notably the experience of the Diplock courts in Northern Ireland and the collapse of cases such as those involving the Official Secrets Act. But the black experience in this respect is frequently neglected and needs to be emphasised.

Sentencing

Many people have pointed to the disproportionate numbers of black people, especially those of Afro-Caribbean origin, in prisons, borstals and detention centres. The first results of the Prison Department's monitoring of the ethnic origin of prioners were published in June 1986 (Home Office, 1986) and showed that:

304   *P. Gordon*

—about 8 per cent of the male prison population and 12 per cent of the female prison population were of West Indian or African origin, whereas they made up only between 1 and 2 per cent of the general population. They accounted for about 10 per cent of the male remand population, 7 per cent of the adult male sentenced population and 8·5 per cent of sentenced male young offenders.

—the proportion of prisoners of Asian origin was similar to or lower than their proportion in the general population. Overall they accounted for about 2·5 per cent of the male prison population and 2 per cent of the female prison population compared with about 3 per cent of the population as a whole.

—in the case of prisoners under sentence the disproportions were even greater. Thus black people made up 12 per cent of young offenders and 11·5 per cent of adult prisoners, but only 6 and 5 per cent respectively in the comparable age groups in the general population. For women, the corresponding proportions were 12 and 16 per cent compared with 6 and 5 per cent respectively for the comparable age groups.

— the average sentence length of black prisoners was also longer than that of white prisoners. In the case of under 21-year-olds, the average sentence of white prisoners was nine months, but for those of West Indian/African origin it was 12 months and for those of Asian origin it was 11 months. In the case of those prisoners over the age of 21, the average sentence length for white prisoners was 13 months, but for those of West Indian/African origin it was 16·5 months and for those of Asian origin it was 26 months.

—black prisoners, whether of West Indian/African or of Asian origin had fewer convictions than white people sentenced for the same type of offence. For example, 38 per cent of whites had 11 or more previous convictions compared with 22 per cent of West Indian/African origin prisoners and only 8 per cent of Asians; 62 per cent of whites had six or more convictions, but only 48 per cent of West Indian/African originating prisoners and 20 per cent of prisoners of Asian origin.

The first thing to be said about these figures is that they confirmed what black people and prisoners' groups (such as the National Prisoners Movement, PROP) had been saying for a long time: that black people were grossly over-represented in the prison population. These claims had always been denied by the prison authorities. That said, what conclusions can be drawn from these bare statistics about the operation of the criminal law and the criminal process in relation to black people? The answer must be very little. For instance, there is little information about the seriousness of the offences for which people have been sentenced, so it is not possible to know why black people are serving longer sentences than whites, other than that a high proportion of black people are convicted of offences involving illegal drugs which tend to carry higher than average sentences. In addition, it is known that a higher proportion of black people are either tried or sentenced in Crown Court which has greater sentencing powers than the lower magistrates courts. This may reflect differences within each offence group of the seriousness of the offences involved. It may also reflect differences in the proportion opting for trial in the Crown Court for offences which can be tried in either the magistrates court or the Crown Court, or the decisions made by magistrates courts in deciding whether an offence is more suitable for trial at a magistrates court or the Crown Court. In other words, black people may be facing more serious charges which can only be dealt with at Crown Court, or they are electing trial at Crown Court, perhaps in the belief that they will get a fairer trial there, or they are being sent to Crown Court by magistrates who feel their own powers are insufficient to deal with them.

Few studies have looked at the sentencing process and black people, and those that have are open to criticism on a number of grounds. Fludger, for instance, in his study of black people in borstal between 1974 and 1976, found that black inmates had fewer convictions than their white counterparts. They had, he said, arrived in borstal "at an earlier stage in their criminal careers". This could not be explained by their having been convicted of more serious offences but no alternative explanation was offered (Fludger, 1981). Since then only three studies have looked at the sentencing process in relation to black defendants. In the first study, McConville and Baldwin, using data gathered for other studies in Birmingham in 1975 and 1976 and London in 1978 and 1979, looked at just under 1400 contested and guilty plea cases in Crown Courts, including 339 cases involving black defendants. Matching the black and white defendants as closely as possible according to age, sex, criminal record and previous sentence, the authors concluded that "there appears to be no evidence, of direct, systematic bias on racial lines in sentencing in the Crown Courts". This finding, the authors described as "tentative, but important" (McConville & Baldwin, 1982). This research, however, is open to criticism on a number of grounds. First, the research data had been gathered some years previously and for a different purpose. Second, the research looked only at Crown Courts and not at magistrates courts where most criminal cases are heard. Third, and most important, the study did not look at whether the criteria used to match the defendants were themselves influenced by race. For example, it might be the case that the black defendants had more previous convictions as a result of police harassment. There was a danger, one anonymous critic said at the time, that the findings would "achieve a publicity they do not deserve".

The second study, by Crow and Cove, did look at magistrates courts, examining 668 cases, including those of just over 100 black defendants. The authors concluded that there was no basis for concluding that 'non-Whites' were likely to receive different sentences than 'Whites'. In criminal justice terms, they said, the cases of the different ethnic groups in the sample were handled "in similar ways and the sentences they are given are similar". But unlike McConville and Baldwin, who had at least stated that their findings were tentative, Crowe and Cove concluded their article with a claim, certainly not justified by such a small scale piece of research, that their findings "may serve to contribute to the development of confidence in the court system among ethnic minorities' (Crowe & Cove, 1984, p. 417).

A third, even smaller study was that carried out by Mair as a pilot study for a more detailed piece of research. Mair collected data in two magistrates courts in Leeds and Bradford, covering 1173 cases, but including only 123 black defendants. Mair found no significant differences in the sentencing of black and white defendants except that black people were considerably less likely than whites to be given probation orders and more likely to be given community service orders. He also found that Asian defendants were less likely than whites to be referred for social inquiry reports before sentence, while defendants of Afro-Caribbean origin were more likely to be so referred. This is a point of some importance to which I return later. Mair concluded that although it was difficult to draw any firm conclusions, the evidence did not support the "more optimistic assessment" made by Crowe and Cove (Mair, 1986, p. 134).

The evidence on the sentencing of black people, such as it is, raises more questions than it answers. Above all, what none of the studies has been able to explain is the disproportionate number of black people in the prisons and other penal establishments. This has implications for future research, a point to which I return at the conclusion of this article.

Probation

One area of possible differential treatment which might result in black people running a higher risk than white defendants of being sentenced to imprisonment is that of probation. As mentioned above, for example, Mair (1986) found in his small sentencing survey that black people were less likely to be given probation than white defendants, while an earlier study of the West Midlands showed that black adults were significantly under-represented on probation, but that children and young people were over-represented on supervision. In addition, black people were, in general, significantly more likely to be under supervision after release from imprisonment or detention, but less likely to be on supervision before release (Taylor, 1981). A few small studies illustrate some of the reasons for these findings.

For example, one study of probation officers' perceptions concluded that probation staff lacked an adequate understanding of Rastafarianism, seeing it either in psychological terms as a form of deviance which stemmed from 'inadequate socialisation', or in sociological terms seeing it as an ethnic solution to a supposed 'identity crisis'. Hardly any officers even considered the possibility that black people might adhere to Rastafarianism because of their material situation, while most saw it as an individual, psychologically-determined phenomenon. It was hardly surprising that all the probation staff interviewed said they had encountered 'problems' in their dealings with Rastas. Not surprisingly either, only 1 of 15 social enquiry reports examined in this study recommended that the subject be placed on probation (Carrington & Denney, 1981).

Other studies, albeit also on a small scale, have looked at the social enquiry reports prepared for courts by probation officers. One such study found that a number of reports included a range of racist attitudes and sentiments. One report looked at, for example, spoke of the subject's "mild paranoid attitude which I believe to be part of a cultural more [sic] associated with his ethnic propensities" (Whitehouse, 1983). The potential effect of such remarks is considerable and could well result in black defendants being more likely to be given a custodial sentence.

A more recent study, again carried out in the West Midlands, found that black defendants were more likely than whites to be given an immediate custodial sentence, 35 per cent compared to 21 per cent, and that considerably fewer black defendants received community service orders, although again this was a small scale study covering 222 cases, a quarter of them involving black defendants. An analysis of the social enquiry reports concluded that reports on black defendants were more likely to include negative comments. These, the report noted, were often the result of attempts to describe clients objectively but such attempts were based on implicit assumptions of normality and which ignored the consequences of structural inequality, for instance, that black people were more likely than their white counterparts to be unemployed or homeless. In addition, many of the reports made unnecessary references to the subject's mental state. Although recommendations for non-custodial sentences were made in 90 per cent of the reports on black defendants compared with 88 per cent of the reports on white defendants, the courts were less likely to follow the recommendations on black defendants than on whites. The courts accepted the probation workers recommendations in 43 per cent of the cases involving black defendants and in 58 per cent of the cases involving white defendants. Where the recommendation was not followed, black defendants were more likely to receive a custodial sentence, 50 per cent of such cases compared with 35 per cent of white defendants. This difference could not be explained by black defendants having been convicted of more serious offences. If anything, the report said, it was the white defendants who had been convicted of proportionately more serious offences (Pymm & Lines, 1987).

Through a combination of overt racism, a patronising attempt to 'understand' black clients and a failure to understand the material situation of black defendants, the probation service has not only failed black defendants but has put them at risk and contributed to their criminalisation by the courts.

Racial Violence: Victimisation and Criminalisation

At the same time as black people have been criminalised by the criminal justice system, they have received little by way of protection from the criminal justice system against racial violence. Indeed, this is yet another area where

308   *P. Gordon*

black people, even though they are the victims of crime, are turned into criminals.

The nature and the seriousness of the problem of racial violence in Britain cannot be denied. There are now, according to one survey, about 70,000 racially activated incidents in any one year, ranging from murder and arson and physical assault to nuisance and verbal abuse. Few of these will be reported to the police (Brown, 1983). The situation is so serious in some areas that many black organisations have started to speak not of racial violence but of racial terrorism. Nor is this a new phenomenon: there have been racial attacks for as long as there have been black people in Britain and certainly since the late 1960s and early 1970s black people have been complaining of official apathy and inaction in the face of a steadily worsening situation (Gordon, 1986). But it was only in 1981 that a Home Office report belatedly acknowledged the seriousness of the situation. Despite this, little in the way of remedial or preventive action appears to have followed. For this, the blame must lie with the police for it is they who are responsible for preventing crimes and offences—including the various forms of racial violence and harassment. The list of unsolved murders, along with the clear reluctance of victims even to report incidents, must stand as a clear indictment. The police, it is clear from numerous reports and studies over the years, have with a remarkable consistency denied the racist nature of attacks, played down the seriousness of attacks, often treated victims with hostility and lack of sympathy, allowed alleged attackers to go free and, until recently, refused to make use of their powers to prosecute alleged offenders except in very serious assault cases.

The problem here is not, as some have argued recently, that the law itself is inadequate and ineffective. It is not that the law does not give the police power to deal with racial attacks and harassment but they have failed to exercise their powers. It is therefore a mistake to argue, as some have done, for a new law on racial harassment, which would among other things, create a new specific criminal offence of racial harassment. The problem with such measures is that they suggest that the law cannot at the moment deal with racial violence and harassment. Yet, virtually all forms of racial violence and harassment are already criminal acts.

At the same time as they have failed to protect black people from racial violence, the police have actively criminalised those who have sought to defend themselves in the face of official apathy. In this, they have been supported by the prosecuting authorities and by the courts. In a series of cases such as those of the Virk brothers in 1977, the Bradford 12 in 1981/82, the Newham 8 in 1983 and the Newham 7 in 1984, black people have been prosecuted and, in the case of the Virks, sent to prison for nothing other than defending themselves against racial attacks. In this respect again, the rhetoric of the law—of a supposed right to defend oneself against physical attack—is at odds with the reality of law enforcement (Gordon, 1986).

The police are not, of course, the only people responsible for the prevention of racial violence and harassment and the apprehension and prosecution of offenders. Housing departments of local authorities also have responsibilities in this respect in that many incidents take place on local authority housing estates. Here again the problem is *not* that local authorities do not have the power to take action against those alleged to be responsible for racial attacks or harassment, but that they *do not*. Local authorities have extensive powers in this respect and there is no reason why proceedings should not be brought under the law on behalf of victims of racial harassment. The problem here, as with the police, has not been the absence of powers but a failure to use and test such powers in the courts. Although there have been some attempts in this respect in 1986 and 1987, most of these have been ill-prepared and have, not surprisingly, failed to convince courts reluctant to take the drastic step of eviction. To date there have been only two successful attempts by local authorities to bring proceedings against tenants believed to be responsible for the harassment of black tenants (South Islington Law Centre, 1987; Wright, 1987). Not only have local authorities done little to protect black people from racial violence through taking effective legal action against those responsible, they have also adopted an individualised victim-centred approach which "coupled with a conception of black people solely as passive sufferers ... has slipped into a *victimist* approach that refuses to acknowledge black resistance". In this context, black people are seen "almost as suffering from a *condition* and not an event or series of events" and a political struggle against racial violence is therefore turned into a "problem of social-welfare management in a manner that suggests that victims of racist violence are actually victims of some self-induced pathological condition" (Bhatt, 1987, p. 8).

Conclusion

Black people's experience of the British criminal justice system shows clearly that the rhetoric of the law does not accord with the reality of its practice. The law is not colour-blind, but a means by which black people have been subject to a process of criminalisation. Yet, this process has gone largely unrecognised and undocumented by organisations supposedly concerned with the advancement of civil liberties, the protection of rights and the achievement of justice. Black people have been invisible in their work. At the same time, the 'race relations industry' must itself be indicted in this respect as must academics and other researchers who have, with few exceptions, failed to investigate the many issues which the black experience has thrown up and the many problems this has posed for liberal democratic theory of the rule of law and an impartial judiciary [2]. Two particular issues stand out. First, throughout the 1970s and early 1980s, black activists (and some white prison campaigners such as those in PROP, the National Prisoners Movement) pointed to the growing numbers of black people in British prisons, borstals and detention centres and at the racist treatment of black people in prisons. Yet there was little recognition in-

310   *P. Gordon*

deed of this issue outside the black community itself. Secondly, we might note
the failure—by academics, civil liberties groups, race relations organisations or
whatever—to monitor the treatment by the criminal justice system of those
arrested and charged after the urban disturbances in 1981 and 1985 and
thereby call power to account. In both cases, the concerns of black people
went unheeded. (None of this is to suggest that black people have been alone
in their experience of the reality of the criminal law. The 'rule of law' has been
rather less than reality for numerous other groups in society. It is to emphasise
the particular black experience and to offer a corrective to accounts—even
critical ones—which would ignore it.)

Since the 1981 urban riots, of course, this lack of interest in black people
appears to have changed as organisations (and some academics) have fallen
over themselves in a rush to 'take race seriously'. Yet, appearances can be, and
often are, deceptive. The dominant response in recent years to the interaction
of race and the criminal justice system has mirrored that adopted by many
other professions in Britain. This is an approach which is best described as
'multi-cultural' in which the 'answer' is seen to lie in greater 'sensitivity'
towards black people, greater understanding of their cultures and lifestyles,
and so on—usually to be achieved through multifarious forms of 'training'—
combined with 'equal opportunity' policies and the recruitment of more black
personnel, whether as lawyers, probation officers, magistrates or whatever.
Such an approach ignores the central question of racism, the institutional
practices of a society based on unequal social, economic and power relations.
It avoids the fundamental issue of the political economy of black labour in
Britain in the late 1980s.

This political economy sought the presence of black workers from the
colonies and former colonies for the purposes of post-war economic reconstruction, as units of labour which would depart when their labour was no longer
needed. But when it became clear that the new immigrants would not simply
lift up their tools and go, their presence was defined as a problem in successive
immigration laws. These both defined black people as a problem whose
numbers therefore had to be controlled and erected barriers in the way of
family reunification, thus encouraging the departure of those already here
(Sivanandan, 1982). At the same time, the enforcement of the law turned
increasingly inwards, redefining breaches of the law and leading to increasing
numbers of deportations and removals, and challenging the rights of those
settled here to welfare benefits and other services (Gordon, 1985).

Just as immigration law defined black people as a problem whose numbers
had to be controlled, so black people already settled in Britain (and determined to stay here) were increasingly seen as a problem, particularly by the
police who imposed their own definition—of a 'law and order' problem. Black
people, particularly but not exclusively black youth, were portrayed as openly
disorderly and criminal, as requiring special policing practices and as deserv-
ing the treatment they received in the rest of the criminal justice system. The

police, as Stuart Hall has said in the quotation at the start of this article, have undertaken to police the "social crisis of the cities", a social crisis in which there is no place for black labour, especially that of black youth, and little pretence that black people are here on anything but sufferance and on condition that they accept their subordinate status in British society without complaint. At the end of a long line of agencies and programmes aimed at the forceable assimilation, containment and control of black people—from schools to Manpower Servicedom to urban programmes—stand the police and behind them the force of the criminal law and the criminal justice system. Black people, it seems, must be disciplined and punished if they will not be contained.

At the same time, the association of black people with crime so firmly made by the police and sections of the mass media and the criminalisation of black people by the agencies of the criminal justice system have become central to racist ideology. Criminality and disorder took the place of disease, sexuality and miscegenation which had previously been the central themes in public discussion of race in Britain: these supposed features have increasingly been identified as essential parts of black culture, emphasising the supposed 'otherness' of blacks in Britain, and serving as common-sense explanations for national crisis and decline (Gilroy, 1987; Hall *et al.*, 1978).

It is always tempting to conclude accounts of this nature by calling for further research and study. Those of us involved in research have a tendency (to put it mildly) always to be looking for new areas of work. Yet, in this case, there *is* a need for further research, for further knowledge. How, for instance, do the courts deal with black defendants before them, not just in the major trials of the kind described in this article but, equally important, on a day-to-day basis? Why are there many more black people in prison than might be deduced from their numbers in the population as a whole? How do the courts respond to serious urban disturbances? These are all important questions to which we have only the most partial answers. Such research should not be considered an end in itself, nor should it be allowed to be a means of assisting the management of the 'black problem', as most race relations research has been (Bourne, 1980). It can be, and needs to be, seen as a means of understanding the parameters of contemporary racism, a racism which has been central to the movement towards authoritarianism in Britain at least since the late 1960s. In so doing it can also be a means of empowering black people in their struggles against criminalisation.

Notes

1 I use the word 'black' throughout this article to mean people of Afro-Caribbean *or* Asian origin, the predominant use in Britain, particularly by black people themselves. Where a particular report or document uses other terminology I have followed this, even though it makes for some inconsistency.
2 In this respect it is a matter of some regret that a major research project on black

312   *P. Gordon*

people and the criminal justice system, to have been carried out by Maureen Cain, failed to secure the necessary funding.

Acknowledgement

I am indebted to Joe Sim for his constructive criticisms of an earlier draft of this article and for his encouragement and numerous suggestions.

References

Bhatt, C. (1987) Racial violence and the local state. *Foundation* 2.

Bourne, J. (1980) Cheerleaders and ombudsmen: the sociology of race relations in Britain. *Race & Class* 21(4).

Brown, C. (1983) *Black and White Britain: The Third PSI Survey*. Heinemann: London.

Burnham, M. (1987) *The Burnham Report of International Jurists in Respect to the Broadwater Farm Trials*. Broadwater Farm Defence Campaign: London.

Carrington, B. & Denney, D. (1981) Young Rastafarians and the probation service. *Probation Journal* 28(4).

Crowe, I. & Cove, J. (1984) Ethnic minorities and the courts. *Criminal Law Review*, July 1984.

Denning, Lord (1982) *What Next in the Law?* Butterworths: London.

Fludger, N. (1981) *Ethnic Minorities in Borstal*. Home Office Prison Department: London.

Gilroy, P. (1987) *'There Ain't No Black in the Union Jack': The Cultural Politics of Race and Nation*. Hutchinson: London.

Gordon, P. (1983) *White Law: Racism in the Police, Courts and Prisons*. Pluto Press: London.

Gordon, P. (1985) *Policing Immigration: Britain's Internal Controls*. Pluto Press, London.

Gordon, P. (1986) *Racial Violence and Harassment*. Runnymede Trust: London.

Hil, R. (1980) Black kids, white justice. *New Society* 24 January 1980.

Hall, S. (1979) *Drifting into a Law and Order Society*. Cobden Trust: London.

Hall, S. *et al.* (1978) *Policing the Crisis: Mugging, The State and Law and Order*. MacMillan: London.

Home Office (1982) *The Outcome of Arrests during the Serious Incidents of Public Disorder in July and August*. Home Office: London.

Home Office (1986) *The Ethnic Origins of Prisoners: The Prison Population on 30 June 1985 and Persons Received, July 1984–March 1985*. Home Office: London.

Jones, P. (1985) Remand decisions at magistrates courts. In *Managing Criminal Justice: A Collection of Papers* (Moxon, D., Ed.). HMSO: London.

Joshua, H. *et al.* (1983) *To Ride the Storm: The 1980 Bristol 'Riot' Trial and The State*. Heinemann: London.

Lewis, R. (1980) *Real Trouble: A Study of Aspects of the Southall Trials*. Runnymede Trust: London.

McConville, M. & Baldwin, J. (1982) The influence of race on sentencing in England. *Criminal Law Review*, October 1982.

Mair, G. (1986) Ethnic minorities, probation and the magistrates' courts. *British Journal of Criminology* 26(2).

Black people and the criminal law 313

National Association for the Care and Resettlement of Offenders (1986) *Black People and the Criminal Justice System*. NACRO: London.

Pymm, L. & Lines, P. (1987) *Report on the Birmingham Court Social Enquiry Report Monitoring Exercise*. West Midlands Probation Service: Birmingham.

Rose, B. & Kavanagh, S. (1987) Co-operative defence work. *Legal Action*, January 1987.

Sivanandan, A. (1982) *A Different Hunger: Writings on Black Resistance*. Pluto Press: London.

South Islington Law Centre (1987) Evicting the racist: the Islington experience. *Foundation* 2.

Spicer, R. (1981) *Conspiracy: Law, Class and Society*. Lawrence and Wishart: London.

Taylor, W. (1981) *Probation and After-Care in a Multi-Racial Society*. Commission for Racial Equality: London.

Whitehouse, P. (1983) Race, bias and social enquiry reports. *Probation Journal* 30(2).

Wright, C. (1987) Camden Council versus Hawkins. *Foundation* 2.

Date received: September 1987

[9]

Contemporary Crises 13: 405–432, 1989.
© 1989 *Kluwer Academic Publishers. Printed in the Netherlands.*

Racially disproportionate prison populations in the United States

An overview of historical patterns and review of contemporary issues

WILLIAM J. SABOL
Afro-American Studies Program, 2169 LeFrak Hall, University of Maryland, College Park, MD 20742, U.S.A.

Abstract. This paper reviews trends in black-white incarcerations in the North and South from 1870 to 1980. Using census data on imprisonments it finds that the degree of disproportionate imprisonment of blacks (relative to their representation in the general population) has been higher in Northern states than in Southern states from the middle of the 19th century through the present, although recently the trends have begun to converge. After reviewing explanations for the higher imprisonment rates of blacks in the North, it reviews black-white patterns of arrests and imprisonments by state for 1960, 1970 and 1980 and finds that the variations in black-white imprisonments are not fully accounted for by arrests. Finally, it comments on appropriate methodologies for examining racial differences in treatment in the criminal justice system.

I. Historical patterns of black-white incarcerations

Sociologists and historians of prison systems in the United States are not unaware of the long-run patterns of the racially-disproportionate composition of U.S. prisons. Nor are contemporary policy analysts unaware of the fact that in 1984 blacks comprised about 47 percent of the prisoners sentenced in state and federal prisons, while comprising only about 12 percent of the general population. What many contemporary observers may be unaware of, however, is the extent of the regional differences in racial disproportionality in prisons and the historic patterns of black-white differences in incarcerations. Casual inspection of those patterns starkly demonstrates the extent to which criminal justice officials in the North consistently removed larger fractions of blacks from the civilian population and incarcerated them than did criminal justice officials in the South.

In Table 1 are listed the incarceration rates for all persons, whites and blacks in northern and southern states from 1850 to 1980; in Table 2 are listed the black to white incarceration ratios, or the disproportionality ratios, for the two regions. (See Appendix A for a detailed discussion of the data used to compute these rates.)

Those striking regional differences revealed on the tables have not always

406

been buried in the historical record. Interestingly enough, however, many of the social commentators who raised this issue, with the exception of Myrdal (1944), were apologists for Southern criminal justice systems. Those apologists, like Alfred Stone (1908), presented data on the regional differences in black-white incarcerations to argue that if incarceration rates were a measure of the discriminatory treatment of blacks, then criminal justice officials in the North were far more guilty of the crimes of which they accused Southerners than were the Southerners who operated the leases.

While arguments about regional differences in black-white incarcerations were tied up with the broader arguments concerning reforming prisons that occurred around the turn of the century (see, for example, any of the annual reports of the National Prison Association meetings around this time for discussions about the nature of correctional reforms, as well as tangential discussions of the regional differences in racially disproportionate prisons), observations and discussions of the issue of higher black incarceration rates in the North than in the South virtually ceased by the late 1920s. The impression created by this historical silence was that it was only in the South that blacks suffered disproportionately at the hands of criminal justice officials and social control institutions.

Early twentieth century observers of the regional differences in black-white incarceration rates were interested in a few basic issues. Among them were first, the reasons behind the higher black than white incarceration rates in both regions of the country. Second, they were interested in the factors producing changes in the levels of those incarceration rates. Third, they were concerned with how changes in black and white crime rates affected changes in (particularly) black incarceration rates, and why changes in black crime rates seemed to be insufficient to explain the changes in black incarceration rates. Moreover, acknowledging the problematic criminal statistics available at that time, they attempted to determine the degree to which the sources of the biases that characterized criminal statistics also characterized the treatment of black offenders. All of this is to say, that in addition to focusing on criminal justice outcomes, early 20th century researchers were intent on determining the social origins of both differences in black-white criminal involvement and differences in the two groups respective criminal justice outcomes.

Social commentators, especially black scholars, attempted to understand the complex relationships between black crime and punishment and economic and social conditions like poverty, ignorance, urbanization, the social disorganization of the areas in which blacks were highly concentrated, or the subordinate status of blacks in American society, as Frazier (1949) observes. Indeed, one striking element common to the many analyses of the 1900 through 1940 period was the role that the marginalization of black men played in generating black crime rates. Certainly Dubois' (1973) "criminal class" or

Wright's (1969) detailed considerations of the poverty that characterized social conditions of blacks in the North were no less comments on the effects of marginality than Frazier's remark that "Negro men are constantly faced with unemployment and constantly live on the fringe of a marginal existence. As a result of these social and economic factors Negro men constitute a disproportionately large part of the criminal element in cities" (1949: 642).

The crux of the matter, in terms of explaining racial differences in incarcerations, lay not merely in a consideration of the racial differences in official measures of criminal involvement, but it lay in a consideration of the underlying reasons for those differences. The aim of such elaborate analysis was not to "explain away" the serious problems of crime in the black community; rather, the aim was consistent with the aims of contemporary policy research: to shed light on the problem in the hope of changing the social conditions which spawned the racial differences. That policy hope was best expressed by E. Franklin Frazier:

> This new understanding of the nature of Negro crime and juvenile delinquency has helped to redefine these problems. But whether this knowledge will be utilized to reduce Negro crime and juvenile delinquency will depend partly upon the extent to which the Negro is integrated into American life and partly upon the measures which the American community adopts to deal with these problems. (Frazier 1949: 653)

Given those conclusions, what did the early twentieth century writers have to say about the regional differences in black-white incarcerations?

First, given the caveat on the limits of official measures of crime, they did conclude that the black-white gap in imprisonments was due in part to differential involvement in crime. Monroe Work's (1913) evaluation of black crime in the South demonstrated the lower, four-decade, post-Civil War crime rates of blacks there, compared to blacks in the North. He demonstrated that the black crime rate in the South was lower than that in the North, and the difference was due to the different proportions of urbanized blacks in the two regions. That difference in crime rates accounts for some of the difference between black incarceration rates in the two regions (between, say, 1870 and 1900), but not all of it. (See Table 1.)

Second, and perhaps more importantly, researchers attempted to explain the reasons for the changes in the incarceration rates in the two regions. Here, the analysis focused not only upon differentials in criminal involvement, but also on differentials in treatment of blacks by the respective criminal justice systems. That was because differentials in crime failed to explain increases or decreases in black incarceration rates. For example, in the South, Work's (1913) study documented that the incidence of crime among blacks decreased

408

slightly or remained stable for over a decade at the turn of the century. However, as Table 1 documents, the black incarceration rate in the South did not remain stable from say, 1890 to 1910. It changed in those years, declining first from 252 per 100,000 to 207 (between 1890 and 1900) and then increasing to 287 in 1910.

In the North, Wright's (1969) analysis of black crime in Pennsylvania documented a similar pattern of black crime following the Civil War. Although black arrests increased in the three decades after the Civil War, the black crime rate, as a percentage of the black population in Pennsylvania, was at about the same level in 1900 as it was after the Civil War (Wright 1969: 157). To the extent that results from Pennsylvania can be generalized for the North, the unsettling conclusion with which we are left is that black crime rates per capita did not increase much following the Civil War; however, (as Table 1) displays, the Northern black incarceration rate increased between 1870 and 1900 from 507 per 100,000 to 772. Therefore, factors other than differential involvement in crime alone were responsible for those changes in black incarcerations in the latter part of the 19th and early part of the 20th century.

The major factor used to explain those changes in black incarceration rates was discrimination. Although both DuBois and Wright downplayed the extent to which individual discriminatory behaviors contributed to the changes in the

Table 1. North-South incarceration rates per 100,000 population.

Year	Total	North		Total	South	
		White	Black		White	Black
1850	30.19	26.23	289.81	14.80	18.62	8.34
1870	86.83	80.65	507.36	70.54	42.56	120.35
1880	119.38	112.09	558.98	101.90	51.00	192.26
1890	130.74	121.38	718.10	122.33	55.17	251.85
1900	106.48	94.91	771.86	94.20	39.16	206.88
1910	114.48	102.36	773.11	116.55	48.80	287.31
1920	93.21	77.25	734.30	95.88	49.64	217.07
1940	200.57	162.98	1132.42	264.95	175.66	553.09
1950	149.98	108.68	867.16	184.70	123.19	408.57
1960	148.28	97.83	822.04	214.12	142.45	493.07
1970	121.73	71.83	611.09	181.46	113.46	460.73
1980	161.66	84.41	671.96	292.58	145.72	631.12

Sources: Census documents. Incarceration rates were computed for all persons in all federal, state or local prisons, workhouses, jails, reformatories, etc., counted on the date the census was conducted. See Appendix A for further information.

The rates for 1860 and 1930 were omitted because no racial breakdowns were given in 1860 and there was no report for 1930.

black incarceration rate, they did allude to the role of institutional discrimination, particularly in economic conditions, as important factors. On the other hand. the Chicago Commission on Race Relations (1922) described in detail the effects of individual discrimination. Some judges, for example. threw out guilty verdicts pronounced on black defendants by all-white juries because they were convinced that the jury was influenced by "color prejudice". In other cases, black defendants requested to be tried by judges rather than all-white juries since they knew that they had little chance of a fair trial at the hands of an all-white jury. Other abuses included unfair challenges to the evidence given by black witnesses and hearings of black defendants that were characterized by such laxity and lack of dignity that in "one instance the judge was shaking dice during the hearing of the case" (Chicago Commission 1922: 333).

While the sum of those discriminatory elements might not add up to the degree of the racial disproportionality in imprisonment unexplained by differential involvement in crime, they do indicate that treatment of black defendants by individuals within criminal justice systems in the North was symptomatic of the pervasive attitude by which whites viewed blacks as inferior or second-class citizens. Interestingly, one explanation to which researchers often resorted to explain discrimination was the absence of a viable black. political voice. Although it was Myrdal who formalized the "political empowerment hypothesis" as one means to promote racial equality, these earlier writers also noted that the absence of fear of reprisal by the black community removed one restraint that protected whites against unfair treatment at the

Table 2. North-South disproportionality ratios.

Year	North	South	North/South
1850	11.05	0.45	24.56
1870	6.29	2.83	2.22
1880	4.99	3.77	1.32
1890	5.92	4.56	1.30
1900	8.13	5.28	1.54
1910	7.55	5.89	1.28
1920	9.51	4.37	2.18
1940	6.95	3.15	2.21
1950	7.98	3.32	2.40
1960	8.40	3.46	2.43
1970	8.56	4.06	2.11
1980	7.96	4.33	1.84

Sources: Census documents as in Table 1.

The disproportionality ratio is the black incarceration rate divided by the white incarceration rate.

410

hands of criminal justice officials. Because of their fewer resources, the
Chicago Commission remarked, black have less influence with which to insure
fair treatment, and "so are more likely to be subjected to annoyance" (1922:
335).

But those explanations that focused only on individual discriminatory actions failed to grasp the extent to which social discrimination accounted for
changes in the racial disproportionality of prisons in the two regions. Most of
these analyses have come from contemporary researchers who have rekindled
interest in the long-term patterns of black-white differences in incarcerations.
Sellin's *Slavery and the Penal System* (1976) was one pioneering study that
attempted to account for the changes in black incarcerations in the South
before and after the Civil War. Sellin depicts, with a fascinating degree of
horror, the way in which white Southerners re-enslaved blacks following the
Civil War through the convict lease system. Although that form of punishment
actually incapacitated only small fractions of the black population in the
South, it was part and parcel of the broader efforts, such as the black codes,
vagrancy laws, peonage, sharecropping arrangements, tenant agreements,
violence and intimidation, which white Southerners inflicted upon blacks. As a
labor-driven form of punishment, the convict lease system, justified by the
13th Amendment which outlawed slavery or involuntary servitude *except* as
punishment for crime, provided a select group of Southern businessmen with a
secure source of cheap labor (when cheap agricultural labor was scarce) while
filling the treasuries of Southern states with profits derived from the labor of
black, leased convicts.

Similarly, Adamson (1983) uses a model of a labor-driven prison system to
explain changes in black incarcerations in the South. Adamson argues that
crime control efforts in the South between 1865 and 1890 were directed
primarily at blacks. Newly-freed blacks represented a "problem population"
for Southern whites. As a group emancipated blacks represented both a threat
to the existing political and economic system, since they could compete directly with white labor to fulfill the needs of the plantation economy, and they
represented a potential resource. Crime control became synonymous with
race control, and the convict lease system provided one means to exploit the
labor of blacks both for the state's benefit and the benefit of the lessors.

Hawkins' (1985) analysis of racial differences in incarcerations in North
Carolina between 1870 and 1980 elaborates upon the theme of a labor-driven
penal system. Hawkins was concerned with testing whether changing conceptions of race or changes in the form of social control better explained the
changes in the racial composition of North Carolina's prisons. By considering
the use of the convict lease system there in the 1880s and 1890s, the subsequent
changes in penal policy in which the state established prison farms and chain
gangs (between 1890 and 1920) and in which black convicts were dispropor-

tionately involved on the chain gangs (hard labor) while whites were (almost exclusively) used on the farms, and the eventual demise of dehumanizing prison work (with the elimination of road-camp work in the mid-1960s) combined with the increased use of prison industries and the gradual acceptance of that type of prison work for whites. Hawkins concludes that the form of labor embodied in the penal system explained the long-run changes in the racial composition of North Carolina's prison. As prison work became more acceptable, the state was able to gradually accept a policy of greater incarcerations of whites.

While the labor component of the penal system changed, that is, as the existing type of labor in the penal system was perceived as acceptable for whites in the South and so white incarcerations increased there, for the North, Myers and Sabol (1987) extend further the linkage between the prison and the labor market. In their model the form of prison labor is less important in explaining racial differences in incarcerations than are the respective labor market conditions of blacks and whites. Myers and Sabol develop a model in which imprisonments are driven by unemployment, which is itself a function of longer-run changes in manufacturing output, or the swings in the trend in growth characteristic of industrial economies. Although they are hampered by the absence of crime data for the entire period which they investigate (1890 to 1980) they show that the growth in imprisonments in the North were driven by black unemployment and that the growth of imprisonment was inversely related to swings in manufacturing output. The swings in black unemployment in the manufacturing sectors provide the linkage to the marginality of black men, the social conditions which generate crime. Thus Myers and Sabol conclude that changes in the black incarceration rate in the North also were labor driven, but in this case, the labor market experiences of blacks was tied to crime and imprisonment.

This brief survey of explanations of the long run differences between black-white incarcerations in the North and South has attempted to show two things. First, comparing racial differences in official measures of crime alone is insufficient to explain the racial differences in black-white imprisonments between the two regions. Second, a full understanding of the racial disproportionality of prisons in the U.S. requires explanations which attempt to uncover the factors underlying the changes in black-white incarcerations. Those broader explanations are necessary not only for fuller understanding, but also from a policy perspective. By limiting the discussion simply to differential involvement in measures of crime, the only policy options available are incapacitation and increased use of sanctions, policies which certainly are important and applicable in some contexts. But those policies can have only limited effects if, as the studies of the historical trends in incarcerations show, the causes of the racial gap in imprisonments reside outside the criminal justice

412

system. Moreover, as will be shown later, today's policies of "sentencing by number" take on the aura of race control even though they are applied in an ostensibly racially neutral fashion.

II. Contemporary patterns of racial disproportionality in prisons

Research on recent periods of black-white differences in incarcerations is markedly different from that in which investigators explain the longer-run changes. Contemporary researchers have framed the problem in terms of differential involvement in crime versus differential treatment of offenders (or discrimination). Generally, they tend to find support for the differential involvement hypothesis, but once finding that, they fail to step outside the criminal justice system to attempt to isolate the factors of social discrimination which generate the differential involvement.

The differential involvement tradition began with Blumstein's (1982) pioneering study on the racial disproportionality of prisons. It has been continued more recently by Langan (1985) and Wilbanks (1987). In addition to reconceptualizing the debate around the contemporary racial disproportionality of prisons, Blumstein devised a new measure of disproportionality. Previous researchers such as Dunbaugh (1979) and Christianson (1981) used the ratio of black to white incarceration rates per 100,000 population as the measure of racial disproportionality. Since they found that ratio to be about eight, they concluded that the overrepresentation of blacks in prison, compared to blacks in the general population, could be due only to widespread discrimination. Blumstein countered first, on logical grounds, that it was not necessary to draw that conclusion based upon comparisons with the general population. Second, he devised a measure of disproportionality based upon the disproportionality in arrests.

Blumstein used a decomposition method common to demographers to calculate the expected fractions of blacks in prison by crime type. The logic of his method rests upon the fact that offenders convicted of different crimes have different probabilities of imprisonment, and that aggregate imprisonment probabilities mask the racial differences in the distribution of crime by crime type. To review briefly his method, Blumstein computes a variable (B_j) representing the black arrest percentage by crime type j. He then computes the expected percentage of prisoners (by crime type) that should be black (R_j) by multiplying B_j by F_j which is the actual distribution of offenders in state prisons by offense type. For all black prisoners the expected percentage is arrived at by summing over the crime types. Because his expected fractions of black prisoners are produced by weighting the distribution of black arrestees by the probability of imprisonment for different crime types, his expected fraction of black prisoners is different from the fraction that would be expected if he had used only aggregate arrests. (For example, using the UCR data for 1974 from his Table 3, p. 1266, the expected percentage of blacks in prison if only aggregate arrests were used would be 29.7; his expected percentage, derived from the decomposition method, was 42.7.)

After calculating the expected percentage of black prisoners, Blumstein develops his disproportionality measure. He defines X, the disproportionality measure, as the ratio of the expected black-to-white incarceration rates based only on arrest disproportionalities to the ratio of black-to-white incarceration rates actually observed. Calculating the disproportionality measure for two years, 1974 and 1979, Blumstein finds that in both years, 80 percent of the disproportionality in prisons is accounted for by the disproportionality in arrests. In other words, he does not find evidence of "flagrant" discrimination in the criminal justice system.

There are a number of criticisms of Blumstein's work. Apart from measurements of arrests, i.e., that the entire U.S. population is not included in the UCR reports, problems which hound all users of UCR data, there are more serious criticisms which need to be discussed. Three of them will be considered here; others which apply to Blumstein's and Langan's follow-up work will be considered later. First, Blumstein assumes that arrests are good measures of criminal involvement. That assumption, however, has not been verified by research which documents the propensity of the police to overarrest (particularly) blacks, particularly in mixed neighborhoods (Smith 1986; Smith, Visher and Davidson 1984), the propensity of prosecutors to decide to seek more serious charges, or at least not reduce charges from the arrest charge, for blacks (Farrell and Swigert 1978) or in their decisions on how to prosecute in homicide cases (Radelet and Pierce 1985), or by the consistent set of differences in the treatment of whites and blacks at every stage throughout the criminal justice process (Petersilia 1983). Those differences are increasingly difficult to account for except by omitted variables (Klepper, Nagin and Tierney 1983) or by reference only to race.

Second, Blumstein uses stock measures of imprisonment, the respective census of prisons conducted by the Department of Justice. The number incarcerated, however, is not strictly comparable to the numbers arrested since the latter is a flow concept. The importance of weighting incarceration data to devise a comparable flow measure was demonstrated by Peterson and Braiker (1980) in their work at RAND. The issue revolves around the differences between an incoming cohort of offenders that parallels the incoming arrestees. That incoming cohort differs from an in-prison sample primarily because anyone in prison for a long period of time is more likely to be found in an in-prison sample than is a person who is in prison for a short period of time. For example, males convicted of homicide constituted between 8 and 11

414

percent of incoming prisoners between 1969 and 1975 in California, but they comprised 17.9 percent of all males in prison in 1976 (Peterson and Braiker 1980: 224). The bias introduced by using the in-prison sample might be one reason for the better fit between the expected and actual fractions of blacks in prison for crimes with longer sentences, like homicide, rape and robbery, and the poorer fit for crimes like burglary, as Blumstein found.

Third, in calculating his standard for *no post-arrest discrimination*, his variable F_j, Blumstein assumed that the existing offense distribution of state prisoners, both black and white, was itself *not* produced by discrimination. In other words, he used the actual distribution of prisoners, which may itself have been produced both by historical and contemporary, individual and social discriminatory forces to prove that there was not much discrimination in the processing of offenders through the criminal justice system to produce the actual distribution of offenders in prison.

In spite of those limitations (and a few others which will be mentioned after considering Langan's work), Blumstein's general conclusion cannot be overlooked. There is a link between racial differences in arrests and the racial disproportionality of the prisons, although the extent to which that link is based solely on criminal involvement versus discrimination is still an incompletely answered empirical question.

Langan (1985) attempted to correct for some of the flaws in Blumstein's work. Using National Crime Survey data on the race of offenders as perceived by victims, he generated distributions of the expected fractions of blacks by crime type that should be admitted into state prisons if blacks and whites were treated similarly. Note, his standard was not based upon existing prison outcomes, as was Blumstein's standard for post-arrest discrimination; rather, Langan compared the treatment of blacks with that of whites. To the degree that the expected fractions of blacks admitted into prison, based on the white probability of being admitted into prison, differed from the actual fractions of blacks (by crime type) admitted into prison, Langan measured racial differences in criminal justice processing or discrimination. Like Blumstein, Langan found little effect of discrimination. Fully 85 percent of the difference between the expected and actual numbers of blacks admitted into prison was accounted for by differential involvement in crime.

Langan uses the National Crime Survey victims' assessment of the race of their assailants to measure criminal involvement. Those data give better assessments of the racial differences in criminal involvement than do arrest data, however, we do not know which of the offenders described by NCS victims are actually arrested and processed through the criminal justice system. In other words, what difference does it make if the NCS offender data give the "true" picture of black crime, when the criminal justice system does *not* process that "true" picture but only a truncated sample that is produced by the behavior of the police? Although Langan justifies his choice of measure by reference to Hindelang's (1978) work comparing the fractions of blacks arrested with the fractions of blacks described as offenders by their victims, except in the case of robbery. it has been demonstrated elsewhere (Myers and Sabol 1988) that there is not necessarily a close association between racial differences in arrests and racial differences in the descriptions of assailants by victims. In any case, only those offenders actually arrested and processed are of interest, not the entire population of offenders.

Second, while Langan's sample of victims who could describe the race and sex of their assailants is quite large for personal crimes, for the property crimes he used, burglary, larceny and auto theft. only five, five and three percent respectively of the victims in the NCS could describe the race of their assailants. That sample of victims was not a random sample; it was based on the likelihood that the victims observed the offender. Moreover, those three porperty crimes accounted for 52, 54 and 60 percent respectively (in 1973, 1979 and 1982, the three years he used) of the seven crimes Langan used to generate his distributions of prisoners. Also, white offenders convicted of those three crimes were responsible for 62, 60 and 66 percent, in the respective years, of white prison admissions and 41, 48 and 53 percent of black prison admissions. again, in the respective years. The nature and extent of the bias introduced by such a sample is impossible to calculate, and (consistent with Blumstein) since the greatest discrepancy between expected and actual fractions of blacks in prison occurs with those crimes. confidence in Langan's results must be cautionary.

Next, as Langan points out (1985: 683), another issue confounding the differential involvement versus differential treatment test is the question of the incidence versus the prevalence of crime among blacks and whites. While some studies show that the races differ more on the prevalence of crime than on the incidence (Blumstein and Graddy 1982), others show that there are little differences in prevalence but that whites have higher incidences of crime (Peterson and Braiker 1980). If the racial differences in criminal involvement stem from differences in incidence. then the absence of comparative data on the criminal records of black and white offenders is of paramount concern.

But if one considers the issue of the incidence versus the prevalence of criminal involvement as it relates to imprisonment differentials. we are led to another conclusion. If the conventional wisdom, which suggests that racial differences in criminal involvement are due to the prevalence of crime among blacks, then a problem arises. Since the probability of imprisonment increases with the number of convictions – or the incidence of crime – but there are no racial differences in incidence, then low-rate black offenders must have a higher probability of receiving a prison sentence than do white offenders, regardless of their incidence. (This is what the Peterson and Braiker findings

416

suggest when, commenting on California, they state, "the California criminal justice system may be characterized by a bias toward more likely incarceration of occasional offenders if they are Mexican-American or particularly if they are black. However, ... it may be that white offenders are both more active and less likely to be arrested and incarcerated" (1980: 65).) In other words, the criminal justice system treats blacks differently from whites *if*, as the conventional wisdom suggests, the differences are due to the prevalence of crime. That differential treatment could be synonymous with discrimination.

Finally, aggregate data do not contain measures which adequately reflect the severity of crime or which reflect an individual offender's habitual involvement in crime. Those two factors were cited by the NAS panel on sentencing (Blumstein et al. 1983) as key determinants of imprisonment. Absent those measures, one can only speculate about the extent to which the racial differences in imprisonment are accounted for by individual involvement in crime versus differential treatment in the criminal justice system.

But even with aggregate data, the decomposition method is not the best way to test for discrimination in the criminal justice system. The method is analogous to a regression model with a single independent variable. Thus users of the decomposition method will not be able to account for other factors, or more importantly, for racial differences on other factors. Since blacks and whites may not have identical or even similar background characteristics or criminal justice experiences, more than one factor must be considered simultaneously and controls must be made for important variables.

One powerful method available to test for effects of discrimination is the residual difference technique pioneered by labor econometricians to test for labor market discrimination. The advantage of the residual difference technique is that it permits researchers to distinguish between the effects of different characteristics (such as racial differences in criminal involvement) and differences in treatment on similar characteristics.

The procedure involves estimating separate regression equations for blacks and whites for the relevant criminal justice outcome.

$$O^A = X^A b^A + e^A$$
$$O^B = X^B b^B + e^B \tag{1}$$

where O^i is the relevant criminal justice outcome for members of group i, X^i is a vector of characteristics for members of groups i, b^A is a vector of parameters for the group i equation, and e^i is the error term for the group i equation. The model assumes that in the absence of discrimination the parameters of the two equations are identical for the two groups. In other words, the characteristics X are treated the same on the relevant criminal justice outcome, O. In the absence of discrimination criminal justice outcomes depend only on relevant legal factors and not on membership in a particular group.

The differences in outcomes, (for example. time served) between the two groups can be decomposed into two parts:

$$\bar{O}^A - \bar{O}^B = (\bar{X}^A - \bar{X}^B)b^A + \bar{X}^B(b^A - b^B) \qquad (2)$$

where the first term on the right-hand-side is called the endowment effect and the second term is called the residual difference. The endowment effect measures that portion of the difference in average outcomes which is due to differences in characteristics. The residual difference measures the difference in average outcomes due to the differences in the parameters of the criminal justice outcome equations. The residual difference is defined as a measure of discrimination (Blinder 1973) because it is a measure of the difference in average outcomes which would persist with an identical set of characteristics for the two groups. In other words. if blacks were identical to whites on legally-relevant and criminal justice background characteristics. the second term on the right-hand-side of the above equation would measure the differences in their outcomes due to differences in treatment by criminal justice decision makers.

Extending the logic of this technique one step further. it is possible to use it to produce evidence of whether or not differences in practice amount to "irrational" differences in treatment that are analogous to the legal requirement that a necessary condition for discrimination is irrationality in. for example. sentencing. The second step amounts to applying the residual difference technique to determine if observed differences in treatment (assuming of course that such differences are found in the first step) are justifiable on grounds of necessity. By way of example. the procedure involved in this second step goes as follows. Suppose the variable of interest was sentence length. and suppose that in the first step residual differences in the treatment of whites and blacks were found. Suppose further that an argument was posited that those differences were justifiable on the grounds that black crime rates are higher than white crime rates and that longer or more severe sentences were warranted on deterrence grounds. In that case. the natural question would be. if the differences in treatment between blacks and whites were eliminated. that is, if blacks were treated identically to whites and given the same. lower average sentence as whites. would the black crime rate increase? If it were to increase, then the differences in treatment could be justified on grounds of necessity or in pursuit of other criminal justice aims. If the black crime rate did not increase upon the elimination of the gap in average sentences. then the necessity justification for the gap would disappear. In Myers'

418

Journal of Quantitative Criminology (1985) article, this test was performed on differences in parole release using the U.S. Board of Parole data for 1972. Upon estimating an economic crime-supply model, the results demonstrated that eliminating the racial punishment disparity did not result in increased crime among blacks.

Evidence produced by applying the residual difference technique to criminal justice data sets can begin to address more clearly the issue of differential involvement versus differential treatment. Findings stemming from the second step can determine whether, if observed, longer sentences for blacks are justifiable in relation to pursuing criminal justice goals. If, on the other hand, they are inefficient, that is, they fail to produce the expected reductions in black crime rates, then it is possible to demonstrate that differential treatment was unwarranted. That would be tantamount to demonstrating that outcomes were produced by discrimination.

The essence of the residual difference technique boils down to the following. One simply cannot test hypotheses about discrimination by first assuming that there is no differential treatment of race-neutral characteristics. Only a method capable of distinguishing between characteristics and treatment effects is capable of solving the differential treatment versus differential involvement dilemma.

III. Regional differences in disproportionality

Finally, this discussion of the racial disproportionality in imprisonment is concluded by returning to the regional differences considered at the outset of this section. Here, however, rather than considering disproportionality solely in relation to population, it is considered as the excesses of black-white imprisonments over the ratio of black-white arrests. The aggregate measure used here differs from the disproportionality values used by Blumstein and Langan since it does not include arrest data by crime type to weight the respective distributions of offenses by those crimes with higher probabilities of imprisonment. Nonetheless, the measure of the overall differences between arrest and imprisonment ratios in each of the fifty states and the District of Columbia points out the extent of the variability in differential treatment and differential involvement across regions and states and over time.

In Tables 3, 4 and 5 are displayed the fractions of black arrests (of total), the fractions of black sentenced prisoners (in state and federal prisons) and the ratio of black arrests to black imprisonments for each state in 1960, 1970 and 1980. The arrest and imprisonment data for 1960 actually are measures for nonwhites, since the census statistics on imprisonment used that racial designation. Arrest data were obtained from the FBI's Uniform Crime Reporting

Program. (See Appendix B for details on the computation of arrest rates by race.)

Looking first at the black proportion of all arrests (Table 3), the largest fractions are in the South Atlantic region in each period. The Middle Atlantic states followed the South Atlantic in each period except 1980, and while the East South Central had the third highest percentage of black arrests in 1960, by 1970 and 1980 the East North Central region had climbed to the third position. Overall, for the United States, the fraction of black arrests declined from 1960 to 1970 and then increased again in 1980.

The increase from 1970 to 1980 in the black fraction of total arrests for the United States is notable principally because *in only one region did the black fraction of total arrests increase.* And that region, the comprising the Mountain states, accounted for too few arrests in order to make a difference nationally. How could this be? Quite simply the regional changes from 1970 to 1980 reflect opposing trends among states within a region. Take for example the Mid-Atlantic region. The black fraction of arrests rose in New York from 0.256 to 0.320 in the 1970–80 decade. It fell in Pennsylvania from an unusually high 0.418 in 1970 to a regional low of 0.251 in 1980. The net impact was to lower the regional average. Other examples of these intra-regional variations in proportions of black arrests can be found. In the East-North Central region, the black fraction of total arrests rose in Illinois and Indiana but fell considerably in Ohio. For the region as a whole, it fell. In the South Atlantic region, the black fraction of arrests rose in Maryland and Washington D.C.; it fell in North Carolina, South Carolina, Georgia and Florida. The net impact in the region? The black proportion of total arrests fell. Across the entire United States then, the black share of total arrests seemed to rise, even though in every region save for the Mountain states the black share of total arrests was on the decline from 1970 to 1980. The large numbers of black arrests in states like Maryland, New York and Illinois account for the tilting of the scales nationally.

With respect to the black proportion of those incarcerated in state and federal prisons (Table 4), except for 1970 the South Atlantic states had the largest fractions, with well over 50 percent of their prison populations consisting of black offenders in all three periods. Close behind the South Atlantic was the Middle Atlantic, again, except for 1960, with over 50 percent of their prisoners being black. As with arrests, the regions with the third and fourth highest fractions of black prisoners fluctuated between the East South Central and the East North Central. While in the East South Central blacks were consistently about 45 percent of the prisoners, in the East North Central, prisons have become increasingly black, so that by 1980 over 50 percent of the prisoners there were black. Finally, for the United States as a whole, prisons have become increasingly black. The fraction black has grown since 1960 (which includes nonwhites other than blacks) when blacks (nonwhites) were

420

Table 3. Fraction black arrests.

State/Region	1960	1970	1980
New England	0.136	0.167	0.130
Maine	0.028	0.008	0.007
New Hampshire	0.004	0.009	0.004
Vermont	0.003	0.004	N.A.
Massachusetts	0.115	0.120	0.154
Rhode Island	0.167	0.125	0.118
Connecticut	0.272	0.303	0.233
Mid Atlantic	0.392	0.346	0.298
New York	0.247	0.256	0.320
New Jersey	0.365	0.328	0.297
Pennsylvania	0.475	0.418	0.251
E.N. Central	0.297	0.327	0.319
Ohio	0.287	0.309	0.167
Indiana	0.200	0.223	0.277
Illinois	0.349	0.427	0.467
Michigan	0.354	N.A.	0.326
Wisconsin	0.165	0.163	0.139
W.N. Central	0.253	0.178	0.094
Minnesota	0.108	0.048	0.043
Iowa	0.088	0.054	0.040
Missouri	0.419	0.384	0.208
North Dakota	0.167	0.006	0.005
South Dakota	0.222	0.007	0.009
Nebraska	0.228	0.141	0.117
Kansas	0.187	0.161	0.150
S. Atlantic	0.472	0.382	0.348
Delaware	0.429	0.466	0.435
Maryland	0.476	0.434	0.476
DC	0.681	0.809	0.884
Virginia	0.422	0.360	0.297
West Virginia	0.075	0.049	0.070
North Carolina	0.444	0.418	0.380
South Carolina	0.469	0.437	0.387
Georgia	0.536	0.454	0.395
Florida	0.391	0.311	0.262
E.S. Central	0.382	0.296	0.266
Kentucky	0.220	0.156	0.112
Tennessee	0.402	0.343	0.274
Alabama	0.459	0.415	0.374
Mississippi	0.562	0.539	0.516

Table 3. (Continued).

State/Region	1960	1970	1980
W.S. Central	0.318	0.275	0.175
Arkansas	0.378	0.305	0.318
Louisiana	0.465	0.480	0.414
Oklahoma	0.261	0.144	0.126
Texas	0.289	0.248	0.145
Mountain	0.205	0.067	0.074
Montana	0.154	0.010	0.010
Idaho	0.212	0.011	0.007
Wyoming	0.146	0.036	0.012
Colorado	0.128	0.099	0.155
New Mexico	0.303	0.036	0.055
Arizona	0.272	0.071	0.070
Utah	0.165	0.040	0.034
Nevada	0.165	0.125	0.100
Pacific	0.218	0.160	0.158
Washington	0.181	0.086	0.035
Oregon	0.155	0.056	0.010
California	0.207	0.185	0.177
Alaska	0.461	0.040	0.069
Hawaii	0.838	0.037	0.035
United States	0.316	0.267	0.319

N.A. means not available

The data on arrests were obtained from the FBI's Uniform Crime Reporting Program. We are thankful to J. Harper Wilson for his help in providing these data.

about 38 percent of the prisoners to 1980 when blacks made up over 44 percent of prisoners in state and federal prisons. Thus, with respect to the racial composition of incarcerations there are no illusions. In the vast majority of states, the black percentage of the totals increased continuously from 1960 until 1980.

What can be said about racial disproportionality of incarcerations in light of the data on arrests? Looking only at the national figures, the response is conventional: Much of the increase in the black representation in America's prisons must be a result of the increase in the black representation among those arrested. But a closer region by region analysis or state by state analysis points up a puzzle. In which states and in which regions are rising black arrests causing the increase in the black imprisonment? The calculations discussed below provide convincing evidence that the national increase in black impris-

422

Table 4. Fraction black in state and federal prisons.

State/Region	1960	1970	1980
New England	0.151	0.238	0.331
Maine	0.011	0.010	0.000
New Hampshire	0.000	0.041	0.031
Vermont	0.010	0.000	0.014
Massachusetts	0.147	0.181	0.348
Rhode Island	0.112	0.216	0.274
Connecticut	0.262	0.361	0.421
Mid. Atlantic	0.463	0.539	0.537
New York	0.449	0.529	0.528
New Jersey	0.531	0.625	0.598
Pennsylvania	0.452	0.488	0.515
E.N. Central	0.374	0.429	0.503
Ohio	0.363	0.448	0.501
Indiana	0.222	0.346	0.360
Illinois	0.519	0.509	0.549
Michigan	0.442	0.449	0.565
Wisconsin	0.187	0.294	0.399
W.N. Central	0.243	0.257	0.317
Minnesota	0.179	0.148	0.192
Iowa	0.078	0.169	0.189
Missouri	0.345	0.391	0.442
North Dakota	0.186	0.000	0.041
South Dakota	0.376	0.013	0.000
Nebraska	0.212	0.236	0.325
Kansas	0.246	0.256	0.380
S. Atlantic	0.523	0.519	0.543
Delaware	0.680	0.590	0.574
Maryland	0.628	0.682	0.724
DC	0.000	0.850	0.944
Virginia	0.612	0.491	0.586
West Virginia	0.211	0.267	0.359
North Carolina	0.554	0.533	0.513
South Carolina	0.544	0.501	0.562
Georgia	0.489	0.489	0.560
Florida	0.420	0.488	0.447
E.S.Central	0.449	0.445	0.460
Kentucky	0.220	0.296	0.319
Tennessee	0.353	0.439	0.462
Alabama	0.564	0.541	0.518
Mississippi	0.661	0.583	0.678

423

Table 4. (Continued).

State/Region	1960	1970	1980
W.S. Central	0.362	0.432	0.431
Arkansas	0.507	0.536	0.518
Louisiana	0.569	0.662	0.692
Oklahoma	0.285	0.267	0.247
Texas	0.303	0.383	0.391
Mountain	0.159	0.150	0.150
Montana	0.192	0.000	0.057
Idaho	0.105	0.000	0.000
Wyoming	0.039	0.000	0.033
Colorado	0.123	0.179	0.177
New Mexico	0.120	0.102	0.074
Arizona	0.249	0.203	0.207
Utah	0.065	0.131	0.059
Nevada	0.204	0.180	0.275
Pacific	0.247	0.224	0.274
Washington	0.194	0.186	0.173
Oregon	0.103	0.104	0.094
California	0.249	0.243	0.317
Alaska	0.436	0.066	0.072
Hawaii	0.844	0.000	0.073
United States	0.381	0.404	0.444

onment *cannot* be the result of uniform increases in black arrests across the nation. In most states and regions the black share of arrests has been falling! And yet, in almost every region black representation among those incarcerated has increased continuously.

Table 5 displays the ratios of the fractions of blacks arrested (the expected fractions of blacks in imprison) with the actual fractions of blacks in prison. The closer this ratio is to one, the closer the correspondence between arrest and imprisonment disproportionalities. Smaller arrest to imprisonment ratios mean that less of the racial composition of prisons is explained by the racial composition in arrests. Thus, for example, the gap between arrests and imprisonment was relatively low for the South Atlantic in 1960 when 90 percent of the racial composition of prisons was explained by the racial composition in arrests. On the other hand, only about 30 percent of the racial composition of prisons in the West North Central in 1980 was explained by the racial composition in arrests.

The South Atlantic and East North Central regions lead the way with the

424

Table 5. Imprisonment disproportionality explained by arrest disproportionality.

State/Region	1960	1970	1980
New England	0.896	0.701	0.394
Maine	2.546	0.840	–
New Hampshire	–	0.214	0.129
Vermont	0.304	–	N.A.
Massachusetts	0.780	0.662	0.443
Rhode Island	1.486	0.578	0.430
Connecticut	1.037	0.838	0.553
Mid. Atlantic	0.846	0.641	0.555
New York	0.550	0.484	0.606
New Jersey	0.688	0.525	0.497
Pennsylvania	1.050	0.856	0.487
E.N. Central	0.794	0.762	0.633
Ohio	0.791	0.690	0.334
Indiana	0.900	0.644	0.769
Illinois	0.672	0.840	0.850
Michigan	0.800	N.A.	0.578
Wisconsin	0.882	0.554	0.348
W.N. Central	1.039	0.695	0.296
Minnesota	0.607	0.327	0.222
Iowa	1.123	0.320	0.214
Missouri	1.216	0.984	0.471
North Dakota	0.902	–	0.125
South Dakota	0.590	0.553	–
Nebraska	1.076	0.597	0.359
Kansas	0.762	0.630	0.394
S. Atlantic	0.902	0.736	0.639
Delaware	0.631	0.790	0.758
Maryland	0.758	0.637	0.658
DC	–	0.953	0.936
Virginia	0.690	0.733	0.507
West Virginia	0.356	0.184	0.196
North Carolina	0.802	0.785	0.741
South Carolina	0.863	0.872	0.689
Georgia	1.097	0.929	0.706
Florida	0.932	0.637	0.586
E.S. Central	0.850	0.666	0.578
Kentucky	1.000	0.527	0.351
Tennessee	1.140	0.781	0.593
Alabama	0.814	0.766	0.721
Mississippi	0.850	0.925	0.761

425

Table 5. (Continued).

State/Region	1960	1970	1980
W.S. Central	0.878	0.638	0.405
Arkansas	0.746	0.570	0.614
Louisiana	0.817	0.725	0.599
Oklahoma	0.916	0.539	0.510
Texas	0.954	0.649	0.370
Mountain	1.311	0.466	0.492
Montana	0.802	–	0.166
Idaho	2.028	–	–
Wyoming	3.691	–	0.364
Colorado	1.044	0.552	0.876
New Mexico	2.533	0.352	0.733
Arizona	1.092	0.350	0.337
Utah	2.551	0.308	0.568
Nevada	0.809	0.697	0.364
Pacific	0.882	0.715	0.578
Washington	0.934	0.461	0.202
Oregon	1.512	0.542	0.102
California	0.829	0.760	0.559
Alaska	1.056	0.630	0.950
Hawaii	0.992	–	0.477
United States	0.831	0.661	0.719

N.A. means that the arrest data were not available.
– means that the fraction of blacks in prison was zero.

The data used in these calculations came from the FBI's Uniform Crime Reporting Program and from the Bureau of the Census counts of institutionalized persons.

closest correspondence between arrests and imprisonments. In two of the three periods, 1960 and 1980, the South Atlantic had the highest fractions of imprisonment explained by arrests, and while there is only a slight difference between the South Atlantic and East North Central in 1980, in 1970 the East North Central had the highest amount explained. Over time, however, in both regions, consistently smaller fractions of the racial composition of prisons could be explained by arrests. The drop was not as dramatic in the East North Central as in the South Atlantic, but it was sharp enough to place it below the South Atlantic in 1980.

Similarly, in all regions (except the Mountain region where the fraction of the black population is quite small) the percentages of the racial composition of prisons explained by arrests declined, as it did for the United States as a

426

whole. In the other regions with large black populations, the East South Central and the Middle Atlantic, the declines paralleled each other. In all periods, the South Atlantic had smaller fractions explained than did the East South Central. By 1980 only about 55 percent of the discrepancy between black arrests and black imprisonments in the Middle Atlantic could be explained.

Other regional differences in the disproportionality between arrests and imprisonments are apparent. For example, whereas in 1960 there was a 90 percent correspondence between arrests and imprisonments in New England, by 1980 that correspondence had dropped to about 40 percent. The West North Central also experienced a similar decline between 1960 and 1980. And yet, despite the fact that each region's (except the Mountain) racial disparity in arrests explained less and less of the racial disparity in incarcerations between 1970 and 1980, for the United States as a whole the apparent ability of arrests disparities to "explain" imprisonment disparities improved.

It is undisputed that nationally the black percent of total arrests rose from 1970 to 1980. It is also unquestioned that nationally the black percent of total incarcerations increased. What is now very much in dispute and of great question is the causal link between disparities in arrests and disparities in imprisonment. Since the very states that accounted for much of the increased racial disparities in imprisonment *did not* contribute to increased racial disparities in arrests, it is problematic as to how current levels of black imprisonment can be attributable to blacks' alleged criminality, measured by their arrest rates.

While it is difficult to build a strong case for discrimination or to reject the differential involvement hypothesis based on the aggregate data in Tables 3, 4 and 5, and in light of the problems with aggregate data, it is possible to point out the wide regional variation that the use of aggregate statistics for the U.S. as a whole masks. Thus while Blumstein and Langan found little evidence for discrimination in the U.S., we have shown wide variations across states and regions. Additionally, the aggregate data hide the fact that while overall there is an appearance of improvement, as the increase from 66 to 72 percent in the proportion of the variation in the racial disproportionality of prisons explained by the racial distribution of arrests, for the U.S. between 1970 and 1980, in actuality each region's experience was the opposite, that is, in each region we were able to explain less of the disproportionality.

In short, this discussion points out the need to consider more closely the issue of the racial disproportionality in prisons, especially from a policy perspective. Since state prisoners comprise the bulk of the prison populations used here, and since individual state sentencing laws and criminal codes and practices differ, the policy implications for the differential involvement versus differential treatment thesis can only be derived by considering the state and local patterns of crime and punishment. Only at that level, and not necessarily at the national level, will we be able to develop usable results and knowledge that can answer the questions relating to the observed discrepancies and, if necessary, devise policies to eliminate differential treatment and discrimination regardless of the forms or locations in which it is manifest.

One final issue merits consideration. In the recent movement toward sentencing reform begun in the early- to mid-1970s, the rehabilitative *cum* administrative model of sentencing and corrections was dismantled. Standard practices like parole and indeterminate sentencing were eliminated. (See Tonry 1988, for an excellent review.) Determinate sentences, guidelines, either of the mandatory or suggestive type were adopted by more than a few states. No states were untouched by the reforms. Even those which kept their indeterminate and rehabilative modes adopted at a minimum mandatory sentences for repeat or habitual offenders or for offenders committed crimes with guns (Shane-DuBow 1985).

In the rush to get the right numbers to structure the guidelines, sentence reform groups generally adopted the same method. They gathered a sample of past cases, analyzed them and given different mixes of legally-relevant characteristics predicted outcomes. Those outcomes given the mix of characteristics provided the basis of the guidelines. In other words, the patterns or decision rules used by judges in sentencing during the pre-guideline period were cemented into the guidelines. If, for example, judges used extra-legal factors in deciding marginal cases, such as giving imprisonment with greater propensity to unemployed versus employed offenders, that bias was built into the guidelines. Similarly, the characteristics of black offenders which determined their pre-guideline outcomes were built into the guidelines used to determine sentences for all offenders, white and black.

While that practice may have resulted in a diminution of the disparities in sentences between whites and blacks, as nearly evaluations of Pennsylvania's guidelines seems to suggest (Kramer and Lubitz 1985), that diminution in disparities may have come at the expense of longer sentences for whites rather than shorter ones for blacks. But more importantly, if in the pre-guideline practices race was an important predictor of sentencing outcomes, and evidence seems to suggest that it played a larger role than usually deemed to be appropriate in Anglo-American legal traditions, then a pattern of discriminatory sentencing has been institutionalized in the guidelines themselves. This means that the application of the guidelines contributes to institutional discrimination. In other words, race may no longer be a directly important indicator of sentencing outcomes, but decisions based on factors that are racially neutral but which are highly correlated with race will perpetuate and perhaps exacerbate existing disparities.

This institutionalization of discrimination process may be most pronounced

428

in the use of pre-sentence reports, particularly in determining whether or not an offender should receive probation versus a prison sentence. A probation officer investigates the background of the offender, focusing on extra-legal factors like unemployment, family structure and the like. For blacks, particularly blacks who have been defined as the underclass (e.g. Wilson 1982; Darity and Myers 1984; Wilson and Neckerman 1986), unemployment and female-headed family structure are highly correlated with race. Thus, presentence reports need not contain any information about the race of the offender, yet due to the correlation between race and those characteristics deemed to be significant predictors of probation failure, blacks will systematically be incarcerated at higher levels than whites because they will receive probation at lower rates than whites. This pattern of institutionalized discrimination does not portend well for the future racial composition of U.S. prisons.

Acknowledgement

Special thanks to Samuel L. Myers, Jr. for helpful comments on an earlier version of this paper.

Appendix A

Imprisonment data and population data were gathered from the decennial census. Since 1850 the Census Bureau conducted special surveys of prisons, counting the numbers of prisoners by race and sex, for every decade except 1930. That year's report was replaced by the National Prison Statistics *Statistics of Prisoners in State and Federal Prisons and Reformatories*, an annual report begun in 1926. Additionally, in 1860 the data were not reported by race; there observations for that year were ommitted. The data used to compute incarceration rates consisted of observations by state by decade for the total number of persons incarcerated in federal, state, local prisons, jails or workhouses on the date the respective census was taken.

Observations were collected on 31 states, 17 of which were used to comprise the South and the other 14 the North. Southern states were Virginia, Delaware, West Virginia, Georgia, North Carolina, South Carolina, Florida, Maryland, the District of Columbia, Texas, Louisiana, Arkansas, Oklahoma, Kentucky, Tennessee, Alabama and Mississippi. The Northern states were Connecticut, Rhode Island, Massachussetts, Vermont, New Hampshire, Maine, Pennsylvania, New York, New Jersey, Michigan, Wisconsin, Ohio, Indiana and Illinois. The respective region's average incarceration rates were computed as weighted sums of each state's incarceration rates; the weight used was the fraction of the region's population comprised by each state.

Researchers (e.g., Cahalan 1979) and the census bureau itself have commented on the noncomparability of the census data on incarcerations. Strictly speaking, those criticisms are quite valid. Bad or incomplete reporting procedures, different definitions of crimes and different sentences for the same crime among various states, was well as different uses of a particular type of facility (e.g., local jails that housed both convicted and sentenced felons as well as individuals awaiting trial) in various states are factors which confound strict comparability. For those reasons data on all persons – whether sentenced or not, although the largest fractions are sentenced prisoners – were used to attempt to avoid those problems. The measures of "gross" incarcerations indicate outcomes of the respective criminal justice systems in the states regardless of the peculiarities of those processes. If, for example, one state used prisons to house only sentenced felons while another used county jails for that purpose also, then the measures of the regional differences in black-white incarcerations are unaffected by those differences.

Next, the primary concern is with black-white differences; however for the 1940, 1950 and 1960 census reports, race was reported as "nonwhite" rather than "Negro" or "black". The "non-white" designation included blacks, American Indians, Japanese, Chinese, Filipinos, Koreans, Hawaiians, Asian Indians, Eskimoes, etc. The direction of the bias introduced by the nonwhite designation can be assessed from the general population data which broke down the nonwhite category into ethnic and racial groups. First, the magnitude of the bias in the South is so small as to be negligible. The fraction of the nonwhite population that was not black in those three decades averaged about one percent.

In the South the non-black, nonwhite population consisted largely of Indians concentrated in North Carolina, Mississippi and Oklahoma. Indians were from 50 to 90 percent of that one percent non-black, nonwhite, and their geographic concentrations remained relatively constant over the 1940 to 1960 period. Consequently, any bias introduced into the measure of the black in-carceration rate for those years was not important.

In the North the majority of the non-black, nonwhites were Japanese or Chinese. Their incarceration rates were known to be lower than black incarcerations, and since they comprised about three percent of the non-black, nonwhite population, the effect is to bias downward, slightly, the estimate of the Northern black incarceration rates. In other words, the true black incarceration rates for the North between 1940 and 1960 were probably higher than reported. Thus the regional disparities in black incarcerations was probably slightly higher than actually reported.

Regardless of those slight differences in adjusting the rates for 1940, 1950 and 1960, the overall pattern of incarcerations is clear. Larger fractions of the Northern black population were placed under the control of the prison systems there than were controlled by penal systems in the South.

Appendix B

Special thanks to J. Harper Wilson, Chief of the FBI's Uniform Crime Reporting Program for providing the aggregate arrest data by state for 1950, 1960 and 1970. The UCR arrest data recorded racial breakdowns only for the agencies which reported racial breakdowns for all 12 months in the respective year.

The number of arrests received from the UCR Program underestimates the true number of black and white arrests. However, one method used by the FBI in calculating black arrests is to compute the fraction of black arrests of the total for the agencies which reported racial break-downs in arrests and then to multiply that fraction by the total number of arrests reported by all agencies. If that number, the "true" number of black arrests, is used to compute the fraction of black arrests of all arrests, one arrives at the same fractions which we have reported since:

$$FBA = BA/(BA + WA) \tag{B.1}$$

where FBA is the fraction of black arrests and BA and WA are black and white arrests, respectively. That fraction, which we reported, is equal to the fraction of black arrests estimated by the FBI since:

430

$$NBA = FBA * TA \qquad (B.2)$$

where NBA is the number of black arrests and TA is total arrests reported by all agencies.
But

$$TFBA = NBA/TA \qquad (B.3)$$

where TFBA equals the true fraction of black arrests. By substituting eq. (B.2) into eq. (B.3) and solving,

$$TFBA = FBA * TA/TA$$
$$NBA/TA = FBA * TA/TA$$
$$FBA * TA/TA = FBA * TA/TA$$

So,

$$FBA = FBA$$

Having comparable fractions of black arrests, one can now look at the regional differences in disproportionality between arrests and imprisonments. Note that unlike the earlier section, in which racial disproportionality was measured in relation to representation in the general population, here it is measured in relation to arrest populations. The fraction of black arrest was used as a proxy for the "expected fractions" of sentenced black prisoners as discussed in the body of the article.

References

Adamson, Christopher, R., "Punishment after Slavery: Southern Penal Systems, 1865–1890," *Social Problems* 1983 (Vol. 30, June), 555–569.

Blinder, Alan S., "Wage Discrimination: Reduced Form and Structural Estimates," *Journal of Human Resources* 1983 (Vol. 4), 436–455.

Blumstein, Alfred, "On the Racial Disproportionality of United States' Prison Populations," *Journal of Criminal Law and Criminology* 1982 (Vol. 73), 1259–1281.

Blumstein, Alfred and Elizabeth Graddy, "Prevalence and Recidivism in Index Arrests: A Feedback Model," *Law and Society Review* 1982 (16: 2), 265–290.

Cahalan, Margaret, "Trends in Incarceration in the United States Since 1880: A Summary of Reported Rates and the Distribution of Offenses," *Crime and Delinquency* 1979 (Vol. 25, January), 9–41.

Chicago Commission on Race Relations, *The Negro in Chicago: A Study of Race Relations and a Race Riot in 1919* (Chicago: University of Chicago Press, 1922) Reprinted by Arno Press and the New York Times: New York, 1968.

Christianson, Scott, "Our Black Prisons," *Crime and Delinquency* 1981 (Vol. 27), 364–375.

Darity, William A., Jr. and Samuel L. Myers, Jr., "Does Welfare Dependency Cause Female Headship? The Case of the Black Family," *Journal of Marriage and the Family* 1984 (Vol. 46, November), 765–780.

Dunbaugh, Frank M., "Racially Disproportionate Rates of Incarceration in the United States," *Prison Law Monitor* 1979 (Vol. 1, March), 205, 219–222.

431

DuBois, W.E.B., *The Philadelphia Negro*, 1899 (Reprinted by Millwood, NY: Kraus-Thomson Organization Limited, 1973).

Farrell, Ronald A. and Victoria Lynn Swigert, "Prior Offense Record as a Self-Fulfilling Prophecy," *Law and Society Review* 1978 (Vol. 12), 436–454.

Frazier, E. Franklin, *The Negro in the United States* (New York: The MacMillan Co., 1949).

Hawkins, Darnell F., "Trends in Black-White Imprisonment: Changing Conceptions of Race or Changing Patterns of Social Control?" *Crime and Social Justice* 1985 (No 24, December), 187–207.

Hindelang, Michael J., "Race and Involvement in Common Law Personal Crimes," *American Sociological Review* 1978 (Vol. 43, February), 93–109.

Klepper, S., D. Nagin and T.J. Tierney, "Discrimination in the Criminal Justice System: A Critical Appraisal of the Literature," in A. Blumstein et al. (eds.), *Research on Sentencing: The Search for Reform* (Washington DC: National Research Council, National Academy of Sciences, 1983), 55–128.

Kramer, John H. and Robin L. Lubitz, "Pennsylvania's Sentencing Reform: The Impact of Commission-Established Guidelines," *Crime and Delinquency* 1985 (Vol. 31, October), 481–500.

Langan, Patrick A., "Racism on Trial: New Evidence to Explain the Racial Composition of Prisons in the United States," *Journal of Criminal Law and Criminology* 1985 (Vol. 76), 666–683.

Myers, Samuel L., Jr., "Statistical Tests of Discrimination in Punishment," *Journal of Quantitative Criminology*, Vol. 1 (1985): 191–218.

Myers, Samuel L., Jr. and William J. Sabol, "Business Cycles and Racial Disparities in Punishment," *Contemporary Policy Issues* 1987 (Vol. 5, October), 46–58.

Myers, Samuel L. Jr. and William J. Sabol, *Crime in the Black Community: Issues in the Understanding of Race and Crime in America*. Report to the National Research Council, National Academy of Sciences, Committee on the Status of Black Americans (Washington DC. January, 1988).

Myrdal, Gunnar, *An American Dilemma: The Negro Problem and Modern Democracy* (New York: Pantheon Books, 1944).

Petersilia, Joan, *Racial Disparities in the Criminal Justice System* (Santa Monica, CA: Rand Corporation, 1983).

Peterson, Mark A. and Harriet B. Braiker with Suzanne M. Polich, *Doing Crime: A Survey of California Prison Inmates* (Santa Monica, CA: Rand Corporation, 1980).

Radelet, Michael L. and Glenn L. Pierce, "Race and Prosecutorial Discretion in Homicide Cases," *Law and Society Review* 1985 (Vol. 19), 587–621.

Sellin, Thorsten, "The Negro and the Problem of Law Observances and Administration," in Charles S. Johnson, *The Negro in American Civilization* (New York: Henry Holt and Company, 1930), 311–329.

Sellin, Thorsten, *Slavery and the Penal System* (New York: Elsevier, 1976).

Shane-DuBow, Sandra, Alice P. Brown, and Erik Olsen. *Sentencing Reform in the United States: History, Content and Effect* (U.S. Department of Justice, Washington DC: National Institute of Justice, 1985).

Smith, Douglas A., "The Neighborhood Context of Police Behavior," in Albert J. Reiss, Jr. and Michael Tonry, (eds.), *Communities and Crime, Crime and Justice: An Annual Review of Research*, Vol. 8 (Chicago: University of Chicago Press, 1986), 313–342.

Smith, Douglas A., Christy A. Visher and Laura A. Davidson, "Equity and Discretionary Justice: The Influence of Race on Police Arrest Decision," *Journal of Criminal Law and Criminology* 1984 (Vol. 75), 234–249.

432

Stone, Alfred Holt, *Studies in the American Race Problem* (New York: Doubleday, Page and Co., 1908).

Tonry, Michael, "Structuring Sentencing," in Michael Tonry and Norval Morris, (eds.), *Crime and Justice: An Annual Review of Research*, Vol. 10 (Chicago: University of Chicago Press, 1988), 267–337.

Wilbanks, William, *The Myth of a Racist Criminal Justice System* (Monterey, CA: Brooks/Cole Publishing Company, 1987).

Wilson, William J., *The Declining Significance of Race*, Second Edition (Chicago: University of Chicago Press, 1980).

Wilson, William J. and Katherine Neckerman, "Poverty and Family Structure: The Widening Gap between Evidence and Public Policy Issues," in S. Danziger and D. Weinberg, (eds.), *Fighting Poverty: What Works and What Doesn't* (Cambridge, MA: Harvard University Press, 1986).

Work, Monroe N. "Negro Criminality in the South," in *The Negro's Progress in Fifty Years* (Philadelphia, PA, 1913).

Wright, Richard R., Jr., *The Negro in Pennsylvania: A Study in Economic History*, 1912 (Reprinted by Arno Press and the New York Times, 1969).

[10]

Racial Politics, Racial Disparities, and the War on Crime

Michael Tonry

Racial disparities in the justice system have steadily gotten worse since 1980, primarily because of politically motivated decisions by the Reagan and Bush administrations to promote harsh drug and sanctioning policies that, existing research and broad agreement among practioners concur, could not significantly reduce crime rates or drug use. It is difficult to imagine a persuasive ethical defense of promotion of policies that were unlikely to achieve their ostensible goals but were foreseen to have an adverse disparate effect on Blacks.

Racial disparities in arrests, jailing, and imprisonment steadily worsened after 1980 for reasons that have little to do with changes in crime patterns and almost everything to do with two political developments. First, conservative Republicans in national elections "played the race card" by using anticrime slogans (remember Willie Horton?) as a way to appeal to anti-Black sentiments of White voters. Second, conservative politicians of both parties promoted and voted for harsh crime control and drug policies that exacerbated existing racial disparities.

The worsened disparities might have been ethically defensible if they had been based on good faith beliefs that some greater policy good would thereby have been achieved. Sometimes unwanted side effects of social policy are inevitable. Traffic accidents and fatalities are a price we pay for the convenience of automobiles. Occupational injuries are a price we pay for engaging in the industries in which they occur.

The principal causes of worse racial disparities have been the War on Drugs launched by the Bush and Reagan administrations, characterized by vast increases in arrests and imprisonment of street-level drug dealers, and the continuing movement toward harsher penalties. Policies toward drug offenders are a primary cause of recent increases in jail and prison admissions

MICHAEL TONRY: Sonosky Professor of Law and Public Policy, University of Minnesota.

This article draws on Tonry's *Malign Neglect: Race, Crime, and Punishment in America* (1994).

CRIME & DELINQUENCY, Vol. 40 No. 4, October 1994 475-494

and populations. Racial disparities among drug offenders are worse than among other offenders.

It should go without saying in the late 20th century that governments detest racial injustice and desire racial justice, and that racial disparities are tolerable only if they are unavoidable or are outweighed by even more important social gains. There are no offsetting gains that can justify the harms done to Black Americans by recent drug and crime control policies.

This article presents data on racial trends in arrests, jailing, and imprisonment; examines the rationales for the policies that have produced those trends; and considers whether the adoption of policies known to have disparate adverse effects on Blacks can be ethically justified. First, the evidence concerning the effectiveness of recent drug and crime control policies that have exacerbated racial disparities is examined. Next, data on arrests, jail, and imprisonment trends are presented and demonstrate that racial disparities have worsened, but not because Blacks are committing larger proportions of the serious offenses (homicide, rape, robbery, aggravated assault) for which offenders were traditionally sent to prison. Finally, the reasons why recent policies were adopted and whether they can be ethically justified are considered.

CRIME REDUCTION EFFECTS OF CRIME CONTROL POLICY

There is no basis for a claim that recent harsh crime control policies or the enforcement strategies of the War on Drugs were based on good faith beliefs that they would achieve their ostensible purposes. In this and other countries, practitioners and scholars have long known that manipulation of penalties has few, if any, effects on crime rates.

Commissions and expert advisory bodies have been commissioned by the federal government repeatedly over the last 30 years to survey knowledge of the effects of crime control policies, and consistently they have concluded that there is little reason to believe that harsher penalties significantly enhance public safety. In 1967, the President's Commission on Law Enforcement and Administration of Justice observed that crime control efforts can have little effect on crime rates without much larger efforts being directed at crime's underlying social and economic causes. "The Commission . . . has no doubt whatever that the most significant action that can be taken against crime is action designed to eliminate slums and ghettos, to improve education, to provide jobs. . . . We shall not have dealt effectively with crime until we have alleviated the conditions that stimulate it."

In 1978, the National Academy of Sciences Panel on Research on Deterrent and Incapacitative Effects, funded by President Ford's department of justice and asked to examine the available evidence on the crime-reductive effects of sanctions, concluded: "In summary, we cannot assert that the evidence warrants an affirmative conclusion regarding deterrence" (Blumstein, Cohen, and Nagin 1978). Fifteen years later, the National Academy of Sciences Panel on the Understanding and Control of Violent Behavior, created and paid for with funds from the Reagan and Bush administration departments of justice, surveyed knowledge of the effects of harsher penalties on violent crime (Reiss and Roth 1993). A rhetorical question and answer in the panel's final report says it all: "What effect has increasing the prison population had on violent crime? Apparently very little. . . . If tripling the average length of sentence of incarceration per crime [between 1976 and 1989] had a strong preventive effect," reasoned the panel, "then violent crime rates should have declined" (p. 7). They had not.

I mention that the two National Academy of Sciences panels were created and supported by national Republican administrations to demonstrate that skepticism about the crime-preventive effects of harsher punishments is not a fantasy of liberal Democrats. Anyone who has spent much time talking with judges or corrections officials knows that most, whatever their political affiliations, do not believe that harsher penalties significantly enhance public safety.

Likewise, outside the United States, conservative governments in other English-speaking countries have repudiated claims that harsher penalties significantly improve public safety. In Margaret Thatcher's England, for example, a 1990 White Paper (an official policy statement of the government), based on a 3-year study, expressed its skepticism about the preventive effects of sanctions:

> Deterrence is a principle with much immediate appeal. . . . But much crime is committed on impulse, given the opportunity presented by an open window or an unlocked door, and it is committed by offenders who live from moment to moment; their crimes are as impulsive as the rest of their feckless, sad, or pathetic lives. It is unrealistic to construct sentencing arrangements on the assumption that most offenders will weigh up the possibilities in advance and base their conduct on rational calculation. (Home Office 1990)

Canada is the other English-speaking country that has recently had a conservative government. In Brian Mulroney's Canada, the Committee on Justice and the Solicitor General (in American terms, the judiciary committee) proposed in 1993 that Canada shift from an American-style crime control system to a European-style preventive approach. In arguing for the shift in emphasis, the committee observed that "the United States affords a glaring example of the limited effect that criminal justice responses may have on

478   CRIME & DELINQUENCY / OCTOBER 1994

crime. . . . If locking up those who violate the law contributed to safer societies then the United States should be the safest country in the world" (Standing Committee on Justice and the Solicitor General 1993). Six years earlier, the Canadian Sentencing Commission (1987) had reached similar conclusions: "Deterrence cannot be used, with empirical justification, to guide the imposition of sanctions."

There is no better evidentiary base to justify recent drug control policies. Because no other western country has adopted drug policies as harsh as those of the United States, a bit of background may be useful before I show why there was no reasonable basis for believing recent policies would achieve their ostensible goals. In drug policy jargon, the United States has adopted a prohibitionistic rather than a harm-reduction strategy and has emphasized supply-side over demand-side tactics (Wilson 1990). This strategic choice implies a preference for legal threats and moral denunciation of drug use and users instead of a preference for minimizing net costs and social harms to the general public, the law enforcement system, and drug users. The tactical choice is between a law enforcement emphasis on arrest and punishment of dealers, distributors, and importers, interdiction, and source-country programs or a prevention emphasis on drug treatment, drug-abuse education in schools, and mass media programs aimed at public education. The supply-side bias in recent American policies was exemplified throughout the Bush administration by its insistence that 70% of federal antidrug funds be devoted to law enforcement and only 30% to treatment and education (Office of National Drug Control Policy 1990).

It has been a long time since most researchers and practitioners believed that current knowledge justifies recent American drug control policies. Because the potential income from drug dealing means that willing aspirants are nearly always available to replace arrested street-level dealers, large-scale arrests have repeatedly been shown to have little or no effect on the volume of drug trafficking or on the retail prices of drugs (e.g., Chaiken 1988; Sviridoff, Sadd, Curtis, and Grinc 1992). Because the United States has long and porous borders, and because an unachievably large proportion of attempted smuggling would have to be stopped to affect drug prices significantly, interdiction has repeatedly been shown to have little or no effect on volume or prices (Reuter 1988). Because cocaine, heroin, and marijuana can be grown in many parts of the world in which government controls are weak and peasant farmers' incentives are strong, source-country programs have seldom been shown to have significant influence on drug availability or price in the United States (Moore 1990).

The evidence in support of demand-side strategies is far stronger. In December 1993, the President's Commission on Model State Drug Laws, appointed by President Bush, categorically concluded, "Treatment works." That conclusion is echoed by more authoritative surveys of drug treatment evaluations by the U.S. General Accounting Office (1990), the National Institute of Medicine (Gerstein and Jarwood 1990), and in *Crime and Justice* by Anglin and Hser (1990). Because drug use and offending tend to coincide in the lives of drug-using offenders, the most effective and cost-effective way to deal with such offenders is to get and keep them in well-run treatment programs.

A sizable literature now also documents the effectiveness of school-based drug education in reducing drug experimentation and use among young people (e.g., Botvin 1990; Ellickson and Bell 1990). Although there is no credible literature that documents the effects of mass media campaigns on drug use, a judge could take judicial notice of their ubiquity. It is not unreasonable to believe that such campaigns have influenced across-the-board declines in drug use in the United States since 1980 (a date, incidentally, that precedes the launch of the War on Drugs by nearly 8 years).

That the preceding summary of our knowledge of the effectiveness of drug control methods is balanced and accurate is shown by the support it receives from leading conservative scholars. Senator-scholar Daniel Patrick Moynihan (1993) has written, "Interdiction and 'drug busts' are probably necessary symbolic acts, but nothing more." James Q. Wilson (1990), for two decades America's leading conservative crime control scholar, observed that "significant reductions in drug abuse will come only from reducing demand for those drugs. . . . The marginal product of further investment in supply reduction is likely to be small" (p. 534). He reports that "I know of no serious law-enforcement official who disagrees with this conclusion. Typically, police officials tell interviewers that they are fighting either a losing war or, at best, a holding action" (p. 534).

Thus a fair-minded survey of existing knowledge provides no grounds for believing that the War on Drugs or the harsh policies exemplified by "three strikes and you're out" laws and evidenced by a tripling in America's prison population since 1980 could achieve their ostensible purposes. If such policies cannot be explained in instrumental terms, how can they be explained? The last section answers that question, but first a summary of recent data on racial trends in arrests, jailing, and incarceration.

RACIAL DISPARITIES IN ARRESTS, JAIL, AND PRISON

Racial disparities, especially affecting Blacks, have long bedeviled the criminal justice system. Many hundreds of studies of disparities have been

480   CRIME & DELINQUENCY / OCTOBER 1994

conducted and there is now widespread agreement among researchers about causes. Racial bias and stereotyping no doubt play some role, but they are not the major cause. In the longer term, disparities in jail and prison are mainly the result of racial differences in offending patterns. In the shorter term, the worsening disparities since 1980 are not primarily the result of racial differences in offending but were foreseeable effects of the War on Drugs and the movement toward increased use of incarceration. These patterns can best be seen by approaching the recent increases in racial disparities in imprisonment as a mystery to be solved. (Because of space limitations, jail data are not discussed here at length, but the trends parallel those for prisons. Between 1980 and 1991, e.g., the percentage of jail inmates who were Black increased from 40% to 48%.)

Figure 1, showing the percentages of prison inmates who were Black or White from 1960 to 1991, reveals two trends. First, for as long as prison population data have been compiled, the percentage of inmates who are Black has by several times exceeded the percentage of Americans who are Black (10% to 13% during the relevant period). Second, since 1980 the Black percentage among prisoners has increased sharply.

Racial disproportions among prison inmates are inherently undesirable, and considerable energy has been expended on efforts to understand them. In 1982, Blumstein showed that around 80% of the disproportion could be explained on the basis of racial differences in arrest patterns. Of the unexplained 20%, Blumstein argued, some might represent bias and some might reflect racial differences in criminal history or arguably valid case-processing differences. Some years earlier, Hindelang (1976, 1978) had demonstrated that racial patterns in victims' identifications of their assailants closely resembled racial differences in arrests. Some years later, Langan (1985) skipped over the arrest stage altogether and showed that racial patterns in victims' identifications of their assailants explained about 80% of disparities in prison admissions. In 1990, Klein, Petersilia, and Turner showed that, after criminal history and other legitimate differences between cases were taken into account, the offender's race had no independent predictive effect in California on whether he was sent to prison or for how long. There the matter rests. Blumstein (1993a) updated his analysis and reached similar conclusions (with one important exception that is discussed below).

Although racial crime patterns explain a large part of racial imprisonment patterns, they do not explain why the Black percentage rose so rapidly after 1980. Table 1 shows Black and White percentages among people arrested for the eight serious FBI Index Crimes at 3-year intervals from 1976 to 1991 and for 1992. Within narrow bands of fluctuation, racial arrest percentages have been stable since 1976. Comparing 1976 with 1992, for example, Black

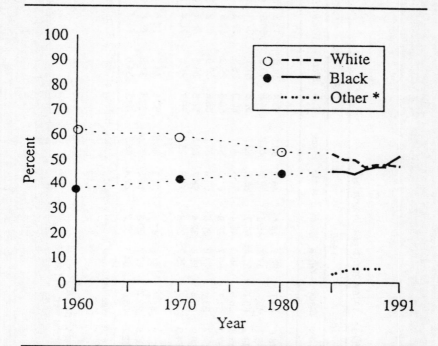

Figure 1:   Prisoners in State and Federal Prisons on Census Date by Race, 1960-1991
SOURCES: For 1960, 1970, 1980: Cahalan 1986, table 3.31; for 1985-1991: Bureau of Justice Statistics 1993, 1991a, 1991b, 1989a, 1989b, 1987.
* = Hispanics in many states, Asians, Native Americans.

percentages among people arrested for murder, robbery, and burglary were slightly up and Black percentages among those arrested for rape, aggravated assault, and theft were slightly down. Overall, the percentage among those arrested for violent crimes who were Black fell from 47.5% to 44.8%. Because prison sentences have traditionally been imposed on people convicted of violent crimes, Blumstein's and the other analyses suggest that the Black percentage among inmates should be flat or declining. That, however, is not what Figure 1 shows. Why not?

Part of the answer can be found in prison admissions. Figure 2 shows racial percentages among prison admissions from 1960 to 1992. Arrests of Blacks for violent crimes may not have increased since 1980, but the percentage of Blacks among those sent to prison has increased starkly, reaching 54% in 1991 and 1992. Why? The main explanation concerns the War on Drugs.

TABLE 1: Percentage Black and White Arrests for Index I Offenses 1976-1991 (3-year intervals)[a]

	1976		1979		1982		1985		1988		1991		1992	
	White	Black	White	Black	White	Black	White	Black	White	Black	White	Black	White	Black
Murder and nonnegligent manslaughter	45.0	53.5	49.4	47.7	48.8	49.7	50.1	48.4	45.0	53.5	43.4	54.8	43.5	55.1
Forcible rape	51.2	46.6	50.2	47.7	48.7	49.7	52.2	46.5	52.7	45.8	54.8	43.5	55.5	42.8
Robbery	38.9	59.2	41.0	56.9	38.2	60.7	37.4	61.7	36.3	62.6	37.6	61.1	37.7	60.9
Aggravated assault	56.8	41.0	60.9	37.0	59.8	38.8	58.0	40.4	57.6	40.7	60.0	38.3	59.5	38.8
Burglary	69.0	29.2	69.5	28.7	67.0	31.7	69.7	28.9	67.0	31.3	68.8	29.3	67.8	30.4
Larceny-theft	65.7	32.1	67.2	30.2	64.7	33.4	67.2	30.6	65.6	32.2	66.6	30.9	66.2	31.4
Motor vehicle theft	71.1	26.2	70.0	27.2	66.9	31.4	65.8	32.4	58.7	39.5	58.5	39.3	58.4	39.4
Arson	—	—	78.9	19.2	74.0	24.7	75.7	22.8	73.5	25.0	76.7	21.5	76.4	21.9
Violent crime[b]	50.4	47.5	53.7	44.1	51.9	46.7	51.5	47.1	51.7	46.8	53.6	44.8	53.6	44.8
Property crime[c]	67.0	30.9	68.2	29.4	65.5	32.7	67.7	30.3	65.3	32.6	66.4	31.3	65.8	31.8
Total crime index	64.1	33.8	65.3	32.4	62.7	35.6	64.5	33.7	62.4	35.7	63.2	34.6	62.7	35.2

SOURCES: Sourcebook of Criminal Justice Statistics. Various years. Washington, DC: Department of Justice, Bureau of Justice Statistics; FBI 1993, Table 43.

a. Because of rounding, the percentages may not add to total.
b. Violent crimes are offenses of murder, forcible rape, robbery, and aggravated assault.
c. Property crimes are offenses of burglary, larceny-theft, motor vehicle theft, and arson.

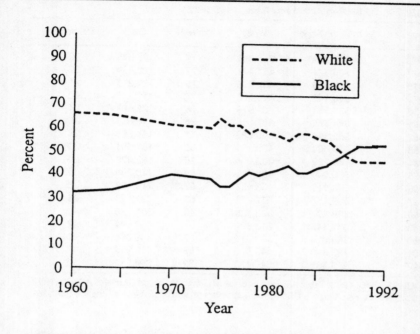

Figure 2:   Admissions to Federal and State Prisons by Race, 1960-1992
SOURCES: Langan 1991; Gilliard 1992; Perkins 1992, 1993; Perkins and Gilliard 1992.
NOTE: Hispanics are included in Black and White populations.

Table 2 shows racial percentages among persons arrested for drug crimes between 1976 and 1992. Blacks today make up about 13% of the U.S. population and, according to National Institute on Drug Abuse (1991) surveys of Americans' drug use, are no more likely than Whites ever to have used most drugs of abuse. Nonetheless, the percentages of Blacks among drug arrestees were in the low 20% range in the late 1970s, climbing to around 30% in the early 1980s and peaking at 42% in 1989. The number of drug arrests of Blacks more than doubled between 1985 and 1989, whereas White drug arrests increased only by 27%. Figure 3 shows the stark differences in drug arrest trends by race from 1976 to 1991.

Drug control policies are a major cause of worsening racial disparities in prison. In the federal prisons, for example, 22% of new admissions and 25% of the resident population were drug offenders in 1980. By 1990, 42% of new admissions were drug offenders as in 1992 were 58% of the resident population. In state prisons, 5.7% of inmates in 1979 were drug offenders, a figure

484   CRIME & DELINQUENCY / OCTOBER 1994

TABLE 2:   U.S. Drug Arrests by Race, 1976-1992

Year	Total Violations	White	White %	Black	Black %
1976	475,209	366,081	77	103,615	22
1977	565,371	434,471	77	122,594	22
1978	592,168	462,728	78	127,277	21
1979	516,142	396,065	77	112,748	22
1980	531,953	401,979	76	125,607	24
1981	584,776	432,556	74	146,858	25
1982	562,390	400,683	71	156,369	28
1983	615,081	423,151	69	185,601	30
1984	560,729	392,904	70	162,979	29
1985	700,009	482,486	69	210,298	30
1986	688,815	463,457	67	219,159	32
1987	809,157	511,278	63	291,177	36
1988	844,300	503,125	60	334,015	40
1989	1,074,345	613,800	57	452,574	42
1990	860,016	503,315	59	349,965	41
1991	763,340	443,596	58	312,997	41
1992	919,561	546,430	59	364,546	40

SOURCES: FBI 1993, Table 43; *Sourcebook of Criminal Justice Statistics—1978-1992.*
Various tables. Washington, DC: U.S. Department of Justice, Bureau of Justice Statistics.

that by 1991 had climbed to 21.3% to become the single largest category of prisoners (robbers, burglars, and murderers were next at 14.8%, 12.4%, and 10.6%, respectively) (Beck et al. 1993).

The effect of drug policies can be seen in prison data from a number of states. Figure 4 shows Black and White prison admissions in North Carolina from 1970 to 1990. White rates held steady; Black rates doubled between 1980 and 1990, rising most rapidly after 1987. Figure 5 shows prison admissions for drug crimes in Virginia from 1983 to 1989; the racial balance flipped from two-thirds White, one-third non-White in 1983 to the reverse in 1989. Similarly, in Pennsylvania, Clark (1992) reports, Black male prison admissions for drug crimes grew four times faster (up 1,613%) between 1980 and 1990 than did White male admissions (up 477%). In California, according to Zimring and Hawkins (1994), the number of males in prison for drug crimes grew 15 fold between 1980 and 1990 and "there were more people in prison in California for drug offences in 1991 than there were for *all* offences in California at the end of 1979" (p. 89; emphasis in original).

Why, if Blacks in their lives are no more likely than Whites to use illicit drugs, are Blacks so much more likely to be arrested and imprisoned? One possible answer, which is almost certainly wrong, is that Blacks are proportionately more likely to sell drugs. We have no representative surveys of drug

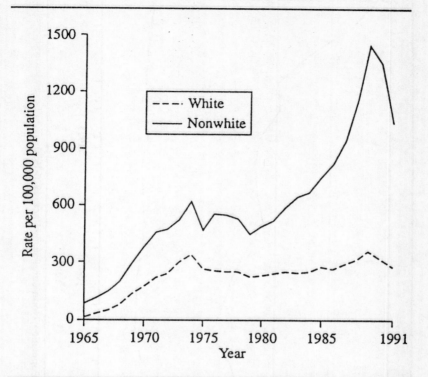

Figure 3:   Arrest Rates for Drug Offenses by Race, 1965-1991
SOURCE: Blumstein 1993b.

dealers and so cannot with confidence paint demographic pictures. However, there is little reason to suspect that drug crimes are more interracial than are most other crimes. In addition, the considerations that make arrests of Black dealers relatively easy make arrests of White dealers relatively hard.

Drug arrests are easier to make in socially disorganized inner-city minority areas than in working- or middle-class urban or suburban areas for a number of reasons. First, although drug sales in working- or middle-class areas are likely to take place indoors and in private spaces where they are difficult to observe, drug sales in poor minority areas are likely to take place outdoors in streets, alleys, or abandoned buildings, or indoors in public places like bars. Second, although working- or middle-class drug dealers in stable areas are unlikely to sell drugs to undercover strangers, dealers in disorganized areas have little choice but to sell to strangers and new acquaintances. These

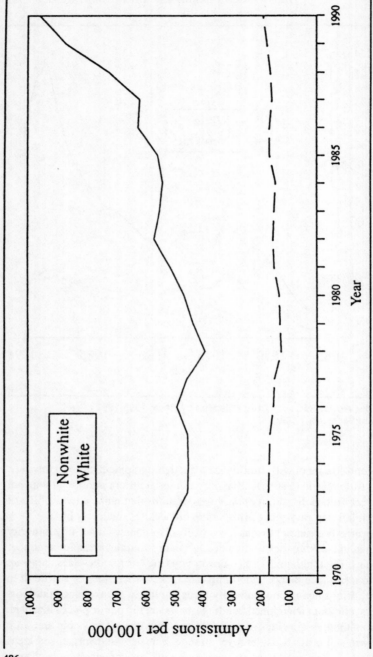

Figure 4:   Prison Admissions per 100,000 General Population, North Carolina, by Race, 1970-1990
SOURCE: Clarke 1992.

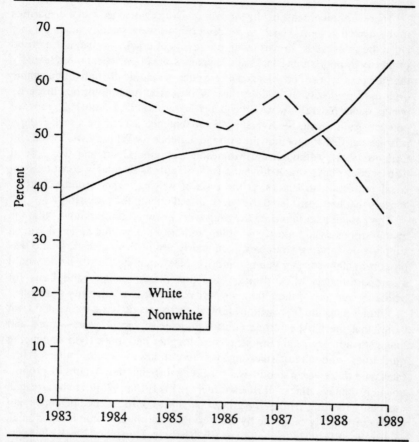

Figure 5: Percentage of New Drug Commitments by Race, Virginia, Fiscal Years 1983-1989
SOURCE: Austin and McVey 1989.

differences mean that it is easier for police to make arrests and undercover purchases in urban minority areas than elsewhere. Because arrests are fungible for purposes of both the individual officer's personnel file and the department's year-to-year statistical comparisons, more easy arrests look better than fewer hard ones. And because, as ethnographic studies of drug trafficking make clear (Fagan 1993; Padilla 1992), arrested drug dealers in disadvantaged urban minority communities are generally replaced within days, there is a nearly inexhaustible potential supply of young minority Americans to be arrested.

488   **CRIME & DELINQUENCY / OCTOBER 1994**

There is another reason why the War on Drugs worsened racial disparities in the justice system. Penalties for drug crimes were steadily made harsher since the mid-1980s. In particular, purveyors of crack cocaine, a drug used primarily by poor urban Blacks and Hispanics, are punished far more severely than are purveyors of powder cocaine, a pharmacologically indistinguishable drug used primarily by middle-class Whites. The most notorious disparity occurs under federal law which equates 1 gram of crack with 100 grams of powder. As a result, the average prison sentence served by Black federal prisoners is 40% longer than the average sentence for Whites (McDonald and Carlson 1993). Although the Minnesota Supreme Court and two federal district courts have struck down the 100-to-1 rule as a denial of constitutional equal protection to Blacks, at the time of writing, every federal court of appeals that had considered the question had upheld the provision.

The people who launched the drug wars knew all these things—that the enemy troops would mostly be young minority males, that an emphasis on supply-side antidrug strategies, particularly use of mass arrests, would disproportionately ensnare young minority males, that the 100-to-1 rule would disproportionately affect Blacks, and that there was no valid basis for believing that any of these things would reduce drug availability or prices.

Likewise, as the first section showed, there was no basis for a good faith belief that the harsher crime control policies of recent years—more and longer mandatory minimum sentences, tougher and more rigid sentencing guidelines, and three-strikes-and-you're-out laws—would reduce crime rates, and there was a good basis for predicting that they would disproportionately damage Blacks. If Blacks are more likely than Whites to be arrested, especially for drug crimes, the greater harshness of toughened penalties will disproportionately be borne by Blacks. Because much crime is intraracial, concern for Black victims might justify harsher treatment of Black offenders if there were any reason to believe that harsher penalties would reduce crime rates. Unfortunately, as the conservative national governments of Margaret Thatcher and Brian Mulroney and reports of National Academy of Sciences Panels funded by the administrations of Republican Presidents Ford, Reagan, and Bush all agree, there is no reason to believe that harsher penalties significantly reduce crime rates.

JUSTIFYING THE UNJUSTIFIABLE

There is no valid policy justification for the harsh drug and crime control policies of the Reagan and Bush administrations, and for their adverse differential effect on Blacks. The justification, such as it is, is entirely political. Crime is an emotional subject and visceral appeals by politicians to people's fears and resentments are difficult to counter.

It is easy to seize the low ground in political debates about crime policy. When one candidate campaigns with pictures of clanging prison gates and grief-stricken relatives of a rape or murder victim, and with disingenuous promises that newer, tougher policies will work, it is difficult for an opponent to explain that crime is a complicated problem, that real solutions must be long term, and that simplistic toughness does not reduce crime rates. This is why, as a result, candidates often compete to establish which is tougher in his views about crime. It is also why less conservative candidates often try to preempt their more conservative opponents by adopting a tough stance early in the campaign. Finally, it is why political pundits congratulate President Clinton on his acumen in proposing federal crime legislation as or more harsh than his opponents. He has, it is commonly said, "taken the crime issue away from the Republicans."

Conservative Republican politicians have, since the late 1960s, used welfare, especially Aid to Families with Dependent Children, and crime as symbolic issues to appeal to anti-Black sentiments and resentments of White voters, as Thomas and Mary Edsall's *Chain Reaction: The Impact of Race, Rights, and Taxes on American Politics* (1991) makes clear. The Edsalls provide a history, since the mid-1960s, of "a conservative politics that had the effect of polarizing the electorate along racial lines." Anyone who observed Ronald Reagan's portrayal in several campaigns of Linda Evans, a Black Chicago woman, as the "welfare queen" or George Bush's use of Black murderer Willie Horton to caricature Michael Dukakis's criminal justice policies knows of what the Edsalls write.

The story of Willie Horton is the better known and makes the Edsalls' point. Horton, who in 1975 had been convicted of the murder of a 17-year-old boy, failed to return from a June 12, 1986, furlough. The following April, he broke into a home in Oxon Hill, Maryland, where he raped a woman and stabbed her companion.

Lee Atwater, Bush's campaign strategist, after testing the visceral effects of Willie Horton's picture and story on participants in focus groups, decided a year later to make Horton a wedge issue for Republicans. Atwood reportedly told a group of Republican activists that Bush would win the presidency "if I can make Willie Horton a household name." He later told a Republican gathering in Atlanta, "there's a story about a fellow named Willie Horton who, for all I know, may end up being Dukakis's running mate." Atwood for a time denied making both remarks but in 1991, dying of cancer, recanted: "In 1988, fighting Dukakis, I said that I would . . . make Willie Horton his running mate. I am sorry."

490   CRIME & DELINQUENCY / OCTOBER 1994

The sad reality is that tragedies like the crimes of Willie Horton are inevitable. So are airplane crashes, 40,000 to 50,000 traffic fatalities per year, and defense department cost overruns. Every person convicted of a violent crime cannot be held forever. Furloughs are used in most corrections systems as a way to ease offenders back into the community and to test their suitability for eventual release on parole or commutation. Horton had successfully completed nine previous furloughs, from each of which he had returned without incident, under a program established in 1972 not by Michael Dukakis but by Governor Francis Sargent, a Republican.

Public discourse about criminal justice issues has been debased by the cynicism that made Willie Horton a major participant in the 1988 presidential election. That cynicism has made it difficult to discuss or develop sensible public policies, and that cynicism explains why conservative politicians have been able year after year successfully to propose ever harsher penalties and crime control and drug policies that no informed person believes can achieve their ostensible goals.

Three final points, arguments that apologists for current policies sometimes make, warrant mention. First, it is sometimes said to be unfair to blame national Republican administrations for the failures and disparate impacts of recent crime control policies. This ignores the efforts of the Reagan and Bush administrations to encourage and, through federal mandates and funding restrictions, to coerce states to follow the federal lead. Attorney General William Barr (e.g., 1992) made the most aggressive efforts to compel state adoption of tougher criminal justice policies, and the Bush administration's final proposed crime bills restricted eligibility for federal funds to states that, like the federal government, abolished parole release and adopted sentencing standards no less severe than those in the federal sentencing guidelines. In any case, as the Edsalls' book makes clear, the use of crime control issues (among others including welfare reform and affirmative action) to elicit anti-Black sentiments from White voters has long been a stratagem of both state and federal Republican politicians.

Second, sometimes it is argued that political leaders have merely followed the public will; voters are outraged by crime and want tougher policies (DiIulio 1991). This is a half-truth that gets the causal order backwards. Various measures of public sentiment, including both representative surveys like Gallup and Harris polls and work with focus groups, have for many years consistently shown that the public is of two minds about crime (Roberts 1992). First, people are frustrated and want offenders to be punished. Second, people believe that social adversity, poverty, and a troubled home life are the principal causes of crime, and they believe government should work to rehabilitate offenders. A number of surveys have found that respondents who would oppose a tax increase to pay for more prisons would support a tax increase to pay for rehabilitative programs. These findings of voter ambivalence about crime should not be surprising. Most people have complicated views about complicated problems. For example, most judges and corrections officials have the same ambivalent feelings about offenders that the general public has. Conservative politicians have seized upon public support of punishment and ignored public support of rehabilitation and public recognition that crime presents complex, not easy, challenges. By presenting crime control issues only in emotional, stereotyped ways, conservative politicians have raised its salience as a political issue but made it impossible for their opponents to respond other than in the same stereotyped ways.

Third, sometimes it is argued that disparate impacts on Black offenders are no problem and that, because much crime is intraracial, failure to adopt tough policies would disserve the interests of Black victims. As former Attorney General Barr (1992) put it, perhaps in ill-chosen words, "the benefits of increased incarceration would be enjoyed disproportionately by Black Americans" (p. 17). This argument also is based on a half-truth. No one wants to live in unsafe neighborhoods or to be victimized by crime, and in a crisis, people who need help will seek it from the police, the public agency of last resort. Requesting help in a crisis and supporting harsh policies with racially disparate effects are not the same thing. The relevant distinction is between acute and chronic problems. A substantial body of public opinion research (e.g., National Opinion Research Center surveys conducted throughout the 1980s summarized in Wood 1990) shows that Blacks far more than Whites support establishment of more generous social welfare policies, full employment programs, and increased social spending. The congressional Black and Hispanic caucuses have consistently opposed bills calling for tougher sanctions and supported bills calling for increased spending on social programs aimed at improving conditions that cause crime. Thus, in claiming to be concerned about Black victims, conservative politicians are responding to natural human calls for help in a crisis while ignoring evidence that Black citizens would rather have government support efforts to ameliorate the chronic social conditions that cause crime and thereby make calls for help in a crisis less necessary.

The evidence on the effectiveness of recent crime control and drug abuse policies, as the first section demonstrated, cannot justify their racially disparate effects on Blacks, nor, as this section demonstrates, can the claims that such policies merely manifest the peoples' will or respect the interests of Black victims. All that is left is politics of the ugliest kind. The War on Drugs and the set of harsh crime control policies in which it was enmeshed were adopted to achieve political, not policy, objectives, and it is the adoption for political purposes of policies with foreseeable disparate impacts, the use of disadvantaged Black Americans as means to the achievement of White politicians' electoral ends, that must in the end be justified. It cannot.

REFERENCES

Anglin, M. Douglas and Yih-Ing Hser. 1990. "Treatment of Drug Abuse." In *Drugs and Crime*, edited by M. Tonry and J. Q. Wilson. Chicago: University of Chicago Press.

Austin, James and Aaron David McVey. 1989. *The Impact of the War on Drugs*. San Francisco: National Council on Crime and Delinquency.

Barr, William P. 1992. "The Case for More Incarceration." Washington, DC: U.S. Department of Justice, Office of Policy Development.

Beck, Allen et al. 1993. *Survey of State Prison Inmates, 1991*. Washington, DC: Bureau of Justice Statistics.

Blumstein, Alfred. 1982. "On the Racial Disproportionality of United States' Prison Populations." *Journal of Criminal Law and Criminology* 73:1259-81.

———. 1993a. "Racial Disproportionality of U.S. Prison Populations Revisited." *University of Colorado Law Review* 64:743-60.

———. 1993b. "Making Rationality Relevant—The American Society of Criminology 1992 Presidential Address." *Criminology* 31:1-16.

Blumstein, Alfred, Jacqueline Cohen, and Daniel Nagin. 1978. *Deterrence and Incapacitation*. Report of the National Academy of Sciences Panel on Research on Deterrent and Incapacitative Effects. Washington, DC: National Academy Press.

Botvin, Gilbert J. 1990. "Substance Abuse Prevention: Theory, Practice, and Effectiveness." In *Drugs and Crime*, edited by M. Tonry and J. Q. Wilson. Chicago: University of Chicago Press.

Bureau of Justice Statistics. 1987. *Correctional Populations in the United States, 1985*. Washington, DC: U.S. Department of Justice, Bureau of Justice Statistics.

———. 1989a. *Correctional Populations in the United States, 1987*. Washington, DC: U.S. Department of Justice, Bureau of Justice Statistics.

———. 1989b. *Correctional Populations in the United States, 1986*. Washington, DC: U.S. Department of Justice, Bureau of Justice Statistics.

———. 1991a. *Correctional Populations in the United States, 1989*. Washington, DC: U.S. Department of Justice, Bureau of Justice Statistics.

———. 1991b. *Correctional Populations in the United States, 1988*. Washington, DC: U.S. Department of Justice, Bureau of Justice Statistics.

———. 1993. *Correctional Populations in the United States, 1991*. Washington, DC: U.S. Department of Justice, Bureau of Justice Statistics.

Cahalan, Margaret Werner. 1986. *Historical Corrections Statistics in the United States, 1850-1984*. Washington, DC: U.S. Department of Justice, Bureau of Justice Statistics.

Canadian Sentencing Commission. 1987. *Sentencing Reform: A Canadian Approach*. Ottawa: Canadian Government Publishing Centre.

Chaiken, Marcia, ed. 1988. *Street Level Enforcement: Examining the Issues*. Washington, DC: U.S. Government Printing Office.

Clark, Stover. 1992. "Pennsylvania Corrections in Context." *Overcrowded Times* 3:4-5.

Clarke, Stevens H. 1992. "North Carolina Prisons Growing." *Overcrowded Times* 3:1, 11-13.
DiIulio, John J. 1991. *No Escape: The Future of American Corrections*. New York: Basic Books.
Edsall, Thomas and Mary Edsall. 1991. *Chain Reaction: The Impact of Race, Rights, and Taxes on American Politics*. New York: Norton.
Ellickson, Phyllis L. and Robert M. Bell. 1990. *Prospects for Preventing Drug Use Among Young Adolescents*. Santa Monica, CA: RAND.
Fagan, Jeffrey. 1993. "The Political Economy of Drug Dealing Among Urban Gangs." In *Drugs and the Community*, edited by R. C. Davis, A. J. Lurigio, and D. P. Rosenbaum. Springfield, IL: Charles C Thomas.
Federal Bureau of Investigation. 1993. *Uniform Crime Reports for the United States—1992*. Washington, DC: U.S. Government Printing Office.
Gerstein, Dean R. and Henrik J. Jarwood, eds. 1990. *Treating Drug Problems*. Report of the Committee for Substance Abuse Coverage Study, Division of Health Care Services, National Institute of Medicine. Washington, DC: National Academy Press.
Gilliard, Darrell K. 1992. *National Corrections Reporting Program, 1987*. Washington, DC: U.S. Department of Justice, Bureau of Justice Statistics.
Hindelang, Michael. 1976. *Criminal Victimization in Eight American Cities: A Descriptive Analysis of Common Theft and Assault*. Washington, DC: Law Enforcement Assistance Administration.
———. 1978. "Race and Involvement in Common Law Personal Crimes." *American Sociological Review* 43:93-108.
Home Office. 1990. *Protecting the Public*. London: H. M. Stationery Office.
Klein, Stephen, Joan Petersilia, and Susan Turner. 1990. "Race and Imprisonment Decisions in California." *Science* 247:812-16.
Langan, Patrick A. 1985. "Racism on Trial: New Evidence to Explain the Racial Composition of Prisons in the United States." *Journal of Criminal Law and Criminology* 76:666-83.
———. 1991. *Race of Persons Admitted to State and Federal Institutions, 1926-86*. Washington, DC: U.S. Department of Justice, Bureau of Justice Statistics.
McDonald, Douglas and Ken Carlson. 1993. *Sentencing in the Federal Courts: Does Race Matter?* Washington, DC: U.S. Department of Justice, Bureau of Justice Statistics.
Moore, Mark H. 1990. "Supply Reduction and Drug Law Enforcement." In *Drugs and Crime*, edited by M. Tonry and J. Q. Wilson. Chicago: University of Chicago Press.
Moynihan, Daniel Patrick. 1993. "Iatrogenic Government—Social Policy and Drug Research." *American Scholar* 62:351-62.
National Institute on Drug Abuse. 1991. *National Household Survey on Drug Abuse: Population Estimates 1990*. Washington, DC: U.S. Government Printing Office.
Office of National Drug Control Policy. 1990. *National Drug Control Strategy—January 1990*. Washington, DC: Author.
Padilla, Felix. 1992. *The Gang as an American Enterprise*. New Brunswick, NJ: Rutgers University Press.
Perkins, Craig. 1992. *National Corrections Reporting Program, 1989*. Washington, DC: U.S. Department of Justice, Bureau of Justice Statistics.
———. 1993. *National Corrections Reporting Program, 1990*. Washington, DC: U.S. Department of Justice, Bureau of Justice Statistics.
Perkins, Craig and Darrell K. Gilliard. 1992. *National Corrections Reporting Program, 1988*. Washington, DC: U.S. Department of Justice, Bureau of Justice Statistics.
President's Commission on Law Enforcement and Administration of Justice. 1967. *The Challenge of Crime in a Free Society*. Washington, DC: U.S. Government Printing Office.

President's Commission on Model State Drug Laws. 1993. *Final Report.* Washington, DC: U.S. Government Printing Office.

Reiss, Albert J., Jr. and Jeffrey Roth. 1993. *Understanding and Controlling Violence. Report of the National Academy of Sciences Panel on the Understanding and Control of Violence.* Washington, DC: National Academy Press.

Reuter, Peter. 1988. "Can the Borders Be Sealed?" *Public Interest* 92:51-65.

Roberts, Julian V. 1992. "Public Opinion, Crime, and Criminal Justice." In *Crime and Justice: A Review of Research*, vol. 16, edited by M. Tonry. Chicago: University of Chicago Press.

Sourcebook of Criminal Justice Statistics. 1978-1992. Washington, DC: Department of Justice, Bureau of Justice Statistics.

Standing Committee on Justice and the Solicitor General. 1993. *Crime Prevention in Canada: Toward a National Strategy.* Ottawa: Canada Communication Group.

Sviridoff, Michele, Susan Sadd, Richard Curtis, and Randolph Grinc. 1992. *The Neighborhood Effects of Street-Level Drug Enforcement.* New York: Vera Institute of Justice.

Tonry, Michael. 1994. *Malign Neglect: Race, Crime, and Punishment in America.* New York: Oxford University Press.

U.S. General Accounting Office. 1990. *Drug Abuse: Research on Treatment May Not Address Current Needs.* Washington, DC: U.S. General Accounting Office.

Wilson, James Q. 1990. "Drugs and Crime." In *Drugs and Crime*, edited by M. Tonry and J. Q. Wilson. Chicago: University of Chicago Press.

Wood, Floris W. 1990. *An American Profile: Opinions and Behavior, 1972-1989.* New York: Gale Research.

Zimring, Franklin E. and Gordon Hawkins. 1994. "The Growth of Imprisonment in California." *British Journal of Criminology* 34:83-95.

Part II
Crime, Policing and Racial Unrest

[11]

BRIT. J. CRIMINOL. Vol. 23 No. 2 APRIL 1983

SELECTING DELINQUENTS FOR CAUTIONING IN THE LONDON METROPOLITAN AREA

SIMHA F. LANDAU* AND GAD NATHAN† (*Jerusalem*)

EXAMINATION of the literature related to the labelling theory (also called by various writers societal reaction hypothesis, social definition hypothesis, interactionist theory, etc.) reveals the great impact that the theoretical writings in this field have had on empirical research on deviance in the last two decades. The emphasis in these writings on the power of social response in causing deviance (see among others Becker, 1963; Erikson, 1962; Hartjen, 1978; Kitsuse, 1962; Lemert, 1951 and 1967; Matza, 1969; Quinney, 1970; Schur, 1971) has "triggered" a wealth of empirical research. An assumption derived from labelling theory is that contingencies other than the criminal act itself affect the chances of being officially labelled as a delinquent by social control agencies. In particular, attention has been drawn to the systematic contingencies stemming from inequalities in society—hence the over-representation of less powerful social groups (*e.g.* those of lower income and/or of certain ethnic origin) in the criminal statistics.

A large number of studies have tested the above assumption by analysing decisions made by the agencies of the criminal justice system in general and those of the juvenile justice system in particular. However, the findings of these studies are rather inconsistent (for a detailed analysis see Landau, 1981). In his review, Landau stresses the need for more comparative research in this field, since most studies on this topic were conducted in the United States. Among the few exceptions (also reviewed by the above author) are studies conducted in Israel (Landau, 1978 and 1979) and England (Bennett, 1979; Landau, 1981; Stevens and Willis, 1979).

The most recent of the three English studies (Landau, 1981) investigated police decisions at the first of two decision-making stages in which the police are involved with juveniles in the London Metropolitan area: whether to charge the juvenile immediately or to refer him (her) to the juvenile bureau. It was found that, while legal variables (previous criminal record and type of offence) play a major role in police decision-making, some extra-legal variables (area, age and ethnic group) also have a significant effect. With regard to area, the findings indicate that juveniles involved in burglary are treated more severely in the Outer London Area, those involved in auto-crime receive harsher treatment in North Inner London, while those in-volved in crimes of violence and "public disorder and other offences" are

* Director, Institute of Criminology, Faculty of Law, Hebrew University of Jerusalem.
† Associate Professor, Department of Statistics, Hebrew University of Jerusalem.
  The authors would like to thank Joy Mott of the Home Office Research Unit and Chief Super-intendents Leslie Sharp and John Robinson of the Metropolitan Police for their assistance in obtaining the data. Thanks are also due to Menachem Amir, Stanley Cohen, Maya Landau and Leslie Sebba for their valuable remarks. The study was made possible through the support pro-vided by the Research Fund of the Faculty of Law of the Hebrew University and the Posnansky Trust of the British Friends of the Hebrew University.

SELECTING DELINQUENTS FOR CAUTIONING

dealt with more severely in South Inner London. With regard to ethnic group, it was found that blacks involved in crimes of violence, burglary and " public disorder and other offences " are treated more harshly than their white counterparts.

The implicit assumption underlying the dichotomy between legal and non-legal (or extra-legal) variables is that the juvenile justice system should be guided by the principles of formal rationality (Weber, 1954), according to which like cases should be treated in a like manner (*i.e.* seriousness of offence and prior record should be the major criteria for decision-making). However, formal rationality or formal justice which might be quite appropriate for adults are generally regarded as much less appropriate in the juvenile justice system, in which much greater discretionary power is granted to the court and other agencies (such as the juvenile bureaux) in order to attain what Matza (1964) calles individualised justice.

Horwitz and Wasserman (1980), using Weber's concept of substantive rationality, emphasise that the principle guiding the juvenile justice system is substantive justice rather than formal justice. Accordingly they make a distinction within the so-called non-legal variables between discriminatory and substantive variables. Ethnic group and social class are typical examples of discriminatory variables, while variables relating to the character and social circumstances of the juvenile are of a substantive nature. These latter variables, considered as extra-legal by the formal justice model, are appropriate and important within a substantive justice model. The few previous studies which did include such variables in their analysis found that they were indeed more related to juvenile court dispositions than were the discriminatory variables of ethnic group and class. Thomas and Cage (1977) analysed home situation and school enrolment, Cohen and Kluegel (1978) examined whether the juvenile was working and/or in school, while Horwitz and Wasserman (1980) investigated the juvenile's problems in school and/or with parents as the substantive variables in their study

It should be noted, however, that the use of substantive criteria in the juvenile justice system has been the topic of much debate in recent years. Two main issues are raised in this context: first, there is considerable doubt as to whether substantive criteria are being applied appropriately; secondly, even if they are appropriately applied, whether this might not lead to the erosion of civil liberties and legal protection from juveniles (Hellum, 1979; Morris *et al.*, 1980; Rubin, 1979). The first of these issues was specifically mentioned by Horwitz and Wasserman (1980), who raise the question whether the use of substantive criteria indirectly leads to unwarranted discrimination against powerless youths (pp. 105–106). This speculation, together with doubts regarding the use of substantive criteria within the juvenile justice system call for more rigorous empirical research into this topic. In the London study previously mentioned (Landau, 1981), substantive variables were not analysed as they are not systematically available to the police at the first stage of their processing of the juveniles. It is, therefore, the purpose of the present study to continue and investigate the second stage of this process, *i.e.* decisions made by the juvenile bureaux in

SIMHA F. LANDAU AND GAD NATHAN

the London Metropolitan area. At this stage the effect of legal, discriminatory variables, as well as substantive ones, on police decision-making will be analysed.

The Police Decision-Making Process

The following diagram describes the two-stage decision-making process in which police are involved with juveniles in the Metropolitan Area:

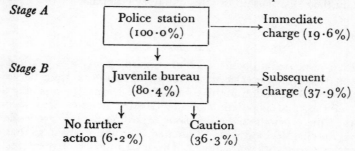

Stage A — Police station (100·0%) → Immediate charge (19·6%)

Stage B — Juvenile bureau (80·4%) → Subsequent charge (37·9%) → No further action (6·2%) / Caution (36·3%)

The percentages in brackets refer to the total number of decisions (1,708) on which the analysis in the previous London study (Landau, 1981) was based. In that study, only decisions made at stage A were analysed.

As seen in the diagram, most juveniles arrested are not charged immediately but are referred to the juvenile bureau (see also Oliver, 1973). At the bureau, a detailed investigation is conducted on the juvenile's alleged offence as well as his background. This usually includes a home visit as well as the gathering of information from the local authority social services, educational welfare services, etc. The investigating officer prepares a detailed report about the case and recommends an appropriate course of action. The report is presented to the senior officer of the bureau who makes the final decision as to treatment of the juvenile. He has to choose between three possible alternatives: to take no further action (NFA), to caution the juvenile or to charge him/her. Cautioning is considered as one of the diversionary alternatives available to prosecution (Ditchfield, 1976), thus avoiding the stigma of being brought to court. Moreover, a cautioned juvenile does not receive a criminal record number (Bennett, 1979). It should be noted regarding stage A that police standing orders specify that type of offence and previous criminal record (legal criteria) should be the main criteria for decision, although discretion may be used to override this general directive (Landau, 1981). On the other hand, in stage B no reference is made in the standing orders to any legal criteria. In practice, the cautioning procedure is adopted particularly in the case of a first offender with what is considered to be a " satisfactory background report " (Oliver, 1973). However, the head of the juvenile bureau has very wide discretionary powers as to the final decision; there are no established levels of recidivism beyond which a juvenile may not be cautioned. Similarly, the fact that a juvenile is referred to a juvenile bureau for the first time does not preclude

SELECTING DELINQUENTS FOR CAUTIONING

a decision to send him/her to juvenile court. The only formal conditions for
the administration of a caution are: (1) the offender must admit the offence;
(2) the parents must agree to the child being cautioned; (3) the person
aggrieved, or loser, must be willing to leave the decision to the police
(Oliver, 1973). In stage B, therefore, we have a set of official guidelines that
point to the crucial importance of substantive criteria at that stage. The aim
of this study is to see how these substantive criteria are in fact applied and
to ascertain their relationship to discriminatory criteria.

The Study

This study investigated all police decisions regarding juveniles, made during
the last quarter (October–December) of 1978, in the juvenile bureaux of
five Divisions of the London Metropolitan Police District (comprising about
one-fifth of the total population of the Greater London area—Landau,
1981). As in the previous study, decisions regarding the same juvenile subsequent to the first decision were eliminated from the analysis, so that each
decision relates to a different subject. The total number of these decisions
was 1,373.

The data were collected from the standard official registration forms
used by the Metropolitan Police for statistical purposes. The independent
variables were divided into two groups, non-legal and legal. The six non-
legal variables were:

1. *Area of Offence*—The five Divisions covered by the study were divided
into three areas: 1, Lambeth and Wandsworth, two adjacent boroughs
in Inner London, south of the River Thames (two Divisions); 2,
Camden and Hackney, two closely situated boroughs in Inner London
noth of the River Thames (two Divisions); 3, Brent and Harrow, two
adjacent boroughs in the outer London Area (one Division).

2. *Age.* Juveniles were divided into two age groups: (1) 10–14; (2) 15–16.

3. *Sex.*

4. *Ethnic group* This variable was dichotomised into: (1) white; (2)
black.[1]

5. *Tenure of accommodation* of the juvenile's family. The two categories of
this variable were: (1) owned (owner-occupier); rented (from council,
housing association or privately). Since the data available to us did
not provide any direct information as to the socio-economic status of
the juvenile's family, tenure of accommodation was used here as an
indirect or approximate measure of that status. The figures provided
by the National Dwelling and Housing Survey (Department of the
Environment, 1979) confirm our assumption as to the strong (although

---

[1] *i.e.* juveniles of Negro (mainly West Indian) origin. The two ethnic groups included in this
study comprise 95·7 per cent. of our sample. Due to the very small proportion (4·3 per cent.) of
juveniles of other ethnic origin (Indian, Pakastani, Chinese, Japanese, Arabian and dark-skinned
European) only whites and blacks were included in the study. For detailed analyses of the low rate
of criminality among Asians see Mawby, McCulloch and Batta (1979) and Stevens and Willis (1979).

SIMHA F. LANDAU AND GAD NATHAN

not absolute) relationship between tenure of accommodation and several class-related variables.[2]

6. *Latch-key child.* This term, used in the official form, relates to children who are left on their own without parental control, on a regular basis. The two categories here are: (1) latch-key child[3]; (2) non-latch-key child. This substantive variable was included in our analysis owing to the importance ascribed to perental control in a considerable number of studies and theories on delinquency causation (Hirschi, 1969; Glueck and Glueck, 1970; Elliot, Ageton and Canter, 1979).

The two legal variables in the study were:

7. *Offence.* (1) crimes of violence; (2) burglary; (3) auto-crime[4]; (4) theft; (5) public disorder and similar offences[5]; (6) traffic and other offences.[6]

8. *Previous criminal record.* (1) no previous referrals; (2) one or more previous referrals but no previous convictions; (3) one or more previous convictions.

The dependent variable was the police decision. However, in 105 cases (7·6 per cent.) no further action (NFA) was taken by the police.[7] These cases were eliminated, so that the outcomes of the dependent variable were only " charge " and " caution ". This reduced the number of decisions analysed from 1,373 to 1,268. The elimination of subjects on the basis of ethnic origin (see n. 1), and of those for which no information was available regarding variables 5 or 6 from the present analysis, further reduced the number of cases included in the study from 1,268 to 1,146. All results reported are based on the latter number of subjects.

Results

Table 1 presents the frequency distribution of the independent variables, as well as the proportion of cases cautioned in each category. Table 1 shows that the chances of a caution are considerably higher when the juvenile in

[2] The comparison between " owner-occupiers " and persons who live in rented accommodation reveals that among the former there is a much higher proportion of: (a) heads of households who are professionals, employers, managers and other non-manual workers (Table 4 in the Survey); (b) households with one or more cars available (Table 6 in the Survey); (c) households with above-standard number of bedrooms (Table 2 in the Survey); (d) centrally heated accommodation (Table 6 in the Survey).

[3] The official police instruction defines them as children who: " (1) regularly return home from school to an empty house; (2) are regularly left on their own during school holidays, for a substantial part of the day ". These instructions proceed to operationalise the above definition in greater detail: " This condition is usually due to the fact that both parents are working. ' Substantial part of the day ' should be taken to mean a minimum of three hours. ' Regularly ' should be taken to mean a minimum of three days in each working week. Any child who is thought to fall into either category should be included ".

[4] The offences included in auto-crime are: the unauthorised taking of motor vehicles, thefts of or from motor vehicles and thefts of other conveyances, mainly bicycles.

[5] " Similar offences " include criminal damage, offensive weapon, drunkenness, suspected person, etc.

[6] " Other offences " include obstructing the police, threatening words or behaviour, hoax calls to fire brigade or police, obstructing highway, throwing stones, etc.

[7] The specified reasons for the 105 NFA decisions were as follows: insufficient evidence (51·4 per cent.), victim declines to prosecute (15·2 per cent.), trivial offence (8·6 per cent.) and other reasons (24·8 per cent.).

SELECTING DELINQUENTS FOR CAUTIONING

TABLE 1

Distribution of the Independent Variables and Percentage of Cases Cautioned in each Category

Variable			Distribution N	%	Percentage of cases cautioned*
Area:	1.	Lambeth/Wandsworth	503	43·9	52·6
	2.	Camden/Hackney	295	25·7	42·4
	3.	Brent/Harrow	348	30·4	49·1
Age:	1.	10–14	594	51·8	56·9
	2.	15–16	552	48·2	40·2
Sex:	1.	Male	995	86·8	46·5
	2.	Female	151	13·2	64·2
Ethnic group:	1.	White	753	65·7	53·7
	2.	Black	393	34·3	39·7
Tenure of accommodation:	1.	Owned	265	23·1	59·2
	2.	Rented	881	76·9	45·7
" Latch-key child ":	1.	Yes	332	29·0	38·3
	2.	No	814	71·0	53·2
Offence: 1.		Crimes of violence	84	7·3	28·6
2.		Burglary	191	16·7	48·2
3.		Auto-crime	199	17·4	35·7
4.		Theft	382	33·3	59·7
5.		Public disorder and similar offences	154	13·4	39·0
6.		Traffic and other offences	136	11·9	62·5
Previous record: 1.		No previous referrals	630	55·0	73·8
2.		One or more previous referrals but no previous convictions	248	21·6	23·0
3.		One or more previous convictions	268	23·4	14·2
		Total	1,146	100·0	48·9

* There is a significant association between each variable and police decision. The χ^2 values for *all* variables are significant at least at the 0·02 level. (Most are significant at the 0·001 level.)

question is a female, has no previous referral, is involved in " traffic and other offences ", or is below the age of 15. There is also a higher chance of a caution if the offence is committed in area 1 (Lambeth/Wandsworth), if the juvenile's family owns its accommodation, if he/she is not a latch-key child, or if he/she is white. Factors associated with a lower chance of being cautioned are: previous conviction or referral, involvement in crimes of violence, age 15 or above, being male, living in rented accommodation, being a latch-key child, committing the offence in area 2 (Camden/Hackney), or being black.

It should be noted that, of all eight independent variables in Table 1, the one which seems to be most strongly related to police decision is previous record. In other words, the descriptive analysis of stage B decision reveals that, despite the official emphasis on substantive criteria, nevertheless on the surface previous record is the most significant predicting variable of the key decision whether to charge or caution.

In order to determine the relative contribution of each variable presented in Table 1 to police decision, a logistic regression analysis was utilised. This is a multivariate technique designed to assess the effect of a number of

SIMHA F. LANDAU AND GAD NATHAN

TABLE 2

*Summary of Stepwise Results**

1. Step No.	2. Term entered	3. Degrees of freedom	4. Log likelihood	Goodness of Fit		Improvement	
				5. Chi-Square	6. p value	7. Chi-Square	8. p value
Main Effects							
0	Constant	—	−794·052	915·728	<0·001	—	—
1	Previous criminal record	2	−605·365	538·355	<0·001	377·373	<0·001
2	Offence	5	−579·851	487·327	0·003	51·028	<0·001
3	Ethnic group	1	−569·566	466·757	0·018	20·569	<0·001
4	"Latch-key child"	1	−563·761	455·146	0·040	11·611	0·001
5	Age	1	−560·742	449·109	0·056	6·038	0·014
6	Area	2	−556·690	441·023	0·082	8·086	0·018
Interactions							
7	Offence by area	10	−544·312	416·249	0·182	24·774	0·006
8	Offence by ethnic group	5	−536·716	401·056	0·288	15·193	0·010
9	Previous record by ethnic group	2	−532·625	392·875	0·366	8·181	0·017

* Significance levels of 0·05 were used for entering and for removal of terms.

SELECTING DELINQUENTS FOR CAUTIONING

independent variables on a qualitative dependent variable (see full details in Cox, 1970).

As it was reasonable to assume that the independent variables may contribute not only separately as main effects but also jointly, interactions between these variables had to be taken into consideration. However, for the sake of simplicity only two-way interactions were considered for potential inclusion in the model.

In order to choose between alternative models, a stepwise method was utilised on the basis of the BMDPLR computer programme (Dixon and Brown, 1979). This method adds at each step to the model that term which maximises the likelihood function. Terms are added hierarchically in the sense that interactions are added only if their component main effects are also included. At each step, checks are made to ensure that terms previously included in the model still contribute significantly to the goodness of fit. The process stops when the inclusion of no additional terms would significantly increase the likelihood.

The application of the above stepwise method to our data is summarised in Table 2. In Table 2 each line represents a step. Column 4 gives the log of the likelihood and shows its increase from step to step. The chi-squared goodness of fit to the model at each step is given in column 5 and its p value in column 6. Columns 7 and 8 show the improvement in goodness of fit at each step and its p value, respectively.

From Table 2 it is seen that all the main effects of all variables, except sex and tenure of accommodation, are included in the final model which fits the data adequately ($p = 0.366$). Only three two-way interactions are required: offence by area, offence by ethnic group and previous record by ethnic group. Table 2 reveals that previous criminal record is the variable that contributes most to the goodness of fit and is therefore entered at the first step. The second main effect term to enter the model is the only other legal variable—offence. These two legal variables together account for about 82 per cent. of the total reduction in chi-square goodness of fit attained by the model.[8]

The main conclusions that can be drawn from the statistical analysis are as follows:

1. Previous criminal record has a significant effect on police decision to caution, *i.e.* the police were more likely to caution a juvenile instead of charging him/her, if he/she had not previously been referred.

2. With regard to offence, the results indicate that the six offences can be divided into three hierarchical groups: 1. " traffic and other offences " (offence 6); 2. burglary and theft (offences 2 and 4); 3. crimes of violence, auto-crime and " public disorder and similar offences " (offences 1, 3 and 5). The results show that juveniles committing the offences in group 1 are significantly more likely to be cautioned than those committing the offences in the other two groups. The offences in

[8] Full details on the model obtained, estimates of the parameters for main effects, for interactions and for their standard errors can be found in the full research report obtainable from the first author.

SIMHA F. LANDAU AND GAD NATHAN

group 2 are treated significantly more leniently than those in group 3. Within groups 2 and 3 there are no significant differences as to the probability of a caution decision.

3. As to ethnic group, white juveniles were significantly more likely to be cautioned than their black counterparts.
4. Latch-key children were less likely to be cautioned, compared to non-latch-key children.
5. Juveniles of the younger age group (10–14) have greater chances of being cautioned.
6. As to area, although areas 1 (Lambeth/Wandsworth) and 3 (Brent/Harrow) seem to be associated with a higher probability of cautioning, the individual differences between the areas are not significant.

TABLE 3

Predicted Probabilities of Cautioning

3.1: Offence by area and ethnic group

Offence	Area			Ethnic group		All
	1	2	3	White	Black	categories
1. Crimes of violence	0·243	0·353	0·300	0·400	0·182	0·286
2. Burglary	0·491	0·333	0·667	0·489	0·460	0·482
3. Auto-crime	0·333	0·452	0·263	0·418	0·189	0·357
4. Theft	0·709	0·456	0·542	0·670	0·506	0·597
5. Public disorder and similar	0·381	0·257	0·482	0·480	0·232	0·390
6. Traffic and other	0·630	0·600	0·636	0·595	0·800	0·625
All categories	0·525	0·424	0·491	0·537	0·397	0·489

3.2: Previous criminal record by ethnic group

Previous record	Ethnic group		All categories
	White	Black	
1. No previous referrals	0·788	0·640	0·738
2. 1 + previous referrals; no previous convictions	0·252	0·191	0·230
3. 1 + previous convictions	0·194	0·043	0·142
All categories	0·537	0·397	0·489

Table 3 presents the predicted probabilities of a cautioning decision for combinations of categories of variables included in the model. The results in Table 3 present the combined effect of both the main and interaction effects of the variables in the model on police decision to caution. From Table 3·1 it can be seen that the largest difference between areas is in the offence of burglary, for which the chances of juveniles being cautioned are twice as great in area 3 (Brent/Harrow) as in area 2 (Camden/Hackney). On the other hand, juveniles involved in " traffic and other offences " have very similar (high) chances of being cautioned in the three different areas.

As to the combination of offence and ethnic group it is seen in Table 3.1 that only in " traffic and other offences " are black juveniles more likely to be cautioned. All other differences between the two groups are in the opposite direction. The most salient differences between the two ethnic groups are found in " public disorder and other offences ", auto-crime, and crimes of violence, where the chances of white juveniles being cautioned are more than twice those of their black counterparts.

As to the interaction between previous criminal record and ethnic group, it is seen in Table 3.2 that the largest difference between the two groups is in

SELECTING DELINQUENTS FOR CAUTIONING

TABLE 4

Salient Differences Between Ethnic Groups in the Probability of a Cautioning Decision

Profile No.	Area	Age	"Latch-key child"	Offence	Previous record	Probability for ethnic group		Difference between White and Black
						White	Black	
1	3	15-16	No	Traffic and other	1 + previous referrals / No previous convictions	0·361	0·771	−0·410
2	1	10-14	No	Crimes of violence	None	0·663	0·271	+0·392
3	2	10-14	Yes	Crimes of violence	None	0·642	0·253	+0·389
4	2	10-14	No	Crimes of violence	None	0·761	0·376	+0·385
5	3	15-16	No	Crimes of violence	None	0·793	0·420	+0·373
6	1	15-16	Yes	Crimes of violence	None	0·567	0·198	+0·369
7	2	10-14	Yes	Crimes of violence	None	0·544	0·184	+0·360
8	1	10-14	Yes	Crimes of violence	None	0·525	0·173	+0·352
9	2	10-14	No	Public disorder and similar	None	0·696	0·351	+0·345
10	3	10-14	No	Crimes of violence	None	0·852	0·522	+0·330
11	3	15-16	No	Public disorder and similar	None	0·766	0·436	+0·330
12	1	10-14	Yes	Public disorder and similar	None	0·770	0·442	+0·328
13	1	10-14	No	Theft	1 + previous convictions	0·417	0·101	+0·316
14	1	15-16	No	Public disorder and similar	None	0·798	0·484	+0·314
15	1	15-16	Yes	Crimes of violence	None	0·424	0·122	+0·302
16	3	10-14	No	Public disorder and similar	None	0·831	0·537	+0·294

SIMHA F. LANDAU AND GAD NATHAN

cases of juveniles with previous convictions. A white juvenile with previous convictions is over four times more likely to be cautioned than his/her black counterpart.

The respective predicted probabilities for the main effects of age and " latch-key child " can be obtained from the proportions of cases cautioned, presented in Table 1: thus, the predicted probability of obtaining a caution for a juvenile in the younger age group (10–14) is 0·569, while in the older age group (15–16) this probability is only 0·402. " Latch-key children " have a predicted probability of 0·383 of being cautioned, in comparison to a predicted probability of 0·532 for juveniles who are not so defined by the police.

To illustrate the use of the model we shall consider the effect of the juvenile's ethnicity on police decision by looking at those profiles for which the absolute differences between the two ethnic groups in the predicted probability of caution are the largest. Table 4 presents 16 of these profiles. It should be noted, however, that these profiles represent the extreme differences provided by the model. As can be seen, the largest absolute difference is found in the only profile (out of 16) which includes " traffic and other offences " (Profile 1). The chances of a black juvenile in that profile getting a caution are much greater than those of his/her white counterpart. In the other 15 profiles in Table 4, however, the differences between the two groups are in the opposite direction. Analysing profiles 2–16 in Table 4 (in which black juveniles have smaller chances of being cautioned), it can be seen that:

1. all juveniles with these profiles (except for one) have no previous record;
2. most (9 out of 15) are in the younger age group (10–14);
3. two-thirds of these profiles (10 out of 15) are of juveniles who are not defined as latch-key children;
4. juveniles with these profiles are involved mainly in crimes of violence (9 out of 15) and to a lesser extent in " public disorder and similar offences " (5 out of 15). Theft is the only other offence represented in these profiles (1 out of 15);
5. area 1 is slightly over-represented in these profiles (7 out of 15) while areas 2 and 3 are under-represented (4 each).

Discussion

The findings of the present study will now be discussed and the effect of various variables on police decision-making at the two stages in which they are involved with juveniles in the London Metropolitan area (Landau, 1981) will be analysed.

The main conclusion that can be drawn from the findings of the present study is that, while legal variables (especially previous criminal record) play a major role in police decisions regarding the cautioning of juveniles, some non-legal variables also have a significant effect on them. Of the six non-legal variables included in this study, sex and tenure of accommodation were the only ones that did not contribute significantly to the police decision.

SELECTING DELINQUENTS FOR CAUTIONING

The finding regarding sex is consistent with the previous London study (Landau, 1981) which also failed to show any contribution of this variable to police decision. One can conclude, therefore, that the juvenile's sex has no effect on police decision in either of the two stages in which they are involved with juveniles in the Metropolitan area. This finding runs counter to a number of American studies demonstrating sex differences in decision-making in the juvenile justice system (*e.g.* Chesney-Lind, 1973; Cohen and Kluegel, 1978; Cohn, 1963; Terry, 1967).

The interpretation of the finding regarding tenure of accommodation is somewhat less straightforward. It should be remembered that this variable was included in the study as an indirect or approximate measure of the socio-economic status of the juvenile's family (in the absence of a more direct measure). Our finding that tenure of accommodation of the juvenile's family has no effect on police decision indicates that police are not biased in their decision by the juvenile's socio-economic status. This finding contradicts that of Bennett (1979) who found that police do discriminate against working-class juvenile offenders. However, one should be cautious in comparing the findings of the two studies, for the following reasons: (1) Bennett's findings have been seriously questioned on methodological grounds (Landau, 1981). (2) Different measures for socio-economic status were utilised in the two studies. The measure used by Bennett was father's occupation (manual as opposed to non-manual occupation), which would seem to be a more direct indicator of the juvenile's socio-economic status than tenure of accommodation. In view of these points, it may be concluded that, although our data do not indicate that the juvenile's socio-economic status affects police decision regarding cautioning, further research would be necessary to substantiate this finding. It is recommended that such research should employ a more direct measure of socio-economic status.

The significant contribution of age to police decision (found also in the previous London study—Landau, 1981) is hardly surprising, as there are good reasons to regard age as a semi-legal variable owing to the strong association between it and behavioural maturity of juveniles in the age groups investigated in this study.

Latch-key children

Police policy towards " latch-key children " reflects an attitude on their part that cautioning is a less effective means of treating juveniles who are lacking (to a certain degree) in parental control (those defined by police as " latch-key children "). This attitude is in line with control theories (Hirschi, 1969; Elliot *et al.*, 1979) which claim a causal relationship between lack of (or reduced) parental control and delinquent behaviour. Thus, juvenile bureaux, in adopting this approach, select " latch-key children " more frequently for the more authoritarian and formal treatment provided by the juvenile court.

Further analysis of our data reveals that reduced parental control (indicated by the term " latch-key child ") is significantly associated with

SIMHA F. LANDAU AND GAD NATHAN

other indicators of actual or potential " problem family " background.
(1) Family disruption[9] is found to be more frequent among latch-key
children.[10] (2) These children, more frequently than those not so defined,
are brought up in family settings other than those of their natural parents.[11]
(3) Latch-key children were also more frequently known to local authority
services[12] as well as to education welfare services.[13]

These additional findings provide us with a wider perspective regarding
the independent effect of the " latch-key child " variable on police decision.
It is not just the lack of sufficient parental control as such that decreases
considerably the chances of a caution: it is, to a large extent, the additional
substantive variables, perceived by police as " criminogenic " conditions
that " go together " with this insufficient control. Some of these conditions
can be seen as the causes of or contributing factors to insufficient control
(*e.g.* family disruption or not living with both natural parents), while others
may be the result of insufficient control (*e.g.* " known to educational welfare
services "). What these conditions have in common, however, is that they
contribute to (or justify) the police perception of latch-key children as bad
risks for cautioning.

Type of offence and area

As the findings have shown, the type of offence committed by the juvenile
strongly affects the chances of cautioning. These chances are highest for
juveniles involved in " traffic and other offences " and lowest for crimes of
violence, auto-crime and " public disorder and similar offences ". However,
what is of particular interest are the interactions found between offences
and the two non-legal variables, area and ethnic group.

The probabilities based on both the main and interaction effects of
offence by area (Table 3) indicate that juveniles involved in crimes of
violence have the lowest chances of being cautioned in Lambeth/Wands-
worth (area 1); those involved in burglary, theft and " public disorder and
similar offences " have the lowest chances of obtaining a caution in Camden/
Hackney (area 2); while those involved in auto-crime receive harsher
treatment (lowest chances of a caution) in Brent/Harrow (area 3)

Turning to the lenient side of police decisions—in Brent/Harrow (area 3)
the highest chances of a caution are found for burglary and " public disorder and similar offences "; crimes of violence are dealt with most leniently

[9] Defined in the official J.B. form as families in which one of the following was found: parents
divorced or separated; either parent is dead; parent absent through illness or prison; parent ill or
handicapped; father out of work.

[10] More than two-thirds (70 per cent.) of the latch-key children in our sample come from " disrupted families " as compared to just above one-third (37 per cent.) of the children not so defined
($\chi^2 = 93 \cdot 98$; d.f. $= 1$; p $= 0 \cdot 0001$).

[11] Most latch-key children in our sample (59 per cent.) live in settings not including both natural
parents (parent and step-parent or cohabitee, single parent, foster parents, community home or
other environment). The equivalent proportion among non-latch-key children is only 34 per cent.
($\chi^2 = 61 \cdot 07$; d.f. $= 2$; p $= 0 \cdot 0001$).

[12] More than half (54 per cent.) of latch-key children were known to local authority social
services in comparison to only 38 per cent. of the non-latch-key children ($\chi^2 = 24 \cdot 37$; d.f. $= 1$:
p $= 0 \cdot 0001$).

[13] Forty-four per cent. among latch-key children as compared to only 30 per cent. among
those not so defined ($\chi^2 = 20 \cdot 44$; d.f. $= 1$; p $= 0 \cdot 0001$).

SELECTING DELINQUENTS FOR CAUTIONING

in Camden/Hackney (area 2); while juveniles involved in theft are treated most leniently in Lambeth/Wandsworth (area 1).

It is of interest to compare the interaction between offence and area in the present study with the interaction between these two variables found in the previous London study (Landau, 1981). In doing this one has to keep in mind the hierarchical nature of the two stages in the police decision-making process. At stage A, the investigating police-station officer singles out the more severe cases for immediate charge, while the less severe cases are referred to the juvenile bureau (Landau, 1981). At the bureau (stage B) a further distinction is made between the less severe cases who are cautioned and the more severe ones who are brought to court. According to this analysis, if at stage A the police are particularly strict regarding a certain offence, then only the relatively minor offences of this type will reach the juvenile bureau, where they have, as such, a higher probability of being dealt with quite leniently. Therefore, one would expect an inverse (or complementary) relationship between the decisions at the two stages. Offences for which juveniles are more frequently charged immediately at the police station would be dealt with more frequently by cautioning at the juvenile bureau.

A comparison of the interaction between area and offence at the two stages reveals that in three out of the four offences for which such a comparison was possible[14] (crimes of violence, burglary, auto-crime and " public disorder and similar offences "), this expected inverse (or complementary) relationship is indeed found:

(1) At stage A, juveniles involved in burglary have the highest chances of being charged immediately in area 3 (Brent/Harrow) (Landau, 1981) while at stage B (in the present study) juvenile burglars in that area are the most likely to be cautioned.

(2) At stage A, juveniles involved in auto-crime have the highest chance of being charged immediately in area 2 (Camden/Hackney) (Landau, 1981) while in the present analysis (stage B) juveniles involved in this offence have the highest chances of obtaining a caution in area 2.

(3) At stage A, juveniles involved in " public disorder and similar offences " have the highest chances of being charged immediately in area 1 (Lambeth/Wandsworth) (Landau, 1981) while at the juvenile bureau (stage B) the probability of cautioning for this offence in area 1, although not the highest, is considerably higher than in area 2. It should be noted, however, that the differences between areas regarding this offence do not reach statistical significance. Only with regard to crimes of violence was the expected inverse relationship between the two stages of police decisions not found; juveniles in area 1 (Lambeth/Wandsworth) have the highest chances of being sent to court both at the police-station level (stage A: Landau, 1981) and at the level of the juvenile bureau (stage B: present analysis). A possible explanation for this unexpected consistent pattern at the two stages may be that in this area police at all levels (including the juvenile

[14] Regarding theft there were hardly any differences between the areas at the first stage, while " traffic and other offences " were excluded from the previous analysis (Landau, 1981).

SIMHA F. LANDAU AND GAD NATHAN

bureau) treat crimes of violence more harshly due to their actual and/or perceived greater prevalence in this part of the Metropolitan District. The statistical figures support this explanation: in 1977 the rate[15] of recorded crimes of violence per 1,000 population committed by juveniles in Lambeth/ Wandsworth (0·86) was considerably higher than the rate in Camden/ Hackney and Brent/Harrow (0·61 and 0·44, respectively). It seems, there-fore that the lower probability of cautioning for juveniles involved in crimes of violence in Lambeth/Wandsworth (in spite of the higher probability of immediate charge for this offence in that area at stage A) is affected by the greater prevalence of these offences in that area. It should be noted, how-ever, that the differences between areas regarding crimes of violence are small and do not reach statistical significance.

Ethnic group

As to the variable of ethnic group, our findings reveal that except for " traffic and other offences " the chances of white juveniles obtaining a caution are considerably greater than the chances of their black counterparts. This is particularly true in relation to crimes of violence, auto-crime, and " public disorder and similar offences ". With regard to auto-crime, this finding is in accordance with the assumption that there is an inverse re-lationship between police decisions at the two stages. At the first stage of police decision-making (Landau, 1981) black juveniles have a slightly increased probability (in comparison with white juveniles) of receiving a more lenient decision (referral to the juvenile bureau). As to the other two offences (crimes of violence and " public disorder and similar offences ") blacks are treated more harshly by police at both stages of decision-making; they are less frequently referred to the juvenile bureau (Landau, 1981) and at the bureau they are less frequently cautioned than whites (present study).

Our findings regarding these two offence categories are in line with those of Stevens and Willis (1979) who found that blacks in London had par-ticularly high arrest rates for two offences ("other violent theft" and " being a suspected person "). These two offences fit exactly into our two offence categories mentioned above: " other violent theft " is part of crimes of violence in our study, while " being a suspected person " is included within " public disorder and similar offences " in the present analysis (see n. 5). This similarity between the findings of the three studies (Stevens and Willis, 1979; Landau, 1981 and the present study) cannot be overlooked. Unless alternative explanations are provided, a bias on the part of the police against blacks involved in these offences cannot be ruled out. More-over, in the Scarman report on the riots in Brixton (an area belonging to the borough of Lambeth, included in this study) racial bias on the part of the police was specifically mentioned: ". . . there were instances of harass-ment and racial prejudice among junior officers on the streets of Brixton which gave credibility and substance to the arguments of the police's

[15] For the computation of this rate, the number of crimes of violence committed by juveniles in each area was taken from the juvenile bureau figures and the figures regarding the population in these areas were taken from *London Facts and Figures* (1978).

SELECTING DELINQUENTS FOR CAUTIONING

critics " (Scarman, 1981, p. 73). Tuck and Southgate (1981) found (in Manchester) that West Indians were more likely than whites to express hostility towards the police.

In the context of the present analysis, some explanation is still needed for the almost general practice of the juvenile bureaux to grant cautions less frequently to black juveniles.[16] Several possible explanations (not necessarily mutually exclusive) can be put forward for this practice:

(1) It is possible that the categories of some legal independent variables included in our study were not sensitive enough to differences which may exist between black and white juveniles. For instance, for the variable measuring record, dichotomies were used (distinguishing between those without and those with one or more previous referrals or convictions). It is quite possible that among those juveniles with previous records, blacks have more previous referrals and/or convictions than their white counterparts, thus explaining the greater proportion of harsher decisions made for these juveniles by the police. However, a more sensitive re-analysis failed to show any significant difference between the black and white juveniles on this legal variable.[17]

(2) The number of non-legal variables covered in this study is somewhat limited. A wider knowledge of more background variables might explain, to some extent, the differences found between the two ethnic groups. As the decision at the juvenile bureau is made after a home visit and/or other inquiries, such wider background information is available. Comparing the two ethnic groups on some of these variables we found that black juveniles came more frequently from disrupted families than do their white counterparts,[18] a greater proportion of them (in comparison to whites) are brought up in family settings not including both natural parents[19] and among them latch-key children are found more frequently than among white juveniles.[20] Black juveniles come also from larger families.[21] Given this additional background information it seems that the harsher treatment (less cautioning) of black juveniles at the juvenile bureau can be explained in terms of their more detrimental family conditions, *i.e.* the juvenile bureau, guided by substantive considerations, perceives blacks more frequently as bad risks for cautioning; thus their higher representation among those brought to court.

[16] The only exception is " traffic and other offences ". However, the number of black juveniles involved in this offence category was not more than 20.

[17] As to previous referrals, those with such referrals were divided into three groups (1, 2–3 and 4 or more previous referrals.) It is of interest to note that among white juveniles there was a slightly *higher* proportion of cases in the most severe category (4 or more) than among their black counterparts: 11·4 per cent. as opposed to 8·1 per cent. Regarding previous convictions the findings were quite similar. Here juveniles with previous convictions were re-divided into those with only one and those with two or more convictions. It was found that the proportion of white juveniles with two or more convictions (12·4 per cent.) is greater than that among black juveniles (9·4 per cent.).

[18] Among the black juveniles in this study, 53 per cent. are from disrupted families in comparison to 42 per cent. among their white counterparts ($\chi^2 = 10\cdot54$; d.f. $= 1$; p $= 0\cdot0012$).

[19] More than half (51 per cent.) of the black juveniles in this study do not live with both natural parents. The equivalent proportion among white juveniles is only 36 per cent. ($\chi^2 = 23\cdot22$; d.f. $= 1$; p $= 0\cdot0001$).

[20] More than one-third (36 per cent.) of the black juveniles in the study are defined as latch-key children, in comparison to about one-fourth (26 per cent.) of their white counterparts. ($\chi^2 = 12\cdot38$; d.f. $= 1$; p $= 0\cdot0004$).

[21] More than half (57 per cent.) of the black juveniles' families in the study have four children or more. Among the white group this percentage is only 42 ($\chi^2 = 23\cdot52$; d.f. $= 1$; p $= 0\cdot0001$).

SIMHA F. LANDAU AND GAD NATHAN

These conditions may also reduce the likelihood of full co-operation between the juvenile's parents and the juvenile bureau. It should be remembered that such co-operation is one of the conditions for administering a caution (Oliver, 1973; Ford, 1975, p. 173). In the absence of this co-operation, the juvenile bureau officer is more likely to decide that it would be in the best interest of the juvenile to refer the case to the juvenile court. This point of co-operation provides an excellent example of the difficulty of sustaining the distinction between substantive and discriminatory criteria. What appears to be a reasonable and fair criterion (co-operation) may frequently be related to a discriminatory variable (ethnic group).

As mentioned earlier, another necessary condition for a caution to be granted is that the juvenile must admit the offence, and the offence must, in the opinion of the officer, be fully capable of proof in court if need be (Ford, 1975, p. 173). It is quite possible that black juveniles, more frequently than white, deny the offences of which they are accused. This denial may be due to more mistaken arrests of blacks for certain offences,[22] to greater antagonism of blacks towards the police[23] or to a combination of both. Whatever the case, the result is the same—an increased tendency to refer blacks to the juvenile court.

Another possible factor which may contribute to the lower chances of blacks being cautioned has to do with the third necessary condition for a caution to be administered: that the person aggrieved, or loser, must be willing to leave the decision to the police. In other words, a caution cannot be granted if the complainant or victim of the offence insists on the prosecution of the juvenile in court. It is quite possible, therefore, that complainants insist more frequently on a court charge when a black juvenile is involved. This possibility is in accordance with the findings of Black and Reiss (1970) who report that ". . . it is evident that the higher arrest rate for Negro juveniles in encounters with complainants and suspects is largely a consequence of the tendency of the police to comply with the preferences of complainants. This tendency is costly for Negro juveniles, . . . While police behaviour follows the same patterns for Negro and white juveniles, differential outcomes arise from differences in citizen behaviour." It should be noted, however, that in this study the great majority of encounters between complainants and juveniles were racially homogeneous. These findings of Black and Reiss (1970) lead them to the following conclusion: " Given the prominent role of the Negro complainant in the race differential, then, it may be inappropriate to consider this pattern an instance of discrimination on the part of policemen."

Summing up the discussion regarding the variable of ethnic group: we identified three factors which help to explain the harsher way in which black juveniles are dealt with by the juvenile bureau:

(1) The strong association in police records between blacks and certain

[22] Such as for crimes of violence and " public disorder and similar offences ", in which black juveniles are treated more harshly at both stages of the police decision-making process.
[23] This was the opinion expressed by some police officers dealing with juveniles in England (Landau, 1981). This opinion (correct or false) if widely held may in itself increase the likelihood of mistaken arrests of blacks. Thus, these two possible reasons might be closely connected.

SELECTING DELINQUENTS FOR CAUTIONING

types of offences (particularly crimes of violence and " public disorder and similar offences ") found in several studies conducted in London.[24]

(2) The greater prevalence of " problem family " backgrounds among black juveniles, leading the juvenile bureaux officers to perceive them (more frequently than whites) as bad risks for a caution.

(3) The formal necessary conditions for a caution might be more difficult to obtain in cases involving black juveniles.

These factors may not be totally independent of one another and all three require further and more direct investigation.

The second factor mentioned above brings us back to the topic of " unwarranted discrimination against powerless youths as a result of the extensive use of substantive criteria by the juvenile justice system " (Horwitz and Wasserman, 1980). Official figures (similar to our findings) reveal that a large proportion of the total black population in the country live in conditions very likely to be defined as detrimental or problematic by juvenile justice agencies. Among blacks a very large proportion of children are born outside marriage,[25] blacks are of a much lower economic status[26] and their families are larger[27] and much less well-housed than white households.[28] The *combination* of all these facts results in the almost certain prediction that juvenile justice agencies, guided by substantive criteria, will be less lenient towards black juveniles " in the best interest of the child ". These were precisely the findings reported by Horwitz and Wasserman (1980): " Members of minority groups are slightly more likely than whites to have community problems and are more likely to be placed on probation for this reason. Therefore, it is possible that the use of substantive criteria leads members of minority groups . . . to receive harsher dispositions than they would in a system of formal rationality " (p. 114). Findings of this sort strongly support the claims of the critics of the juvenile justice system, well represented by the following statement: ". . . the entire conception of ' individualised justice ' requires reassessment. In combination with the vagueness of delinquency statutes, the enormous amount of discretion vested in officials at the various stages of delinquency-processing invites uncertainty and confusion and sets the stage for discriminatory practices. Nor does the basic notion of ' treating ' the child's broad problems, rather than reacting to a specific law violation, appear to further the aim of

24 The source of this association is far from being clear-cut. It deserves a separate detailed study in which the wider perspective of race relations, ethnic stereotypes, as well as real involvement of blacks in these offences should be considered.

25 In 1976, almost half (48 per cent.) the British children born to mothers who immigrated from the West Indies were born outside marriage. The equivalent figure regarding the total population of Great Britain was only 9 per cent. (Thompson and Peretz, 1979, p. 67).

26 The figures provided by Table 7 in the National Dwelling and Housing Survey (Department of the Environment, 1979) show that of heads of households with identified socio-economic group, only 3 per cent. of West Indians were either professional or employers and managers as against 23 per cent. of whites; and 42 per cent. of West Indians were semi-skilled or unskilled manual workers as against 21 per cent. of whites. West Indian heads of households were also more likely to be unemployed than whites.

27 The average size of households was 3·7 persons for West Indian households and 2·7 persons for white households (Table 7 in the Survey).

28 In response to the question on satisfaction with accommodation, over one quarter (27 per cent.) of West Indian households expressed a degree of dissatisfaction with their accommodation, compared with 8 per cent. of white households (Table 8 in the Survey).

SIMHA F. LANDAU AND GAD NATHAN

' rehabilitation ' in any meaningful way. In fact the sense of injustice to
which this approach gives rise may, as we have seen, actively reinforce
attitudes that breed delinquency " (Schur, 1973, pp. 168–169). While the
ideal of individualised justice remains strong in the juvenile justice system,
recent years have seen a trend towards increasing the formality of decision-
making in the various agencies of that system (President's Commission,
1967; Schur, 1973; Horwitz and Wasserman, 1980; Morris *et al*., 1980). It
seems appropriate for the juvenile bureau to follow this trend and adopt a
more formal approach based more directly on the juvenile's previous
record and on the severity and circumstances of the offence. We strongly
believe that, by doing this, the representation of blacks among juveniles
sent to court will be more balanced.

Future Research

Future research should investigate more directly the substantive as well as
other variables taken into consideration by the juvenile bureau officers when
recommending a caution or prosecution. This should be done by adding
participant observation and direct interviewing of the law-enforcing
officers to the collection of official data. As the distinction between substantive and other non-legal variables may not always be clear, this issue
should also be clarified in future research. It might be that the exact weighting of " substantive " *vs*. " discriminatory " *vs*. " legal " variables is less
important in predicting decisions than the overall composites or " typifica-
tions " used by police officers. When the juvenile is black, is lacking in
parental control and is involved in crimes of violence or " public disorder
and similar offences " he is regarded as a bad risk for a caution and thus a
suitable candidate for court prosecution.

Given the important role of the juvenile bureau as one of the major
" gate-keepers " to the criminal justice system, the effectiveness of the
decisions made by this agency should be studied in a well-controlled follow-
up research. In research of this type, the relative success of cautioning, as
opposed to the more stigmatising decision of prosecution, in preventing
future delinquency should be compared. Such research would not be easy
from the methodological point of view. However, if well done, it would
provide us with valuable and much needed information as to the long
range effect of the decisions made within this important social control
agency.

Summary

This study investigated the contribution of legal and non-legal variables to
police decisions at the second of the two decision-making stages in which
the police are involved with juveniles in the London Metropolitan area—the
decision whether to caution the juvenile or to prosecute him (her) in the
juvenile court. For this purpose, decisions regarding 1,146 juveniles referred
to the juvenile bureaux in five Divisions of the London Metropolitan Police
District were investigated, utilising a multivariate logistic regression analysis.

SELECTING DELINQUENTS FOR CAUTIONING

It was found that, while legal variables (previous criminal record and type of offence) play a major role in police decisions regarding the cautioning of juveniles, some non-legal variables (age, area, ethnic group and parental control) also have a significant effect on the decision. Juveniles with reduced parental control have lower chances of being cautioned. Reduced parental control was found to be associated with other indicators of actual or potential problematic family background. An interaction between type of offence and area was identified. As to ethnic group, the findings reveal that except for " traffic and other offences ", the chances of black juveniles obtaining a caution are considerably smaller than those of their white counterparts. Particular attention is focused on crimes of violence and " public disorder and similar offences ", for which blacks are treated more harshly at both stages of police decision-making. A distinction is made between substantive non-legal variables (*e.g.* parental control) as opposed to discriminatory non-legal variables (*e.g.* ethnic group). Data from the present study together with data from national surveys suggest that the harsher treatment given to black juveniles is a result of the extensive use of substantive criteria by the juvenile bureaux. It is recommended, therefore, that the juvenile bureaux adopt a more formal approach, based more directly on the juvenile's previous record and on the severity and circumstances of the offence. As a result, a more balanced representation of blacks among juveniles sent to court may be achieved. Suggestions were made regarding further research on this topic.

REFERENCES

BECKER, H. S. (1963). *Outsiders: Studies in the Sociology of Deviance.* New York: Free Press.

BENNETT, T. (1979). " The social distribution of criminal labels". *British Journal of Criminology,* **19,** 134–145.

BLACK, D. J. and REISS, A. J. (1970). " Police control of juveniles ". *American Sociological Review,* **35,** 63–77.

CHESNEY-LIND, M. (1973). "Judicial enforcement of the female sex role: The family court and the female delinquent ". *Issues in Criminology,* **8,** 51–67.

COHEN, L. E. and KLUEGEL, J. R. (1978). "Determinants of juvenile court dispositions: Ascriptive and achieved factors in two metropolitan courts." *American Sociological Review,* **43,** 162–176.

COHN, Y. (1963). " Criteria for the probation officer's recommendation to the juvenile court judge ". *Crime and Delinquency,* **9,** 262–275.

COX, D. R. (1970). *The Analysis of Binary Data.* London: Methuen.

DEPARTMENT OF THE ENVIRONMENT. (1979). *National Dwelling and Housing Survey.* London: Government Statistical Service, HMSO.

DITCHFIELD, J. A. (1976). *Police Cautioning in England and Wales.* Home Office Research Study No. 37, London: HMSO.

DIXON, W. J. and BROWN, M. B. (1979). *BMDP-79.* Berkeley, Calif.: University of California Press.

SIMHA F. LANDAU AND GAD NATHAN

ELLIOT, D. S., AGETON, S. S. and CANTER, R. J. (1979). " An integrated theoretical perspective on delinquent behaviour ". *Journal of Research in Crime and Delinquency*, **16,** 3–27.

ERIKSON, K. T. (1962). " Notes on the sociology of deviance ". *Social Problems*, **9,** 307–314.

FORD, D. (1975). *Children, Courts and Caring*. London: Constable.

GLUECK, S. and GLUECK, E. (1970). Working mothers and delinquency. In: *The Sociology of Crime and Delinquency* (2nd ed.), ed. by M. E. Wolfgang, L. Savitz and N. Johnston. New York: Wiley, pp. 496–498.

HARTJEN, C. A. (1978). *Crime and Criminalisation*, (2nd ed.). New York: Praeger.

HELLUM, F. (1979). " Juvenile justice: The second revolution ". *Crime and Delinquency*, (1969). **25,** 299–317.

HIRSCHI, T. (1969). *Causes of Delinquency*, Berkeley, California: University of California Press.

HORWITZ, A. and WASSERMAN, M. (1980). " Formal rationality, substantive justice and discrimination". *Law and Human Behavior*, **4,** 103-115.

KITSUSE, J. I. (1962). " Societal reaction to deviant behavior: Problems of theory and method ". *Social Problems*, **9,** 247–256.

LANDAU, S. F. (1978). " Do legal variables predict police decisions regarding the prosecution of juvenile offenders? " *Law and Human Behavior*, **2,** 95–105.

LANDAU, S. F. (1979). " Discrimination in the handling of juvenile offenders by the police: Some Israeli findings ". *Delinquency and Social Deviance*, **7,** 159–168 (Hebrew).

LANDAU, S. F. (1981). " Juveniles and the police: Who is charged immediately and who is referred to the juvenile bureau? " *British Journal of Criminology*, **21,** 27–46.

LEMERT, E. M. (1951). *Social Pathology: A Systematic Approach to the Theory of Sociopathic Behavior*. New York: McGraw-Hill.

LEMERT, E. M. (1967). *Human Deviance, Social Problems and Social Control*. Englewood Cliffs, N.J.: Prentice Hall.

London Facts and Figures (1978), No. 5, Greater London Council.

MATZA, D. (1964). *Delinquency and Drift*. New York: Wiley.

MATZA, D. (1969). *Becoming Deviant*. Englewood Cliffs, N.J.: Prentice-Hall.

MAWBY, R. I., McCULLOCH, J. W. and BATTA, I. D. (1979). " Crime amongst Asian juveniles in Bradford ". *International Journal of the Sociology of Law*. **7,** 297–306.

MORRIS, A., GILLER, H., SZWED, E. and GEACH, H. (1980). *Justice for Children*. London: Macmillan.

OLIVER, I. T. (1973). " The Metropolitan Police Juvenile Bureau Scheme ". *Criminal Law Review*. August, 499–506.

President's Commission on Law Enforcement and Administration of Justice (1967). *Task Force Report: Juvenile Delinquency and Youth Crime*. Washington D.C.: U.S. Government Printing Office.

QUINNEY, R. (1970). *The Social Reality of Crime*. Boston: Little Brown.

RUBIN, H. T. (1979). " Retain the juvenile court? Legislative developments, reform directions and the call for abolition ". *Crime and Delinquency*, **25,** 281–298.

SELECTING DELINQUENTS FOR CAUTIONING

SCARMAN, LORD. (1981). *Report of an Inquiry: The Brixton Disorders, 10–12 April 1981.* London: HMSO.

SCHUR, E. M. (1971). *Labelling Deviant Behavior: Its Sociological Implications.* New York: Harper and Row.

SCHUR, E. M. (1973). *Radical Non-Intervantion: Rethinking the Delinquency Problem.* Englewood Cliffs, N.J.: Prentice-Hall.

STEVENS, P. and WILLIS, F. (1979). *Race, Crime and Arrests.* Home Office Research Study No. 58. London: HMSO.

TERRY, R. M. (1967). Discrimination in the handling of juvenile offenders by social control agencies," *Journal of Research in Crime and Delinquency,* **4,** 218–230.

THOMAS, C. W. and CAGE, R. J. (1977). " The effect of social characteristics on juvenile court dispositions ". *Sociological Quarterly.* **18,** 237–252.

THOMPSON, E. J. and PERETZ, J. (1979). *Social Trends,* No. 9 (1979 ed.). Central Statistical Office. London: HMSO.

TUCK, M. and SOUTHGATE, P. (1981). *Ethnic Minorities, Crime and Policing.* Home Office Research Study No. 70. London: HMSO.

WEBER, M. (1954). *Max Weber on Law in Economy and Society,* ed. by M. Rheinstein Cambridge Mass: Harvard University Press.

[12]

Black Mayors and Police Policies

Grace Hall Saltzstein
University of California, Riverside

This study examines the impact of black mayors on police department policies of interest to black citizens in 105 municipal governments in the United States. The correlates of community-oriented policing, minority recruitment, black representation among sworn officers, citizen controls over department policies, and departmental responses to public disorder incidents are examined, and the presence of a black mayor during the time frame in question is found to be associated with both black representation among sworn officers and adoption of citizen controls over the department. The implications of these findings for the study of black mayoral influence are explored.

A substantial body of literature now exists assessing the correlates of black representation in federal, state, and local bureaucracies (Meier and Nigro, 1976; Dye and Renick, 1981; Eisinger, 1982), on city school boards (Welch and Karnig, 1978; Robinson and England, 1981), and on city councils (Engstrom and McDonald, 1981; MacManus, 1978; Karnig and Welch, 1982). Consequently, though a number of controversies remain unresolved, we now know quite a bit about the socioeconomic, political, and structural factors which facilitate or impede the representation of blacks in such institutions.

What we still know little about is the impact of black representation on policy. While the symbolic value of black political representation is hardly to be discounted in a system of representative democracy, most advocates for and analysts of black political representation have assumed that increases in such representation ultimately will find expression in public policy. The research issue in this regard concerns whether and to what extent "passive" or descriptive representation (which depends upon representatives' characteristics, such as sex or race) is linked with "active" or substantive representation of the interests of those groups represented.

While active representation can take a variety of forms, such as representative-constituent policy agreement, or service, allocative, or symbolic responsiveness (Eulau and Karps, 1977), most analysts have looked for evidence of the provision of collective benefits to blacks (allocative responsiveness) to suggest the presence of such representation. Case studies have suggested that black officials can and do allocate benefits to the black community (Keech, 1968; Campbell and Feagin, 1975; Nelson and Meranto, 1977), but, as Eisinger notes (1982, p. 381), ". . . they have not always been able to distinguish with precision those consequences that occurred as a direct function of black power . . . nor have they sorted out in any systematic way alternative or contributing explanations for black gains." Yet attempts to test for a link between passive and active representation of blacks' interests across a large number of jurisdictions have been limited and, with a few notable exceptions (Eisinger, 1982; Meier and England, 1984; Browning, Marshall, and Tabb, 1984), have done little to clarify the problem.

Those studies which have looked at the impact of black mayors on policy illustrate some of the difficulties. For example, Keller (1978), in studying public expenditures over several years in three cities with black mayors and three cities with white mayors, concludes that "it is not clear" that black mayors spend more on welfare-type functions or programs. Yet Karnig and Welch (1980) find that black mayors in a sample of 135 cities did spend more for social welfare but spent less for most physical facilities, protective services, and community amenities. Such apparently contradictory findings are common, and critics argue that the fault lies, at least in part, with reliance on expenditures as policy indicators. As Meier and England (1984) note, conceptualization of allocative responsiveness to blacks requires policy indicators which are clearly linked to black wishes or needs and which can be altered or affected by the actions of government officials. Expenditure data have been criticized on both grounds (Schuman and Gruenberg, 1972; Eisinger, 1982; Meier and England, 1984; Ostrom, 1983), as being too dependent on law, history, or economics, and thus not subject to short-term influences of government officials; and as requiring "some questionable assumptions about which broad areas are of greater or lesser importance to the black electorate and black politicians" (Eisinger, 1982, p. 382).

A number of analysts have sought to avoid the perils of assigning black interests to expenditure categories by focusing upon the possible link between black officials and employment representation of blacks within the governmental workforce (Dye and Renick, 1981; Eisinger, 1982; see Stein, 1986, on minorities). While still subject to the constraints of law, history, or economics (see Ostrom, 1983; Schneider, 1980, on police employment), public employment is less subject to such influences than are expenditures (Wanat, 1976). Further, employment of blacks is clearly a tangible, unambiguous benefit to those employed and can be of great benefit to the black community in general. A link between black or minority officials and municipal employment of minorities has been established by analysts (see Eisinger, 1982; Stein, 1986), yet we are left with the question as to whether such a link represents simply some contemporary form of a "spoils system" or whether it is part of a broader form of ethnic politics influencing a wide variety of municipal programs and policies. To date, we know very little about whether or

Black Mayors and Police Policies   527

under what circumstances black mayors are linked with nonemployment, nonexpenditure policy outputs.

Some related research suggests what could be done to examine this question. Meier and England (1984) build on the work of Bullock and Stewart (1979) regarding "second generation discrimination" by exploring the link between black school board representation and black versus white students' involvement in various educational programs. Browning, Marshall, and Tabb (1984) examine the impact of black and Hispanic political incorporation on a variety of policy outputs in ten California cities. However, school governance is quite distinctive and black/white participation ratios are not so readily created in other program arenas, so we can't be sure how the active and passive representation links identified by Meier and England would hold up in regard to black mayors and municipal government policies. Similarly, Browning, Marshall, and Tabb do not look at the impact of black mayors and, because of their small sample, are not able to control for the potentially confounding effects of a variety of social, economic, and political factors.

BLACK MAYORS AND POLICE POLICIES

This study seeks to explore questions of black mayoral influence in the context of municipal police departments' programs and policies. For some time, urban police departments have been a focus of pressures for policies more responsive to minorities. The possible police role in contributing to or exacerbating racial tensions, triggering riots, blocking legitimate minority aspirations, and shaping minority perceptions of justice and equity in contemporary society have been a subject of interest to broad segments of society at numerous times (Altshuler, 1970; Hahn, 1971; Rossi, Berk, and Eidson, 1974).

Police departments have been accused of blatantly racist and repressive practices in so many black communities (Levine, 1974; Nelson and Meranto, 1977) that it is not surprising that many black majors have campaigned on explicit pledges to "control" the police by pushing for adoption of specific programs and policies designed to better serve the needs or wishes of the black community. Yet, black mayors have often found it difficult to alter police/minority relations when confronted with socially-polarized, majority-dominated police bureaucracies and unions (e.g., Eisinger, 1980). Programs which have been advanced to enhance police/minority group relations are many and varied and meet with differing levels of support in black communities. Yet, if black mayors are inclined toward the practice of ethnic politics, we should certainly expect to see that inclination manifested in the adoption of at least some police practices, unless other factors intervene.

The sample utilized to test for such a link represents the universe of U.S. municipal police departments employing at least 100 full-time personnel in

528   Grace Hall Saltzstein

cities with a black population equal to at least 5% of the total as of 1970 ($N =$ 169).[1] Individual departments were surveyed by mail regarding specific department programs, procedures, and organizational characteristics. One hundred thirty-six departments responded to the survey; complete data for this analysis were obtained for 105 of those (62.1% of the total sample). The final data set includes departments in cities which range in size from 37,000 to 1.6 million (1970 population) and have black populations comprising between 5.2% and 7% of the total population of the city.[2] A complete list of the cities in which sample departments are located can be found in the appendix, with cities having black mayors during some or all of this period denoted by asterisks.

RESPONSIVE POLICE OUTPUTS

As noted earlier, analysts have experienced difficulties in selecting policy indicators which are clearly linked to race and subject to influence by specific elected or appointed officials. Further, few analysts have looked at more than one or a small number of policy indicators, thus limiting their ability to generalize about representation. Hence, this analysis seeks to tap an array of police policies widely supported by blacks to see which, if any, appear linked to the presence of a black mayor. In that regard, individual departments were questioned about the presence or absence, as of 1984, of a wide variety of programs and policies as well as basic features of implementation and adoption dates. In addition, departments were asked to provide copies of reports detailing the representation, as of 1984, of blacks in the ranks of full-time sworn officers.[3]

Table 1 lists the policies considered and their incidence in these departments as of 1984. As is evident, there is considerable variation in the utilization of different programs. Some, such as neighborhood watch programs and formal restrictions on the use of fatal force, have achieved such widespread use as to foreclose their ability to differentiate departments,[4] while others, such as team policing (designed to make police operations more responsive to localized needs),[5] are not as widely used.

[1] The range was selected so as to include departments large enough to provide a full range of police services and have established routines.

[2] Respondents were compared with non-respondents in terms of department size, city population, geographic region, form of government, and a number of other features. No significant differences were evident, though the sample appears to slightly overrepresent mayor-council cities and to underrepresent the very largest cities.

[3] Employment data are listed on EEO-4 reports filed annually with the Federal government.

[4] Much more subtle differences in the nature of those formal restrictions on the use of fatal force must be charted to differentiate departments.

[5] Team policing provides "an attempt to decentralize the policy organization to make it more responsive to the localized needs and interests of neighborhood and community group" and

Black Mayors and Police Policies 529

TABLE 1

PRESENCE OF MINORITY-ORIENTED COMMUNITY OUTREACH PROGRAMS
IN MUNICIPAL POLICE DEPARTMENTS, 1984

	Number of Departments	Percent of Total ($N = 136$)
Team Policing in Minority Neighborhoods	25	21.6
Development of Neighborhood Watch Programs in Minority Neighborhoods	113	97.4
Regular Meetings with Minority Groups	88	75.9
Formal Departmental Restrictions on the Use of Fatal Force	115	99.1
Creation of Civilian Review Board	16	13.8
Storefront Offices in Minority Communities	31	26.7
Use of Integrated or All-Black Recruitment Teams	67	53.2
Recruitment Visits to Minority Community Centers	77	61.1
Advertising Job Openings in Minority News Media	84	66.7
Providing Pre-exam Counseling and Training to Black Applicants	45	35.7
Use of Special Selection Standards for Minority Applicants	16	12.7
Existence of Department AA Plan	84	67.7

	Minimum	Maximum	$\bar{X}$
Black/Nonblack Ratio Among Sworn Police Officers ($N = 114$)	.08	56.4%	11.8

One output which is singled out for examination here is the establishment of a Civilian Review Board to oversee selected police activities. Browning, Marshall, and Tabb (1984) find adoption of such boards, in their sample of ten California cities, to be linked to minority incorporation into the dominant governing coalition, noting that minority leaders throughout the country "often advocated the creation of civilian review boards as a means of publicizing and investigating incidents of excessive use of force by police" (p. 152). As of 1984, less than 15% of the sample cities examined here had a Civilian Review Board in place; fewer than 70% of those had authorization to investigate citizen complaints against the department and fewer than 40%

---

usually involves "stability of patrol through permanent assignment of police teams to small areas or neighborhoods" (Johnson, Misner, and Brown, 1981, p. 135).

had authorization to review most or all department policies. As an indicator of the extent of citizen oversight into departmental affairs, the Civilian Review Board measure is assigned one point each for the presence of a Civilian Review Board as of 1984, authorization to investigate citizen complaints, and authority to review most or all department policies.

Because so many other programs and policies were considered and many appear to be similar type of policies, correlations between policies were examined for possible patterns of incidence. While some policies are intercorrelated, not all are, so data reduction techniques were employed to search for the presence of clusters of policies. Individual programs were first coded as a zero if the program was not provided at any time between 1975 and 1984, a one if it had been adopted by 1984, a two if it had been in existence since 1980, and a three if it had been adopted as early as 1975. The coding scheme thus assumes that early adoption is a sign of greater responsiveness.[6]

Factor analysis was employed to indicate appropriate groupings of programs. Two separate factors accounted for 33% and 23% of the variance, respectively, with three different programs loading highly on each factor. No other factors were significant, and the remaining program indicators did not load highly on either of these two factors. The first factor shows high loadings for regular meetings with black community groups, utilization of team policing, and operation of storefront offices in minority communities. It is thus assumed to represent a style of community-oriented policing geared to the specific needs of the black community, an approach to policing that finds strong support in black communities. The second factor clearly represents minority recruitment efforts, with high loadings on the use of integrated recruitment teams, advertising in minority media sources, and provision of pre-exam counseling for minority applicants to the police department. Factor scores are utilized throughout the analysis to represent community-oriented policing and minority recruitment efforts.

While demands for more expansive efforts to recruit blacks have been strong, black communities have also pressed demands for immediate, tangible results in terms of greater black representation among the ranks of sworn officers. Because so many formal and informal barriers to employment in police departments disproportionately affect black applicants, it has been assumed that much can be done to increase black representation in the ranks of uniformed officers even in the absence of an expanded black applicant pool (Preston, 1977) and black mayors have moved to do just that (Eisinger, 1982). Consequently, expanding minority recruitment and increasing black representation are efforts which can be and are pursued simultaneously,

---

[6]Similarities to assumptions made by Browning, Marshall, and Tabb (1984) are evident, as they code adoption of a Police Civilian Review Board as zero for no board, one for consideration without adoption, and two for consideration and adoption.

Black Mayors and Police Policies   531

with the latter not entirely dependent on the former.[7] Representation here is measured by the percentage of blacks among the ranks of full-time, sworn police officers as of 1984.[8]

One final dependent variable is included in the analysis to represent a policy which does not engender a clear position from the black community. Police departments generally exercise a fair amount of discretion in handling incidents such as drunk and disorderly, vagrancy, loitering, noise, and similar offenses (known generally as public disorder offenses), and responses can vary from the quite informal (verbal admonitions, driving a drunk home, etc.), somewhat less informal (referral or transport to an appropriate social service agency), to the more formal (official diversion to a public or private program, or arrest). Yet, police and public officials in general get mixed signals from the minority community as to the "appropriate" or desired response to such incidents. Given the crowded housing patterns and unemployment rates in predominantly black communities, blacks are more likely than whites to be part of public disorder incidents. If the usual department policy is one of arrest in such circumstances, critics may (and do) interpret that response as police harassment or discrimination. On the other hand, other members of minority communities (especially the elderly and homeowners), who may be disturbed by incidents of public disorder in the neighborhood, often object to what they perceive as a more lax standard of treatment of such incidents. Consequently, black mayors would have to look to their black community for clearer signals as to how to respond.

Considerable pressures arose during the late sixties and early seventies to "decriminalize" such incidents, and many police departments were constrained by law to handle incidents with informal responses, such as diversion. Departments were queried regarding their usual response to such incidents and any legal constraints on that response,[9] and the first measure is used as a dependent variable in an analysis which subdivides the sample between those cities with above-average rates of black homeownership (linked to demands for formal responses to public disorder) and those with below-average rates of black homeownership.

INDEPENDENT VARIABLES

Any given set of police policies is likely to emerge as a consequence of a variety of forces internal and external to the police organization. In order to

[7] Further support for this assumption is evident in the low correlation between scores on the minority recruitment factor and actual levels of black representation ($r = -.04$).

[8] While some indicator of parity in representation might be utilized (by dividing black employment representation by the percentage of blacks in the city), the interest here is to test for any such linkages. Further, in many cases, the pressure from black communities has been for more police jobs, not simply the proper share of those jobs.

[9] The legal requirements are included as a control variable in subsequent statistical analyses.

assess the impact of black mayors on police policies across a large number of cities, we must attempt to account for all plausible competing explanations for the presence of any given policy. Consequently, we must consider a variety of community, political, and organizational characteristics associated with police outputs.

Virtually any analysis of responsiveness to black demands assumes that such responsiveness is likely to have some connection with the percentage representation of blacks in a community population, either as a consequence of the sheer weight of demands, the needs which those numbers represent, or of the potential electoral mobilization inherent in population shares. The black population percentage in each city as of 1980 is thus included as an indicator of black community characteristics on the assumption that cities with larger proportions of black citizens will be more likely to provide police policies to benefit the black community.

However, it does not seem likely that urban police departments would respond to their black communities as undifferentiated masses, significant only in their size. Studies of both micro- and macro-level providers suggest that service providers at any level are more responsive to certain types of citizens or clients. Agencies and street-level bureaucrats appear to be more receptive to claims from stable, responsible clients (Stone, 1977; Lipsky, 1979); for other reasons, cities may tend to be more responsive to property-taxpayers (Peterson, 1981). Given the sociology of urban policing (Skolnick, 1966), it seems that police departments might be more likely to respond to the wishes of the black community if that community includes a large number of what are perceived to be stable, responsible citizens (e.g., homeowners). Further, the size of the black homeowning population is likely to provide an essential clue to black mayors and police departments as to how the police should respond to public disorder incidents. The percentage of the black population which are homeowners is thus assumed to be linked to more responsive policies.

Employment studies and studies of police accountability both suggest that an important intervening variable in the translation of black demands into police outputs might be the form of government in the city. After years of research on the question, analysts still assume that "reform" governments are likely to be "sluggish" in responding to newer political forces (Levine, Rubin, and Wolohojian, 1981). Those features which professionalize the operations of government under such systems also insulate those operations from external influences, including the influences of elected municipal officers. Some analysts thus see government form acting as a constraint on mayoral influence on city outputs (Kuo, 1973; Karnig and Welch, 1980; Saltzstein, 1986), while studies of police accountability similarly have postulated a more limited impact of elected officials on police programs and policies in non-machine or weak-machine settings (see Kahn, 1979). Reformism is represented in this analysis as each city's score on a scale representing council-manager form of government, nonpartisan local elections, and mostly or all at-large elections.

Because the analysis focuses upon the outputs of a single municipal department, it is necessary to control also for organizational features which might lead to particular outputs. Analysts attest to the considerable autonomy of municipal bureaucracies in general (Lowi, 1967; Sayre and Kaufman, 1965; Banfield and Wilson, 1963), while numerous studies emphasize the singular autonomy of urban police departments in particular (Skolnick, 1966; Nardulli and Stonecash, 1981). A significant component of the literature on police behavior and outputs stresses the importance of internal organizational characteristics and procedures in determining outputs (Skolnick, 1966; Wilson, 1968a; Goldstein, 1977). Within that genre of research, an emphasis on "styles" of policing is clearly evident, with departments arrayed along a continuum between professional and nonprofessional organizations (Skolnick, 1966; Neiderhoffer, 1969; Wilson, 1968b). Operations of professional departments are presumed to be "characterized by frequent use of arrests to settle disputes, formalistic applications of the law, low levels of corruption, efficiency in handling routine matters, and high levels of skill in the use of equipment" while less professional departments are presumed to be "more flexible and informal in defining and carrying out their responsibilities" (Henderson, 1975).

Thus, though not a direct measure of police performance, professionalism is presumed to be related significantly to police performance and policy. A wide variety of police department characteristics have been associated with professionalism (Feuille and Juris, 1976; Rudoni, Baker, and Meyer, 1978). An array of such variables were subjected to factor analysis here, producing a single factor with high positive loadings on department reliance on civilian employees, use of numerous entry requirements, higher education requirements for entry-level personnel, and the presence of specialized police personnel functions separate from city personnel systems. Factor scores on this measure are utilized throughout the analysis as indicators of professionalism, with an assumption that professionalism will be associated with a propensity to arrest in public disorder cases, more limited acceptance of community-oriented (i.e., particularistic) policing, and lower levels of minority recruitment and minority representation among sworn officers.[10]

Another major organizational characteristic which is presumed to inter-

---

[10] Low levels of minority representation in the sworn ranks is presumed to be an unintended consequence of professionalism. While the universalistic criteria evident in professional departments would limit the effect of overt racism in hiring, the more rigid standards and entry requirements of professional departments are likely to have a disproportionate negative impact on black applicants (Feagin and Feagin, 1978).

vene in the translation of pressures into outputs reflects the extent of organizational insulation from outside influences. Just as reform features serve to buffer the larger municipal organization from the pressure of residents and elected officials, some specific institutional practices of police departments can serve to insulate the department from the influence of residents, elected officials, and the larger municipal bureaucracy. The influence of elected officials, black or white, on police operations is clearly diminished by placing control over appointments and dismissals in the hands of "neutral" managers according to objective standards, with merit appointments and civil service tenure. Highly-developed civil service systems, thus, have been presumed to insulate departments from external pressures (Nardulli and Stonecash, 1981; Thompson, 1975; Stein, 1986). Factor analysis was used to identify a single factor indicating departmental insulation from influence through the personnel process, with high positive loadings on the extensiveness of police civil service coverage, the restrictiveness of hiring certification rules, and the extent of reliance on formal, written exams for ranking candidates. It is assumed that greater insulation provides departments with the capacity to exercise their own preferences in regard to policy; the likely direction of that response depends upon which other factors influence department preferences.

Analysts have noted resource constraints as a major limitation on the ability of black mayors "to translate their policy initiatives into policy" (Karnig and Welch, 1980, p. 114). Because many, if not all, police policies and programs require resources, some measures of resource availability are needed in the analysis. Resource expenditures, in the form of equipment, personnel, and money, have been linked to several measures of police effectiveness (The Urban Institute, 1972; Skogan, 1976). Larger departments are more likely to be able to redeploy personnel to staff a new program, even if additional positions cannot be obtained.[11] Similarly, departments which spend more, relative to the size of the community, are likely to have greater slack resources to use to begin a new program or augment an existing one. Consequently, the log of department size and the per capita expenditures of the

---

[11] Similar arguments could be advanced regarding the potential impact of department growth or decline on programs and policies, especially in the case of minority recruitment and actual black representation among sworn officers. However, department growth (in terms of employment change from 1976 to 1983) is highly negatively correlated with 1975 department size ($r = -.68$), such that both variables cannot be used in the same equation. A duplicate analysis, using employment change instead of department size in each equation, was performed with nearly identical results to those presented here. In the case of 1984 black representation among sworn officers, then, it does not appear that employment declines are consistently associated with lower representation levels in 1984. It is most likely that employment declines are reflected in declines in black employment representation over time in cities rather than in general representation levels at a single point in time.

Black Mayors and Police Policies 535

department as of 1975 are included here on the assumption that greater resources at the beginning of the time period in question (1975–1984) are likely to be positively associated with the adoption during this period of policies responsive to the black community.

An additional variable considered in the case of minority recruitment and employment representation only is the presence or absence of some form of legal pressure to increase minority representation among sworn officers. Legal pressure is coded as a one if the department operated under either a court order or a consent decree affecting minority hiring at any time during the period from 1973 through 1983.

The final independent variable considered in the analysis represents the potential influence of black mayors. Twenty-four cities in the sample had black mayors in office at some time during the ten-year period from 1974 through 1983; five of these had one or more black mayors in office during the entire period. Because it is assumed that opportunities to influence police policies increase with the number of years during which blacks hold office, black mayoral influence is assigned one point for each year during which a black held the position of mayor. The count is adjusted for each dependent variable so that black mayoral presence is counted only for the years preceding adoption of any given policy. Thus, in those cases in which a black did not hold the mayor's office until some time after a particular program or policy had been adopted, black mayoral influence is coded as a zero.

ANALYSIS

Multiple regression analysis is utilized to examine the impact of black community characteristics, government characteristics, departmental characteristics, and black mayors on the various indicators of responsiveness in policing. In the case of police responses to public disorder incidents, two separate regressions are run, one for cities with above-average rates of black homeownership and one for cities with below-average rates. The findings are presented in table 2.

Nearly all of the equations are significant and do provide some insight into the variability of correlates of different police policies and into the role of black mayors.[12] In the aggregate, black mayors appear to exert an influence independent of other factors in only a limited number of cases of police policies examined here. In those cases where the influence of black mayors is not significant, other influences clearly outweigh any potential mayoral influence. Consequently, a closer examination of those outputs which are not linked, at the aggregate level, to black mayoral influence may suggest some of the limits on that influence.

[12] Though the explained variation is modest in all but a couple of cases, that is not unexpected in dealing with programmatic output variables (see Meier and England, 1984).

TABLE 2

IMPACT OF COMMUNITY, POLITICAL, AND ORGANIZATIONAL FACTORS ON POLICE POLICIES

Independent Variable	Community-Oriented Policing	Minority Recruitment	Black Representation among Sworn Officers	Citizen Control over Department	Usual Response to Public Disorder[b]	
					Cities w/Above-Average Homeownership	Cities w/Below-Average Homeownership
% Black Population	.32[a]*	.19	.59*	-.04	-.35*	.02
% Black Homeowners	-.05	-.04	-.06	-.15	—	—
Reformism	.04	.10	.04	-.02	.09	.04
Legal Pressure	—	.15	.06	—	—	—
Department Size	.25*	.23*	-.02	.10	-.03	.06
Per capita Department Expenditures	.11	.15	-.20*	-.17	.10	.10
Department Insulation	.14	.08	.02	.07	-.29*	-.20
Department Professionalism	.09	.08	.16*	.21*	.07	-.04
Legal Requirements	—	—		—	.31*	.52*
Black Mayor	-.13	.04	.31*	.30*	-.15	-.19
R^2	.22*	.23*	.77*	.20*	.37*	.19

[a] Standardized regression coefficients.
[b] Responses range from -2 (arrest in most cases) to +2 (very informal responses in most cases).
* Significant at .05 or less.

Black Mayors and Police Policies   537

Community-oriented approaches to policing, as measured here, appear to be most closely associated with a substantial black percentage in the community and, secondarily, with greater departmental resources in the form of larger numbers of police personnel. The link with black population representation does suggest some attempt to meet black community needs or wishes through these types of programs though it may also suggest that a relatively large black population is required before departments are likely to feel that such particularistic resource expenditures are justified. The correlation with department size similarly suggests that programs which are resource intensive, such as team policing or meetings with minority groups, are also necessarily dependent upon resource availability. Hence, their provision will depend upon the availability of slack personnel resources and will be less susceptible to mayoral influence.

A similar pattern applies to minority recruitment efforts. While the extent of recruitment has little to do with the representation of blacks in the community and is not significantly linked to court pressure, recruitment efforts like community-oriented programs are dependent upon the presence of departmental resources. Larger departments, even those under no legal pressure to do so, are more likely to provide an extensive array of minority recruitment techniques, an act which may have a lot to do with having the personnel to run such programs but which may not mean much in terms of actual representation.

While black mayors also are not linked to specific responses to public disorder incidents, the correlates of alternative responses differ somewhat from the previous examples. First, black homeownership does provide a significant cue as to what response is desired by the black community, but this appears to be true primarily for cities with higher-than-average rates of black homeownership. Only the legal requirements prove significant in explaining police response in cities with below-average rates of homeownership, and the equation in that subsample is insignificant.

For cities with above-average black homeownership, however, the situation is more complex. Legal constraints (which almost always require an informal response) play a significant role but are actually less powerful a predictor than the black population percentage and are only slightly more significant than the extent of police department insulation. Both black population and department insulation are associated with a greater propensity to arrest or otherwise resolve disorder incidents in a formal fashion. Thus, more insulated departments in communities with above-average rates of black homeownership are more likely to treat such incidents as crimes and exercise what might be considered the traditional propensity of police departments to resolve disputes through arrest. Even more important, where high rates of black homeownership are combined with relatively large black populations, departments are much more likely to respond to public dis-

order by arresting the offenders. The cue-giving function served by black
population size and homeownership, irrespective of the race of the mayor, in
this case proves the best predictor of police department action in an ambiguous policy setting. The lack of an independent impact of black mayors on
policy response in this case may suggest that black mayors feel more cross-
pressured in this instance and, when looked at in the aggregate, are somewhat less likely to view their representational responsibilities solely in terms
of representing the interests of homeowners, even black ones.

Though black mayors are not significantly associated, in aggregate terms,
with the policies considered thus far, it is not too surprising to find a link
between black mayors and black representation among sworn police. If black
mayors focus "on jobs that count" (Eisinger, 1982, p. 387), then they should
certainly emphasize high-paying, high-visibility sworn police positions; and
if they want to "control the police," creation of a more representative bureaucracy provides a mechanism for asserting internal control (Fairchild,
1978). As always, however, the primary determinant of black employment
representation is the percentage representation of blacks in the community.
Nonetheless, the amount of representation among sworn police accounted
for in this fashion (39%) is lower than that explained in studies of general
municipal employment (Stein, 1986), indicating the greater restrictiveness of
police hiring which impedes the direct translation of population representation into job shares.

Yet, even after controlling for the availability of black recruits, the presence of a black mayor accounts for an additional, significant increment in the
representation of blacks among sworn police ranks. Each year a black holds
the mayor's office translates into a 1.5% higher level of black representation
among the ranks of sworn officers, as compared to cities with comparable
black populations. Black mayors obviously emphasize black representation
in police departments and are associated with higher levels of representation
even though they do not, apparently, pursue expanded black recruitment
efforts.

The other two variables which are related significantly to employment
representation prove to be associated with such shares in a fashion other
than that predicted. Contrary to expectations, per capita expenditures are
negatively associated with black representation among sworn officers, while
professionalism is positively related. However, these may not be anomalous
findings at all but rather suggest a need for rethinking the original hypotheses in the context of employment allocations. In such a context, it is important to note that police activity is extremely personnel-intensive, with higher
per capita expenditures linked to higher police salaries (Schneider, 1980).
Thus, departments with high per capita expenditures pay higher salaries,
which are most likely more attractive to nonblack applicants. Such a setting

Black Mayors and Police Policies   539

is conducive to a competitive employment arena, in which blacks are more likely to lose out to white applicants.

Similarly, the original hypothesis that the rigidities and higher standards of professional departments would disadvantage blacks to a greater extent than would traditional, informal barriers may underestimate the extent and importance of informal barriers to black representation among sworn officers. The fact that black mayors are linked to increases in black employment without making changes in personnel procedures lends credence to the notion that informal barriers have operated to exclude blacks. If so, professional departments, with their impersonal, impartial standards, would be more likely to fairly represent blacks within their ranks. Additional analysis, accounting for more specific effects of informal barriers and professional procedures, is warranted in regard to this issue.

Another significant impact of black mayoral influence is evident in regard to the presence of citizen controls over the police department. Here, the presence of black mayors is the single best predictor of the adoption of Civilian Review Boards with authority to investigate citizen complaints. Further, this relationship appears quite independent of black community characteristics, with no link evident between the size of the black population or the black homeownership rate and citizen control over the police department. In fact, the only significant factor other than black mayoral presence is department professionalism, with more professional departments somewhat more likely to have adopted such provisions by 1984.

Thus, in examining the array of policies considered here, we find statistically significant evidence of black mayoral influence in two cases but not in others. This does not mean that individual black mayors in specific cities did not pursue such policies, but only suggests that there was no clear, consistent connection between the presence of black mayors and the adoption of such policies across a large number of cities during this time frame. The apparent lack of a link between black mayoral power and policy outputs could occur for a variety of reasons—black mayors or black communities might not consider these consistently high-priority issues in all communities; black mayors might not be successful in getting even high-priority policies adopted; or resource or demographic factors simply may be much more important in the aggregate than political power in getting certain kinds of policies adopted.

Numerous analysts have noted significant constraints on mayoral power in general (Kuo, 1973) while others have delineated serious limitations on black mayoral power (Karnig and Welch, 1980; Nelson and Meranto, 1977). Given the resource restraints in most municipalities, it perhaps should not be surprising to find no independent influence of black mayors on programs which require significant increases in personnel or other expenditures. Thus, as

was evident here, provision of such resource-intensive programs as community-oriented policing and special minority recruitment efforts should be expected only in departments with sufficient slack resources to pay the costs
without diverting resources from other programs.

Resource restraints are not as important in regard to police employment
or civilian review mechanisms. Mayors have a variety of ways to encourage
hiring of certain groups, through appointment of sympathetic personnel officials and department heads, alteration of personnel policies and rules, or
changes in the entire employment climate. Especially where informal practices have inhibited black access to employment, as in police employment,
black mayoral pressure and suasion may be sufficient to achieve substantial
gains in black representation. With ongoing new hiring and replacement
hiring, gains in employment shares may be possible with no specific resource
outlays to achieve that outcome.

CONCLUSIONS

This analysis does provide some limited support for the possibility of a
practice of a politics of ethnicity in American cities which would include not
just provision of divisible benefits, such as jobs, to blacks but also would provide programs and policies of interest to the black community in general.
While black mayoral influence is evident here only in regard to black police
employment and adoption of Civilian Review Boards, those linkages, when
examined in conjunction with policies where black mayoral influence is not
significant, suggest a number of features of black mayoral influence and of
approaches to studying that influence.

To some extent, analysts who have looked at black representatives' impact
on policy outputs across a large number of cities have been seeking to determine whether there is something which can be thought of as a black political
agenda in American cities (as has been suggested in some case studies) and to
determine the conditions under which that agenda has been or can be
achieved. Expenditure data have proven unsatisfactory to test such questions, while employment outputs have allowed for only a partial test. By
focusing on police employment *and* police programs, this analysis has sought
to explore these questions in a hotly-contested municipal policy arena,
where the outlines of a black policy agenda might be expected to be
discernable.

The analysis suggests that discerning such an agenda across a large number
of cities is difficult. While individual black mayors undoubtedly do respond
to black preferences with policy adoptions in specific cities, those responses
are sufficiently diverse as not to form a clear pattern when aggregated. Further, many policy alternatives have achieved such currency that they may be

adopted or implemented by police departments in response to stimuli other than the presence of a black mayor.

Thus, policies which have been identified as desirable to black communities in general may be provided in various communities simply because the black community is sufficiently large to justify such particularistic service provision or because sufficient resources are available to do so. When aggregated across a large number of cities, the presence of a black mayor in such cases may appear superfluous, constituting neither a necessary nor sufficient impetus to policy adoption.

A somewhat different problem is apparent in those cases in which the preferences of the black community might vary between cities. While police departments in general might be expected to respond more positively to the wishes of stable, "responsible" members of the black community, we shouldn't expect black mayors to define their representational roles in such simple terms. Black mayors may be cross-pressured in circumstances in which community preferences conflict, responding one way in one case and another way in others. Across a large number of cities, we would also expect to find differences between black mayors in their perceptions of their primary representational loyalties, such that responses where preferences vary would cancel one another out when aggregated.

Yet, despite all these difficulties, black mayors are linked, clearly and significantly, to at least two sets of police policy outputs examined here—police employment and the adoption of citizen controls over police department actions. While neither output need require significant resource expenditures, both might be expected to engender significant opposition from some members of the municipal organization and the community. Yet, black mayors apparently are able to overcome any political opposition in regard to at least two policy outputs desired by blacks, lending further support to a linkage between passive and active representation and suggesting that any "politics of ethnicity" practiced by black mayors may include more than the provision of public sector employment.

Manuscript submitted 28 March 1988
Final manuscript received 15 January 1989

APPENDIX

CITIES HOUSING SAMPLE POLICE DEPARTMENTS

*Birmingham, AL	Rockford, IL	Winston-Salem, NC
Huntsville, AL	Springfield, IL	Oklahoma City, OK
Mobile, AL	Anderson, IN	*Cincinnati, OH
Montgomery, AL	*Gary, IN	Columbus, OH
Fort Smith, AR	South Bend, IN	*Dayton, OH
Bakersfield, CA	Des Moines, IA	Toledo, OH
*Berkeley, CA	Topeka, KS	Portland, OR
*Compton, CA	Lexington, KY	Erie, PA
Fresno, CA	Louisville, KY	Reading, PA
Inglewood, CA	Baton Rouge, LA	Harrisburg, PA
Long Beach, CA	*New Orleans, LA	Charleston, SC
*Oakland, CA	Shreveport, LA	Greenville, SC
Pomona, CA	Boston, MA	Chattanooga, TN
*Richmond, CA	Cambridge, MA	Knoxville, TN
Sacramento, CA	*Grand Rapids, MI	Nashville, TN
San Bernardino, CA	*Saginaw, MI	Memphis, TN
San Diego, CA	*Ann Arbor, MI	Austin, TX
San Francisco, CA	Jackson, MS	Beaumont, TX
Stockton, CA	Omaha, NE	Dallas, TX
Denver, CO	Las Vegas, NV	Fort Worth, TX
*Hartford, CT	Elizabeth, NJ	Houston, TX
Wilmington, DE	*Newark, NJ	Lubbock, TX
*Gainesville, FL	*Plainfield, NJ	San Antonio, TX
Jacksonville, FL	Trenton, NJ	Waco, TX
Miami, FL	Buffalo, NY	Alexandria, VA
Orlando, FL	New Rochelle, NY	Chesapeake, VA
*Tallahassee. FL	Niagara Falls, NY	Hampton, VA
Tampa, FL	Rochester, NY	Norfolk, VA
*West Palm Beach, FL	Syracuse, NY	*Richmond, VA
Albany, GA	White Plains, NY	*Roanoke, VA
*Atlanta, GA	Yonkers, NY	Virginia Beach, VA
*Augusta, GA	Charlotte, NC	Tacoma, WA
*Macon, GA	Greensboro, NC	Huntington, WV
Evanston, IL	High Point, NC	Racine, WI
Peoria, IL	*Raleigh, NC	Milwaukee, WI

*Black mayor in office during some or all of the period 1974–1983.

REFERENCES

Altshuler, Alan. 1970. *Community Control.* New York: Pegasus.

Banfield, Edward C., and James Q. Wilson. 1963. *City Politics.* Cambridge: Harvard University Press.

Browning, Rufus P., Dale Rogers Marshall, and David Tabb. 1984. *Protest is Not Enough.* Berkeley: University of California Press.

Bullock, Charles S., III, and Joseph Stewart. 1979. Incidence and Correlates of Second-Generation Discrimination. In Marion L. Palley and Michael Preston, eds., *Race, Sex, and Policy Problems.* Lexington: Lexington Books.

Black Mayors and Police Policies 543

Campbell, David, and Joe R. Feagin. 1975. Black Politics in the South: A Descriptive Analysis. *Journal of Politics*, 37:129–59.

Dye, Thomas R., and James Renick. 1981. Political Power and City Jobs: Determinants of Minority Employment. *Social Science Quarterly*, 62:475–86.

Eisinger, Peter. 1980. *The Politics of Displacement*. New York: Academic Press.

———. 1982. Black Employment in Municipal Jobs: The Impact of Black Political Power. *American Political Science Review*, 76:380–92.

Engstrom, Richard L., and Michael McDonald. 1981. The Election of Blacks to City Councils. *American Political Science Review*, 75:344–54.

Eulau, Heinz, and Paul D. Karps. 1977. The Puzzle of Representation: Specifying Components of Responsiveness. *Legislative Studies Quarterly*, 2:233–54.

Fairchild, Erika. 1978. Enforcement of Police and Law Enforcement Policy. *Policy Studies Journal*, 7:442–49.

Feagin, Joe, and Claireece Feagin. 1978. *Discrimination American Style*. Englewood Cliffs: Prentice Hall.

Feuille, Peter, and Hervey Juris. 1976. Police Professionalization and Police Unions. *Sociology of Work and Occupations*, 3:88–113.

Goldstein, Herman. 1977. *Policing a Free Society*. Cambridge: Ballinger Publishing.

Hahn, Harlan. 1971. Local Variations in Urban Law Enforcement. In Peter Orleans and William R. Eillis, Jr., eds., *Race, Change and Urban Society*. Beverly Hills: Sage.

Henderson, Thomas A. 1975. The Relative Effects of Community Complexity and of Sheriffs upon the Professionalism of Sheriff Departments. *American Journal of Political Science*, 19:107–132.

Johnson, Thomas, Gordon E. Misner, and Lee P. Brown. 1981. *The Police and Society*. Englewood Cliffs: Prentice-Hall.

Kahn, Ronald. 1979. The Politics of Police Accountability: A Test of the Bureaucratic-State Approach to Political Change in Machine Cities. In Fred Meyer, Jr., and Ralph Baker, eds., *Determinants of Law-Enforcement Policies*. Lexington: D. C. Heath.

Karnig, Albert K., and Susan Welch. 1980. *Black Representation and Urban Policy*. Chicago: University of Chicago Press.

———. 1982. Electoral Structure and Black Representation on City Councils. *Social Science Quarterly*, 63:99–114.

Keech, William R. 1968. *The Impact of Negro Voting*. Chicago: Rand McNally.

Keller, E. J. 1978. The Impact of Black Mayors on Urban Policy. *The Annals*, 439:40–52.

Kuo, Wen. 1973. Mayoral Influence on Urban Policy-making. *American Journal of Sociology*, 79:620–28.

Levine, Charles H. 1974. *Racial Conflict and the American Mayor*. Lexington: D. C. Heath.

Levine, Charles H., Gene S. Rubin, and George G. Wolohojian. 1981. Resource Scarcity and the Reform Model: The Management of Retrenchment in Cincinnati and Oakland. *Public Administration Review*, 41:619–28.

Lipsky, Michael. 1979. *Street-Level Bureaucracy*. New York: Russell Sage Foundation.

Lowi, Theodore J. 1967. Machine Politics—Old and New. *Public Interest*, 9:83–92.

MacManus, Susan. 1978. City Council Election Procedures and Minority Representation: Are They Related? *Social Science Quarterly*, 59:153–61.

Meier, Kenneth J., and Robert E. England. 1984. Black Representation and Educational Policy: Are They Related? *American Political Science Review*, 78:392–403.

Meier, Kenneth J., and Lloyd G. Nigro. 1976. Representative Bureaucracy and Policy Preferences. *Public Administration Review*, 36:458–70.

Nardulli, Peter F., and Jeffrey Stonecash. 1981. *Politics, Professionalism, and Urban Services: The Police*. Cambridge: Oelgeschlager, Gunn and Hain.

Nelson, William E., and Phillip J. Meranto. 1977. *Electing Black Mayors*. Columbus: Ohio State University Press.

Niederhoffer, Arthur. 1969. *Behind the Shield: The Police in Urban Society.* Garden City: Doubleday.

Ostrom, Elinor. 1983. Equity in Police Services. In Gordon P. Whitaker and C. D. Phillips, eds., *Evaluating the Performance of Criminal Justice Agencies.* Sage Criminal Justice System Annual, 19. Beverly Hills: Sage.

Preston, Michael B. 1977. Minority Employment and Collective Bargaining in the Public Sector. *Public Administration Review,* 37:511–15.

Peterson, Paul. 1981. *City Limits.* Chicago: University of Chicago Press.

Robinson, Ted P., and Robert E. England. 1981. Black Representation on Central City School Boards Revisited. *Social Science Quarterly,* 62:495–502.

Rossi, Peter, Richard Berk, and Bettye Eidson. 1974. *The Roots of Urban Discontent.* New York: Wiley.

Rudoni, Dorothy, Ralph Baker, and Fred Meyer, Jr. 1978. Police Professionalism: Emerging Trends. *Policy Studies Journal,* 7:454–60.

Saltzstein, Grace H. 1986. Female Mayors and Women in Municipal Jobs. *American Journal of Political Science,* 30:140–64.

Sayre, Wallace, and Herbert Kaufman. 1965. *Governing New York City: Politics in the Metropolis.* New York: W. W. Norton.

Schneider, Mark. 1980. Resource Reallocation, Population Movement and the Fiscal Condition of Metropolitan Communities. *Social Science Quarterly,* 61:545–66.

Schuman, Howard, and Barry Gruenberg. 1972. Dissatisfaction with City Services: Is Race an Important Factor? In Harlan Hahn, ed., *People and Politics in Urban Society.* Beverly Hills: Sage.

Skogan, Wesley G. 1976. Efficiency and Effectiveness in Big City Police Departments. *Public Administration Review,* 36:278–86.

Skolnick, Jerome. 1966. *Justice without Trial.* New York: Wiley.

Stein, Lana. 1986. Representative Local Government: Minorities in the Municipal Workforce. *Journal of Politics,* 48:694–713.

Stone, Clarence. 1977. Paternalism among Social Agency Employees. *Journal of Politics,* 39:794–804.

Thompson, Frank J. 1975. *Personnel Policy in the City.* Berkeley: University of California Press.

The Urban Institute. 1972. *Improving Productivity Measurement and Evaluation in Local Government: A Four-Part Study.* Washington: The Urban Institute.

Wanat, John. 1976. Personnel Measures of Budgetary Interaction. *Western Political Quarterly,* 29:295–97.

Welch, Susan, and Albert K. Karnig. 1978. Representation of Blacks on Big City School Boards. *Social Science Quarterly,* 59:162–72.

Wilson, James Q. 1968a. *Varieties of Police Behavior.* Cambridge: Harvard University Press.

———. 1968b. The Police and the Delinquent in Two Cities. In James Q. Wilson, ed., *City Politics and Public Policy.* New York: Wiley.

Grace Hall Saltzstein is assistant professor of political science at the University of California, Riverside, CA 92521.

[13]

JOURNAL OF LAW & SOCIETY
VOLUME 9, NUMBER 1, SUMMER 1982

COMMENTS

Racism, The Police and Community Policing: A Comment on the Scarman Report

MAUREEN CAIN AND SUSAN SADIGH

INTRODUCTION

In this comment we consider three matters. First, we present the results of research in a south London magistrates' court which have a bearing on the question of institutionalized racism. These data were submitted as evidence to Lord Scarman's enquiry. Secondly, we consider the Scarman report and the way in which it dealt with allegations of racism. Thirdly, we examine critically Lord Scarman's proposals for community policing and offer some alternative suggestions.

BLACK PEOPLE IN COURT[1]

Research Method

The data derive from two periods of research in a south London court. A schedule was designed for recording events and information available in court. This was used to carry out pre-coded observations during weeks beginning 13th March, 10th April, 17th April, and 24th April 1978. The second research period covered eight weeks during November and December 1978, and January 1979. During the second period (apart from the Christmas break) pre-coded observations were recorded in alternate weeks, and an attempt was made to record a verbatim account of the proceedings in the other alternate weeks. Pre-coded observations were recorded on weeks beginning 20th November, 4th December, and 18th December 1978, and 15th January 1979. Data presented here are derived largely from the statistical analysis of the pre-coded observations.

Great care was taken to avoid bias in drawing the sample. A rota with a random starting position was devised for each research period, so that the research worker (Ms Sadigh) circulated between the three open courts on different days and, also by pre-arrangement, attended sometimes in the morning and sometimes in the afternoon. This prior choice, before the lists were known, precluded bias on our part, and also minimized any possible observer effect upon the court staff. On the half days when the researcher was in court every case, of whatever kind, was recorded. During the first four-week period 129 cases were recorded, and during the second period 167. Two hundred and sixty-nine cases, involving 368 defendants, were thus systematically recorded. (A further 145 cases were covered by the detailed conversational records kept on the alternate weeks in the second period.)

How Defendants get to Court

West Indians are charged with different offences from white people. They appear before the court charged with victimless crimes, as a result, that is, of pro-active policing, far more frequently than white defendants. These data are set out in Table 1. Of the West Indian defendants 46.6% (27) were charged as a result of pro-active policing, compared with 30.1% (83) of the white defendants. Examples of such charges which depend on police officers rather than victims taking the initiative are motoring offences, drunkenness, being a suspicious person, or obstructing the police. We did not include the last offence unless it were the most serious offence with which the defendant was charged, and could not, therefore, have occurred while the defendant was being arrested for something else.

These figures in themselves are striking, but the differences between black and white defendants are even more marked if drinking and driving offences (for which there is an objective measure of evidence) and other drunkenness offences, are excluded. The West Indian figure then remains at 46.6%, while that for white defendants charged as a result of police initiatives drops to 18.8%.

While it could be that these results reflect the offences that people of different colours 'commit', it is at least equally possible that they are brought about by differential patrolling and charging practices on the part of the police. The results are certainly entirely consistent with black people's view that they are objects of police harassment on the streets. They really are charged as a result of police activity more often than other people: in drawing attention to this they are simply stating a fact.

Another frequent allegation made in black communities is that young men in particular are vulnerable to police harassment. We did not study police activity on the streets, but nearly half of the West Indians charged and brought to court were under 21 (28 out of 60, i.e., 46.66%). This contrasts with only 12.36% of white defendants (34 of 275)[2]

Our evidence from this south London court is therefore entirely consistent with the view that young blacks are indeed disproportionately harassed.

Allocation of Defendants to Magistrates

At the time of the investigation there were three stipendiary magistrates, all male, who sat regularly in the court, in addition to the benches of lay

Table 1 Most serious charge by ethnic group

		Against the person	Property offences	Drunkenness	Public order	Motoring	Drunk in charge of motor vehicle	Other	Total	Unknown
"West Indian"	No.	12	18	—	11	16	—	1	58	2
	%	20.7	31.0	0.0	19.0	27.6	0.0	1.7	100.0	
"White"	No.	25	151	25	9	43	6	17	276	9
	%	0.9	54.7	9.0	3.3	15.6	2.2	6.2	100.0	
Other	No.	—	11	—	—	7	2	3	23	—
	%	0.0	47.8	0.0	0.0	30.4	8.7	13.1	100.0	

χ^2 40.02 $P < 001$

[In calculating this chi-square the two drunkenness categories were amalgamated, and the "other" and "unknown" categories were omitted].

Table 2 *Magistrate by defendants' colour*

	Magistrate 1 "tough"		Magistrate 2 "soft"		Magistrate 3		Extra Magistrate		Lay Justice		Total		Missing observations
	No.	%	No.	%	No.	%	No.	%	No.	%	No.	%	
West Indian	15	25.0	1	1.7	5	8.3	11	18.3	28	46.7	60	100.0	—
Other black	5	21.7	3	13.0	1	4.4	1	4.4	13	56.5	23	100.0	—
White	72	25.4	43	15.2	42	14.8	16	5.7	110	38.9	283	100.0	2

χ^2 14.67 $P < .01$

magistrates. Some of the lay chairpeople were female. During the second research period a fourth stipendiary magistrate, also male, sat in the court to help out. A number of West Indian defendants appeared before him, but he has not been included in the analysis of stipendiary magistrates for two reasons: first, he was a relatively unknown quantity to those responsible for listing, so they could not have taken his reputation into account in their allocation of cases, even had they wished to; secondly, because this magistrate was sitting on only one half day during the second phase of the study, including his cases would have made the statistics very difficult to interpret, there being too few cases for significant comparison. (His inclusion would, however, have considerably strengthened our argument about the differential distribution of cases, as Table 2 shows.)

Table 2 reveals a consistent administrative practice of allocating black defendants' cases disproportionately to lay justices. In large part this resulted from the different offences with which black defendants were charged.

However, if lay justices are excluded from the analysis[3] a different pattern emerges, and one which is consistent with a racist practice on the part of court administrators.

Among the regular magistrates there was one who had the reputation among court staff for being 'tough' and another who was regarded as 'soft'. These are the terms used by the court workers, which we have found it useful to retain in the analysis. The research workers heard the designations made by probation staff, police officers, and a local press reporter, who added that the 'tough' magistrate had a reputation for not granting bail. There were few comments about the third regular magistrate, or about the lay magistrates and lay chairpeople.

Throughout both phases of the research a far higher proportion of black defendants than of white defendants who were brought before the three regular stipendiaries were allocated to the reputedly 'tough' magistrate. This evidence is presented in Table 3.

Table 3 Stipendiary magistrate by defendants' colour

	Magistrate 1 "tough"		Magistrate 2 "soft"		Magistrate 3		Total	
	No.	%	No.	%	No.	%	No.	%
West Indian	15	71.4	1	4.8	5	23.8	21	100.0
Other black	5	55.6	3	33.3	1	11.1	9	100.0
White	72	45.9	43	27.4	42	26.7	157	100.0

Significance: West Indian and white only calculated

χ^2 6.35 $P<.05$

It must also be said, in fairness, that our data do not provide evidence of differences in the severity of sentences awarded by these magistrates. On this point we have no evidence either way, for many of the cases observed were remanded rather than sentenced.[4]

However, when the style of conducting the proceedings is considered the reason for the magistrate's tough reputation becomes clear. The research worker, who as an anthropologist had no previous experience of magistrates' courts, selected the following comments as typical of the three magistrates from the verbatim records kept during phase 2 of the research. In summarizing her analysis it could be said that Magistrate 1 was offensively authoritarian; Magistrate 2 tried to create a rapport with defendants; Magistrate 3's style was to say hard things in a colloquial way.

Magistrate 1: 'tough'

(a) Whatever you do in your country I don't know, but you don't tell lies in this country, get that into your thick head. If you're going to live in England you're going to behave like an Englishman and tell the truth or you can leave.

(b) We're sick of you and your like.

Magistrate 2: 'soft'

(a) That's a small fine. If you had come before a lay bench it would be 50% higher. I make my fines considerably lower: ask any officer who is aware of the situation in other courts.[5]

(b) I have some sympathy for you.

Magistrate 3

(a) You're a bit of a fool aren't you? People who pay their insurance foot the bill for charlies like you.

(b) You're going inside.

Thus the experience of black defendants appearing before stipendiary magistrates in the court which we studied would, more often than for white defendants, be one in which they were subjected to verbal abuse.

Research Conclusions

These data support the possibility of institutionalised racism, that is, of racist practices which are endemic and normal. The charging figures which we have presented could result from different on-street offence patterns by black and white people. Alternatively, and given the extensive literature on police patrol practices we think more probably, the figures result from a systematic bias in the use of police discretion.[6] Such bias, as McBarnet has recently argued, is made possible by the law, even encouraged by it.[7] Such bias cannot readily be identified, since the police officers concerned are making separate, 'one off', case-by-case decisions, exercising in each case a lawful discretion or even, as is sometimes argued, a professional judgment. For racism to operate in this way spectacular or flagrant instances of 'prejudice' are not necessary (although there is evidence that these too occur).[8] Racism in this form is hidden embedded in the discourse governing police practice, a part of normal unemotional routine. In other words, racism in this form may be institutionalised.

While our own data cannot prove the existence of institutionalized racism, although they are consistent with such an interpretation, they can disprove the alternative rotten apple theory of the occasional prejudiced officer. The occasional prejudiced officer would have had to work round the clock to produce so dramatic a difference in the offences with which black people are charged! And if he or she had done so, of course, a senior officer could and probably would have spotted this deviant racist practice and stopped it. This being so those who argue that there are only occasional prejudiced officers are implying collusion by supervisory personnel. Without such collusion these occasional and therefore highly visible officers would be moved or otherwise dealt with by the organisation. The alternative argument is that it is precisely because police racism is likely to be institutionalised and normal that it is usually not identifiable in any particular case, and not readily amenable to normal supervisory practices. The ideology which argues that police officers are individually (and professionally) accountable for each separate and discrete decision simply exacerbates the situation, which can only be made apparent if *patterns* of decision, or systematic practices, are identified.[9]

Our data about the administrative practices in the court are less directly relevant to a consideration of Lord Scarman's report, although these too were made available to him. What they do show is the possibility of institutionalized and hidden racism among court officials, and the reasonableness of black defendants who claim that courts are prejudiced against them. They may be wrong in the case of magistrates — for the practice of each magistrate was consistent as between the different colours of defendants appearing before him: the 'tough' man was universally tough, etc. — but the situation is so structured that for black people to impute racism to the court is at least a reasonable interpretation of their experiences there.

THE SCARMAN REPORT

The problem formulated

There is much to cheer in the report of Lord Scarman[10]: recommendations for the penetration of police stations by members of police committees, the establishment of an independent complaints procedure, improved police training at all levels, and not least the opening up of a major debate about community policing, are all to be welcomed. But the fact that within the police establishment there is resistance to the full implementation of these proposals should not prevent us from recognizing that Scarman's analysis of the situation and the proposals to which it gave rise are based on conservative and theoretically questionable premises.

The formulation of the problem in the first three pages of the Report provides a warning. The 'policing problem' which is the object of Scarman's Section 32 Enquiry is a problem *with* the police. By the next paragraph "it is necessary before attempting an answer to the policing problem to understand the social problem"[11] because the characteristics of the area, the social problems, will "set the standards for successful policing". Now we know that standards are variable, and are given a hint that police failures by one set of standards may be understandable by others.

But by page 3 we have a complete reversal, for now Lord Scarman is concerned to understand: "the background of the disturbances and . . . the policing problems to which they gave rise."[12] Thus the problem *with* policing has now become a problem *for* policing. And throughout the Report Lord Scarman retains this latter stance: in general terms his aim is to make policing more effective by securing the co-operation of the community. The community poses problems for the police: but what about the problems which the police pose for the community?[13]

Within this formulation of the problem Scarman accounts for the street confrontations in three interrelated ways. We are offered (i) the *displacement theory*; (ii) the *misperception theory*; and (iii) the familiar *rotten apple theory*[14] albeit in an attenuated form.

The displacement theory
According to this view

> it takes little, or nothing, to persuade them [young blacks] that the police, representing an establishment which they see as insensitive to their plight, are their enemies.[15]

The problem here is located outside the police, who are the relatively blameless victims of displaced and misplaced aggression. On page 37 there is an even clearer formulation

> The inference is irresistible that many young people, and especially many young black people, were spoiling for a row as a result of their frustrations. . .[16]

Two points must be made about the displacement theory. First, it exonerates the police as an institution from responsibility for the antagonism which all agree existed. In so doing it creates theoretical space for the misperception theory and the rotten apple theory.

Secondly, the society at large which is, apparently, responsible is not given any form but remains amorphous. So the racism to which young male blacks (and others) are subject cannot be explained. They are 'underprivileged' as a result of their own starting point and the individual attitudes they meet in various walks of life. Thus Scarman can wish that more black people were middle class and so had 'a real stake' in the community, but he cannot offer a class theory of racial oppression;[17] nor, indeed, does he offer a structural theory of any kind. As a result his suggested solutions must inevitably deal with symptoms rather than causes. The problem, therefore, has been displaced onto a shapeless social order in which everyone and no-one is responsible. The specific practices of police officers are relatively unimportant. The question is why they led to a riot (p. 38), and the answer there lies in the beyond.

The misperception theory

Scarman is a tolerant man. Because of their 'frustrations' he finds the misperceptions of the black community understandable. That Lambeth Council should endorse the view of its Working Party that "this situation is created by the nature of the police force and basic policing methods" is less tolerable, indeed dangerous. None the less it accurately "reflected attitudes, beliefs, and feelings [but not facts] widely prevalent in Lambeth. . ."[18]

Sometimes the perception is self evidently false, as when

> people conclude that the police are present purely to protect those marching and are therefore in agreement with their political beliefs.[19]

These views "clearly are not" justified.

On other occasions, however, a minority of immature police officers may provide grounds for the mistaken perception. Thus

> incidents of misconduct are not as numerous as some would have me believe; but they did occur, particularly when an officer was young, inexperienced, and frightened[20]

Or, again

> there were instances of harassment, and racial prejudice, among junior officers on the streets of Brixton which gave credibility and substance to the arguments of the police's critics[21]

This time the problem is located not in society at large, but in the subjectivities, false perceptions, of black people which society at large causes. Again the police are exonerated.

The consequences of this style of theorizing are therefore serious. But there are also no grounds for it. Even with reference to the small study outlined above there is evidence:

1. that black perceptions of discriminatory treatment by the police are reality based;
2. that harassment is probably routine and widespread and normal.

There is also evidence, from McBarnet's work, that the lawfulness of police activities is not a good criterion to use when identifying on-street harassment of black or other 'marginal' groups. Harassment is lawful, although selecting one ethnic group to harass may not be. But certainly a search for illegal behaviour by police officers will lead to the view that the problem is a minority one. But that completely by-passes the problem of on-street harassment of blacks. The misperception, therefore, is Lord Scarman's.

The Rotten Apple Theory

Examples of the reduction of the problem to that of a minority of inexperienced officers have been given above. Just as the misperception theory is made possible by the displacement theory, so the rotten apple theory is integrally related to misperception. This view enables Scarman to assert that there is no racism among senior ranks, that is, police racism is not institutionalized.

> Racial prejudice does manifest itself occasionally in the behaviour of a few officers on the street . . . I am satisfied, however, that such a bias is not to be found amongst senior police officers.[2]

In itself the argument is a simple one, and it is more important that time be spent tracing its ramifications.

First, because prejudice is rare specific police behaviours and practices must be accounted for in other ways. Thus throwing missiles at demonstrators (rioters) "was understandable, and excusable, when in self-defence".[33] That may be so. It is more dangerous when the argument is extended to cover matters of policy. Thus crime statistics for Brixton were used to justify saturation policing, and Lord Scarman accepted the reasonableness of this position, although he came to the conclusion that the effectiveness of such a strategy might be short-lived, and its costs in terms of community relations too high. If there is no institutionalized racism and no prejudice amongst senior officers then decisions to use saturation tactics were plainly not racially motivated: they could not have been. Rather, they were policy decisions made on sound policing grounds with reference to the crime figures.

This leaves no room for an examination of possible racism in the *construction* of the crime figures: no room either for the presence or absence of any policy guidelines about whom should be stopped, when and with what to charge, and so on. The publication in March by the Metropolitan Police of victims' allegations that the majority of street thieves and attackers were black[24] shows the dangers of this style of theorizing. Scarman might well deplore the decision selectively to announce this questionable statistic. But the insistence that there is no need to identify and eliminate racism among senior officers or as an institutionalized practice means that behaviour of this kind will remain organizationally possible.

Secondly the rotten apple theory individualizes the problem and therefore individualizes the possible solutions.[25] It leads to an emphasis on improved recruitment, improved training, and an improved complaints procedure for dealing with the deviant minority and with occasional lapses. All these are good suggestions, but the first and last are concerned solely with the quality of individuals, and certainly can have no impact on a structural practice which may be deeply embedded; improved training will not help if it is denied that racism may be embedded in police discourse. A

96

paternalistic understanding of the problems of blacks is surely an improvement on no understanding: but until the police understand that black people may be right in identifying them as oppressive there is no chance that they can train individual officers to recognize this and to overcome it.

The individualizing rotten apple theory also leads to a quaint conception of a balance between good and bad qualities. Thus the racism of some may be offset by the "courage and dedication"[26] of others. Courage and dedication are as commonly found among fascists as among freedom fighters, but individualization means that character traits too are assessed in terms of a de-contexted morality, which is also inevitably non-political. Such accolades tell us little.

Finally we come to the most dangerous part of the rotten apple theory — dangerous because it directs rather than merely inhibits change. We mean of course the ideology of police discretion/police professionalism. This dangerous ideology makes the rotten apple theory and its concommitant individual focussed remedies necessary. It is not generated by the rotten apple theory: rather the ideology of discretion/professionalism is consistent with it, and renders structural solutions unthinkable as well as inappropriate. Lord Scarman argues

> The exercise of police judgement has to be as independent as the exercise of professional judgement by a doctor or a lawyer[27]

Furthermore police ". . . are now professionals with a highly specialised set of skills and behavioural codes of their own".[28]

In the first part of this paper we pointed out how the law regarding the direct common-law powers of the constable and the more recent ideology of a zone of non-accountable professional judgement go hand in hand, and together effectively preclude the identification of racism in police practice. Police officers are not alone in making such claims to occupational autonomy. Recently, however, it has been argued that professionalism subverts rather than protects democracy, imports unacceptable ideologies into the decision-making process, and may well work to the disadvantage of those who are supposed to benefit from the service.[29] This is not the place to rehearse those arguments and that evidence. What is certain is that "the idea of the professional of expert judgement creates a non-accountable organisational space for discretionary decision"[30] and that in the case of the police entitlement to make non-accountable decisions is supported by the legal rhetoric of the so-called original powers of the constable.

While we have demonstrated that racist practices within the police are probably of such a kind that they are legal, normal, and not amenable to the usual case by case supervisory measures, Lord Scarman, in support of the ideology of discretion/professionalism rejected the Commission for Racial Equality's proposals for a *statistical* check on police practices whereby such endemic racism could be dealt with.[31] One can only repeat that the low visibility of the constable, the character of pro-active policing which is not delegated or directly capable of checking by management, coupled with the rhetorics of original powers and professional autonomy make supervision peculiarly difficult at any time. We argue in addition that the normalcy of the racism which our data imply renders effective supervision impossible if efforts to identify statistical patterns are not made. Adherence to the rotten apple theory and individualistic accounts therefore make it impossible for effective supervision to be advocated or implemented.

In other words, these theories which are designed to explain and combat racism ultimately sustain it because they sustain the institutional and legal spaces within which it can flourish.

Police priorities and police failures

Because of the way he theorised the problem Lord Scarman was able to identify only a limited number of police failures. Apart from the failures of immature and nervous individuals already alluded to there were failures in judgement by senior officers, for example in persisting with Swamp '81. But the two main failures identified were the failure to give due primacy to maintaining the Queen's Peace[32] and order on the streets, and the tactical failure to placate potential rioters.

The primacy of keeping order on the streets over law enforcement is significant. Brogden has shown that this has always been the major police task.[33] In spite of rhetorics about dealing with crime the police exist primarily as a force of order, a force of opposition to collective changes to the existing structure whether organized or disorganized, as in a riot. Because of this primary function control of the streets has a more than symbolic importance. Thus sociological theory and evidence can come full circle: for we know that certain marginal populations are most vulnerable to arrest; that there are organizational and informal pressures that encourage this; that the law allows and encourages the practice; and now that control of the streets is the official primary task of policing. This helps to explain why most resources are devoted to street users rather than to rapists, housebreakers, and fraudspeople. It even helps explain why traffic-control departments are so large and traffic offences so frequent, although even sociologists have regarded such matters as trivial. Street disorders "put the nation in peril"[34] and control of the streets is therefore paramount at all times.

That control is best achieved by gaining compliance seems unquestionable. But again, given the way the problem is posed, we learn that effective stops and searches require "courteous and carefully controlled behaviour by the police".[35] It is not suggested that given the low success rate (75 charges from 943 stops)[36] either the practice of stopping and searching should be reduced, or the powers restricted or rescinded.

COMMUNITY POLICING

Lord Scarman's most positive proposals concern community policing, or rather statutory consultation. He draws a distinction between accountability and consultation.[31] His main recommendation is for a strengthening of the latter. Police accountability is a separate discussion, worthy of more space. A few points only will be listed here, in particular those which have bearing on the preceding discussion.

1. It is necessary first of all to scotch the myth of the "traditional 'bobby on the beat'".[38] Not only do historical studies indicate an original analogism and a continuing ambivalence on the part of the working class[39] but there is also sociological evidence[40] that in the presumed hey-day of bobbies on beats, before the 1964 Police Act, police officers in both cities and small towns were divorced from the population policed. Certainly they applied their own values and standards of practice, and both by their answers in interviews and by their activities on patrol demonstrated that they were largely immune to community 'role definitions'. As then predicted, technical and organizational charges have since exacerbated this situation. But there is no evidence that police officers (with the exception of those in remote rural areas) were policing to communal or democratic standards before the days of panda cars: quite the contrary.

This point needs making because both in Liverpool and Leicestershire it has been assented that 'putting policemen back on the beat' meets the need for community policing. It does not.

2. Lord Scarman has argued that "accountability is . . . the key to successful consultation and socially responsive policing".[41] We agree. For this reason changes in the constitution of police authorities are necessary, to eliminate the statutory ⅓ magistrates, to make them committees of the local council (i.e. committees of democratically elected people) and to give them positive powers to make policing policy. Lord Scarman's report implies that decisions about the strength and use of the Special Patrol Groups, for example, is something outside the scope of his accountability or consultative structures. He implies this by making recommendations on these matters with no reference to local views. But policing policy must precisely be policy to decide on the allocation of resources as between different areas of work and different specialist units. If a re-constituted police authority determines policy then of course it can hold Chief Constables to account. If it does not determine policy it does not control the criteria in terms of which such an account might be rendered. A purely *ex post facto* or negative accountability is therefore a logical impossibility.

Lord Scarman has suggested that police authorities already have wide powers.[42] Certainly they are empowered to call for reports. It must be made clear that this power includes power to call for statistical reports and to determine the categories in terms of which the statistics are collected. Then information relevant to the presence of absence of racist practices can be collected and made public.

3. If the primary locus of accountability is the local authority and its police authority, this does not preclude national parliamentary accountability. As schools policy is made centrally and interpreted and administered locally so too should policing policy. This would have the advantage that the Home Secretary would be answerable in parliament for policing policies, whereas at the moment his answerability is ambiguous.[43] In addition, the economics of policing are effectively national because of the complexities of the Common Services Fund. Local authorities contribute to this in proportion to their police establishments, and half the cost is paid directly by the Treasury.[44] The fund pays for supra-local squads of various kinds, centralized training schemes, and various forensic and information services. Only the Home Secretary can adequately answer for these activities.

4. Forthly, a centralized anti-discrimination inspectorate, responsible to the Parliamentray Commissioner, may at some time be necessary.[45] The police should fall within the responsibilities of such an inspectorate.

Within such a framework of accountability statutory consultation might work. Consultation does not involve establishing policies or, indeed, any directive power. Its merits therefore, would be that it would help to articulate citizen demands, and that it would make them public. Thus police authorities would have to make decisions in relation to such public demands from their constituents. The power of consultative bodies would be indirect and political; their influence, as Scarman envisaged, might well be direct and day to day.

The question that arises here concerns the membership. We suggest that groups and organizations request representation, and that police authorities be required to accede to such requests unless they can show good reason. As far as possible criteria for membership would have to be public. And as far as possible the precise local forms of the consultative bodies would be various and experimental.[46]

CONCLUSION

Building constitutions in the air can be indeed an empty pass time. These suggestions, however, are intended to be fed into an ongoing debate. We think that their merits are these:-

(a) they offer a possibility of democratic control and grassroots influence which makes sense in terms of an analysis of existing locations of power;

(b) they go beyond public relations exercises, offering real directive power as a basis for accountability. They are therefore less likely to fold up through apathy than experiments in 'community policing' in the United States;[47]

(c) because the police authority would have policy directive powers the consultative committees would have a safeguard against being used by the police to collect information or to promulgate and shape a set of values. They would be democratic agencies, not agencies which the state makes use of to co-opt to its service the 'chaosmic powers' of society;[48]

(d) they undermine the ideology of discretion/professionalism by making the police answerable for *patterns* of behaviour as well as for single decisions;

(e) they would make it possible directly to counter racism.

100

Thus we would achieve a genuinely *democratic* policing structure, not dependent on any myths of communities or 'bobbies'. It would be a structure which would be responsive to genuinely articulated political demands from recognized groups of citizens. Then indeed we might all work together to reduce street crime, domestic assaults, the abuse of information, housebreaking, violence by state employees, and other matters which concern the populace.

NOTES AND REFERENCES

[1] The research presented as the first section of this comment was part of a larger pilot investigation on the theme of black people and the law which was financed by The Nuffield Foundation. The research team was based at the London School of Economics and included J. E. Hall Williams as well as the authors of this paper. Thanks are due both to the School and to The Nuffield Foundation. Thanks are also due to Monica Walker and Susannah Brown who offered statistical advice. The second and third sections were written subsequently by the two named authors, who alone accept responsibility for the views expressed. Thanks are also due to the Cambridge Institute of Criminology for the use of their facilities.

[2] In ten cases the defendant's age was not recorded. But even if all ten are assumed to be under 21, the proportion of such young people among white defendants is still only 15.44% (44 out of 285).

[3] Benches and chairpeople of lay justices varied so frequently that no statistical analysis of any particular bench was possible.

[4] Magistrate 1 sentenced 25 defendants in the sample, Magistrate 2 sentenced 23, and Magistrate 3 sentenced 27.

[5] There is no evidence that this was so in the research court.

[6] E. Bittner, "The police on skid row" (1967) *Am. Sociological Rev.* 32; M. Cain, *Society and the Policeman's Role* (1973); M. Chatterton, "Police in social control" in *Control Without Custody* (1976; ed. J. King); R. Fogelson, *Big City Police* (1977); S. Hall *et al.*, *Policing the Crisis* (1978); I. Piliavin and S. Briar, "Police encounters with juveniles" (1964) *Am. J. of Sociology* 70; A. Stinchombe, "Institutions of privacy in the determination of police administrative practice" (1963) *Am. J. of Sociology* 69; D. James, "Police–black relations: the professional solution" in *The British Police* (1979; ed. S. Holdaway).

[7] D. McBarnet, *Conviction: Law, the State and the Construction of Justice* (1981).

[8] Police Community Relations (London Area) Harold Road Centre, E13, *Policing London: A Study in the London Borough of Wandsworth* (1980).

[9] M. Cain and P. Fitzpatrick, *Report for UNESCO on Formal and Informal Means of Ameliorating Racism and Racial Prejudice with Special Reference to the United Kingdom (as a Common Law Country) and to Legal Measures (1982)*.

[10] Lord Scarman, *The Brixton Disorders 10th–12th April 1981* (1981; Cmnd 8427).

[11] *Ibid.*, para. 1.6.

[12] *Ibid.*, para. 1.11.

[13] I acknowledge in general terms a debt to F. Burton and P. Carlen, *Official Discourse* (1980) whose careful reading of official discourses has sensitised us to their logical structures.

[14] W. Knapp, *The Knapp Report on Police Corruption* (1972)

[15] *Op. cit*, para. 2.37.

[16] *Ibid.*, para. 3.76.

[17] *Ibid.*, para. 6.27.

[18] *Ibid.*, para. 4.33.

[19] *Ibid.*, para. 2.26.

[20] *Ibid.*, para. 43.

[21] *Ibid.*, para. 4.97.

[22] *Ibid.*, para. 4.63.

[23] *Ibid.*, para. 3.60.

[24] *Guardian* 26 March 1982.

[25] M. Cain, "Trends in the sociology of police work" (1979) *Int. J. Sociology of Law* 145.

[26] *Op. cit.*, para. 4.98.

[27] *Ibid.*, para. 4.59.

[28] *Ibid.*, para. 5.3.

[29] M. Cain, "Police professionalism: its meaning and consequences" (1972) *Anglo-Am. Law Rev.* 2; M. Cain and P. Fitzpatrick *loc. cit.*; M. Foucault, *Language, Counter-Memory, Practice* (1977); M. Foucault, *The History of Sexuality Vol. 1* (1978); M. Foucault, *Power/Knowledge* (1980); I. Illich, *The Disabling Professions* (1977); T. Johnson, *Professions and Power* (1972); R. Littlewood and M. Lipsedge, *Aliens and Alienists* (1982); D. Rosenthal, *Lawyer and Client: Who's in Charge?* (1974).

[30] M. Cain and P. Fitzpatrick, *op. cit.*, n. 9, p. 19.

[31] *Op. cit.*, para. 5. 39.

[32] *Ibid.*, p. 62.

[33] M. Brogden, *The Police: Autonomy, Power and Consent* (1982).

[34] *Op. cit.*, p. 15.

[35] *Op. cit.*, para. 4. 67.

[36] *Ibid.*, para. 4. 40.

[37] *Ibid.*, para. 5. 57.

[38] *Ibid.*, para. 4. 10.

[39] M. Brogden, *loc. cit.*

[40] M. Cain, *loc. cit.*, (1973).

[41] *Op. cit.*, para. 5. 57.

[42] *Ibid.*, para. 5. 61.

[43] M. Cain, *loc. cit.*, (1972).

[44] W. Hewitt, *British Police Administration* (1965).

[45] M. Cain and P. Fitzpatrick, *loc. cit.*

[46] These ideas owe much to M. Cain and P. Fitzpatrick, *loc. cit.*

[47] L. Cooper, "Controlling the police" in *The Police in Society* (1975; eds. E. Viano and J. Reiman); G. Washnis, *Citizen Involvement in Crime Prevention* (1976).

[48] B. de Sousa Santos, "Law and community: the changing nature of the state power in late capitalism" (1980) *Int. J. Sociology of Law* 4.

102

[14]

LEE BRIDGES

Policing the urban wasteland

> There are ... limitations on the power of the police. First and foremost, the law. The police officer must act within the law: abuse of power by a police officer, if it is allowed to occur with impunity, is a staging post to a police state.
>
> *The Scarman Report, 1981*[1]

> The police are ... the thick end of the authoritarian wedge, and in themselves so authoritarian as to make no difference between wedge and state. That authoritarianism had been perfected in the colonies, in Ireland, in the fields of British racism, and, as it grew, it found ways to by-pass its political masters and become accountable to no one but itself ...
>
> *A. Sivanandan, 'From resistance to rebellion', 1981*[2]

In the wake of the urban rebellions of 1981, the British state was quick to re-arm its police with new weaponry in the form of plastic bullets, CS gas and mobile water cannons in order to quell any further outbreaks of major disorder. But the 'riots' also set in train a more fundamental review of urban policing policy. The results of this rethinking appeared only fitfully at first by way of specific innovations in police tactics and localised experiments in 'community policing', but

Lee Bridges is a lecturer in judicial administration at the University of Birmingham.

Race & Class, XXV, 2(1983)

32   *Race & Class*

more recently the pace and scope of change have increased significantly. Thus, the government has moved in its Police Bill* to enshrine
within the very citadel of the law authoritarian powers for the police,
while the police themselves, most notably in the plan of London's new
Metropolitan Commissioner, Sir Kenneth Newman, have set about re-
organising their forces the better to penetrate and spy on the community and to suppress social and political unrest.

In these measures we can see the main parameters of the policing
strategy required to uphold the monetarist economic and social order,
in which the new technology and Thatcher/Reaganite policies of
enforced inquality combine to produce permanent mass unemployment, growing social polarisation and spreading urban decay. Such
conditions must inevitably result in the short-term in all types of social
disintegration, including rising rates of crime. But, more significantly,
they imply a shift in the focus of opposition in society away from the
point of production and the representative institutions of the still-
working classes in the trade unions and Labour Party, and more into
the community and towards the extra-parliamentary politics of
previously marginalised groups such as women and blacks and the
swelling ranks of the unemployed and never-employed youth. In order
to meet this threat to what Lord Scarman refers to as 'the normal state
of society',[3] the state must take extraordinary measures in gearing up
the police physically, legally and ideologically, not only to crush such
opposition when it surfaces on the streets, in demonstrations and other
popular forms of protest, but also to pre-empt it by extending their influence and tentacles of surveillance ever wider into the community, its
schools and social and political institutions, and even the family, in-
stilling 'discipline' and keeping tabs on increasingly large sections of
the population.

As in the past, it has been the black population locked within the
inner city wastelands – because of their structural position in the
economy, the effects of institutional racism, and their traditions of
community-based political resistance[4] – that have been the first to experience the harsh realities of this new policing strategy. Of course,
there is a long history of systematic police harassment of the black
community in Britain, as evidenced by a series of reports dating back to
the mid-1960s and culminating in 1979 in the Institute of Race Relations *Police against black people*[5] and the 1980 *Report of the working*

---

* *Originally introduced in Parliament under the full title of the Police and Criminal
Evidence Bill in November 1982, this legislation subsequently completed its Committee
Stage in the House of Commons, only to fall as a result of the calling of the General Election in June 1983. However, the Tory government, returned to office with an increased
and even more right-wing majority, is fully committed to re-introducing the Bill in the
current parliamentary session.*

party into community police relations[6] published by Lambeth Borough Council in London. *Police against black people*, for example, documented 150 separate incidents from different parts of the country concerning police malpractices in such areas as raids on black clubs and meeting places; mass stop-and-search operations conducted against black communities by Special Patrol Groups and the Illegal Immigration Intelligence Unit; arbitrary and violent arrests of black individuals and entry of black homes; and the subjecting of black persons held at (or even visiting) police stations to violence and verbal abuse, long periods of detention without access to lawyers and relations or even basic medical attention, forced confessions and fabricated evidence, and routine fingerprinting and photographing. It is precisely in these areas that it is now proposed to confer extensive new powers on the police under the Police Bill.

But legal powers, as much as they may contribute to police harassment of individuals or particular groups, do not in themselves create a police state. It is through the medium of police organisation and training, backed by an ideology of repression and a political culture that identifies certain sections of the community as a temporary or permanent threat to society, that police powers become translated into instruments of oppression. The point is well illustrated by the powers in the Immigration Act to detain and deport persons suspected of being 'illegal immigrants'. Although similar provisions have been in force for many years in respect of aliens, their statutory extension in the 1971 Immigration Act was itself underpinned by a political culture defining immigrants as 'swamping' British society and, more specifically, by the creation of the specialist Illegal Immigration Intelligence Unit, supported by modern surveillance techniques and computer technology, to effect their enforcement. It is this combination of factors, further backed by an amenable judiciary, that has enabled the Immigration Act to be used as the basis for mass raids and passport checks, resulting in the detention of thousands of persons over recent years, and serving generally to oppress the Asian community.[7] Similarly, in order to grasp the full significance of the Police Bill and how its powers are likely to be implemented as part of the wider political control of the community, it is necessary to locate it within the politics of policing, particularly as they have developed since the 1981 rebellions, and to relate its provisions to other changes already taking place in police organisation and tactics towards inner-city, working-class communities generally.

The politics of policing: From Mark to Newman

As shown elsewhere,[8] the ideological confrontation of black youth has formed a key element in police politics in Britain and their pressures for

34   *Race & Class*

increased powers, at least since the period of Sir Robert Mark's tenure
as Metropolitan Police Commissioner in London in the early 1970s.
While promoting a reactive, 'fire-brigade' style of policing on the
ground, involving the use of mobile patrols backed by advanced
technology and specialist centralised squads, Mark also sought
through his cultivation of both politicians and the media to project the
police into a position where they might influence more directly the content of the law itself.[9] One eventual outcome of this was the setting up
of the Royal Commission on Criminal Procedure (RCCP) in 1978 and
the highly pre-emptory evidences presented to it by Sir David McNee,
Mark's successor as Metropolitan Commissioner, and bodies such as
the Association of Chief Police Officers (ACPO) and the rank-and-file
Police Federation. The RCCP Report, published in January 1981,
went a considerable way in conceding to these police demands for new
powers.[10]

The rebellions that took place in over thirty British cities in the
spring and summer of 1981 temporarily placed the police politically on
the defensive. The government, while re-arming the police and backing
their harsh methods in suppressing the uprisings, nevertheless held
back from an immediate increase in police legal powers, deciding instead to set up and await the outcome of the Scarman Inquiry. The
government's reaction owed little to the strength or nature of the
British Left's response to the rebellions. The general reaction of the
Labour party was to exploit the 'riots' as an occasion for further condemning the government over its economic policies, while being fairly
muted in its criticisms of the police. It was only among more radical
elements in Labour-controlled local authorities such as the Greater
London Council, whose campaign for police accountability was given
popular impetus in the community by the rebellions, that the opportunity was taken to re-open the debate on police powers and the RCCP
proposals in this area. By contrast, the main intellectual response to the
'riots' from the Left came from those sociologists and 'radical'
criminologists who used them to put forward highly invidious theories
of the socio-cultural proclivities of black youth towards crime, thereby
rationalising long-held police prejudices in this regard.[11]

But it was the Scarman Report, published in November 1981, that
prepared the ground for a renewed political assertiveness by the police
and for the eventual emergence of a new policing strategy combining
the openly repressive tactics of 'fire-brigade' policing with the more in-
sidious, and pervasive (but nominally supportive) methods of community policing. This the Report did by not only baldly denying the
existence of institutional racism in Britain, but also by treating as
analytically separate issues of police organisation, powers and conduct
from the question of 'racial disadvantage' in society. To Scarman, this
latter term signified not systematic discrimination but a set of general

processes of social and cultural deprivation, many seemingly with their origin within the black community itself. Thus, Scarman's description of the black community in Brixton[12] notably starts off with the traditional stereotype of the 'matriarchal' West Indian family in which men are 'seldom dominant' or 'of little or no significance' and even women, because of their wage-earning commitments, are frequently 'absent from the family home'. This is seen as leading to high rates of West Indian illegitimacy and children in care, followed in turn by their low achievement at school and eventual failure in the job market, where Scarman does at least admit to their facing some additional problems of discrimination. But significantly absent from this list is any notion of police racism, other than the individual prejudices of a few officers, or of selective policing policies as having contributed to the oppression of the black community

Indeed, to Scarman the police were more victims than perpetuators of 'racial disadvantage', having to deal with its effects in the West Indian community in terms of 'hostile and resentful ... young people' and an idle 'street culture' with opportunities for 'endless discussions of grievances' and for involvement in crime. And whatever the need for social ameliorative measures, it was this propensity towards crime and disorder in the black community that Scarman saw as posing the most immediate threat to the 'normal state of society'. Scarman's endorsement of the government's decision to provide the police with extra riot-control equipment and training and of the RCCP proposals for increased police powers followed from this, as did his support for special saturation policing operations in the black community and the retention of the heavily criticised Special Patrol Group. His main concern was that these powers and operations be carried out in future with greater discretion, especially so as to ensure that the anger created among black youth did not continue to infect 'the attitudes and beliefs of older, more responsible, members of the community'.[13] So he proposed the introduction of multiculturalism in police training, the better to alert the police to the peculiar sensitivities of the black community. This boost to the 'racial awareness' training of police cadets, combined with the 'ethnic' stereotypes on which Scarman based his arguments, significantly complemented and reinforced the culturalist approach to race matters. Other measures included to the same end were the recruitment of additional black police, statutory police 'consultations' with the community and the disciplining of racially-prejudiced conduct among police officers.

Scarman's refusal to link these proposals to a need to combat institutional police racism or to limit their powers enabled the police subsequently to portray them as special pleading and the whole of his Report as a recipe for the 'soft' policing of black areas. In fact, any idea of 'soft' policing was belied by the tactics adopted in inner city-areas

36   *Race & Class*

following the 1981 rebellions, involving saturation foot patrols backed by newly formed Instant Response Units, consisting of teams of specially trained and equipped mobile riot police based in each local police district in London. At the same time, the police followed up the Scarman Report with a major political counter-offensive against their critics and the black community generally in the form of a highly publicised release in March 1982 of racialised crime figures, carefully manipulated to show both a further dramatic rise in 'muggings' and a predominant involvement of black people in such offences. If the release of the racial crime statistics and the general 'law and order' campaign that followed were designed to counter the Scarman Report's more liberal proposals,[14] then they also served to reinforce his identification of crime and disorder as the most pressing social problems of black, inner-city areas. Clearly, this view supported renewed demands for greater police powers, while at the same time providing a rationale for a 'community' or 'multi-agency' approach to policing in which the police themselves would take a more active role in coordinating the work of statutory agencies and community-support services, redirecting their activities towards the control of crime and unrest.

One immediate result of the March 'law and order' campaign was the government's appointment of Sir Kenneth Newman to take over as Metropolitan Police Commissioner from October 1982. Newman's assumption of office itself coincided with renewed rank-and-file police pressure for tougher policing measures against the black community. Thus, in a speech to a fringe meeting at the Tory Party conference a Police Federation vice-chairman said:

> In every urban area there is a large minority of people who are not fit for salvage. They hate every form of authority – whether it is the police or anybody else. The only way that the police can protect society is, quite frankly, by harassing these people so that they are afraid to commit crime.[15]

And lest there be any doubt about the identity of such persons in the minds of the police, this was later confirmed by another Police Federation spokesman:

> There are two conflicting demands. One is to stop harassing young blacks in the inner cities. The other is to stop young blacks harassing other people in the inner cities. Which demand do you respond to? It has to be the second.[16]

Once in office, Newman quickly responded to this pressure, announcing a new system for 'targeting' street criminals which would involve the building up of intelligence on specific persons and subjecting them to constant surveillance. At the same time, 'community representatives' would be enlisted to work alongside increased beat patrols in the more sensitive inner-city locations, no doubt to provide better intelligence on which to 'target' particular individuals.

The Police Bill: licensing police oppression and non-accountability

It was in this context of a rapid intensification of policing in inner-city areas developing in conjunction with a more vociferous and explicitly racist police politics that the government published its original Police Bill in November 1982. The Bill was found to go well beyond the recommendations of the RCCP in its proposals for extending police powers, being based rather on the various police evidences to the RCCP and on their well-entrenched practices in policing the black community. Certainly, in legitimating such practices and extending police powers, the Bill represented an open invitation by the Thatcher government to the police to continue their 'post-riot' clamp-down on inner-city areas and their black population in particular. Of equal if not greater significance, however, is the capacity these new powers will give the police to increase their surveillance and political control of the community at large and the Bill's overall effect in statutorily safeguarding police discretion and the autonomy of local police commanders in pursuing selective policing policies against certain areas and groups. In these latter respects, the Bill will establish a legal basis for attacks on organisations now campaigning to protect the community from police abuse and harassment and stand in future as a constitutional barrier against the establishment of more effective, democratic control of the police.

Although it is not possible here to review in detail the contents of the Police Bill,* it provides for massive extensions in police powers across the full range of their operations. To begin with, it will establish for the first time on a national basis a power for the police forcibly to stop and search persons and vehicles on 'reasonable suspicion' of carrying not only stolen goods (as currently exists in a few localities, including London) but also 'offensive weapons' and articles for use in stealing – the legal definition of both being open to arbitrary interpretation and widescale abuse by the police. The police will also be empowered to set up roadblocks, sealing off an area for up to seven days, whenever a local police superintendent considers that 'the pattern of crime in that area' justifies it. It has been widely noted that these provisions will give legal sanction to such mass stop-and-search operations as Swamp 81,

---

* Although some changes to the Bill when it is re-introduced may be expected, especially as regards police powers to search confidential professional records (see below), it is assumed that the main provisions will remain the same as before.

in which nearly 1,000 persons were stopped on the streets of Brixton in the days immediately preceding the April 1981 uprising, or that carried out over several weeks by the Special Patrol Group in Lewisham in South London in 1975 that resulted in no less than 14,000 stops and over 400 arrests.[17] Nor should it be overlooked that stop-and-search and roadblocks have become an increasingly routine part of policing in inner-city areas, the more so under the saturation foot patrolling and operations of localised Instant Response Units introduced since the 1981 rebellions. Already in 1978 the Metropolitan Police were stopping an estimated 40,000 persons each month in London under their existing powers,[18] and recently published Home Office research has confirmed that black men are three times more likely to be stopped than whites.[19] This discriminatory use of stop-and-search powers and the very low proportion of those stopped who are subsequently arrested, let alone legally convicted, has led some critics to question their usefulness in directly combating crime. On the other hand, constant stop-and-searches directed at increasingly large sections of the population are crucial to the building-up of intelligence on the community and in providing a basis for 'targeting' operations against particular individuals or groups, a factor which no doubt explains the government's persistence in seeking to extend police powers in this field.

In their operations on the street, the police will be further backed up by new statutory powers of arrest and to enter and search premises. The Bill defines a very wide range of offences as 'arrestable' and the police will also be able to arrest a person committing even the most minor offences where certain highly subjective 'arrest conditions' apply, such as that the person concerned is obstructing the highway or that the police do not trust the name and address he or she has given. The police will also be empowered forcibly to enter premises to arrest a person for one of the 'arrestable offences' or subsequently to search their premises, and they will have power immediately to search premises on which an arrest for *any offence* has taken place. These provisions need to be seen in the light of the long history of police tactics in which black community events, social facilities and political meeting places are placed under constant surveillance and the making of arrests for minor offences is used as a pretext for frequent large-scale raids and searches.[20] Again, this type of police operation has intensified in the 'post-riot' period, especially in what the police have identified as the politically sensitive 'symbolic locations' in the inner city.

The police's capacity for political control of the community will also be greatly enhanced by a new legal power to conduct general searches for evidence in premises of organisations and persons not themselves suspected of any crime. This was the element in the original Police Bill that attracted the greatest controversy, particularly in its application to

the confidential records held by professional persons, and it is likely
that in an attempt to separate their critics among the professional
bodies and other elite pressure groups off from more popular opposition to the Bill, the government will make further concessions in this
area. If so, then non-professional advisors and all other individuals
and organisations in the community will still be liable under the Bill to
general searches of their records and premises on the warrant of a
single magistrate. A telling sign of the possible future targets against
which these general search powers may be used can be found in Sir
Kenneth Newman's recent, widely publicised outburst against the
'small minority of police watchers' and other 'activists on the Left'
whom he accused of 'a campaign of dedicated denigration of the
police', including 'zealous dredging for any incident that can be exploited as a cause célèbre and tendentious accounts of complaints
against the police'.[21] In singling out community-based defence campaigns and local police monitoring groups in this way, and further officially labelling them as a 'destabilising influence and a threat to
public order', Newman would appear to have given a clear lead to his
forces on the ground to attack these groups, and one means of undermining their work would be to subject them to regular searches of their
offices and seizure of files and other documents.

The final area in which the Bill provides the police with extensive
new powers is in the detention and interrogation of suspects. Thus, the
police will be empowered to hold a person without charge in order 'to
secure or preserve evidence ... or to obtain such evidence by questioning him', and they will also be granted increased powers forcibly to
search, fingerprint and take body samples from detainees. In most
cases, such detention can extend for up to thirty-six hours on the
police's own authority, during which the detainee may be denied access
to a lawyer or relations, and for a further sixty hours on order of a local
magistrates' court. Of course, these new powers of detention will
operate alongside the Bill's other provisions giving the police a wider
scope to gather evidence in the community, and they will therefore be
in a much stronger position than at present to obtain and use information about detainees or their families and friends in order to induce
them into making confessions. And even where it is not possible using
the vastly increased powers in the Bill to induce confessions or obtain
other evidence upon which to secure a legal conviction, the ability to
detain innocent persons over long periods, to subject them to often
humiliating searches, and continually to re-arrest them on new 'suspi-
cions' will constitute a powerful weapon of summary punishment in
the hands of the police.

Apart from these specific new powers, an important feature of the
Bill is that, far from clarifying the law in this field and establishing a
firmer basis for challenging police abuses through the courts, it will

40   *Race & Class*

actually entrench police discretion more deeply by giving it statutory backing and make judicial review of police activities even more tenuous than at present. A good example of how the Bill achieves this effect is to be found in the concept of a 'serious arrestable offence'. The exercise of various of the more exceptional powers in the Bill is technically restricted to situations involving a 'serious arrestable offence'. Yet, as originally drafted, the Bill defined this as 'an arrestable offence which the person contemplating the exercise of the power considers to be sufficiently serious to justify his exercising it', thereby turning a supposed safeguard for the protection of the citizen into a license for the police arbitrarily to extend their powers at will. In an attempt to remedy the self-legitimating nature of this definition, the government later added a list of criteria against which police decisions as to 'seriousness' might subsequently be reviewed, including such generalised conditions as 'the harm caused or likely to be caused to the security of the state, the administration of justice or public order' or 'the prevalence of similar offences' in an area. Given the example of Sir Kenneth Newman's recent labelling of police critics and other 'activists' as just such a 'threat to public order' and the widely-held police and judicial conceptions (evidence the Scarman Report) of inner-city neighbourhoods as 'high-crime' areas and their populations as prone to disorder, it is not difficult to see that these additional criteria will serve only to reinforce the Bill's effect in licensing a very wide degree of police discretion in their operations against such areas and groups.

In view of the current campaign for greater accountability of the police to elected local authorities, it is also important to note the level within the police hierarchy at which this wide discretion will be located, especially in relation to the structure of local government itself. In the Metropolitan Police area covering Greater London, for example, there are twenty-four police districts, most of which include the area of one or more London boroughs, the smallest unit of elected local government in the capital. However, police operations are further sub-divided into seventy-five local police divisions in London (with a further 250 in other parts of the country), and as a recent report on the Metropolitan Police has noted:

> it is the Chief Superintendent, in charge of each local division, assisted by a Superintendent, who decides how to deploy the officers under his command and what operations to mount. It appears that the Chief Superintendent has considerable autonomy.[22]

Significantly, it is the Superintendent who, under the Police Bill, will wield substantial legal discretion, being empowered on his own accord to authorise such measures as roadblocks, detention for up to thirty-six hours, and the forcible taking of fingerprints and body samples, while it will require only an Inspector, based at each local police station, to sanction the entry and search of an arrested person's premises. Even in those few instances where the police will require the prior permission of an external body before exercising their new powers, relating to detention for up to four days and searches of innocent parties' premises, this will be from local magistrates who can be expected readily to endorse police operational decisions. Thus, the present informal autonomy of divisional and lower level police commanders will be given legal force, and in this respect the Bill will provide them with a statutory umbrella beneath which they will be able to maintain full control of their operations, even in the unlikely event of formal structures of accountability to local authorities being imposed above them.

The Newman plan: mobilising the police state

Even before its introduction in Parliament, the government had anticipated the Police Bill in their appointment of Sir Kenneth Newman as Metropolitan Police Commissioner. Newman's own career spans all aspects of the authoritarian tradition of British policing, from his initial service with the Palestine Police Force, to his earlier period with the Metropolitan Police when he was responsible in the late 1960s for policing anti-Vietnam War demonstrations and introducing new methods of crowd control, through to his six years in Northern Ireland in the 1970s, including a period as Chief Constable from 1976 to 1979. In this latter capacity, Newman 'developed one of the most sophisticated intelligence networks of any police force in Western Europe'[23] and also introduced a new regime of interrogation which led to several adverse reports on the maltreatment of detainees. Newman is also well versed in 'community policing' as a former commander of the Metropolitan Police's Community Relations Branch and, most recently, as head of the national Police Staff College, where he re-oriented courses for senior police officers towards the study of a 'multi-agency' approach to the problems of crime control and 'order management' in inner-city 'ethnic flashpoints'.[24] Newman was, therefore, a perfect choice to forge on behalf of the state a new policing strategy drawing together these different elements, a task he was given immediately on taking office by Home Secretary Whitelaw in his capacity as the police authority for London.

At first sight the Newman plan, announced in January 1983, seems to represent a compilation of recent diverse innovations in police tactics such as 'targeting' and police-community consultative committees, with some additional imported ideas like neighbourhood watch schemes, all combined under the cloak of corporate planning/management and actively sold by way of public opinion surveys

42   *Race & Class*

and the Commissioner's own 'give-away' newspaper.* Beneath the
rhetoric, however, lies an acute awareness, born of the 1981 rebellions
and Newman's experience in Northern Ireland, of the contradictions in
urban policing thrown up by spreading economic and social decay and
the need to make strategic choices in police priorities, as well as to combat the growing popular opposition to the police in certain sections of
the population. Indeed, this latter objective is made quite explicit in
Newman's introduction to his plan:

> the social and political demands on the police in the Metropolis have
> changed and developed. In recent years, there has been a substantial
> increase in the number of formally constituted associations and
> groups representing a range of special interests ... while the police
> still stand high in opinion polls, these are pitched at a very general
> level, and perhaps obscure the fact that the pattern in London is
> variable ... it is already apparent that the Metropolitan Police must
> guard against a deterioration in public confidence, and that there is
> a problem with young people, particularly young West Indians ... In
> some areas, there is a brand of obstruction and hostility which has
> led to deliberately engineered confrontations with the police. It is,
> therefore, *a priority to restore order to such areas* (emphasis ad-
> ded).[25]

In translating this political objective into operational terms, Newman
has followed the logic of the Scarman Report and the prejudices of the
rank-and-file police and popular press in directly associating the problems of political and social disorder with specific categories of crime,
singling out localities with a high incidence of 'street robberies, street
disorders and burglary' for the heaviest concentration of police
organisation, manpower and other resources. Of course, these 'high-
crime' locations are precisely the inner-city areas with substantial black
populations that have been subject in the past to exceptional policing
measures, particularly in the operations of centralised squads such as
the Special Patrol Group. Under the Newman plan, however, there is
to be a shift in emphasis away from centralised operations, which are
seen to have produced 'a serious imbalance in the deployment of manpower between New Scotland Yard and police districts' and have also
become a focal point for political opposition to the police. In their
place, Newman is promoting a more comprehensive policing strategy
encompassing three key elements: the reorganisation of the crime control and public order functions of the police so as to be permanently

---

* *Strategy 83*, a monthly supplement now being distributed free with the Metropolitan
Police's in-house newspaper, *The Job*. In his attack on 'police watchers', Newman spoke
of their campaigns being 'bolstered by a variety of hostile broadsheets and give-away
newspapers', this latter a clear reference to the Greater London Council Police Com-
mitee Support Unit's *Policing London*.

and even more intensively 'targeted' on the inner-city 'high-crime' areas and the dissident elements in their populations; the vast expansion of police surveillance and intelligence-gathering through a combination of increased foot patrolling and various 'community policing' initiatives; and the more open and sophisticated legitimation of police priorities and activities, again through 'community policing' and such measures as divisional policing plans and localised crime and public opinion surveys.

Thus, the previous role of the Special Patrol Group is being displaced in part by new Intelligence and Surveillance Units operating in each of the four areas, into which the Metropolitan Police District as a whole is divided, and by new plainclothes crime squads being set up in each local police district. It is on these units that the new 'targeting' strategy of dealing with street crime, involving 'improved information-gathering, analysis and targeted action' against both individuals and particular locations, will be centred. This tactic is drawn directly from Newman's Northern Ireland experience in combating the IRA and its political supporters in the community, and it is notable that when the first such area-based 'targeting' squad was created in south London late in 1982, it drew officers from the centralised Criminal Intelligence Branch and Anti-Terrorist Squad. In addition, under the Newman plan the Instant Response Units set up in each police district following the 1981 uprisings are to be renamed as District Support Units (DSUs) and made permanent. While retaining their riot-control capabilities, the DSUs will have their functions expanded, almost in direct parallel with the new powers contained in the Police Bill, to include 'anti-burglary patrols, rowdyism patrols, searches, roadblocks, observations, [and] execution of warrants'. In effect, then, the DSUs will become localised versions of the Special Patrol Group, carrying out stop-and-search operations, manning roadblocks and conducting raids on premises. Indeed, figures recently released by the Metropolitan Police indicate not only the scale of DSU operations, but also how, in line with the political objectives behind Newman's strategy, their activities are directed primarily at controlling social and political 'disorder' rather than conventional crime. Thus, in only the first four months of 1983, DSUs were responsible for 5,735 arrests (about one-sixth of the Metropolitan Police's normal total of arrests), of which only thirty nine were for street robbery and 207 for burglary, but no less than 4,000 for what is described as 'street disorder', despite this having been a period of relatively few major disturbances. For its part, the Special Patrol Group is being retained with its role also re-defined in terms of 'anti-burglary patrols', possibly to be directed more at the large, 'problem' housing estates on the edges of the inner city.

The aim in future will be to ensure that these strategic-level crime control and public order operations impinge on the community and

44   *Race & Class*

dissident groups within it more selectively, and to achieve this divisional-level police commanders are to be given a more prominent role in managing and coordinating police activities in their localities. The Newman plan speaks of the need to re-examine the role of Chief Superintendents and Superintendents, and this is echoed in a recent Police Training Board report which points to these ranks as requiring 'a thorough and sympathetic knowledge of the political context in which they work' and proposes training in such topics as 'cultural relativism and equality before the law' and 'the basic sociology of different social and racial groups'.[26] Given the police's rejection of anti-racism in their training at other levels* and the general context in which such 'multiculturalism' and sociology will be taught, it is not difficult to imagine its effects in confirming police stereotypes and informing their prejudices about the propensities of certain sections of the population towards crime and disorder. Moreover, in line with their position under the Police Bill, this type of training may serve only the better to educate local police commanders to treat all policing problems in inner-city areas as 'serious' and therefore as potentially justifying the fullest exercise of their new legal powers.

But the effectiveness of strategic police operations will depend on more than the social or political sophistication of divisional-level commanders. These operations will also be tied in directly with what is termed the 'ground cover and crime prevention' aspects of the Newman strategy, under which an expanded system of surveillance and intelligence-gathering on the community and its political activities is being put into operation. At the heart of this system lie new beat patrols in the inner cities, including saturation coverage for areas of 'special difficulty', which will serve to build up a picture of each street and locality and their inhabitants, feeding this information up through a computerised network to be used as a basis for area and district-level crime control and public order operations and those of other specialist squads such as the Illegal Immigration Intelligence Unit. A telling picture of the modern 'bobby on the beat' now operating in one area of London emerged recently:

> Working as part of reliefs and responsible to the duty officers, they will nevertheless be directed to patrol a grid square. And as an additional aid to their task they will be carrying a concertina-fold plastic-encased 'crib' which provides them with a pocket guide:
> – map of the grid square they're covering;

---

* Most notably in the case of John Fernandes, a black lecturer at the Metropolitan Police's Cadet Training School, whose attempts to introduce anti-racism into the curriculum were rejected. He was subsequently barred from teaching at the school when he exposed wide-spread racist attitudes among police cadets as evidenced by a set of their essays.

– list of the key points needing a special eye ...
– priority days and priority names;
– names, addresses and PHOTOGRAPHS of active criminals living
in the square being patrolled.[27]

But if the beat patrolmen are thus linked directly with 'strategic' police
operations, they will also be at the centre of an extension of police
influence and spying deeper into the community itself. The Newman
plan calls for the specific 'tasking' of individual officers to promote
and become involved with neighbourhood watch schemes, victim support groups, tenants' associations and inter-agency links with other
service organisations and professionals working in the community. Of
course, such initiatives can serve to supplement police manpower,
especially in the 'low priority' outer urban areas and in terms of police
public assistance functions where Newman admits that police activity
will need to be curtailed in order to concentrate resources on the inner
city. But these aspects cannot be isolated from the primary role of
'community policing' in improving police intelligence on society at
large, for example, by recruiting 'community representatives' to assist
in beat patrolling of the more sensitive 'symbolic locations' identified
in a recent police statement[28] or in organising schools, local authority
housing and social services departments and other statutory and voluntary agencies to provide regular information on their clients and to pick
out potentially 'disruptive' elements in the community.

Of course, another purpose behind 'community policing' is to
activate media and public opinion in support of police operations. This
legitimating function is to be expanded under the Newman plan with
consultative committees, soon to be made statutory under the Police
Bill, singled out as a 'vehicle for directing overall strategy', albeit
under the careful direction of the District Commander who will 'identify specific problems *to the committee*' (emphasis added). For this
purpose, local policing plans are now being prepared in each division
and district in London, with all the accoutrements of 'participation' by
lower-ranked officers and 'consultations' with the public through local
crime and opinion surveys. In a situation of monetarist cutbacks in
community-support services and general social disintegration in the
inner cities, these surveys will inevitably result in 'findings' of growing
concern over rising levels of crime, and therefore provide further
rationalisation for increases in police activity. Also, by concentrating
on specific forms of intra-communal crime, they will serve to promote
generational, ethnic and other political divisions in the community on
policing issues. In a similar vein, Newman has now made it clear that
only the views of the 'law abiding community' need to be considered,
presumably intending to exclude from public consultations those
groups who are most active in defending the community against police

abuse and harassment. In this respect, Newman has recently issued instructions for a more 'open' information policy to improve the general image of the police with the local press and other media and has also urged local police commanders to follow his lead in directly attacking the political legitimacy of monitoring groups and other campaigns on policing issues in their areas.[29]

It is important to bear in mind the overall political context in which this attempted de-legitimation of police critics is taking place. The Thatcher government, in its pursuit of the new monetarist economic and social order in Britain, has entered its second term of office even more firmly committed to attacking and, if necessary, abolishing all institutional forms of opposition to its authority. Already there have been massive inroads into the independence of local government and the trade unions, as well as a general undermining of welfare state support for the community at large. And the government is now pledged to the direct abolition of the Greater London Council and other Labour-controlled metropolitan county authorities on which the campaign for the democratic accountability of the police has been based. Even in advance of this, as shown above, the Police Bill will undercut claims for formal police accountability by providing statutory authority for a vast increase in police powers and for the extensive operational discretion of local police commanders.

Newman's strategy for policing London represents the application of Thatcherite authoritarianism to the inner cities as the location of growing, non-institutional protest and opposition in society. Put another way, Newman has set out to marshall the racist prejudices and reactionary politics of the police rank-and-file and harness them to the requirements of monetarism for increased repression and for surveillance and political control over ever larger sections of the population. In doing so, Newman has recognised that, with Labour Party and trade union abilities to protect basic civil liberties substantially eroded (their will to do so in relation to black people's rights was never strong) and the campaign for formal accountability being rapidly eclipsed, the main challenge to his strategy and that of the state lies, as in 1981, in the community and their continuing resistance to the police state being imposed over their lives. It is, therefore, imperative on him not only to crush popular expressions of that resistance on the street when they arise, but also to defeat those groups struggling to create a more organised, political opposition to police repression. By the same token, in their campaigns against the Police Bill and the general policing policies that lie behind it, and beyond this in beginning to forge a new popular politics of resistance to the ravages of monetarism and Thatcherism, these groups are waging a struggle that has much wider significance for the anti-racist and socialist movements as a whole.

References

1   Cmnd. 8427, *The Brixton Disorders 10-12 April 1981* (London, 1981) para. 4.60.
2   A. Sivanandan, 'From resistance to rebellion' in *A Different Hunger* (London, 1982), pp. 49-50.
3   Scarman Report, *op. cit.*, para. 4.57.
4   See Sivanandan, *op. cit.*
5   Institute of Race Relations, *Police against black people* (London, 1979).
6   London Borough of Lambeth, *Final report of working party into community police relations in Lambeth* (London, 1980).
7   P. Gordon, *Passport raids and checks* (London, 1980).
8   See Cecil Gutzmore's article (pp 13-30) in this issue.
9   Sir Robert Mark, *In the office of Constable* (London, 1978), especially chapters 11 and 21.
10 Cmnd. 8092, *Report of the Royal Commission on Criminal Procedure* (London, 1981).
11 The writers concerned are Ian Taylor, Jock Young and John Lea. For a critical review of their work, see Lee Bridges, 'The British Left and law and order', *Sage Race Relations Abstracts* (February 1983).
12 Scarman Report, *op. cit.*, paras. 2.16-2.22.
13 *Ibid.*, para. 4.77.
14 For a detailed account of the release of the racial crime statistics and the following 'law and order' campaign, see Joe Sims, 'Scarman: The police counter attack', *The Socialist Register 1982*.
15 *Guardian* (7 October 1982).
16 *Guardian* (20 November 1982).
17 *Police against black people, op. cit.*, pp. 11-12.
18 RCCP Report, *op. cit.*, Vol. 2, Appendix 3.
19 C. Willis, *The use, effectiveness and impact of police stop and search powers* (London, 1983).
20 *Police against black people, op. cit.*, pp. 6-9.
21 Cmnd. 8928, *Report of the Commissioner of Police of the Metropolis for the year 1982* (London, 1983), p. 3.
22 *A New Police Authority for London — A Consultation Paper on Democratic Control of the Police in London* (London, Greater London Council Police Committee, 1982), p. 28.
23 Peter Taylor, *Beating the Terrorists* (Harmondsworth, 1980).
24 A conference entitled 'Policing inner cities' was held at the Police Staff College in July 1982.
25 *Report of the Commissioner ..., op. cit.*, Appendix 31. All further references to Newman's plan, unless otherwise cited, are taken from this source.
26 *Report of the Police Training Council Working Party on community and race relations training for the police* (London, 1983), para. 7.21.
27 *Strategy 83* supplement to *The Job* (June 1983).
28 'Towards the contract', New Scotland Yard Press Release (29 June 1983). In addition to Railton Road, Brixton, these include All Saints Road, Notting Hill; the Broadwater Farm Estate, Tottenham; and the Finsbury Park area.
29 *Strategy 83* supplement to *The Job* (July 1983).

[15]

International Journal of the Sociology of Law 1988, **16**, 521–539

Race, Crime and Policing: Empirical, Theoretical and Methodological Issues

TONY JEFFERSON

Centre for Criminological and Socio-Legal Research, University of Sheffield, U.K.

Introduction

> As culture displaced anxiety about the volume of black settlement, crime came to occupy the place which sexuality, miscegenation and disease had held as the central themes and images in the earlier discourses of 'race' (Gilroy, 1987, p. 109).

> It is the rough, difficult and potentially violent aspects of multi ethnic areas that oblige police units having a more robust capability (Newman, 1983).

The relationship between race, crime and policing in the U.K. has been the contested heart of the debate about law and order from the mid-1970s onwards, a debate to which the inner city riots of the 1980s—and a third term of Conservative Government under Thatcher—has added a new intensity. The political import and relevance of the debate, as the decline of Britain's economic, political and social landscapes continues, is clear. What, however, is less clear is what a radical politics of law and order in this area might look like; consequently we need to look to the coherence of the intellectual resources at hand to guide such a project. What I intend, therefore, is to attempt such a task, namely, to examine 'What we know' and identify core problems. For clarity's sake, I intend first to summarise the available (empirical) evidence, then compare contrasting (theoretical) interpretations of the data, and subsequently spell out certain (methodological) implications for adequate research strategies in this area. I end, finally, by offering a sketch—a 'theoretical case-study' of contemporary police–black relations—which is based on my attempt at the lineaments of a resolution of the problem identified.

0194–6595/88/040521 + 19 $03.00/0

522   *T. Jefferson*

The Evidence

> On empirical issues the gulf between ... positions may be unimportant
> (Banton, 1987, p. 166).

Two issues which need to be borne in mind throughout are the inconsistent
terminology employed in the literature and the difference between attitudes
and behaviour. On the question of terminology, sometimes the literature dis-
tinguishes between Asians, that is, persons from the Indian Subcontinent, not
those from China, etc., and Afro-Caribbeans, that is, persons of African or
West Indian origin, and at other times the single term 'black' is used, either as
a synonym for Afro-Caribbean (not always explicitly) and/or to reference both
ethnic groups (other non-white ethnic groups tend to be either ignored or
assimilated). I can only follow this terminology, but will try to highlight the
different experience of Asians where it is possible. To highlight the distinction
between attitudes and behaviour, I will start with the literature on attitudes
and then move to that on behaviour.

Attitudes and Prejudice

Police Attitudes

Though we lack survey data, all the major British and North American
studies, from the early post-war period on, agree that negative, stereotypical,
prejudiced and hostile attitudes to blacks are rife amongst police officers (cf.
Westley, 1970; Skolnick, 1975; Lambert, 1970; Policy Studies Institute, 1983).
Asians may be singled out for exemption (albeit regarded as 'liars if suspected
of wrong doing', Southgate, quoted in Benyon) (1986, p. 55) and young West
Indians for particular calumnies. If one single utterance can sum up the sheer
'taken-for-grantedness' of racist language (and the underlying racist assumptions and attitudes) within the police, it has to be the extraordinary gaffe from
a public platform committed by a police community-relations officer, the publicity surrounding which cost him his career, and public ostracism from the
Federation. Speaking at the 1984 Police Federation Conference he referred
blithely to "our coloured brethren or nig nogs".

Some have argued that the origins of such attitudes lie in the peculiarly
"conservative and authoritarian personalities" that the police force attracts
(Coleman & Gorman, 1982; p. 1; Potter, 1977; Cook. 1977); others that police
recruits largely reflect the 'normal' prejudices of the social group (overwhelmingly the manual working class. cf. Cain, 1973; Reiner, 1978) from which
police are drawn (Skolnick, 1975; Bayley & Mendelsohn, 1969). There is also
some evidence that prejudicial attitudes are learned on the job, through contact with the macho action-oriented conservatism of the occupational subculture, and/or the 'reality-shock' of street encounters. Ironically, some of the best

evidence for this comes from those who also see the police attracting authoritarian personalities (Coleman & Gorman, 1982, p. 1). Of course, these explanations are not all mutually exclusive; as Reiner says—in a conclusion I endorse—police prejudice is probably "a reflection of the racism prevalent in British society and the social groups from which the police are drawn, *as well as* the situations in which many police–black encounters occur (themselves the product of racism within Britain)" (Reiner, 1985, p. 161, italics added).

Black (*i.e. Afro-Caribbean and Asian*) Attitudes

Police hostility to blacks is mirrored in the well-documented black antipathy to police, a finding of long-standing and as true of the North American as the British experience. But though blacks are more hostile to the police than are other groups, and more critical of police performance, this is not to say that a majority of black people are hostile, nor that they subject police performance to blanket criticisms. Reiner, for example, thought that, on the evidence, "by the late 1970s ... a clear majority of black Americans had a positive image of the police" (1985, p. 160); and the Policy Studies Institute (hereafter PSI) that the hostile views of West Indians (in London) "by no means amount to a complete rejection of the system" (PSI, 1983, Vol 4, p. 332).

Hostility is more marked among the young (thus reciprocating greater police hostility), and especially "among those low income or unemployed young black males who are the special targets of heavy policing" (Walker, 1983, on the North American evidence, quoted in Reiner, 1985, pp. 100–101). The situation in London is no different. There the PSI described "the lack of confidence in the police among young West Indians ... as disastrous" (PSI, 1983, Vol 1, p. 326), a result of the much greater likelihood of West Indians believing that "the police regularly engage in abuse of powers and excessive force, and that they fabricate evidence" (Reiner, 1985, p. 173). Asians tend to be less critical than West Indians (except with regard to racial attacks), though more so than Whites (Reiner, 1985, p. 173).

The relationship of these attitudes to experience is not straightforward. The fact that hostility is most concentrated amongst the young unemployed and heavily policed males might suggest a *direct* connection between these hostile attitudes and their experiences of oppressive policing: and the PSI did indeed find a positive relationship between contact (of any kind) with the police and a critical view of them (PSI, 1983, Vol 1, p. 326). However, the PSI data also revealed that "for the most part" personal experience could not explain "the hostility to the police among West Indian Londoners". Rather, such hostility stemmed *indirectly* from a perception of the police as "the most obvious symbol and representative of an oppressive white authority" (Smith, 1986, p. 11). Of course, these explanations need not be exclusive: direct experience might harden and amplify an existing indirectly acquired hostility.

Behaviour and Discrimination

The complex relationship between (prejudiced) attitudes and (discriminatory or racist) behaviour is revealed in the PSI's observationally-based finding "that police officers tend to be hostile to black people in general terms, and certainly indulge in much racialist talk, but often have friendly and relaxed relations with individual black people in specific instances" (PSI, 1983, Vol. 4, p. 334). What such a finding may tell us about the significance of race (as against other factors) in encounters, and the question of discrimination, we must postpone until the next section. For the moment we need to outline what we know about, first, the police treatment of blacks as suspects and, second, as victims.

Black Suspects

(i) *Stop and Search*

Disproportionate stopping of young black males emerges from both the North American and the British evidence. Reiner's summary of the North American evidence—"the police stop and question young, low-income, ethnic minority males more frequently than any other group" (1985, p. 157)—holds true, with one exception, for the British evidence. Here, Willis (1983), Field & Southgate (1982), the British Crime Survey (Southgate & Ekblom, 1984), the PSI (1983) and the Metropolitan Police (in its evidence to Scarman on stops in Lambeth) provide the 'rule' of disproportionate stopping of blacks, especially young black males, to which Tuck & Southgate (1981) prove the single exception (to which we return below in the discussion). The PSI findings serve well to demonstrate the importance of both age and ethnicity:

> Younger people were much more likely to be stopped than older people, by a factor of about 11 to 1 in terms of the proportion of people stopped or about 30 to 1 in terms of the mean number of stops per person (PSI, 1983, Vol 1, p. 95).

> the difference between West Indians and white people is not very striking (24 per cent for West Indians, 17 per cent for white people). However, the mean number of stops is nearly three times as high among West Indians as among white people ... largely because those West Indians who are stopped tend to be stopped repeatedly (*ibid.*).

Asians, by contrast, have a comparatively low stop rate (PSI, 1983, Vol 1, pp. 96, 98).

(ii) *Arrests*

The pattern for arrests is similar to that for stops. Scotland Yard's revelation to the Select Committee on Race Relations, 1976–1977, that 12% of those arrested (in the Metropolitan Police District) for indictable crime in 1975 were Afro-Caribbean, anticipated the findings of Stevens & Willis (1979) based on the same MPD figures. They found that the arrest rate for Afro-Caribbeans "was higher than that for whites and Asians for every category of offence" (Benyon, 1986, p. 17). When age was controlled for, however, it was found that blacks were disproportionately arrested mainly in four offence categories: assault, robbery, "other violent theft", and "other indictable offences" (Reiner, 1985, p. 166). Asians, it should be added, were under-represented in all categories except assault. This pattern was repeated, with even greater over-representation, in the 1983 figures (Home Office statistics quoted in Walker, 1987, p. 40), and found general confirmation (for young (i.e. 15–24) West Indians only) in the PSI results, and in figures based on victim identification (in the minority of cases where these were available). Again, 'robbery' and 'other violent theft' were particularly heavily over-represented, according to victims.

I return later to discuss the role of discrimination in explaining these arrest patterns. For the moment, I want simply to draw attention to the fact that "other violent theft" allows "considerable scope for selective perception" (Stevens & Willis, 1979, p. 41) as does its near neighbour 'robbery' (cf. Blom Cooper & Drabble, 1982). Moreover, the black arrest rate for the highly discretionary offence of 'sus' was 14 or 15 times the white rate (an important factor in its eventual abolition).

The North American studies endorse the finding of blacks being disproportionately arrested (cf. Black & Reiss, 1967; Lundman, Sykes & Clark, 1978), though there is disagreement as to whether blacks are also disproportionately subject to "uncivil treatment" and physical abuse. Skolnick (1975) felt uncivil treatment was routine for 'negroes' (sic), whereas Reiss (1971, p. 14) thought the police "did not treat negroes uncivilly more often than whites". As to physical abuse, the Black–Reiss (1967) study concluded that whites fared worse than 'negroes'; a conclusion at odds with the figures for police killings of citizens, which reveal blacks as hugely over-represented (though police shootings have dropped significantly since 1977 after policy and training were tightened and improved, as Reiner (1985, p. 159) reminds us).

(iii) Prosecution

Here the general picture is similar to that on stops and arrests. Landau's two studies on the cautioning of juvenile offenders in London (Landau, 1981; Landau & Nathan, 1983) found that at the two stages where decisions are made about juveniles—the decision to refer to the Juvenile Bureau and the Bureau's decision on whether to caution—Afro-Carribean juveniles were more likely to be charged (an outcome regarded as the harshest) at least for some offences crimes of violence, burglary and a range of public order offences in the case of the initial decision to charge immediately, and all "except for 'traf-

526   *T. Jefferson*

fic and other offences'" (Landau and Nathan, 1983, p. 142) in the case of the
Bureau decisions). This conclusion is not supported by the similar work of
Farrington & Bennett (1981), who found no significant differences in the
cautioning of whites and non-white juveniles (n = 907). Certain differences
between the studies may well account for this finding, for, as Monica Walker
(1987) points out, the Farrington & Bennett study included "almost as many
Asians as West Indians" was "conducted 5 years earlier" and "dealt only with
those aged under 15" (Walker, 1987, p. 50). Whilst we do not know the effect
of the large number of Asians in the non-white category, we do know from the
study by Batta, Mawby & McCulloch (1978) on cautioning in Bradford that
Pakistanis there were significantly more likely to be cautioned than Indians or
non-Asians (though the figures for the small number of West Indians involved
were not analysed separately).

Cain & Sadigh's study of 269 cases in a south London magistrate's court
during 1978–1979 provided further evidence of disproportionate charging of
West Indians in the case of 'victimless' crimes, i.e. those resulting from pro-
active policing (Cain & Sadigh, 1982, p. 87). The same study also showed that
this applied to 'reactive' offences too, as Reiner (1985, p. 169) has subsequently pointed out.

Black Victims

(i) Victims

The flip side of over-heavy policing is under-protection, especially in the case
of racial attacks. The extent of this racial violence—ranging from insults and
minor assaults to arson and murder—has been documented in a number of
studies (Bethnal Green and Stepney Trades Council, 1978; Klug, 1982;
Greater London Council (GLC), 1984; Fryer, 1984), but it was the Home
Office study of 1981 that produced official statistical confirmation of its disproportional effect. This found, for instance, that for all racially motivated incidents (including insults, harassment, etc., as well as offences), Asians were 50
times and blacks 37 times as likely to be victims as whites.

The sequel to such attacks, according to blacks, is police indifference or hostility (GLC, 1984, p. 18). Yet moves towards community self-defence are either
directly penalised, with the 'defendants' ending up as the accused, often after
clashes with the police, or indirectly so, as when general 'calls for assistance'
are turned into 'fishing expeditions' for illegal immigrants (Benyon, 1986,
p. 51; Gordon, 1983, p. 37). The fact that the trials have proved largely (but
by no means wholly) successful in arguing the case that 'self-defence is no
offence', and that Sir Kenneth Newman added racial attacks to his list of
special priorities (in his January, 1985 Report), as did his successor, Peter
Imbert (*Guardian*, March 1st, 1988, p. 2), should not lead anyone down the
road of complacency: the charges against the youths meant they went into the

courtroom with the prospect of lengthy custodial sentences, the 'reward' of failure; and it remains to be seen whether Newman's high level concern can be turned into effective, practical action on the ground, given the way the present structure of accountability only permits ultimately discretionary policy making in operational areas (see Grimshaw & Jefferson, 1987, pp. 195–265).

(ii) Complaints against the police

If everybody feels hard-done-by when it comes to complaints against the police, blacks, in line with the above pattern, have good reason to feel more so, as Reiner (1985, p. 170) says, summarising the material, "blacks are more likely to make formal complaints, but less likely to have these upheld". And according to the most comprehensive analysis, a Home Office study of complaints against the Metropolitan police during the 1970s (Stevens & Willis, 1981), blacks are more likely to make *serious* complaints. Yet the PSI (1983) found (Vol 1, pp. 269–72) that West Indians are *less* likely to complain than either whites or Asians, which suggests that the disparity in rates "understates the difference in grievances" (Reiner, 1985, p. 171). What may account for the lower substantiation rate is the fact that blacks were more likely to be under arrest at the time of the complaint or have a 'record'—both "discrediting factors" according to Box & Russell (1975). It should of course be remembered that substantiation rates for all groups is low (1979, first quarter: 1·5% blacks, 3·6% Asians, 4·6% whites, Stevens & Willis, 1981, p. 16).

Before turning to the discussion of the data, it may be useful to summarise the broad consensus of the foregoing. Benyon's gloomy words, summarising his own review of the literature, are as good as any:

> The data show that black people are stopped and searched, and arrested, far more frequently than other people, and were far more likely to be charged with being a 'suspected person' before the relevant section of the Vagrancy Act 1824 was repealed. Many young black people feel they have been 'hunted irrespective of their innocence or guilt' (Scarman, 1981, para 4.22). There are also numerous allegations of racial abuse, harassment and assault by the police, but only a few of these, such as the case of the Whites, have ever been proved. Although the number of formal complaints against the police has risen, few of these are substantiated either. (Benyon, 1986, p. 53).

Interpreting the Data

The key points of contention underlying competing interpretations can be expressed in the form of two questions, namely:

(1) Is *race*, rather than *other factors* of known significance such as age, class, demeanour, etc., the central determinant of police behaviour?

528   *T. Jefferson*

(2) Is *different* treatment necessarily *discriminatory* treatment?

The following discussion will be focused through these questions.

(1) Is Race the Real Issue?

This question has two components: (a) whether the key determinant is structural or situational and (b) if structural, which structural feature—age, race, class, etc.—is central. Taking (a) first, Reiner makes the point that whereas the statistical studies reveal the 'disproportional' patterns which suggest discrimination at work, the observational studies on both sides of the Atlantic "suggest that police handling of blacks is largely to be explained by situational variables (where the encounter occurred, what sparked it, complainants' wishes, etc.) and interactional variables (i.e. co-operativeness of citizens), rather than any observable element of discrimination" (Reiner, 1985, p. 171). Thus, although the Black–Reiss observational study (1967) in the United States confirmed the disproportionate rate of black arrests, they put this down not to race but to "the greater rate at which blacks show disrespect for police" (Reiner, 1985, p. 157), and to their greater likelihood of being involved in incidents when complainants (usually black) demanded arrest. A replication study found that the disrespect could have been a *consequence* of the officers' behaviour in about half the cases (Sykes, Fox & Clark, 1976); and a re-analysis of the Black–Reiss data showed that blacks were still disproportionately arrested even when complainant preferences are controlled for (Sherman, 1980; see also Smith & Visher, 1981). These subsequent studies suggest then that not all of the difference in arrest rates can be accounted for by interactional or situational factors, even if much of it can be. But the Black–Reiss observations find support in the British-based work of James who argues that policing blacks is essentially 'normal policing', that is policing which is determined by the subcultural values of action, control, excitement, etc. However, James does concede that if blacks are subject to normal policing *more often*, this could make for a qualitative change in police–black relations (James, 1979, p. 82).

The question of 'demeanour', i.e. whether blacks are regarded as more disrespectful, may also have been a factor in the Landau cautioning studies. For, if black juveniles are seen generally as a worse risk because of a perceived disrespectful 'stroppiness', or if they or their parents are less willing to accept a caution (because they intend to plead not guilty and acceptance requires an admission of guilt) this will adversely affect their cautioning rate. Unfortunately, the Landau studies had no information of this sort.

For all who admit the presence, whether weak or strong, of structural features, there remains the issue of which structural feature is the key determinant. Put another way, since structures rarely operate in isolation, the question is, in any given situation, what is the element of purely *racial* as opposed to other kinds of discrimination (on grounds of age or class, for example)? The PSI talks of "four characteristics that are strongly related to the likelihood of being stopped: age, sex, ethnic group and ownership or use of a vehicle" (1983, Vol 1, p. 94). Age and sex are relatively easy to control for statistically so that the degree to which 'race' is operative in particular situations can be relatively precisely calibrated. Not so with class, which is in any case much harder to control for since it is notoriously difficult to define, let alone measure. The result is that most studies conveniently overlook it, as does the PSI, though where analysis is conducted using class related factors (such as unemployment and type of jobs) it emerges as a relevant structural characteristic (for examples, see below).

It is this aspect that may account for the apparently aberrant findings of the Moss Side 'stops' study, the only one, remember, not to find disproportionate stops of blacks. Monica Walker makes the point that these results were obtained from small homogeneous areas within Manchester, whereas the figures for all the other studies were based on much larger more heterogeneous areas in London. This means, effectively, that the Manchester figures have been controlled for class, but not so the London figures. So, the 'racial' differences in stop rates found in London could be the result of class, for when class *is* controlled for, as in the Manchester study, the 'racial' difference disappears. It is a criticism Monica Walker makes more generally; thus, the higher arrest rates found for blacks in London may be a consequence of their social class position. Since offenders come disproportionately from manual workers, the unemployed and the socially deprived, and since black people are overrepresented in these categories, then "for London as a whole it is not surprising that black people have higher arrest and offender rates" (Walker, 1987, p. 43). She makes the point, for example, that the PSI study found that the unemployed are more likely to be stopped than those in work and that unskilled manual workers were twice as likely to be stopped in a vehicle as professional and managerial workers. So, she concludes, "a more detailed analysis, controlling for these (class) factors, would enable a more valid comparison to be made between the black and white groups" (Walker, 1987, p. 49). This failure to control for social class is a point she also makes about the Landau cautioning studies.

If it is so that blacks are differently policed, more because of their age and class than their ethnicity, they are still *more* policed overall because they are, as a group, more youthful and more working class. But, it seems unlikely that there is not a racial factor over and above a class factor at work. For, whereas being middle class can place a white person above certain kinds of police suspicion, being black can be sufficient to *lower* even the most 'respectable' and middle class into the 'suspicious' category. To put it more graphically, middle class Nigerian students or diplomats are still more often 'mistakenly' stopped/arrested, etc. than their white counterparts. The overall result is that if a pure racial factor is difficult to disentangle, this is partly because (working) class and race are tightly connected, even if wrongly, in the 'suspicious' eyes of white police officers. This reading is in line with the findings of a recent unpublished analysis, which shows that blacks were more likely to be stopped than whites of similar employment status and social class (Drew, personal communication).

(2) Is Different Treatment the Same as Discriminatory Treatment?

If race, directly or indirectly, is a factor in policing, the question still remains, is the different 'over-policing' of blacks a product of *discrimination* (i.e., unfair), or a product of the different 'over-offending' behaviour of blacks, and therefore *appropriate* to the circumstances. The traditional line, supported broadly by the police (where it is not actively initiated by them), is that black crime levels—as evidenced by figures for arrests, prosecutions and supported by victim identification where available—are disproportionately high and therefore *require* disproportionate attention.

There is of course, as we have seen, evidence for this view. Apart from the MPD's own statistics, the Stevens & Willis (1979) arrest figures suggest a higher rate of black offending. And careful though they are to discuss the range of factors affecting the higher arrest rate, they are forced to conclude that at least part of it has to be attributed to more offending behaviour. Monica Walker calculates that, if offender rates were equal, black people would have to be four and a half times more likely to be arrested for burglary, and 14 times more likely for robbery, than whites (Walker, 1987, p. 40). If these figures are regarded as 'implausible' then, again, at least part of the higher arrest rate has to be a function of higher offending. The notion that part of the higher arrest rate has to be related to higher offending behaviour is shared by the PSI (1983) and both Reiner (1985) and Benyon (1986), after their careful overviews of the available evidence. But the case has been put most strongly and controversially by Lea & Young in a series of articles, and most fully in a book, *What is to be done about Law and Order*, written on behalf of the Socialist Society (Lea & Young, 1984). Their argument, in brief, talks of black deprivation leading to higher offending, of police stereotyping leading to a 'ready' response to such offending, and of the two processes reinforcing each other in the form of a "vicious circle" (Lea & Young, 1984, pp. 166–167).

Opposition to this case—but in particular to the idea that the higher black arrest rate is connected with a higher rate of offending—has come most vociferously from the Institute of Race Relations (cf. Bridges, 1983a and b; Gilroy, 1982, 1983; Gutzmore, 1983). Refusing to 'haggle' over the official crime statistics, the upshot apparently is to regard the higher black crime figures as *simply* the result of police prejudice.

To see the question thus starkly is, as Benyon (1986, p. 24) says, 'unusual'. And indeed, most of those whose work we have been reviewing opt for an explanation which sees police behaviour as partly discriminatory and partly a response to higher black crime rates. Thus Stevens & Willis suggest that the higher arrest rates for blacks can be explained by a combination of 'intrinsic' and 'extrinsic' factors. The former include indices of deprivation and greater offending behaviour; the latter things like more time spent on the streets, greater visibility, and police stereotyping. The PSI interpretation broadly follows this mixture of deprivation, offending and stereotyping. Even Scotland Yard mention the disproportionate youth and social deprivation of West Indians making their higher offending unsurprising—though, not surprisingly, they do not regard police stereotyping as a factor. Reiner's 'mixed' interpretation couches itself in structural, historical and cultural terms. Structural processes operate so "that ethnic minorities figure disproportionately in the young 'street' population which has always been the prime focus of police 'order maintenance' work", and this may include involvement in "specific kinds of street crime". And things are worse in a recession. Police prejudice provides the accentuating "cultural factors". The result is a vicious circle of conflict (Reiner, 1985, pp. 175–176).

Situating Interpretations

Whatever the answers given to the two questions which provided the focus of the above interpretations, the question of their *sufficiency* remains. Is it enough, in other words, to identify race as a significant determinant of police behaviour and/or to conclude that treatment is racially discriminatory? If orthodox sociologists tend to think so, marxists tend not to. As Banton puts it, once marxism had issued its challenge to orthodox sociology in this area, this meant that "it [racism] had become the *explanadum* (that which is to be explained) instead of being part of an *explanans* (that which explains)" (Banton, 1987, p. 148).

The reason why the simple identification of racism is insufficient as an explanation is because it fails to address the question of transformation: how racism arises, and the circumstances under which it changes over time. This requires that racism be situated historically. Understanding historical conjunctures, like all other theoretical understandings, is never an innocent nor uncontested affair, nor is it unproblematic. It is always achieved via a critique which displaces other understandings. For reasons of space, I intend to rely on a summary of an existing critique (Gilroy, 1987, pp. 15–42), as a prelude to my critique of the critique.

Gilroy's trenchant dual-critique simultaneously berates the sociology of race relations and the more politically inspired discussions of race and racism. In both cases the faults are similar: racism is regarded *either* as a property of structure *or* as a source of meaning. In the former instance race is reduced to an effect of more fundamental structures—relations of production in the case of Marxists like Sivanandan (1982), market relations in the case of Weberians like Rex and Tomlinson (1979). In the latter instance (racism as a source of meaning), racial discourses become sets of autonomous ideas, or ideologies in the marxist sense, depending on political persuasion. Either way, the connection with other structures is either completely severed (Banton and Harwood, 1975), or effectively so, under the attenuating influence of the idea of relative autonomy (Gabriel and Ben-Tovim, 1979). Thus the 'economism' of the former approaches is matched by the idealism of the latter ones. Finally, there is a 'culturalist' tendency which reduces race to ethnicity and provides warrant for the study of race as the study of ethnically distinct, separate cultural collectivities (Lawrence, 1982).

Whilst I have some reservations about the characterisation of the 'ideological' reading of race by Gramscian Marxists like Gabriel and Ben-Tovim (1979), since it is clear that Gilroy himself is also heavily reliant on a non-reductive Gramscian marxism, I shall not pursue that here. Having thus concisely seen off rival accounts, Gilroy, citing Bhaskar (1979; 1980), suggests a processual model of society which effectively *links* structures, agents and meanings. In this model, societies are both structuring and the products of human agency, as humans act to transform existing structures and hence societies. Culture, in this model, provides the crucial mediation between the two: it becomes "a field articulating the life-world of subjects (albeit de-centred) and the structures created by human activity" (Gilroy, 1987, p. 17). This transformative model of society, combined with a demand for a reconstructed class theory which can encompass the new political realities and struggles of the late 20th century, places struggle centre stage. "Objective conditions structure the range of possibilities, but precise outcomes emerge directly from struggles" (*ibid.*, p. 30). This unpredictability of outcome affects both class formation ("class in concrete historical conditions is ... the effect of struggles", *ibid.*) and race formation ("'race' is a political category that can accommodate various meanings which are in turn determined by struggle", *ibid.*, p. 38).

This 'open-ended' perspective, plainly echoes Hall's "Marxism without guarantees":

> Understanding 'determinacy' in terms of setting limits ... rather than in terms of the absolute predictability of particular outcomes, is the only basis of a 'marxism without final guarantees'. (Hall, 1986, p. 43).

And it means that:

> The primary problem for analysis of racial antagonism which occurs within the broad framework of historical materialism must be the manner in which racial meanings, solidarity and identities provide the basis for action. (Gilroy, 1987, p. 27).

In the present period, "one of the definitive characteristics of contemporary racism is its capacity first to define blacks in the problem/victim couplet and then expel them from historical being altogether" (Gilroy, 1987, p. 26). The chapter on "lesser breeds without the law" goes on to demonstrate how the 'problem' side of the couplet has come to mean, from the 1970s on, 'black criminality'.

> As culture displaced anxiety about the volume of black settlement, crime came to occupy the place which sexuality, miscegenation and disease had held as the central themes and images in the earlier discourses of 'race'. Crime, in the form of both street disorder and robbery was gradually identified as an *expression of black culture* which was in turn defined as a cycle in which the negative effects of 'black matriarchy' and family pathology wrought destructive changes on the inner city by literally breeding deviancy out of desperation and discrimination (Gilroy, 1987, pp. 109–110, italics in original).

Given this, the role of anti-racism, to which Gilroy contributes admirably in the book, "must be ... to respond by revealing and restoring the historical dimensions of black life ... outside the categories of problem and victim" (*ibid.*, p. 27).

There is much here with which to agree. The rejection of approaches reliant on either the reductive or the idealistic; the attempt to offer a processual model of society in which objective conditions structure but do not determine precise outcomes; the recognition of the need to reconstruct class theory in the light of contemporary realities; and the attention to the profanity of the (historical) particular. To characterise it in a way with which the author might take issue, it seems to be a highly laudable attempt to wed a Gramscian focus on the centrality of conjunctural struggle (albeit under determinate conditions) to a Foucauldian emphasis on the irreducibility of particular discourses (be they of race, or class, or whatever).

One of the (ironical) problems this open-ended marxism turns up, I shall call 'the return of the repressed'. If concrete struggles within particular (discursive) locations produce indeterminate outcomes, the question is posed: what are the concepts we need to make sense of particular outcomes? Or, to put it another way, how are outcomes to be explained in terms of the determinations actually operating in particular instances. To say that struggle produces indeterminate outcomes is not to deny the role of determinations as such—for that would be to abandon the realm of the social altogether, an odd position for Marxists to adopt. Rather, it is to say that the notion of struggle *alone* cannot specify the determinations in play. It follows that the notion of 'struggles' has to be specified: in terms of the participants, their respective institutional locations, their informing 'ideologies-in-use', and so on. Which brings us full circle, to those sociological studies examining encounters between police and black youth, arrest decisions, the cautioning 'moment', etc. Re-enter the repressed.

Of course the explanations offered by a historically informed approach, and one that is not, do ultimately differ (and significantly so), a point I shall demonstrate later. But, there is a level—the discursive if you like—at which agreement is not only possible but to be expected. The competing common-senses police and black youth bring to street level encounters, for example. This helps explain, I think, the current promiscuous intermingling of research findings from very different theoretical approaches: nothing is forbidden when traditionalism meets post-modernism in the cosmopolitan thoroughfares of the discursive. Problems arise when the (partial) discursive explanation is *either* seen as sufficient *or* mistaken for the whole. Avoiding such problems requires that discursive explanations be situated historically.

Methodological Implications

The methodological implications of the above can be spelled out briefly, for they follow on from the conclusions just drawn. Attention to particular discourses necessarily entails concrete, empirically based research. And if it is just the discursive level that is of interest, the methods adopted—quantitative, observational etc.—can be selected according to traditional criteria, namely, which can best shed light on the particular object of inquiry. The theoretical promiscuity at the discursive level is consonant with a corresponding methodological promiscuity. But, once again the question of (historical) adequacy intervenes. And, if this is sought, there are methodological implications.

In the first place, the methodology has to be able to shed light on the historical process somehow. That means, in practice, the object of inquiry cannot be so narrowly focused that the historical process remains invisible, or only partially so. (The corollary, of course, is that the focus should not be so broad that *particular* determinations escape notice.) Elsewhere, we have called this approach a "theoretical case study": an approach characterised by "methods ... capable of illuminating in one movement the form of the structures *and their inter-relationship*" (Grimshaw & Jefferson, 1987, p. 27, italics in original).

Such an approach is distinctive in relation to three core methodological approaches, namely, representative sampling, the conventional case-study, and historical documentation. The former, which attempts through sampling to produce empirical generalisations, requires for its success, "an analytical framework of sufficient clarity to make the results adequately comprehensible" (*ibid.*, p. 28). In other words, findings produced through this (positivistic) approach can only be made proper sense of where an analytical framework already exists. The irony is that the positivism of the approach precludes the production of the necessary starting point.

The methodological limitations of the conventional case-study, broadly associated in this area with interactionist observational studies, tend to follow from the theoretical limitations of interactionism, namely, over-attention to observable interactions and processes, and to the accounts of participants. In other words, the theoretical predelictions of interactionism produce a methodological focus on the 'seen and heard', and the absence of a methodological strategy to uncover the hidden structures and processes at work 'behind all our backs'.

The problems with the 'historical documentation' approach, a methodological approach which "entails an accumulation of instances based on case studies and records" (*ibid.*, p. 31), tend to be those associated with reductionist marxism more generally, that is to say, the characteristic raiding of historical and contemporary records, for instances of abuse and discrimination say, is over-attentive to the 'class' significance of events and under-attentive to *other* "determinations necessary to comprehend fully ... particular events" (*ibid.*).

Whilst the precise range of methods associated with theoretical case studies will vary, the above comments point towards a combination of methods—statistical, observational and documentary—and a case chosen with "a sufficient range of empirical differences and interconnections to constitute a starting point for the task of elucidating theoretical concepts generated through a critique of existing theory" (*ibid.*, p 32). (For a fuller elaboration, see Grimshaw & Jefferson, 1987, pp. 27–34).

Conclusion: Holding on to Both Ends of the Chain

Of course it was Althusser who first talked of the necessity of holding on to 'both ends of the chain'. And even as we slough off the overly rationalist structuralist strait-jacket he bequeathed us, we should not forget our considerable debts to him for tackling so boldly erstwhile stifling marxist shibboleths. The following is my attempt, based on a critical reading of all the literature here reviewed, to hang on to both ends of the chain. It is an historically located account of contemporary police–black relations, which attempts to be alert to the discursive determinations in play—though for reasons of space these can only be touched upon here. It constitutes the rudiments of a 'theoretical case-study'.

1 We do not *know* what the *real* rate of black crime is, nor whether it is on the increase. Take robbery for instance. The British Crime Survey reveals that only 8% of robberies were recorded. If these figures applied to London this would mean that there is a suspect for only 1 in 100 robberies. The comparable figure for burglaries would be 5 in 100 (Walker, 1987, p. 39). This means that *whatever* the arrest figures, and whatever the victim identifications, the 'unknown' element is so great, *especially* for these crimes where black 'over-representation' is seen as greatest, as to make all estimates of black offending strictly conjectural.

2 We should not, however, be especially *surprised* if the black crime rate is higher, even if we cannot *know* this. This is because of the known link between certain kinds of crime, deprivation and unemployment (cf. Farrington *et al.*, 1986), and the over-representation of blacks suffering from deprivation as a consequence of structural racism (cf. Brown, 1984). We

should not be surprised either if there is an *increase* in certain kinds of 'survival' crime during a period of recession, such as the present one, whose immediate roots go back at least to the early 1970s.

3 During a recession, crime can become a symptom of the crisis, amongst the authorities and in the popular imagination. The link between the two is often secured through a 'moral panic', which serves to recast the crisis in terms of 'law and order' and provide convenient 'folk devils' to blame. The moral panic also serves to sensitise both police and the public to the 'folk devil' in question, leading to a possible increase in stereotyping, and in public reporting and police targeting behaviour. This can amplify the relevant statistics, which themselves become used to justify the 'law and order' campaign initiated by the moral panic. All of these features have in fact been associated with the present recession. The "moral panic" about mugging of 1972–1973 led to an increased sensitivity to the folk devil of black youth "street criminals", "public concern", police targeting, and the production of legitimating statistics (Hall, *et al.*, 1978). The release of racially coded crime statistics from the mid 1970s onwards by Scotland Yard has clearly been a part of the ideological battle to justify their 'tough' policing of black areas. The most notorious example of this was the release of racially coded figures for 'robbery' and 'other violent theft' suspects in March, 1982. Many saw this as the Metropolitan Police's reply to Scarman. (cf. Sim, 1982).

4 A recession also increases the police role in 'order maintenance' in various ways, as greater conflict—industrial, political or social—makes police life generally tougher. This serves to harden police attitudes. The development of paramilitary policing, and the corresponding switch from defensive to offensive crowd-control tactics, has exacerbated this hardening through the 1970s and 1980s (cf. *State Research* and *Policing London* generally). Those cast as 'folk devils' become victims not only of targeting, but also of this new hardening of attitudes. The clear evidence of worsening relations between police and black youth durng the 1970s fits with such a reading.

5 From the perspective of disadvantaged groups, including black youth, crime is liable to become a more necessary part of a survival strategy during a recession. The consistently higher rates of youth unemployment during the present structural recession (from the late 1960s onwards), and the even higher rates for black youth (cf. Brown, 1984, pp. 151–152), make such groups currently amongst the most socially disadvantaged. (On black youth 'survival strategies', see Pryce, 1986.)

6 The attitudes of those most affected by the recession will tend to harden, especially towards those state institutions held to be responsible for the increased difficulties of 'life on the margins'. The most visible of the state institutions—such as the police—become symbolic of the heightened oppression, and liable to become hated. The attitudes of black youth to the police provide evidence of this hardening, as do their actions, most obviously in the riots of the 1980s (cf. Hall, 1985; Sivananden, 1985). This reading squares

with the PSI evidence, mentioned earlier, that personal experience alone could not account for the degree of hostility to the police found among West Indian Londoners (Smith, 1986, p. 11).

7 The combination of points 3, 4, 5 and 6, brings police and the most disadvantaged and stigmatised groups into constant and increasingly conflictual contact. Black youth increasingly become part of the police problem; and the police increasingly become part of the problem for black youth.

8 At this point the self-fulfilling prophecy, the vicious circle, the amplification of deviance (both police and youth deviance) is set in motion. Police enter encounters expecting trouble and act aggressively to pre-empt it. Black youth similarly expect trouble and create the necessary ('disrespectful') mind set to cope. The resulting 'trouble' demonstrates well how the increased racist oppression of a society in crisis is reproduced, in street level encounters, between the state's agents and a chosen folk devil, in what can be a deadly dynamic of mutual distrust, tension, hostility, and, eventually, hatred.

I would like to thank Stuart Hall and Monica Walker for their comments on an earlier draft of this paper.

References

Banton, M. (1987) *Racial Theories*. Cambridge University Press: Cambridge.

Banton, M. & Harwood, J. (1975) *The Race Concept*. David & Charles: Newton Abbott.

Batta, I. D., Mawby, R. I. & McCulloch, J. W. (1978) Crime, social problems and Asian immigration: the Bradford experience. *International Journal of Contemporary Sociology* **18**, 135–168.

Bayley, D. & Mendelsohn, H. (1969) *Minorities and the Police*. Free Press: New York.

Benyon, J. (1986) *A Tale of Failure: Race and Policing*. Policy Papers in Ethnic Relations, No. 3. University of Warwick: Warwick.

Bethnal Green and Stepney Trades Council (1978) *Blood on the Streets*. Bethnal Green and Stepney Trades Council: London.

Bhaskar, R. (1979) *The Possibility of Naturalism*. Harvester: Hassocks.

Bhaskar, R. (1980) Scientific explanation and human emancipation. *Radical Philosophy* **26**, autumn.

Black, D. & Reiss, A. J. (1967) *Studies of Crime and Law Enforcement in Major Metropolitan Areas*, vol 2. Government Printing Office: Washington DC.

Blom-Cooper, L. & Drabble, R. (1982) Police perception of crime. *British Journal of Criminology* **22**, No. 1, 184–187.

Box, S. & Russell, K. (1975) The politics of discreditability. *Sociological Review* **23**, No. 2, 315–346.

Bridges, L. (1983a) Policing the urban wasteland. *Race and Class* **25**, No. 2, 31–47.

Bridges, L. (1983b) Extended views: The British left and law and order. *Sage Race Relations Abstracts*, February, 19–26.

Brown, C. (1984) *Black and White Britain: the Third PSI Report*. Heinemann: London.

538   *T. Jefferson*

Cain, M. (1973) *Society and the Policeman's Role*. Routledge: London.
Cain, M. & Sadigh, S. (1982) Racism, the police and community policing; a comment on the Scarman Report. *Journal of Law and Society* **9**, No. 1, 87–102.
Coleman, A. M. & Gorman, P. L. (1982) Conservatism, dogmatism, and authoritarianism in British police officers. *Sociology* **16**, No. 1, 1–11.
Cook, P. M. (1977) Empirical survey of police attitudes. *Police review* **85**, 1042, 1078, 1114, 1140.
Farrington, D. P. & Bennett, T. (1981 Police cautioning of juveniles in London. *British Journal of Criminology* **21**, No. 2, 123–135.
Farrington, D. P., Gallagher, B., Morley, L., St. Ledger, R. J. & West, D. J. (1986) Unemployment, school leaving and crime. *British Journal of Criminology* **26**, No. 4, 335–356.
Field, S. & Southgate, P. (1982) *Public Disorder*. Home Office Research Study No. 72. HMSO: London.
Fryer, P. (1984) *Staying Power: The History of Black People in Britain*. Pluto: London.
Gabriel, J. & Ben-Tovim, G. (1979) The conceptualisation of race relations in sociological theory. *Ethnic and Racial Studies* **2**. No. 2.
Gilroy, P. (1982) The myth of black criminality. In *The Socialist Register 1982* (Eve, M. & Musson, D. Eds). Merlin: London.
Gilroy, P. (1983) Police and thieves. In *The Empire Strikes Back* (Centre for Contemporary Cultural Studies, Ed.). Hutchinson: London.
Gilroy, P. (1987) '*There Ain't no Black in the Union Jack*'. Hutchinson: London.
Gordon, P. (1983) *White Law: Racism in the Police, Courts and Prisons*. Pluto: London.
Greater London Council (GLC) (1984 *Racial Harassment in London*. GLC: London.
Grimshaw, R. & Jefferson, T. (1987) *Interpreting Policework*. Allen & Unwin: London.
Gutzmore, C. (1983) Capital, 'black youth' and crime. *Race and Class* **25**, No. 2, 13–30.
Hall, S. (1985) Cold Comfort Farm. *New Socialist* **32**, 10–12.
Hall, S. (1986) The problem of ideology — marxism without guarantees. *Journal of Communication Inquiry*, **10**, No. 2, Summer. 28–44.
Hall, S., Critcher, C., Jefferson, T., Clarke, J. & Roberts, B. (1978) *Policing the Crisis*. Macmillan: London.
Home Office (1981) *Racial Attacks*. HMSO: London.
James, D. (1979) Police black relations: the professional solution. In *The British Police* (Holdway, S. Ed.). Blackwell: Oxford.
Klug, F. (1982) *Racist Attacks*. Runnymede Trust: London.
Lambert, J. (1970) *Crime, Police and Race Relations*. Oxford University Press: Oxford.
Landau, S. (1981) Juveniles and the police. *British Journal of Criminology* **21**, No. 1, 27–46.
Landau, S. & Nathan, G. (1983) Selecting delinquents for cautioning in the London Metropolitan Area. *British Journal of Criminology* **28**, No. 2, 128–149.
Lawrence, E. (1982) In the abundance of water the fool is thirsty: sociology and black pathology. In *The Empire Strikes Back* (Centre for Contemporary Cultural Studies, Ed.). Hutchinson: London.
Lea, J. & Young, J. (1984) *What is to be Done About Law and Order?* Penguin: Harmondsworth.
Lundman, R. J., Sykes, R. E. & Clark, J. P. (1978) Police control of juveniles: a replication. *Journal of Research in Crime and Delinquency* **15**, No. 1, 74–91.
Newman, Sir K. (1983) Policing and social policy in multi-ethnic areas in Europe.

Keynote speech to Cambridge Colloquium on 'Policing and Social Policy in Multi-Ethnic Areas in Europe', 30 August, 1983.

Policy Studies Institute (PSI) (1983) *Police and People in London*, Vol 1: Smith, D. J. *A Survey of Londoners*. Vol 2: Small, S. *A Group of Young Black People*. Vol 3: Smith D. J. *A Survey of Police Officers*. Vol 4: Smith, D. J. & Gray, J. *The Police in Action*. PSI: London.

Potter, L. J. (1977) Police officer personality. *M. Ed. thesis*. University of Bradford: Bradford.

Pryce, K. (1986) *Endless Pressure*. 2nd Edn. Bristol Classical Press: Bristol.

Reiner, R. (1978) *The Blue Coated Worker*. Cambridge University Press: Cambridge.

Reiner, R. (1985) Police and race relations. In *Police: The Constitution and the Community*. (Baxter, J. & Koffman, L. Eds). Professional Books: Abingdon.

Reiss, A. J. (1971) *The Police and the Public*. Yale University Press: New Haven.

Rex, J. & Tomlinson, S. (1979) *Colonial Immigrants in a British City*. Routledge: London.

Scarman, Lord (1981) *The Brixton Disordes 10–12 April 1981*. Cmnd 8427. HMSO: London.

Sherman, L. W. (1980) Causes of police behaviour: the current state of quantitative research. *Journal of Research in Crime and Delinquency*, **17**, No. 1, 69–100.

Sim, J. (1982) Scarman: the police counter attack. In *The Socialist Register 1982* (Eve, M. & Musson, D. Eds). Merlin: London.

Sivanandan, A. (1982) *A Different Hunger*. Pluto: London.

Sivanandan, A. (1985) Britain's gulags. *New Socialist* **32**, 13–15.

Skolnick, J. (1975) *Justice without Trial*. 2nd Edn. Wiley: New York.

Smith, D. (1986) West Indian hostility to the police in relation to personal experience. Unpublished. Policy Studies Institute: London.

Smith, D. & Visher, C. (1981) Street level justice: situational determinants of police arrest decisions. *Social Problems* **29**, No. 2, 167–177.

Southgate, P. (1982) *Police Probationer Training in Race Relations*. Research and Planning Unit, Paper 8. Home Office: London.

Southgate, P. & Ekblom, P. (1984) *Contacts between Police and Public: Findings from the British Crime Survey*. Home Office Research Study No. 77. HMSO: London.

Stevens, P. & Willis, C. (1979) *Race, Crime and Arrests*. Home Office Research Study No. 58. HMSO: London.

Stevens, P. & Willis, C. (1981) *Ethnic Minorities and Complaints against the Police*. Research and Planning Unit Paper 5. Home Office: London.

Sykes, R. E., Fox, J. C. & Clark, J. P. (1976) A socio-legal theory of police discretion. In *The Ambivalent Force*, 2nd Edn (Niederhoffer, A. & Blumberg, A. S. Eds). Dryden Press: Hinsdale, Illinois.

Tuck, M. & Southgate, P. (1981) *Ethnic Minorities, Crime and Policing*. Home Office Research Study No. 70. HMSO: London.

Walker, M. A. (1987) Interpreting race and crime statistics. *Journal of The Royal Statistical Society*, Series A (General) 150, Part 1, 39–56.

Walker, S. (1983) *The Police in America*. McGraw Hill: New York.

Westley, W. (1970) *Violence and the Police: A Sociological Study of Law, Custom and Morality*. MIT: Cambridge, Mass.

Willis, C. (1983) *The Use, Effectiveness and Impact of Police Stop and Search Powers*. Research and Planning Unit, Paper 15. Home Office: London.

Part III
Black Crime: Personality, Culture or Structural Circumstances?

[16]

In my opinion . . .   **À mon avis . . .**

Lombrosian Wine in a New Bottle: Research on Crime and Race[1]

JULIAN V. ROBERTS
AND
THOMAS GABOR
DEPARTMENT OF CRIMINOLOGY
UNIVERSITY OF OTTAWA
OTTAWA, ONTARIO

Les médias canadiens ont consacré beaucoup d'attention aux recherches de Philippe Rushton qui visent à montrer l'existence d'une influence génétique sur les taux de criminalité. L'article examine les données relatives à la relations entre race et criminalité. Nous notons, au début, que la surreprésentation des noirs dans les taux de criminalité se limite à un petit nombre d'infractions par rapport à l'ensemble des crimes. Il existe aussi des infractions où les noirs sont sous-représentés ainsi qu'une grande catégorie d'infractions où la race est sans effet. En outre, même dans le cas des infractions où les noirs sont surreprésentés, leur surreprésentation est fort exagérée. Quoi qu'il en soit, cette conclusion, tirée de la recherche corrélationnelle, n'étaie guère une explication génétique de la criminalité. Quand nous nous penchons sur la criminalité transculturelle de n'importe quelle catégorie raciale (la pureté raciale est, elle aussi, en question), nous constatons que la positon génétique est constamment réfutée. A notre avis, les théories environnementales de la criminalité fournissent une explication beaucoup plus vraie des variations temporelles et transculturelles des taux de criminalité. En résumé, même si les travaux du Pr Rushton ont capté l'attention des médias, il n'existe guère de bases scientifiques à ses assertaions en matière de criminalité et de génétique.

Considerable attention has been devoted by the Canadian news media to the research of Philippe Rushton, which purports to show a genetic influence upon crime rates. This article examines the evidence pertaining to the relationship between race and crime. We begin by noting that the over-representation of blacks in crime rates is restricted to a small number of offences relative to all crimes. Also, there are offences in which blacks are under-represented, as well as a large category of offences in which there is no race effect. Moreover, even for those offences in which blacks are over-represented, the extent of this over-representation has been greatly exaggerated. In any event, this finding — drawn from correlational research — offers little support for a genetic explanation of crime. When we turn to cross-cultural crime patterns of any racial category (racial purity, too, is in question), we find that the

CANADIAN JOURNAL OF CRIMINOLOGY/REVUE CANADIENNE DE CRIMINOLOGIE   APRIL/AVRIL 1990

genetic position is consistently refuted. Environmental theories of crime, we believe, offer a far more powerful explanation of temporal and cross-cultural variations in crime rates. In summary, although the work of Professor Rushton has caught the attention of the news media, there is little scientific basis for his assertions in the area of crime and genetics.

"In our civilized world, to note the proof of the influence of race upon crime is both easier and more certain. We know that a large number of the thieves of London are of Irish parentage or are natives of Lancashire" (Lombroso 1899: 16).

"While comprising 13% of the population of London, African-descended people account for 50% of the crime" (Rushton 1988: 1016).

"it is certainly great nonsense to speak of criminal and non-criminal races. Such things do not exist and are not even to be imagined" (Bonger 1943: 28).

Canadian criminologists have been challenged recently by the work of a professor of psychology, Philippe Rushton, who claims to have uncovered evidence of significant inter-racial differences in many areas of human behaviour, including criminality (Rushton 1987; 1988; 1989). In January 1989, Professor Rushton delivered a paper at the American Association for the Advancement of Science conference in San Francisco (Rushton 1987). Rushton proposed a genetically-based hierarchy in which blacks (who supposedly evolved earlier than whites or orientals) were, *inter alia*, less intelligent and law-abiding than whites and orientals. Rushton asserts that there are substantial inter-racial differences in crime rates, and that these are accounted for by genetic factors. We shall examine later the credibility of genetic explanations of variations in crime rates. First, it is important to address the context of these assertions, and their likely impact upon society.

Rushton's speculations about race and crime have achieved national coverage exceeding that accorded any research project undertaken by criminologists (Globe and Mail 1989). Part of the reason for this is the aggressive posture adopted by Rushton: he has been interviewed in several newspapers and has appeared on several television programmes with national audiences. In contrast, the reaction from criminologists, but not other professional groups (Globe and Mail, 1989), has been muted. His monopolization of media coverage may, we believe, have had a detrimental impact upon public opinion. It is important, therefore, that criminologists in Canada respond to his statements. While Rushton's claims

about racial influences upon intelligence have been challenged, his assertions about crime have not.

The Effect of Rushton's Views on Public Theories of Crime Causation

The race-crime controversy has important consequences for public
opinion in the area of criminal justice. Many of the important questions
in the field of criminology — such as the relative deterrent effect of
capital punishment — cannot be addressed by experiments. Accordingly,
criminologists have used sophisticated correlational procedures to untangle
the relative effects on crime of correlated variables such as genetic and
environmental factors. The existence of a simple statistic then, such as
the over-representation in some crime statistics of certain racial minorities, will by itself convince few scholars. Criminologists have become
sensitized to the possibility of alternative explanations for apparently
straightforward relationships. Members of the public, however, are not
so sophisticated in drawing inferences from statistical information. In
fact, a great deal of recent research in social psychology has documented
numerous ways in which the layperson is led into making unjustified
inferences from material such as that which appears in newspapers (Fiske
and Taylor 1984; Nisbett and Ross 1980).

Rushton's theories may affect public opinion in this area for several
reasons. First, as already noted, the average layperson may not readily
seek alternative (i.e., non-genetic) explanations for the over-representation
of blacks in certain types of crime. Second, laypersons are less likely to
realize that studies on race and crime are essentially correlational, rather
than causal in nature. Third, the race/crime hypothesis comes from a
highly-credible source, namely a well-published and tenured university
professor. Fourth, it is vital to remember that, to the average member of
the public, crime is a relatively unidimensional phenomenon: it usually
involves violence, loss of property, and is a consequence of a "criminal
disposition". Members of the public tend to regard offenders as a relatively homogeneous group (Roberts and White 1986) varying somewhat
in their actions but not their motivations. Criminologists have long been
aware of the deficiencies of this perception of crime; the multi-dimensional
nature of crime and the complexity of motivation render sweeping statements about the etiology of crime invalid. Finally, but not last in impor-

293

CANADIAN JOURNAL OF CRIMINOLOGY/REVUE CANADIENNE DE CRIMINOLOGIE   APRIL/AVRIL 1990

tance, some people may be particularly receptive to racial explanations of crime. Thus, views, such as those expressed by Professor Rushton, may have the unintended effect of inflaming racism in Canada.

Furthermore, Rushton's views received what many laypersons might interpret as substantial support within days of the news media's coverage of his San Francisco address. On February 16, a representative of the Toronto Police Force released statistics showing that blacks were over-represented in the crime statistics in the Jane-Finch area of Toronto (Toronto Star 1989). These data are likely to be misinterpreted by members of the public to constitute evidence supporting a genetic explanation of crime.

For the vast majority of the public, the mass media constitute their primary source of information about crime and criminal justice. Public conceptions of deviance are a consequence of what people read, hear, and see in the media. An abundance of research has demonstrated a direct correspondence between public misperceptions of crime and distorted media coverage of criminal justice issues (Doob and Roberts 1982). Since criminologists have failed to refute Rushton in the news media, we have also relinquished access to the one means of influencing public opinion on this issue. Criminologists may be highly skeptical of Rushton's opinions in the area of crime, but the only way that this skepticism can affect the public is though coverage in the news media. Once again, we note that while Rushton has been criticized by various behavioural geneticists (such as David Suzuki), his assertions regarding race and crime have remained uncontested.

We believe, therefore, that it is important to address the hypothesis that inherited racial traits affect crime rates. For the rest of this paper, we shall examine some methodological issues relating criminality to race. A comprehensive survey of the literature on this topic would occupy a whole issue of a journal; with the length restrictions upon a single article, we can only highlight the research findings and point out what we perceive to be the principal flaws in Rushton's argument. We shall draw upon data from Canada, the United States, and the United Kingdom. Finally, it should be made clear from the outset that we are addressing Rushton's theory as it pertains to the phenomenon of crime. We are not behavioural geneticists, to whom we cede the question of whether the general theory of racial differences withstands scientific scrutiny.

The Scientific Argument: Empirical Research on Race and Crime

1. *Problems with the Definition of Race*

Rushton relates an independent variable (race) to a dependent variable (crime). The inter-racial comparisons cited by Rushton are predicated on the assumption that people are racially pure. Each racial "category" is held to be homogeneous, but this is now accepted by contemporary anthropologists and biologists to be an antiquated and dangerous myth. Centuries of inter-breeding reduce Rushton's rather crude tripartite classification (black, white, oriental) to the level of caricature. For example, Radzinowicz and King (1977) note that in the United States, close to 50% of those classified as black are over half white by lineage (see also Herskovits 1930; and, for a study of the offenders, Hooton 1939). Many American whites, as well, have some black ancestry: Haskell and Yablonsky (1983: 95) note that:

> Estimates of the number of blacks who have "passed" into the white society run as high as 7 million. In addition to those millions who have introduced an African mixture into the "white" population of the United States in the relatively recent past, there must have been millions of Africans who were assimilated into the population of Spain, Portugal, Italy, Greece, and other Mediterranean countries. Descendants of those people are now part of the "white" population of the United States.

Wolfgang and Cohen (1970) cite data showing that no more than 22% of all persons designated as black, in the United States, were of unmixed ancestry. Fully 15% of persons classified as black were more white than black (Wolfgang and Cohen 1970: 7). The pervasiveness of such racial overlap calls genetically-based racial theories of crime into question. (For the rest of this article, for convenience only, we shall continue to refer to inter-*racial* differences. This does not mean we endorse the racial trichotomy of blacks, orientals and whites advanced by Professor Rushton.) Finally, it is important to bear in mind that crime statistics deal with race as a sociological and not a biological category. In short, the independent variable, as it were, is highly problematic. Now we turn to the dependent measure, official and unofficial measures of crime.

CANADIAN JOURNAL OF CRIMINOLOGY/REVUE CANADIENNE DE CRIMINOLOGIE   APRIL/AVRIL 1990

2. *The Issue of Over-Representation in Official Crime Statistics*

Rushton's evidence for a genetic influence consists of the over-representation of blacks in official statistics of crime in the United States, the United Kingdom, and elsewhere. Specifically he asserts that:

> African descended people, for example, while constituting less than one-eighth of the population of the United States or of London, England, currently account for over 50% of the crimes in both places. Since about the same proportion of victims say their assailant was black, the arrest statistics cannot really be blamed on police prejudice (Rushton 1987: 3).

There are at least two factually incorrect elements here, but first we offer a general comment regarding the issue of over-representation.

A simple correlation between two variables does not constitute evidence of a *causal* relationship. A multitude of other confounding factors must be ruled out before one can contemplate a causal relationship. Even if the relationship between race and crime holds up after careful secondary analyses, this is hardly convincing evidence of genetic influences. The fact that parental alcoholism is correlated with alcoholism in the offspring does not prove a genetic component to alcoholism. Alcohol abuse can be a learned behaviour as well. The same argument applies to the race-crime relationship.

Another point is relevant to the issue of a disproportionate involvement in crime. Virtually every society contains racial and ethnic groups, usually minorities, who are more criminally active in certain crimes than the rest of the population. According to Rushton's theory of criminal behaviour, native Canadians should display lower, not higher, crime rates than non-natives. Unfortunately for the theory, this is not true. The over-representation of native offenders in the criminal justice statistics has been apparent for some time (Griffiths and Verdun-Jones 1989; Laprairie 1989). Explanations in terms of the social strata in our society occupied by indigenous peoples can easily explain these findings; Rushton's racial theory cannot. According to Rushton's typology this group, being oriental or mongoloid, should display lower, not higher rates of criminality.

According to Rushton's genetic explanation of crime, the crime rates for blacks should be higher than the white crime rates, *and* the rates for native Canadians should be *lower* than the non-native population. The two categories (blacks; natives) are genetically dissimilar; their rates of criminality should reflect this difference (relative to the white population). The fact is that both black Americans and native Canadians share an elevated risk of certain kinds of criminality (relative to the comparable white populations in their respective countries). Such an outcome is, of course, perfectly consistent with a sociological explanation: both minority groups share a protracted history of constrained social opportunity, as well as overt discrimination.

Also in Canada, French Canadians are the most active in the crime of robbery (Gabor, Baril, Cusson, Elie, LeBlanc and Normandeau 1987). In England, Irish immigrants have been over-represented in crimes of assault for years (Radzinowicz and King 1977). In Israel, the Arab population and non-European Jews are more criminally active in conventional crimes than the European Jews (Fishman, Rattner and Weimann 1987). Such over-representation, then, is the rule rather than the exception across different societies.

To return to Rushton's suggestion, two errors can be identified. First, he cites data published in the *Daily Telegraph* (a British newspaper) showing that blacks account for over 50% of the crimes in the United States and the United Kingdom (Rushton 1988). By any measure, this is a considerable exaggeration. If he refers to all reported crimes and not merely index crimes, blacks account for about 29% of all persons charged in the United States (United States Department of Justice 1989).

As well, aggregate statistics based on index crimes alone misrepresent the true picture. Crime is not, as suggested by Rushton's publications, a homogeneous category of behaviours. While blacks in the United States account for over 60% of arrests for robbery and almost 50% of arrests for murder, they account for about 30% of arrests for burglary and theft, less than 24% of those arrested for arson and about 20% of those arrested for vandalism (U.S. Department of Justice 1987). Using Rushton's own data, blacks are under-represented in crimes like tax fraud and securities violations. In fact, arrest statistics for white-collar crimes such as fraud and embezzlement are significantly higher for whites. Treating crime as a unitary phenomenon obscures this diversity. These variations reflect differential opportunities for offending, and not, we submit, offence-specific genetic programming.

297

CANADIAN JOURNAL OF CRIMINOLOGY/REVUE CANADIENNE DE CRIMINOLOGIE   APRIL/AVRIL 1990

Differential treatment of blacks by the criminal justice system

Finally, arrest statistics reflect, to a degree, the more rigorous sur-veillance by police to which minorities are subject. Data on this point are hard to obtain; the magnitude of the problem is hard to quantify. Nevertheless, the recent release of the "Guildford Four" in England, after 15 years of imprisonment following a wrongful conviction based upon fabricated police evidence, reveals the dangers posed to minorities by an over-zealous police force.

Research in the United States sustains the view that the police are more likely to arrest and charge blacks (Black and Reiss 1967; Lundman, Sykes and Clark 1978). Wolfgang and Cohen (1970: 71) summarize some of this research:

> In comparing arrest statistics for blacks and whites, it is important to remem-ber, then, that one reason for the high arrest rates among blacks is that they are more likely to be stopped, picked up on suspicion and subsequently arrested.

Furthermore, the bias does not remain at the police station: British data (Landau 1981; Landau and Nathan 1983) show that prosecution is more likely for persons of Afro-Caribbean origin. Bias persists at most critical stages of the criminal justice process. As Paul Gordon (1988: 309) noted, summarizing data on the issue:

> Black peoples' experience of the British criminal justice system shows clearly that the rhetoric of the law does not accord with the reality of its practice. The law is not colour-blind, but a means by which black people have been subject to a process of criminalization.

Most recently, Albonetti and her colleagues (1989) have demonstrated that while the influence of race upon pre-trial decisions is complicated, white suspects have the edge over black suspects.

To summarize the data on contact with the criminal justice process, American blacks are clearly over-represented in violent crime statistics, slightly over-represented in property crimes, and under-represented in white-collar crimes. In order to explain this diverse pattern, one has to strain the genetic explanation beyond the breaking point. Are blacks genetically pre-disposed towards street crimes while whites are pro-grammed to commit white-collar crimes? A far more plausible explana-tion exists: social groups commit crimes as a consequence of their social situations and in response to prevailing criminal opportunities. This environmental perspective explains more findings and requires fewer assumptions. The law of parsimony, then, clearly favours environmental over genetic theories of crime. In short, Rushton's explanation of crime by reference to genetic influences requires acceptance of the position that specific antisocial behaviours are directly related to genetic structure. Modern behavioural geneticists would undoubtedly reject this view.

3. *Over-Representation and Alternative Source of Crime Statistics: Victimization Surveys and Self-Reported Criminality*

There is convincing evidence that arrest data exaggerate the true incidence of black criminality. Two alternative sources of information on crime make this clear. Overall, FBI data indicate that 46.5% of all violent crimes reported to the police are committed by blacks. However, the victimization survey conducted by the U.S. Department of Justice found that blacks account for only about 24% of violent crimes (U.S. Department of Justice 1986). Which source presents a more accurate picture of crimes actually committed? With regard to crimes of violence, data derived from victims would appear to be more accurate than arrest data. But it is not just victimization surveys that cast doubt upon the official statistics. A third source of information on crime patterns also shows discrepancies. Rojek (1983) compared police reports with self-reports of delinquency. In the police data-base, race was a significant factor in several offence categories, but this was not true for the self-reports. Other studies using the self-report approach (Williams and Gold 1972) have found a similar pattern: no difference between black and white respondents (Pope 1979) or only slight differences (Hirschi 1969).

Unreported versus reported crime

Another explanation for the elevated incidence of black offenders in official crime statistics concerns the issue of unreported crimes. As we have noted, official crime data indicate that blacks are more likely than whites to commit certain crimes (personal injury offences) and less likely than whites to commit other types of crimes. The problem with crime statistics is that the reporting rate is highly variable, depending upon the offence. The types of offences committed by blacks are more likely to be reported than the offences committed by whites. Any examination of aggregate crime statistics is going to over-estimate the true

CANADIAN JOURNAL OF CRIMINOLOGY/REVUE CANADIENNE DE CRIMINOLOGIE   APRIL/AVRIL 1990

incidence of crime committed by blacks relative to the amount of crime committed by whites.

To conclude, the extent of over-representation of blacks, even in those offences where it occurs, has been exaggerated. In perhaps the most comprehensive study to date which relates crime to race, Michael Hindelang (1982) tested various theories which attempted to explain inter-racial differences. He concluded that the theories of delinquency that best explain the patterns of data were sociological rather than biological. These included Merton's re-formulation of anomie theory (Merton 1968), Cloward and Ohlin's opportunity theory (Cloward and Ohlin 1960), and Wolfgang's sub-culture of violence theory (Wolfgang and Ferracuti 1982).

A final word on the crime statistics utilized by Rushton consists of a caveat: recorded crime is exactly that; it is only a small fraction of all reported and unreported crime. A recent article by Tony Jefferson (1988: 535) makes the point succinctly:

> We do not *know* what the *real* rate of black crime is, nor whether it is on the increase. Take robbery for instance. The British Crime Survey reveals that only 8% of robberies were recorded. If those figures applied to London this would mean that there is a suspect for only 1 in 100 robberies. The comparable figure for burglaries would be 5 in 100 (Walker, 1987, p. 39). This means that *whatever* the arrest figures, and whatever the victim identifications, the 'unknown' element is so great, *especially* for those crimes where black 'over-representation' is seen as greatest, as to make all estimates of black offending strictly conjectural.

When there is sound reason to suppose that the police are more vigilant with regard to black suspects and offenders, it is clear that if we were able to replace reported with unreported crime rates, the inter-racial differences would diminish still further.

Self-report studies provide insight in another area as well. While Professor Rushton associates "lawlessness" with being black, there is overwhelming evidence indicating that most people, at one point or another, commit acts for which they could be prosecuted. As an example, in a now classic study, Wallerstein and Wyle (1947) surveyed 1700 New York City residents without a criminal record. Fully 99% admitted to involvement in at least one of 49 offences. This evidence suggests that rule-breaking is normal activity on the part of most citizens in Western societies. The selection of norm violators to be prosecuted therefore is critical to an understanding of who becomes officially classified as a criminal. Many observers of the criminal justice system believe that race may be a key factor affecting that selection process. Another classic study, Hartshorne and May's (1928) investigation of children, also showed that dishonesty was both pervasive and situation-specific. There was little cross-situational consistency: children that were dishonest in one situation were honest in others. This emphasis on the social situation as the determinant of behaviour is consistent with an environmental view of crime, and inconsistent with Rushton's genetic theory. (A large body of evidence, drawn from longitudinal, self-report, experimental, and observational research, suggests that law-breaking is widespread in North American Society. For a comprehensive review of this literature see Gabor, forthcoming).

4. Within race comparisons

(a) Comparisons over time

In the next two sections, we examine variation in crime rates within race, but across time and cultures. If genetic factors have an important impact upon crime, rates should be relatively stable within race, across both time and cultures. This, however, is not the case. Further undermining Rushton's thesis are the temporal and cross-cultural variations in crime patterns for the black population. Street crime by blacks in the United Kingdom has only recently increased significantly. Just over a decade ago Radzinowicz and King (1977) were able to write that, with the exception of prostitution and other victimless crimes, the black community was as law-abiding as other Britons. Any increase in crime rates within a generation obviously cannot be attributed to genetic factors. This point was made recently by Anthony Mawson (1989) in the context of explanations of homicide in terms of Darwinian selection (Daly and Wilson 1988). Mawson (1989: 239) notes the inability of biological explanations of homicide to account for fluctuations in homicide rates over a short period of time:

> Thus, it seems doubtful whether a selectionist explanation can be applied to changing homicide rates, even those occurring over a thousand years.

301

CANADIAN JOURNAL OF CRIMINOLOGY/REVUE CANADIENNE DE CRIMINOLOGIE   APRIL/AVRIL 1990

The same argument applies in the context of Rushton's work: increases in offending by blacks over a period of ten to fifteen years cannot possibly be explained by reference to genetic influence.

In the United States as well, the proportional involvement of blacks in crime has risen over the past few decades. One major factor in this rise has been the proliferation of illicit drug usage. Heroin use became pervasive in the 1950s and "crack" cocaine is creating an explosion of violent crime in this decade. As well, the erosion of taboos relating to inter-racial crimes has been associated with increased victimization of whites by blacks (Silberman 1978). A third major development has been the greater accessibility of firearms. These are three potent environmental factors affecting black criminality. One would be hard-pressed to find a genetic explanation for the changing criminal activity pattern of a race over such a short period of time.

(b) Comparisons across jurisdictions

The variations in black, white, and oriental crime from one society to another also demonstrate the potency of environmental factors in the etiology of crime. Levels of violent crime in the American South are greater for both blacks *and* whites than they are in other parts of the country. As well, there is substantial variation in the homicide rates for blacks in different American states. For example, in Delaware the homicide rate for blacks is 16.7 per 100,000. This is considerably lower than the homicide rate for black residents of other states; in Missouri, for example, the rate is 65 per 100,000 (Carroll and Mercy 1989).

Cross-national, within-race comparisons make the same point. Black Americans have a higher homicide rate than their more racially-pure counterparts in Africa: this fact directly contradicts Rushton's thesis. The author (Bohannan 1960: 123) of a study of African homicide concludes:

> if it needed stressing, here is overwhelming evidence that it is a cultural and not biological factor which makes for a high homicide rate among American negroes.

More recent data (International Criminal Police Organization 1988) demonstrate the same variations: the homicide rate per 100,000 inhabitants varies from .01 (Mali) to 29 (Bahamas) and 22.05 (Jamaica). It is noteworthy also that the Caribbean homicide rates are far in excess of even the African countries with the highest rates (e.g., Rwanda, 11 per 100,000; Tanzania 8 per 100,000). This despite the fact that residents of the Caribbean are more racially mixed than blacks from Africa. According to Rushton's theory, homicide rates should be higher not lower in the more racially pure African states.

Furthermore, orientals do not constitute a monolith of law-abiding citizens. The homicide rates in the Far East also vary considerably, from 39 per 100,000 residents in the Phillipines to 1.3 per 100,000 in Hong Kong. In Thailand, the homicide rate exceeds the rate of homicide in Japan by a factor of twelve (International Criminal Police Organization 1988). In all these comparisons, the genetic explanation falls short. The magnitude of these *intra*-racial differences suggests that the potency of environmental factors to explain crime rates far exceeds that of genetic factors. In statistical terms, these data imply that the percentage of variation in crime rates explained by genetic factors is negligible, if it exists at all.

5. *Victimization Patterns*

There is another form of over-representation of which Professor Rushton appears unaware: blacks are at much higher risk of becoming the victims of violent crime. In the United States, black males are 20 times more likely than whites to be shot, cut, or stabbed, and black females are 18 times more likely to be raped than white women (Wolfgang and Cohen 1981). Black Americans are also more likely than whites to be victims of burglary, motor vehicle theft, assault, robbery and many other offences (U.S. Bureau of Justice Statistics 1983). Although blacks constitute only 12% of the general United States population, over 40% of homicide victims are black. See Barnett and Schwartz (1989) for recent data showing black victimization rates to be approximately four times higher than white rates. The same trends are apparent in other countries, such as England. The over-representation of blacks as victims is substantial, yet no-one has posited that such over-representation is due to a genetically-based susceptibility to criminal victimization. While this finding is not inconsistent with an explanation based upon genetic factors, it does underscore the importance of environmental factors such as propinquity and accessibility. Violent crimes are a result of an interaction between offender and victim. To posit an over-riding genetic

CANADIAN JOURNAL OF CRIMINOLOGY/REVUE CANADIENNE DE CRIMINOLOGIE   APRIL/AVRIL 1990

basis of crime is to ignore the role of the victim and situational factors (Boyd 1988; Wolfgang 1958). When we examine the dynamics of the violent crime most commonly associated with blacks — armed robbery — we readily see the importance of situational determinants. Actually, recourse to physical violence occurs only in a small minority of robberies. Usually the violence that does occur arises in response to victims who resist the robbers' demands (Gabor *et al.*, 1987). The violence, therefore, is often instrumental and situation-specific.

If blacks are more likely to be both offenders and victims in relation to certain types of crime, then a plausible explanation for their over-representation on both counts is that they tend to live in areas in which violence is a normal consequence of stress, threat, and frustration. This essentially is Wolfgang and Ferracuti's (1982) subculture of violence thesis. Aside from living in environments where violence is normative behaviour, blacks tend disproportionately to live in poverty. Furthermore, they are over-represented among urban dwellers. Economic status and urban residence are linked to a number of crime indices. A fair examination of black and white criminality would therefore necessitate comparison between persons situated similarly in society.

But even the presence of a correlation between race and certain indices of crime, after other plausible environmental factors have been partialled out, does not demonstrate a genetically-based race/crime link. As Charles Silberman (1978) has pointed out, the experience of black Americans has been very different from the experience of any other disadvantaged group. The generations of violence, deprivation, disenfranchisement, and exclusion from educational and vocational opportunities to which they have been subjected has not been shared by any other ethnic or racial group. Moreover, much of this racial discrimination persists, to this day, and in this country, as recent research has documented (Henry and Ginsberg 1985). Discrimination of this kind can engender social patterns and attitudes towards authority that lead to law breaking.

Careful epidemiological research can result in samples of black and white citizens that are "matched" on many important background variables such as social class, income, education, age, family size and composition. Comparisons between such groups is preferable to comparison based upon unmatched samples, but the effects of long-term discrimination, brutality, and oppression over generations cannot be captured by the most rigorous multiple regression analysis. As John Conklin (1989: 140) notes:

> to argue that blacks and whites of similar backgrounds will have the same crime rate is to argue that centuries of discrimination have had no long-term effects on blacks that are conducive to criminal behaviour.

Our opposition to Rushton's views should not be interpreted to mean that we deny the existence of any genetic influences upon human behaviour. Rather, we take issue with the attribution of racial differences in criminality to genetic factors. In our view, there is little scientific basis for his rather sweeping assertions about the relative "law-abidingness" of different racial groups. The few statistics he provides are susceptible of a multitude of highly probable alternative explanations derived from an environmental perspective. Given the incendiary nature of the theory and its policy implications, we feel that the burden of proof is upon Professor Rushton to provide more convincing data than the few ambiguous statistics he has to date brought forth. We leave it to others (Lynn 1989; Zukerman and Brody 1988) to evaluate the scientific credibility of Professor Rushton's genetic explanation of other phenomena such as: intelligence, sexual restraint, personality, political preferences, and the efficacy of the German army in World War II (Globe and Mail 1989). In the area of criminality, his evidence, in our view, falls short of discharging a scientific burden of proof.

The Born Criminal is Born Again

Racial explanations of differences in crime rates are of course hardly new; many criminologists will read Professor Rushton's statements with a sense of déjà vu. The attempt to relate crime and race clearly echoes the writings of Cesare Lombroso, both in method and conclusion. The quotes preceding this article underline the parallels between the two theories separated by almost a century. Ironically, given Rushton's research focusing on the head-sizes of different races, Lombroso was also preoccupied with the study of offenders' skulls. His primary research tool was a craniometer. In his instructions regarding the physical examination of criminals, Lombroso notes:

CANADIAN JOURNAL OF CRIMINOLOGY/REVUE CANADIENNE DE CRIMINOLOGIE   APRIL/AVRIL 1990

"careful examination of this part [i.e. the skull] is of the utmost importance"
(Lombroso-Ferrero 1911/1972: 238-239).

The same failure to distinguish a causal from an associative relationship permeates Lombroso's writings. For example, in the chapter
devoted to racial influences on crime in his major work, he makes
statements such as the following:

> "I have found that in the departments [i.e. in France] where dark hair
> predominates the figures for murder reach 12.6%, while the light haired
> departments give only 6.3%" (Lombroso 1899/1968: 35).

The reader should not interpret this as an example of mere muddle-
headed empiricism on Lombroso's part, the product of unscientific but
benign inquisitiveness. Lombroso's biological theory has a danger common to all such theories — it led him to misinterpret data and to write
statements that are shocking even to today's reader, inured to racialism
by the events of the 20th century. For example, after dealing with Jews
("synonymous with usurer"), Lombroso (1899/1968: 38-39) notes that
gypsies are:

> the living example of a whole race of criminals and have all the passions and
> all the vices of criminals.

And in another work (Lombroso-Ferrero, 1911/1972: 40) on this occasion edited by his daughter:

> In the gypsies we have an entire race of criminals with all the passions and
> vices common to delinquent types: idleness, ignorance, impetuous fury, van-
> ity, love of orgies, and ferocity.

He then accuses them of all manner of vice, including cannibalism.

Early Research on Polygeny

Stephen Jay Gould (1981), in a highly acclaimed review of research
linking race and heredity to human behaviour and intelligence, has
identified countless flaws in logic and method of some of the seminal
works in this area. Gould shows that both polygeny (the doctrine that
the races could be ordered from the most primitive to the most advanced)
and craniometry predated Lombroso.

Gould begins by asking whether inductive science contributed to
the emergence of racial ranking or whether an *a priori* commitment to
ranking generated the research and conclusions that, not so surprisingly,

buttressed the pre-existing commitment to racial hierarchies. The evidence Gould presents strongly favours the latter hypothesis. He shows that American polygeny, for example, was at its apex when the racial caste system in the United States was under assault. Gould also shows that the protagonists of racial theories tended to unabashedly speak about the natural inferiority of the "Negroid" race. The research examining such things as cranial differences between the races, therefore, was far from value-neutral science.

It is interesting to note that one of the foremost empiricists of polygeny, Samuel Morton, on the basis of measures of cranial capacity, rated whites ahead of orientals on his racial hierarchy; whereas Rushton considers orientals the most advanced of races, with respect to both intelligence and temperament.

Also interesting is the disparity between Rushton's descriptions of the behavioural inclinations of blacks and those offered in the 19th century. Louis Agassiz, the Swiss naturalist who immigrated to America and was a leading theorist of polygeny, referred to the "Negro" as "submissive, obsequious, and imitative" (Gould, 1981: 46). These adjectives are inconsistent with the image of blacks portrayed by Rushton. Are the discrepancies between present day and earlier polygenists based on inductive science or changing cultural stereotypes? Is it genetic mutation or social change that is responsible for the violence currently attributed to blacks by people like Rushton?

Gould further identifies some methodological weaknesses undermining cranial measures. Samuel Morton (in Gould, 1981: 53) proceeded in the following way:

> He filled the cranial cavity with sifted white mustard seed, poured the seed back into a graduated cylinder and read the skull's volume in cubic inches. Later on, he became dissatisfied with mustard seed because he could not obtain consistent results. The seeds did not pack well, for they were too light and still varied too much in size, despite sieving. Remeasurements of single skulls might differ by more than 5 percent.

Gould (1981: 53-54) observes that Morton's measures

> matched every good Yankee's prejudice — whites on top, Indians in the middle, and blacks on the bottom; and, among whites, Teutons and Anglo-Saxons on top, Jews in the middle, and Hindus on the bottom. . . . Status and access to power in Morton's America faithfully reflected biological merit.

CANADIAN JOURNAL OF CRIMINOLOGY/REVUE CANADIENNE DE CRIMINOLOGIE   APRIL/AVRIL 1990

Gould reanalyzed Morton's data and catalogued a multitude of methodological shortcomings; for example, his skull measures failed to control for sex and body size. Skull measures, of course, also assume that skull size and mental ability are related. As a bottom line, Gould (1981: 54) asserts that, "to put it bluntly, Morton's summaries are a patchwork of fudging and finagling in the clear interest of controlling a priori convictions." Speculating about the discrepancies in Morton's data, Gould (1981: 65) states that

> Plausible scenarios are easy to construct. Morton, measuring by seed, picks up a threateningly large black skull, fills it lightly and gives it a few desultory shakes. Next, he takes a distressingly small Caucasian skull, shakes hard, and pushes mightily at the foramen magnum with his thumb. It is easily done, without conscious motivation; expectation is a powerful guide to action.

The tendency of craniometricians and criminal anthropologists to fit any finding into their explanatory models of crime is shown by their reactions to "anomalies" in brain size:

> The large size of many criminal brains was a constant source of bother to craniometricians and criminal anthropologists. Broca [the famous French craniometrician] tended to dismiss it with his claim that sudden death by execution precluded the diminution that long bouts of disease produced in many honest men. In addition, death by hanging tended to engorge the brain and lead to spuriously high weights (Gould, 1981: 94).

Broca also argued that brain size increased with the advancement of European civilization. When he found that the brain size of people buried in common graves in the 18th century was, on the average, larger than those buried in the 19th century, he argued that the earlier sample included higher status individuals (Gould, 1981: 96).

Our intention is not to impugn the personal integrity of researchers, such as Rushton, who have advanced genetic theories linking race and human behaviour. Rather, we have attempted to show, by reviewing some of the earlier work of polygenists, that the area of race and crime, given the emotionalism permeating it, may easily lend itself to ideological bias.

Conclusion

To conclude, there are some important lessons to be learned from research on race and crime. First, it is clear that the news media are particularly sensitized to controversial research. Most empirical work in criminology is at once more substantive and less controversial. Accordingly, it escapes the attention of the news media and thereafter the public. Second, the importance of addressing the methodological shortcomings of a genetic explanation of crime cannot be over-stated. Although Professor Rushton has steered clear of speculating about the policy implications of a theory linking race and crime, Lombroso was not so reticent. In "Criminal Man" we find the following:

> When we realize that there exist beings, born criminals, who reproduce the instincts common to the wildest savages and . . . are destined by nature to injure others . . . we feel justified in demanding their extermination (Lombroso, 1899/1968: 202).

People who accept the view that variations in crime rates reflect genetic factors may also embrace an underlying message about crime prevention. There is an unmistakable message conveyed by a view asserting a race-crime relationship predicated on genetic differences. Social programs aim to eradicate educational, social, and economic inequities. These efforts can only be undermined by statements stressing the importance of genetic factors in determining criminality.[2]

We end with a quote from Elliot Currie (1985: 219):

> The real issue is whether we regard the evidence on the persistence of family problems and the continuity of troubling behaviour from childhood to adult life as indicative of predispositions that are largely unrelated to their social context and that we are virtually powerless to alter. For many conservative writers, the dark conclusion to be dawn from this evidence . . . is that there are sharp limits to what we can do for either troubled children or the troubled adults they often become. That conclusion lends support to the ever more intensive search for new methods of screening and incapacitation and to the simultaneous neglect of policies to reduce economic and racial disadvantage.

Notes

1. The authors would like to acknowledge that this manuscript has benefitted from the comments of Michael Petrunik, from the University of Ottawa, the editorial committee of the Canadian Journal of Criminology, and two anonymous reviewers.

2. The same line of reasoning applies to the more controversial debate on intelligence. The danger is that if we accept the position that a great deal of variation in IQ scores is due to genetic factors, it makes less sense to invest in programs designed to affect the pedagogical environment.

CANADIAN JOURNAL OF CRIMINOLOGY/REVUE CANADIENNE DE CRIMINOLOGIE   APRIL/AVRIL 1990

References

Albonetti. Celesta. Robert Hauser, John Hagan and Ilene Nagel
  1989   Criminal justice decision making as a stratification process: The role of race and stratification resources in pe-trial release. Journal of Quantitative Criminology 5: 57-82.

Barnett. Arnold and Elliot Schwartz
  1989   Urban homicide: Still the same. Journal of Quantitative Criminology 5: 83-100.

Black. D. and Albert Reiss
  1967   Studies of Crime and Law Enforcement in Major Metropolitan Areas. Washington: Government Printing Office.

Bohannan. Paul
  1960   African Homicide and Suicide. Princeton, N.J.: Princeton Univ. Press.

Bonger. Willem
  1969   Race and Crime. New Jersey: Patterson Smith. (Originally published 1943).

Boyd. Neil
  1988   The Last Dance: Murder in Canada. Toronto: Prentice Hall.

Carroll. Patrick and James Mercy
  1989   Regional variation in homicide rates: Why is the west so violent? Violence and Victims 4: 17-25.

Cloward. Richard A. and Lloyd Ohlin
  1960   Delinquency and Opportunity: A Theory of Delinquent Gangs. New York: The Free Press.

Conklin. John
  1989   Criminology. (Third edition) New York: Macmillan.

Curie. Elliot
  1985   Confronting Crime. New York: Pantheon.

Daly. Martin and Margo Wilson
  1988   Homicide. New York: Aldine.

Doob. Anthony N. and Julian V. Roberts
  1982   Crime: Some Views of the Canadian Public. Ottawa: Department of Justice

Fishman, G.. Arye Rattner, and Gabriel Weimann
  1987   The effect of ethnicity on crime attribution. Criminology 25: 507-524.

Fiske. Susan T. and Shelley E. Taylor
  1984   Social Cognition. Reading, Mass.: Addison-Wesley.

Gabor. Thomas
  In Press   Crime by the public. In Curt Griffiths and Margaret Jackson (eds), Introduction to Canadian Criminology. Toronto: Harcourt Brace Jovanovich.

Gabor. Thomas. Micheline Baril, M. Cusson, D. Elic, Marc LeBlanc, and Andre Normandeau
  1987   Armed Robbery: Cops, Robbers, and Victims. Springfield, Illinois: Charles C. Thomas.

Globe and Mail
  1989   February 11, 14.

Gordon. Paul
  1988   Black people and the criminal law: Rhetoric and reality. International Journal of the Sociology of Law 16: 295-313.

Gould. Stephen Jay
  1981   The Mismeasure of Man. New York: W.W. Norton.

Griffiths, Curt and Simon Verdun-Jones
  1989   Canadian Criminal Justice. Toronto: Butterworths.

Hartshorne, M. and May, M.A.
  1928   Studies in Deceit. New York: Macmillan.

Haskell, M.R. and L. Yablonsky
  1983   Criminology: Crime and Criminality. Boston: Houghton Mifflin.

Henry, F. and E. Ginsberg
  1985   Who Gets the Work: A Test of Racial Discrimination in Employment. Toronto: Urban
         Alliance on Race Relations and the Social Planning Council.

Herskovits, Melville J.
  1930   The Anthropometry of the American Negro. New York: Columbia University Press.

Hindelang, Michael
  1982   Race and Crime. In Leonard D. Savitz and N. Johnston (eds.), Contemporary Criminol-
         ogy. Toronto: John Wiley.

Hirschi, Travis
  1969   Causes of Delinquency. Berkley: University of California Press.

Hooton, Ernest A.
  1939   Crime and the Man. Cambridge, Mass: Harvard University Press.

International Criminal Police Organization
  1988   International Crime Statistics 1985-86.

Jefferson, Tony
  1988   Race, crime and policing: Empirical, theoretical and methodological issues. International
         Journal of the Sociology of Law 16: 521-539.

Landau, Simha
  1981   Juveniles and the police. British Journal of Criminology 21: 27-46.

Landau, Simha and G. Nathan
  1983   Selecting delinquents for cautioning in the London metropolitan area. British Journal of
         Criminology 28: 128-149.

LaPrairie, Carol
  1989   The role of sentencing in the over-representation of aboriginal people in correctional
         institutions. Ottawa: Department of Justice.

Lombroso, Caesare
  1968   Crime. Its Causes and Remedies (English Edition) Montclair, New Jersey: Patterson
         Smith. (Original publication: Le Crime, causes et remèdes 1899).

Lombroso-Ferrero, Gina
  1972   Criminal Man According to the Classification of Cesare Lombroso. Montclair, N.J.:
         Patterson Smith. 1972 (Originally published 1911).

Lundman, R., R. Sykes and J. Clark
  1978   Police control of juveniles: A replication. Journal of Research in Crime and Delinquency
         15: 74-91.

Lynn, Michael
  1989   Race difference in sexual behaviour: A critique of Rushton and Bogaert's evolutionary
         hypothesis. Journal of Research in Personality 23: 1-6.

Mawson, Anthony
  1989   Review of Homicide (Daly and Wilson, 1988). Contemporary Sociology March 238-240.

CANADIAN JOURNAL OF CRIMINOLOGY/REVUE CANADIENNE DE CRIMINOLOGIE   APRIL/AVRIL 1990

Merton, Robert K.
    1968   Social Theory and Social Structure. Glencoe: The Free Press.

Nisbett, Richard and Lee Ross
    1980   Human Inference: Strategies and Shortcomings of Social Judgement. Englewood Cliffs, N.J.: Prentice Hall.

Pope, Carl E.
    1979   Race and crime re-visited. Crime and Delinquency 25: 345-357.

Radzinowicz, Leon and Joan King
    1977   The Growth of Crime: The International Experience. London: Penguin.

Roberts, Julian V. and Nicholas R. White
    1986   Public estimates of recidivism rates: Consequences of a criminal stereotype. Canadian Journal of Criminology 28: 229-241.

Rojek, Dean G.
    1983   Social status and delinquency: Do self-reports and official reports match? In Gordon P. Waldo (ed), Measurement Issues in Criminal Justice. Beverly Hills: Sage.

Rushton, J. Philippe
    1987   Population Differences in Rule-Following Behaviour: Race Evolution and Crime. Paper presented to the 39th Annual Meeting of the American Society of Criminology, Montreal, November 11-14.

    1988   Race differences in behaviour: A review and evolutionary analysis. Personality and Individual Differences 9: 1009-1024.

    1989   Race differences in sexuality and their correlates: Another look and physiological models. Journal of Research in Personality 23: 35-54.

Silberman, Charles
    1978   Criminal Violence, Criminal Justice. New York: Vintage.

Toronto Star
    1989   February 17, 20.

United States Department of Justice
    1983   Sourcebook of Criminal Justice Statistics. Washington, D.C.: Bureau of Justice Statistics.

    1986   Criminal Victimization in the United States. Washington, D.C.: Bureau of Justice Statistics.

    1987   Sourcebook of Criminal Justice Statistics. Washington, D.C.: Bureau of Justice Statistics.

    1989   Sourcebook of Criminal Justice Statistics. Washington, D.C.: Bureau of Justice Statistics.

Wallerstein, James S. and Clement J. Wyle
    1947   Our law-abiding lawbreakers. Probation 25: 107-112.

Williams, Jay and Martin Gold
    1972   From delinquent behaviour to official delinquency. Social Problems 20: 209-229.

Wolfgang, Marvin
    1958   Patterns in Criminal Homicide. Philadelphia: University of Pennsylvania Press.

Wolfgang, Marvin and Bernard Cohen
    1981   Crime and race: The victims of crime. In Burt Galaway and Joe Hudson (eds.), Perspectives on Crime Victims. St. Louis: C.V. Mosby.

    1970   Crime and Race. Conceptions and Misconceptions. New York: Institute of Human Relations Press.

Wolfgang, Marvin and Franco Ferracuti
    1982   The Subculture of Violence. Beverly Hills, Cal.: Sage.

IN MY OPINION . . . À MON AVIS . . .

Zuckerman, Marvin and Nathan Brody
1989   Oysters, rabbits and people: A critique of "race differences in behaviour" by J.P. Rushton. Personality and Individual Differences 9: 1025-1033.

[17]

Race and Crime: A Reply to Roberts and Gabor

J. Philippe Rushton
Department of Psychology
University of Western Ontario
London, Ontario

Afin de permettre une évaluation adéquate de ma théroie, je a) présente des données déjà publiées ailleurs qui montrent que, en moyenne, les mongoloïdes l'emportent sur les caucasoïdes et ceux-ci sur les négroïdes en ce qui concerne la grosseur du cerveau et l'intelligence, le retard maturationnel, la retenue sexuelle, le tempérament tranquille et l'organisation sociale, b) analyse de nouvelles données qui montrent que la criminalité présente des différences raciales d'ordre international, c) traite de la valeur prédictive de la race quant au comportement, d) fait voir l'existence de traits de caractère durables, e) montre que Lombroso est juste dans certaines de ses convictions touchant les bases biologiques de la criminalité, f) examine des données qui tendent à montrer que les différences de la criminalité ont une base génétique, et g) propose que la recherche se penche sur la question des bases neurohormonales de la criminalité.

To allow an adequate of my theory, I (a) tabulate previous data showing that, on average, Mongoloids > Caucasoids > Negroids in brain size and intelligence, maturational delay, sexual restraint, quiescent temperament, and social organization; (b) analyze new data demonstrating that race differences in crime occur internationally; (c) discuss the predictive power of race for behavior; (d) show the existence of enduring traits of character; (e) show Lombroso to have been correct in some of his beliefs about the biological basis of crime; (f) review evidence suggesting that the race differences in crime have a genetic basis; and (g) propose that future research investigate the neurohormonal basis of crime.

Roberts and Gabor (1990) seriously misrepresent my position. They manoeuvre around the main argument and so deconstruct the crime figures into particulars that readers may fail to see the forest for the trees. To appreciate what I have said, therefore, it is necessary to consider the data in Table 1. The crux of the matter — and I wish to emphasize that this is the essential point — is that any theory proposed to explain the many differences among human races must be judged by its ability to account for the overall pattern of correlated variables in which the Caucasoid average so consistently falls between those of Mongoloids and Negroids. It is not simply differences in crime that require explanation.

CANADIAN JOURNAL OF CRIMINOLOGY/REVUE CANADIENNE DE CRIMINOLOGIE   APRIL/AVRIL 1990

Table 1

Average Racial Differences in Life History Variables

	Mongoloids	Caucasoids	Negroids
Brain weight and intelligence			
Cranial capacity	1448 cc	1408 cc	1334 cc
Brain weight at autopsy	1351 g	1336 g	1286 g
Millions of "excess neurons"	8900	8650	8550
IQ test scores	107	100	85
Maturation rate			
Gestation time	?	Medium	Early
Skeletal development	?	Medium	Early
Age of walking	Late	Medium	Early
Age of first intercourse	Late	Medium	Early
Age of first pregnancy	Late	Medium	Early
Life-span	Long	Medium	Short
Personality and temperament			
Activity level	Low	Medium	High
Aggressiveness	Low	Medium	High
Cautiousness	High	Medium	Low
Dominance	Low	Medium	High
Impulsivity	Low	Medium	High
Sociability	Low	Medium	High
Reproductive efforts			
Multiple birthing rate	Low	Medium	High
Size of genitalia	Small	Medium	Large
Secondary sex characteristics	Small	Medium	Large
Intercourse frequencies	Low	Medium	High
Permissive attitudes	Low	Medium	High
Sexually transmitted diseases	Low	Medium	High
Androgen levels	Low	Medium	High
Social organization			
Law abidingness	High	Medium	Low
Marital stability	High	Medium	Low
Mental health	High	Medium	Low

For over 70 years, the psychological study of race focused mainly on the differences between blacks and whites in the United States, especially in educational achievement and intelligence. My research broadened the data base on race by (a) including Mongoloid samples (one third of the world's population), (b) including other Negroid samples (most black people live in post-colonial Africa), and (c) considering other life-history variables including speed of physical maturation, brain size, longevity, personality traits, rate of twinning, reproductive behaviour, and social organization. I concluded that the average racial group differences are to be found worldwide, in Africa and Asia as well as in Europe and North America (Rushton 1988a).

316

Before proceeding further, I emphasize that considerable variability exists within each major group, as well as within numerous subdivisions. Thus there are important individual differences to be considered over and above the average tendencies. Racism is the failure to acknowledge such within-group variation and to treat (usually mistreat) people in a category as though they were all the same. When Roberts and Gabor (1990) make such outlandish statements as "Professor Rushton associates 'lawlessness' with being black", they seriously misrepresent my views.

The central scientific question then is: Why should Caucasian populations average between Negroid and Mongoloid populations on so many variables? While socialization obviously has a significant role to play in achievement, sexuality, and social organization, other observations such as the speed of physical maturation, morphology, and the production of gametes imply the presence of evolutionary and therefore genetic influences.

r/K Evolution Theory

The racial pattern found in Table 1 may be explained by an ecological theory of why traits covary in animal life-histories in which Mongoloids are more *K*-selected than are Caucasoids and Negroids. *K*-selected life-histories emphasize parenting effort as contrasted with *r*-selected life-histories which emphasize mating effort, the bioenergetic tradeoff between which is postulated to underlie cross-species differences in speed of maturation, body size, reproductive effort, and mortality rate (Ruston 1985, 1988a, 1988b; following E.O. Wilson 1975). Selection for increased brain size, for example, typically leads to fewer and slower maturing offspring, greater parental care per each offspring, stronger parental bonding, increased social organization, and a longer life span.

Within species of plants, insects, birds and non-human mammals, many of the life-history variables are found to covary as theoretically expected and to be genetic in origin. There is, therefore, good biological reason to apply such analyses to differences among humans. One analysis of reproductive effort within the Caucasoid population contrasted the characteristics of the mothers of dizygotic twins who, because they ovulated more than one egg at a time can be considered to represent the *r*-strategy, with the mothers of singletons representing the *K*-strategy.

317

CANADIAN JOURNAL OF CRIMINOLOGY/REVUE CANADIENNE DE CRIMINOLOGIE   APRIL/AVRIL 1990

Predictably, the former mothers were found to have, on average, a lower age of menarche, a shorter menstrual cycle, a higher number of marriages, a higher rate of coitus, a greater fecundity, more wasted pregnancies, an earlier menopause, and an earlier age of death (Rushton 1987).

Of critical importance to the current debate is the work of Ellis (1987a, 1987b, 1989, forthcoming) directly applying r/K theory to crime. Ellis (1987a) contrasted the characteristics of criminals who, because they are lower in altruism and social organization, can be considered to represent the r-strategy, with the general population representing the K-strategy. The criminals were found to have, on average, shorter gestation periods (more premature births), a more rapid development to sexual functioning, a greater copulatory rate outside of bonded relationships (or at least a preference for such), less stable bonding, a lower parental investment in offspring (as evidenced by higher rates of child abandonment, neglect and abuse), and a shorter life expectancy. Ellis (1989:94) also analyzed rape from an r/K perspective linking forced copulation to an r-reproductive strategy. Regarding race differences, he theoretically derived the prediction that "blacks should have higher rape rates than whites, and whites in turn should have higher rates than Orientals". As we shall see from international data, Ellis's prediction is confirmed.

International Crime

Stable social organization depends on individuals following rules, a construct which can be indexed through marital functioning, mental durability, and law abidingness. On each of these measures, the rank-ordering within American populations is Mongoloid > Caucasoid > Negroid, and cross-cultural studies suggest these findings may be internationally generalizable (Rushton 1988a). Individually motivated and capricious assault and murder is universally condemned and clearly provides a good index of social disorganization. With homicides, the U.S. has the highest rate in the industrialized world, but 49% are committed by Negroids and 13% by Hispanics.

Roberts and Gabor (1990) deny the international generalizability of the crime data and argue that because some African countries report lower homicide rates than do some Asian countries that: "the genetic position is consistently refuted''. Before dealing with whether genetic explanations fit the data, it is important to consider just what are the data. To establish them, I consulted International Crime Statistics for 1983-1984 and 1985-1986 which provided data on nearly 100 countries in 14 crime categories (International Criminal Police Organization 1988). Because the figures for some crimes are highly dependent on a country's laws (e.g. ''Sex Offences'') or on availability (e.g. ''Theft of Motor Cars''), I focussed on the three most serious crimes which are relatively unambiguous: *Murder*, ''Any act performed with the purpose of taking human life, in whatever circumstances. This definition *excludes abortion but includes infanticide*'' (Preface, emphasis in original); *Rape*; and *Serious Assault*, ''An injury whereby life could be endangered, including cases of injury involving the use of a dangerous instrument. Cases where instruments are used merely to threaten people without causing injury are to be excluded.''

I collated the figures per 100,000 population for 1984 and 1986 (or the next nearest year) and aggregated across the three categories (see Table 2). Countries for which data could not be found in all three categories were dropped. Countries were then grouped by primary racial composition with only Fiji and Papua New Guinea being eliminated due to uncertainty as to their racial status. For 1984, complete data were available for 71 countries: 9 Mongoloid (including Indonesia, Malaysia, and the Philippines), 40 Caucasoid (including Arabic North Africa, the Middle East, and Latin America), and 22 Negroid (sub-Saharan Africa including Sudan, and the Caribbean); for 1986, complete data were available for 88 countries (12 Mongoloid, 48 Caucasoid, and 28 Negroid). Obviously, these groupings do not represent in any sense ''pure types'' and there is enormous racial and ethnic variation within almost every country; moreover, each country undoubtedly differs in the procedures used to collect and disseminate the crime figures. Certainly, within each racial grouping are to be found countries reporting both high and low crime rates. The Philippines, for example, a country grouped as Mongoloid, reported one of the highest homicide rates in the world, 43 per 100,000 in 1984; Togo, a country grouped as Negroid, had the lowest reported crime rate in the world, a ''rounded down'' 0 per 100,000 in all 3 crime categories in 1984.

Race, Crime and Justice

CANADIAN JOURNAL OF CRIMINOLOGY/REVUE CANADIENNE DE CRIMINOLOGIE   APRIL/AVRIL 1990

Table 2

International Crime Rates per 100,000 Population for Countries
Categorized by Predominant Racial Type

	Homicide		Rape		Serious Assault		Total	
	Mean	SD	Mean	SD	Mean	SD	Mean	SD
1984								
Mongoloid (N = 9)	8.0	14.1	3.7	2.6	37.1	46.8	48.8	50.3
Caucasoid (N = 40)	4.4	4.3	6.3	6.5	61.6	66.9	72.4	72.5
Negroid (N = 22)	8.7	11.8	12.8	15.3	110.8	124.6	132.3	139.3
F(2.69)	1.92		3.99*		3.16*		3.59*	
1986								
Mongoloid (N = 12)	5.8	10.9	3.2	2.7	29.4	40.2	38.4	42.7
Caucasoid (N = 48)	4.5	4.6	6.2	6.3	65.7	91.2	76.4	95.4
Negroid (N = 28)	9.4	10.6	14.4	15.9	129.6	212.4	153.3	223.8
F(2.86)	3.04		7.54*		2.87		3.55*	

*P < 0.05

The means and standard deviation for the three racial groups broken down by type of crime are shown in Table 2. If each country is treated as an independent entry, the results of one-way ANOVAs reveal that the races differ significantly in crime production. Using the aggregates, significant linear trends show Mongoloids > Caucasoids > Negroids for both 1984 ($F(1,69) = 5.20$, $P < 0.05$) and 1986 ($F(1,86) = 4.99$, $P < 0.05$). For readers objecting to the parametric analysis of these ratio figures, the exact probability of getting this particular ranking twice in a row is $1/6 \times 1/6 = 0.027$. Thus, despite enormous variation within each group, trends emerge in the direction predicted by Ellis (1989) and Rushton (1988a) and not as predicted by Roberts and Gabor (1990).

A similar racial pattern of social organization is found when assessed historically. Two and a half thousand years ago, China governed 50 million people via an imperial bureaucracy with universally administered entrance exams leading to the Inner Cabinet (Bowman 1989), an achievement which may have surpassed those of equivalent European civilizations, including that of the Roman Empire. In Africa, however, written languages were not invented and the degree of bureaucratic organization necessarily limited (Baker 1974). Post-colonial African social organization still lags significantly behind the rest of the world (Lamb 1987).

The Predictability of Race

Many consider the use of racial terminology to be poorly justified. Especially following World War II, it has been argued that the phrase "ethnic group" be substituted for race, thereby shifting the emphasis away from a "question begging . . . biologistic bias" (Montagu 1960: 697). This position, however, obscures higher level conceptual order. It is not just crime which is predictable by race. The rate per thousand births of two-eggs twins is less than 4 for Mongoloids, about 8 for Caucasoids, and more than 16 for Negroids, regardless of which country the samples are taken from (Bulmer 1970). This is because the tendency to double-ovulate is inherited largely through the race of the mother, independently of the race of the father, as observed in Mongoloid-Caucasoid crosses in Hawaii and Caucasoid-Negroid crosses in Brazil (Bulmer 1970). Similarly in sexual behavior and its consequences (intercourse frequencies, sexually transmitted diseases including AIDS), the Japanese are similar to the Chinese and Koreans, whether assessed in their home countries, Hawaii, or the U.S. mainland, but are different from Russians, Israelis, and European-Americans, who in turn are similar to each other but are different from Kenyans, Nigerians, and African-Americans (Rushton and Bogaert 1987, 1989). The unit of analysis with the highest explanatory power, therefore, is the higher order concept of race, within which cluster the different ethnic groups and, ultimately, individuals.

The relation between race and antisocial behavior has been found even for children in a unique Canadian setting. In Montreal, 825 4-to-6-year-olds from 66 different countries speaking 30 different languages were assessed by 50 teachers. All the children were in preschool French language immersion classes to enable better integration into the school system. The Negroid children often came from French language countries like Haiti, the Caucasoid children from Spanish-speaking countries like Chile, and the Oriental children from Vietnam and Kampuchea. Teachers reported better social adjustment and less hostility-aggression from Mongoloid children than from Caucasoid children than from Negroid children (Tremblay and Baillargeon 1984).

Race is also correlated with brian size. Roberts and Gabor make much of the endocranial data and analyses by S.J. Gould, the Harvard paleontologist and anti-sociobiological ideologue. Consider, therefore,

CANADIAN JOURNAL OF CRIMINOLOGY/REVUE CANADIENNE DE CRIMINOLOGIE   APRIL/AVRIL 1990

the data in Table 3. The first column presents the "corrected" figures from a paper alleging "unconscious . . . finagling" and "juggling" of internally measured cranial capacity measures in the work of S.G. Morton (1799-1851), America's great 19th century contributor to physical anthropology (Gould 1978). The second column presents an update of these figures after Gould explicitly acknowledges that his biases incline him to making directional errors (Gould 1981). In both, Gould dismissed the differences in Table 3 as "trivial". When the principle of aggregation is applied to Gould's figures, however, the results show that in size-of-brain case, Mongoloids (Native Americans + Mongolians) > Caucasoids (Modern Caucasians + Ancient Caucasians) > Negroids. After excluding "Malays" due to uncertainty as to their racial category, the figures from column 1, in cubic inches, average 85.5, 84.5, and 83, respectively, and from column 2, 86.5, 85.5, and 83, respectively. (The figures do not change appreciably if Malays are included as either Mongoloids or Caucasoids). Endocranial differences of 1 or more cubic inch (16 cm³) should not be dismissed as "trivial". Gould's analysis and conclusions are misleading.

Table 3

S.J. Gould's "Corrected" Final Tabulation of Morton's
Assessment of Racial Differences in Cranial Capacity

Population	Cubic inches	
	1978 Version	1961 Version
Native Americans	86	86
Mongolians	85	87
Modern Caucasians	85	87
Malays	85	85
Ancient Caucasians	84	84
Africans	83	83

The evidence for racial differences in brian size includes an enormously greater amount of data than that shown in Table 3, with thousands of converging data points from (a) internally measured cranial capacity, (b) brain weight assessed at autopsy, and (c) cranial volume estimated from external head measures (Rushton, Forthcoming). For example, Beals, Smith and Dodd (1984) computerized the entire world data base of 20,000 crania gathered by 1940 (after which data collection virtually ceased because of its association with racial prejudice), grouped them by continental area, and found statistically significant differences. The sex-combined brain cases from Asia averaged 1380 cm^3 (SD = 83), those from Europe averaged 1362 cm^3 (SD = 35), and those from Africa averaged 1276 cm^3 (SD = 84). When body size was accounted for, the differences remained or became even larger because Mongoloids are typically smaller than Caucasoids and Negroids, except for their heads.

Aggregation and Moral Character

Roberts and Gabor so jumble the crime figures into type, region, generation and subpopulation with no discernible pattern being seen that it seems as if only a hodge-podge of unspecified post-hoc "situational" and "interaction" factors *could* fit the data! Perhaps though, Roberts and Gabor have missed an important point when they state "Any examination of aggregate crime statistics is going to over-estimate the true incidence of crime committed by blacks relative to the amount committed by whites". They do not say why it is that aggregation should produce an overestimate.

Emphasizing the context-dependent nature of criminal behavior has led many theorists to argue that situational determinants and person × situation interactions are so powerful that it is not useful to analyze crime from the perspective of enduring traits of character (Campbell and Gibbs 1986). It has seemed self-evident from such an "interactionist" perspective that, if people alter their behavior with varying circumstances, they cannot be said to have enduring characteristics that reliably differentiate them from others. In support, situationalists point to the alleged low level of behavioral consistency across contexts. This is the position endorsed by Roberts and Gabor who cite a classic study by Hartshorne and May (1928) to the effect that there is very little cross-situational consistency in honesty. As Roberts and Gabor put it: "children that were dishonest in one situation were honest in others".

The cross-situational consistency issue is pivotal in the search for human nature and the definitive study is the enormous "Character Education Inquiry" carried out by Hartshorne and May in the 1920s and published in three books (Hartshorne and May 1928; Hartshorne, May and Maller 1929; Hartshorne, May and Shuttleworth 1930).

323

CANADIAN JOURNAL OF CRIMINOLOGY/REVUE CANADIENNE DE CRIMINOLOGIE   APRIL/AVRIL 1990

Hartshorne and May gave 11,000 elementary and high school students some 33 different behavioral test of altruism (referred to as the "service" tests), self-control, and honesty in home, classroom, church, play, and athletic contexts. Concurrently, ratings of the children's reputations with teachers and classmates were obtained. Altogether more than 170,000 observations were collected. Scores on the various tests were correlated to discover whether behavior is specific to situations or consistent across them.

The results showed that any one behavioral test correlated, on average, only 0.20 with any other test. If, however, the measures were aggregated into batteries, then much higher relationships were found either with other combined behavioral measures, with teachers' ratings of the children, or with the children's moral knowledge scores. Often these correlations were on the order of 0.50 to 0.60. For example, the battery of tests measuring cheating by copying correlated 0.52 with another battery of tests measuring other types of classroom cheating. Thus, depending on whether the focus is on the relationship between individual measures or on the more representative relationship between averaged groups of behaviors, situationalism and consistency are both supported. Which of these two conclusions is more accurate?

A major error is involved in focussing on correlations between just two situations. The more accurate assessment is to use a *principle of aggregation* and average across a number of measures (Rushton, Brainerd and Pressley 1983). The argument for aggregation becomes particularly obvious to university professors in the context of multiple-choice examinations. Imagine how unreliable assessing undergraduates' course performance with a single multiple-choice item would be. Such items only intercorrelate 0.15. Aggregating across many items, however, typically provides a reliable index of a student's performance. Similarly, single items on IQ tests only correlate 0.15, subtests based on 4 to 6 items correlate 0.30 to 0.40, and batteries of items comprising verbal and performance subscales correlate 0.80. In psychometric parlance, aggregation effects occur because specificity variance and error variance cancel out, leaving only true score variance to remain.

Figure 1 presents data applying the principle of aggregation to an aggression questionnaire where correlations increase as a function of the

Figure 1

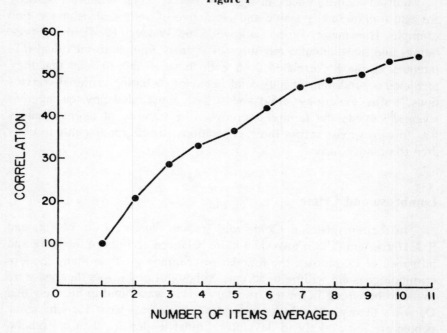

Relation between number of aggressive items aggregated and the predictability of other aggressive occasions. As shown, the greater the amount of aggregation, the greater the predictability.

Source: Rushton and Erdle 1987.

number of items involved. As the number of items being correlated increase from 1 to 7 to 11, the corresponding predictabilities increase from 0.10 to 0.44 to 0.54 (Rushton and Erdle 1987). Clearly, if the goal is to predict aggressiveness, aggregated estimates provide increased utility. Similar results occur with group differences. The percentage of variance accounted for by sex differences in the aggression data shown in Figure 1 increased from 1% to 3% to 8% as the number of questionnaire items increases from 1 to 5 to 23. Parallel results occur when age and socio-economic status differences were examined. When age, sex, and SES were combined, the Multiple R increased from an average of 0.18 for single items to 0.39 for the 23 items. Similar results occur when official crime figures are used.

325

CANADIAN JOURNAL OF CRIMINOLOGY/REVUE CANADIENNE DE CRIMINOLOGIE   APRIL/AVRIL 1990

Individual differences in aggressiveness, when reliably assessed, are also longitudinally stable and predictive of antisocial behavior. For example, Huesmann, Eron, Lefkowitz and Walder (1984), using peer ratings and questionnaire measures of aggression, found individual differences at age 8 correlated 0.46 with those at age 30, and that they predicted a syndrome of antisocial behavior including criminal convictions, traffic violations, child and spouse abuse, and physical aggressiveness outside the family. Moreover, the stability of aggressiveness was found to exist across three generations, from grandparents to children to grandchildren.

Lombroso and Crime

In their magisterial *Crime and Human Nature*, J.Q. Wilson and R.J. Herrnstein (1985) provide a more balanced account of the work and influence of Lombroso, the founder of criminology, than many modern criminologists are willing to accept. Although Lombroso's theories were found to be wrong in most particulars, value was found in his view that Darwin's theory of evolution provides a biological basis for why some people are more likely to develop criminal tendencies than are others, and why physical indicators may exist to allow prediction. Foremost among recent developments is the work in behavioral genetics.

According to American, Danish, and Swedish adoption studies, children who were adopted in infancy were at greater risk for criminal convictions if their biological parents had been convicted than if their adoptive parents had been (Mednick, Brennan and Kandel 1988). In one study of all 14,427 nonfamilial adoptions in Denmark from 1924 to 1947, it was found that siblings and half-siblings adopted separately into different homes were concordant for convictions. Convergent with this adoption work, twin studies of adults have found that identical twins were roughly twice as much alike in their criminal behavior as fraternal twins. In a study by Rowe (1986) for example, the heritability of self-reported antisocial behavior was about 50%. A unique study comparing sets of identical and fraternal twins raised together *and* apart on the same tests has confirmed the typical heritability of 0.50 across diverse traits, including those under consideration, such as aggression, behavioral restraint, and traditional morality (Tellegen, Lykken, Bouchard, Wilcox, Sagel and Rich 1988).

Perhaps the least appreciated aspect of twin studies is the information they also provide about environmental effects. The important environmental factors influencing development turn out not to be shared by siblings but to be unique to each child. Such factors as social class, family religion, parental values, and child-rearing styles are not found to have a common effect on siblings. The important environmental variance turns out to be within a family, not between families (Plomin and Daniels 1987). This is true even of traits such as altruism and aggression, which parents are expected to socialize heavily. In a study of 573 pairs of adult twins, 50% of the variance on each scale was found to be associated with genetic effects, virtually 0% with the twin's common environment and the remaining 50% with each twin's specific environment (Rushton, Fulker, Neale, Nias and Eysenck 1986). These results are shown in Table 4.

Table 4

Variance Components from an Analysis of Altruism and Aggressiveness
Questionnaires From 573 Adult Twin Pairs

Trait	Additive genetic variance	Common environmental variance	Specific environmental variance
Altruism	51%	2%	47%
Empathy	51%	0%	49%
Nurturance	43%	1%	56%
Aggressiveness	39%	0%	61%
Assertiveness	53%	0%	47%

Source: Rushton, Fulker, Neale, Nias, and Eysenck 1986.

No one believes genes code for social behaviors directly. Rather, genes code for enzymes which, under the influence of the environment, lay down tracts in the brains and neurohormonal systems of individuals, thus affecting people's minds and the choices they make about behavioral alternatives. In regard to aggression, for example, people may inherit nervous systems that differentially predispose them to anger or irritability, or impulsivity, or a lack of conditionability (Ellis 1987b).

327

CANADIAN JOURNAL OF CRIMINOLOGY/REVUE CANADIENNE DE CRIMINOLOGIE   APRIL/AVRIL 1990

There are many plausible routes from genes to behavior, and collectively these routes may be referred to as epigenetic rules.

Because cultural practices and social learning play such an important role in human behavior, epigenetic rules may explain how social influences are genetically channelled. (Lumsden and Wilson 1981; Rushton, Littlefield and Lumsden 1986). Consider, for example, the important observation in Table 4 that common family environment has little impact on longer-term personality. Thus, within the same rearing environment, genetically different siblings are biased to learn different items of information because they have different sets of epigenetic rules channeling their common environments in individual ways. In an illustrative study on television effects, Rowe and Herstand (1986) found that although same-sex siblings resemble one another in their exposure to violent programs, it is the more aggressive sibling who (a) identifies more with aggressive characters, and (b) views the consequences of the aggression as positive. Within-family studies of delinquents find that both intelligence (Hirschi and Hindelang 1977) and temperament (Rowe 1986) distinguish delinquent siblings from those who are not delinquent. It is not difficult to imagine how intellectually and temperamentally different siblings might seek out different social environments.

Within the constraints allowed by the total spectrum of cultural alternatives, people create environments maximally compatible with their genotypes, and choosing friends and spouses is one of the most important ways they do this (Rushton, Littlefield and Lumsden 1986). Thus, epigenetic rules, by influencing preferences, might explain the well known tendency for aggressive and delinquent personalities to seek each other out for friendship and marriage. In a study of delinquency among 530 adolescent twins by Rowe and Osgood (1984), path analysis revealed not only that antisocial behavior was about 50% heritable, but that the correlation of 0.56 between the delinquency of an individual and the delinquency of his friends was mediated genetically, that is, that students genetically disposed to delinquency were also genetically inclined to seek each other out for friendship.

Genetic "influence", however, not genetic "determinism", is the appropriate catch-phrase when it comes to social behavior. Genes affect a person's threshold for activation; for some people a small stimulus is

328

needed to produce behavior while for others a greater stimulus is required. An analogy may be drawn from the field of health. If someone has a genetic disposition for flu, they may never catch it in a benevolent environment. The obverse is also true; a person genetically resistant to flu may continually suffer from it in a hostile environment. In many cases, the environment is powerful enough to override genetic differences; at present about 50% of the variance in social behavior seems to be of genetic origin, leaving another 50% to the environment. As environments become less impeding and more equal across people, however, the genetic contribution becomes larger; over the last 50 years the heritability of both academic attainment (Heath, Berg, Eaves, Solaas, Corey, Sundet, Magnus and Nance 1985) and longevity (Scriver 1984) has increased. The generational changes in crime discussed by Roberts and Gabor may similarly be due to the easing of social constraints on underlying genotypes. If my genetic analysis is correct then, as environments equalize, racial differences in crime will increase further.

Finally, consider the Lombrosian concept of "stigmata". During gestation, an insult that disturbs fetal brain development in an unobservable way may simultaneously produce a minor physical anomaly (MPA) on the external body surface. Mednick et al. (1988) provide the example of ear development. The ears start low on the neck of the fetus and gradually drift into their accustomed positions. If an insult occurs and development is affected, the ears' drift upward may end prematurely, resulted in low-seated ears — an observable MPA. The number of MPAs can be counted as an index of hidden central nervous system anomalies. Utilizing longitudinal data for 129 males, Mednick et al. (1988) found that for children raised in an unstable family, the number of MPAs at age 12 years were related to violent offending by age 21.

Race, Crime and Genetics

But how much of the variance in crime among the races is of genetic origin? At the moment this is unknown. That some of it is, however, is highly likely from several lines of reasoning. First, all the data in Table 1 are explained by a gene-based evolutionary theory of racial differentiation, and it would be implausible and unparsimonious to make an exception for just one of the dimensions unless good evi-

CANADIAN JOURNAL OF CRIMINOLOGY/REVUE CANADIENNE DE CRIMINOLOGIE   APRIL/AVRIL 1990

dence was provided for doing so. Indeed, there is evidence of genetic linkage between the various dimensions, e.g. between law abidingness and temperament (Rowe 1986) and between law abidingness and sexual behavior (Rowe, Rodgers, Meseck-Bushey and St. John 1989).

A second line of evidence comes from generalizing the 50% heritability found *within* populations to the between-group differences. While it is often thought that heritabilities are specific to particular populations, recent evidence shows they are generalizable across distinct ethnic and cultural groups. For example, genetic estimates calculated in Japan for Wechsler IQ subtests predict the magnitude of the black-white differences on the same subtests in the United States (Rushton 1989b). This directly implies that the racial differences in intelligence are partly genetic in origin and indirectly increases the likelihood that those in crime are also.

Then, as in the discussion of Table 4, the crucial environmental variables influencing postadolescent behavior are found to be within families, not between them. This important discovery implies that since the environmental variables usually proposed to explain racial differences in crime, such as social class, religious beliefs, cultural practices, father absence, and parenting styles account for so little variance *within* race, they are unlikely to *between* races. This leaves genetic and within-family explanations to account for the differences.

Finally, the heritability of racial differences has been suggested more directly. With respect to both social deviancy and IQ, preliminary data indicate that black children adopted into white families are found to not resemble the adoptive siblings with whom they were raised for 17 years (Scarr, Weinberg and Gargiulo 1987). When the children were 7 years of age the results had shown that black IQ was comparable to white IQ, but a 10-year follow up indicates that black IQ and educational achievement has significantly declined while social deviance and psychopathology has increased.

Future Research

It is useful to conjecture about the physiological basis for the racial differences in crime, for regardless of how much the cause is environmental or genetic, both influences must have a representation in the central nervous system. It is completely incorrect to juxtapose the environmental with the biological when one intends to contrast the environmental with the genetic; *both* sources must inevitably be mediated biologically.

Rushton and Bogaert (1987) suggested that testosterone may be one such biological mediator. Several studies have related circulating testosterone in blood and free testosterone in saliva to antisocial and aggressive behavior (Dabbs and Morris, Forthcoming). Moreover, Lynn (1989) has reviewed evidence showing that the races differ in testosterone in the direction Mongoloids < Caucasoids < Negroids. Also, Ellis (Forthcoming) has hypothesized that platelet MAO activity is a biological marker for some of the key neurochemistry underlying crime, and that blacks have significantly lower MAO activity levels than whites.

A more central locus for research attention is brain functioning. It is of interest, for example, to wonder where the 15-20 cm^3 of grey matter that differentiates the races is located. Gordon (1987) has demonstrated that black-white differences in the prevalence of delinquency can be accounted for by their differences in mean IQ and suggested that the same relation may hold for adult criminality. One agenda now, therefore, is to go beyond the racial differences in genetically based covarying traits and to identify the underlying physiological mechanisms. Explaining racial differences in crime may thus become a crucible for understanding individual differences, for the former constitute an aggregate of the latter.

References

Baker, J.R.
1974   Race. Oxford: Oxford University Press.

Beals, K.L., C.L. Smith, and S.M. Dodds
1984   Brain size, cranial morphology, climate and time machines. Current Anthropology 25: 301-330.

Bowman, M.L.
1989   Testing individual differences in ancient China. American Psychologist 44: 576-578.

Bulmer, M.G.
1970   The Biology of Twinning in Man. Oxford: Clarendon Press.

Campbell, A., and J.J. Gibbs
1986   Violent Transactions: The Limits of Personality. Oxford: Blackwell.

CANADIAN JOURNAL OF CRIMINOLOGY/REVUE CANADIENNE DE CRIMINOLOGIE   APRIL/AVRIL 1990

Dabbs, J.M. Jr., and R. Morris
   Forthcoming
          Testosterone and antisocial behavior in a large sample of normal men. Psychological
          Science.

Ellis, L.
   1987a Criminal behavior and *r/K* selection: An extension of gene-based evolutionary theory.
          Deviant Behavior 8: 149-176.

   1987b Neurohormonal bases of varying tendencies to learn delinquent and criminal behavior. In
          E.K. Morris and C.J. Braukmann (eds.), Behavioral approaches to crime and delin-
          quency. New York: Plenum.

   1989   Theories of Rape. New York: Hemisphere.

   Forthcoming
          Monoamine oxidase and criminality: Identifying an apparent biological marker for anti-
          social behavior. Journal of Research in Crime and Delinquency.

Gordon, R.A.
   1987   SES versus IQ in the race-IQ-delinquency model. International Journal of Sociology and
          Social Policy 7: 30-96.

Gould, S.J.
   1978   Morton's ranking of races by cranial capacity. Science 200: 503-509.

   1981   The Mismeasure of Man. New York: Norton.

Hartshorne, H. and M.A. May
   1928   Studies in the Nature of Character: Vol. 1. Studies in Deceit. New York: Macmillan.

Hartshorne, H., M.A. May and J.B. Maller
   1929   Studies in the Nature of Character: Vol. 2. Studies in Self Control. New York: Macmillan.

Hartshorne, H., M.A. May and F.K. Shuttleworth
   1930   Studies in the Nature of Character: Vol. 3. Studies in the Organization of Character. New
          York: Macmillan.

Heath, A.C., K. Berg, L.J. Eaves, M.H. Solaas, L.A. Corey, J. Sundet, P. Magnus and W.E. Nance
   1985   Education policy and the heritability of educational attainment. Nature 314: 734-736.

Hirschi, T. and M.J. Hindelang
   1977   Intelligence and delinquency: A revisionist review. American Sociological Review 42:
          571-587.

Huesmann, L.R., L.D. Eron, M.M. Lefkowitz and L.O. Walder
   1984   Stability of aggression over time and generations. Developmental Psychology 20: 1120-1134.

International Criminal Police Organization
   1988   International Crime Statistics, 1983-1984, 1985-1986.

Lamb, D.
   1987   The Africans. New York: Vintage.

Lumsden, C.J. and E.O. Wilson
   1981   Genes, Mind and Culture: The Coevolutionary Process. Cambridge, MA: Harvard Uni-
          versity Press.

Lynn, R.
   1989   Testosterone and gonadotropin levels and *r/K* reproductive strategies. Unpublished manu-
          script. Department of Psychology, University of Ulster, Northern Ireland.

Mednick, S.A., P. Brennan and E. Kandel
   1988   Predispositions to violence. Aggressive Behavior 14: 25-33.

Montagu, M.F.A.
 1960   An Introduction to Physical Anthropology (3rd ed.). Springfield, Ill.: Charles C. Thomas.

Plomin, R. and D. Daniels
 1987   Why are children in the same family so different from one another? Behavioral and Brain Sciences 10: 1-60.

Roberts, J.V. and T. Gabor
 1990   Lombrosian wine in a new bottle: Research on crime and race. Canadian Journal of Criminology 32.

Rowe, D.C.
 1986   Genetic and environmental components of antisocial behavior: A study of 256 twin pairs. Criminology 24: 513-532.

Rowe, D.C. and S.E. Herstand
 1986   Familial influences on television viewing and aggression: A sibling study. Aggressive Behavior 12: 111-120.

Rowe, D.C. and D.W. Osgood
 1984   Heredity and sociological theories of delinquency: A reconsideration. American Sociological Review 49: 526-540.

Rowe, D.C., J.L. Rodgers, S. Meseck-Bushey and C. St. John
 1989   Sexual behavior and deviance: A sibling study of their relationship. Developmental Psychology 25: 61-91.

Rushton, J.P.
 1985   Differential K theory: The sociobiology of individual and group differences. Personality and Individual Differences 6: 441-452.

 1987   Toward a theory of human multiple-birthing: Sociobiology and r/K reproductive strategies. Acta Geneticae Medicae et Gemellologiae 36: 289-296.

 1988a Race differences in behaviour: A review and evolutionary analysis. Personality and Individual Differences 9: 1009-1024.

 1988b The reality of racial differences: A rejoinder with new evidence. Personality and Individual Differences 9: 1035-1040.

 1989a The evolution of racial differences: A response to M. Lynn. Journal of Research in Personality 23: 7-20.

 1989b Japanese inbreeding depression scores: Predictors of cognitive differences beween blacks and whites. Intelligence 13: 43-51.

 Forthcoming
      Race, brain size and intelligence: A rejoinder to Cain and Vanderwolf. Personality and Individual Differences.

Rushton, J.P. and A.F. Bogaert
 1987   Race differences in sexual behavior: Testing an evolutionary hypothesis. Journal of Research in Personality 21: 529-551.

 1989   Population differences in susceptibility to AIDS: An evolutionary analysis. Social Science and Medicine 28: 1211-1220.

Rushton, J.P., C.J. Brainerd and M. Pressley
 1983   Behavioral development and construct validity: The principle of aggregation. Psychological Bulletin 94: 18-38.

Rushton, J.P. and S. Erdle
 1987   Evidence for an aggressive (and delinquent) personality. British Journal of Social Psychology 26: 87-89.

CANADIAN JOURNAL OF CRIMINOLOGY/REVUE CANADIENNE DE CRIMINOLOGIE   APRIL/AVRIL 1990

Rushton, J.P., D.W. Fulker, M.C. Neale, D.K.B. Nias and H.J. Eysenck
    1986   Altruism and aggression: The heritability of individual differences. Journal of Personality
           and Social Psychology 50: 1192-1198.

Rushton, J.P., C.H. Littlefield and C.J. Lumsden
    1986   Gene-culture coevolution of complex social behavior: Human altruism and mate choice.
           Proceedings of the National Academy of Science of the US.A. 83: 7340-7343.

Scarr, S., R.A. Weinberg and J. Gargiulo
    1987   Transracial adoption: A ten year follow-up. Abstract in Program of the 17th Annual
           Meeting of the Behavior Genetics Association, Minneapolis, Minnesota, U.S.A.

Scriver, C.R.
    1984   An evolutionary view of disease in man. Proceedings of the Royal Society of London, B
           220: 273-298.

Tellegen, A., D.T. Lykken, T.J. Bouchard Jr., K.J. Wilcox, N.L. Segal and S. Rich
    1988   Personality similarity in twins reared apart and together. Journal of Personality and Social
           Psychology 54: 1031-1039.

Tremblay, R.E. and L. Baillargeon
    1984   Les difficultés de comportement d'enfants immigrants dans les classes d'accueil, au
           préscolaire. Canadian Journal of Education 9: 154-170.

Wilson, E.O.
    1975   Sociobiology: The New Synthesis. Cambridge, MA: Harvard University Press.

Wilson, J.Q. and R.J. Herrnstein
    1985   Crime and Human Nature. New York: Simon & Schuster.

[18]

CECIL GUTZMORE

Capital, 'black youth' and crime

The phenomenon of 'youth' (white and largely male) has had an extraordinary hold over the attention of both popular writers and social scientists in Britain since the Second World War. And, since the late 1960s, a great deal of notice has been taken of the apparently related phenomenon called 'black youth', who have been effectively constituted as a special social category by some of the crucial ideological and repressive apparatuses of the British state. These include the House of Commons, acting through its Select Committee on Race Relations and Immigration (SCRRI), later a sub-committee of the Standing Home Affairs Committee; the Community Relations Commission/Commission for Racial Equality (CRC/CRE), a quasi-governmental body controlled by the Home Office; the Home Office itself, through the CRC/CRE, the Home Office Research Unit and *Bulletin,* parliamentary answers and White Papers, particularly those replying to reports of the SCRRI, etc., the Metropolitan Police, which has exploited a specially nurtured relationship with the media; the media themselves; and, not least in importance, for they increasingly provide the objective academic authority for all of this, various university departments of sociology, and units of the Social Science Research Council. According to Fisher and Joshua, the category 'black youth' was

> primarily intended for a special class (sic) of West Indian youngsters, usually in conflict with their parents' generation; 'often

Cecil Gutzmore is a black political activist who is also a researcher and writer.

Race & Class, XXV, 2(1983)

14   *Race & Class*

kicked out of their homes'; 'who do not register for work, who are aimless, rootless drifters; concerned with "hustling" for a living' ...; [in] 'culture conflict', 'alienated' and 'adrift from society' and 'from the instruments of law and order' ... As a group they had partly evolved and partly readopted Jamaican Rastafarian ideologies, symbols and practices, then constructing within the British environment a distinctive and compensating subculture.[1]

Fisher and Joshua go on to treat the uses of this categorisation in relation to British social policy. But such policies primarily evolved in the context of a deepening structural crisis both for British national capital and the international capitalist economy. That is the framework within which the use of the concept 'black youth' has to be examined.

Capital and the criminal justice system

In approaching the issue of 'black youth' and the criminalisation of the black community, one has to begin with the middle years of the 1960s, when the long-term comparative decline of British capitalism began to demand fundamental changes in the domestic economy as well as in some aspects of that economy's relationship to international capital. Internationally, relations with the British Commonwealth – the basis of a 'cheap food' for British workers policy – were to be altered in favour of closer ties with western European capital, primarily, and with United States and Japanese capital secondarily.

Domestically, it became imperative to intensify the use of state power against the working class. A complex anti-working-class project which took effect at both the economic and the political-ideological levels was accordingly evolved. At the level of the economy, the key words signifying the trend in policy included the 'technological revolution', 'ministry of technology', 'selective employment tax', 'corporation tax', 'labour shake-out', 'national plan', 'national economic development council(s)', etc. This trend began in the final years of the Tory government of Macmillan, but was fundamentally the task assumed by Harold Wilson's Labour governments. In addition, there was a major attempt to shift the terms of the economic class struggle against the working class by disrupting or outlawing forms of workers' action (initially, those spoken of as 'illegal' or 'wildcat' strikes, 'restrictive practices', etc.)

The heightened role of the state in directly confronting workers was first demonstrated in Wilson's politically charged intervention against the (in fact official) strike of the National Union of Seamen in 1966. But it was his second government's attempt to legislate on the industrial relations proposals set out in its White Paper 'In Place of

Strife' which was central. From it, a passage can be charted directly from Edward Heath's Industrial Relations Act and the political battles with the National Union of Mineworkers, through the social contract of the Wilson-Callaghan governments with the Trades Union Congress, to the current assault, aided by the mass unemployment of monetarism, on the forms and structures of the economic class struggle of British workers.

At the political-ideological level, from the 1960s onwards, the beginning of a long-term movement can be traced to use the criminal justice system to increase the state's power over workers in their communities and in their 'political' organisations. This was justified ideologically in terms of the need to 'modernise' the legal system in 'society's interest' and in the face of the 'rising tide of crime'. It can be traced back to R.A. Butler's creation of the Criminal Law Revision Committee (CLRC) in 1959, and specifically to his successor Henry Brooke's request to it in 1964:

> to review the law of evidence in criminal cases and to consider whether any changes are desirable in the interest of the fair and efficient administration of justice; and in particular what provision should be made for modifying rules which have ceased to be appropriate in modern conditions.[2]

The difficulty was that there was no evidence to support the case for tightening up the criminal justice system at the expense of ordinary citizens. Lord Devlin might state that:

> If the success of a system of criminal prosecution is to be measured by the proportion of *criminals* whom it convicts and punishes, the English system must be regarded as a failure. Far too many people who have in fact committed crimes escape punishment.[3]

But, in reality, there was no good evidence for this assertion, assuming, of course, that Devlin was not referring to the failures of the police — detection rates were low even then. The problem was how to get round the stubborn fact that only 8 per cent of those brought before British courts were ever acquitted. If it could be solved, the path would be substantially eased towards the desired changes in the criminal justice system.

To find out how this solution was achieved, it is necessary to focus attention on one of the most influential Commissioners of Police in post-war years, who clearly recognised above all the importance of the connection between the ideological and repressive functions of the state. As Chief Constable of Leicestershire in the mid-1960s, Robert Mark had secured some national attention as a result of much-publicised work on Leicester's traffic problem which had left him:

'firmly established with ... my force, my watch committee, the city council and not by any means least important, the press'.[4] Invited, in the wake of this, to give a lecture at Oxford in October 1965, he called for four far-reaching changes in the criminal law: 'majority verdicts in jury trials; pre-trial disclosure of defence alibis; abolition of the caution against self-incrimination, and the requirement for the accused to enter the witness box'.[5]

It was, however, a book sent to him for review that set Mark working on the use of statistics — statistics which could be used to give substance to the claim that there was a type of 'criminal', 'clever', 'mobile' and 'knowledgeable-as-to-legal-rights', who was able to escape justice even after being caught, charged and brought before the courts; statistics which, in other words, could supply an important and necessary ideological justification for tightening up the criminal justice system.

What Mark discovered, in that book, was that 'of all those tried on indictment for crimes of violence 39 per cent were acquitted'. Did this then mean that there were areas of acquittal which, if given special attention and publicity, could be used to stymie the inconvenient truth that 'the proportion of acquittals was so low [only 8 per cent of the total] that there could be no possible justification for shifting the balance of the criminal trial in favour of the prosecution'? In *contested* cases, he discovered, after some investigation, that '80 per cent plead guilty, 20 per cent plead not guilty and of those 40 per cent are acquitted'. Very close, it seemed, to Mark's newly discovered 39 per cent acquittal figure for 'crimes of violence'. It would thus be possible to shift attention away from the objectively low acquittal rate overall by turning the glare of publicity on to another aspect of that rate: taken as part of a smaller whole, that 8 per cent became 40 per cent. But more 'evidence' was needed first. Mark therefore asked for figures from his fellow Midlands Chief Constables who, with one exception, obliged — they too had 40 per cent of the 'criminals' their forces took to the crown courts acquitted by juries bound by the need for unanimous verdicts. Their 'findings' were obligingly published by the *Guardian* in May 1965. Mark, with the help of the Home Office, then arranged for his statistical manoeuvre to be extended to England and Wales generally, thus making his 40 per cent figure national. The 'national' results were published in a report in the *New Law Journal* in the middle of 1966.[6]

Mark had succeeded in demonstrating that a little statistical manipulation backed up by good publicity goes a very long way. In subsequent years, the technique was repeatedly extended to other areas of the criminal justice system, and the ramifications of this initial 'break-through' are now inescapably with us almost twenty years later

Capital, 'black youth' and crime   17

– most strikingly in the provisions of, and the justifications provided for, the Police and Criminal Evidence Bill.

Mark himself was to claim that the results of his efforts included legislation brought forward by the then (Labour) Home Secretary, Roy Jenkins, to require the pre-trial disclosure of alibi defences and the adoption of majority verdicts by juries. The jury system has since been subjected to intermittent attacks: the defendant's right to peremptory challenge of jurors was drastically cut by the Criminal Law Act 1977.[7] Ex-Master of the Rolls Lord Denning continued the attack with his libellous outbursts against black jurors who served in the trial that followed the Bristol uprising in 1980.

There have been other important related changes in the criminal justice system. Perhaps the most comprehensive are those included in the Scottish Criminal Justice Act 1980.[8] Mention can also be made of the substantial reduction in the right to trial by jury. Defendants' rights in respect of the choice of their own legal representatives and to have assistance under the Legal Aid scheme have been greatly reduced in recent years by a series of Regulations. Instances in which it has been determined that Legal Aid shall be withheld at the discretion of magistrates' courts include many which result directly from police operations ostensibly directed at reducing crime, but actually intended to increase their control of the streets. Sentencing policy also has been changed to the disadvantage of ordinary people. Thus there has been a deliberate attempt to reduce the use of custodial sentences against certain types of offenders (white-collar crime) while increasing its use for other types of offence such as assaults on the police (too often proved merely on the word of police officers) and the possession of offensive weapons (ranging from combs to bangles). The most outrageous uses of sentencing policy were seen in the aftermath of the April 1979 demonstration in Southall and again after the July 1981 uprisings, when persons swept up in droves from the streets by the police were herded into the prisons (some of them specially opened) with scant regard to legal niceties.[9] And the revival of old laws for use in current circumstances has been quite common. 'Sus'[10] is perhaps the best known: but the revival of 'affray', 'conspiracy' and even 'blasphemy' laws is now prevalent.

In other words, since the mid-1960s there has been a steady increase in the use of the state to reduce the rights of the working-class people. Except for the objections raised by the 'civil liberties lobby' and by certain political formations in and of the black communities, including Black People Against State Harassment and the Institute of Race Relations,[11] these changes have not been contested.

18 *Race & Class*

'Mugging': the creation of a black crime
'Mugging' and the police

Statistical manipulation generally is the base upon which the major aspect of the criminalisation of the black community, connected to so-called 'mugging'/'robbery and other violent thefts'/'street crime' /'crime against the person', has rested.

'Mugging', as has been demonstrated by Stuart Hall and others,[12] is a crime without legal status or definition. The term was imported from the US in the late 1960s; around 1972-3 (the time also at which Mark became Commissioner of the Metropolitan Police) it began to be blown up into the 'crime' which most menaces urban Britain. It must be noted, though, that it was the news media — especially the press — and the courts, rather than the police, who initially orchestrated the popular campaign about 'mugging'. It was also they who first suc-cessfully presented the link between 'mugging' and 'black youth'. This was to take us beyond the period when the criminal stereotyping of the black community was limited to its alleged connection with drugs (ganja/marijuana), prostitution (pimping) and the illegal selling of drink or gambling in unlicensed premises — a stereotyping which was largely confined to local newspapers. It inaugurated a new period in which the national news media came to present the whole black com-munity in terms of the posited involvement of a part of it ('black youth') in the perpetration of a 'bestial' (read black) crime menacing 'society' (read white).

Both the media and the courts initially built the campaign about 'mugging' around dramatic 'deterrent' sentences passed on specific cases. What was still lacking was the statistical evidence, as Mark realised. Accordingly, in his 1972 Annual Report he presented what one commentator has generously referred to as ' "reconstructed" statistics for its ['mugging'] incidence back to 1968'.[13] These 'reconstructed' figures were instrumental in inducing the then Home Secretary into asking police forces nationally to provide similar statistics — almost a repeat of what had occurred in the mid-1960s in relation to acquittal rate statistics. The 'reconstructed' 1968-72 figures had said nothing about the 'race' or 'colour' of those allegedly perpetrating the 'muggings' — this had to be interpreted from the press coverage. The only way to fill that lacuna henceforth would be with racially coded statistics.

Within three years it was to be revealed (at a major trial in 1975 following a police raid on the black Carib Club in North London) that a 'race code' was in use on the Metropolitan Police's criminal record office form which comprised the following categories: IC 1 White-skinned European type; IC 2 Dark-skinned European type;

Capital, 'black youth' and crime 19

IC 3 Negroid type; IC 4 Asian type; IC 5 Oriental type; and IC 6 Arabian type.

There were still a number of further unsolved problems. First, police perception and practice were to be the determinant of the 'race' of offenders. Second, it has never been clear that the 'race code' on the criminal record office form is completed in respect of all persons charged: if it has, then the question: 'Why have the published statistics shown the breakdown of only those "crimes" in which blacks are purportedly over-involved?' gains added force. Thirdly, the forms as described above are only used for persons actually charged with specific offences. They are/were, therefore, not a source of crime statistics for offences where no one has been charged. Yet, if the alleged disproportionate black participation in 'mugging' was to be fully dramatised, a higher figure than that for either black people (however dubiously 'coded') actually charged and/or convicted of relevant offences needed to be presented to the public.

Mark's Metropolitan Police solved this in three ways. In the first place, it continued the practice of conflating crimes which neither logically nor actually belonged together.[14] Second, since even after such conflations the crimes in which black people were allegedly over-involved remained no more than a miniscule proportion of actual crime, every conceivable means had to be exploited in order to highlight them and to suggest their peculiarly menacing nature. Third, the source of such statistics was shifted away from the criminal record office form to the crime report sheet, to which the practice of 'race coding' was extended. The Met was thus able to ask the victims of 'muggings' to supply information as to their perception of the 'race'/colour of their assailants. Such information was then formally recorded for statistical processing.[15]

By the mid-1970s, the Met was in a position to release statistics which were used to persuade the public that 'mugging' was increasing massively, that black youth were principally involved in such 'mugging' and that the victims were mainly elderly white women. Crucially, the Met had complete discretion as to how and when these figures were used, 'made available', published, leaked, submitted to appropriate bodies, etc. It also began to develop a more sophisticated, and would-be academic, body of work, based on its own figures and according by and large with its own interpretations. These were carried out either by its own statisticians, or undertaken on its behalf.[16] The most substantial of them, by an ex-police official turned sociologist, Pratt's *'Mugging as a social problem'*, was published in 1980, and generated massive media publicity of the most simplistic and scare-mongering kind.

In March 1976 the Met submitted a memorandum to the Select Committee on Race Relations and Immigration. It made two key claims. The first was that criticism of the police by the black community was

totally 'unjustifiable' and only put 'most officers on the defensive'.
This was put forward in all seriousness, despite the weight of testimony
and evidence – recorded in local newspapers, the black press, ad hoc
pamphlets, memoranda submitted to Select Committees, radio and TV
programmes – documenting lawless police behaviour against the black
community from the 1950s on.[17] The memorandum acknowledged 'a
growth of the tendency for members of London's West Indian communities to combine against police ... In the last 12 months forty such
incidents have been recorded.' And it identified that 'unjustifiable
criticism' together with a number of other factors – prominently
'socially alienated, unemployed black youth', along with 'political
demagogy' – as making the 'potentiality for conflict ... inherent in
every law enforcement situation between police and West Indian ...
currently a source of considerable concern'. There, then, was 'black
youth' again – identified in contrast to the 'vast majority of West Indians, who are hard-working, law-abiding people' – somewhere near
the source of the trouble.

The second key claim was over 'West Indian crime rates'. In its
1971-72 Report on Police/Immigrant Relations, the Select Committee
on Race Relations and Immigration had stated that: 'coloured immigrants are no more involved in crime than others: nor are they
generally more concerned in violence, prostitution and drugs. The
West Indian crime rate is much the same as that of the indigenous
population.'[18] This, insisted the Met, was wholly wrong and the
mistake was entirely the fault of the Select Committee, for in 1972 its
attention had been drawn, by police officers, to 'the disproportionate
involvement of black youth in crimes of "theft from the person" and
"robbery" ',[19] though in 1971-2 that force can have had no racially
coded statistics on which to base this assertion. In any event it was *now*
(in 1976) possible 'from police records to categorise persons arrested by
racial type and in respect of certain crimes to classify offenders by skin
colour from the evidence given by the victim of the crime'. It will be
noted that this distinction accords with the account, given above, of
the two sources of police statistics evolved by the Met under Mark.

The memorandum went on to present its figures – first based on the
criminal record office forms (i.e., figures of those arrested and
charged). Aware of the weaknesses of such figures, it immediately raised the possibility of the counter-argument that 'police discriminate
against black people when enforcing the law'. The Met was therefore
not going to rely exclusively on those arrest-based figures: the second
source – the criminal record sheets (based on victims' perceptions) –
would be brought into play. In order to give weight to this source, the
following claim was made:

> During 1974 [following] concern [which] began to grow both in
> police and community circles about the degree of involvement by

black youth in robbery and theft [from the] person in some areas ...
an internal study was undertaken by officers of the Community
Relations Branch.

The result of this was to show 'that 79 per cent of robberies were alleged to be committed by people described by their victims as "black",
"coloured" or "West Indian" ', while in respect of 'theft from the
person offences', 83 per cent were similarly desribed. The memorandum went on to claim: 'Further analysis showed that 70 per cent of the
victims were females and 20 per cent were aged over 60 years ... Of the
victims, 89 per cent were white' (figures completely at variance with
Pratt's later study of the same evidence). The memorandum expressed
no doubts whatsoever about these victim-perception based statistics
which were, in the eyes of the Met, necessarily acceptable in so far as
they 'avoid the charge of discimination by the police which could be
raised in the use of arrest figures'. Indeed, 'it also provides a yardstick
for testing the validity of the [police] discrimination charge'. Having
said this, the memorandum then presented figures (arrest/CRO based)
for robbery: '62 per cent were black ... for theft from the person 82 per
cent were black'. The inevitable effect of the memorandum's open
publication was massive media coverage in which 'black crime against
old white victims' was the main object of extensive press descriptions.
This was one of the ways in which the Met's control of the release of
'crime figures' served to orchestrate the campaign for the ideological
criininalisatioii of the black community. Identical figures could be used and re-used to fuel intermittent but always dramatic coverage of the
'black youth'-'black crime' issue.

'Mugging' and the press

The Met's next tactic regarding 'black crime' figures was to release
them for specific areas – those know to contain large concentrations of
black people (Hackney, Lambeth, Lewisham, Peckham, etc.). These
were then taken up by the press (and the media generally) both locally
and nationally. Such figures were used, for example – again to confirm
the menace of black youth – in the aftermath of the defensive battle
fought against the police at the 1976 Notting Hill Carnival. There was
also an intention to engender more basic day-to-day fears than those
which could be squeezed from the image invoked by Mark after Notting Hill, of black people trying to establish 'no go areas' in London.

The press teemed with 'black crime' stories. Pearson Phillips wrote
of 'mugging':

What makes this activity a social hot potato is the fact that an
estimated 80 per cent of recorded instances in some parts of inner
London are the work of black teenagers ... Peckham police entered

22 *Race & Class*

the arena on Monday with a hand out issued from Scotland Yard's press bureau headed: 'Police Crackdown on Peckham Muggers'. It stated: 'From January to June this year, there were on average about 25 muggings in the area each month. But the figure has risen steeply to over 50 a month ... most of the victims are elderly women ... the muggers, who are almost exclusively coloured youngsters between the ages of 12 and 17, appear to hunt in gangs of twos and threes ... of 339 "muggings" between January and September ... 285 of the victims said that their attackers were non-European.'[20]

That same story made the *South East London and Kentish Mercury* (14.10.76), the *Daily Telegraph* (12.10.76), the *London Evening News* ('Muggings: MPs Demand Inquiry', 13.10.76) and the *Daily Mail, Guardian, South London Press* and *Sunday Telegraph* within the space of a few days. The *Daily Mail* on 13 October 1976 ran not only an editorial on 'mugging' entitled 'The Sad Ballad of Peckham Rye', but also a 'Portrait of an old woman living dangerously. She had an evening out in Peckham.' The *Sunday Telegraph* of 17 October 1976 was able to report on virtually London-wide figures and characterised the 'vast majority of muggers' as 'second generation immigrant West Indian teenagers without job prospects, many of them homeless, without recreation or any sense of purpose'. As October wore on new twists were to be given to this single story. The *London Evening Standard* (21.10.76), for example, stressed that a person ('you') who is burgled in Brixton is unlikely to have the thief caught 'because so many of the policemen there are otherwise engaged, fighting the muggers'.

A few days earlier the CRC had chosen to publish its rebuttal of the 'evidence' put forward by the Metropolitan Police in its memorandum. But this, given the bias of the media and its virtually one-way coverage of such issues, simply added fuel to the fire. The *Daily Telegraph*, for example, first reported the CRC's views under the headline 'Police accused of "arranging" figures on black crime'[21] – in other words, it was framed as an attack on police integrity which might be thought guaranteed to go down badly with *Telegraph* readers. Set beside the police, the CRC had little if any credibility in such quarters. Even so, the opportunity was taken to restate the figures given by the police as well as presenting the CRC's case through long, quasi-academically argued quotations. In addition, on the following day the *Telegraph* returned to the issue: 'Yard denies race chief's "predictable charges" '. It quoted Scotland Yard on its inability to 'suppress information' which was felt to be 'in the public interest' as a matter of 'duty', despite its 'dilemma' over whether to 'expose experience and facts to public debate' with the attendant risks of 'feeding prejudice' or, alternatively, losing the 'definition of social problems and consequently apathy about their resolution'.

Capital, 'black youth' and crime   23

In the context of the press campaign of October 1976, the judiciary re-entered the fray – most notably in the person of Judge Gwyn Morris – but not as they had done in the 1972-3 'mugging scare', that is, by passing excessive sentences which were themselves the object of sensational media reporting. Gwyn Morris's approach was one of deep 'concern'. The *Standard* on 22 October gave its front page over to him: 'Judge takes weekend to ponder sentence ... What should I do with mugger pack?' As he put it: 'the facts speak for themselves. The youths – aged 16 and 17 – are all black and their victims were all white women.' The massive publicity generated over the weekend ensured that he received

> hundreds of letters from women in that area about this type of conduct. It is pitiful to read them. One elderly lady wrote to me saying she lived two streets away from her married daughter but could not go out at night to visit her and nor could her daughter come to visit her mother.

Gwyn Morris's 'agony' also made many national newspapers including *The Times* which devoted many column inches to it under the headline: 'Packs of thieves part of immense social problem, says judge'.

Again, in the context of the press campaign of October 1976, the Home Office caught the attention of the press when one of its ministers of state in a written answer stated that 'mugging' offences had risen by nearly half in three years. He reminded the House of Commons that the Met kept a log of such offences, defined as 'offences of robbery of personal property which follow sudden attack in the open where there is not previous association between the victim and the assailant'. He also confirmed that despite a request, said to have been made four years earlier, by the Home Office to police forces for figures on 'mugging', 'Manchester and Liverpool police do not keep statistics for mugging alone. Liverpool could only supply overall figures for robberies, while Manchester lumped together a range of crimes from murder to rape.'[22] This tends to confirm the role of Sir Robert Mark and the Metropolitan Police in generating the inordinate attention paid to statistics for so-called 'mugging' and 'robbery and other violent crime' in the London area, and, in essence, providing a statistical base for the state's campaign of criminalisation.

But such almost ad hoc announcements are by no means the whole of the Home Office story. Through its research unit it has had a considerable additional impact. Among its reports have been studies on 'stops, searches and arrests' (one of which purported to show no significant differences between 'West Indian' and white experiences); and on 'public disorder' carried out in Handsworth, Birmingham, in the aftermath of the 1981 uprisings. One of the most significant was a study on 'race, crime and arrest'. The study had been conducted despite the fact that:

24   *Race & Class*

Published material available, much of it from police sources, appeared to suggest that towards the beginning of the decade, ethnic minority involvement in crime, taken as a whole, was similar to that of the population at large in areas of predominantly West Indian settlement ... In areas of predominantly Asian settlement the crime rate of ethnic minorities was thought to be below average.'[23]

The research was accordingly directed to the one area of the country where considerable 'evidence' apparently contradicting the general situation was known to exist, that is to the Metropolitan Police District. 'The research therefore examines Metropolitan Police District arrest data for the year 1975, the first year for which reliable information about the racial or ethnic identity of persons arrested by the Metropolitan Police was available.' They supplied no criteria whatever that such data was 'reliable'. For after all, as we have already seen, the Met itself acknowledged at least one major basis of doubt about its figures. Despite this, the publication attracted considerable press, radio and TV coverage for its 'findings' which amounted to nothing more – quite literally – than a regurgitation of police statistics.

*   *   *

The campaign to criminalise the black community through 'mugging' and the emphasis on 'black youth' continues unabated in the 1980s. In 1982 the Metropolitan Police released crime statistics (racially coded for certain categories) which aroused the predictable press campaign; the same obtained for the 1983 figures, except that this time they were released through an MP and not directly by the police themselves.

But the crucial feature of the use of such statistics, indeed of the whole criminalisation campaign in the early 1980s, is that its objectives have changed. It is part, it will be recalled, of an overall restructuring of the state and its apparatuses in the context of an economic decline. That decline has intensified despite the discovery of oil in the North Sea and the oil price revolution. At the political-ideological level, however, this restructuring has achieved significant success. Both failure and success alike necessitate an even more ruthless pursuit of the capitalist project. The effects of this necessity have for some years been visible in the monetarist policies both of the former Labour and current Tory governments (mass unemployment, cuts in social benefits and services, etc.) and in more repressive legislative and other state practices (Police Bill, Data Protection Bill, the retention and proposed extension of the Prevention of Terrorism Act, a more militarised police force.) Now, given further that these measures, vis-à-vis the black communities, are pursued in the context of a racism which permits almost unbridled lawlessness in police behaviour towards them, as well as ensuring that many of the effects of monetarism (especially chronic unemployment) disproportionately affect them, and that no solution has been found to the political demands of the Irish national movement in the Six

Counties of Northern Ireland, there will almost inevitably be increased physical resistance to the British state.

Such has been the resistance seen on the streets of mainland Britain since 1976, when black youth at Notting Hill, on the occasion of the huge annual black carnival held there, fought a pitched battle against a police force which had for two days, in huge numbers, heavily and aggressively policed the affair. (Earlier carnivals far less menacingly patrolled had always been peaceful.) It culminated in the generalised uprisings of April through to July 1981 and continues in smaller scale outbreaks — primarily spontaneous, sometimes more organised and which go virtually unreported — in Liverpool 8, Brixton, Notting Hill, Stoke Newington, etc. Nowhere can it be truly said to have been mindless or pointless violence — violence 'for its own sake' as it were. Everywhere it has been of a defensive nature, being prompted and produced by the aggression of the state as expressed largely through lawless policing practices.

The response of the various apparatuses of the state has been to intensify the criminalisation campaign, increasingly through mobilising the 'black youth'-'black crime' couple. The purpose here has been and is to legitimate the increasingly aggressive machinery of suppression which since 1976 has been adopted by the police, to say that the resistance has no justification and can only be explained by the unremitting attempts of 'black youth' to keep the streets free of police so as to indulge in their 'criminal activity'. This approach was first developed in 1976 when, shortly after the Carnival uprising in Notting Hill, post hoc evidence of 'muggings' from the previous Carnival (1975) was produced by a Metropolitan Police Inspector in a letter to *The Times* in early September. This, he said, explained the style of policing in 1976 — a style which had directly contributed to the defensive violence directed against the Met and which had, up until the publication of that letter, been justified in terms of the size of the event and its location, which made it a threat to public order requiring massive numbers of police to control. Since then, the alleged involvement in 'crime' by 'black youth' has become the explanation for the whole plethora of police misdemeanours and police practices characterised as 'hard' policing.

It was precisely for this reason that first, Counsel to the Scarman Inquiry into the uprisings and second, the Metropolitan Police itself set out to convince Lord Scarman that it was the rising tide of 'crime' by 'black youth' in Brixton (Lambeth) which drove the police into acting like 'an army of occupation'[24] against the local black community. Certain black 'community leaders' supported the 'rising crime' line of argument:

> Young people around the streets all day, with nothing to do ... and the 'successful' criminal has a story to tell. So one evil has bred

26   *Race & Class*

another, and as unemployment has grown in both older and
younger generations crime has become more commonplace and
more acceptable. This is a vicious circle to which there is no present
end in sight.[25]

Whatever the effect of such 'evidence' on Scarman, he certainly made
the 'rising tide of black crime' the cornerstone of what he termed 'the
policing dilemma', as well as of his account of the 'Brixton story'.
Essentially then, it is the police line on 'black crime' which informed
Scarman's authorised version of the 1981 uprisings and their causes.

'Mugging' and the sociologists

The criminalisation process, however, has not rested solely with the
police, the media and the institutions of government. It depends in a
very real sense for its validity on the work of a number of sociologists,
not only of the right but self-proclaimed 'radicals'. Their work is an
important and increasingly prominent element of the criminalisation
process as it is being carried out in the 1980s, and for that reason merits
further examination. They have made use of, and further refined, a
cultural approach to the study of social reality which is not merely
compatible with the police's own ideology but is informed by it – the
academics share both language and concepts with police ideologues.
Exponents from both groups speak and write in such a way that 'black
youth' is confirmed as the key image in a framework in which the alleged 'violent proclivities' of black people are taken as an established fact
– established on the basis of the purported practices of the youth. It is a
culturalism which on occasion goes over into a quasi-geneticism.
   On one side of the coin is Sir Kenneth Newman, who has been
described as using 'the language of sociology and "preventative policing" as fluently as John Alderson, its best known exponent',[26] and who
is on record as having stated that, 'In the Jamaicans you have a people
who are constitutionally disorderly. It's simply in their make-up.
They're constitutionally disposed to be anti-authority.'[27] On the other,
are two sociologists, self-identified as radical, who go even further:

> There is a penchant for violence within West Indian culture,
> possibly stemming from the days of slavery when the only method
> of retaliation was doing physical damage to the overseer, agent or
> even slave-master ... Whatever the source of this proclivity there can
> be no denying its existence: black youth do have a certain fascina-
> tion for violence. The almost incredible enthusiasm for movies in
> the Kung Fu idiom and the massive numbers involving themselves in
> the martial arts (as well as more conventional contact sports) tells us
> something about young blacks' interest in violence, as do their

celebrations of a range of archetypical violent anti-heroes, 'Dirty Harry', Chuck Morris and the late Bruce Lee.'[28]

The quick shift away from the initial apparently culturally deterministic explanation; the revelation on their part of a consciousness in which slave resistance is seen as having been no more than 'retaliation'; the swift dance from 'penchant' to 'proclivity', 'fascination', etc.; the daring suggestion that sport and preferences for types of movies can be talked of as 'violence' are all worthy of the yellow press and exemplify a strange notion of what amounts to social scientific evidence. This is capped by their eagerness to add a splash of sexually differentiated colour, in asserting, with no greater regard for evidence, let alone proof, that 'Street attacks used to be the sovereign operation of black boys, but more recently, girls have organised themselves into gangs and have demonstrated a willingness to engage in such tactics.'

In the face of such an identity of language and perspective, it is difficult even to begin to distinguish between the function in the class struggle in Britain of those, on the one hand, whose role is openly that of repression* and those, on the other, whose ostensible role is that of objective academic research. The 'black youth'-'black crime' linkage, with its undertones and overtones of violence, is crucial to the research framework of two other self-proclaimed radical academics, whose published work sets them squarely in line with the criminalisation process being carried out against the black community:

> the fact that inner-city black youth culture is a counter culture of despair and resistance to discrimination and deprivation and the fact that it involves simultaneously soaring rates of crime ... set the scene for the development of a vicious circle whereby the relations between police and community deteriorate in such a way that each step in the deterioration creates pressure for further deterioration. Changes in police tactics in recent years (increasing use of stop and search, 'sus' etc.) cannot be seen as the result of gratuitous police prejudice. Such a view would assume that the basis of consensus policing still existed.[30]

Lea and Young quite explicitly quote police testimony to Scarman as their main evidential source. Their work revolves around a myth that 'consensus policing' once existed and that 'black crime' then drove the police away from it towards 'hard policing'. 'Consensus policing' is certainly a socio-historical myth. 'Hard policing' is equally mythical. It in no way encompasses the range of brutalities and lawlessness committed against black people by the police which

---

* Witness the evidence, validated by Amnesty International, the European Court of Human Rights and even in part by the British government's Committee of Inquiry into Police Interrogation in Northern Ireland,[29] of the torture of suspects.

28   *Race & Class*

have centrally framed the relationship between us and the police. Since
Lea and Young do not admit the overwhelming weight of evidence in
this area, it follows that the police are not seen as racist and that
therefore racism does not explain in any significant way the police
behaviour towards black people or the latter's defensive – if
dramatically explosive – response.

Given such an approach, it is not surprising that their concern is to
help focus attention on the effects of 'street crime'. They are currently
attempting to carry out a so-called Criminal Victimisation Survey,
under the auspices of several of the Labour-controlled inner city
boroughs of London.* This 'survey' has as its main object that other
creature of the criminalisation campaign, the 'victims', (old, white)
women and 'Asians', who, they say, are being attacked not only by
white thugs but also by 'black youths'. We have already seen above the
type of conceptual framework which would give shape and form to
their findings. In so far as their findings, however shakily grounded,
create an impression of a rise in street crime, their result will be to
justify even more intensive policing. As for 'black youth', Lea and
Young see them as their own worst enemies: they have allowed
themselves to become hopelessly 'marginalised' by shunning the traditional options of the white working class and adopting a violence which
appears mindless. Lea and Young go on to speak of:

> the relatively less acute marginalisation of Asian youth compared to
> West Indians. It has been observed that the Southall violence of
> 1981 was of a different order to that of Brixton and Toxteth. Asian
> youth in Southall were on the streets for an explicitly organised pur-
> pose: to defend their community against gangs of violent hooligans
> from outside the area.[31]

Apart from the fact that the black people of Liverpool 8 have become
'West Indians', worse things are happening in that text. Lea and
Young's conceptual framework forces them to put foward the image of
a non-racist, almost blameless police. They therefore extract them
from Southall 1981: the Asian community was organised solely to defend itself from external gangs. But this flies in the face of the
evidence. In Southall, Coventry and East London, there is a
documented history of police condoning racist violence against Asian
communities.[32] On 23 April 1979 the Asian community of Southall suffered an organised attack by the Metropolitan Police, and in July 1981
Asians did not merely protect themselves against civilian hooligans,
they also defended themselves against police thugs. Even Scarman
acknowledges this. It is hard to comprehend how Lea and Young can
suggest that the other major uprisings of 1981 were not similarly

---

* To date these attempts have been resisted by the local black communities.

Capital, 'black youth' and crime 29

defensive. No amount of talk about 'black youth', 'crime' or 'marginalisation' can change this. Instead, it only demonstrates how such sociology serves capital and its ruling class against workers (black and white).

Summary and conclusion

'Black youth', as we have seen, is a social category that has been fabricated and manipulated by the British state. Both its creation and its use have to be understood in terms of a project by capital developed at the economic level and the political-ideological level to save itself from chronic decline. A significant element in it involves the tightening up of the criminal justice system and the criminalisation of the black communities. The alleged disproportionate involvement of 'black youth' in 'crime' has been fundamental to that criminalisation, which has been carried out in a campaign which is now entering its second decade. The essence of it is the use of bogus statistics, developed on the basis of techniques of manipulation first used by Sir Robert Mark in the mid-1960s. The measure of his success is that these techniques, deployed in close co-operation with the media and a variety of other state apparatuses, can contrive to make less than 1 per cent of crime in London more important than the 99 per cent plus there, and all crime in the rest of the country. In recent years – since the mid-1970s – the intensified pursuit of capital's project has led to physical resistance of a defensive sort against state aggression. The state and its apparatuses have not hesitated to use the 'black youth'-'black crime' couple in a new way, that is to explain such resistance so as to shift the blame for it back on the the black communities and legitimate forms of militarisation of the police which have been adopted on a wide scale. The crisis of capital remains. The aggression of the state is undiminished. The defensive resistance of the black working class (employed and unemployed) is very likely to continue and to take on subtler and more deadly forms.

References

1 G. Fisher and H. Joshua, 'Social Policy and black youth', in E. Cashmore and B. Troyna, *Black youth in crisis* (London, 1982); see also the review of *Black youth in crisis* by Errol Lawrence in this issue.
2 *Criminal Law Revision Committee Report*, Cmnd. 4991 (London, 1972).
3 Quoted in Robert Mark, *In the office of Constable* (London, 1978).
4 Ibid.
5 Ibid.
6 Ibid.
7 It should be noted that the beginning of the attack on the jury system appears to have coincided almost exactly with the extension of the right of service to virtually all adult citizens.

30 *Race & Class*

8   See *State Research Bulletin* (No. 28, 1982), p.70.
9   See *Legal Action Group Bulletin* (November 1982), pp. 10-12.
10 'Sus' was, in fact, replaced by the Criminal Attempts Act 1980, and evidence of its misuse by the police is beginning to emerge.
11 See, for example, BASH (Black People Against State Harassment), Briefing paper on the proposals ... of Sir David McNee to the Royal Commission on Criminal Procedure, 29 September, 1978, and Institute of Race Relations, *Police against black people* (London, 1979).
12 S. Hall et al, *Policing the crisis: mugging, the state and law and order* (London, 1978).
13 Ibid.
14 Ibid., pp. 13-18.
15 M. Pratt, *Mugging as a social problem* (London, 1980), pp. 14, 93-6.
16 T.D. Jones, 'Crime and race: a report by the statistical adviser to the Metropolitan Police' (unpublished, Scotland Yard, 1974), see also R.R. Crump and J.F. Newing, 'Footpad crime and its community effects in Lambeth' (unpublished report of the A7 division, Scotland Yard, 1974); and Pratt, op. cit.
17 It is not possible to give a comprehensive listing here, but mention should be made of J. Hunte, *Nigger hunting in England?* (London, 1966); N. Dawes, *Points of concern: police and black workers: the boroughs of Greenwich and Lewisham* (London, 1972); D. Humphrey and G. John, *Police power against black people* (London, 1972); S. Pullé, *Police-immigrant relations in Ealing* (London, 1973); *Under heavy manners: report of the labour movement enquiry into police brutality and the position of black youth in Islington, held on Saturday, 23 July 1977* (London, 1977); S. Hall, op. cit.,; Institute of Race Relations, op. cit.
18 Quoted in the Metropolitan Police memorandum of March 1976 to the Select Committee on Race Relations and Immigration.
19 This and the following quotations in the section are taken from the Metropolitan Police memorandum, ibid.
20 *Observer* (17 October, 1976).
21 *Daily Telegraph* (21 October 1976).
22 *The Times* (21 October 1976).
23 P. Stevens and C.F. Willis, *Race, crime and arrests* (London, 1979). A preliminary report was published in the *Home Office Research Bulletin* (No. 8, 1979).
24 *Final report of the working party into police community relations in Lambeth* (London, 1981).
25 *The Brixton disorders 10-12 April 1981: report of an inquiry by the Rt Hon Lord Scarman*, Cmnd 8427 (London, 1981).
26 Report by David Leigh in the *Observer* (21 March 1982).
27 Quoted in Bruce Porter, 'The British Riots: hatred of the police was the common thread', in *Police Magazine* (January 1982).
28 Cashmore and Troyna, op. cit.
29 *Report of the committee of inquiry into police interrogation procedure in Northern Ireland*, Cmnd. 7497 (London, 1979).
30 J. Lea and J. Young, 'The riots in Britain 1981: urban violence and political marginalisation', in Cowell, Jones and Young (eds), *Policing the riots* (London, 1982).
31 J. Lea and J. Young, 'Urban violence and political marginalisation: the riots in Britain, summer 1981', in *Critical Social Policy* (Vol 1, no. 3, 1982).
32 See, for example, K. Leech, *Brick Lane* (Birmingham, 1978); National Council for Civil Liberties, *Report of the unofficial committee of inquiry into Southall, 23 April 1979* (London, 1980); Bethnal Green and Stepney Trades Council; *Blood on the streets* (London, 1978); *Racial attacks: report of a Home Office study* (London, 1981).

[19]

RACE AND IDEOLOGY IN THE 1980S

The Black "Underclass" Ideology in Race Relations Analysis

Leslie Inniss and Joe R. Feagin

Introduction

CONSIDER THIS CITY SITUATION. A central city with 25% unemployment. One-third of the residents have moved out. There are
many young men with no jobs collecting welfare checks and on the
streets or playing pool with friends most of the day. There are many young
women watching television all day. There are numerous unemployed adult
children living with an unemployed parent. Many of these city residents have
a problem with alcohol and drugs. Older men who once did heavy labor have
been laid off; most have been out of work for years. Many young unmarried
women, especially teenagers, in the public housing complexes are pregnant or
have already had illegitimate children. Most of the young do not expect to
work in the near future. They seem resigned, angry, or fatalistic about their
lives. They feel no one in government cares about them. These people certainly fit the definitions of the underclass used in recent literature in the United
States.

Where is this "underclass"? What city are we describing? What are the
likely racial characteristics of these urbanites? Many would guess the city is
Chicago, New York, or Atlanta, but this city is actually Liverpool, England,
once a prosperous city and the second great city of the British Empire. Interestingly, the people described are the *white* and British residents of a troubled
city. Not one is Black. Many have educations and skills but no jobs in this
northern England city, which has been neglected by the Conservative government ensconced in London in the affluent south of England ("Frontline,"
1986).

LESLIE INNISS is in the Department of Sociology, University of Texas at Austin, Austin, TX
78712–1088.
JOE R. FEAGIN is in the Department of Sociology, University of Texas at Austin, Austin, TX
78712–1088.

Reflection on these Liverpool data suggest some of the serious problems with the current discussions of the "Black underclass" by scholars and journalists in the United States. Few U.S. scholars would seriously discuss these white, formerly middle-income families and individuals in Liverpool as some type of "underclass," as a new or distinctive class characterized by problematical values, a "subculture of poverty and deviance," teen pregnancies, crime-oriented males, and better-off families moving out.

To explain the tribulations of the white, formerly middle-income residents of Liverpool there is no need to use the interpretive language of individualized pathology and value aberration that is the focus of the Black underclass discussion in the United States. There is no need to consider these people as a self-reproducing subculture of pathological behavior that contrasts with the "healthy" behavior of their better-off counterparts elsewhere. Nor is there good reason to view the poor young women of Liverpool, with their illegitimate children and single-parent status, as major contributors to the larger underclass problem. The principal reason for the personal and family troubles in Liverpool is the flight of capital to more profitable locations outside the north of Britain; disinvestment is the cause of most unemployment and underemployment. Investors decide where the jobs go. Unemployment is reproduced from one generation to the next not by values, but rather through the working of capital investment markets.

The concept of the "underclass," as it has developed in the last decade in the United States, is not only ahistorical and noncomparative, but also highly ideological and political. It represents a casting about for a way of defining the problems of the poor, and particularly the Black poor, without substantial reference to the actions of U.S. investors and capital flight. A number of social scientists have testified before state legislatures and Congress on the problems of the underclass. The "underclass" problem thereby became politically defined and bureaucratized. An adequate interpretation of the underlying causes of the unemployment and poverty-related problems of Liverpool lies in the decisions of investors to invest or disinvest. And there is no reason not to interpret similar "underclass" phenomena in U.S. cities in the same fashion. There is no need for a new conceptual framework called the "Black underclass" theory which explains the Black situation as culturally distinctive. American scholars have largely failed to put the situation of Black Americans in proper international and comparative perspective.

In this article we will examine the origins of the underclass theory, assess why this wrongheaded viewpoint has taken such hold on the (mostly white) American mind, and provide a more accurate view of what is wrong in Black and white America.

* * * * *

The Concept of the Underclass

Early Conceptions of the Black Lower Class

The concept variously labelled the "rabble," the "dangerous class," the "lumpenproletariat," and the "underclass" has a long history in Western intellectual thought. Many European analysts have feared the cities because of the growth of sizeable, or organized, working populations. And this perspective migrated to North America. In the 1830s one of the founders of sociology, the French government official Alexis de Tocqueville, visited U.S. cities and wrote perhaps the first white assessment of the Black lower class; he noted that

> the lower ranks which inhabit these cities constitute a rabble even more formidable than the populace of European towns. They consist of freed blacks, in the first place, who are condemned by the laws and by public opinion to a hereditary state of misery and degradation.... [T]hey are ready to turn all the passions which agitate the community to their own advantage; thus, within the last few months, serious riots have broken out in Philadelphia and New York (de Tocqueville, 1945: 299).

These words are from *Democracy in America*, an influential sociological analysis of the United States, and they reflect the fears of many educated whites about the "rabble" of Blacks and immigrants in the cities. This rabble is seen by white observers as disturbed, emotional, and dangerous. Note, too, that free Blacks in the cities are highlighted as a central part of the urban rabble. Thus, the idea of the Black underclass is not new with the debates of the 1960s or 1980s; the idea is at least a century and a half old. It is also interesting to note that while de Tocqueville saw free Blacks as dangerous and threatening, he also recognized the role of laws and public opinion in perpetuating the oppressive conditions of freed Blacks, a recognition of discrimination missing in much of the current discussion of the underclass.

Recent Discussions of the Black Underclass: The 1960s

According to *The Oxford English Dictionary*, the word "underclass" was first used in English in 1918 (Burchfield, 1986: 1069). Its initial use was as a description of a process — for example, a "society moves forward as a consequence of an under-class overcoming the resistance of a class on top of them." It was not until 1963, in Gunnar Myrdal's *Challenge to Affluence*, that the term was used to describe in some detail a population — "an 'underclass' of unemployed and gradually unemployable persons and families at the bottom of society." The link between Blacks and the underclass was apparently first made in 1964. A January 1964 issue of the *Observer* noted that "the Negro's protest today is but the first rumbling of the underclass." Again in 1966 a connection between Blacks and the underclass was made in the August 19 *New Statesman*: "The national economic growth has been bought at the expense of industrial workers and the poor (largely Negro) underclass" (Burchfield, 1986: 1069).

Moreover, by the 1960s U.S. scholars were writing on the subject of the Black underclass, although the more common terms then were "the poor," "the lower class," and "the culture of poverty." The view of poor communities accenting pathological traits was particularly influenced by the culture-of-poverty generalizations of anthropologist Oscar Lewis. His culture-of-poverty perspective emphasizes the defective subculture of those residing in slum areas, at first in Latin America, and by the 1960s in the United States. Developing the "culture of poverty" concept for the U.S. poor in the book *La Vida*, Lewis (1965) argues that this culture is "a way of life which is passed down from generation to generation along family lines." The poor adapt in distinctive ways to their oppressive conditions, and these adaptations are transmitted through the socialization process.

During the 1960s the acceptance of this view by both scholars and policymakers was given greater legitimacy by its being featured in federal government publications. Published by the government, Catherine Chilman's scholarly publication entitled *Growing Up Poor* in effect gave governmental sanction to the culture-of-poverty portrait, with emphasis on personal disorganization, superstitious thinking, impulsive behavior, inadequate childrearing practices, and a lack of ability to defer gratification (Chilman, 1966). A second government publication, entitled *The Negro Family* (1965), focused on the alleged lack of social integration and pathology in *Black* communities. Here social scientist (later U.S. Senator) Daniel Patrick Moynihan argued that:

> at the heart of the deterioration of the fabric of Negro society is the deterioration of the Negro family. It is the fundamental source of the weakness of the Negro community at the present time (Moynihan, 1965: 5).

The typical lower-class Black family was broken or disintegrated. Moynihan proceeded to argue that, in contrast, the typical white family "had maintained a high degree of stability." Black family disorganization was, in turn, tied to disintegration in other aspects of Black lower-class life. Moynihan accentuated the "tangle" of pathology and crumbling social relations — which in his view characterized Black communities — and argued further that "there is considerable evidence that the Negro community is, in fact, dividing between a stable middle class group that is steadily growing stronger and more success-

ful and an increasingly disorganized and disadvantaged lower class group"
(*Ibid.*, 1965: 5–6).

The policy impact of this lower-class-pathology emphasis in the social science literature can also be seen in the major government reports on Black/white conflict in the 1960s, including the *Report of the National Advisory Commission on Civil Disorders*. Writing about Black America under a heading of "Unemployment, Family Structure, and Social Disorganization," the authors of this report used a variety of disorganization codewords:

> The culture of poverty that results from unemployment and family breakup generates a system of ruthless, exploitative relationships within the ghetto. Prostitution, dope addiction, and crime create an environmental "jungle" characterized by personal insecurity and tension (National Advisory Commission on Civil Disorders, 1968: 7).

Critics of the Culture of Poverty View

There was much debate over the lower-class-pathology perspective during the 1960s and 1970s. Anyone returning to the discussion of the period will have a strong feeling of *déjà vu*. For example, in *Lower-Class Families* Hyman Rodman argues that the lower-class view is a stereotyped view emphasizing negative aspects. Rodman contends that there are numerous responses made by lower-class persons in adapting to deprivation other than the lower-class-pathology adaptation. One response, the "lower-class value stretch," can be seen in the fact that many poor people share dominant middle-class values and aspirations and reflect these in actions, while at the same time reflecting lower-class values; their repertoire of values is usually greater than for middle-class individuals. Thus when conditions change, such as an availability of employment, most of the poor can rapidly adapt.

In the late 1960s and early 1970s, the junior author of this article also developed a critique. One point made then was that, although types of criminal behavior and drug use exist to a disproportionate degree in many Black communities, the extent of this behavior is exaggerated in many assessments of day-to-day life. It is too easy to move from characteristics of a minority of the Black residents of a given urban community, however unconventional or criminal, to ungrounded generalizations about Black areas overall. In addition, there is much unheralded white-collar crime and drug use in white suburban communities, but scholars have not developed a deviant subculture perspective for these communities. Moreover, the quick typification of Black areas in pathological organization terminology, with its overtones of character flaws and individual blame, tends to play down the intimate relationship between these areas and the larger racial system surrounding them (Feagin, 1974: 123–146).

The Lower Class Becomes the Underclass

The Underclass Debate

In the 1970s and 1980s, the debates between the neoconservatives and liberals over the character and constitution of the underclass have mirrored the debates of the 1960s. Numerous analysts have underscored the significant growth in the problems confronting central city Blacks since the 1970s. The emphasis on Black problems has coincided with a major economic crisis (for example, disinvestment in many cities) and, thus, a legitimacy crisis for U.S. capitalism. This crisis of legitimacy has involved ordinary Americans questioning the actions and legitimacy of U.S. elites. Commentators and social scientists such as Charles Murray, Glenn Loury, Ken Auletta, Nicholas Lemann, Nathan Glazer, and Daniel P. Moynihan have played an important role in refurbishing the legitimacy of the existing system of inequality by moving the public discussion away from such issues as decent-paying jobs, capital flight, racism, and militarism and back onto the old 1960s' issues of crime, welfare, illegitimacy, ghetto pathologies, and the underclass. For example, in his 1975 book entitled *Affirmative Discrimination*, Nathan Glazer described a "tangle of pathology in the ghetto" which cannot be explained by "anything as simple as lack of jobs or discrimination in available jobs." Although Glazer does not use the term underclass, he does conjure up its image with comments that suggest that many Black youth prefer illicit activities because they do not want to work at regular jobs. From his perspective, neither rapid economic growth nor affirmative action will benefit unskilled and culturally impoverished Black males reluctant to do low-wage work (Glazer, 1975: 71–72).

A Cover Story in Time

One of the first national discussions of the underclass appeared in the cover story of *Time* magazine in August 1977, not long after the burning and looting of a store by unemployed Blacks during the New York City electrical blackout in July 1977. The *Time* portrait anticipates that which appears later in both scholarly and journalistic sources: "The underclass has been...left behind.... Its members are victims and victimizers in the culture of the street hustle, the quick fix, the rip-off, and, not least, violent crime" (*Time*, 1977: 14). Although the article tends to focus on the culture, welfare involvement, illegitimacy, street values, and feelings of hopelessness among the members of the underclass, it does also discuss the impact of long-term unemployment on the Black underclass' self-esteem and identification. However, the increasing conservatism of the late 1970s can be seen in the emphasis on individual and private sector initiatives. Asserting that there is no political consensus for governmental job creation or War-on-Poverty programs — which the journalists argue would increase inflation — the article retreats to the mostly conservative strategies of education, tougher law enforcement, a lower minimum wage, work requirements for welfare recipients, and giving private business control of job training programs. The conservative tone of much subsequent discussion of the underclass was foreshadowed in this mass media article.

In the late 1970s prominent intellectual magazines began to carry articles defining the situation of the Black poor in terms of the "underclass." For example, Ken Auletta produced an influential series of articles for the *New Yorker*, which he later developed into a book called *The Underclass*. For Auletta the underclass only includes the nine million people who are permanently poor. Auletta discusses the Black, white, and Hispanic underclasses, but the emphasis is on impoverished Blacks. The central issue is class culture. The underclass is grouped by Auletta into four distinct categories: the passive poor, hostile street criminals, hustlers, and the drunks, homeless, and released mental patients who roam city streets (Auletta, 1982: 198–304). (He leaves out the underemployed and unemployed poor.) For Auletta, racism plays no significant part in the formation of the underclass. Auletta uses "Black underclass" to describe those with a lifestyle characterized by poverty and antisocial behavior: "The underclass suffers from behavioral as well as income deficiencies" (*Ibid.*, 1982: 28). These behavioral deficiencies include immorality, broken families, and a poorly developed work ethic. Auletta's accent on the old "culture of poverty" characteristics is linked to his argument that the plight of the Black underclass has little to do with racial discrimination but instead is the product of cultural deprivation. While he makes occasional concessions to environmental factors, the general tone of this analysis indicates that he prefers the culture-of-poverty perspective.

Similarly, in a 1980 *New York Times Magazine* article, Carl Gershman argued that it is the worsening condition of the underclass, not racial discrimination, which requires the greatest policy attention (Gershman, 1980: 24–30). Critical to his argument is the old idea that the conditions of poorer Black Americans are due to the "tangle of pathology" in which they find themselves. He, too, argues that poor Black Americans are locked into a lower-class subculture, a culture of poverty, with its allegedly deviant value system of immorality, broken families, juvenile delinquency, and lack of emphasis on the work ethic.

Moreover, in a widely read 1986 article in the *Atlantic Monthly*, Nicholas Lemann wrote that:

every aspect of the underclass culture in the ghettos is directly trace-
able to roots in the South — and not the South of slavery but...in the
nascent underclass of the sharecropper South.... In the ghettos, it appears that the distinctive culture is now the greatest barrier to
progress by the black underclass rather than either unemployment or
welfare (Lemann, 1986: 35).

The culture of the underclass is seen as the greatest barrier to Black advancement. The poor Black communities lack positive values. In the 1970s,
the ghettos went from being diversified to being "exclusively Black lower-
class" and this resulted in complete social breakdown. "Until then the strong
leaders and institutions of the ghetto had promoted an ethic of assimilation,"
but with the movement away of institutions and leaders there was a "free fall"
into "social disorganization." Echoes of the 1960s arguments can again be
heard in these views; the criminalized underclass flourished because there was
no middle class to reign it in.

Moreover, a 1988 article in the *Chronicle of Higher Education* reviewed
the research on the underclass and concluded:

Although the underclass constitutes a minuscule portion of the total
U.S. population and a very small proportion of all those living in
poverty, the lives of the ghetto poor are marked by a dense fabric of
what experts call "social pathologies" — teenage pregnancies, out-of-
wedlock births, single-parent families, poor educational achievement,
chronic unemployment, welfare dependency, drug abuse, and crime
— that, taken separately or together, seem impervious to change
(Coughlin, 1988: A5).

The language of pathology was given legitimacy in this important journal of
higher education.

The Mass Media Picks Up the Underclass

Not only the intellectual magazines but also the mass media proclaimed
the culturally oriented underclass theory in the mid–1980s. Using social science scholarship, the journalistic accounts had their own special twist. For example, a 1987 *Fortune* magazine author commented as follows:

Who are the underclass? They are poor, but numbering around five
million, they are a relatively small minority of the 33 million Americans with incomes below the official poverty line. Disproportionately
Black and Hispanic, they are still a minority within these minorities.
What primarily defines them is not so much their poverty or race as
their behavior — their chronic lawlessness, drug use, out-of-wedlock

births, welfare dependency, and school failure. "Underclass" describes a state of mind and a way of life. It is at least as much a cultural as an economic condition (Magnet, 1987: 130).

An *Esquire* article excerpted in a 1988 *Reader's Digest* put it this way:

The heart of the matter is what has come to be called the underclass — those nine million impoverished black Americans (of a total of 29 million blacks), so many of whom are trapped in welfare dependency, drugs, alcohol, crime, illiteracy, and disease, living in isolation in some of the richest cities of the earth (Hamill, 1988: 105).

A Leading Scholar: William J. Wilson

In the late 1970s and 1980s, the University of Chicago sociologist William J. Wilson, a leading Black scholar, became an effectual exponent of the Black underclass perspective. Wilson's 1980 work, *The Declining Significance of Race*, had a major influence on the misconceptions surrounding the "Black underclass." Wilson contended that affirmative action programs had actually widened the gap between the Black middle class and the rest of Black America and had produced a Black underclass that has fallen behind the larger society in every aspect. Wilson's book opened the door for assumptions that racial discrimination had little significance for those who were moving up into the Black middle class and, by extension, that class (status) discrimination was more important than racial discrimination. The Black middle class had become a central part of the underclass argument. Racial discrimination, in employment at least, was not considered to be significant for middle-class Black Americans.

More recently, Wilson has argued that the underclass is composed of individuals who lack training and skills and who either experience long-term unemployment or are not a part of the labor force; individuals who engage in street criminal activity and other aberrant behavior; and families who experience long-term spells of poverty or welfare dependency. He developed these ideas most extensively in a widely discussed 1987 book, *The Truly Disadvantaged*. There Wilson targets the underclass and demonstrates numerous fallacies in the recent neoconservative analysis of the Black poor. Wilson shows, for example, that there is no consistent evidence that welfare programs decrease work effort or increase dependency and that the growing percentage of out-of-wedlock Black births is not the result of immorality or welfare, but instead results from the declining birth rate among married women as well as young women's difficulty in finding marriageable Black men — young men who are not chronically unemployed. In reply to the neoconservative emphasis on the subculture of poverty, Wilson develops the concepts of *social isolation* and *concentration effects.* A central Black underclass dilemma is the departure of stable middle-class families from traditional ghetto areas into better residential neighborhoods farther away. The poor thus face social isolation unlike that of the past. Not only are there fewer role models, but there are also fewer supportive institutions, including family stores, churches, and other voluntary associations. This deterioration brings a decline in sense of community, neighborhood identification, and norms against criminal behavior. Coupled with isolation are the concentration effects of having single-parent families, criminals, and the unemployed crowed into one area. Wilson rejects the neoconservative notion that the causes of current Black problems lie in self-perpetuating cultural traits.

Other Black Scholars

By the 1980s the term "underclass" was being used by white and Black social scientists. A number of Black scholars have made use of, and thereby helped to legitimate, the terminology of the Black underclass. However, although they accept the language of pathology, they have tended to accent the structural causes of the underclass dilemma. For example, in a 1984 book Pinkney has argued that

> Perhaps two of the major defining characteristics of the black underclass are their poverty and the social decay in which they are forced to survive.... Often they are forced to engage in criminal activities, a rational response to the circumstances in which they find themselves. And it must be noted that since these people are treated as animals, they frequently respond in kind (Pinkney, 1984: 117).

He goes on to place emphasis on the structural conditions faced by Black Americans. Moreover, in a 1987 analysis of the Black family, Billingsly notes in passing the growth of the underclass:

> The black underclass continues to grow, due in part to extensive poverty, unemployment, and family instability.... Composed of those families and individuals at the bottom of the economic and social scales — perhaps a third of all black families — this sector of the population experiences an enormous portion of suffering (Billingsly, 1987: 101).

Douglas G. Glasgow published *The Black Underclass* in 1981; his book has been unnecessarily neglected. Although Glasgow uses the underclass terminology by defining the underclass as a "permanently entrapped population of poor persons, unused and unwanted," his analytical focus is on structural factors. He addresses institutional racism as it operates in the educational system and the job market. Programs like affirmative action have failed to improve life for the inner-city poor because these programs have been "aimed at correcting superficial inequities without addressing the ingrained societal factors that maintain such inequities." Moreover, in a recent article Glasgow notes that the concept of the Black underclass has become widespread and generally has negative connotations. The portrait is one of ne'er-do-well welfare recipients and irresponsible fathers of illegitimate children on the dole. Glasgow takes issue with three of the major assumptions in underclass theory: the implication that there is a value deficiency in the Black community which created the underclass; the notion that the underclass problem is mainly a female/feminization problem rather than a racial one; and the notion that it was antipoverty programs that created the underclass. Nonetheless, he does accept the concept of the underclass as useful and suggests that the underclass concept adds another dimension to the traditional class structure of upper, middle, working, and lower class (Glasgow, 1987: 129–145).

A Report by Local Government

Just as in the 1960s, governmental reports in the 1980s have picked up on the underclass theory in analyzing urban problems. A report of the New York City Commission on the Year 2000, established by Mayor Ed Koch, reviews the health of that city and finds it to be "ascendant," with a strong economy and the "exuberance of a re-energized city." While this Koch report does recommend some job creation and development control actions, one section provides an underclass interpretation of poverty in the city. Contrasting conditions of earlier immigrants with the contemporary poor, it portrays the latter as not having the churches and other institutions that aided the mobility of earlier immigrants:

> A city that was accustomed to viewing poverty as a phase in assimilation to the larger society now sees a seemingly rigid cycle of poverty and a permanent underclass divorced from the rest of society.

The report takes a limited "the city can only do so much" attitude to the solution of the poverty problem; the first two solutions proposed are for the "city to do what it can to discourage teenagers from becoming pregnant" and to provide troubled families at an early point with a caseworker. Some attention is given to the need to find job training programs for the welfare mothers, and a brief paragraph outlines how the city needs to develop programs to employ in its own division young unemployed males. As in many previous governmental reports, education is accented as the long-term solution to poverty in the city. There is no attention to the role of racial discrimination in Black poverty, nor is there any analysis of urban capital investment and disinvest-

24   INNISS AND FEAGIN

ment. From the beginning the orientation is "to make more sections of the city attractive to business" (Commission on the Year 2000, 1988: 33).

A Critique of the Underclass Theory

A Politicized Theory

The concept of the underclass, as it has developed in the last decade, is highly political and represents a defining of the problems of the Black poor in ways that do not involve an indictment of the existing structure of U.S. society. Neoconservatives use a reconstituted culture-of-poverty explanation, while liberals like Wilson mix some of the culture-of-poverty language with an emphasis on the social isolation and concentration of the Black poor. All theories, including the underclass theory, reflect the bias and societal situations of the theorists. Much of the underclass theorizing of the neoconservative theorists — and the white policymakers propagating it — is replete with white fears, assumptions, and biases. Liberal analysts, moreover, have generally fallen into the trap of accepting the language of the underclass theory even though they may place emphasis on demographic or structural factors.

The Problem of Definition

A major indicator of the problems in underclass theory is the ambiguity in various definitions. Auletta, for example, excludes the underemployed and includes street criminals, welfare mothers, hustlers, and the homeless. Wilson includes those who are among the long-term unemployed or who lack skills. For some, the underclass includes both rich criminals and the very poor. Most, but not all, see the underclass as made up primarily of minorities.

Behavior seems to be a common theme. Gephart and Pearson (1988: 3) claim that "most current definitions center around the concepts of concentrated and persistent poverty and/or a profile of 'underclass behaviors' that are judged dysfunctional by their observers." Neoconservatives and liberals alike use the language of illegitimacy, disorganization, and pathology. Many use income to count the underclass, but use behavior as the focus of the discussion. This means that the working poor and the elderly are sometimes included in the total count of those in the underclass, but are not part of the behavioral discussion. Even putting numbers on the size of the underclass has been problematical. Some estimates of the underclass include only a small share of the poor, while others expand the notion to include a much larger population. In a 1988 policy journal article, Ricketts and Sawhill have tried to make the definition of the underclass more concrete and specific, and thus to make it more useful for policymakers. They noted that "estimates of the underclass vary widely — from 3% to 38% of the poor. Persistence-based measures generally lead to higher estimates than location-based measures" (Ricketts and Sawhill, 1988: 318). They develop a definition using census data for geographical areas of cities:

> an underclass area [is] a census tract with a high proportion of (1) high school dropouts...; (2) prime-age males not regularly attached to the labor force...; (3) welfare recipients...; and (4) female heads (Ricketts and Sawhill, 1988: 321).

They found that 2.5 million Americans live in these census tracts, although they admit that many nonpoor also live in there. Their final estimate is that there are about 1.3 million non-elderly adults living in underclass areas.

There is also a problem with the use of "class" in the term "underclass." The underclass distinction is not really a class distinction, because it does not focus on the hierarchy of classes or the relationship of classes, as does the tradition of class analysis since Karl Marx and Max Weber. While some argue that the underclass is outside the production (work) system, this is not actually the case, as we will see below. Moreover, if there is a Black underclass, presumably there is an "overclass." Yet the mainstream discussion does not discuss this "overclass."

Capitalism and Capital Flight

The underclass theory has arisen during an era when American capitalism is undergoing great change. There has been much capital flight out of central cities into suburban areas, cities in the Sunbelt, and foreign countries. Capital and corporate flight is at the heart of Black joblessness and poverty. Workers, Black or white, do not have the same ability to flee the community as do large corporations (Feagin and Parker, 1990: 37–50). Indeed, the threat of corporate flight has become a type of coercion, in that it forces workers to agree to wage reductions and other concessions — or in some cases to accept low-wage jobs. In addition, social scientists have functioned to legitimate a view of the U.S. capitalist system which suggests that Black workers should accept low-wage jobs.

Perhaps the strongest feature of Wilson's book, *The Truly Disadvantaged*, is the emphasis on joblessness as an important causal factor in the isolation of the Black underclass. Wilson argues that the scarcity of young Black males with regular jobs substantially accounts for the growing numbers of female-headed households and the increase in out-of-wedlock births. If young men and women cannot afford to get married, rent an apartment, and live together in a stable economic situation, young women set up their own households, raise their children, and often depend on welfare benefits. Wilson concludes his analysis with a call for a traditional job training and full employment policy, coupled with macroeconomic policy to generate a tight labor market and growth.

Among leading industrial nations the U.S. government has provided the weakest job training and creation programs. One important reason for this is that the U.S. state is substantially under the control of corporate capital, whose leadership seeks the freedom to invest or disinvest wherever profit margin and market control dictate and, thus, to weaken labor, cut taxes, and reduce employment programs. Wilson and other liberal analysts generally do not deal critically with the structure and operation of the contemporary capitalist system. The movement of jobs from northern cities to the Sunbelt cities and overseas, which Wilson does note, is not just part of a routine fluctuation in U.S. capitalism, but rather signals that investors are moving much capital, on a long-term basis, to areas with cheap labor and weak state regulation. Without a radical new policy restructuring the undemocratic investment policy of U.S. capitalism, it is not possible to deal fundamentally with job problems of central city dwellers. In *Black in a White America*, Sidney Willhelm has pointed to the major problem facing large nonwhite groups concentrated in racially stratified low-wage jobs — the abandonment of whole populations as capitalism restructures to meet the chronic need for renewed profits. The U.S. economy no longer needs the majority of Black workers for full-time jobs (Willhelm, 1983).

Neoconservative and liberal analysts suggest that either the private sector or the government can provide enough jobs to solve the Black underclass problem. Yet, to quote from Adolph Reed (1988: 170),

> what if there is no upward mobility queue — or at least not one either fat enough to accommodate the large populations of marginalized blacks and Hispanics or sturdy enough to withstand the dynamics of racial and class subordination?

Contemporary Discrimination: The Matter of Race

For most underclass analysts the concept of the Black underclass accents class culture or social isolation and downplays racial discrimination. A major weakness in Wilson's book is the rejection of current race discrimination as a significant reason for Black problems. Underclass analysts fail to consider the ways in which current discrimination perpetuates the effects of past discrimination. This results in, among other misconceptions, an ahistorical analysis, a too positive evaluation of the situation of middle-income Black Americans, and insufficient attention to the effect of discrimination on the Black underclass.

The discrimination of the past is much more substantial and thoroughgoing for Black Americans. There is a view among some neoconservative scholars that "blacks today are like white immigrants yesterday," and that there is no need for governmental intervention on behalf of Blacks. In an article in the *New York Times Magazine* in 1966, social scientist Irving Kristol argued that "The Negro Today is Like the Immigrant of Yesterday" (Kristol, 1966: 50–51, 124–142). In his view the Black experience is not greatly different from that of white immigrant groups, and Black Americans can and will move up, just as the white immigrants of yesterday did. Similarly, Glazer argues that there are some important differences between the experiences of Blacks and those of white immigrants, but that there are more similarities than differences. He emphasizes that the difference is one of degree: "the gap between the experience of the worst off of the [white] ethnic groups and the Negroes is one of degree rather than kind. Indeed, in some respects the Negro is better off than some other groups" (Glazer, 1971: 458–459). Glazer further avers that, for the most part, the employment conditions faced by Black migrants to Northern cities were no worse than those encountered by white immigrant groups.

Yet historical research by Hershberg, Yancey, and their associates has demonstrated that economic conditions at the time of entry into cities and the level of anti-Black racism at that time made the experiences of Blacks far more oppressive and difficult than those of white immigrant groups in northern cities. In the case of white immigrant groups, and of their children and grandchildren, group mobility was possible because:

1.   Most arrived at a point in time when jobs were available, when capitalism was expanding and opportunities were more abundant;

2.   Most faced far less severe employment and housing discrimination than Blacks did; and

3.   Most found housing, however inadequate, reasonably near the workplaces (Hershberg, 1981: 462–464).

From an historical perspective there is no new underclass of the Black poor. For more than half a century there have been many Blacks in and outside cities without jobs; from the beginning of urban residence many Blacks have been locked into the segregated housing in cities.

Moreover, much "past" discrimination that reduced Black resources and mobility is not something of the distant past, but rather is recent. *Blatant* discrimination against Blacks occurred in massive doses until 25 years ago, particularly in the South. All Blacks (and whites) over the age of 30 years were born when the U.S. still had massive color bars both North and South. Most Blacks over 40 years of age were educated in *legally* segregated schools of lower quality than those of whites, and many felt the weight of massive *blatant* racial discrimination in, at least, the early part of their employment careers. And the majority of those Black Americans under the age of 30 have parents who have suffered from blatant racial discrimination. Moreover, most white Americans have benefited, if only indirectly, from past racial discrimination in several institutional areas.

A second misconception can be seen in the conceptualization of the Black middle class. By focussing on the middle class, scholars and other writers can argue that the problem of "race" is solved, that the only problem is that of the underclass, which is not racially determined. For example, it is often assumed that Black women hold favored positions in the labor market because affirmative action programs and equal opportunity programs have been most beneficial to middle-class Black women. This in turn leads to the assumption that Black professional women have experiences, interests, and concerns which are very substantially at variance with Black women who belong to the underclass (i.e., welfare mothers). However, whatever their class position, there are certain fundamental commonalties of experiences and perceptions shared by Black women as a racial-gender group.

Research on upper-middle-income Blacks in corporate America shows them to be suffering from widespread discrimination. Jones' research on Black managers has found that the predominantly white corporate environment, with its intense pressures for conformity, creates regular problems. Jones describes one Black manager working his way up the executive ranks. One day he met with other Black managers who wanted his advice on coping with discrimination:

> Charlie concluded that this should be shared with senior management and agreed to arrange a meeting with the appropriate officers. Two days before the scheduled meeting, while chatting with the President at a cocktail affair, Charlie was sobered by the President's disturbed look as he said, "Charlie I am disappointed that you met with those black managers. I thought we could trust you" (Jones, 1986: 89).

Jones has also reported racial climate data from his nationwide survey of a large number of Black managers with graduate-level business degrees. Nearly all (98%) felt that Black managers had not achieved equal opportunity with white managers, and more than 90% felt there was much anti-Black hostility in corporations. The leaders in white (male) oriented organizations are willing, often grudgingly, to bring Blacks and women into important positions but in token numbers and under the existing rules (Jones, 1985).

In addition, members of the Black middle class do not have the same long-term financial security of comparable whites. Thus, a 1984 Census Bureau study of wealth found that the median Black household had a net worth of about $3,400, less than one-tenth of the median white household's net worth.

This means that a crisis could easily wipe out most Black middle-class families (U.S. Bureau of the Census, 1987: 440–441).

Moreover, in the 1980s many Black workers at all status levels have faced layoffs and sharp reductions in income, including auto and steel workers. A Federal Service Task Force study found that in the early 1980s minority workers were laid off at 50% higher rate than whites. As Robert Ethridge of the American Association for Affirmative Action put it in 1988: "There are a lot [of Blacks] in peripheral areas like affirmative action and community relations, but as companies downsize, restructure, and merge, they want to cut off those fluff areas" (Ellis, 1988: 68). The eight years of attacks on affirmative action under the Reagan administration took their toll. There is today less commitment to affirmative action in the business community.

The Reality of Discrimination

White Americans tend not to see the actual racial discrimination that exists in U.S. society, while Black Americans are acutely aware of it. In reply to an early 1980s Gallup poll question ("Looking back over the last ten years, do you think the quality of life of Blacks in the U.S. has gotten better, stayed the same, or gotten worse?"), over half of the nonwhites in the sample (mostly Blacks) said "gotten worse" or "stayed the same" (Gallup Opinion Index, 1980: 10). Yet only a fifth of the *white* respondents answered in a negative way. Three-quarters of the whites said "gotten better." The survey also asked this question: "In your opinion, how well do you think Blacks are treated in this community: the same as whites are, not very well, or badly?" Sixty-eight percent of the whites in this nationwide sample said Blacks were treated the same as whites; only 20% felt they were not well treated or were badly treated.

In the spring of 1988, a *Business Week* article reported on a national survey showing that about half of the Blacks interviewed felt that they had to work harder than whites; just 7% of whites agreed. Over half the Blacks interviewed felt that most Blacks are paid less than whites "doing the same job." The comparable percentage for whites was 18%; 70% of the whites interviewed felt there was pay equality. Eighty percent of the Black respondents, and just 32% of the whites, felt that if an equally well qualified Black and white were competing for the same job, that the Black applicant would be less likely to be hired. Furthermore, 62% of Black respondents said that the chances for Blacks to be promoted to supervisory jobs were not as good as those for whites; even 41% of whites agreed (Ellis, 1988: 65).

Residential Dispersion and Desegregation

Current theories of the Black underclass emphasize the importance of Black middle-class flight from previously all-Black areas and into all-white areas. Underclass theorists argue that middle-class Blacks can and do abandon the ghetto to "move on up" to integrated suburban neighborhoods. The implication is that there is widespread housing integration, at least at the middle-class level. However, theories that focus on middle-class abandonment cannot explain the overwhelming statistical evidence of continuing residential segregation at all class levels (Newman, 1978; Peterson, 1981; Johnston, 1984). To take one example, in the city of New Orleans most Blacks at all income levels remain in traditionally Black areas; the four census tracts with the largest concentrations of Blacks are three public housing projects and one large Black suburban subdivision adjacent to poor Black areas (Inniss, 1988).

Black suburbanization has been low. Only one-tenth of Black Americans live in the suburbs today. Housing segregation data suggest that many stable-income, middle-income Black families have not moved far from ghetto areas, but rather live in nearby suburbs on the ghetto fringe. Thus, one study conducted in the 1980s of New Jersey found that most of the increase in Black suburban population in that state occurred in or near existing Black neighborhoods (Lake, 1981). A 1988 study by Denton and Massey also questioned the middle-class abandonment thesis. Using data from the 1980 census, Denton and Massey found that within the 20 metropolitan areas with the largest Black populations, Blacks continue to be highly segregated residentially, at all socioeconomic levels. Even for the best-educated Blacks, those with one year or more of postgraduate work, the index of segregation was very high. They conclude that if the Black middle class is abandoning the Black poor, "they are not moving to integrated Anglo-Black neighborhoods" (Denton and Massey, 1988: 814).

Moreover, in a recent national survey the majority of the whites interviewed said that the percentage Black in their neighborhood had stayed the same or gone down in the past five years; only 29% said the percentage Black had increased — even a little. Among the Black respondents only 10% reported that the percent Black in their neighborhood had gone down in the last five years. Thirty-five percent reported that the percentage had gone up (Ellis, 1988: 65). The surveys suggest no great changes in the mid–1980s.

Conclusion

The solution to the problem of Blacks in America is neither obscure nor novel. The vestiges and badges of slavery are still very much in evidence in the terrible statistics that the underclass theorists repeat. But these statistics are not the result, at base, of some underclass subculture or isolation from the Black middle class. They reflect past and present discrimination. One problem is that most commentators have gotten so used to Black poverty that their language of pathology and ghettos seems relatively accurate and harmless. Yet like other forms of discrimination and segregation Black "ghettos" go back to, and are a residue of, slavery; we should not speak of them cavalierly as though they were just areas of cities somehow comparable to other areas such as "suburbs." Ghettos are terrible places reflecting the *result* of white racism, no less.

To get rid of these badges and vestiges of slavery, we not only need some broad restructuring of modern capitalism to meet the needs of ordinary workers, Black and white, but in our view we also require race-specific solutions such as expanded — and aggressive — affirmative action. In theory at least, the concept of affirmative action is radical; affirmative action recognizes that past wrongs are structured-in and must be specially addressed with race-specific structural programs. Some previous affirmative action plans have been successful in opening up institutions for Black Americans.

The opponents of equal opportunity and affirmative action have scored a brilliant coup by getting the mass media to discuss affirmative action in terms of the simplistic phrase "reverse discrimination." Yet the term is grossly inaccurate. Traditional discrimination has meant, and still means, the widespread practice of blatant and subtle discrimination by whites against Blacks in most organizations in all major institutional areas of society — in housing, employment, education, health services, the legal system, and so on. For three centuries now, tens of millions of whites have participated directly in discrimination against millions of Blacks, including routinized discrimination in the large-scale bureaucracies that now dominate this society. The reverse of traditional discrimination by whites against Blacks would mean reversing the power and resource inequalities for a long time: for several hundred years, massive institutionalized discrimination would be directed by dominant Blacks against most whites. That societal condition would be "reverse discrimination." It has never existed.

Moreover, Kenneth Smallwood (1985) has argued that white America has historically benefited from huge federal "affirmative action" plans for whites only, programs which laid the foundation for much of white prosperity in the United States. To take one major example, from the 1860s to the early 1900s, the Homestead Act provided free land in the West for whites, but because most Blacks were still in the semislavery peonage of Southern agriculture, most could not participate in this government affirmative action program giving land to U.S. citizens. That billion-dollar land giveaway became the basis of economic prosperity for many white Americans and their descendants. Recent affirmative action plans for Black Americans pale in comparison with that single program. Moreover, most New Deal programs in the 1930s primarily subsidized white Americans and white-controlled corporations. Thus, Federal Housing Administration (FHA) actions helped millions of white American families secure housing while that agency also encouraged the segregation of Black Americans in ghetto communities. Massive New Deal agricultural programs and the Reconstruction Finance Corporation kept many white American bankers, farmers, and corporate executives in business, again providing the basis for much postwar prosperity in white America.

Yet similar, massive multibillion dollar aid programs have never been made available to most Black Americans. Preferential treatment for white Americans has always been legitimate, and was for more than three centuries an essential part of government development in U.S. society. If so, one might add, why not provide three centuries of equivalent, legitimate, large-scale affirmative action to build up the wealth of the Black American victims of white discrimination?

REFERENCES

Auletta, Ken
    1982   The Underclass. New York: Random House.
Billingsly, Andrew
    1987   "Black Families in a Changing Society." The State of Black America 1987.
                    New York: National Urban League.
Burchfield, R.W. (ed.)
    1986   A Supplement to the Oxford English Dictionary. Oxford: Clarendon Press.
Chilman, Catherine S.
    1966   Growing Up Poor. Washington, D.C.: U.S. Government Printing Office.
Commission on the Year 2000
    1988   New York Ascendant. New York: Harper and Row.
Coughlin, Ellen K.
    1988   "Worsening Plight of the Underclass Catches Attention." The Chronicle of
                    Higher Education (March): A5.
de Tocqueville, Alexis
    1945   Democracy in America. Phillips Bradley (ed.), Vol. I. New York: Random
                    House.
Denton, Nancy A. and Douglas S. Massey
    1988   "Residential Segregation of Blacks, Hispanics, and Asians by Socioeconomic
                    Status and Generation." Social Science Quarterly 69 (December): 797–817.
Ellis, James E.
    1988   "The Black Middle Class." Business Week (March 14): 68.
Feagin, Joe R.
    1974   "Community Disorganization: Some Critical Notes." Marcia Pelly Effrat (ed.),
                    The Community: Approaches and Applications. New York: Free Press:
                    123–146.
Feagin, Joe R. and Robert E. Parker
    1990   Building American Cities. Englewood Cliffs, N.J.: Prentice-Hall.
"Frontline"
    1986   "Will There Always Be an England?" Public Broadcasting System.
Gallup Opinion Index
    1980   "Whites, Blacks Hold Different Views of Status of Blacks in U.S." Report No.
                    178 (June): 10.
Gephart, Martha A. and Robert W. Pearson
    1988   "Contemporary Research on the Urban Underclass." Social Science Research
                    Council Items 42: 3.

The Black "Underclass" Ideology   33

Gershman, Carl
    1980   "A Matter of Class." New York Times Magazine (October 5): 24–30.
Glasgow, Douglas G.
    1987   "The Black Underclass in Perspective." The State of Black America 1987.
                New York: National Urban League, Inc.
    1980   The Black Underclass. San Francisco: Jossey-Bass.
Glazer, Nathan
    1975   Affirmative Discrimination: Ethnic Inequality and Public Policy. New York:
                Basic Books.
    1971   "Blacks and Ethnic Groups." Social Problems 18: 458–459.
Hamill, Pete
    1988   "America's Black Underclass: Can It Be Saved?" Excerpt from Esquire in
                Reader's Digest (July): 105.
Hershberg, Theodore et al.
    1981   "A Tale of Three Cities: Blacks, Immigrants, and Opportunity in Philadelphia:
                1850–1880, 1930, 1970." T. Hershberg (ed.), Philadelphia. New York: Oxford
                University Press: 462–464.
Inniss, Leslie
    1988   "Segregation in New Orleans." Unpublished paper. Austin: University of
                Texas.
Johnston, R.J.
    1984   Residential Segregation, the State and Constitutional Conflict in American
                Urban Areas. London: Academic Press.
Jones, Ed
    1986   "What It's Like to Be a Black Manager." Harvard Business Review
                (May–June): 84–93.
    1985   "Beneficiaries or Victims? Progress or Process." Unpublished Research Re-
                port. South Orange, New Jersey (January).
Kristol, Irving
    1966   "The Negro Today Is Like the Immigrant of Yesterday." New York Times
                Magazine (September 11): 50–51; 124–142.
Lake, Robert W.
    1981   The New Suburbanites: Race and Housing in the Suburbs. New Brunswick,
                N.J.: Center for Urban Policy Research, Rutgers University.
Lemann, Nicholas
    1986   "The Origins of the Underclass." The Atlantic Monthly (June): 31–55.
Lewis, Oscar
    1965   La Vida. New York: Random House.
Magnet, Myron
    1987   "America's Underclass: What to Do?" Fortune (May 11): 130.
Moynihan, Daniel P.
    1965   The Negro Family: The Case for National Action. Washington, D.C.: U.S.
                Government Printing Office.
National Advisory Commission on Civil Disorders
    1968   Report of the National Advisory Commission on Civil Disorders. Washington,
                D.C.: U.S. Government Printing Office.
Newman, Dorothy K. et al.
    1978   Protest, Politics, and Prosperity: Black Americans and White Institutions
                1940–1975. New York: Pantheon.
Peterson, Iver
    1981   "Judge Appoints Overseer to Integrate Ohio Suburb." New York Times
                (January): A–12.
Pinkney, Alphonso
    1984   The Myth of Black Progress. Cambridge: Cambridge University Press.
Reed, Adolph
    1988   "The Liberal Technocrat." Nation (February 6): 170.

Ricketts, Erol R. and Isabel V. Sawhill
    1988   "Defining and Measuring the Underclass." Journal of Policy Analysis and
                      Management 7: 318.
Smallwood, Kenneth W.
    1985   "The Folklore of Preferential Treatment." Southfield, Michigan. Unpublished
                      manuscript.
Time
    1977   "The American Underclass." (August 29): 14.
U.S. Bureau of the Census
    1987   Statistical Abstract of the United States: 1988. Washington, D.C.: U.S. Gov-
                      ernment Printing Office.
Willhelm, Sidney
    1983   Black in a White America. Cambridge: Schenkman.
Wilson, William J.
    1987   The Truly Disadvantaged: The Inner City, the Underclass, and Public Policy.
                      Chicago: University of Chicago Press.
    1980   The Declining Significance of Race. Chicago: University of Chicago Press.

[20]

BRIT. J. CRIMINOL. VOL. 33 NO. 2 SPRING 1993

RACIAL HARASSMENT AND THE PROCESS OF VICTIMIZATION

Conceptual and Methodological Implications for the Local Crime Survey

BENJAMIN BOWLING*

Victimization surveys, like crime statistics and the criminal law, tend to treat racial harassment and other forms of crime as though they were static events or incidents. Racial victimization, however, does not occur in an instant and is more dynamic and complex than the notion of a 'racial incident' can imply. Events-oriented criminological research has yet to capture the experience of repeated or systematic victimization; the continuity of violence, threat, and intimidation: or the complex relationships among all the social actors involved. It is argued that if racial harassment and other forms of crime are to be described and explained adequately and controlled effectively, they should be conceptualized as processes set in geographical, social, historical, and political context. Surveys should be complemented by other methods of enquiry to enable an examination of the social processes which give rise to criminal incidents.

This paper arose from reflection upon the value and shortcomings of a local survey of racial violence commissioned by the Home Office in 1989 as part of the North Plaistow Racial Harassment Project (Bowling and Saulsbury 1992; Saulsbury and Bowling 1991).[1] The project aimed to develop joint police, community, and local authority strategies to combat racial violence. It employed a problem-solving approach consisting of problem description, initiative development, implementation, and evaluation. Two components of the 'problem description' phase were agency-based: an analysis of official records and interviews with local officers. A third component was a victimization survey based on the methodology of earlier surveys such as the Newham Crime Survey (London Borough of Newham 1987) and the 1988 British Crime Survey (see Mayhew *et al.* 1989). Rather than researching crime in general, it focused solely on racially motivated attacks and harassment.

The aims of the survey were to describe the nature and extent of the problem in the project area and to identify where and when it occurred, and who the victims and offenders were. It sought to uncover the degree to which attacks and harassment were

* Home Office Research and Planning Unit. This paper is © Crown copyright.

An earlier version of this paper was presented at the 'Realist Criminology' conference, Simon Fraser University, Vancouver, Canada in May 1990. The author would like to thank all those who have commented on various drafts of the paper, and, in particular, John Lowman, Brian MacLean, Karim Murji, Bill Saulsbury. Jim Sheptycki, Sandra Walklate, Roy Walmsley, the anonymous reviewers, and the editor of the *British Journal of Criminology*.

[1] There are a range of terms used to describe the expression of racism in violence. For the purposes of this paper 'racial violence' will be used as a generic term to refer to violence motivated partly or wholly by racism. The more precise terms of 'racial harassment' and 'racial attack' will be used where appropriate. Despite the use of the term 'racial' rather than 'racist' violence, it should be made clear that the violence which forms the subject matter for this chapter pertains to racism, rather than to 'race' *per se*. Thus, the problem is not simply one of neutral conflict between races but, rather, one of *racism*—the 'ideologies and social processes which discriminate against others on the basis of their putatively different racial membership' (Solomos, 1989: xiii; see also note 2 below).

BENJAMIN BOWLING

reported and to examine how statutory and voluntary agencies responded when they were. The survey demonstrated that racial violence was widespread in the project area and that it was having a severe impact on specific members of the local community. It showed that Afro-Caribbean and Asian people were those most likely to be victimized, that groups of young white men were most often identified as the aggressors involved, and that incidents occurred most frequently in the vicinity of the victim's home. The survey also suggested that very few people reported their victimization to the police or any other agency and that when they did, they were rarely very satisfied with the outcome (Saulsbury and Bowling 1991: appx. 4).

However, as we argued in the final report on the project, many of these facts were already well known to the local statutory agencies, as was the concern about the problem expressed by many of those surveyed (Saulsbury and Bowling 1991: 26–9). The survey left no doubt that action to tackle the racial violence was needed. But the answers to the descriptive questions we had asked did not really stimulate ideas about how to tackle the problem. We lacked what seemed to be vital explanatory inform-ation—*how* and *why* racial attacks and harassment were occurring in the locality, and *why* statutory agencies seemed not to be responding appropriately to reported incidents. We still knew little about what processes underpinned these incidents or what happened after they had occurred. Still obscure were the nature of the relationships between minority and majority communities and how racism and violence influenced the behaviour patterns of these communities. While racial victim-ization seemed to be a dynamic phenomenon, the survey had reduced the process to a static and decontextualized snapshot.

In this paper I will argue that specific forms of crime may best be understood when set in their social, historical, and political context. The first task, therefore, will be to provide the reader with a brief history of the emergence of racial violence as a social problem in Britain, the process by which it became defined as a specific form of crime, and of the role of surveys in highlighting the problem during the 1980s. The paper will go on to argue that racial violence and other forms of crime may be conceptualized more profitably as processual rather than as incidental. It will then examine some of the conceptual and methodological problems which arise when trying to reconcile a dynamic, processual conception of victimization with an inherently static, events-oriented methodology, namely the victimization survey (Genn 1988). The paper argues not that local victimization surveys should be abandoned, but that future surveys should be complemented by qualitative data that may illuminate the processes by which forms of crime are perpetrated and experienced. Racial violence is used as an example in this article not because it is a special case, different from all other forms of crime, but simply because it is from the experience of conducting policy-oriented research into racial violence that this paper draws its lessons.

Racial Violence: The Emergence of a Social Problem

Some authors have argued that racial violence has for centuries formed an integral part of the experience of black- and brown-skinned people living in Britain (Gordon 1984; Fryer 1984). There is certainly evidence of violence directed specifically against ethnic minority individuals and communities in Britain since the 1950s (Klug 1982; Layton-

232

RACIAL HARASSMENT AND THE PROCESS OF VICTIMIZATION

Henry 1984).[2] Several academic and journalistic accounts document outbreaks of racial violence in various parts of England during the 1950s and 1960s. There were, for example, 'anti-black riots' in Nottingham and London in 1958 (Layton-Henry 1984; Fryer 1984: 376–83; Solomos 1989) and in midland and northern towns such as Dudley, Smethwick, Wolverhampton, Middlesborough, Accrington, Leeds, and elsewhere in the early 1960s (Pearson 1976; Reeves 1989: 44). Each of these outbreaks involved large gangs of white men targeting isolated black families and individuals. In some places the attackers belonged to 'racialist' youth cultures such as the Teddy Boys. Others involved far right, anti-immigration political movements such as Oswald Mosley's British Union of Fascists (Hall *et al.* 1978; Layton-Henry, 1984).

During the 1970s what became known as 'Paki-bashing' was increasingly reported in numerous locations across the country (Layton-Henry 1984; Reeves 1989: 125–52; Gordon 1990). Gangs of white men targeted Afro-Caribbeans, Asians, and others who 'looked foreign'. Again, some attacks were perpetrated by youths allied to racist youth cultures such as the skinheads, while others involved racist political organizations such as the National Front (Gordon 1990; Tompson 1988). Towards the end of the 1970s it was widely believed that racial violence was escalating dramatically. There were some well-publicized violent episodes involving the NF, such as those in Brick Lane in 1978 and Southall in 1979. From around this time community organizations, trade unions, and anti-racist groups began to document racist outbursts, persistent campaigns of harassment, and the effects of violence on black communities (Bethnal Green and Stepney Trades Council 1978; Commission for Racial Equality 1979; Institute of Race Relations 1987).

Defining Racial Violence as Crime

In February 1981, the Joint Committee Against Racialism (JCAR) presented a report on racial violence to the Home Secretary.[3] In response, central government acknowledged the anxieties expressed by JCAR and commissioned the first official study of

---

[2] In the British context, critical analysts would use the language of 'race' and racism to identify the subordination of black people (i.e. people from the Caribbean, Africa, and the Indian subcontinent) and to articulate strategies of resistance to such subordination (e.g. Smith 1989). It has been said that the language of 'ethnicity' has been useful neither theoretically nor politically. However, in a broader geographical context, the term 'black' does not resonate with the identity of many victimized minorities. Additionally, in a global political context the terms of 'ethnicity' have recently gained renewed impetus. Simple black/white divisions cannot explain, for example, the violence directed against 'ethnic' Romanians living in Poland, or the targeting of all 'foreigners' by the German neo-Nazis. It may be that the language of culture, identity, and politics needs to be rethought (Hall 1992). For the purposes of this paper, the term 'ethnic minority' will be used to refer to people subject to violence or other forms of oppression because of their skin pigmentation, language, or cultural or geographical background. The use of this terminology acknowledges that in some circumstances *non-black* ethnic minorities may be the subject of violence expressed by majority communities. Despite the use of the terms of ethnicity, a critical perspective would retain its focus on racism as a term to investigate the structures which place people from ethnic minorities in a subordinate position; and to analyse the racialized ideologies which serve to justify such subordination (see Smith 1989).

[3] JCAR is an umbrella organization representing the major political parties and the largest ethnic minority pressure groups, including representatives of the Board of Deputies of British Jews. JCAR's representation was the event which precipitated action by the Home Office (Home Office 1981). However, pressure had been mounting for some time from a variety of sources. A number of organizations campaigned against racism and racial violence during the 1970s. Organizations such as the Anti-Nazi League and Rock Against Racism were concerned with issues such as police violence, immigration laws, and the rise of the National Front and other neo-fascist organizations. Monitoring groups such as Lewisham Action on Policing in south-east London and the Southall Monitoring Group were active specifically in organizing and demonstrating against racial attacks (see Layton-Henry 1984: 108–21).

BENJAMIN BOWLING

racial attacks and harassment (*Hansard*, 5 Feb. 1981, col. 393). The report of the Home Office study dramatically altered the status of racial violence as a policy issue. The study consisted of two complementary research strategies—a survey of reported incidents in selected police areas across the country and interviews with the police, local community organizations, and local officials in each area.

The information contained in the report which had the greatest impact was the quantitative '*factual* survey of racial attacks' based on incidents recorded by the police (Home Office 1981: 6, emphasis added). Here, incidents in which victim and offender were of 'different ethnic origin' were collected from eight police forces across England and Wales for two months. The resulting 2,630 'inter-racial incidents' were then categorized on the basis of 'the certainty with which it could be assumed that the primary motive was racial' (Home Office 1981: 7). In half of the incidents collected, police records indicated that neither the police nor the victim thought that the incidents were racially motivated. In one quarter there was 'insufficient evidence to decide', while in 15 per cent there were 'some indications of a racial motive'. The remaining 10 per cent with 'strong evidence of a racial motive' amounted to 289 incidents.

This two-month sample of racially motivated incidents is not particularly large, given that the incidents were drawn from police force areas (including Merseyside, Manchester, Leicestershire, Lancashire, and London) with a total population of over 17 million. Racial incidents, the report estimated, formed less than one-quarter of one per cent of all recorded crime. In total, the report estimated that there would be '7,000 or so racially motivated incidents . . . reported in England and Wales in a year'. However, the report concluded that because of under-reporting, these recorded racial incidents probably represented only a small proportion of those that took place (Home Office 1981: 14).

The finding that has been most frequently cited by reports which followed (e.g. GLC 1984; Brown 1984; Kinsey *et al.* 1987) was that the rate of racially motivated victimization was 'much higher for the ethnic minority population, particularly the Asians, than for white people. Indeed the rate for Asians was 50 times that for white people and the rate for blacks was 36 times that for white people.' The report also commented on the types of incidents suffered by different ethnic groups: 'Figures for Asians were particularly suggestive: 12 of the 13 victims of arson were Asian, as were 16 of the 25 recipients of abusive telephone calls, and 57 of the 72 victims of racially motivated window-smashing. On the other hand, 20 of the 24 victims of handbag snatches or theft from persons, which were judged to be racially motivated, were white' (Home Office 1981: 12).

This statistical description overshadowed the qualitative 'views and opinions' gleaned from interviews with community groups and local officials. The primacy given to statistical 'fact' directed attention away from the subjective experience of racial harassment:

In most places, it was said that the problem had deteriorated significantly within the space of the last year, and that the main perpetrators were of the skinhead fraternity. Assaults, jostling in the street, abusive remarks, broken windows, slogans daubed on walls—these were among the less serious kinds of racial harassment which many members of the ethnic minorities (particularly Asians) experience, sometimes on repeated occasions. The fact that they are interleaved

RACIAL HARASSMENT AND THE PROCESS OF VICTIMIZATION

with far more serious racially-motivated offences (murders, serious assaults, systematic attacks by gangs on people's homes at night) increases the feeling of fear experienced by the ethnic minorities. It was clear to us that the Asian community widely believes that it is the object of a campaign of unremitting racial harasssment which it fears will grow worse in the future. In many places we were told that Asian families were too frightened to leave their homes at night or to visit the main shopping centre in town at weekends when gangs of young skinheads regularly congregate. (Home Office, 1981: 16)

The impact of the report was considerable. In the foreword to the report, the then Conservative Home Secretary William Whitelaw declared that racial attacks were 'wicked crimes which can do our society great harm'. He stated that 'the study has shown clearly that the anxieties expressed about racial attacks are justified. Racially motivated attacks, particularly on Asians, are more common than we supposed; and there are indications that they may be on the increase' (Home Office 1981: iii). The study was of particular importance because it demonstrated that although police forces in England and Wales had no means of recording crimes with racial motivation, such crimes could be found in their records. Additionally, by identifying these acts as 'wicked crimes' the Home Secretary ensured that henceforth it was impossible to deny that racial violence was an object for policing.[4]

A direct result of the production of this report was the introduction of an 'operational definition' and recording and monitoring procedures within the Metropolitan Police (see House of Commons 1982).[5] The publication of this report marks a dramatic increase in police and local and central government activity directed at controlling racial violence. Indeed, if one were to rely solely on police and central and local government sources of knowledge, it might appear that at the beginning of the 1980s a new form of crime emerged. This crime—termed variously racial (or racist) violence, racial attacks, racial harassment, and racial incidents—became, quite suddenly, a policy issue. It is only since 1981 that any local or central government agency kept records of racist violence or began to develop policies to control it. It is only since this time that any have considered it necessary to ponder the definition of the problem and to carry out resarch on the extent and nature of the problem and the effectiveness of the statutory response to it.[6]

[4] Although this is the first official recognition of racial violence as crime, clearly some of these incidents have been defined as crimes previously. Indeed, the most serious of them (such as murder, arson, and serious assult) would certainly have been recorded as crimes, even if they were not recorded as racial (Institute of Race Relations 1987). For example, Gordon (1990) lists 74 racist murders in Britain between 1970 and 1990. Many of the more mundane events involved in racial harassment would also come within legal and police definitions of crime. The offences of assault, criminal damage, and threatening behaviour are broad enough to cover all types of racial violence (see Forbes 1988). The 1965 Race Relations Act created the criminal offence of incitement to racial hatred and the 1986 Public Order Act Pt III also includes a number of offences which deal with the stirring up of racial hatred. A private member's Bill to make racial harassment a specific form of crime was defeated in 1985 (GLC 1985).

[5] The Metropolitan Police was the only force to start routinely collecting 'racial incident' statistics at this time. It was not until 1985, when the Association of Chief Police Officers (ACPO) issued *Guiding Principles* for the response to 'racial incidents'. that other large urban forces began to follow suit (see Home Office 1986).

[6] Numerous reports on racial violence and the statutory response to it were produced in the 1980s and early 1990s. Many were conducted by Labour local authorities (e.g. GLC 1984; Hesse *et al*. 1992), Councils for Racial Equality (e.g. CRE 1981, 1987*a,b*, 1988), anti-racist pressure groups (e.g. Institute of Race Relations 1987; Newham Monitoring Project 1990; Hounslow Community Relations Council 1986) and central government (e.g. Ekblom and Simon 1988; Home Office 1989, 1991; Sampson and Phillips 1992). Recent reports have concentrated on police service delivery (Cutler and Murji 1990), housing policy (Ginsburg 1989), and services for victims (Kimber and Cooper 1991). Recent reviews include Gordon (1990), FitzGerald (1989), and FitzGerald and Ellis (1990).

BENJAMIN BOWLING

Surveys of Racial Violence

In the introduction to the second Islington Crime Survey, Crawford *et al*. state that 'the major purpose of victimization surveys is to gain a more accurate estimate of the true extent of crime than that provided by the official crime statistics compiled by the police which are subject to widely acknowledged problems of accuracy, the most serious of which is the failure of a high proportion of victims to report criminal incidents to the police' (1990: 2). Obviously, some forms of crime are more likely to be reported than others. For example, most car thefts are reported because, by law, they must be insured against. On the other hand, official crime statistics reflect only a small proportion of racial attacks because of the unwillingness of victims to report to the police (Home Office 1981). It seems that the need to look to sources beyond police records to estimate the 'true extent' of crime is particularly acute for racial violence.

A number of crime surveys have attempted to make quantitative estimates of racial violence. The Policy Studies Institute (PSI) study of *Black and White Britain* estimated that the frequency of racial attacks might be over ten times the figure calculated by the Home Office using police records, bringing the number closer to 70,000 (Brown 1984: 256). The first Islington Crime Survey (Jones *et al*. 1986: 64) estimated that '17% of all assaults which were aimed at Islington residents [in the previous year] were racist in nature', amounting to around 870 cases per year. The authors suggest that despite the likelihood that this estimate was low, only about 4.5 per cent of these cases were recorded by the police.

The Newham Crime Survey was undertaken specifically to challenge police statistics which Newham Council believed grossly underestimated racial violence. The survey included a 'Racial Harassment Questionnaire' that was presented only to Afro-Caribbean and Asian respondents.[7] They found that '1 in 4 of Newham's black residents had been the victims of some form of racial harassment in the previous 12 months' (London Borough of Newham 1987: 34). They also found that two in three victims had been victimized more than once (p. 50) and that the 116 victims of racial harassment gave details of a total of 1,550 incidents which they had experienced in the previous twelve months. Of these, eighty-five (or just over 5 per cent) were said to have been reported to the police.

The first two sweeps of the British Crime Survey (BCS) (Hough and Mayhew 1983, 1985) paid little attention to the problems of racial harassment or attacks. Reflecting growing criticism of this omission, the 1988 BCS specifically attempted to measure 'ethnic minority risks', including racially motivated offences (Mayhew *et al*. 1989). Facilitated by a booster sample of Afro-Caribbeans and Asians, the survey found that black people were more at risk than whites for many types of crime, even after taking account of social and demographic factors.[8] It was also found that 'Afro-Caribbeans and particularly Asians see many offences against them as racially motivated. Being threatened and assaulted because of race is common' (Mayhew *et al*. 1989: 50). Forty-

---

[7] In the British context the term 'Asian' usually refers to people whose origins lie in the Indian subcontinent. In Newham the largest proportion of Asians are from India, though there are also numbers of Pakistani, Bangladeshi, and Chinese residents.

[8] Some of the factors which are 'taken account of' in this survey are themselves influenced by racially discriminatory practices. People from ethnic minorities are to be found in low socio-economic status and income groups; the areas in which they live and the quality of their housing are influenced by racially discriminatory policies and practices in housing and employment. This means that such aspects should not be factored out of an understanding of 'race'

RACIAL HARASSMENT AND THE PROCESS OF VICTIMIZATION

four per cent of assaults directed against Asians and a third of those directed against Afro-Caribbeans were thought by respondents to be racially motivated, as were about half of the incidents involving threats. When an incident was thought to be racially motivated, 'the use of racist language was the main reason given by both Afro-Caribbeans and Asians, particularly the former. Asians were rather more likely than Afro-Caribbeans to see an incident as racially motivated because they felt that it was something only committed against their minority group, or that it had happened to them before, involving the same people' (Mayhew *et al.* 1989: 48).

Crime Surveys and the Prioritization of Racial Violence

The nature of the questions asked in the nationwide BCS reflects the change in the prioritization of racial violence which occurred in the 1980s. Since the middle of that decade, the surveys described above have produced quantitative evidence of racial violence and of the degree to which it is under-reported. There seems little doubt that these data and their use as a means to apply pressure on police and on local and central government agencies brought about change in the official view of racial violence.

In 1985 racial incidents became a Metropolitan Police 'force priority' and the Association of Chief Police Officers (ACPO) issued national *Guiding Principles* (Metropolitan Police 1985: 130–1; ACPO 1985). In 1986 a government Home Affairs Committee report referred to racial attacks and harassment as 'the most shameful and dispiriting aspect of race relations in Britain' (House of Commons 1986: iv). The prioritization of racial attacks and harassment has been the subject of several Home Office circulars (e.g. Home Office 1986, 1989, 1991) and Metropolitan Police orders (June 1987; November 1990). Most recently, a 'multi-agency approach' to racial violence has been developing which advocates that the police should work in a co-ordinated fashion with other local agencies (Home Office 1989; Kinsey *et al.* 1987: 125). Now, racial violence is a priority for six central government agencies, the police, the prosecuting authorities, the courts, and local government services including housing, education, and social services (Home Office 1989, 1991; Bowling and Saulsbury 1992).

During the 1980s, surveys contributed to the movement of racial violence from the margins to the centre of national and local political agendas. Now many statutory agencies have recording and monitoring procedures and operational guidelines. But despite these very real changes, there is little evidence that statutory policies directed at tackling perpetrators, assisting victims, or preventing racial violence have been effective. In 1989, the central government interdepartmental racial attacks group found 'few examples of effective multi-agency liaison . . . [and] . . . relatively few examples of effective unilateral action by individual agencies' (Home Office 1989: para. 34). Despite a decade of statutory activity there is little evidence that racial violence is being controlled. There is little evidence indeed that it has decreased in incidence, prevalence, or in its effect on minority communities in Britain (FitzGerald 1989; Ginsburg 1989; Cutler and Murji 1990; Gordon 1990).

---

differences in victimization rates—rather, these disadvantages are the very dimensions of racism. Susan Smith (1989) describes racism as a set of *mutually reinforcing* structures or processes. Finding people from ethnic minorities in social groups which are prone to victimization is a feature of, not incidental to, racism.

BENJAMIN BOWLING

Criminal Incidents and Criminology

Until recently, criminology has been content to conceive of crime as a collection of criminal incidents—as events of norm violation (MacLean 1986). Although feminists and critical criminologists have developed more dynamic accounts of crime (of which more below), the dominant approach to the study of victimization is still events-oriented (Skogan 1986; Genn 1988). In this respect both conventional and 'left realist' surveys reflect the orientation of the criminal justice system. Criminal incidents are the stock-in-trade of the crime control sector of government and of administrative criminology. Estimates of the size of the problem, and descriptions of where it is located and who the actors are, are necessarily based on such counting exercises, as are measurements of police performance such as the clear-up rate. Indeed, the *modus operandi* of the criminal justice system is based upon and shaped by the processing of individual events.

The criminal justice system attempts to deal with racial violence as individual acts in the same way that it deals with other forms of crime. British law recognizes only the event defined as the criminal offence (Smith and Hogan 1983; Forbes 1988). The police definition of crime reflects the legal structure of police work (Grimshaw and Jefferson 1987), and, like the rest of the criminal justice system, is ordered around the reification of human experience into discrete events (Manning 1988). To become an object for policing or the courts, an aspect of human behaviour or interaction must be fixed in space and time and be definable as an offence (Young 1990). Police policy documents often stress that the object for policing is a racial *incident* rather than attack or harassment (e.g. House of Commons 1986: 1). The policing systems, consisting of racial incident forms, incident report books, and methods for calculating response times and detection rates, reflect their concern with discrete events.

The orientation of the criminal justice system and of criminology towards counting individual events also reflects the quantitative emphasis of social science more generally. Qualitative data are often considered soft, anecdotal, or, as in the 1981 Home Office study on racial attacks, merely 'views and opinions'. Quantitative data, by contrast, are considered hard, objective, or 'factual'.

Racial Victimization as a Process

Despite the primacy of incident-based accounts of crime and racial violence, some authors have argued that crime should be seen not as an event, but as a process. As MacLean suggests, 'crime is not an *event* or "social fact", but a social *process* which includes a number of social events each of which is inextricably bound up with the other[s]' (1986: 4–5, emphases in original). Conceiving of racial violence and other forms of crime as processes implies an analysis which is dynamic; includes the social relationships between all the actors involved in the process; can capture the continuity across physical violence, threat, and intimidation; can capture the dynamic of repeated or systematic victimization; incorporates historical context; and takes account of the social relationships which inform definitions of appropriate and inappropriate behaviour.

Racial victimization is, like other social processes, dynamic and in a state of constant movement and change, rather than static and fixed. While individual events can be

RACIAL HARASSMENT AND THE PROCESS OF VICTIMIZATION

abstracted from this process, fixed in time and place and recorded by individuals and institutions, the process itself is continuous. Much can be learned from studying criminal events; but, just as it is impossible to understand the content of a movie by looking at only one still frame, 'it is impossible for us to understand crime or any other process by looking at an individual event or moment' (MacLean 1986: 8).

The process of racial victimization involves a number of social actors, each of whom has a dynamic relationship with the others. It is usual, first, to look at victim and offender and at the relationship between them. Obviously, an investigation of racial violence should include an analysis of the characteristics of the people who set out to attack or harass ethnic minorities and of their motivation for doing so. Equally, it should include an analysis of the characteristics of the people under attack and of the effects that victimization has on them. But when an individual is attacked, the process of victimization is not confined to him or her alone, but may extend to immediate and extended families, friends, and 'community'. When a serious incident occurs—a racially motivated arson attack or murder, for example—the impact may be felt among people in locations far away from where the incident itself occurred. Similarly, there is a relationship between perpetrators of racial attacks and their families, friends, and community. The expression of racial violence and the victimization to which it gives rise is underpinned by the relationships between different *communities* in particular localities and within society as a whole. Exploring these relationships and the part they play in condoning or condemning racial outbursts seems crucial to an understanding of the process of racial victimization. As yet, however, we know much less about offenders in cases of racial violence than about victims.

Also of importance are the roles of the police and other state agents such as social workers and public housing managers. For those cases that come to be defined as crimes and for which a prosecution is initiated, criminal justice professionals (such as court officials, prosecutors, defence lawyers, magistrates, and judges) play their part. These actors intervene in the process of racial and other forms of victimization in ways which have the potential for escalation as well as amelioration of its effects. A dynamic account of the impact of state action and reaction is important for comprehending the totality of the process of victimization. Finally, local and national news media play their part in communicating knowledge of attacks or about the quality of the statutory response to various sections of the community.

Clearly, the notion of process applies to all forms of crime. Car theft is no less dynamic and bound up with wider social processes than is racial violence. However, the few qualitative accounts that exist point to racial violence often taking the form of multiple victimization (Sampson and Phillips 1992), repeated attacks (Home Office 1981), and a constant (Walsh 1987) or 'unrelenting barrage of harassment' (Tompson 1988). In this sense, racial victimization may be compared with wife battery, which is very often prolonged and habitual (Genn 1988; Stanko 1988). Victimization which constitutes repeated physical violence or continuous threat and intimidation may be distinguished by its enduring quality. As Stanko (1990) suggests, these forms of violence create 'climates of unsafety' which transcend individual instances of violence. Attempting to reduce multiple victimization to a series of incidents means that much of this experience will be lost (Genn 1988: 90; Farrell 1992; Sampson and Phillips 1992).

Thinking about how events may be connected so as to illuminate underlying social processes leads on to a consideration of the connections between different forms of

BENJAMIN BOWLING

violence in the experience of an individual who is being victimized. Kelly (1987) argues that women experience sexual violence as a continuum—'a continuous series of events which pass into one another and which cannot be readily distinguished' (1987: 77). Making these connections seems equally important with regard to the experience of racial violence. As Pearson *et al.* suggest:

For white people, for example, racial harassment and racial attacks are undoubtedly merely incidental, one-off events which are rarely, if ever, encountered. For black and minority ethnic groups, on the other hand, these are areas of experience which are part and parcel of everyday life. A black person need never have been the actual victim of a racist attack, but will remain acutely aware that she or he belongs to a group that is threatened in this manner. In much the same way that the high levels of 'fear of crime' among women can be better understood when experiences of subordination and daily harassments, from the subliminal to the blatant are re-connected (Stanko, 1987), so the re-connected experiences of racism from a black and minority ethnic perspective shift the ground of how to define a 'racial' incident and what it is to police 'racism'. (1989: 135)

Although the implications of such an approach have yet to be pursued in research practice, survey research has hinted at its importance. The authors of the first Islington Crime Survey, for example, concluded from one interview that: 'some segments of the population are so over-exposed to this kind of behaviour [racist assaults] that it becomes part of their everyday reality and escapes their memory in the interview situation' (Jones *et al.* 1986: 63).

MacLean (1986) argues that crime is underpinned by broader social, political, and economic processes. Of importance for violence directed specifically against ethnic minority individuals and communities are the social, political, and cultural processes of racism and racial exclusion. Susan Smith has argued that forms of political and 'common sense' racism have permeated all levels of British society (1989: 146). Certainly the politics of the New Right have racist ideas at their core (Barker 1981; Fielding 1981; Gilroy 1987: 11; Solomos 1989). These ideas, some have suggested, influence public opinion in the form of 'low level racism' (Husbands 1983), 'a sentiment which infuses daily life and is widely but abstractly expressed by a broad cross-section (perhaps a majority) of the population' (Smith 1989: 148). In a similar vein, Solomos argues that as 'race' became an important variable in British politics, so the terms of debate about migration, civil unrest, crime, and the 'inner city' became subtly infused with racialized stereotypes and symbols (1989; see also Miles and Phizacklea 1984). As well as 'top down' racism, it has been argued that there are 'bottom-up' influences. This 'experiential racism' is 'a reaction by white Britons to those broad patterns of local socio-economic change that are outside their control and that coincide with (but of course have no necessary causal relationship with) the presence of black people' (Smith 1989: 149). Clearly, widespread racial antipathy does not determine the expression of racial violence. But, as Smith argues, racist sentiments 'provide a reservoir of procedural norms that not only tacitly inform routine activity, but are also able to legitimatize more purposive explicitly racist practices' (Smith 1989: 150).

The influences of popular and politically organized racism on the manifestation of racial violence are complex and have yet to be charted fully. It seems that the factors which influence the time, place, and form of an 'outbreak' of racial hatred into violence

240

RACIAL HARASSMENT AND THE PROCESS OF VICTIMIZATION

are many; but some trends have been discerned. Some commentators have identified the contiguity of media-generated 'moral panics' about the presence and behaviour of ethnic minority people and spates of racial attacks (Tompson 1988; Gordon 1990). Others have identified factors influencing the geographical distribution of racial violence (e.g. the ethnic composition and stability of the local population, changes in the local economy, and variations in the strength of local identity (Husbands 1983)). In some specific locations (such as the east end of London) racial antipathy and territorial defensiveness are deep-seated and reflected in support for racist politics (Husbands 1983). Dick Hobbs describes racism as 'part of East London's ideological inheritance'. (1988: 11). The high incidence of racial violence reported in specific locations must be examined in the context of popular and political racist sentiment.

The Process of Racial Harassment: Research and Policy Development

So far in this paper I have charted the emergence of the issue of racial violence, and the part played by local and national surveys in this process. I have pointed to the role of the survey in directing attention to the problem of racial violence and its utility in describing patterns of victimization. I have also illustrated that racial violence is neither expressed nor experienced in an instant, but that it is more diffuse, contextually bound, and dislocating for its victims than a notion such as 'racial incident' can imply. For both criminological research and criminal justice practice, this throws up the question of whether the 'events orientation' has served to limit an understanding of, and an appropriate response to, the process of racial violence.

Implications for survey research

The problem facing those wishing to conduct survey research into racial violence is that of developing ways to capture victimization *as a process* from the events that surveys describe. This means developing ways of investigating repeat victimization, focusing on all the elements of the crime process and incorporating social context. Some aspects of the process of victimization may be captured by the creative use of the survey method. Capturing other aspects may require the use of supplementary or complementary methodologies.

The difficulty faced by surveys in capturing repeated victimization has been commented on by numerous authors (Farrell 1992; Genn 1988; Kelly 1987). In a valuable paper on 'multiple victimization', Genn argues that:

Although the experiences of multiple victims ought in theory to represent an important part of the total picture of criminal victimisation and might provide useful insights into the conceptualization of 'crime', victims surveys have largely failed to provide any detailed information on multiple victimisation. This failure stems primarily from the general orientation of crime surveys and partly from the inherent limitations of the survey method as a means of understanding complex social processes. (1988: 90)

A survey could attempt to describe repeated racial victimization by rigorously counting every definable event in an episode of harassment or attack. If, for example, an individual or family is being harassed regularly, a complete account could be made of each violent, threatening, or intimidatory act, together with each graffito and other

BENJAMIN BOWLING

property damage experienced. However, this would create serious methodological problems; victimization surveys have tended to produce aggregate statistics and do not deal well with statistical outliers (Genn 1988). Further problems arise in defining how salient an event must be to merit being either mentioned by a victim or recorded by the survey (e.g. Biderman 1981). Having reached a definition of a relevant event, in some cases the counting task would be a formidable one (Genn 1988). Some cases of racial harassment span a period of years and would include a huge number of salient events (Tompson 1988). These problems are apparent even for surveys designed sensitively enough to capture racial harassment. If the remit of the survey is broader than this, the chances are that any description of this form of victimization will be submerged beneath aggregate victimization statistics (Genn 1988). It must be acknowledged that the general orientation of contemporary victimization surveys has tended to marginalize the experience of those suffering forms of repeated victimization such as racial violence, wife battery, and child abuse. There is an urgent need for research to develop creative means of measuring and describing repeated, systematic, and enduring victimization (Farrell 1992). It may be that survey research can be adapted so that it is sensitive to this dynamic. Or it may be that surveys should be used for purposes for which they are better suited, leaving repeated victimization to be investigated by supplementary or alternative methods of research.

Surveys of racial violence have focused mainly on the experience of crime victims, and of their experiences of reporting to the police. There has been almost no research on perpetrators. While the most basic of descriptions have been formulated (racial attackers tend to be young white men), they remain something of an effigy in the criminological literature. In order for a holistic account of victimization to be developed, account must be taken of all the actors in the process, and of the relationships among them. While they would be sensitive and difficult to conduct, surveys of perpetrators and their associates could be conducted in parallel with surveys of victims. It might be possible to conduct surveys of offending using the 'self-report method' in localities with high rates of racial victimization. Another approach would be to extend surveys of racist attitudes (e.g. Husbands 1983) to cover racially motivated violence and attitudes towards it.

Surveys, like official statistics, tend to produce static descriptions of crime, and it is not immediately apparent how a dynamic description can be developed from these still images. This stasis has meant that the descriptions produced have missed many moments in the crime process. Among the elements missing are accounts of the relationship between victim and perpetrator and of their relationships to the communities to which they belong; also the moments other than the short time-slice that comes to be defined as the criminal event. Notably missing, too, is information about the events subsequent to reporting to the police, such as how criminal and civil justice processes affect both victim and offender. Surveys have told us little about alternative responses to victimization such as self-defence, retaliation, forgiveness, restitution, or conciliation. While an investigation of these processes could be included in an elaborated survey methodology, they are precluded by the survey's inherent emphasis on the criminal event.

While surveys (like any other method) can be presented in their geographical, historical, and social context, most often they are not. As a result, descriptions of patterns of victimization are divorced from wider social processes. Indeed, it may be

RACIAL HARASSMENT AND THE PROCESS OF VICTIMIZATION

that the survey research process tends more towards decontextualization than other methods. Some crime survey researchers (and 'left realists' in particular) have stressed the importance of both social context and social process to an investigation of crime (e.g. MacLean 1991). However, how they are to be incorporated in practice into an empirical research programme has yet to be fully addressed (Walklate 1989, 1990, 1992).

Implications for policy development

With respect to policy development, where surveys have had most influence has been on the place of the victim in the criminal justice process (Hough and Mayhew 1985; Rock 1990: 317–24). Surveys have shown that victims of racial violence are many and that victimization has a debilitating effect on their lives. Now, racial harassment victims may be seen as genuine targets for specialist service provision (see Kimber and Cooper 1991). However, while surveys have identified the people who are most likely to be victimized, other methods of research are required to illuminate ways in which people have survived or resisted this victimization. Similarly, while surveys have identified the people most likely to be perpetrators, other methods may be of more help to identify the social, political, and economic factors which give rise to racial hatred, or the factors which lead to its expression in violence.

Because surveys alone cannot capture the dynamic of crime as a social process, the policies to which they have given rise have tended to be one-dimensional, focusing on the event of norm violation. As a result, policies have tended to emphasize reactive police and local authority responses rather than community-based preventive measures. However, there seems to be a contradiction between the idea that racial victimization is a dynamic process and the idea that the problem may best be tackled by responding to a disconnected incident. As Pearson *et al.* argue, the police definition referring specifically to racial *incidents* implies that 'racial harassment and attacks are "one off" events . . . something which happens casually and which remains disconnected from the dominant forms of life within our society' (1989: 134). This conception, they argue, fails to match with black people's experience of victimization. The apparent contradiction between police definition and subjective experience perhaps explains why research studies report the police response to racial violence frequently to be inappropriate (e.g. Smith and Gray 1983: 409–12; Gordon 1990; Dunhill 1989: 68–79; Institute of Race Relations 1987; Newham Monitoring Project 1990; Hesse *et al.* 1992).

There is a similar contradiction between the experience of victimization and legal practice. Forbes has identified the limitations to tackling racial harassment imposed by a legal system which understands crime only as a single event: '[In presenting a case] only facts relevant to the particular offence which can be proved may be mentioned. Thus, it is not usually permissible to refer to other offences that have been committed by the perpetrator. This means that the offence cannot be set in context as part of a sustained campaign of racial harassment' (1988: 17–2). In court, as with policing, the focus on a single event renders the process of victimization invisible. It seems that reducing the complex processes of racial exclusion (Husbands 1983) and the expression of violence to a racial incident strips it of meaning for the victim and for those to whom

243

the incident must be described (such as a police officer, judge, or jury). By rendering earlier episodes in the process of victimization 'inadmissible evidence' or irrelevant to police investigation, neither the effect on the victim nor the implications for the rest of the 'community' can be described. This undermines the ability of statutory agents to understand the meaning of the event (from the victim's perspective in particular) and therefore to respond appropriately to it. Again, this point applies more broadly than to racially motivated crime. Indeed, it underlines one of the major dissatisfactions of victims and communities with criminal justice agencies—that they look only at the incident, not at its history and setting (Genn 1988; Shapland *et al.* 1985).

Ways Forward

If racial victimization (and other forms of crime) may best be conceptualized processually, it follows that the social response to the problem must tackle the underlying processes as well as responding to the reported incidents to which these processes give rise (Goldstein 1990). In order to develop such a response, research is required that is dynamic, takes account of all moments in the crime process, can capture the dynamic of repeated victimization, and is set in geographical, social, historical, and political context. Some of these data may be provided by the next generation of crime, victimization, and offending surveys. However, as has been argued by many authors, qualitative as well as quantitative research methods are required to procure a holistic analysis (Bell and Newby 1977; Walklate 1989, 1990).

There are innumerable ways in which methods could be combined. Surveys could be complemented by ethnography, life history research, case studies, and other methods to research aspects of victimization and offending. The combination of methods will clearly be contingent on the nature of the research subject. Different combinations will have advantages for different forms of crime and for different moments in crime processes. Local circumstances of funding and access will also dictate which methods are possible in any given setting. What is important is that the research should allow for the relationships between victim, offender, and statutory agents (police, courts, housing authority, etc.) to be charted; and that these relationships should be set in the context of family, 'community' and neighbourhood, race, class, and age divisions.

One approach which has been useful in criminology and other spheres is the case study. According to Yin, 'a case study is an empirical inquiry that: investigates a contemporary phenomenon within its real-life context; when the boundaries of the context are not clearly evident; and in which multiple sources of evidence are used' (1989: 23). These features lend themselves to an empirical, holistic, and processual account of crime. Surveys alone can try to deal with phenomenon and context, but by dint of the need to limit the number of variables to be analysed, their ability to investigate context is extremely limited (Yin 1989: 23). Context, history, and process can best be captured using evidence from sources such as historiographical material, depth interviews, and observation as well as official records and surveys. In British criminology, case studies have produced some excellent descriptive and theoretical books (e.g. Smith and Gray 1983; Grimshaw and Jefferson 1987).

Case studies combining surveys with other methods of inquiry offer good theoretical possibilities. Such a holistic methodological approach provides the opportunity for

RACIAL HARASSMENT AND THE PROCESS OF VICTIMIZATION

developing explanations of specific types of crime. Explanation—asking how and why—requires tracing processes over time as well as describing frequencies and incidence. Ethnographic or life-history accounts of people identified in a survey seem to have tremendous potential in this respect. They offer the opportunity for the research subjects to describe their experiences in their own terms. This appplies as much to research on victims (e.g. Kelly 1988 on sexual violence; Stanko 1990 on danger) as it does to research on perpetrators (e.g. Pearson 1976 on machine-smashing and 'Paki-bashing' in Lancashire).

To understand offending, victimization, and state intervention, the actions and experiences of the social actors involved, and the points at which they intersect, must be charted. In order to achieve this, interviews with survey respondents could be expanded to follow through the whole process of offending and victimization. Starting with the historical context of any given instance, data could be collected on the events involved in the commission of the offence, its immediate aftermath, and long-term consequences for those involved. Qualitative accounts of the subjective reality of each actor in particular instances will help flesh out the skeletal descriptions provided by surveys.

In providing a multi-faceted account of the expression and experience of violence, a case study can identify multiple sites for intervention. It offers the potential for evaluating the effectiveness of policing and the criminal justice system. By charting the moments at which criminal justice agents intervene in the process of victimization and survival, the impact of their actions can be assessed. At present, the police and criminal justice system appear only fleetingly in survey descriptions. And yet both victim and offender may have to interact with them over an extended period (totaliing hours, if not days and weeks) after the event. Surveys could ask respondents what happened *after* the initial response, but would soon become cumbersome in the attempt. The case study, with its historical element, is suited to exploring some of these connections and could retain quantitative verification if it incorporates a survey.

Expanding a local survey into a case study need not present resource problems. Relative to the costs of a survey, the supplementary qualitative research components present value for money. The four-volume PSI study *Police and People in London* is a good example. This study included a survey of police officers, a survey of Londoners, in-depth observation of the police in action, and participant observation with a group of young black men (see Smith 1983*a*, *b*; Smith and Gray 1983; Small 1983). A recent 'local inquiry' into racial violence conducted by the London Borough of Waltham Forest (Hesse *et al.* 1992) illustrates the potential of the case study method for researching this particular problem. The report primarily draws on evidence presented to a panel of inquiry—testimony from victims and their advocates, vitriolic counter-blasts from local racists, and records from the police and the local authority housing department. This contemporary material is then set in the context of the local history and geographical spread of racial violence. The key disadvantage of this approach is the risk of being thought unscientific or actually failing to bring sufficient rigour to the collection and analysis of data. Incorporating a survey into a case study would overcome this problem and may mean that researchers can have their cake and eat it too. Such a study would have the validity and reliability that stem from representative sampling while incorporating an investigation of the context necessary to comprehend racial violence as a process.

BENJAMIN BOWLING

Conclusion

Accounts of outbreaks of racial violence and increasing numbers of reported racially motivated incidents in England and elsewhere featured prominently in British media sources at the end of the 1980s and the beginning of the 1990s.[9] These reports are troubling in and of themselves. As I have argued in this paper, however, these events reflect wider processes that have a profound effect upon ethnic minority individuals and communities who live under the threat and fear of victimization. Moreover, the process of racial victimization has serious implications for all who live in societies affected by racial hatred and its expression in violence.

In Britain, crime surveys have produced objective evidence of the existence and manifestation of racial violence. This, together with media reports and the work of monitoring organizations and of the anti-racist lobby, has ensured a place for racial violence on the research and policy agendas of local and central government and the police. Local and central government politicians and officials have also played their part in this process of prioritization. The pressing need now is for quantitative research to be complemented by more qualitative and idiographic accounts of racial violence, thus facilitating description and explanation of their manifestation in specific locations. It is now time to move beyond static, events-oriented methods of describing racial violence and other forms of crime to a methodologically pluralist approach in which the complex social processes involved can be explored in their real-life context. With such material to hand, how and why racism is expressed in violence may be explained and effective means of controlling this singularly divisive form of crime and victimization may be developed.

REFERENCES

ACPO (1985), *Guiding Principles Concerning Racial Attacks*. London: Association of Chief Police Officers.

BARKER, M. (1981), *The New Racism*. London: Junction.

BELL, C., and NEWBY, H. eds. (1977), *Doing Sociological Research*. London: Allen and Unwin.

BETHNAL GREEN AND STEPNEY TRADES COUNCIL (1978), *Blood on the Streets*. London: Bethnal Green and Stepney Trades Council.

BIDERMAN, A. D. (1981), 'When Does Interpersonal Violence become Crime? Theory and Methods for Statistical Surveys', in R. G. Lehnen and W. Skogan, eds., *The National Crime Survey: Working Papers*, vol. 1: 48–51. Washington DC: US Department of Justice Bureau of Statistics.

[9] Between 1989 and 1992, violence involving skinheads, far right political groups (such as the National Front and British National Party), and other racists was reported in the English towns of Oldham, Manchester, Sheffield, Bradford, Leeds, Huddersfield, Batley (West Yorkshire), Birmingham, Leicester, Edmonton, and Norwich. In London there have been spates of racial attacks reported in the boroughs of Newham, Tower Hamlets, Waltham Forest, Southwark, Camden, Islington, Greenwich, Sutton, and Hackney. At least twenty mosques were fire-bombed during the Gulf conflict *Guardian*, 6 Feb. 1991; *Times*, 17 Jan. 1991). Further afield, increases in racial violence and far-right activity have been reported across both eastern and western Europe including Scotland, France, Sweden, Germany, Poland, Italy, and Spain. These reports resonate with recent accounts of a rise in far right activity and racist violence in the USA, Canada, South Africa, and elsewhere. There have also been many reports of the desecration of Jewish cemeteries and attacks on Jewish children and homes, the most notable of which was the destruction of graves and the exhumation of a body in a Jewish graveyard in May 1990 in Carpentras, France (*Times*, 15 Aug. 1990; *Independent* and *Telegraph*, 29 Aug. 1990). In Britain attacks on Jewish cemeteries have occurred in Leeds, Manchester, and Edmonton *Daily Mail*, 5 Aug., 26 Aug. 1990; *Express, Mirror, Times, Independent*, 30 July 1990).

RACIAL HARASSMENT AND THE PROCESS OF VICTIMIZATION

BOWLING, B., and SAULSBURY, W. E. (1992), 'A Multi-agency Approach to Racial Harassment', *Home Office Research Bulletin*, no. 32.

BROWN, C. (1984), *Black and White Britain: The Third PSI Survey*. London: Heinemann.

CRE (1979), *Brick Lane and Beyond: An Inquiry into Racial Strife and Violence in Tower Hamlets*. London: Commission for Racial Equality.

—— (1981), *Racial Harassment on Local Authority Housing Estates*. London: Commission for Racial Equality.

—— (1987a), *Living in Terror: A Report on Racial Violence and Harassment in Housing*. London: Commission for Racial Equality.

—— (1987b), *Racial Attacks: A Survey in Eight Areas of Britain*. London: Commission for Racial Equality.

—— (1988) *Learning in Terror: A Survey of Racial Harassment in Schools and Colleges in England, Scotland and Wales, 1985–87*. London: Commission for Racial Equality.

CRAWFORD, A., JONES, T., WOODHOUSE, T., and YOUNG, J. (1990), *The Second Islington Crime Survey*. Middlesex: Middlesex Polytechnic Centre for Criminology.

CUTLER, D., and MURJI, K. (1990), 'From a Force into a Service? Racial Attacks, Policing and Service Delivery', *Critical Social Policy*, March/April.

DUNHILL, C. (1989), 'Women, Racist Attacks and the Response from Anti-Racist Groups', in Dunhill, C., ed., *The Boys in Blue: Women's Challenge to the Police*. London: Virago.

EKBLOM, P., and SIMON, F., with BIRDI, S. (1988), *Crime and Racial Harassment in Asian-run Small Shops: The Scope for Prevention*, Crime Prevention Unit Paper no. 15. London: Home Office.

FARRELL, G. (1992), 'Multiple Victimisation: Its Extent and Significance', *International Review of Victimology*, 2: 85–102.

FIELDING, N. (1981), *The National Front*. London: Routledge.

FIENBERG, S. E. (1977), 'Deciding What and Whom to Count', in R. G. Lehnen and W. Skogan (1981), *The National Crime Survey: Working Papers*, vol. 1: 59–60. Washington DC: US Department of Justice, Bureau of Statistics.

FITZGERALD, M. (1989), 'Legal Approaches to Racial Harassment in Council Housing: The Case for Reassessment', *New Community*, 16/1: 93–106.

FITZGERALD, M., and ELLIS, T. (1990), 'Racial Harassment: The Evidence', in C. Kemp, ed., *Current Issues in Criminological Research*, British Criminology Conference, vol. 2. Bristol: Bristol Centre for Criminal Justice.

FORBES, D. (1988), *Action on Racial Harassment: Legal Remedies and Local Authorities*. London: Legal Action Group.

FRYER, P. (1984), *Staying Power: The History of Black People in Britain*. London: Pluto.

GENN, H. (1988), 'Multiple Victimization', in M. Maguire and J. Pointing, eds., *Victims of Crime: A New Deal?*: 90–100. Milton Keynes: Open University Press.

GILROY, P. (1987), *There Ain't no Black in the Union Jack: The Cultural Politics of Race and Nation*. London: Hutchinson.

GINSBURG, N. (1989), 'Racial Harassment Policy and Practice: The Denial of Citizenship', *Critical Social Policy*, 26: 66–81.

GLC (1984), *Racial Harassment in London: Report of a Panel of Inquiry Set Up by the GLC Police Committee*. London: Greater London Council.

—— (1985), *Racial Harassment: Time to Act* (Report of the Conference held on 17 November 1985). London: Greater London Council and Racial Harassment Bill Group.

GOLDSTEIN, H. (1990), *Problem-Oriented Policing*. New York: McGraw-Hill.

BENJAMIN BOWLING

GORDON, P. (1984), *White Law*. London: Pluto.

—— (1990), *Racial Violence and Harassment*, 2nd edn, Runnymede Research Report. London: Runnymede Trust.

GRIMSHAW, R., and JEFFERSON, T. (1987), *Interpreting Policework*. London: Allen and Unwin.

HALL, S. (1992), 'New Ethnicities', in J. Donald and A. Rattansi, *'Race', Culture and Difference*. London: Sage.

HALL, S., CRITCHER, C., JEFFERSON, T., CLARKE, J., and ROBERTS, B. (1978), *Policing the Crisis: Mugging, the State, and Law and Order*. London: Macmillan.

HESSE, B., RAI, D. K., BENNETT, C., and McGILCHRIST, P. (1992), *Beneath the Surface: Racial Harassment*. Aldershot: Avebury.

HOBBS, D. (1988), *Doing the Business*. Oxford: Oxford University Press.

HOME OFFICE (1981), *Racial Attacks: Report of a Home Office Study*. London: Home Office.

—— (1986), *Home Office Good Practice Guide for the Police: The Response to Racial Attacks*. London: Home Office.

—— (1989), *The Response to Racial Attacks and Harassment: Guidance for the Statutory Agencies*, Report of the Inter-Departmental Racial Attacks Group. London: Home Office.

—— (1991), *The Response to Racial Attacks and Harassment: Sustaining the Momentum*, 2nd Report of the Inter-Departmental Racial Attacks Group. London: Home Office.

HOUGH, M., and MAYHEW, P. (1983), *The British Crime Survey: First Report*, Home Office Research Study no. 76. London: Home Office.

—— (1985), *Taking Account of Crime: Key Findings from the 1984 British Crime Survey*, Home Office Research Study no. 85. London: Home Office.

HOUNSLOW COMMUNITY RELATIONS COUNCIL (1986), *The Nature and Extent of Racial Harassment in the London Borough of Hounslow*. London: Hounslow Community Relations Council.

HOUSE OF COMMONS (1982), Home Affairs Committee, 2nd Report, *Racial Attacks*. London: HMSO.

—— (1986), Home Affairs Committee, 3rd Report, *Racial Attacks and Harassment*. London: HMSO.

HUSBANDS, C. (1983), *Racial Exclusionism and the City: The Urban Support for the National Front*. London: Allen and Unwin.

INSTITUTE OF RACE RELATIONS (1987), *Policing against Black People*. London: Institute of Race Relations.

JOINT COMMITTEE AGAINST RACIALISM (1981), *Racial Violence in Britain*. London: Joint Committee Against Racialism.

JONES, T., MacLEAN, B. D., and YOUNG, J. (1986), *The Islington Crime Survey: Crime, Victimisation and Policing in Inner-City London*. Aldershot: Gower.

KELLY, L. (1987), 'The Continuum of Sexual Violence', in J. Hanmer and M. Maynard, eds., *Women, Violence and Social Control*: 46–60. London: Macmillan.

—— (1988), *Surviving Sexual Violence*. Cambridge: Polity.

KIMBER, J., and COOPER, L. (1991), *Victim Support Racial Harassment Project*. London: Community Research and Advisory Centre, Polytechnic of North London.

KINSEY, R., LEA, J., and YOUNG, J. (1987), *Losing the Fight Against Crime*. Oxford: Blackwell.

KLUG, F. (1982), *Racist Attacks*. London: Runnymede Trust.

LAYTON-HENRY, Z. (1984), *The Politics of Race in Britain*. London: Allen and Unwin.

LEHNEN, R. G., and SKOGAN, W. (1981), *The National Crime Survey: Working Papers*, vol. 1: *Current and Historical Perspective*. Washington DC: US Department of Justice Bureau of Statistics.

RACIAL HARASSMENT AND THE PROCESS OF VICTIMIZATION

LONDON BOROUGH OF NEWHAM (1987), *The Newham Crime Survey*. London: London Borough of Newham.

MACLEAN, B. D. (1986), 'Critical Criminology and Some Limitations of Traditional Inquiry', in B. D. MacLean, ed., *The Political Economy of Crime: Readings for a Critical Criminology*. Scarborough, Ontario: Prentice-Hall.

—— (1991), 'In Partial Defence of Socialist Realism: Some Theoretical and Methodological Concerns of the Local Crime Survey', *Crime, Law and Social Change*, 15: 213–54.

MAGUIRE, M., and POINTING, J., eds. (1988), *Victims of Crime: A New Deal?* Milton Keynes: Open University Press.

MANNING, P. K. (1988), *Symbolic Communication*. London: MIT Press.

MAYHEW, P., ELLIOTT, D., and DOWDS, L. (1989), *The British Crime Survey*, Home Office Research Study no. 111. London: HMSO.

METROPOLITAN POLICE (1985), *Report of the Commissioner of Police of the Metropolis for the year 1984*. London: HMSO.

MILES, R., and PHIZACKLEA, A., (1984), *White Man's Country: Racism in British Politics*. London: Pluto.

MORGAN, R., and SMITH, D. J., eds. (1989), *Coming to Terms with Policing: Perspectives on Policy*. London: Routledge.

NEWHAM MONITORING PROJECT (1990), *Newham Monitoring Project Annual Report 1989*. London: Newham Monitoring Project.

PEARSON, G. (1976), ' "Paki-bashing" in a North Eastern Lancashire Cotton Town: A Case Study and its History', in J. Mungham and G. Pearson, *Working Class Youth Culture*. London: Routledge.

PEARSON, G., SAMPSON, A., BLAGG, H., STUBBS, P., and SMITH, D. J. (1989), 'Policing Racism', in R. Morgan and D. J. Smith, eds., *Coming to Terms with Policing: Perspectives on Policy*. London: Routledge.

REEVES, F. (1989), *Race and Borough Politics*. Aldershot: Avebury.

ROCK, P. (1990), *Helping Victims of Crime*. Oxford: Oxford University Press.

SAMPSON, A., and PHILLIPS, C. (1992), *Multiple Victimisation: Racial Attacks on an East London Estate*, Police Research Group Crime Prevention Unit Series Paper 36. London: Home Office Police Department.

SAULSBURY, W. E., and BOWLING, B. (1991), *The Multi-Agency Approach in Practice: The North Plaistow Racial Harassment Project*, Home Office Research Study no. 64. London: Home Office.

SHAPLAND, J., WILLMORE, J., and DUFF, P. (1985), *Victims in the Criminal Justice System*. Aldershot: Gower.

SKOGAN, W. G. (1986), 'Methodological Issues in the Study of Victimisation', in E. Fattah, ed., *From Crime Policy to Victim Policy*: 80–116. London: Macmillan.

SMALL, S. (1983), *Police and People in London*, vol. 2: *A Group of Young Black People*. London: Policy Studies Institute.

SMITH, D. J. (1983a), *Police and People in London*, vol. 1: *A Survey of Londoners*. London: Policy Studies Institute.

—— (1983b), *Police and People in London*, vol. 3: *A Survey of Police Officers*. London: Policy Studies Institute.

SMITH, D. J., and GRAY, J. (1983), *Police and People in London*, vol. 4: *The Police in Action*. London: Policy Studies Institute.

SMITH, J. C., and HOGAN, B. (1983), *Criminal Law*. London: Butterworth.

BENJAMIN BOWLING

SMITH, S. J. (1989), *The Politics of 'Race' and Residence: Citizenship. Segregation and White Supremacy in Britain*. Cambridge: Polity.

SOLOMOS, J. (1989), *Race and Racism in Contemporary Britain*. London: Macmillan.

STANKO, E. A. (1987), 'Typical Violence. Normal Precautions: Men, Women and Interpersonal Violence in England, Wales, Scotland and the USA', in J. Hanmer and M. Maynard, eds., *Women. Violence and Social Control*. London: Macmillan.

—— (1988), 'Hidden Violence Against Women', in Maguire and Pointing, eds.: 40–6.

—— (1990), *Everyday Violence*. London: Pandora.

TOMPSON, K. (1988), *Under Siege: Racial Violence in Britain Today*. Harmondsworth: Penguin.

WALKLATE. S. (1989). *Victimology: The Victim and the Criminal Justice Process*. London: Unwin Hyman.

—— (1990). 'Researching Victims of Crime: Critical Victimology', *Social Justice*, 17/3.

—— (1992). 'Appreciating the Victim: Conventional, Realist or Critical Victimology?', in R. Mathews and J. Young. eds., *Issues in Realist Criminology*. London: Sage.

WALSH, D. (1987), *Racial Harassment in Glasgow*. Glasgow: Scottish Ethnic Minorities Research Unit.

YIN, R. K. (1989), *Case Study Research*. London: Sage.

YOUNG, M. (1990), *An Inside Job*. Oxford: Clarendon Press.

Part IV
Race and Gender

[21]
The Criminalisation and Imprisonment of Black Women

Black women suffer the double disadvantage of being stereotyped according to race and gender, readily labelled as deviant in the community and over-represented in prison. They now represent 18% of the rising female prison population, yet little is known of their experience. Ruth Chigwada, post-graduate student at LSE and part-time Lecturer in Criminology, interviewed ten Black women ex-prisoners concerning their treatment in the penal system and concludes that they are criminalised because of their lifestyle and by racist, class-biased attitudes.

lack women are more likely to suffer social factors which are brought to bear in sentencing. An example taken from the *Hornsey Journal* highlights the problem. It reported that Broadwater Farm Estate was occupied by 'problem families' and that the sight of 'unmarried West Indian mothers walking about the estate' aggravated racial tensions. Such remarks serve to criminalise Black women and contribute to their image as suspects, the end result being that they are frequently given custodial sentences for relatively minor offences.

Again, an *Evening Standard* article stated that young Black men commit a disproportionately high number of violent crimes in London because 'most black mothers when young girls ... have children out of wedlock and are not supported by the fathers. There appears to be less stigma attached to single parenthood in the Black community. The only hope is that somehow the West Indian marriage can be encouraged and supported.'

The implication of the reports is that Black women, as single parent mothers, deviate from the norm and are a problem to society. Yet it may be that a society that practices racial and gender discrimination in school and the labour market encourages them to have children as one way of demonstrating control over at least one aspect of their lives.

Of the ten women I interviewed, eight were born in the UK and 9 had received only one prison sentence. Eight were single parents, two were unmarried without children. Eight were of Caribbean origin and two West African. Nine felt that the Criminal Justice system was unjust. Eight felt that the police had no respect for Black women and spoke of police harassment and checks on their immigration status.

Fumi's Story

'One morning at 7 a.m. six policemen came to my flat to arrest my boyfriend. They ransacked the whole place and left the place in a big mess. When they did not find anything they turned to me and asked to see my passport. After showing them they told me to get dressed and go with them to the police station to answer questions about a forged passport. I said, 'But you have just seen my passport. I don't have a forged passport.' They said, 'Yes, you have.'

'They took me to the police station and when we got there they showed me a passport with a picture. The picture looked nothing like me. I said it was not my passport and it wasn't me on that picture. They said, 'We know you Black people, you disguise yourselves.' They wouldn't let me go.

'The following morning they said to me, 'Let's talk about your marriage.' They started asking me questions about my marriage. They asked for my husband's name and everything about him and many other questions. They asked me if he was a Black or white man. They said to me that because of the fact that my husband is white 'we are suspicious'. One of them said, 'It's one of these marriages Black women get involved in — isn't it? — to get a permit to stay in this country. I said,

'The only way to tell an illegal Black from a legal one is to suspect the lot.'

'But we have been married now for three years, it's just that things didn't work.'

'By the second day in police custody I was feeling very weak and depressed about the whole thing. I was worried sick about my daughter who was 18 months at the time. The police had made arrangements for her to be taken into care and I was wondering how she was coping without me as it was the first time she had ever been separated from me. I had not had anything to eat from the day before. No food was offered to me.

'The police officers kept firing questions at me about my marriage, saying that I should agree that it was a marriage of convenience. They then said to me if I agreed that it was a marriage of convenience they would let me go and be with my daughter. For my daughter's sake I signed the statement.

'The next thing they did was to ask me to get into a car. The car was an ordinary car with two men at the back and a driver — all were in their ordinary clothes. I honestly believed they were taking me to my flat as they had said. I was shocked when I found myself at Holloway. I said to them, 'But this is not my flat', and one of them told me to shut up. By then I was crying my eyes out.

'When I got to Holloway some women asked me what I was in for and I told them everything and that I was worried about my daughter. They told me that I was allowed a phone call.

'When two Black women fight the prison officers tend to take no action.'

When the priest came to see me he agreed to make a call to my cousin. My cousin, even though she had two children of her own, agreed to look after my daughter and collected her from the social services.'

Racist Assumptions

This is just one case in which the police tricked a Black woman into signing statements against her better judgement and neglected to inform her

about her rights to see a solicitor and make a phone call. In the end the police dropped the passport forgery charge on the second day of hearing.

The case supports Paul Gordon's argument that all Black people are seen as 'immigrants'. Given that some are illegal, it is common to hear comments such as: 'the only way to tell an illegal Black from a legal one is to suspect the lot.'[1] The upshot of this attitude is that many Black families do not report racist attacks to the police because they fear unfounded immigration checks and threats of deportation.

In addition to the humiliation of immigration status checks, is the even more traumatic experience of arrest procedure. Eight of the women with whom I spoke mentioned the strip search to which every prisoner is subjected on their first day in prison and whenever they are transported from one prison to another. One woman said: 'I did not like to be strip-searched in front of other women. It is very embarrassing and humiliating'. They all felt that there should be a private room for strip searching. Five of the women claimed that Black visitors were subjected to strip searches more often than non-Blacks. 'When it's a Black woman they really do a thorough search. I did not have many visitors in prison. Who would want to come and be strip-searched like that?'

Under the *Police and Criminal Evidence Act 1984* the police have been given extended powers to carry out strip searches and intimate body searches at the station — and this seems to have encouraged an aspect of racial and sexual discrimination to creep into policing. Consider the case of Mrs Lorna Lucas, reported in *South London Press,* 7 February 1986. In August 1981 Mrs Lucas was arrested and assaulted by police following an incident in a builders' office and was kept in police custody overnight. While in police custody a police officer looked up her skirt and said, 'What a sight this is before breakfast'. Mrs Lucas eventually sued the police for assault, false imprisonment and malicious prosecution and was awarded £26,000 in damages.

Privileges and Discretion

Other examples of racism were cited in each interview. All the women talked about privileges in prison and how they could be withdrawn for trivial things. Six of the women believed that racism played a part. 'I was put on report for taking three slices of bread at breakfast time. They felt I was too greedy but I was hungry.' 'I feel that if an officer takes a dislike to you or if she is racist — you have your privileges withdrawn more. The officers abuse their power.'

Nine of the women felt that racism affected work assignments and that it was particularly difficult for a Black woman to be allocated a place on an education class. 'A lot of people want to go to the education unit. I put my name down for education. I put an application in five times and each time I was told the class was full. But I noticed that some people who came after me got places on education classes — and all of these women were white.'

This statement was confirmed by a Black woman prison teacher I interviewed. She said she never had any Black women in her class and that each time she asked about the Black women who had put forward their names for her class she was told that there were not enough officers to escort them. Considering that the authorities view education as one of the easier activities to administrate, the implication was that, because of authorities' preconceived notions that Black women are problematic, they are seen to require more officers' attention. Another woman said: 'I could not get a place in education class so I ended up doing

sewing. You have to do something otherwise you would be locked up for 23 hours a day.'

The same prison teacher also expressed her concern that Black women are viewed as troublemakers in prison. For instance, when a Black woman fights with a White woman, the Black woman tends to be put on report and

'You are lucky to have a toilet. In your country you would have to go to the bush.'

punished. However, when two Black women fight the prison officers tend to take no action.

Lack of Concern

All the women I interviewed expressed their concern about the physical conditions of prison. They found the prison very dirty and infested with cockroaches. Complaints were often met with racist rebuffs, as when one woman complained about the state of the toilet. The prison officer said: 'You are lucky to have one — in your country you would have to go to the bush.'

According to six of the women, maltreatment of Black non-British women was not uncommon. One woman said: 'They were horrible to foreign Black women, reminding them all the time about where they came from and saying how lucky they were to have this and that.' 'They really looked down on African women and one White woman was put on report for calling an officer a racist.'

The women felt that some of the prison officers were nice, but had to behave differently and look tough in front of their colleagues. On the other hand, one woman explained, 'Some officers were not interested in your problems, only gossip. They wanted to know the business of other inmates.'

According to six of the women the lack of concern on the part of prison officers contributed to the occurrence of self-mutilation by prisoners. They believe that prison officers should have listened to and reassured troubled women. 'When you are in there a lot of things get you down. Women worry about their children, about losing their homes. The officers should sit down and talk to the women.'

Longer Sentences

Seven of the women claimed that Black women are given relatively longer sentences for similar offences than non-Black women. They also assert that non-British Black women are handed even longer sentences: 'Foreign Black women have it tough in prisons — some of them can't speak English and the prison officers don't bother to explain the rules to them. Most of these women don't know their rights.' This view was confirmed by a Black woman prison teacher who maintains that women should be allowed to choose their own solicitor: 'I have known of a case where a woman wanted to change the solicitor because he was no good but was not allowed.'

Conventional Gender Role

Some feminist criminologists have found that middle-class notions regarding appropriate behaviour for women affect sentencing decisions as well as the processes of arrest and trial. Pat Carlen, in her Scottish prison study,[2] discovered that appropriate gender role, wifehood and domesticity, are factors likely to affect sentencing decisions.

The Black woman whose gender role does not match middle class expectations is likely to receive rougher treatment by the authorities. Black women are often viewed as aggressive, in part because of their powerlessness to conform to what British society sees as correct behaviour. Social work practice and social enquiry reports are deeply influenced by the values of the dominant culture. For example, Black women may be seen as over-protective, over-religious or over-punitive, and labelled as 'bad' mothers. Expressions of emotions, whether anger or affection, may be misinterpreted. Similarly, value judgements concerning issues such as sexual or family relationships, work status, parental responsibility based on a Eurocentric view of society, are then used to justify prison sentences. This might partially explain why Black women are thirteen times more likely than white women to be incarcerated in psychiatric hospitals (*The Guardian*, 31 September 1987). Attempts to educate authorities concerning the customs and habits of other cultures might elicit a more just sentence.

Accelerated Criminal Career

Other disquieting evidence reveals that Black women receive custodial sentences at a far earlier stage in their 'criminal' careers than other offenders. As the Commission for Racial Equality found in 1981, alternatives to custody are rarely offered to Black women, resulting in an increase in those sentenced to custody.

The fact that many Black women are unemployed and reside in rented flats also contributes to their over-representation in prisons and mental hospitals. Sentencers often take into account employment status when determining which sentence to impose. Employment increases the chance of avoiding custody, as the courts do not wish to jeopardise income. Similarly, housing situations are also considered. However, bad housing has been found to cause depression which can result in sentencing to psychiatric hospitals.

When Black women are sent to prison, they often suffer more than white counterparts, precisely because of their social situation. Most Black women are unemployed, single parents, living below the poverty line and in poor housing facilities. It is likely that they will be seen as 'unfit' mothers and that their children will be taken away, and it will be very difficult to regain custody. This is further complicated by the fact that when Black women go to prison they often lose their council flats because of rent arrears. When they attempt to regain custody of their children they no longer have accommodation for them. Moreover, loss of their council flats while in prison makes it difficult for them to gain parole as they no longer have homes.

In Conclusion

It can be concluded that Black women are not only unduly criminalised, but are often maltreated by the police. Repercussions have been widespread as is evidenced by the Review Panel set up by West Midlands County Council in the wake of the Handsworth disturbances which concluded that the maltreatment of a Black woman was of primary importance to an understanding of the circumstances leading to the 'riot'. The Panel found that many citizens of Handsworth were convinced the assault and intimidation of Black women was a general police policy.

To eradicate racism in the Criminal Justice system, generally and in prisons specifically, the present government must take seriously the problem of race and poverty. Laws protecting the rights of Black people must be enforced. Money should be appropriated to rebuild these poor communities where a large percentage of Black women live. Existing education and training programmes should be expanded and new ones created to enable Black women to develop the skills necessary to compete in the job market.

Until these aims are achieved several remedies will help alleviate the current problems. Black women should be considered far more vigorously for non-custodial measures. Police and judges should be made aware of their racist and sexist attitudes. Affirmative action efforts should be enhanced to increase the number of Black people in all levels of the criminal justice system. However, it should be recognised that more representation does not,

'When it's a Black woman they really do a thorough search.'

in itself, compensate for race discrimination. Black administrators are often forced to participate in or tolerate racially discriminating treatment.

Finally, the subordination of Black women to white people in this society is largely responsible for the disproportionate numbers of Black women in prisons. In order to reduce the number of Black women who enter prisons each year their criminalisation by the police and Press must stop. Because Black women often remain unmarried and have children, they should not be criminalised for it. Black women should not be judged according to standards of white, middle class female roles. The Criminal Justice system should be able to take into account the different cultures and to accept that the era of female subservience to men has passed.

References:

1. Paul Gordon, *White Law*, Pluto Press, 1983.

2. Pat Carlen, *Women's Imprisonment: A Study of Social Control*, RKP, 1983.

[22]

Minority and Female:
A Criminal Justice Double Bind

Coramae Richey Mann

THIS ARTICLE ADDRESSES THE STATUS of minority (Black, Hispanic, Native American) women offenders from arrest to incarceration. As such, it examines and synthesizes the scattered information on a group that is doubly discriminated against because of their gender and race/ethnicity status.[1] For many decades the study of women's deviance was rare and the reports available were limited to examinations of prostitution and other sexual deviance thought to be "typical" female offenses. It was gradually recognized that all women offenders did not fit this stereotype and that women were involved in a wide variety of activities that are labeled "criminal." In the 1970s, and more so in the 1980s, criminological inquiry and research turned to women as offenders, but there is still a dearth of studies of the processing of women at each level of the criminal justice system. This neglect is exacerbated in the case of minority or nonwhite women, especially Black women, who comprise the largest proportion of women caught in the criminal justice double bind. The scarcity of documented sources necessarily circumscribes the discussion presented here.

The Criminal Justice Processing of Minority Women:
Arrest, Prosecution, and Sentencing

The Crimes

The Uniform Crime Reports (UCR) compiled by the Federal Bureau of Investigation are the most frequently utilized sources of arrest information in the United States today.[2] Unfortunately, the UCRs are not crosstabulated by gender and race, which makes it impossible to isolate the offenses for which minority women are arrested. Nonetheless, the parameters of the incidence of female crime can be estimated from aggregated data on race and gender when combined with a number of studies specifically addressing minority female offenders.

CORAMAE RICHEY MANN teaches in the Department of Criminal Justice, Indiana University, Bloomington, IN 47405. She would like to thank Darnell Hawkins and Dragan Milovanovic for their helpful comments on earlier versions of this article.

RICHEY MANN

The latest available data reveal that in 1987, 31.3% of the total arrests were of minority persons, 29.7% of whom were Black (U.S. Department of Justice, 1988: 183). Blacks also made up 47.3% of persons arrested for Index violent crimes in 1987, yet comprised only 13% of the U.S. population.[3] Women, on the other hand, accounted for 17.7% of total 1987 arrests and 11.1% of Index violent crime arrestees (UCR, 1988: 181). Clearly, women make up a small proportion of arrests, especially for serious offenses, a pattern that has persisted since 1960 when female arrests were first recorded in a separate category (Rans, 1978). Of course, these statistics tell us little about the crimes of minority women, but a number of research efforts suggest that when each subgroup is compared with their white counterparts, the Black woman is as likely to be involved with the law as is the Black man.[4] Homicide and drug offenses are serious crimes of contemporary public concern and, excluding prostitution, are probably the offenses involving women that are most frequently examined.

Early studies of criminal homicides by gender and race reveal that Black females are second to Black males in frequency of arrests (Wolfgang, 1958; Pokorny, 1965) and their conviction rates have been reported as 14 times greater than those of white females (Sutherland and Cressey, 1978: 30). More recent efforts tend to corroborate the previous studies by Wolfgang and Pokorny in showing extremely high proportions of Black females as both victims and offenders. As homicide offenders, Black females have been found to predominate in every major study where women offenders were included (e.g., Suval and Brisson, 1974; Biggers, 1979; Riedel and Lockhart-Riedel, 1984; Weisheit, 1984; Block, 1985; Formby, 1986; Goetting, 1987; Mann, 1987). Black men are their principal victims, since homicide is not only an intraracial, but also an intergender event. Homicide has been reported as the leading cause of death among young Black males from 15 to 24 years of age (Mercy, Smith, and Rosenberg, 1983). Since the average age of the Black male homicide victim is older in cases of domestic homicide (about 38 years old) and in instances of nondomestic killing by a Black female assailant (about 29 years old, see Mann, 1988a), it is clear that Black men are at a high risk of death throughout their lifetimes. Thus, it is not surprising that homicide has been designated by the U.S. Public Health Service as the primary public health risk for Black men in the U.S.

In 1970, Williams and Bates reported an overrepresentation of Black females in female admissions to the Public Health Service Hospital in Lexington, Kentucky, for narcotic addiction. Most of these women (63.8%) were urban residents from New York, Chicago, and Washington, D.C., compared to only 22.8% of the white female addicts. More recently, Pettiway (1987: 746) found female heroin and other opiate users to be ethnically split: Blacks were 35%, whites 33.8%, and Hispanics 31.2% (Puerto Rican 16.4% and Cuban 14.8%). Both studies found a strong correlation between women's drug usage and crime. Mann (1988b) compared random samples of female homicide offenders in six major U.S. urban areas on the basis of drug and nondrug use. Few differences were found between the two groups; the majority of whom were Black (77.7%). This led to the conclusion that women who kill are similar to each other on a number of important characteristics, regardless of their substance abuses (alcohol or narcotics). While there were proportionately fewer Blacks in the homicide user group, Mann found there were almost twice the proportion of Hispanic assailants in the abuser group, compared to the nonabuser Hispanic group.

Arrests

Black women are seven times more likely to be arrested for prostitution than women of other ethnic groups (Haft, 1976: 212). Yet, it cannot be empirically established that Black prostitutes are more prevalent than prostitutes in other female racial/ethnic groups. One possible explanation for the disproportionate number of arrests is that Black prostitutes are forced to practice their profession on the streets instead of under the benevolent protection of a hotel manager or in luxury apartments, as predominantly white call girls are able to do. "Street walking" increases the likelihood of police contact and harassment as well as possible law enforcement racial bias:

> As might be expected, the largest proportion of arrests of Black prostitutes takes place in the inner cities where living standards are low, the level of desperation high, and police prejudice endemic (*Ibid.*).

Are harassment and readiness to arrest indicative of police reactions to Black women offenders? A study of incarcerated female offenders reveals that Black women are more likely than white women to perceive police officers as excessively brutal, harassing, and unlikely to give them a break through nonarrest (Kratcoski and Scheuerman, 1974). The researchers conclude that the police discretionary power not to arrest was used more liberally with white women than with Black women.

Moyer and White (1981) hypothesized that police officers would apply more severe sanctions to a Black woman than to a white woman, especially if the Black woman was "loud, boisterous, aggressive, vulgar, and disrespectful" — characteristics seen by some whites as typical of Black people. In the second instance, the researchers reasoned, demeanor could also potentially predict law enforcement bias. While neither hypothesis was supported, type of crime in association with demeanor strongly influenced decisions of police officers where women were concerned, more so than with male offenders.

Pre-Trial, Prosecution, and Sentencing

In minority communities it is generally believed that in addition to the racial prejudice exhibited by the police toward minorities, the white-dominated judicial system also treats them more stringently (Deming, 1977). The few studies of the criminal justice processing of men and women appear to indicate differential treatment of nonwhite women offenders at every stage of the process.

According to earlier studies, at the pre-trial stage minority women are frequently unable to make bail and are held in jail until their court hearing, or they are excessively detained relative to the type of offense committed (see, e.g., Barrus and Slavin, 1971; Nagel and Weitzman, 1971). Many judges deny bail or insist upon higher and higher bail for each prostitution arrest, and since 53% of arrested prostitutes are Black women, the impact upon this minority group is obvious (DeCrow, 1974). An analysis of grand larceny and felonious assault cases sampled from criminal cases in all 50 states isolated a *disadvantaged pattern* of discrimination which resulted in adverse treatment of Black women at virtually all stages of the criminal justice process, including the likelihood of being jailed before and after conviction more so than white women (Nagel and Weitzman, 1971).

Recent research suggests that, in some jurisdictions, the detention status of women offenders may not be related to race/ethnicity. Mann (1984: 168) reports that in the Fulton County (Georgia) criminal courts,

> no overall relationship was found between race and whether a defendant was held in detention before the court hearing, since 66.7% of the Black women and 63.6% of the white women were in jail at the time of their court hearing.

Mann did find that not a single Black female was released on her own recognizance compared to nine percent of non-Blacks and that there was a slight tendency for higher bails set for Black women.

A court study by Daly (1987) compared Seattle and New York City jurisdictions and found that in both jurisdictions the Black and Hispanic female detention rates were lower than those of white women. And apparently being married was found to mitigate more strongly against detention for Black women than Hispanic women in New York City, where 62.6% of the female defendants were Black (a higher proportion than for Black men) and 28.8% were Puerto Rican (*Ibid.*: 161).

The poverty of most minority women offenders may contribute to either a lack of legal counsel or the necessity to rely upon public defenders instead of private attorneys for the defense of their cases. There are as many excellent public defenders as there are inept private attorneys, but it is generally acknowledged that the overwhelming case loads of public defenders permit little attention to individual defendants.[5]

Bias on the part of judges may also affect the appointment of free legal counsel. In one Alabama study, 42% of the white female defendants were afforded court-appointed counsel compared to only 26% of the Black females (Alabama Section, 1975). The reverse should have been indicated, since at that time the median income of Black families in Alabama was one-half that of white families.

A Washington, D.C., study noted the "Black-shift phenomenon," that is, 63% of the adult female population of the District of Columbia was Black. Yet the proportion of first bookings into detention was 73% Black, with Black women comprising 83% of those returned to jail from the initial court hearing, 92% of them receiving 30 days or more. For those given prison sentences, 97% were sentenced for three months or more (McArthur, 1974). For the District's white females, the comparable proportions were in descending order: 37% of adult female population, 27% of first detention bookings, 17% of returns to jail, eight percent 30 days or longer sentence, and only three percent sentenced to three months or longer (Adams, 1975: 185). In a re-analysis of these data, Adams did not find that the type of offense adequately explained the racial differences, but rather that "compared with whites, black women seem underdefended and oversentenced." Further, "they may have been overarrested and overindicted as well" (Ibid.: 193).

Foley and Rasche (1979: 104) found that "differential treatment is definitely accorded to female offenders by race." Over a 16-year period, they had studied 1,163 women sentenced to the Missouri State Correctional Center for Women. Their comparison of sentence lengths for all offenses, combined, showed no significant differences between Black and white female sentence lengths, but Black women did receive longer sentences (55.1 months) than white women (52.5 months). An examination of individual crimes revealed that Blacks received significantly longer sentences (32.8 months) than whites (29.9 months) for crimes against property, and served longer periods in prison. Although white women were accorded lengthier sentences for crimes against the person (182.3 months) at almost double the length for Black women (98.5 months), the actual time served was longer for Black women (26.7 months versus 23 months). In fact, the white women imprisoned for murder served one-third less time than did Black women who committed the same offense. The same held true for the analysis of drug offenses between the two groups. There was no significant difference in mean sentence length between them, yet Black women served significantly more time in prison (20.4 months) when compared with white female drug law violators (13.2 months).

Sentencing outcomes based on the race of the victim and offender are a source of much controversy where men are concerned,[6] but little attention has been devoted to the interracial homicides of women and the sentences received. Two recent studies suggest that the race of the victim influences sentencing of women homicide offenders. In a study of female homicide offenders in six U.S. cities for 1979 and 1983, Mann (1987) found modest (although not statistically significant) support for a devaluation hypothesis.[7] When Black women killed other Blacks, 40% of them received prison sentences, but if the victim was non-Black, 66.7% were imprisoned. Conversely, if both the victim and offender were non-Black, 45.3% of the female offenders were incarcerated, while 50% of non-Black women who killed Blacks went to prison. The other study, conducted by Shields (1987), examined female homicide in Alabama from 1930 to 1986. He found that in the few cases which crossed racial lines, the offenders — who were all Black — received severe sentences. In fact, the majority of convicted Black females received life sentences.

The Punishments

Another method of investigating the relationship between gender, race, and the criminal justice system is through examining the crimes for which women are imprisoned.

According to a national survey by the U.S. General Accounting Office (1979), of the women offenders released from prison in 1979, almost two-thirds (64.3%) were minorities, and more than one-half (50.2%) were Black. As seen in Table 1 (found at the end of the article along with all subsequent tables), each minority group is disproportionately represented in the inmate population according to its proportion in the general female population. On the other hand, as an incarcerated group, white females are substantially less populous.

Data excerpted from a national survey of incarcerated women reported by Glick and Neto (1977), shown in Table 2, reveal that Black women were more likely to be imprisoned for drug offenses (20.2%) and murder (18.6%). Drug offenses and forgery/fraud made up almost one-half (44.8%) of the crimes for which Native American women were in prison. Even more startling was the 40.3% of Hispanic women who were incarcerated for drug offenses — twice as frequently as Blacks.

An examination of the prison statistics from states with large numbers of minority women offers a more detailed picture of the offenses of these women. California, for example, incarcerates more women than any other state in the nation. In 1979, 19% of the women cited and arrested were Black, 17.3% were Mexican-American, 0.96% were Native American, and 0.44% were Asian-American (Hegner, 1981). Similar to the national results reported above, excluding the UCR catch-all "all other offenses," Table 3 shows that in California, Hispanic women (in this case, Mexican-American) were more frequently arrested for drug offenses (24.2%), with burglary second (21.8%), and theft third (16.5%). Black women's arrests were primarily for theft (19.6%), assault (17.8%), and drugs (17.8%). Assault was the first-ranked offense of Native American women (30.5%), followed by drugs (11.8%) and theft (11.2%).

Kruttschnitt (1981) examined the sentencing outcomes of a sample of 1,034 female defendants processed in a northern California county between 1972 and 1976. She found that:

> ...in three of the five offense categories either the defendant's race or her income significantly affects the sentence she receives. Specifically, black women convicted of either disturbing the peace or drug law violations are sentenced more severely than their white counterparts; lower-income women convicted of forgery receive the more severe sentences.... [T]he status of welfare is generally given the greatest weight and appears to have a more consistent impact than either race or income alone on the sentences accorded these women (*Ibid*, 256).

In a separate analysis to determine if the relatively severe sentences were due to race, low-income, or welfare status, Kruttschnitt (*Ibid*: 258) found that most of the effect of race on sentencing was direct and not indirect through welfare, or that "the impact of race on sentencing appears to have little to do with the fact that blacks are more likely to be welfare recipients than whites."

In terms of incarceration in the California prison system, Table 4 compares the three major offenses of each minority group with that of white females and gives the proportions of those receiving prison sentences. Although there may be mitigating circumstances involved in the dispositions of individual cases, Table 4 reveals some curious race/ethnic differences between the women felons in California. Whereas 50% of the Mexican-American women arrested for homicide end up in prison, only 30.2% of whites, 24.8% of Blacks, and 20% of Native American women convicted of this offense were sentenced to prison, despite comprising higher proportions of those originally arrested for this crime. Similarly, although Black women accounted for 21.2% of women arrested for drug law violations, only 25.8% of those offenders were sent to prison. Mexican-American women were more likely than Black women to receive a prison sentence for drugs (33.3%) compared to their arrest proportion (13.4%). In contrast, white women drug violators, who represent the primary group arrested for this offense (65.1%), were far less likely to be imprisoned (39.4%) than any minority female group. It seems that in terms of homicide and drug violations, minority women, and particularly Mexican-Americans, are treated differentially by the California criminal justice system. As seen in Table 4, the offenses of robbery, assault, and burglary also show disproportionate prison sentences for Mexican-Americans, when compared to white and other minority females.

It has been demonstrated that the Black female offender is more likely to be arrested and imprisoned than any other female minority group, but the California statistics just cited indicate that the number of arrests of Hispanic women are slowly gaining on those of Black women. The similarities of the crimes of California and New York Hispanic women, who are culturally different and from opposite shores of the country, are provocative. The most frequent offense for which a Puerto Rican woman offender in New York State was sentenced in 1976 was also dangerous drugs (53.8%), with robbery second (17.9%) and homicide third (10.3%) (Wright, 1981). New commitments to the facilities of the New York State Department of Correctional Services in that year reveal that Puerto Rican female commitments comprised 22.1% of all New York State female commitments for drugs compared to 51.5% Black and 25.3% white. Puerto Rican women were also eight percent of the women imprisoned for homicide, while comprising only a portion of the five percent of the national Hispanic female population. Black women were 80% of the women sent to prison for homicide in New York that year; whites were 12%.

One might wonder why it is that in California white women are less likely to be imprisoned for drug law violations than Mexican-American women when this crime is the primary arrest offense for both groups. Are white women referred to drug treatment programs while minority women are sent to prison? Why are white California women more likely to go to prison for robbery than Black women? Could it be because they rob from business establishments and Blacks rob from individual Blacks? Currently there are no hard and fast answers to such questions, but scattered evidence seems to indicate that minority women are not treated equitably by the criminal justice system.

Incarcerated Minority Women

Jails, particularly rural Southern jails are "targets for the sexual abuse" of the women who occupy them, especially Black inmates, according to Sims (1976: 139). Sexual harassment is typical, but cases such as that of Black inmate, Joan Little, who killed the white jailer in Beaufort County, North Carolina, who had sexually molested her, are atypical. Few women in jails kill the jailers and male inmates who sexually humiliate and molest them.

Many jails housing women are dirty and unsanitary. Health care is rare; so are recreational programs. There is no way to separately house women who would participate in work release programs, and, thus, such programs are rare for jailed women. Because of their small numbers in comparison to men, training and education programs for women in jails are generally impossible. Yet a great number of the women in the nation's jails, most of whom are Black, are misdemeanants (43.5%) or unsentenced (46.7%), and have committed victimless crimes (Glick and Neto, 1977: 70). Female offenders of all ages — the sentenced as well as the unsentenced, the mentally ill, the potentially dangerous psychotics, from prostitutes to accused murderers — are confined together in jail because of a lack of housing for female offenders (U.S. General Accounting Office, 1979).

Prisons for women have their own psychologically devastating effects on women, especially for the over 50% minority population occupying them (Goetting and Howsen, 1983). The appalling lack of interest in women's prisons is typically attributed to their small numbers when compared to male felons. Thus, the majority of correctional funds are directed towards men's prisons to the neglect of female prison facilities. As a result, medical and health services — particularly those peculiar to women's special gynecological and obstetrical needs — are poor or lacking. The federal General Accounting Office found that women in prisons have fewer vocational programs at their disposal compared to men, or an average of three compared to the 10 in men's facilities (U.S. General Accounting Office, 1979). The existing programs follow the sex stereotype of the traditional female role — clerical skills, cosmetology, and food services (Glick and Neto, 1977: 77) — and are geared toward lower-paying jobs. Prison industries in women's facilities rarely provide training beyond that leading to employment as a hotel maid, cook, waitress, laundry worker, or garment factory worker (Simon, 1975).

The frequent location of women's prisons in rural areas introduces special problems for a woman offender. To be physically distant from one's children, family, friends, and legal counsel results in a deprivation of communication that reinforces the female inmate's feeling of isolation and powerlessness (Gibson, 1976). Those women who are mothers (variously estimated at 56% to 70% [Glick and Neto, 1977]) — and most minority women in prison are mothers — experience special problems related to custody, support, and other legal matters pertaining to their children (McGowan and Blumenthal, 1976). Because of these distances, an imprisoned woman has greater difficulty obtaining legal counsel or conferring with her attorney.

In an atmosphere that is tense and oppressive, minority women face additional problems related to the rural locations of women's prisons. Most of the staff are whites recruited from the farm and rural areas surrounding the prisons, while the majority of the inmates are nonwhites from urban areas, a mixture that contributes to ever-present friction. A majority of both white and nonwhite (Black and American Indian) female inmates in Kruttschnitt's study (1983) of the Minnesota Correctional Institution for Women felt that race/ethnicity influenced correctional officers' treatment of the female inmates. Over two-thirds of the minority women perceived racial discrimination in the institution and 29.4% felt that job assignments were influenced by race (35.3% had no opinion). Nonwhite women, who comprised 42% of the Minnesota prison population (where 93% of the staff and administration were white) cited "race relations" as the most frequent response for intra-inmate assaults (Kruttschnitt, 1983: 585).

In many institutions for women felons, Hispanic women are not permitted to speak Spanish, to read or write letters in their native language, to subscribe to Spanish-language magazines or newspapers, or to converse with their visitors in Spanish (Burkhart, 1973: 153). Since many Hispanic inmates do not speak English, these customary procedures tend to isolate these women even more than other minorities.

Alejandrina Torres, a Puerto Rican nationalist, who has never been convicted of an act of violence, was arrested in 1983 on charges of possessing weapons and explosives and seditious conspiracy against the government (Reuben and Norman, 1987: 882). Upon conviction in 1985, Ms. Torres received a sentence of 35 years in prison. She and a white self-proclaimed revolutionary, Susan Rosenberg, who has been associated with the Weather Underground group (McMullian, 1988: C1), were put in a new "high security" facility in Lexington, Kentucky, on October 29, 1986. Below is a graphic description of the conditions under which they were housed:

> The two women...are confined to subterranean cells twenty-three hours a day. They are permitted one hour of exercise in a yard measuring fifty feet square; upon their return they are strip-searched. That daily outing is the only time they see sunlight, except when they leave the facility for medical or dental treatment. On those occasions they are handcuffed and manacled by chains around their waists. In their cells they are kept under constant surveillance by guards or television cameras.... They say they are exposed to various forms of sensory deprivation designed to alter their personalities. The lights in their cells glare down on them continuously, and they are forbidden to cover them in any way (Reuben and Norman, 1987: 881).

Distance also denies a woman access to her parole board (Arditi et al., 1973). In the criminal justice system parole is not a right, but a privilege. One earns parole by demonstrating the ability to function in society in an "acceptable way." The criteria parole boards use to grant parole are vague, and both institutional and noninstitutional criteria are used in decisions. In addition to the institutional behavior of a woman, industrial time, meritorious "good time" earned, as well as original and prior offense records may be a part of the release decision. Women convicted of property crimes, drug offenses, or alcohol-related offenses are those who experience less successful parole outcomes (Simon, 1975), yet these are the crimes that usually result in the incarceration of minority women. Parole boards expect higher standards of proper conduct from women than they do from men. A double sex standard which holds that "extra-marital sex is normal for men but depraved for women" might more readily lead to denial or revocation of parole for women (Haft, 1974). Minority women, particularly unwed minority mothers, are frequently viewed by society as being more carefree sexually and of looser moral fiber.

Whatever thoughts occupy the minds of parole board members concerning minority women inmates, there is some evidence that their release from prison differs significantly because of race/ethnicity. Foley and Rasche (1979: 103) found that white women in Missouri more frequently received parole than did Black women (41.3% versus 33.3%), while Black women were more likely to be released from prison through commutation of their sentences. As a result, Blacks served a highly significant 30% more actual time (19.4 months) than whites (14.9%).

Excluding the lynchings of untold numbers of Black females in the early years of this nation, a preliminary inventory of confirmed lawful executions of female offenders from 1625 to 1984, reported by Strieb (1988), reveals that for the 346 female offenders for whom race is known, 229, or 66% were Black women, and 108 were white women (31%). Apparently these proportions have reversed in recent years. In their compilation of a list of the women executed since 1900, Gillispie and Lopez (1986) found that of the 37 women killed, 32% were Black and 68% white. Nonetheless, relative to their numbers in the general population, Black women are disproportionately represented on the death rows of this country. As of August 1, 1988, to the time of this writing, seven of the 22 female death-row inmates are Black (31.8%), and one of the two female inmates under the age of 18 awaiting death is Black.

Conclusions and Recommendations

The most cogent conclusion one can draw from an examination of the minority woman offender in the United States criminal justice system is that despite awakening interest in female criminality, little attention is devoted to the Black, Hispanic, or Native American female offender. Vernetta Young incisively describes the dilemma that confronts Black women in American society, a depiction which is equally applicable to all minority women:

Black women in American society have been victimized by their double status as blacks and as women. Discussions of blacks have focused on the black man; whereas discussions of females have focused on the white female. Information about black females has been based on their position relative to black males and white females. Consequently, black women have not been perceived as a group worthy of study. Knowledge about these women is based on images that are distorted and falsified. In turn, these images have influenced the way

in which black female victims and offenders have been treated by the
criminal justice system (Young, 1986: 322).

The other obvious conclusion is that the few available studies of the minority woman offender tend to document differential treatment due to her
racial/ethnic status. Discrimination and a lack of concern for her needs and
those of her family are witnessed on every level of the system — arrest, pre-
trial, judicial, and corrections.

Since the number of incarcerated women is not large, comprising only a
little over four percent of the inmate population in the United States, a comprehensive national survey of all female offenders in the District of Columbia,
and all 50 states and territories would provide a sound, empirical basis for
policy changes that could ameliorate the status and condition of arrested, incarcerated, probationed, and paroled minority female offenders in this nation.

Law enforcement personnel, on the streets and in the station houses, should
be sensitized to the special situations faced by the minority mothers whom
they arrest. Further, they should be intensively trained in race and community
relations as a part of their academy curriculum, as well as in continuing training sessions throughout their careers. Emphasis in such training should be on
the cultural nuances of the various racial/ethnic groups in the nation, human
relations training, and cross-cultural interactions. Since the majority of police
officers are men, special training should be available in the psychology of
women and intergender relations.

Efforts should be made to release arrested minority women on their own
recognizance, since they are often of low income and cannot make bail. If bail
is felt to be required, it should be within the realm of possibility for the specific female offender. Since a majority of minority woman offenders are heads
of households, any alternatives to outright release of a minority female offender should minimize the disruption of family ties.

Many changes are needed in the laws and the administration of justice by
the criminal courts in regard to all women offenders. The following items
should be considered:

1. Indeterminate sentencing exclusively applied to women should be
   eliminated;

2. Prostitution should be decriminalized, particularly since such laws
   have a discriminatory effect against minority women, while ignoring
   the male customer who is usually white;

3. Other victimless crimes, such as drug and alcohol abuse, should be
   viewed as the diseases they are and decriminalized;

4. Educational programs should be initiated to orient both Native
   Americans and criminal justice personnel to the rights of Native

Americans and the discretion and powers of tribal laws and courts; translators should be provided at every level of the criminal justice system for those minorities who are not English speaking; and

5.   More women and minority judges and other administrators should be installed at every level of the judicial system.

The corrections system is probably the area most in need of change, yet it is the most entrenched and resistant of all the elements of the criminal justice system, despite its potential for administrative policy change due to its strong state control. In their plea for treatment intervention for female offenders, Iglehart and Stein (1985: 152) note that "historically, the female offender has been forgotten, ignored, or merely footnoted when the treatment and rehabilitation of offenders are discussed." Every effort should be made to maintain and strengthen the fragile family ties of minority woman offenders incarcerated in jails and prisons through widened avenues of communication, more home furloughs, conjugal visits, and family life and childcare educational programs. Pregnant inmates should be permitted to keep their new-born infants while in prison to enhance the bonding process. Legal services, law libraries, and access to courts should be afforded to all women in prison to assist them in preparing defenses and appeals and to properly deal with legal problems concerning their children.

All language restrictions should be eliminated and translators should be available for those minority women not proficient in the English language. Corrections officers should be bilingual in those areas with large numbers of Spanish-speaking inmates. More and better medical, vocational, and educational programs should be provided in women's correctional facilities to maintain sound health and prepare women for nontraditional jobs to gainfully support themselves and their families upon release. Finally, minority women offenders should be released from prison under the same conditions and with the same considerations as nonminority women through timely determination by parole boards and commissions containing minority women in equal proportions to those in the prison system of each state.

For over 15 years I have labored over the etiology of crime and thought that understanding female crime would offer the key to a general theory of crime causation based on the political, economic, and social realities of an inequitable society such as ours. The notion of generating theory diminishes in importance with the realization of the injustices perpetrated against *all* racial/ethnic minorities in the U.S. criminal justice system through institutional racism. Particularly distressing is the double discrimination experienced by minority women offenders simply because they are nonwhite and happen also to be female; they are the most powerless of the powerless.

Perhaps in another 15 years, the real meaning of a criminal justice system dominated by white males will be sufficiently documented that the "grand"

108   RICHEY MANN

theory will fall into place. But somehow I doubt it. According to Sophocles, "knowledge must come through action," to which Disraeli would add, "justice is truth in action." The path is clearly demarcated.

Table 1:
Proportions of Incarcerated Women in Federal and State Prisons, 1978, Compared to Proportions in the General Female Population, by Race/Ethnicity*

	% in Prison	% in Female Population
White	35.7	82.0
Black	50.2	11.0
Hispanic	9.1	5.0
Native American	3.2	0.4
All Other	1.8	1.6
TOTALS	100.0	100.0

* *Source*: U.S. Government Accounting Office, Washington, D.C., 1979, p. 8.

Table 2:
Offense Data on U.S. Incarcerated Women by Race/Ethnicity, 1979,* in Percentages

Offense	White	Black	Hispanic	Native American	Total
Murder	12.9	18.6^2	8.6	13.4^3	15.3^3
Other Violent	2.2	2.3	0.9	3.0	2.1
Robbery	9.2	13.8	8.7^3	6.6	11.3
Assault	3.2	7.5	1.6	5.8	5.5
Burglary	6.2	4.2	12.7^2	6.0	5.7
Forgery/Fraud	22.3^{1***}	11.3	8.2	23.8^1	15.6^2
Larceny	8.1	14.1^3	8.6	7.2	11.2
Drugs	20.4^2	20.2^1	40.3^1	21.0^2	22.1^1
Prostitution	1.3	3.1	2.4	0.7	2.4
Other Nonviolent	14.1^3	5.0	8.0	12.5	8.7
TOTALS***	100.0	100.0	100.0	100.0	100.0

* Compiled from Glick and Neto (1977), Table 4.10.14.
** Numbers indicate rank order.
*** Rounded to 100.0.

Table 3:
Arrest Offenses of Woman Felons in California, 1979, by Race/Ethnicity*

Arrest Offense	White N	%	Black N	%	Mexican American N	%	Native American N	%
Homicide								
N=228	86	(0.7)	113	(1.5)	24	(0.7)	5	(2.7)
%=100.0	37.7		49.6		10.5		2.2	
Rape								
N=17	9	(0.07)	4	(0.05)	4	(0.01)	0	----
%=100.0	52.9		23.5		23.5		-	
Robbery								
N=919	355	(3.0)	403	(5.5)	143	(4.2)	18	(9.6)
%=100.0	38.6		43.9		15.6		1.9	
Assault								
N=3,082	1,232	(10.3)	1,310	(17.8)^2	483	(14.2)	57	(30.5)^1
%=100.0	39.9		42.5		15.7		1.9	
Burglary								
N=3,320^3	1,649	(13.7)^3	908	(12.4)	744	(21.8)^2	19	(10.2)
%=100.0	49.7		27.4		22.3		0.6	
Theft								
N=3,793^2	1,771	(14.7)^2	1,437	(19.6)^1	564	(16.5)^3	21	(11.2)^3
%=100.0	46.7		37.9		14.9		0.5	
Auto Theft								
N=845	402	(3.3)	283	(3.9)	147	(4.3)	13	(7.0)
%=100.0	47.6		33.5		17.4		1.5	
Drugs								
N=6,172^1	4,017	(33.4)^1	1,309	(17.8)^3	824	(24.2)^1	22	(11.8)^2
%=100.0	65.1		21.2		13.4		.36	
All Other								
N=4,590	2,502	(20.8)	1,577	(21.5)	479	(14.0)	32	(17.1)
%=100.0	54.5		34.4		10.4		0.7	
Totals								
N=22,966	12,023	(100.0)	7,344	(100.0)	3,412	(100.0)	187	(100.0)
%=100.0	52.4		32.0		14.9		0.8	

* *Source*: California Bureau of Criminal Statistics and Special Services, 1980.
Notes 1–3: Rankings excluding "all other" offense category.

Table 4:
Proportions of California Women Felons Arrested and Imprisoned in 1979, by Race/Ethnicity*

Race/Ethnicity: Offense	White N	%	Black N	%	Mexican American N	%	Native American N	%	Totals N
Homicide									
Arrest	86	(37.7)	113	(49.6)	24	(10.5)	5	(22)	228
Prison	26	(38.8)	28	(41.8)	12	(17.9)	1	(1.5)	67
% Arrest/Prison	--	30.2	--	24.8	--	50.0	--	20.0	--
Rape									
Arrest	9	(52.9)	4	(23.5)	4	(23.5)	--	--	17
Prison	1	(100.0)	--	--	--	--	--	--	1
% Arrest/Prison	--	11.6	--	--	--	--	--	--	--
Robbery									
Arrest	355	(38.6)	403	(43.9)	143	(15.6)	18	(1.9)	919
Prison	41	(51.2)	23	(28.8)	16	(20.0)	--	--	80
% Arrest/Prison	--	11.6	--	5.7	--	11.2	--	--	--
Assault									
Arrest	1,232	(39.9)	1,310	(42.5)[2]	483	(15.7)	57	(1.9)[1]	3,082
Prison	14	(37.8)	21	(56.8)	2	(5.5)	--	--	37
% Arrest/Prison	--	1.1	--	1.6	--	2.3	--	--	--
Burglary									
Arrest	1,649	(49.7)[3]	908	(27.4)	744	(22.3)[2]	19	(0.6)[2]	3,320[3]
Prison	30	(53.9)	12	(36.5)	17	(28.3)	--	--	59
% Arrest/Prison	--	1.8	--	1.3	--	2.3	--	--	--
Theft									
Arrest	1,771	(47.6)[2]	1,437	(37.9)[1]	564	(14.9)[3]	21	(.05)[3]	3,793[2]
Prison	28	(53.9)	19	(36.5)	4	(7.7)	1	(1.9)	52
% Arrest/Prison	--	1.6-	--	1.3	--	0.7	--	4.8	--
Auto Theft									
Arrest	402	(47.6)	283	(33.5)	147	(17.4)	13	(1.5)	845
Prison	4	(57.1)	3	(42.9)	--	--	--	--	7
% Arrest/Prison	--	0.9	--	1.1	--	--	--	--	--
Drugs									
Arrest	4,017	(65.1)[1]	1,309	(21.2)[3]	824	(13.4)[1]	22	(0.36)	6,172[1]
Prison	26	(39.4)	17	(25.8)	22	(33.3)	1	(1.5)	66
% Arrest/Prison	--	0.6	--	1.3	--	2.7	--	4.5	--
All Other									
Arrest	2,502	(54.5)	1,577	(34.4)	479	(10.4)	32	(0.7)	4,590
Prison	74	(55.6)	42	(31.6)	15	(11.3)	2	(1.5)	133
% Arrest/Prison	--	2.9	--	2.7	--	6.7	--	6.3	--

Minority and Female   111

Race/Ethnicity: Offense	White		Black		Mexican American		Native American		Totals
	N	%	N	%	N	%	N	%	N
Totals									
Arrest	12,023	(52.4)	7,344	(32.0)	3,412	(14.9)	187	(0.8)	22,966
Prison	244	(48.6)	165	(32.9)	88	(17.5)	5	(1.0)	502
% Arrest/Prison	--	2.0	--	2.3	--	2.6	--	2.7	--

Source: California Bureau of Criminal Statistics and Special Services, 1980.
Notes 1–3: rankings excluding "all other" category.

NOTES

1. Two groups of female offenders are excluded from this discussion — Asian American women offenders and adolescent female offenders. In the first instance, the small numbers preclude an examination of this offender group, since Asian American women comprise less than one percent of arrested women. Girls present peculiar problems because of their age and the uniqueness of their processing through the juvenile justice system.

2. Reporting problems from the various jurisdictions introduce multiple potential errors, but more importantly, these statistics are based upon the U.S. Census which consistently undercounts minorities, especially Blacks and Hispanics.

3. Beginning in 1987, the UCR program ceased collection of "ethnic origin" data; however, in 1986 Hispanics were listed separately and were 12.7% of total arrests and 14.7% of arrests for Index violent crimes.

4. As the female minority group most studied and most involved in the U.S. criminal justice system, the focus throughout this article is on Black women. However, it is contended that other minority women share the same type of experiences in the system.

5. Observations of women's criminal court cases indicated that the public defenders observed in the 11 courts were sorely pressed for time. Many had only minutes to talk to their clients, most of whom were assigned at the arraignment. As a result, over 95% of the cases were plea bargained.

6. The most cogent example is capital punishment. According to the NAACP Legal Defense Fund, since the 1976 reinstitution of capital punishment, 30.69% of those executed were minority defendants with white victims, but not a single white defendant with a minority victim had been executed as of August, 1988.

7. The idea here is that the criminal justice system "values" white lives and "devalues" Black and other minority lives in the imposition of harsher sentences if the victim is white rather than Black. This devaluation is particularly appropriate in an interracial crime.

REFERENCES

Adams, Stuart N.
    1975   "The 'Black-Shift' Phenomenon in Criminal Justice." The Justice System
                Journal: 185–194.

112   RICHEY MANN

Alabama Section
      1975   "Alabama Law Review Summer Project 1975: A Study of Differential Treat-
                    ment Accorded Female Defendants in Alabama Criminal Courts." Alabama
                    Law Review 27: 676–746.
Arditi, Ralph R., Frederick Goldberg, M. Martha Hartle, John H. Peters, and William R. Phelps
      1973   "The Sexual Segregation of American Prisons." Yale Law Journal 82,6:
                    1229–1273.
Barrus, C. and A. Slavin
      1971   Movement and Characteristics of Women's Detention Center Admissions,
                    1969. Washington, D.C.: District of Columbia Department of Corrections.
Biggers, Trisha A.
      1979   "Death by Murder: A Study of Women Murders." Death Education 3: 1–9.
Block, Carolyn Rebecca
      1985   Lethal Violence in Chicago Over Seventeen Years: Homicides Known to the
                    Police, 1965–1981. Chicago: Illinois Criminal Justice Information Authority.
Burkhart, Kathryn
      1973   Women in Prison. Garden City, N.J.: Doubleday.
Daly, Kathleen
      1987   "Discrimination in the Criminal Courts: Family, Gender, and the Problem of
                    Equal Treatment." Social Forces 66,1:152–175.
DeCrow, Karen
      1974   Sexist Justice. New York: Vintage.
Deming, Richard
      1977   Women: The New Criminals. New York: Thomas Nelson.
Foley, Linda A. and Christine E. Rasche
      1979   "The Effect of Race on Sentence, Actual Time Served and Final Disposition
                    of Female Offenders." John A. Conley (ed.), Theory and Research in Criminal
                    Justice. Cincinnati: Anderson.
Formby, William A.
      1986   "Homicides in a Sem-Rural Southern Environment." Journal of Criminal Jus-
                    tice 9: 138–151.
Gibson, Helen E.
      1976   "Women's Prisons: Laboratories for Penal Reform." L. Crites (ed.), The Fe-
                    male Offender. Lexington, Mass.: D.C. Heath.
Gillispie, L. Kay and Barbara Lopez
      1986   "What Must a Woman Do to Be Executed?" Paper presented at annual meet-
                    ings of the American Society of Criminology.
Glick, Ruth M. and Virginia T. Neto
      1977   National Study of Women's Correctional Programs. Washington, D.C.: Gov-
                    ernment Printing Office.
Goetting, Ann
      1987   "Homicidal Wives: A Profile." Journal of Family Issues 8,3: 332–341.
Goetting, Ann and Roy Michael Howsen
      1983   "Women in Prison: A Profile." The Prison Journal (Fall/Winter): 27–46.
Haft, Marilyn G.
      1976   "Hustling for Rights." L. Crites (ed.), The Female Offender. Lexington,
                    Mass.: D.C. Heath.
      1974   "Women in Prison: Discriminatory Practices and Some Legal Solutions."
                    Clearinghouse Review 8: 1–6.
Hegner, Quinton
      1981   California Bureau of Criminal Statistics and Special Services.
Iglehart, Alfreda P. and Martha P. Stein
      1985   "The Female Offender: A Forgotten Client?" Social Casework: The Journal of
                    Contemporary Social Work 66,3: 152–159.

Kratcoski, Peter C. and Kirk Scheuerman
1974   "Incarcerated Male and Female Offenders' Perceptions of Their Experiences in the Criminal Justice System." Journal of Criminal Justice 2: 73–78.
Kruttschnitt, Candace
1983   "Race Relations and the Female Inmate." Crime and Delinquency (October): 577–591.
1981   "Social Status and Sentences of Female Offenders." Law and Society Review 15,2: 247–265.
Mann, Coramae Richey
1988a   "Getting Even? Women Who Kill in Domestic Encounters." Justice Quarterly 5,1: 33–51.
1988b   "Female Homicide and Substance Use: Is There a Connection?" Paper presented at the annual meetings of the American Society of Criminology.
1987   "Black Female Homicide in the United States." Paper presented at the National Conference on Black Homicide and Public Health.
1984   "Race and Sentencing of Female Felons: A Field Study." International Journal of Women's Studies 7,2: 160–172.
McArthur, Virginia A.
1974   From Convict to Citizen: Programs for the Woman Offender. Mimeo.
McGowan, Brenda G. and Karen L. Blumenthal
1976   "Children of Women Prisoners: A Forgotten Minority." L. Crites (ed.), The Female Offender. Lexington, Mass.: D.C. Heath.
McMullian, Bo
1988   "Women's Wing Part of Prison." The Tallahassee Democrat (February 26): C1–C2.
Mercy, James A., Jack C. Smith, and Mark L. Rosenberg
1983   "Homicide among Young Black Males: A Descriptive Assessment." Presented at the annual meetings of the American Society of Criminology.
Moyer, Imogener L. and Garland F. White
1981   "Police Processing of Female Offenders." L. Bowker (ed.), Crime in America. New York: Macmillan.
Nagel, Stuart and Lenore Weitzman
1971   "Women as Litigants." The Hastings Law Journal 23,1: 171–198.
Pettiway, Leon E.
1987   "Participation in Crime Partnerships by Female Drug Users: The Effects of Domestic Arrangements, Drug Use, and Criminal Involvement." Criminology 25,3: 741–765.
Pokorny, Alex D.
1965   "A Comparison of Homicide in Two Cities." Journal of Criminal Law, Criminology and Police Science 56,4: 479–487.
Rans, Laurel L.
1978   "Women's Crime: Much Ado About...?" Federal Probation (March).
Riedel, Marc and Lillie Lockhart-Riedel
1984   "Issues in the Study of Black Homicide." Paper presented at the annual meetings of the American Society of Criminology.
Reuben, William A. and Carlos Norman
1987   "The Women of Lexington Prison." The Nation (June 27): 881–883.
Shields, Alan J.
1987   "Female Homicide: Alabama 1930–1986." Paper presented at the annual meetings of the American Society of Criminology.
Simon, Rita
1975   The Contemporary Woman and Crime. Washington, D.C.: Government Printing Office.
Sims, Patsy
1976   "Women in Southern Jails." L. Crites (ed.), The Female Offender. Lexington, Mass.: D.C. Heath.

Strieb, Victor L.
      1988   American Executions of Female Offenders: A Preliminary Inventory of
                          Names, Dates, and Other Information (3rd Edition). Xerox, prepared for dis-
                          tribution to research colleagues.
Sutherland, Edwin H. and Donald R. Cressey
      1978   Criminology. Philadelphia: J.D. Lippincott.
Suval, Elizabeth M. and R.C. Brisson
      1974   "Neither Beauty nor Beast: Female Homicide Offenders." International Jour-
                          nal of Crime and Penology 2,1: 23–24.
U.S. Department of Justice
      1988   Crime in the United States 1987. Washington, D.C.: Government Printing
                          Office.
U.S. General Accounting Office
      1979   Female Offenders: Who Are They and What Are the Problems Confronting
                          Them? Washington, D.C.: Government Printing Office.
Weisheit, Ralph A.
      1984   "Female Homicide Offenders: Trends Over Time in an Institutionalized Pop-
                          ulation." Justice Quarterly 1,4: 471–489.
Williams, Joyce and William M. Bates
      1970   "Some Characteristics of Female Narcotic Addicts." International Journal of
                          the Addictions 5,2: 245–256.
Wolfgang, Marvin E.
      1958   Patterns in Criminal Homicide. Philadelphia: University of Pennsylvania
                          Press.
Wright, Emilie D.
      1981   Statistical Analysis Center, Division of Criminal Justice Services, State of
                          New York.
Young, Vernetta D.
      1986   "Gender Expectations and Their Impact on Black Female Offenders and Vic-
                          tims." Justice Quarterly 3,3: 305–327.

[23]

Toward a Structural Theory of Crime, Race, and Gender: The Canadian Case

John Hagan

This article outlines and explores a structural theory of race, gender, and crime. We address past concerns about the use of official data to test theories of crime, and we advocate the renewed use of these data to test such theories. Three structural hypotheses are proposed and tested. Each hypothesis focuses in a different way on the interaction of race, gender, and crime, and the third hypothesis adds a crucial fourth variable—age. Our results support the structural approach proposed and encourage further comparative research.

Race and gender are now securely established correlates of crime. Until recently, there was concern that the correlations of race and gender with crime might be a simple product of biases in official crime data. However, Michael Hindelang (1978; 1979) put these concerns to rest by comparing distributions of offenses using official and victimization data. Overall, these comparisons confirm that race and gender are both strong correlates of crime, regardless of the kind of data used to explore such relationships. Official data surely have their failings, but these failings are not of the size and form sometimes feared. The significance of these contributions probably has not been realized fully. On the one hand, it is now clear that race and gender should be fundamental variables in criminological theory construction. On the other, it is now clear that official sources of data can be used to study the relationships of race and gender with crime. Hindelang's research not only made clear the work that needed to be done; it also pointed the way to the resources for doing it.

But how should official data on crime, race, and gender be used to expand our theoretical and empirical knowledge? We argue below that

JOHN HAGAN: Professor of Sociology and Law at the University of Toronto. He is a member of the editorial boards of the *American Sociological Review*, the *American Journal of Sociology, Criminology, Law & Human Behavior*, and several other American and Canadian journals.

CRIME & DELINQUENCY, Vol. 31 No. 1, January 1985 129-146
© 1985 Sage Publications, Inc.

one important means of doing so involves examining the interaction of race and gender on crime. The challenge is to predict on theoretical grounds the form this interaction will take. The reward for meeting this challenge is a clearer explication of the effects of race and gender on crime. It is one thing to predict bivariate relationships; it is quite another to take such an analysis to the multivariate level. Criminologists have recognized this point for some time. The early writings of the Marxist criminologist, Willem Bonger (1916), make this point. Bonger asserted that the social bases of the relationship between gender and crime could be demonstrated by taking class position into account. Reasoning from Marxist premises, Bonger argued that the relationship between gender and crime should decline with class position. His point was that as economic circumstances declined, the social differences between the sexes would also decline, and so therefore their different levels of criminal involvements. Although Bonger had limited data with which to test these arguments, he nonetheless made preliminary efforts to do so.

The structural theory of race, gender, and crime we outline in this article derives from Bonger's work. We begin with the premise that not only do race and gender divisions stratify our society, but that these divisions crosscut one another in socially significant ways. This point is made most effectively not by beginning with the crime problem itself, but by considering how race and gender separately and together stratify the society in which we live.

The stratification effects of both race and gender are recognized most clearly in terms of labor force participation. Racial minorities and women, of course, are restricted in their levels of participation. But the meaning of reduced participation is much different for minority and majority women. Minority group women are much more likely to rely on such participation for their own or others subsistence. This form of reduced participation is therefore more likely to be seriously disadvantaging. Alternatively, the exclusion of majority group women from labor force participation is more likely to be of a patronizing form. Assuming that crime is at least in part a response to subsistence needs, this should mean that:

H_1: differences between racial minority and majority group crime rates will be greater for women than men; and

H_2: differences between male and female crime rates will be greater within racial majority than minority groups.

Said differently, the race-crime relationship is suppressed among men, and the gender-crime relationship is suppressed among minorities. This is because being male brings the chances of minority and majority group members being involved in crime closer together, whereas being in a minority group brings the chances of men and women being involved in crime closer together. The results are reductions in the crime rate differences indicated above.

Although hypotheses of the above kind were encouraged some time ago by Henry and Short (1954), we are aware of only one partial American test. This is found in Wolfgang's (1958) classic study of criminal homicide. Wolfgang reports in this study of Philadelphia homicide cases that the sex ratio among whites was 8.6 to 1.0, compared to 4.01 to 1.0 among blacks. These data are consistent with our hypotheses, if only for homicide in America.

These arguments can be taken one step further by considering the influence of age. Age also stratifies. Class differences increase with age. Therefore, age should intensify the above patterns. So,

> H3: the differences between racial minority and majority group crime rates will increase faster for women than men with age, as will the differences between male and female crime rates for members of racial majority groups.

This last hypothesis is in some ways the most interesting, because it seems likely to produce the most extreme group differences. For example, older majority group women are extremely unlikely to be involved in crime, whereas more often, older minority group women have little recourse but to be so. It is difficult to see these differences in anything other than structural terms—the economic circumstances of the two subgroups are so dramatically different. In other words, it is this higher order interaction involving age that makes the structural origins of links between race, gender, and crime most apparent. Interestingly, we are not aware that this higher order interaction has ever been explored for theoretical purposes. We do so with Canadian data below.

CRIME, RACE, AND GENDER IN CANADA

The value of considering issues of crime, race, and gender in countries other than the United States is the prospect of analyzing similarities as well as differences in these societal settings, and the outcomes they produce. For the main part of this article, we will emphasize similarities between these societal settings and the groups involved. In the final part of the article, we will consider the differences.

There is little doubt that gender relations are similar in the two countries. In a variety of American studies (Nye and Short, 1957; Wise, 1967; Hindelang, 1971; Cernkovich and Giordano, 1979; Jensen and Eve, 1976; Hindelang et al., 1981), as well as in the important Canadian research of Linden and Fillmore (1981; see also Hagan et al., 1979), males exceed females in self-reported delinquencies by more than two to one. Official data put this ratio at more than three to one. A common explanation for this disparity, of course, is that police are more sensitive and responsive to male delinquencies. However, whether the self-report or official data more accurately reflect gender differences in crime and delinquency, the behavioral differences clearly are large, both in Canada and the United States.

So too are racial differences in crime rates, although the racial groups involved are obviously different. Where attention has focused primarily on the crime problems of black Americans, the focus in Canada is on Native persons. Three broad groupings are often considered Native in Canada. These include persons of Indian, Metis, and Inuit backgrounds. Each grouping requires comment.

The Canadian government draws a consequential legal distinction between treaty and nontreaty Indians. Treaty Indians are those whose ancestors entered into agreements or treaties with the government and who maintain residence on a reserve (known in the United States as reservations) so as to maintain a "registered" status under the *Indian Act* of Canada. Nontreaty Indians are those whose ancestors did not reach negotiated agreements with the government and who retain a registered status regardless of whether they remain in residence on a reserve. There remain many other Indians, in a racial or cultural sense, who fall into neither of the above categories, either because they were never considered as entitled to registration, or because they have lost their right to registration. For our purposes, perhaps the most important of the latter are those Indian women who by law forfeit their registered status when they marry a nonregistered man. This particular form of sex discrimination is an important structural problem that Indian women confront in Canadian society.

The term Metis is used in Canada to refer to persons of partial Indian ancestry. Originally, this term was used to refer to persons of mixed French and Indian backgrounds. However, the term is now used more broadly and has achieved some legal recognition.

The Inuit, or Eskimos, are the remaining grouping included among Canada's Native persons. In a 1939 decision, the Supreme Court of Canada held that the Inuit were to be included within the term "Indian" for purposes of the *British North America Act*. Since then, attention to this group has slowly increased.

The diversity of the above groupings is easily recognized. In strictly legal terms, Canada's Indians form more than 150 politically separate units called Bands located on approximately 2,000 parcels of land called reserves (Kew, 1972). In sociological terms, 10 traditional linguistic groups (Algonquin, Iroquois, Siduk, Athabasca, Kootenay, Salish, Wakash, Tsimish, Haida, and Tlingt) and 6 major cultural areas (Algonquin, Iroquois, Plains, Plateaus, Pacific Coast, and MacKenzie River) have been identified. It is therefore reasonable to ask the question whether any single theory should be used to explain Native criminality, or indeed whether explanatory attention should be focused on this aggregate of persons that is, after all, a creation of the state. Verdun-Jones and Muirhead (1979: 8) make this point well when they note that

> unfortunately, it is only too easy to construct theories about 'native' criminality while nevertheless evading the implications of the fact that the term 'native' applies equally to the Inuit living in an isolated community in the frozen tundra, to the Indian living in a reserve in suburban North Vancouver, B.C., to the Indian living in a small rural reserve in Alberta, and to the migrant Indian passing through the urban skid row.

However, these same authors also note that "the present basis of common identity lies in nation-wide economic deprivation" (1979: 4). The structural theory we wish to explore in this article takes this common base of economic deprivation as its focal point.

THE DATA

Concerns about invidious racial distinctions have increasingly led governments to remove such categories from their official statistics. Federal Canadian crime statistics are a case in point. They no longer include information on racial background. Fortunately, a recent survey of "The Native inmate in Ontario" (Birkenmayer and Jolly, 1981), conducted with the support of the Ontario Ministry of Correctional

Services, includes information on the apparent race of all offenders admitted to Ontario correctional institutions during 1979 and 1980. These data are combined with census figures to calculate the rates and ratios used below to test the hypotheses formulated at the outset of this article. Of course, incarcerated offenders represent only a very small part of the full offender population. In Canada, it is estimated that only 1 out of 600 offenders is ultimately sent to prison. Among the factors that may lead to the overrepresentation of Native offenders in prison is their higher likelihood of defaulting in the payment of fines (Hagan, 1974). As a check on the bias the use of prison data may produce in testing our hypotheses, we also include below a set of calculations based on Winnipeg arrest statistics. Since these data come from another time, place, and stage in the criminal justice process, it would be difficult to be sure which of these differences might be responsible for any differences in outcomes. However, to the extent that Winnipeg arrest statistics replicate the patterns found with Ontario prison statistics, we will have good reason to believe that our findings can be generalized. We turn now to the analysis of these data.

THE ANALYSIS

We begin by considering the bivariate relationship between race and crime, and gender and crime, in Ontario. In Table 1 we see that overall, Native persons have far higher crime rates than nonNative persons. The total Native crime rate is 4.5 times the nonNative rate. There is variation among offenses. For example, whereas Native property and person crimes rates are more than three times the non-Native rates, Native drug and traffic offense rates are actually lower than the non-Native rates. However, the most dramatic source of variation is in alcohol offenses. Here the Native offense rate is more than 16 times the non-Native rate. Alcohol offenses clearly contribute most to differences between Native and non-Native Canadians.

Gender differences are substantially greater than racial differences in Ontario. Overall, the male crime rate is nearly 20 times the female crime rate. Again, there is significant variation across crime categories. Interestingly, the most dramatic of these specific differences is for public order and peace offenses, for which the male rate is more than 30 times the female rate. Our explanation of this extreme difference focuses on

TABLE 1
Race and Sex Offense Rates[a] and Ratios, Ontario Prison Statistics

Offense	Native		Non-Native		Native/ Non-Native Ratio	Male		Female		Male/ Female Ratio
	N	Rate	N	Rate		N	Rate	N	Rate	
Person	387	4.766	4637	1.446	3.296	4709	2.279	315	.152	14.993
Property	1523	18.758	25110	6.198	3.026	25724	12.450	909	.440	28.295
Public order and peace	472	5.813	9484	2.341	2.483	9650	4.671	306	.148	31.561
Public morals and decency	17	.209	647	.160	1.306	613	.300	51	.025	12.000
Liquor	4728	58.233	14357	3.544	16.431	17620	8.528	1465	.709	12.028
Drugs	65	.801	4790	1.182	.678	4592	2.223	263	.127	17.504
Traffic	604	7.439	30841	7.613	.977	29973	14.510	1472	.712	20.379
Miscellaneous	820	10.100	5331	1.316	7.674	5935	2.873	206	.010	287.300
Total	8616	106.120	95197	23.499	4.516	98816	47.827	4987	2.414	19.812

a. In this and subsequent tables, rates are calculated per 1,000 population. Ontario population figures are given in Birkenmayer and Jolly (1981: Appendix B).

women's restriction to the private sphere. Women are more likely to be allocated to the private space of the home; men are more likely to be allocated to public spaces where work as well as leisure activities can lead to officially controlled criminal behavior. This difference helps to account for gender disparities in all of the crime categories of Table 1, as well as for the largest of these differences in public order and peace offenses.

The data contained in Table 1, then, confirm that there are racial as well as gender differences in Canadian crime rates that parallel those found in the United States. Our interest now turns to determining whether these differences vary in theoretically expected ways at the multivariate level. To address this issue, we first calculate (within each offense category) race by sex—and then sex by race—offense rates and ratios. These calculations will allow a test of our first two hypotheses above, namely, that differences between male and female crime rates are greater within majority than minority groups.

Overall, the results presented in Table 2 are supportive of our hypotheses. The total female race ratio is more than five times the total male race ratio. This means that the ratio of Native to non-Native crime rates is much greater among women than men. Similarly, the total non-Native sex ratio is between five and six times the total Native sex ratio. This means that the ratio of male to female crime rates is much greater among non-Native than Native persons. As hypothesized, then, the race-crime relationship is suppressed among men, and the gender-crime relationship is suppressed among Native persons. Both of these suppression effects can be understood as resulting from the structural position occupied by non-Native women, who are restricted from full social and economic participation, but who are less likely to be economically disadvantaged as a result. Alternatively, Native women are also restricted from full social and economic participation, but with much higher levels of economic hardship. The consequences of this difference between the structural positions of Native and non-Native women are reflected in the much higher crime rates of the former. These in turn are reflected in a greater race-crime relationship among women and a smaller gender-crime relationship among Native persons.

We should not leave the impression that the above patterns are uniform across all offense categories. The male and female race ratios are largest among liquor offenses. This reflects the extremely high involvement of male and female Native persons in liquor offenses. However, note further that the female race ratio (115.477) is more than

TABLE 2

Race by Sex and Sex by Race Offense Rates and Ratios, Ontario Prison Statistics

Offense	Male Native		Male Non-Native		Female Native		Female Non-Native		Male Race Ratio	Female Race Ratio	Native Sex Ratio	Non-Native Sex Ratio
	N	Rate	N	Rate	N	Rate	N	Rate				
Person	341	4.200	4368	1.076	46	.567	269	.066	3.896	8.591	7.41	16.33
Property	1365	16.812	24359	6.013	158	1.946	751	.185	2.796	10.519	8.64	32.50
Public order and peace	428	5.271	9222	2.278	44	.542	262	.065	2.314	8.338	9.73	35.05
Public morals and decency	14	.172	599	.148	3	.037	48	.012	1.162	3.083	4.65	12.33
Liquor	3706	45.640	13914	3.435	1022	12.587	443	.109	13.287	115.477	3.63	31.51
Drugs	63	.776	4529	1.118	2	.025	261	.064	.694	.391	31.04	17.47
Traffic	579	7.131	23394	7.256	25	.308	1447	.357	.983	.862	23.15	20.32
Miscellaneous	692	8.523	5253	1.297	128	1.576	78	.109	6.571	82.947	5.41	68.26
Total	7188	88.530	91628	22.618	1428	17.588	3559	.879	3.914	20.009	5.03	25.73

ten times the male race ratio (13.287). The nonNative sex ratio (31.51) is also nearly ten times the Native sex ratio (3.63). Our explanation of these great disparities is that non-Native women rarely are found in structural circumstances that lead them to drink and recover in public.

It is also interesting to note that there are two offenses—drugs and traffic—for which Native rates do not exceed those of non-Natives, for either males or females. These exceptions to the overall pattern can again be explained in structural terms. Native men and women have less access to drugs and cars than non-Native men and women. The former are therefore less likely to be involved in drug and traffic offenses.

Table 3 repeats the calculations of Table 2, using the Winnipeg arrest data and some slightly different offense categories. The result is a nearly complete replication of results. For six of the seven offense categories, the female race ratios exceed the male race ratios and the nonNative sex ratios exceed the Native sex ratios. For these categories of offenses, this again means that the ratio of Native to non-Native crime rates is greater among women than men, and that the ratio of male to female crime rates is greater among non-Native than Native persons. Again, these patterns are particularly pronounced for liquor offenses, with drug offenses providing the single exception to the overall pattern. Indeed, not a single Native person is included among the Winnipeg drug arrests. The only clear difference between the Ontario prison statistics and the Winnipeg arrest statistics involves the category of traffic offenses. We are unable to account for this single difference. Nonetheless, the more general pattern predicted in hypotheses one and two above, involving a greater race-crime relationship among women and a smaller gender-crime relationship among Native persons, apparently can be generalized beyond our Ontario prison data.

Our final test of the kind of structural perspective we are proposing involves the third hypothesis above, namely, that with age differences between Native and non-Native, crime rates will increase faster for women than men, as will differences between male and female crime rates among non-Native as compared to Native persons. Hirschi and Gottfredson (1983) recently have argued that the age distribution of crime is invariant across social conditions. Although generally this may be true, our hypothesis nonetheless predicts an interaction of race, sex, and age on crime that results from the very low criminal involvement of older, nonNative women. Data presented in Table 4 generally confirm this prediction.

Note first in Table 4 that Native rates of crime peak later than non-Native rates. The Native male rate peaks at 32.441 in the 25-35-year-

TABLE 3

Race by Sex and Sex by Race Offense Rates and Ratios, Winnipeg Arrest Statistics

	Male				Female					Male Race Ratio	Female Race Ratio	Native Sex Ratio	Non-Native Sex Ratio
	Native		Non-Native		Native		Non-Native						
Offense	N	Rate	N	Rate	N	Rate	N	Rate					
Property	53.	.867	282.	.653	8.	.130	22	.053	1.328	2.453	6.669	12.320
Person	26.	.422	104.	.242	3.	.061	4.	.010	1.744	6.100	6.918	24.200
Legal justice	8.	.141	38.	.089	5.	.084	1.	.004	1.584	21.000	1.679	21.000
Traffic	94.	1.523	1210.	2.801	1.	.031	16.	.039	.544	.795	49.129	71.821
Drugs	0.	0	61.	.143	0	0	8.	.019	—	—	—	7.526
Liquor	1112.	18.016	1574.	3.642	394.	6.380	111.	.260	4.947	24.539	2.824	14.008
Other	151.	2.460	595.	1.378	59.	.955	40.	.095	1.785	10.053	2.576	14.505

SOURCE: Bienvenue and Latis (1974), reformulated.

139

TABLE 4
Race by Sex and Sex by Race Rates and Ratios for Selected Age Groups, Ontario Prison Statistics

	Male				Female				Male Race Ratio	Female Race Ratio	Native Sex Ratio	Non-Native Sex Ratio
	Native		Non-Native		Native		Non-Native					
Age	N	Rate	N	Rate	N	Rate	N	Rate				
16	128	3.153	2294	1.132	30	.740	231	.114	2.785	6.491	4.261	9.930
17	237	5.838	3787	1.870	42	1.035	304	.150	3.122	6.900	5.641	12.467
18	262	6.454	4116	2.032	40	.985	303	.149	3.176	6.611	6.55	13.638
19-24	1219	30.027	18100	8.936	218	5.369	1203	.594	3.360	9.039	5.59	15.044
25-35	1317	32.441	12566	6.204	266	6.557	922	.455	5.229	14.411	4.498	13.635
36-50	917	22.588	7401	3.654	185	4.557	438	.216	6.182	21.097	4.957	16.917
51+	505	12.395	3301	1.630	106	2.611	120	.059	7.604	44.254	4.747	27.627

old age group, whereas the non-Native male rate peaks at 8.936 in the 19-25-year-old age group. Similarly, the Native female rate peaks at 6.557 in the 25-35-year-old group, whereas the non-Native female rate peaks at .594 in the 19-24-year-old group. However, more significant are the differences between the male and female race ratios and the Native and non-Native sex ratios. As predicted, the female race ratio increases much faster than the Native sex ratio. So while the male race ratio increases from a low of 2.785 in the 16-year-old age group to 7.604 in the 51-year and older age group, for the same age groups the female race ratio increases from 6.491 to 44.254. Again, using the same age groups for comparative purposes, the Native sex ratio increases only slightly from 4.261 to 4.747, whereas the non-Native sex ratio increases from 9.930 to 27.627. We take the extremely high female race ratio in the highest age group (44.254), and the similarly high non-Native sex ratio in the highest age group (27.627), as reflecting the dramatic structural differences in life experiences of Native and nonNative women: the latter almost never commit criminal acts; the former are processed with some frequency for doing so. Given the powerful effects of age that Hirschi and Gottfredson assert, the above differences are all the more striking.

CRIME AND RACE IN THE UNITED STATES AND CANADA

Thus far we have adopted an assumption that minority and majority groups are related to one another in similar ways in the United States and Canada. This assumption follows from the theoretical premise that similar structural conditions of disadvantage should produce problems of similar form across social serttings. However, although there are similarities in these conditions across the United States and Canada, there are also differences that cannot and should not be ignored.

Notice must first be taken of the differences in crime between the countries. Violent crime rates in particular are higher in the United States than in Canada. Indeed, there is growing evidence that the disparity in violent crime rates between these countries is increasing (see Hagan, 1984). Beyond this, there are differences of kind as well as in amount of criminal violence in these two countries. In the United States, for example, about half of all homicides involve handguns; in Canada

142   CRIME & DELINQUENCY / JANUARY 1985

the figure is approximately ten percent. Friedland (1981: 1) illustrates this point with some graphic comparisons:

> In 1971 there were fewer than 60 homicides committed with handguns in all of Canada. Metropolitan Toronto, with more than 2,000,000 persons, had only 4 handgun homicides that year. In contrast, in 1979, handguns were used in almost 900 killings in New York City, and 300 in Metropolitan Detroit, and 75 in Metropolitan Boston. . . . The six New England states had over 200 handgun homicides in 1979; the four Canadian Maritime Provinces did not have a single handgun homicide in 1979. There were over 10,000 handgun homicides in the U.S. in 1979, almost 20 times the Canadian *per capita* rate.

Historically, these differences are widely thought to have a base in the settlement of the American and Canadian west. Quinney (1970) observes that on the American frontier, local authorities were free to develop their own law enforcement policies or to ignore the problem of crime altogether. Similarly, Inciardi (1975) observed that, "the American frontier was Elizabethan in its quality, simple, childlike, and savage . . . . It was a land of riches where swift and easy fortunes were sought by the crude, the lawless, and the aggressive, and where written law lacked form and cohesion." Put simply, the American frontier was also a violent frontier—a model in some ways for the city life that followed (Bell, 1953).

Canada intended to be different. This is one of the reasons Canada chose to have a federal criminal code, with John A. Macdonald (Canada's first Prime Minister) arguing in the confederation debates that "I think this is one of the most marked instances in which we take advantage of the experience derived from our observations of the defects in the Constitution of the neighboring Republic" (cited in Friedland, 1981: 24). The Canadian approach was of initially firmer, but necessarily more strategic, control (McNaught, 1975). MacLeod (1976) notes that by the 1870s, the American government was spending over $20 million a year just fighting the Plains Indians. At the same time, the *total* Canadian budget (of which defense was only a part) was just over $19 million. According to MacLeod (1976: 3), "It is not an exaggeration to say . . . that the only possible Canadian west was a peaceful one." The North-West Mounted Police (NWMP), with powers unparalleled by any other police force in a democratic country, were given responsibility for establishing "peace and order." Kelly and Kelly (1976: 21) contend that the NWMP of the 1890s "attended to the health and welfare problems of Indians and Eskimos," whereas Brown and Brown (1973: 10) write that, "the NWMP were established as a semi-military force designed to keep order on the prairies and to facilitate the transfer of most of the territory of the region from the Indian tribes to the federal government with a minimum of expense and bloodshed."

Whichever of the above accounts of the role of the NWMP is the more accurate, it is clear that Canada's Native people were treated in a significantly different way than were Native people in the United States. America's treatment of both its black and Native minorities was extraordinarily violent. Canada's treatment of its Native people was and may still be socially and economically poor, but it has not been nearly so violent. It seems unlikely from a structural perspective that this difference in the form of mistreatment would not have had behavioral consequences, for example, in rates of violent crime.

One final point should be made before we bring this speculative discussion of national differences to its conclusion in terms of issues of race and crime. This point involves the very different policies the two countries have followed in terms of gun control. Canada has long had tighter and more effective gun control legislation than the United States. We have already noted the different records of handgun homicide found in the two countries. We believe that the above features of Canada's and the United States' past constitute a rather striking set of differences. The United States violently suppressed its black and Native minorities within a society that makes a most democratic instrument of violence— handguns—freely available. Canada socially and economically suppressed its Native people, but much less violently, and made access to instruments of violence, particularly handguns, rather difficult. These are very different structural strategies and they could be expected to produce different behavioral effects. For example, it might be expected that Canada's Native people should be less violent in their criminal behavior than are Native people in the United States. Such comparisons may hold a key to a deeper understanding of the dramatic differences in crime rates that characterize the United States and Canada.

CONCLUSION

In this article we have broadly outlined and explored a structural theory of race, gender, and crime. Our premise has been that official data can be used in significant ways to test explanations of criminal behavior, and that a structural perspective is particularly useful in exploring the meaning of these data. At the outset of the paper, three structural hypotheses were stated, each focusing in a different way on the interaction of race and gender on crime. In many ways, the most crucial of these hypotheses was the third, which adds a fourth variable— age. In an important article, Hirschi and Gottfredson (1983) recently have argued that the age distribution of crime is invariant across social conditions. However, the structural perspective we have proposed predicts that with age, differences between Native and nonNative crime rates will increase faster for women than men, and differences between male and female crime rates will increase faster for nonNative than Native persons. Our data are consistent with this hypothesis. We think this exception to the invariance Hirschi and Gottfredson cite derives in large part from the dramatic structural differences in life experiences of older Native and nonNative women. The latter almost never commit criminal acts; the former are processed with some frequency for doing so. Put differently, the age curve that Hirschi and Gottfredson describe declines much more rapidly for nonNative than Native women. Anyone who has visited a Canadian women's prison will know that this is not a statistical aberration of minor consequence; these prisons contain large numbers of older Native women. The argument is easily made that this is one of the most severely disadvantaged groups in Canadian society.

Whether the hypotheses we have offered and the findings we have described are unique to the problems of Canada's Native population is unclear. We have stated our hypotheses broadly so as to encourage their wider test. However, in the preceding section of this article, we also noted some very important differences between Canada and the the United States. The United States more violently suppressed its minorities and made instruments of violence—particularly handguns—freely available to its citizens. Canada was less violent, if no less discriminatory, in its racial suppression, and has more strictly controlled firearms. Comparative research based on the United States and Canada holds the promise of telling us much about the very different crime experiences of the two countries and their respective minority populations.

REFERENCES

Bell, D.
    1953   "Crime as an American way of life." Antioch Rev. 13: 131-54.

Bienvenue, P. M. and A. H. Latis
 1974 "Arrests, dispositions, and recidivism: A comparison of Indians and whites."
  Canadian J. of Criminology and Corrections 16: 105-116.
Birkenmayer, A. and S. Jolly
 1981 A Native Inmate in Ontario. Toronto: Ontario Native Council on Justice.
Bonger, W.
 1916 Criminality and Economic Conditions. Boston: Little, Brown.
Brown, L. and C. Brown
 1973 An Unauthorized History of the R.C.M.P. Toronto: Lewis and Samuel.
Cernkovich, S. and P. Giordano
 1979 "A comparative analysis of male and female delinquency." Soc. Q. 20: 131-145.
Friedland, M.
 1981 "Gun control in Canada: Politics and impact." Presented to Seminar on
  Canadian-U.S. Relations, Harvard Center for International Affairs: University
  Consortium for Research on North America.
Hagan, J.
 1974 "Criminal justice and Native people: A study of incarceration in a Canadian
  Province." Canadian Rev. of Sociology and Anthropology Special Issue
  (August): 220-36.
 1984 The Disreputable Pleasures: Crime and Deviance in Canada. Toronto:
  McGraw-Hill Ryerson.
Hagan, J., J. Simpson, and A. R. Gillis
 1979 "The sexual stratification of social control: A gender-based perspective on
  crime and delinquency." British J. of Sociology 30: 25-38.
Henry, A. and J. Short
 1954 Suicide and Homicide. Glencoe, IL: Free Press.
Hindelang, M.
 1971 "Age, sex and versatility of delinquent involvement." Social Problems 18:
  522-35.
 1978 "Race and involvement in common law personal crimes." Amer. Soc. Rev. 43:
  93-109.
 1979 "Sex differences in criminal activity." Social Problems 27: 143-156.
Hindelang, M., T. Hirschi, and J. Weis
 1981 Measuring Delinquency. Beverly Hills, CA: Sage.
Hirschi, T. and M. Gottfredson
 1983 "Age and the explanation of crime." Amer. J. of Sociology 89: 552-84.
Inciardi, J.
 1975 Careers in Crime. Chicago: Rand McNally.
Jensen, G. and R. Eve
 1976 "Sex differences in delinquency: An examination of popular sociological explanations." Criminology 13: 427-48.
Kelly, W. and N. Kelly
 1976 Policing in Canada. Toronto: Macmillan.
Kew, M.
 1972 "100 Years of making Indians in B.C." Canadian Dimension 4: 35-40.
Linden, E. and C. Fillmore
 1981 "A comparative study of delinquency involvement." Canadian Rev. of Sociology and Anthropology 18: 343-61.

146   CRIME & DELINQUENCY / JANUARY 1985

MacLeod, R. C.
  1976   The North-West Mounted Police and Law Enforcement 1873-1905. Toronto:
          Univ. of Toronto Press.
McNaught, K.
  1975   "Political trials and the Canadian political tradition," in M. L. Freidland (ed.),
          Courts and Trials: A Multi-Disciplinary Approach. Toronto: Univ. of Toronto
          Press.
Nye, F. I. and J. Short
  1957   "Scaling delinquent behavior." Amer. Soc. Rev. 22: 326-32.
Quinney, R.
  1970   The Social Reality of Crime. New York: Little.
Verdun-Jones, S. and G. Muirhead
  1979   "Natives in the Canadian criminal justice system." Crime & Justice 7: 3-21.
Wise, N.
  1967   "Juvenile delinquency among middle class girls," in E. Vaz (ed.), Middle Class
          Delinquency. New York: Harper.
Wolfgang, M.
  1958   Patterns in Criminal Homicide. New York: Wiley

Name Index